Huawei

Xiaoying Dong · Mengling Yan · Yanni Hu

Huawei

From Catching Up To Leading

北京大學出版社
PEKING UNIVERSITY PRESS

Springer

Xiaoying Dong
Guanghua School of Management
Peking University
Beijing, China

Yanni Hu
China Academy of Information
and Communications Technology
Beijing, China

Mengling Yan
School of Economics and Management
Beijing University of Posts
and Telecommunications
Beijing, China

Translated by
Wang Qiong
Hunan Normal University
Changsha, China

ISBN 978-981-19-4080-4 ISBN 978-981-19-4078-1 (eBook)
https://doi.org/10.1007/978-981-19-4078-1

Jointly published with Peking University Press
The print edition is not for sale in the Mainland of China. Customers from the Mainland of China please order the print book from: Peking University Press.
ISBN of the Chinese edition is 978-7-301-29843-5

This Springer imprint is published by the registered company Springer Nature Singapore Pte Ltd.
The registered company address is: 152 Beach Road, #21-01/04 Gateway East, Singapore 189721, Singapore

Preface

Why Have We Followed Huawei For So Long?

My research team and I started to study Huawei since 2010, and during the past decade, three Ph.D. students, more than 20 master students and MBA students have been involved in the research. The research process was supported by our own funds and the National Natural Science Foundation of China.[1] We had confusion and self-doubt from time to time along the journey but eventually carried it through. What exactly is it that has supported us so long to study a single company? Here are three things that I believe have the most significant impact.

First, in 1999 I joined the EU-China Higher Education Exchange Program and started to study knowledge management in the UK. At that time, knowledge management was something quite new even among the academia, meanwhile many famous multinationals were suffering from the loss of knowledge due to brain drain. As intellectual capital began to play an increasingly important role in value creation, many enterprises began to pay more attention to wealth creation through knowledge management, to avoid repeating mistakes through knowledge reuse, and to enhance innovation capacity by tapping the tacit knowledge. At first, my British mentor did not think much of my research on knowledge management, for he did not see much value in it for a socialist country. However, I was convinced that knowledge management would be big because natural resources can be exhausted, while human creativity and knowledge are inexhaustible, and the potential is far from being fully explored.

When I returned to Peking University in 2000 to teach a course on knowledge management for entrepreneurs, many were not impressed either, saying that their companies could still make a lot of money without relying on knowledge or knowledge management. Therefore, I was particularly impressed by Huawei's refreshingly different perception of the strategic value of knowledge resources when I first came into contact with the company. As early as in 1997 when the *Huawei Basic Law* was

[1] "Research on the impact of strategic leadership and organizational learning on ambidexterity building in high-tech enterprises", 2013–2017, Project No. 71371017.

published, it stipulated that knowledge is the only strategic resource for the development of Huawei. Specifically, Article 6 states that "Huawei had no natural resources to depend upon, but what it did have was the brainpower of its employees. This is its oil, its forest, and its coal…" In Article 17, it specifically states that "by converting knowledge into capital, labor, knowledge, management and the accumulated contributions of entrepreneurs can thus be manifested and rewarded. Equity arrangements can help build the backbone of the company and help the company keep an effective control; this way the company can grow sustainably. The capitalization of knowledge and a dynamic property rights system that adapts to technological and social changes is the direction we need to constantly explore." In the first 20 years of China's reform and opening up, many enterprises focused on the exploitation of tangible resources, and mostly natural resources, with making the first bucket of gold their primary goal. Huawei, on the contrary, explicitly pointed out the strategic value of human capital and intellectual capital to the sustainable development of the enterprise. It regards intellectual capitalization as the key to system design and incentive mechanism so that the company can better unite, stimulate, and motivate its employees and align employees' goals with organizational goals. Such a visionary understanding was not common at the time.

Second, in 2009, I had the opportunity to work as a knowledge management consultant for a well-known private enterprise, which was an industry leader in China with good prospects. The company was quite optimistic about future expansion and had laid out plans for 2018. However, the executives began to tune out different voices and did not care about operational upgrading or organizational change. I remember that when asked about the value of knowledge management, an executive replied, "Knowledge management is like Traditional Chinese medicine; it may help you stay healthy but cannot save your life."

By 2012, the market had not grown as fast as the executives predicted but instead was rather depressed. Due to blind optimism, over-expansion, lagging capacity, inadequate flexibility, and lack of a crisis contingency plan, the company was unable to adapt to the rapid changes in the market, and its products had to be sold for a song, causing serious damage to the company's brand and value. The company plummeted in the market position in a short period of time; its share price depreciated, and its executives left one after another. I was shocked. I asked myself why an industry leader had such a free fall in a matter of two to three years? What was the problem? What kind of entrepreneurs can lead the organization to avoid such a fall and go from strength to strength? When I read Ren Zhengfei's speech, this passage enlightened me. When he talked about Huawei's growth, he said that as a leader, he had "no sense of pride but only a sense of crisis". To survive, a company must constantly engage in self-reflection. "Self-reflection at the organizational level can optimize the process and management; self-reflection at the personal level can also remarkedly improve oneself. Users don't have to worry about the collapse of such companies". It is this all-round self-reflection and self-knowledge that make Huawei deeply aware of its shortcomings and gaps, through the "dissipation structure", it continuously focuses on building new capabilities in no-man's land in a forward-looking manner. From the two disparately different cases, I witnessed first-hand that the thought, mindset, determination, wisdom, rationality, self-reflection, and sense of crisis of the leadership are so critical to the organization in terms of identifying future direction, resources input, and building a viable culture.

Third, between 2009 and 2014, supported by Guanghua-Cisco Leadership Institute at Peking University, I had the opportunity to study with the executives of central SOEs at Cisco in the United States, and had an extensive exchange with Cisco executives and heard a lot of presentations. Cisco, an Internet company founded in 1984, has weathered a number of storms in the past 37 years. During this period, many industry giants (such as Alcatel, Nortel, Motorola, etc.) have successively disappeared or been acquired, but Cisco is still active in the Internet world as a tech optimist. If we consider innovation and operation as the two drives for the sustainable development of the enterprise, Cisco has constructed an efficient business model based on the two competencies, thus making sure it can survive in an environment where radical technologies are frequent.[2] The key elements to sustainable development include the customer-centric philosophy and system design, highly adaptable organizational culture, efficient execution system, operational excellence, and risk management system, and continuous transformation and change. In the early days of development when Huawei had a yawning gap with the industry leaders in terms of R&D, marketing, management, branding, and capital, it decided to prioritize management system and platform. According to Ren: "Management is the core, without which even if talent, technology, and capital are introduced, they will not generate synergy." Such a development path and model of Huawei is based on its reflection on Chinese culture, a thinking about why there was no world-class company in China for thousands of years, and in-depth research and understanding of Western companies. It is also particularly worthwhile to study and explore how Huawei can establish its own ambidexterity model as a follower.

How to Study Huawei?

Researching into Huawei is rather difficult because it always keeps a low profile, and seldom publicizes itself. So, we had no choice but tried everything possible to collect first-hand and second-hand information and material as much as possible.

The first-hand information and material include: (1) speeches by Ren Zhengfei on formal or informal occasions (107 pieces in total, about 350,000 words); (2) postings on the Huawei Voice Community; (3) Huawei's annual reports (2006–2015); (4) books and research papers written by Huawei employees; (5) interviews with Huawei executives and employees, lectures held by Huawei people at Peking University and other places, transcripts of lectures in MBA and EMBA classes, and interviews with its employees at Huawei; (6) interviews with former and current Huawei employees students, their course reports and theses; (7) the comments of executives of foreign and domestic companies (e.g., Siemens, Samsung, etc.) on Huawei (nearly 300,000

---

[2] *Cisco: from innovation to operation*. Peking University Press. 2018.

words in total); and (8) interviews with professionals who have had cooperative or competitive relationships with Huawei (nearly 50,000 words).

Second-hand information and material include: (1) existing books on Huawei; (2) research papers on Huawei on the Chinese academic journal network (https://cnki.net/); (3) domestic and international media coverage on Huawei; and (4) online news and reports on Huawei. Through the systematic analysis of these materials, we confirm the consistency, credibility, and authenticity of these materials to make up for the lack of close-up contact with the company. Time is a good yardstick to help us know more about the words, actions, and results of the company in multiple dimensions, levels, perspectives, and stages. An "unexpected" benefit of this "clumsy" approach is that by looking at Huawei from a distance, we have gained a relatively bigger picture. Of course, the downside is also obvious: we don't have sufficient details for the stories and the motives behind the stories.

In this context, we focus our research on systematically sorting out Huawei's core strategies, ideas, and management methods, using ambidexterity, knowledge management, and information management as theoretical perspectives. In the process of writing, we systematically and structurally sorted out Huawei's development path from a technology follower to a market leader by taking time as the main thread and management issues as the guide. Among them, Ren Zhengfei's speeches are the most important and valuable information. By deconstructing and reconstructing his speeches, we sorted out his views, judgments, and choices as a business leader in different development stages and contexts. On this basis, we then deepened and supplemented the information based on interviews and other first-hand and second-hand sources and confirmed the validity, reliability, and accuracy of the information from informal conversations.

In the interviews, we found that Huawei people are straightforward: they did not hide their shortcomings and rarely sugarcoated or whitewashed their problems. Even junior employees are cool-headed; they are humble to the point of self-deprecating. Huawei is not a perfect enterprise; its growth had its share of "organizational black holes". Huawei has experienced "selection errors," "inadequate research and development," "market failure," "brain drain", "faction conflict", "senior management corruption", and "mounting pressure". Some problems disappeared, some were alleviated, some may be worsened, and meanwhile some new problems emerged. We have no intention to set a model but to describe the journey of Huawei in terms of executive perception, human resources, R&D processes, organizational learning: how it tried, errored, and improved itself. ("What" and "How"). These growth problems that Huawei has experienced are common problems in the process of corporate growth and have some reference significance for other Chinese companies.

The target readers of this book are entrepreneurs and managers, so we focus our research on how Huawei thinks and does, and carry out systematic research, sorting, integration, and analysis. Through a problem-oriented framework and heading, it provides more direct and useful information and clues for managers. Based on a systematic understanding of Huawei's practices, we have summarized and modeled them based on time, data, illustration, and flow chart, etc. The last section of each chapter is a comparison between Cisco and Huawei. We also summarized an "Eagle

Model" to analyze what Huawei has done right. We also discuss the modeling of the ambidexterity of Huawei.

Nevertheless, we are aware that, in terms of breadth, depth, and time span, we still have a lot to dig into and summarize for such a great company with over 30 years of history featured by ups and downs, and what the book can present is only the tip of the iceberg. In the face of future global competition, we need more scholars to study the development path of Chinese enterprises, to provide a reference for entrepreneurs who aspire to develop their enterprises into internationally competitive players.

How We Feel About Huawei?

My team and I have been studying Huawei for nearly 10 years, which humbles, inspires, and touches us. The vision, dedication, tenacity, perseverance, customer centricity, and learning spirit demonstrated by Huawei people have always inspired and motivated us to move forward. Whenever we wanted to give up, wavered, or were distracted by other research and teaching opportunities, it was Huawei's "focus principle" and the principle of "working together towards the same end" that helped us to refocus. It's fair to say that we have benefited a lot from studying Huawei: we are more refreshed with our body and mind in better shape. We learned from the observation and study on Huawei from a technology follower to a market leader that it has been an uphill journey with winding paths. Huawei is particularly admirable in an atmosphere that most companies are impatient, easily tempted by short cuts and immediate profits; many companies focus on seeking fame but lack of long-term vision and investment in key future capabilities.

This year marks the 40th anniversary of reform and opening up. To realize the Chinese dream of national rejuvenation and narrow the gap with the leading countries, with painstaking efforts and great wisdom, generations of Chinese people have created the "Chinese miracle". History is not only a valuable record of this generation but also a valuable asset for future generations.

Since 2019, Huawei has been under unprecedented pressure in the international arena. As we all know, the pressure is closely linked to geopolitics, economic interests, national security, and technological superiority. In the history of mankind, no other companies have ever been at the center of the international political and economic power game, which also reveals the strategic importance of Huawei in the global digital economy landscape. Huawei has gone through punitive measures one after another the US has taken on the market, the operating system, the supply chain of its core technologies and on its key manufacturing process, Huawei survived, thanks to its strategic foresight, a large pool of talent, knowledge, and technology reserves, as well as the strong support from the Chinese market. Huawei further increases its support for basic research, meanwhile rapidly enters new areas and new markets for transformation. As the verse goes, "Hard it is, finally you get gold from sand". So does Huawei. After all these trials and hardships, its belief, culture, and dedication remain unchanged, and it is a role model and benchmark for other Chinese companies to forge ahead in the face of challenges and difficulties.

The writers of this book are as follows: Dong Xiaoying (Introduction, Chaps. 1–6, 8 and 11); Yan Mengling (Chaps. 9 and 12); Hu Yanni (Chaps. 7, 10, and 13). All the figures in the book are based on the teaching materials of Dong Xiaoying's. Please refer to the reference at the end of the book for the published papers on Huawei's ambidexterity by Yan Mengling, who collected a large number of Ren's speeches and articles from the Huawei Voice Community and created the list of typical self-reflection events in Huawei and Huawei's joint innovation centers. Hu Yanni is responsible for organizing and correcting the content and references of the whole book. The authors are especially grateful to Prof. Peng Siqing, Prof. Wu Yajun, Prof. Gong Jiangang, Fang Fei and many students for their contributions. The authors would also like to thank Lin Junxiu and Xu Bing at Peking University Press, our outstanding partners, for their enthusiasm, professionalism, and responsibility. The authors would also like to give special thanks to our families, whose love, trust, encouragement, and support have kept us going this long.

Yanyuan, China
August 2018

Xiaoying Dong

Introduction

Catching-Up Countries

In his book *Economic Backwardness in Historical Perspective*,[3] Alexander Gerschenkron, an economic historian, and professor at Harvard University studied the economic development of Russia, Germany, France, Austria, Bulgaria, and other countries in the 19th century and proposed the core concept of economic backwardness. He found that relative backwardness creates a tension between the promise of economic development, as achieved elsewhere, and the continuity of stagnation. Such tension takes political form and motivates institutional innovation, whose product becomes an appropriate substitution for the absent preconditions for growth. The catching-up countries have different production structures, organizational structures, and system designs from the leading countries. Professor Geshenkelong found that the more backward an economy is at the outset of economic development, the more likely certain conditions are to occur:

- Special institutions, including banks or the state, will be necessary to properly channel physical capital and human capital to industries.
- There will be an emphasis on the production of producer goods rather than consumer goods.
- There will be an emphasis on capital-intensive production rather than labor-intensive production.
- There will be a great scale of production and enterprise.
- There will be a reliance on borrowed rather than local technologies.
- There will be a reliance on productivity growth.

The social approval of entrepreneurs accelerates the process of industrialization. The greater the resistance of the external environment to innovation, the higher the requirements for entrepreneurs' character and willpower. His studies show that economic backwardness is not necessarily a disadvantage; it could be transformed

[3] Alexander Gerschenkron. *Economic Backwardness in Historical Perspective. Beijing:* Commercial Press, 2009.

into an advantage. Professor Gerschenkron found it worthy of study whether the backward economies should follow the model of advanced or industrialized countries. As for the statement by Karl Marx—"The country that is more developed industrially only shows, to the less developed, the image of its own future",[4] it needs to be further explored empirically.

Many economical laggards dream to be leaders. In the past 40 years, China's reform and opening-up program has shown the world a rare success. Since 1977, China has been making huge economic and social progress. As shown in Fig. 1, between 2007 and 2017, the number of Chinese companies on the Fortune Global 500 list has grown substantially while the number of American, Japanese, and German companies was decreasing.

During this period of rapid economic development in China, in addition to the support of the government's policies and strategies, the rapid growth of large firms is mainly driven by the following three factors:

1. The market size. A populous country naturally has a large market, a large number of companies, especially infrastructure, utilities, and resource-based companies. In 2017, six of the top ten companies in the world were resource-based companies (oil, electricity, etc.) and three were from China.
2. New demand. In the past 30 years, Chinese consumption (such as in household appliances, food, automobiles, real estate, etc.) has grown exponentially. To meet the rapid growth of local demand, a large number of fast-growing domestic companies emerged.
3. The speed and scale of the development and application of new technologies. The development of high and new technologies (such as biomedicine, ICT, and

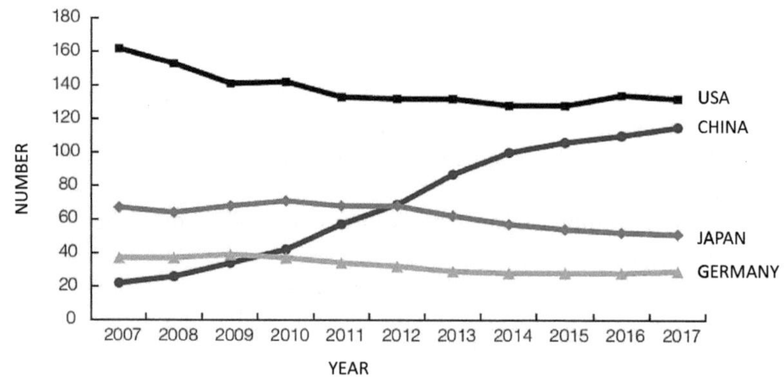

Fig. 1 The number of Fortune Global 500 companies in USA, China, Japan, and Germany (2007–2017)[5]

[4] Karl Marx. *Capital*. Shanghai: SDX Joint Publishing, 2009.

[5] The figure is credited to Professor Emeritus Qiwen Wang, at Guanghua School of Management, Peking University.

Internet technology) has spawned a large number of knowledge-intensive enterprises. Unlike resource-based enterprises, knowledge-intensive enterprises have higher requirements for human capital, knowledge, and innovation capabilities, and face much tougher competition too.

Catching-Up Companies

Catching-up companies and latecomer companies are different concepts: Catching-up companies are categorized according to the time they enter the industry: these companies try to catch up with the first movers under the circumstances that they lack resources and capabilities. However, latecomer companies do not lack resources and capabilities but choose to enter the industry later so that when innovative technologies or products are accepted by the market, they can gain an advantage through product optimization or lower costs. Catching-up companies are also different from startups. Startups usually use niche resources, technologies, business models, or differentiated market positioning to gain a competitive edge, so they have fewer technology or market barriers.

The following are the defining characteristics of catching-up companies:

- In terms of the time of entry, when catching-up companies enter the market, there are already a large number of first movers;
- In terms of strategic intent, catching-up companies, as the name suggests, aim to catch up and surpass;
- In terms of operation mode, catching-up companies are imitators rather than innovators, and are good at using various forms of leverage and resource integration;
- In terms of organizational learning, catching-up companies are fast learners, using the system to accelerate capacity building and continuously improve their competitive status;
- In terms of resources and capabilities, catching-up companies often lack the technical, marketing, managerial, and branding resources, and they need to use limited resources to ensure viability and achieve the maximum value.

When catching-up companies enter the industry, technology and market are their most obvious disadvantages. Their technological disadvantage is manifested in the lack of not only core technology and an R&D system but the ecology for acquiring technological resources. Catching-up companies are usually in developing countries, which are often geographically far away from international R&D and knowledge system centers. Generally, they operate in isolation in places where engineering, technological, and R&D capabilities are lagging, with immature industrial and technological infrastructure, and less developed universities and technical institutions. In contrast, leading companies have large R&D departments and invest profusely in R&D and the commercialization of new technologies. Meanwhile, there are a large number of start-ups around; they constantly strengthen their technological leadership and differentiation through M&As to continuously promote technology and expand the market, thus increasing their competitive edge. Catching-up companies, on the other hand, have to pay a much bigger price to access cutting-edge technologies and knowledge systems.

Catching-up companies usually lack brand recognition, reputation, marketing channels, and customer loyalty. It is not uncommon that tech start-ups from developing countries will face doubts and even contempt when entering markets in advanced countries. So, they will have to pay extra efforts to change the stereotype images and build trust with customers. If catching-up companies are positioned to only serve local customers, they will be drifted even further away from the mainstream international market, causing greater difficulties for subsequent development. Therefore, only after they overcome all the difficulties can they enter the global market and obtain substantive development and recognized competitiveness.

In addition to technological and marketing drawbacks, catching-up companies also face management challenges. They usually have a yawning gap with established companies in the UK, the US, and Germany. It is imperative to enhance their management quickly and effectively so that they will be able to compete with their counterparts in advanced countries in efficiency, process, information system, supply chain management, and other operating systems. In addition, catching-up companies also suffer from inadequate capital and lack of seasoned professionals; these disadvantages may lead to costly trial and error, if not failure. As the Chinese saying goes, good steel should be used in the blade. It is critical for decision-makers of catching-up companies to make the best of the limited resources.

Nevertheless, catching-up companies also have their advantages. They are usually hungrier than industry leaders for knowledge and success and have a greater drive for fast growth. To survive, they usually have a stronger sense of urgency and crisis, which can be translated into investment in future-proof capacities. The lack of resources makes them particularly wary of risks and expect higher returns. These young companies are usually passionate, dynamic, flexible, cost-effective, highly efficient, and highly aware of market segmentation; they cherish development opportunities and are good at making breakthroughs in an unfavorable environment. They study conscientiously and take their competitors more seriously. As they only have limited customers, they cherish available opportunities more, are more willing to take challenging orders, and work harder to build trust with their customers. Unlike some giant firms, they are not arrogant, stubborn, or bureaucratic. Therefore, catching-up companies are striving harder to move forward, embrace changes, and seek breakthroughs. They take every market and technology transformation opportunity seriously so that they can overtake the first movers. When they have sufficient technical resources, they emulate industrial leaders to avoid innovation traps; they are willing to adapt the product or process according to user needs or provide products at a lower price when the customer's budget is tight, or even give away products for free when customers do not trust them. All in all, they will make the best of their limited resources and seek every opportunity to overtake industrial leaders.

Research on the catching-up countries and companies mainly focuses on electronics, semiconductors, and communications industries in the Asia-Pacific region (especially Japan and South Korea). It is found that those that have successfully overtaken the US and European leaders mainly rely on improving their knowledge systems; pathways include differentiation, forming an alliance, organizational learning, integration, benchmarking, reverse engineering and reverse investment, D&R (rather than R&D). The recipe for success is to internalize external resources to form iterative development and absorption and integration capabilities. Meanwhile, as a latecomer, catching-up companies can have the mass production and marketing advantage once they are positive about customers' response to the new product or service. The imitation and follow-up strategy may have a greater advantage than the first-mover advantage.

The entry point is also critical for catching-up companies. According to W. Abernathy and J. Utterback's research,[6] the technological development trajectory of leading countries can be divided into three stages: the fluid phase, the transitional phase, and the specific phase.

In the fluid phase, the rate of disruptive innovation is high, but the new technology is usually rough, expensive, and not reliable, but it can meet the needs of some market segments. Tech start-ups and large firms will invest in these new technologies, but the market is volatile. So, firms need a flexible structure to respond to changes promptly and effectively in the market.

In the transitional phase, a variety of technologies will be eliminated or integrated, and the dominant design will emerge. The focus of the industry will shift to improving the dominant design and mass production of the design. Competition emphasis shifts from product innovation toward process innovation, as process innovation is vital to costs reduction. If newcomers initiate radical business model innovation, they have the chance to reshape the industry.

In the specific phase, as the market matures, and the price war becomes increasingly fierce; production processes are automated, integrated, and systematic, and rigorously standardized high-quality products become more important.

The fluid phase witnesses the high rates of technology elimination and disruptive innovation; the transitional phase, radical process innovation, and business model innovation. The specific phase, on the other hand, witnesses lower disruptive innovation of both products and processes; emerging technologies are developed into mature technologies. Research shows that the technological trajectory of catching-up countries not only covers the specific phase, but also the fluid and transitional phases. It is possible for catching-up companies to lead in the application and diffusion of new technologies after they successfully acquired, absorbed, and improved the mature technologies of leading countries and mastered the core innovative technologies. Then with cost and operational advantage, they may have breakthroughs, overtake leading companies, and become leaders themselves. When a large number of firms in catching-up countries reach this point, the overall economic competitiveness of these countries will catch up with the leading countries.

---

[6] Abernathy, W.J., and M. Utterback. 1978. Patterns of innovation in technology. *Technology Review*, 80 (7): 40-47.

Why Study Huawei?

Professor Geshenkelong's research focuses on the catching up of the former Soviet Union and Eastern European countries in industrialization. In the context of informatization instead of industrialization and globalization instead of localization, how did China catch up? Since the reform and opening up program kicked off, the catching-up process of China in industrialization and informatization has been characterized by fast speed, large scale, and complicated structures. Whether it is the support of government policies, the advancement of state-owned enterprises (SOEs) and private firms, the application of the Internet and mobile Internet, or consumer penetration, China is one of the best performers in the world. The breadth, depth, and speed of the development of the information and Internet industries have had a global impact and have attracted worldwide attention. The vigorous development of the industries has created a favorable external environment but does not guarantee the emergence of large enterprises. In a market of fierce competition, how did Huawei grow from a small company with limited resources into an international giant? What are its philosophy, strategies, and stories? These are the issues of particular interest to us.

Huawei started with 20,000 yuan (about 3000 USD) in 1987. In 2017, Huawei's sales revenue was 603.6 billion yuan (about 87.76 billion USD), ranking 83rd in Fortune Global 500. Together with carriers, Huawei has built over 1,500 networks worldwide, connecting more than one-third of the world's population. It sells over 100 million mobile phones each year. Huawei operates in 170 plus countries, with 19.4 million employees, over 900 branch offices, 14 research centers, and 36 joint innovation centers. According to WIPO, Huawei came out on top of the 2015 Top PCT[7] Applicants; its competitor Samsung ranked fourth and Ericsson, sixth. Its revenue was also growing fast (see Fig. 2). Meanwhile, according to Interbrand's 2017 Best Global Brands Report, Huawei ranked 70th. Huawei is the third fastest-growing company in terms of brand value after Facebook and Adobe. The ranking evaluated not only the financial indicators but also consumer feedback. Also, the company's profit must be expected to be positive over the longer term.

Nevertheless, in terms of assets, Huawei is not one of the largest. And you will not find Ren Zhengfei, the name of its founder, on any richest people list not even in China. For many years, Huawei keeps a low profile, yet it has won more attention and respect from the media, the business circle, and the society at large than any other Chinese company.

After nearly 10 years of data accumulation, verification, and exploration, the author and the research team hope to understand, analyze, and interpret Huawei in a rational, objective, systematic and down-to-earth manner, so as to discover and summarize Huawei's philosophy, strategies, development trajectory, and key success factors. In the last decade, we observed and confirmed various facts from multiple dimensions and collected and sorted out different opinions at multiple levels. Thanks to our curiosity for this great company and thirst for learning, we have maintained our

[7] Patent Cooperation Treaty.

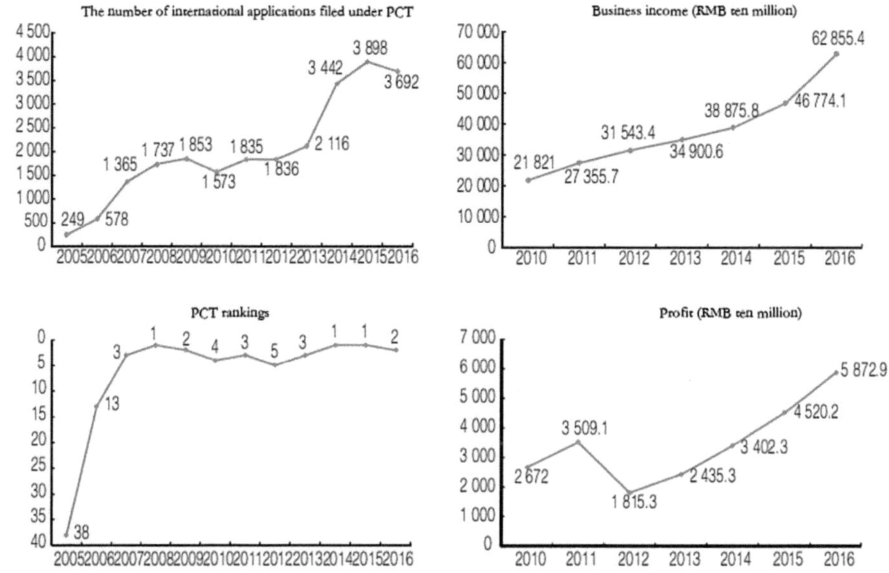

Fig. 2 PCT filings, revenue, and profit of Huawei

research passion. During the research, we followed the principles of independence, neutrality, and objectivity. The author's another book—*Cisco: From Innovation to Operation*, a work product of a 5-year study on the company has provided excellent materials to compare the innovation and management performance of these two ICT giants.

We are aware that in terms of breadth, depth, complexity, and speed of development, the Huawei story is beyond our capacity. But nevertheless, as researchers, we feel like it's our calling to record the story of a group of hard-working "nobodies", who have put Huawei on the world map.

Contents

Part I From Technology Follower to Market Leader: What Did Huawei Do Right?

1 The Eagle Model 3
- 1.1 Thinking Patterns 5
- 1.2 Strategies 7
- 1.3 Corporate Culture 8
- 1.4 Organizational Skills 9
- 1.5 Organizational Change and Capacity Building 10
- 1.6 Human Resources 11
- 1.7 Organizational Learning and Knowledge Management 12
- 1.8 R&D and Innovation System 14
- 1.9 Market Competition System 15
- 1.10 Management System and Platform 16

2 Can Huawei Model Be Copied? 19

Part II Case Studies

3 Huawei's Unique Thinking System and Strategic Leadership 25
- 3.1 Rational Heroism and Noble Realism 26
- 3.2 Adversity Is a Great Treasure 28
- 3.3 The Focus of the Top Leader 29
- 3.4 Strategic Thinking in Uncertainties 32
- 3.5 Paradox Thinking of the Leadership 36
- 3.6 The Power of Unity and Sharing 41
- 3.7 Self-management of Leadership 42
- 3.8 Huawei Versus Cisco 44

4 From a Mom-and-Pop Operation to a World-Class Player 49
- 4.1 Start-up Phase: The Survival Period (1987–1996) 51
- 4.2 Standardization Phase: From a Local Company to a Multinational Company (1997–2007) 57

4.3 Marketing Phase: Toward a Multinational Company (2008–2011) ... 67
4.4 Branding Phase: Building a Consumer-Centric Premium Brand (2012–2016) ... 70
4.5 Digitization Phase: The World's Leading Digital Company (2017–Present) ... 72
4.6 Huawei's Transformation Methodology ... 75
4.7 Success Factors for Huawei's Transformation ... 77
4.8 Huawei Versus Cisco ... 80

5 Corporate Culture and Practice Integrated with Key Interest Groups ... 83
5.1 Service Is at the Heart of Corporate Culture ... 85
5.2 Core Culture I: Customer Centricity ... 86
5.3 Core Culture II: Dedication ... 89
5.4 Core Culture III: Self-reflection ... 91
5.5 Core Culture IV: Openness, Compromise, Grayness ... 100
5.6 Consensus Building Through the *Huawei Basic Law* ... 101
5.7 Huawei Versus Cisco ... 106

6 Rational and Controlled R&D Innovation System ... 111
6.1 The Status and Inputs of R&D ... 113
6.2 The R&D System Development ... 115
6.3 Early R&D Principles ... 118
6.4 R&D Organization Design and Management ... 121
6.5 Innovative Use of Internal and External Resources ... 123
6.6 Innovation Climate ... 126
6.7 A Two-Wheel-Drive: Basic Research and Applied Research ... 129
6.8 Huawei Versus Cisco ... 132

7 A Cobweb Organizational Structure ... 137
7.1 Principles and Methodology of Organizational Design ... 139
7.2 Business Leadership Model for Organizational Change ... 143
7.3 Huawei's Organizational Change Process ... 147
7.4 RJC: A Regional Commissioner Agency ... 153
7.5 Iron Triangle: Customer-Facing Field Operational Units ... 155
7.6 The Elite Team: A Pool of Resources to Assist the Front Line ... 160
7.7 Huawei Versus Cisco ... 162

8 Management Transformation and System Building in Line with International Standards ... 165
8.1 The Strategic Value of the Management System for Catch-up Firms ... 167
8.2 Objectives and Focus of the Management System ... 170
8.3 The Principle of Balance in the Management System ... 174
8.4 Principles and Objectives of Management Change ... 177
8.5 Huawei's IT Capacity Building ... 191

8.6 Risk Management 195
8.7 Huawei Versus Cisco 198

9 A Dynamic and Empowering Organizational Learning System 201
9.1 Organizational Learning Builds Key Competencies 202
9.2 Approach and Evolution of Organizational Learning 204
9.3 Organizational Learning and Knowledge Dissemination 210
9.4 Openness and Diversity of Learning 215
9.5 Formation and Accumulation of Organizational Memory 216
9.6 Construction and Development of Huawei University 218
9.7 Evolution of Organizational Learning 225
9.8 Huawei Versus Cisco 229

10 Human Resource Development System to Unlock Potential 233
10.1 Organizational Talent System 234
10.2 The Value of the Rotating CEO System 236
10.3 Cultivate Talent with Practice-Based Training 238
10.4 The Qualities of Managers 241
10.5 Selecting Managers 246
10.6 A Comprehensive Incentive Mechanism for Continuous Motivation 252
10.7 Huawei Versus Cisco 260

11 Knowledge Management Integrating Organizational Knowledge 263
11.1 Strategic Awareness of Knowledge Assets 265
11.2 Institutionalized Respect for Knowledge 266
11.3 Key Paths to Closing the Knowledge Gap 268
11.4 Evolution of KM at Huawei 272
11.5 KM Platform 277
11.6 Community of Practice 279
11.7 Project-Based KM 281
11.8 Management of Knowledge Content and Assets 286
11.9 Huawei Versus Cisco 287

Part III Research Papers

12 How Huawei Broke Through the Triple Dilemmas to Build Dual Capability? 293
12.1 Triple Dilemmas to Build Dual Capability 293
12.2 Huawei's Dual Capability Model 295
12.3 The Separation Strategy 297
12.3.1 Exploration Activities 297
12.3.2 Application Activities 303
12.3.3 Separation Strategy 1: Job Rotation 308
12.3.4 Separation Strategy 2: Focus Principle 310
12.4 Integration Strategy 311

12.4.1 Self-reflection and the Grayness Principle 312
12.4.2 Resource Integration 315
12.4.3 Customer Centricity 316
12.4.4 Equity Incentive 317
12.4.5 Management Platform 319
12.5 How Huawei Overcame the Triple Dilemma of Dual-Capability Building 320
12.5.1 Getting out of the Resource Contention Dilemma 320
12.5.2 Get out of the Paradigm Conflict 323
12.5.3 Getting out of the Closed Loop Dilemma 325
12.6 Conclusion 327

13 Huawei Phones: From Low-End to High-End 331
13.1 Initiating Products Upgrading (2003–2010) 331
13.2 Upgrading Phase (2011–2013) 332
13.3 Upmarket Brand Phase (2014–Present) 335
13.4 Recipe to Success 337
13.4.1 The Core Role of the Leaders in Product Upgrading ... 338
13.4.2 The Relationship Between Product Innovation and Complementary Assets in Large Companies 340
13.5 From Low-End to High-End: Huawei Stories 343

Appendix A: Representative Self-reflection Events of Huawei 345

Appendix B: Huawei Joint Innovation Centers (JICs) 349

Part I
From Technology Follower to Market Leader: What Did Huawei Do Right?

Chapter 1
The Eagle Model

The harpy eagle, also known as royal-hawk, is the largest and most powerful raptor in the Amazon rainforest. The young eagle has to go through relentless training by its mother not long after it was born. The mother eagle will take the eaglet to a treetop or a cliff, and then drop it. Some timid eaglets will fall and die. The survivors will continue to face the most horrifying test: most of the bones in their wings will be broken by their mother, and then they will be pushed again from the height. Many eaglets die from the test, but the mother eagle will not go soft on the "bloody" training. Some hunters felt sorry for the eaglets with broken wings and secretly brought them home, but only found later that these home-raised eaglets could not fly high, as their two-meter-long wings became a huge burden. It turns out that broken bones are the key to soar. The eagle's wing bones have a strong regenerative ability, as long as the eaglets can endure the pain and continue to fly after their bones have been broken, the wings will continue to be congested, and soon they will be able to recover and soar.

This book systematically summarizes Huawei's development in the past three decades. Based on the comparison between Huawei and Cisco, the book summarizes an Eagle Model (see Fig. 1.1) to explain how Huawei has evolved from a technology follower to a market leader. Each of the ten elements in the Eagle Model has rich meanings and is correlated with other elements. The ten elements form a strong synergy as "the whole is greater than the sum of its parts" and support the "Eagle" to soar under any weather.

As the figure shows, the Eagle Model consists of ten interconnected elements. We can line up these ten elements into one column and three rows. The four elements lined up in the column are thinking patterns, strategies, corporate culture, and management system and platform.

Huawei likes to use military strategies to guide its commercial operations. The leadership's rational, strategic, forward-looking thinking, paradox thinking, critical thinking, as well as values, heroism, and optimism behind all these thinking patterns are essential to Huawei's strategic positioning and path selection. Their thinking

X. Dong et al., *Huawei*,
https://doi.org/10.1007/978-981-19-4078-1_1

Fig. 1.1 The eagle model

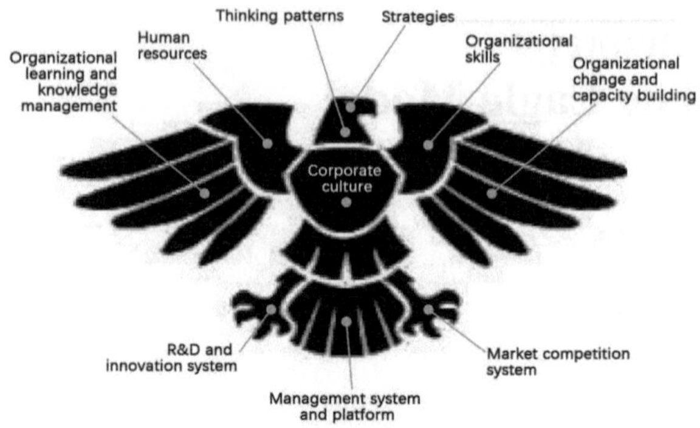

patterns and values determine the center of gravity of Huawei and foster stability, vision, rationality, restraint and focus in its choices and decision-making.

Huawei's thinking patterns determine its strategic focus. That is why Huawei can resist temptations and interference when making investment decisions. Huawei demonstrates a high degree of focus and dedication and refuses to let investment fads go into its head. This is how the company manages to always focus on the long-term goals and moves forward along its main strategic businesses.

The corporate culture represents Huawei's *Tao* (guiding principles). It values "customer-centricity, dedication, and perseverance". It puts people (customers and employees alike) at the core, and regards dedication as the code of conduct, setting the tone of Huawei's corporate culture featured by result-orientation, and down-to-earthiness.

The management system and the platform are the company's tools to build it into "a world-class company". Guided by the principle of rigidifying, solidifying, and optimizing, Huawei used foreign bricks to build China Town", meaning it adopted mature management systems, processes, and methods from overseas leading companies, to lay a solid foundation for resources consolidation and scaled operation. At the "tail" of the "eagle" are the management system and the platform, which are the key for strategic execution, coordination, and balance.

Horizontally, what supports the two wings are three sets of contradictions. Human resources and organizational skills are the most critical forces to ensure the success of a firm; organizational learning and knowledge management are the enabling systems to improve human resources while organizational change and capacity building are the enabling systems to improve organizational skills. With the support of the two wings, the energy of the "eagle" eventually converges on the two "claws": the R&D and innovation system and the market competition system. The former is a comprehensive set of Huawei's products and services while the latter signifies Huawei's overall strength to meet global customer needs.

Huawei's success stems from two aspects. First, the high degree of consistency and alignment between the thinking patterns, strategies, corporate culture, and the management system and the platform, which forms an efficient support system from *Tao* to tools, and from thought to practice. Second, the balance struck between human resources and organizational skills, between their respective enabling systems as well as between the R&D system and the market system.

The so-called paradox refers to two seemingly opposing but correlated elements. The two opposites are not only competing with each other but also interdependent and transforming into each other. The paradox thinking prevents people from going to extremes of black or white (either/or) thinking. It helps people embrace rather than reject contradictions. Paradox thinking emphasizes that a pair of two opposites are also correlated; therefore, conflicts shall not be repressed, excluded, or dismissed. Instead, a proactive management approach should be adopted to balance the two opposites dynamically, and fully tap the potential of mutual transformation. We shall use creative ways to develop both ends while identifying ways to create and increase value between the two opposites.

For example, in the early days when Huawei was dealing with the relationship between the R&D system and the market system, by following the principles of "controlled innovation", "nurturing businessman with an engineering background", "customer-centered innovation", Huawei focused on what's good for both innovation and market. With the ultimate goal of survival in mind, Huawei integrates efforts on both fronts to minimize innovation failure. In recent years, with the changing external competitive environment and its own capacity, Huawei has dynamically adjusted the proportion and total amount of inputs into the R&D system and the market system. Built on product and technology innovation, theoretical innovation and cutting-edge innovation have been reinforced so that its R&D and innovation can lead the market.

Supported by its corporate culture, the goal and interest of the employees and the organization are well aligned and reinforced by a series of systems and governance mechanisms (such as the rotating CEO system, employee stock ownership plan (ESOP), performance evaluation mechanism, etc.), with minimized internal and external risks of conflict and division.

Huawei also strikes a dynamic balance between organizational learning and knowledge management on the one hand and organizational reform and capacity building on the other. That is a balance between inheritance and change. This way it can ensure the stability and sharing of the firm's knowledge system via dynamic mechanisms like empowerment and rotation, and adapt continuously through organizational reforms. During the process, the individual and organizational capabilities have been constantly enhanced while the inertia induced by stability and the chaos brought about by changes can both be reduced.

1.1 Thinking Patterns

In the Eagle Model, the brain represents Huawei's thinking patterns. Thinking patterns reflect the epistemology and compass of the firm's rational thinking and judgment, and its dominant logic system for the interpretation of the external environment and assessment of its capability. Huawei is supported by a sound and profound philosophical system. The leadership's thinking patterns are Huawei's lighthouse.

What is commendable is that the corporate philosophy is systematically manifested by the leader's speeches and organizational documents, which play an essential role in enhancing organizational consensus. Huawei's practice can be regarded as the implementation and manifestation of the corporate philosophy. The organizational memory built on the philosophy and practices is a key force of unity. Therefore, Huawei's success is first and foremost attributed to its philosophy and independent judgment.

Focus and dedication

Survival (especially long-term survival) has always been the core goal of Huawei. Although Huawei has faced enormous investment opportunities and easy money, it is always capable of resisting the temptation, delaying gratification, and staying focus on its core businesses. With honest hard work, down-to-earth practices, ingenuity, perseverance, and focus, Huawei has made a tough choice and made a difference in a road less taken. Some may think that success comes too late with too big a price. However, it is the pioneering spirit that ensures the company stays competitive. Ren Zhengfei believes that the more lucrative the sector is, the competitive it will be, hence a higher rate of failure. Only on the "no man's land", a sector ignored by many, can one's dedication yield to unique competitiveness.

Sense of urgency

In order to survive, the sense of urgency, danger, fear, and insecurity are always part of Huawei's dominant thinking. After studying a large number of failed cases in history, and in both military and industrial sectors, Huawei's leaders hope to spot signals and traps of failures, and carefully and rationally explore business development paths, with the focus on the stability of the current operation and future growth. Ren is never content with past honors; he always has a sense of urgency. He is quite low-key and doesn't mind being left alone. Ren embraces the future and always explores future pain points together with the customers. Huawei's sense of urgency is stemmed from its executives' profound understanding of the industry dynamics and the cutting-throat competition. Huawei leaders have transformed this sense of insecurity both externally and internally. Externally, it is manifested as a high degree of alert to the future and the external world, dynamic scanning, R&D, forward-looking strategic layout, and new capability building. Huawei spares no effort to study its competitors from home and abroad to better understand the gap with the industrial leaders, and avoid strategic misjudgment and blind spots. Huawei has also transmitted the external competitive pressure to internal pressure and continuously motivates the organization and prevents inertia, especially in good times.

Self-reflection and self-knowledge

Even in the early days, Ren was aware of the limitations of the individual's strength. To succeed, it needs to gather all forces possible. To that end, the following is essential. First, gather people that are ambitious, passionate, and enterprising to strive for a common vision. Second, understand people and gratify their hierarchy of needs, including being recognized and valued, self-fulfillment, learning and growth, being treated fairly and respected. Third, use the system or institutional innovation to tap people's potential. Fourth, face problems and deficiencies squarely and improve continuously.

Huawei, from the leadership to the grassroots, always remains sober-headed and keeps a low profile. The corporate culture featured by low profile and self-discipline is critical to the transformation from a technology follower to a market leader. First, it helps to stay focused despite distractions. Second, it provides a relatively safe environment for growth. Third, it reduces unwanted controversy.

1.2 Strategies

Strategic focus

In the Eagle model, guided by rational and forward-looking judgment, Huawei has developed a sound methodology to formulate, break down and execute its strategy and realized an upward spiraling closed loop. Through continuous improvement, Huawei's strategic decoding system proves to be very effective in promoting strategic transformation and reform. Huawei has always been highly focused on its strategic goals and moving forward unwaveringly. The leadership of Huawei is committed to corporate missions and values, with a profound understanding of the ruthless competition in the industry, knowing that a little slack may cause fatal damages. Meanwhile, Huawei has a clear understanding of its own weak links. It always keeps a close eye on the gaps with competitors and weak links in resources and capabilities with constant self-criticism and fully understands that only with the concentration of resources and strengths can it win. That is why Huawei always stays focused on its strategy formulation and execution. With that unwavering focus, Huawei makes the best of its resources and has established its core competitiveness.

In the process of catching up, Huawei realized that only by focusing on its priorities can it go deeper, be more solid and competitive. Strategic focus requires resistance to temptations and avarice. In the development of its key capabilities, Huawei uses its best resources to find breakthroughs, and will not scale up until it has taken a strong foothold. In terms of strategic execution, Huawei has established a set of strategic decoding methods at the organizational level, effectively conveying and breaking down the organization's strategic intent to every team and every employee so that each has a clear performance target.

Strategic transformation

Huawei has a good pace of strategic transformation and has struck a dynamic balance between upgrading and stability. Strategic transformation not only helps the company enter new markets but also upgrades its capability system. Based on the author's observation, over the past 30 years, Huawei has experienced four major transformations.

The first transformation is from a "peasant army" to a "regular army". In 1995 when the communications industry was booming and witnessed fierce competition among domestic and foreign manufacturers, Huawei with less than 1.5 billion USD announced its vision to be a world-class company. Its goal was to make its production and management aligned with international practice in three years, marketing, five years, and become an international technology leader in ten years.

The second transformation is from centralized management to market-oriented management. In 2006, Huawei entered the international market and bridged the gap with its international competitor. However, later the M&As of the giants again widened the gap. Against this background, Huawei launched a new round of restructuring, Ren pointed out that the focus of competition had shifted to competition for customer resources; therefore, Huawei needed to transform from centralized management to truly market-oriented management and let people who can hear the shots call the shots. To achieve this new strategic goal, Huawei launched a new round of reform on finance, IT systems, management processes, and authorization.

The third transformation is from 2B to 2C. In 2011, guided by the strategic "Cloud-Network-End" positioning, Huawei for the first time launched a transformation from 2B to 2C, and vigorously developed its smartphone business. With the focus shifted from engineering to design, from products to branding, Huawei has joined the ranks of the top three smartphone vendors.

The fourth transformation from a brick-and-mortar business to a digital one has just started. In 2017, building on its cloud strategy, Huawei explicitly proposed a digital transformation strategy. In the process of the strategic transformation, Huawei not only conducts meticulous due diligence but also has clear strategic intent. It not only has a methodology of strategy formulation but also has strict execution teams supported by performance evaluation systems. All these elements have made Huawei a fine example of strategic transformation.

1.3 Corporate Culture

Corporate culture is at the heart of the Eagle Model. If the brain determines rationality, the heart generates emotion. The corporate culture focuses on care and warmth.

People-centered

People—both customers and employees—are the center of focus of Huawei. Employees dedicated to meeting customers' needs are recognized by the company. Huawei smartly connects the two most important stakeholders, so that employees can clearly understand the code of conduct and performance standards. Huawei's corporate values are simple, plain, and straightforward, so they are easy to relate to.

Self-criticism

Self-criticism is one of Huawei's driving mechanisms. Criticism and self-criticism are one of the three work styles of the Communist Party of China (CPC). Huawei borrows it as a major method for self-reflection. The value of self-criticism lies in facing the problem head-on, telling the truth, and being humble. Huawei people always focus on the merits of customers and competitors to constantly improve themselves. Thanks to self-criticism, Huawei is able to continuously identify problems, look for ways to effectively solve them, and thus achieve continuous improvement. Self-criticism helps Huawei fly like an eagle under any weather with calmness, play to its strength while avoiding its weakness, and grow. Even when days are good, it will not get smug. Self-criticism is relatively easy at the catching-up phase, as the firm is fully aware of its short links; it will be difficult when the firm grows big. However, self-criticism is exactly what big firms need to stave off arrogance, self-righteousness, and prejudice.

Openness and inclusiveness

Openness, inclusiveness, and flexibility help Huawei to adapt. These values help Huawei to coexist harmoniously with others in all weathers. In a chaotic environment, one should be flexible and identify the right timing in accordance with the time and space. One should abandon recklessness, rigidity, intolerance, single value, the linear mindset, and thinking in absolute terms. Instead, one should explore alternatives, making space for adjustment and recovery for oneself and others.

1.4 Organizational Skills

In the Eagle Model, Huawei's organizational system sits on its right wing as the most important force for its continued success. The system has two essential characteristics: a well-connected organizational network and an activated organizational system.

A well-connected organizational network

Ren once compared Huawei's organizational system to a resilient cobweb and pointed out that it was an important foundation for cross-department collaboration, teamwork, and resilience. A well-connected organizational network first and foremost is knitted with the common vision, the common goal, and common interests. With 30-plus years of painstaking effort, the bonding between a group of founders cemented through brutal competitions has become key nodes of the network. Senior management debriefing sessions, the military-style training system, the zigzag talent training model, and other methods have formed a shared memory of the organization and a diversified network structure, which further strengthens the organizational links. Team performance-based promotion mechanism, the "Iron Triangle Operation Unit" motivates teams to support and assist each other. The three-year rotation system makes it difficult to form self-interested factions and allows every manager to fit in the new position as soon as possible. It is this resilient cobweb-like organizational system that makes Huawei people resilient. That is why Huawei people always toast those who succeed and offer a helping hand to those who fail.

A dynamic organizational system

Passion and vitality were not an issue in the days when Huawei strived to catch up, but with expanding scale and greater visibility, how to maintain passion and vitality is a matter of special concern to senior management. Huawei is always wary of slackness and bureaucracy, common vices of large firms. Ren repeatedly warns all employees to heed risks especially in good times and points out that slackness in thinking is the biggest obstacle to development.

Huawei adopts radical means to restructure the organization system to activate the company and prevent slackness, including a flexible mechanism where the manager should be ready to take a lower as well as a higher post, last-place elimination, sustained high pressure, collective resignation of the marketing department, senior researchers posted to the international market, lower the average age of the employees, but the incentives are always tilted toward the toughest positions.

1.5 Organizational Change and Capacity Building

In the Eagle Model, the capacity system is the enabler of the organizational system. A strong Huawei is not because someone is strong, but because of its strong and self-renewal capacity. Huawei's leadership believes in the theory of dissipative structures. A dissipative structure in a dynamic-orderly operation would be formed in the system far from the equilibrium state under the following condition: the system must be open and far from the equilibrium state. The system exchanges matter, energy, and information with the external environment constantly. When a parameter in the system reaches the bifurcation, the system jumps into a new orderly state from an unstable state and a dissipative structure appears. Huawei needs the dissipative structure to introduce new energy and achieve upward spiraling growth.

Capacity building first

Huawei has always put capacity building first and never cut corners. Even in the early days, Ren has realized that capacity building is much more important than wealth accumulation. He believes that the value of intellectual property and technology know-how outweighs capital, as capital can only maintain or increase its value when it is attached to knowledge. If you don't want to be vulnerable, you need to master the core technology. At the organizational level, the best defense is an offense; to create new advantages, you need to give up existing ones. For the company's strategic development, the most important thing is not just possessing the knowledge, but the ability and vision to obtain and apply knowledge. Under the guidance of this understanding, Huawei's development path is different in the following aspects: First, investing hugely in R&D even when the budget is tight. Second, prioritizing knowledge transfer and capacity building in its globalization. Selling products is not a priority for Huawei. Instead, Huawei would always firstly build a competence center close to an international leader, such as Ericsson and Cisco; it also built one in India and later in Russia, Israel, and France to leverage local strengths. In Ren's view, truly visionary leaders would not be stingy with investment in the future.

Absorptive capacity

Huawei values proven solutions at home and abroad and systematically introduces the world's top solutions and best practices (such as from the US military, international consulting companies, etc.). To build a world-class company, Huawei put management capacity and product quality first, as it recognizes that a strong system that attracts talent, technology, and capital can only be built on good management. Huawei introduced IBM's integrated product development (IPD) process. It follows the principles of rigidifying, solidifying, and optimizing to ensure the comprehensiveness and integrity of the introduction. Based on a systematic understanding of the process, adaptive adjustments will be made according to the practices of the past years so that the capacity building is solid and thorough and Huawei's R&D system can promptly accept, absorb and digest external knowledge and align with international practice as quickly as possible.

1.6 Human Resources

In the Eagle Model, human resources are the most critical factor for Huawei to catch up and take the lead. Life in Huawei can be both lucky and miserable. Lucky, because ambitious young people can have enormous and fair opportunities to learn and grow fast. Miserable, because the work intensity, pressure, and challenges in Huawei are extraordinary, and sometimes people have to work away from their families and homeland. How to give meaning to this hardship is the key to attracting and retaining talents.

Military-like efficiency and courage

Huawei's talents grow up in tough conditions, and have some common qualities: they are hard-working, modest, studious, aggressive, candid, tenacious, inquisitive, self-disciplined, honest, altruistic, self-sacrificing, etc. From these qualities, you may find that Huawei people are as tough, persistent, and courageous as soldiers, and as inquisitive, passionate, and sincere as students. These qualities have everything to do with the following three main mechanisms of Huawei: First, the promotion mechanism. In Huawei, promotion is based on performance and merit. Such a fair, objective, and transparent promotion mechanism helps increase employees' satisfaction and loyalty. People can focus on their work rather than waste their energy on office politics. Second, the incentive mechanism tilted toward positions with the most difficult conditions and best results. The message of Huawei is loud and clear: those who are willing and can work in difficult conditions and rise to challenges will be supported and profusely compensated. Third, the mechanism that taps into the potential and passion of Huawei people. Huawei requires its senior managers have a sense of mission, middle managers, a sense of urgency, and junior managers, a sense of hunger. It is the sense of mission that guides the company to strive and grow.

The governance mechanism and a community of shared interests

Due to various reasons, Huawei does not choose to go public, but the Employee Stock Ownership Plan (ESOP) helps reduce internal frictions. Public companies usually have to take a lot of time and energy to balance the interests between internal and external shareholders, between major and minor shareholders, and between investors and company founders. If the interests of the stakeholders do not align, for example, some pursue short-term gains, while others seek long-term development, strategy formulation will be very consuming. The ESOP scheme of Huawei and the fact that Ren only holds an insubstantial portion of total shares help shape the collective will of the company: the corporate and personal goals are highly aligned, reducing strategic conflicts while gathering collective willpower and knowledge for common development, thus forming a strong community of shared interests. Meanwhile, the company greatly reduces the coordination costs and conflicts between stakeholders without the constraints of external shareholders so that funds can be channeled to the critical fields for future development. In addition, the ESOP scheme serves three purposes: it unifies shareholders; it establishes a highly efficient internal financing mechanism; it also constrains and checks and balances behaviors that might bring harm to the business.

1.7 Organizational Learning and Knowledge Management

In the Eagle Model, organizational learning and knowledge management is the best enabler of human resources. Knowledge and effort are the best friends of hundreds of thousands of hardworking Huawei people with a humble background. Huawei's talent selection mechanism is tilted toward those who can find problems, and explore ways to solve them, and those who grow by drawing on experience and lessons from both failure and success. That is why in Huawei learning is endogenous, and employees are always inquisitive, and learning is a big part of their career.

Work as learning

Unlike many corporate learning systems, Huawei's organizational learning is integrated into every link of work; work as learning has become the norm. The most obvious manifestation of a strong ambition is a strong thirst for knowledge. The top leaders set a good example by writing articles about their learnings and disseminates them throughout the organization. The organizational learning system almost contains everything and penetrates every corner of Huawei. It could be reflections on failed cases in Chinese history or world history; it could be the world's military establishment and military systems; it could be analysis of the global markets or field trips to leading companies around the world; it could be feedback from researchers over a coffee or consumers for product and service improvement; it could be business analysis and R&D framework learned from IBM or summary and methodology based on its own service system and practices; it could be a debriefing session or a self-criticism session...

The humbleness, hunger, competitive learning, knowledge redundancy, the zigzag development of human resources of Huawei all aim to make the organization stay open-minded and innovative, so that the velocity and density of its knowledge flow are greater than its competitors. In particular, the debriefing sessions can help convey the strategic intentions top down.

On-the-job training

Another important feature of Huawei's organizational learning system is on-the-job training. Question-oriented interactive communication helps to make tacit knowledge explicit, and passive experience valuable wealth. It also turns questions and conversations into knowledge in the shortest time frame. Huawei's organizational learning system is targeted, practical, interdepartmental and interregional, competitive, and even confrontational. Targeted means the learning is always question-oriented, the question may be philosophical or realistic. Practical means knowledge impartment and research should effectively solve practical problems and confusions for the team and/or business development. No matter for senior management debriefings, team discussions, or the study groups, the team members must be interdepartmental and interregional, as diversity increases knowledge redundancy as well as ideas and solutions. Meanwhile, the organizational memory formed in the interdepartmental and interregional learning helps to establish and enhance inter-departmental links, cooperation, and collaboration. Competitive means ceaseless competition within and between various teams in Huawei to select the most valuable solutions. In the competitions between the smartest, potentials are tapped into to the extreme, and they appreciate one another; everyone is a winner in such competitions. Confrontational refers to the military-style competitions between the blue and red teams. Through the confrontational competitions, shortcomings and blind spots are identified on both sides, and solutions are perfected.

Knowledge is essential

Expertise is usually the strongest suit for a catching-up company. Huawei's knowledge management has gone through several phases. Phase 1: knowledge acquisition. As a newcomer in the industry, Huawei spared no effort in acquiring knowledge from competitors and customers alike by imitation, copy, and reverse engineering. Phase 2: knowledge absorption and protection-oriented knowledge management. On the one hand, Huawei invested heavily in the introduction of the Western management system to internalize external knowledge effectively. In the process, while carefully evaluating knowledge and introducing the most experienced consultants, by rigidifying, solidifying, and optimizing, Huawei comprehensively absorbs external knowledge and internalize it. On the other hand, with increasing R&D investment and technical accumulation, Huawei also started focusing on the protection of its technology and intellectual property rights. Especially after a number of incidents of knowledge loss, Huawei's effective protection of knowledge later becomes exemplary in the industry. Phase 3: knowledge integration and reuse. With the global expansion, Huawei needs to effectively integrate fragmented knowledge to improve the efficiency of the use and sharing of knowledge; therefore, knowledge platform development was put on the agenda. Huawei attaches great importance to the reuse of knowledge in R&D. It draws an analogy between the flower-manure relationship and the new knowledge-old knowledge relationship. It believes that the effective use of old knowledge can improve the efficiency of R&D and reduces costs. At present, Huawei's knowledge management practices are penetrated in all business links, and Huawei people are all aware of the importance of knowledge management. Activities like knowledge acquisition, knowledge sharing, and knowledge practice community help the company efficiently absorb lessons learned in practice and share them as much as possible within the company, laying a solid foundation for a world-class knowledge-intensive organization.

1.8 R&D and Innovation System

In the eagle model, the R&D and innovation system and the market competition system are the two claws, which are the manifestations of Huawei's core competitiveness. The reasons that Huawei can survive and thrive are two folds: first, its competitive technologies and products; second, its channel and marketing system, which makes its technologies and products visible and recognized by customers in the global market.

Controlled innovation

Huawei's R&D system is built step by step: from imitation to controlled innovation, from progressive innovation focused on product improvement to the 2012 Laboratory for future-oriented disruptive innovation. Huawei's three-decade intensive R&D investment stems from its profound understanding that only by grasping the core technology system can it avoid being at the mercy of others. Meanwhile, Huawei also goes all out to minimize the failure and waste in R&D and improve the return on investment and success rate of R&D. The key is to link R&D with the market while focusing on accumulation, reuse, and passing on of knowledge as well as the development process and quality management. In the development of the R&D system, Huawei has always been wary of excessive innovation. Guided by the paradox thinking, Huawei always examines the two sides of innovation. As Ren said: "Innovation and revolution always involve disruption. So, it is not easy to balance innovation and stability and figure out the appropriate pace and degree of change. In many cases, innovation is just a patching-up. Changes may bring about solutions, but they also may cause failure. That is why we need to be wary of excessive innovation." Huawei's innovations may not be as disruptive as those in Silicon Valley, but they are relevant to the market and customer needs, responsive to industrial development, and highly compatible with and adapted to corporate capabilities and resources, thus constituting a major weapon for the survival of the company.

Global layout

Of Huawei's 180,000 employees, 80,000 are engaged in R&D; it is by far the world's largest research development team. Huawei's competence centers are concentrated to the north of the Tropic of Cancer, in countries like Israel, UK, France, Italy, Sweden, the Netherlands, Ireland, Russia, Japan, Canada, and the US. Of the top 15 research institutes of Huawei, the number of employees ranges from 1000 to over 10,000; many are top experts in the world. They always keep a close eye on the strategic main businesses to ensure that Huawei does not waste resources on non-strategic businesses. Even within its main business the communications sector, every few years, Huawei cuts off non-strategic departments to ensure stay on course.

1.9 Market Competition System

Marketing with a hands-on attitude

Huawei's marketing started from towns and villages to big cities in China; then it started from developing countries to developed countries in Europe. Building trust is not easy, nor is it for any company to earn 70% of its revenue from overseas markets. In the beginning, even customers in developing countries did not trust Chinese telecommunications products, if not totally dismissed them, let alone customers in developed countries. Gradually some tried out, used some for free, found that they were not bad, and began to buy them. Only those who have gone through the journey can get how far Huawei has come. Not only do the products have to be solid, but the services must go all in. Huawei cannot say no to any job, no matter how hard it is, or how thin the profit is. Only by delivering above and beyond, can Huawei earn respect and reputation after been questioned and nitpicked.

An efficient and collaborative vanguard system

Huawei has a lot of innovations in its market system. It values the collaboration and capabilities portfolio of the frontline teams and their interaction with the organization. It involves complex issues such as management, authorization, control, and coordination of the marketing teams. The organization gives people who can hear the shots call the shots. What's important is to make sure the company management platform effectively supports Iron Triangle Operation Units at frontlines so that professional customer service teams can meet complex customer needs better and faster. Huawei's market system has a three-tier support platform from the regional companies, from the headquarters, and the global competence centers. Huawei's success in the fiercely competitive global market is attributable to its accurate judgment and timely response of the "squad leaders" at the frontline as well as the trust, authorization, and effective support of the company platform.

1.10 Management System and Platform

In the Eagle Model, the management system and platform are located in the rear wings. They have two important functions: one is to integrate systematic strength, and the other is to provide platform support. In the development of Huawei, the management system and platform are the first core competency Huawei built. Based on the study of success stories of multinationals, Ren explored the culture and mindset of Chinese companies to understand why China did not produce any business giants in the last century. He realized that the flexibility, ambiguity, and curiosity of Chinese people make it difficult to establish a stable and controllable management system, which is a very important foundation for large enterprises. According to Ren, a company-level management platform is essential to integrate human, capital, and technology resources to form systematic synergy. Despite severe cultural challenges and barriers to change, Huawei did not give up building and continuously optimizing the platform in the last two decades, laying a solid foundation for building a world-class company.

System integration

The system strength refers to Huawei's capacity-building management through the application of processes, IT, and platforms. The system integration covers the resources of the entire enterprise, including information flow, business flow, capital flow, logistics, and knowledge flow. The integration goes both horizontal and vertical: the horizontal integration mainly integrates resources across sectors, regions, and business units, and the vertical integration integrates resources in the market end and the back-office end. When the company effectively integrates resources at all ends, it can greatly enhance the transparency and efficiency of the resources flow, decision support, supply chain monitoring, end-to-end customer service, and cross-departmental collaboration. In the past 30 years, Huawei has invested heavily in building the system strength to integrate resources. This process has not yet been completed, but as the scale and complexity of the enterprise increase, the system strength will become even more important.

Platform support

Support refers to Huawei's management platform that enables front offices. The front offices refer to the vanguard teams in the global markets, and the platform refers to the two-tiered platform of the regional companies and the headquarters that provide support to the efficient and flexible operations of front offices. The global center of competence provides expertise and knowledge sharing. Huawei has long realized that the future business competition is about information and competition between the frontline project managers. The coordination between the frontline project managers and the regional companies and headquarters is a manifestation of the overall organizational capabilities. The frontline project managers are not supposed to fight alone but instead are supported by the platform. Information flow and knowledge sharing are essential. The structure of front offices supported by the company platform works thanks to Huawei's continuous investment and capacity building in processes, IT, and platforms in the past 30 years. As a result, Huawei has acquired strong resource integration capability, dynamic coordination capability, and accurate analysis capability so that it can provide efficient services to frontline operations in the shortest time possible.

In order that people who can hear the shots have the authority to call the shots and win the "battle", Huawei needs to use this management platform to balance business applications at the front ends, and allocate the right resources at the right time, in the right place, to the right people. The biggest challenge in this process is to dynamically understand the dynamic markets, which puts very high requirements on the information management capabilities.

Chapter 2
Can Huawei Model Be Copied?

Huawei's catching up case certainly illustrates the great momentum as a latecomer just as Professor Gerschenkron points out that the more backward an economy is at the outset of economic development, the more rapid rates of industrial growth. The reform and opening-up policy of China certainly inspired Chinese people's pursuit of wealth, success, and a better life. The hunger for success was like a sleeping volcano that suddenly erupted. Many impoverished yet ambitious Chinese seized this window of opportunity, buried themselves in their work, and tenaciously tried to catch up. With the innovation of ideas, policies, systems, mechanisms, and governance, human capital potential and enthusiasm have been unleashed. With teamwork, a sharing spirit, and collectivism, they move forward against obstacles and challenges. These are the most important strategic resources for backward economies.

Gerschenkron's model has been partially proved by the case study of Huawei. On the one hand, Huawei, to a large extend, has a good understanding of and has followed the concepts, rules, methods, and paths of development in industrialized countries. Especially in the development of its management system, R&D system, and product quality system, Huawei has introduced and implemented the processes, systems, and methodologies of developed countries directly or indirectly, built on which it made its own innovation and development. On the other hand, in the catching-up process, with systematic ideological, institutional, personnel, and organizational innovation, Huawei has outpaced its competitors in the speed, strength, and depth of development.

In terms of ideological innovation, every 5–7 years, Huawei will have a strategic upgrading. Each upgrade will adapt the internal capacity to the external environment and be supported by a new round of capacity building. Each step that Huawei has made is steady, and step by step it hits its preset targets.

In terms of institutional innovation, Huawei's senior management smartly links and integrates the interests and demands of stakeholders and minimizes risks that may compromise the organization's strength. The ESOP scheme aligns with the core objectives and interests of the company and employees. The rotating CEO system resolves the selection and retention of senior executives. The principles of

X. Dong et al., *Huawei*,
https://doi.org/10.1007/978-981-19-4078-1_2

customers first and dedication sort out the relationship between external and internal key stakeholders.

In terms of personnel innovation, Huawei puts human capital before monetary capital and generously rewards those who work hard, learn fast and achieve a lot. The result-based talent selection and evaluation system are objective, fair, and transparent. The "target-path-results" trajectory is visible and greatly reduces uncertainties, which helps to stimulate employees' enthusiasm.

In terms of organizational innovation, through strategic upgrading, the 3-year rotation system, and dynamic reforms, Huawei constantly identifies and eliminates comfort zones that may create corporate inertness so as to maintain organizational vitality and a sense of urgency.

From a technology follower to a market leader, Huawei has come a long way: its employees have gone through painful efforts, pressure, challenges, hardship, doubts, and a sense of insecurities. So, it is hard to say whether the Huawei model can be copied or not. Some may be willing to go the extra mile to achieve more, but others may prefer a work-life balance. So, the difference between companies firstly comes down to the difference in their values and goals.

Huawei's success also has something to do with its special historical background. First, Huawei was founded in the early days of China's reform and opening-up program in Shenzhen, a testing ground for reform; therefore, it enjoyed good policy support and an enabling environment. Second, the expanding global communications and Internet industry generates huge demand. Third, when Huawei entered the market, it was faced with fierce international competition. It has enhanced Huawei's international outlook and industry standards, which in turn compels rapid growth. Fourth, Huawei has seized the opportunities after the 2008 global financial crisis when consumers had more demand for inexpensive products; it also benefits from the Snowden leaks as people began to pay more attention to information security. These external conditions cannot actually be copied.

Despite the external conditions, does Huawei's model have some universal value? Different people may have different answers. China's market environment also needs a diversity of practices and explorations. After a systematic study of Huawei, the author would like to share the following five findings.

First, the entrepreneur's philosophy is the most important element constituting a firm's competitiveness. The company's vision, mission, transformation, revolution, culture, and institutions all stem from the outlook of the entrepreneur on the world, life, and the industrial environment. Therefore, to create a great company, first, we need great entrepreneurship, great entrepreneurs, and great entrepreneurial thinking.

Second, the focus is the precondition for greatness. In the three-decade-long development, Huawei leaders have focused on long-term values. They dare to put all the eggs in one basket, without any doubt, wavering, or slack. In an environment that worships quick success, Huawei has resisted temptations, maintained a low profile, and delayed gratification. With focus and dedication, Huawei eventually excels in depth and differentiation, which would not be possible without absolute faith. Despite the distractions and temptations for quick money, Huawei has been focusing on the R&D of communications technology and product quality, patiently making breakthroughs at the technological frontiers and eventually grows into an industry leader. This focus and dedication are impossible to acquire unless one can overcome short-sightedness and the desire for a quick fix.

Third, corporate culture shapes personality. Working in Huawei is by no means easy. The corporate culture that values customers first, dedication, and perseverance is manifested by a group of businesspeople with an engineering background who are responsible, hardworking, dedicated, and down to earth. They expand markets with honest and hard work, win respect with decade-long dedication, and toast success but also offer a helping hand to those who fail. In Huawei, nepotism does not work. Instead, no matter who you are or where you are from, if you work hard enough, you can make your name in the company.

Fourth, the intensity of competition determines how much respect the company wins. In the global market of intensified competition, Huawei chose a hard path. The more competitive the environment is, the higher requirements for the character and willpower of the leader, strategic decision-making, and execution ability of the enterprise and for the organizational network and organizational learning will be. The character of the entrepreneur is closely related to the vision of the entrepreneur; the strategic decision-making and execution ability of the enterprise depends on the cognitive ability and action of the enterprise; the organizational network depends on the management platform, the organizational memory, as well as cross-departmental collaboration and teamwork; the organizational learning is closely related to target-setting, understanding of knowledge gaps and the organizational value of learning. As a latecomer, Huawei is always aware of the urgency, always remains modest, always faces the challenges squarely, and never be contented with past glories. All these qualities are valuable to a latecomer.

Fifth, tapping into potential is the most important catalyst for catching up. All Huawei's institutions are human-centered, and good institutions should be able to release potential. Huawei tries its best to mobilize and tap into human potential and enthusiasm. Huawei as a late mover is more persistent, more hardworking, more inquisitive, more modest, braver, tougher, and a better team player than many other companies. That is what makes Huawei special.

Nevertheless, people still have concerns about Huawei's future. In the Internet and digital age, Huawei has grown into an industry leader and now faces different challenges and problems. What it takes to grow from 1 to 100 is different from 0 to 1? When it has got the hang of integration of a variety of existing technologies, can it make a breakthrough in the development of original technology? When Huawei people have got used to obedience and execution, can they also be good at creation and making breakthroughs? When it has got used to collectivism, can it also embrace individualism? When it has got used to rapid march with high pressure, can it keep calm and carry on? When Huawei people have got used to doing their part, can they build a Huawei system or a Huawei ecology? Whether it is self-transformation, radical and progressive transformation, or separation and integration, Huawei's future will depend on its disruptive innovation in the industry and market transformation. The failure of most leading companies is due to the restrictions of their past success and core competencies. The unbridled greed, hunger for a bigger size and faster growth, being deaf to criticism or inconvenient truth, and listening only to high praises have crippled many leading companies which underestimate the value of disruptive technologies and missed opportunities for corporate transformation. Fortunately, Huawei has the genes of self-criticism, and always has a soft spot for weird talents and gives them opportunities and scope to make breakthroughs. Therefore, we have full confidence in Huawei's future.

Part II
Case Studies

Chapter 3
Huawei's Unique Thinking System and Strategic Leadership

The viability, strength, and size of a company are key indicators of the comprehensive ability and stamina of the entrepreneur. The practical wisdom of an entrepreneur obtained from fierce competition determines the company's ideals, characters, values, and corporate culture; it is directly reflected in the company's strategic development, resource allocation, and human capital development. According to Ikujiro Nonaka,[1] a Japanese organizational theorist, best known for his study of knowledge management, practical wisdom is tacit knowledge acquired from experience that enables people to make prudent judgments and take actions based on the actual situation, guided by values and morals. Practical wisdom is "common sense in an uncommon degree." Practical wisdom is critical to the following four key issues:

First, the company's long-term goals and perseverance to achieve them. Enterprises usually can focus on development in a stable environment, but in a state of flux, people are often attracted by so-called opportunities and tempted to deviate from their original direction. Over the past 30 years, China has experienced rapid development and breathtaking changes. To stay on their original course requires an unswerving focus of the firms. Therefore, the biggest challenge for business leaders is how to effectively stay focused. The focus of leaders is critical to the organization, especially for a centralized organization, as the focus of leaders can bring the most strategic resources and can be translated into KPIs, especially in the early stage of development. However, the focus is limited, and leaders need to balance between the present and the future, and the internal and the external; they should also be able to tell the relevant from the irrelevant, and strategies from tactics. How to strike a balance and how to tell the difference is part of the art of leadership.

---

[1] Nonaka I., Takeuchi H. The Big Idea: The wise leader[J], *Harvard Business Review*, 2011, 89(5)58–67 146.

X. Dong et al., *Huawei*,
https://doi.org/10.1007/978-981-19-4078-1_3

Second, transforming passion into practical wisdom and rational thinking. Entrepreneurs are usually passionate, but passion is a double-edged sword, which may not only lead to perseverance but also irrational expansion and fatal mistakes. Therefore, a balanced entrepreneur needs to have not only passion, but also practical wisdom and rational thinking. Due to the complexity, volatility, and uncertainty of the development environment, corporate leaders need to have diversified thinking patterns, including rational thinking, strategic thinking, forward-thinking, exploratory thinking, critical thinking, holistic thinking, ambidextrous thinking, and reverse thinking, etc. The cognitive complexity of leaders is critical to navigating a complex environment. To gain this cognitive ability, leaders need to be open-minded about learning and good at communication and sharing. They need to study both successful stories and best practices on the one hand and reflect on failures on the other so that they can continuously improve their depth of thinking and maintain the rationality and objectivity of thinking. The critical thinking of the development environment and the internal system of the enterprise helps the organization to continuously push its boundaries.

Third, effective communication and empathy. The leaders need to convey their values, missions, and vision to win understanding, empathy and support so that the employees are willing to align their effort with the organizational goals with a full understanding of the meaning and value of their hard work.

Fourth, self-knowledge, self-reflection, and self-management. Leaders' introspection, self-knowledge, and self-motivation are critical. Introspection helps them recognize their limitations; therefore, in the case of failure, they will not be devastated. It also helps them discover the value of others and consolidate organizational strength for a common goal. Self-evaluation is an important part of self-management and self-discipline. Effective self-management of the leader has an important balancing effect on the organization so that it will not be arrogant in good times or frustrated in bad times.

Leadership is a philosophy, an art, a culture, but also management. Only with a great personality can a great company be created.

3.1 Rational Heroism and Noble Realism

Ren once said: "When we were small, my mother told us the story of the Hercules. We admired him very much. When we were young and ignorant, we admired big heroes like Li Yuanba and Yu Wencheng. When we read the lines of Li Qingzhao, a great female poet during the Song dynasty in our teens: "One ought to live like a hero in this world, and after death, a hero remains", we were touched by her love for Xiang Yu, a prominent warlord that rebelled against the Qin Dynasty. Of course, heroism is not meaningless. It can drive us to achieve more."[2]

[2] Ren Zhengfei: "The river flows eastward in spring". December 2011.

The hero does not to be perfect. At Huawei, being a hero does not mean being perfect. When summing up his life experience, Ren emphasized that what matters is to give full play to one's strength rather than try to be perfect. From the interviews, we found that Huawei people were honest with the existing difficulties, problems, and shortcomings of the company. Perhaps it is because of the tolerance of imperfections, Huawei people are true to themselves, flexible, confident, and do not have many packages. They seek development despite shortcomings, pursue realistic goals, and give full play to their strength.

Ren never stops self-reflection. He understands that logic and not losing sight of the bigger picture rather than language is his strongest suit. Therefore, he does not care about his language skills but gives full play to his logic. Huawei's development and R&D strategies are also about giving full play to the company's strengths to achieve realistic goals.

In Huawei, heroes are those who align their interests and effort with that of the company. According to our research, the word "hero" appeared 143 times in his speeches and three times in his speech titles. ("Do not forget the hero", Call for heroes", and "Don't be a short-lived hero") Ren believes that Huawei should be a cradle of heroes because what pushes Huawei forward should be over 70% of its outstanding employees rather than a couple of leaders. Those who can truly push the company forward are true heroes.

Huawei heroes have the following traits. First, they are hard-working and dedicated. Any employee who works diligently and responsibly in hardship is regarded as a hero at Huawei. Huawei's marketing teams are the best examples. They worked in the cold and harsh mountainous areas in Yunnan, the desert in the northwest, the blizzards of the Greater Khingan Mountains, and throughout Europe and Africa. Second, they are never contented with the past glory or daunted by difficulties. Third, they are upright. They are never shy of correcting their mistakes or bad habits and are willing to be unsung heroes. Fourth, they are dedicated. For example, in 1995, the entire Marketing Department resigned collectively to make way for a competitive elimination mechanism. Fifth, heroes are also part of the organization; heroism and collectivism are not mutually exclusive. Everyone should emulate a hero, and everyone can be a hero.[3] At Huawei, heroes need to keep abreast of the time and constantly improve themselves. Today's success does not guarantee tomorrow's success. To stay as a hero, one must never stop learning, never be complacent and always go above and beyond.[4]

Heroism is not about big empty words. At Huawei, heroism is manifested in its persistent pursuit of company goals. Ren never advocates vanity goals or encourages *kowtow* or a great leap forward. On the contrary, he advocates realistic and rational goals. Rational heroism and noble realism are the two sides of the same coin. He also understands that if Huawei cannot take the lead in the world, it may go down at any time. For Huawei, to survive is a realistic and rational goal. Viability should be the primary goal of any firm so that it can pay taxes, and the state can use the tax revenue

[3] Ren Zhengfei: "Don't forget the heroes". January 23, 1997.

[4] Ibid.

to care for and support more people. Employees work hard to make themselves and their families happy. They go home with bonuses during the Spring Festival, wash their feet for their loved ones and their parents, and express their sincere love.

Guided by rational idealism, Ren puts forward realistic targets so that the company can travel light: "To see the future, we need to jump out of the box. Today we have the capacity, but we shall not be out of touch with reality. We shall not delude ourselves that we can carry the entire humanity, or the entire society, or the great rejuvenation of the Chinese nation. That would be too much for us. Our target should be simple: every step forward is a victory. It does not have to be a giant stride."[5]

3.2 Adversity Is a Great Treasure

Stay calm and resilient in success and failure. Ren's life has witnessed the ups and downs of China in the past 50 years and has its share of frustration and suffering. In his childhood, he endured hunger and his father was investigated because he was a former KMT official. For the same reason, later, the college admission of his younger sibling was denied. He himself only had a three-year college education and then the Cultural Revolution started. His younger siblings didn't even finish high school. Ren was not a Youth League member in college and did not get admitted to the CPC until 1977 when the Cultural Revolution was officially ended. During the Cultural Revolution, no matter how hard he worked or how much he contributed, he was never commended. Even when his subordinates were awarded, he was not. Such hardship and mental ordeal have built his character. He has learned to keep calm and a low profile and not to seek name and fame. All these adversities have eventually translated into driving forces and opportunities.[6] In the hardship, he realized that the value of unity.[7]

In 1976 when the Cultural Revolution came to an end, Ren's life had a seismic change. Because of his inventions, which filled two national gaps, and honors like "Model Soldier" suddenly flooded in and he was even called a hero. By this time, he had grown indifferent to fame and fortune; many prizes were claimed by others on his behalf, and he shared the bonuses with his colleagues. The two-decade military career had a huge impact on his personality and management style. He once said: "From these 20 years, I have learned obedience, endurance, and patience, especially obedience."[8] These qualities are also reflected in Huawei's culture.

Having something to do is a blessing. Ren's father is his role model. Regardless of unfairness and humiliation, his father always found pleasure in doing stuff. This upbeat attitude has an imprint on Ren. Ren's father was a principal of a technical school during the Cultural Revolution, which was a step-down from his previous

[5] The minutes of the 2012 Laboratory Seminar. July 2, 2012.

[6] Ren Zhengfei: "My youth". July 19, 2006.

[7] Ibid.

[8] Ren Zhengfei: "Do not be a perfect man" at a meeting with model CPC members. May 21, 2008.

position. But he never regarded it as a humiliation; instead, he devoted himself to the new job. As a result, the teaching quality of the school soared with an over 90% enrollment rate. He loved his job so much that he did not retire until he was 75 years old in 1984. He hoped that his children would cherish their time and do a good job at their work too. Ren was inspired by his father. In the difficult early days, such a spirit carried him through. And now even in his seventies, he is still a hands-on leader.

Hardship carries strong willpower. The setbacks and hardship experienced in the adversities have given Huawei a strong resistance to pressure, challenges, and grievances, and immunity to rumors. Ren told his employees repeatedly: "Do not fear rumors; live with peace of mind against rumors."[9] In the last 30 years, Huawei has traveled on a bumpy road and had its share of frustrations, pains, and failures. But Huawei believes that "what rises from the ashes is a phoenix and who climbs out of the mud pit is a great people."[10] Adversities have taught Huawei the value of a low profile and self-reflection, which has protected Huawei, especially in the early days.

Ren's story is a good story for Huawei: adversities can be meaningful. Ren once remarked: "Hardship builds character. You should not judge a company or a department when things are good but rather judge them when everything seems wrong, just like the saying 'Adversity tells the character.'"[11] For Huawei, setbacks and failures are simply the compass pointing the way forward. "Hardships are blessings in disguise. If we have not experienced any hardship, it would be our Achilles' heel."[12] Hardship can carry a company forward. "Of all the strengths that one can possibly obtain, the most powerful strength comes from within."[13]

3.3 The Focus of the Top Leader

The sense of urgency and crisis

What Huawei has achieved so far has everything to do with its sense of urgency and crisis, which stems from not only Ren's reflection upon the failures of former industry leaders but also from the trials and tribulations that Huawei has gone through. The sense of urgency can both drive the company forward and carry it through thick and thin. Ren once said "Over the past ten years, I have been thinking of our possible failure and chose to turn a blind eye to our success. I have never felt glorified by our success or proud of myself, instead, I have developed a sense of crisis. This might be the reason for Huawei's survival. If all of us try to figure out how we can survive, we

[9] Ren's remarks at Huawei Shanghai Research Center in 2010.

[10] Ren Zhengfei: "A glowing youth" at the launching of the network product line. June 13, 2008.

[11] Ren Zhengfei: speech on understanding laws of nature, giving play to the core team, continuously improving the per capita benefits, and working together to overcome difficulties, at the Q3 marketing meeting. 2002.

[12] Ren Zhengfei: "Huawei's winter", *Huawei People*. 2001.

[13] Ren Zhengfei: talks with the participants of the 10th Senior Management Seminar held by Huawei Academy. 2011.

may survive for a much longer time. The day will come when we cannot do anything to save the company. I have no doubt about it. Everyone should be prepared. Things have developed this way since the beginning of human history. I don't know if all the employees have ever thought about what we should do if one day the company's sales and profits begin to drop, or if the company goes bankrupt."[14] It is driven by this sense of crisis, Huawei maintains its motivation to improve constantly. Facing the Internet bubble burst and the transformation of the global industries, Huawei organized an extensive discussion on crisis: Was Huawei facing a crisis? Which departments, units, and processes of Huawei were facing a crisis? How to improve? How to increase the per capita benefits? "If we can find answers to those questions, then we shall survive."[15]

Huawei's sense of urgency is not only reflected on the strategic level but penetrated in every detail of the company. Everyone no matter what they do should have a sense of urgency and take charge. Huawei's sense of urgency in this sense is a collective responsibility. "Every employee should always be wary of poor quality and high repair rate and do a good job to prevent these problems."[16] If you ask anyone in Huawei, no matter they are management or not, they will tell you straightforward that Huawei still has many problems, or give you figures or facts of the gap between Huawei and its competitors. Everyone is clear about what needs to change and how to enhance their core competencies. For the same project, Ericsson's offer is 350,000 US dollars, but Huawei can do it for 200,000 US dollars; it is attributable to Huawei's continuous effort to find its deficiencies and improve internal management, and to Huawei's teamwork. The primary reason that Huawei people are good team players is that those who choose to stay usually are not alpha dogs or self-centered. Huawei's culture worships everyday heroes and values organizational management, which greatly reduces the risks brought by the recklessness of individuals.[17]

Viability is the core issue

Ren has pondered hard on the viability issue from the perspectives of history, global technological development, and industrial competition. From a historical perspective, compared with the eras of trains, ships, telegraphs, and faxes in the last 100 years, today's competition is exponentially intensified; companies may go under any day if they are sloppy. That is why Ren requires all employees to focus on the main businesses, work hard, and resist temptations. This is the only way to survive in a fiercely competitive environment.

From the perspective of global technological development, the development of Internet and ICT technology makes dynamic global resource allocation possible, bringing delivery and services closer to customers and R&D closer to where the talent is, providing better services faster and driving down the manufacturing cost. With intensified competition, those companies that have more resources

---

[14] Ren Zhengfei: "Huawei people refuse to fail", at Huawei's annual meeting. December 26, 1995.

[15] Ren Zhengfei: "Huawei's winter", *Huawei People*. 2001.

[16] Ren Zhengfei: speech at the meeting with secretaries. February 22, 1997.

[17] From the interviews with Huawei employees by the author.

and move faster are getting larger and stronger; have-nots and slow movers will be stuck. It is especially true for the electronics industry, which is always in a state of oversupply.

From the perspective of industrial competition, the quality and performance of IT and electronic products are constantly improving, which puts higher requirements for the human capital and of course, drives the salary higher. At the same time, the constant oversupply easily leads to a price war. The good old days are long gone. Some western companies also joined the price war and tried to squeeze the profits. In some cases, they squeezed so much that they could barely squeeze through.[18] As the prices of electronic products constantly drop, only by good management and eliminating waste can the company survive.

Against such a backdrop, Ren keeps asking himself: how can Huawei stand tall? He pointed out three directions for the company: First, continuous change. "The only constant in life is change. If a company cannot change and evolve, it will go under, and it will happen quickly. The reason that Huawei's international competitors lose is not because of the ascent of Huawei, but because they pay their employees too much."[19] Second, continuously improving the core competitiveness. "Huawei should never stop exploring how it can survive, why it needs to survive, and what value it can create. The basis for sustained viability is to continuously improve the core competitiveness, which will bring more profits. This is a closed cycle."[20] Third, think ahead but focus on the present. Ren admitted that he did not have any lofty ideals and only focused on the next two or three years. "I focus more on short-term management improvement instead of long-term strategic objectives." To survive and be a global market leader, Huawei needs to be humble. It needs to study the strengths of its competitors and identify its shortcomings and correct its mistakes. Meanwhile, it should embrace international cooperation. In fact, all Huawei's flagship products are developed with its international partners. For a company to sustain itself, it needs to face its problems and, more importantly, solve them. Only when the problems are solved can it move forward.[21]

How to activate the company's self-driving vitality?

Ren believes that it is the internal mechanisms that have driven Huawei, a private high-tech company, to go this far. That is why Huawei's reforms have always been centered on improving internal mechanisms. These reforms have pushed Huawei to a new high and made its employees, who are selfless, responsible, hardworking, professional, down-to-earth, and good team players, the core of the company. These internal mechanisms can maintain the stability of the company and enhance its ability to withstand risks. These mechanisms attract more and more outstanding talent to join Huawei and work hard for its success.

---

[18] Ren Zhengfei: "Do not be a perfect man" at a meeting with model CPC members. May 21, 2008.

[19] Ren Zhengfei: "Do not be a perfect man" at a meeting with model CPC members. May 21, 2008.

[20] Ren Zhengfei: "Survival is fundamental to an enterprise", Huawei People. 2000.

[21] Ren Zhengfei: remarks at the orientation. November 11, 1999.

3.4 Strategic Thinking in Uncertainties

The thinking patterns of Huawei leaders

The reason that Huawei can move forward sustainably lies in the thinking of its leaders: they are not obsessed with past success but focus on future development. Figure 3.1 shows the two dimensions and six indicators of the thinking patterns of Huawei leaders. The abscissa represents the time variables (past, present, and future); the ordinate represents the space variables (individual, organization, and society). Huawei's leaders are not obsessed with honor or pride or the organization's past glories; instead, they are self-reflective, rational, and crisis-minded. They focus on the present and the viability of the company. They have no political agenda and keep themselves as low-key as possible. They are patient and understand the importance of resisting temptations. They understand the importance of striking a balance between short-term interests and long-term goals with paradox thinking. Huawei leaders are forward-looking when it comes to social, technical, and industrial development trends. They embrace the future despite uncertainties and build future-oriented capabilities through the dissipative structure. They grasp the principal contradiction in uncertainties and focus on the long-term development of the company. They demonstrate strategic thinking, forward-thinking, and innovative thinking.

In the thinking system, how to manage uncertainties is essential.

We cannot predict the future, but we can embrace it

The uncertainty refers to the unknowingness of the future development at the time of decision-making, and limited information about the external environment. The

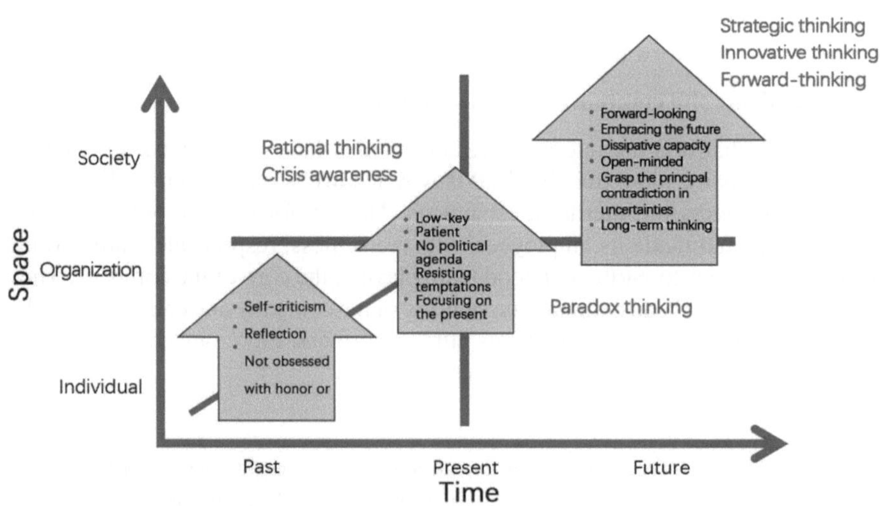

Fig. 3.1 The thinking patterns of Huawei leaders

uncertainty may arise from three main reasons: first, the future development of the company is by nature difficult to predict; second, people lack the information and knowledge to predict the future; third, people's cognition is locked by "specific boundaries" and, thus losing the time window for generating new cognition and adaptation to a new environment. Misjudgment of uncertainty may bring incalculable losses to the firm. In the case of a deviation in the perception of uncertainty, the company can suffer strategic mistakes. Management uncertainty is an important challenge faced by corporate decision-makers. Facing uncertainties, Ren realized: "Historical failures are good lessons. We cannot work on future uncertainties, but we can find a direction by induction and put ourselves in a reasonable organizational structure and be aggressive. Demise is inevitable. This is the law of nature. But our responsibility is to extend the life of Huawei as long as possible."[22] Ren called out: "We cannot predict the future, but we can embrace it. Ups and downs are only natural. Even when our company shrinks significantly, we must not only keep calm but also unswervingly continue to promote the organizational reform that is based on our long-term values. We must reform. More importantly, we must open up. We must not rest on the laureates of the past and free our company from the restraints of old thinking. As long as we can constantly motivate our team, we are hopeful."[23]

Identify development trends and pitfalls

Huawei's response to uncertainties also benefits from forward-looking research on markets and technologies. In 2012, Huawei invested 20 billion USD in 2012 Laboratory for future-oriented basic research. As to the mission of 2012 Laboratory, Ren once used a metaphor, "We bet the future data pipeline will be as wide as the Pacific."[24] The market is always full of temptations and traps. Companies with no clear long-term goals are easily tempted by short-term gains and fall right into the traps. Ren asks his people to pay close attention to changes in the market and be ready even before they take place. He always heeds traps and the adjustments of the market. In the early days, Huawei did not have a product portfolio, so should the company lose the orders for its single product, it would be very difficult indeed. That is why paying close attention to the changes in the market and keeping accurate analysis and judgment are crucial to Huawei. "Before the market changes fundamentally, we need to upgrade our mature products, make them systematic, and make a series of those products. We need to accelerate product diversification and the development of the international market. We need to increase production and cut costs on all fronts with optimized management, simplified procedures, reduced personnel, and improved efficiency. There is no other way."[25]

---

[22] Ren Zhengfei: "The river flows eastward in spring". December 2011.

[23] Ibid.

[24] The minutes of the 2012 Laboratory Seminar. July 2, 2012.

[25] Ren Zhengfei: "Huawei people refuse to fail", at Huawei's annual meeting. December 26, 1995.

The clearer the company's goals, the stronger its ability to deal with uncertainties

In Ren's view, uncertainties are always there. However, a company with clear long-term goals can make more accurate decisions faster and act faster when opportunities present themselves. Ren believes that a company with clear long-term goals should seize the window of opportunity to make profits so as to support the long-term development of the company. We need to cultivate a group of courageous employees to charge forward, and thus continuously stimulating our organization and management system. Those warriors are not directly engaged in the in-depth development of the company, but when they are ready, they can grow into strategists to direct the development of the company. You must dream big to win big. A Chinese proverb says, "Great generals must have risen from the ranks; prime ministers must have served as local officials." Managers and executives must have hands-on experience, otherwise, they are likely to drop the ball at a certain point.[26]

Facing uncertainties, focus on the principal contradiction

Ren believes that supervisors at all levels should focus on the principal contradiction and the principal aspect of the contradiction when facing technology and market uncertainties at home and abroad. They should have clear goals and understand the proper pace and flexibility to achieve these goals. They should also value self-reflection and be aware of the changes around the world.[27] How can we grasp development opportunities in uncertainties? Ren believes that we must first get the pain points of customers. Secondly, we must pay attention to what customers care about. We need to see the future before they do; we can discuss the future needs and pain points with the customers, so that they will also see the future and are willing to work with Huawei to find solutions for the future. We need to convince them that Huawei is their ally, and our services can help them advance into the future. Finally, Huawei's showroom should showcase future technologies instead of history.

Foresight is critical for leaders

Ren and his executive team are capable of not only focusing on the core strategy in a chaotic and uncertain environment but also seeing the light at the end of the tunnel and knowing that winter is coming when flowers are still in full bloom.[28] They can always find a way forward in chaos and uncertainties and a way upward in transformation. Although they have misjudged and made mistakes, their strategic thinking and foresight have always led the company forward.

---

[26] Ren Zhengfei: "Let people who can hear the shots call shots" at the awarding conference of Huawei's sales and service system. January 2009.

[27] Ibid.

[28] Ren Zhengfei: "Huawei's winter", *Huawei People*. 2001.

The first time that Ren realized the importance of foresight was after he participated in the National Science and Technology Award Conference in 1978. Luo Ruiqing, a member of the Standing Committee of the Central Military Commission made a keynote speech at the conference although he was already severely ill at that time. Luo pointed out that the next decade would be a rare period of peace, and we must pay full attention to economic development. The then 33-year-old Ren did not understand the political significance at that moment. A couple of years later, China witnessed massive disarmament. The entire branch where Ren served was let go. At that moment, it was the first time that he understood what foresight was and that the future competition was in the economic rather than political or military fields.

In the early days of Huawei, Ren adopted a laissez-faire management style and gave a lot of leeway to field managers. There was no fixed agenda in meetings and information was obtained in a free, equal, and a bit chaotic atmosphere. But one principle had to be observed, that is, customer-centricity. Every demand from the customer must be responded to and every opportunity appreciated.

The decentralized thinking and decision-making model not only enabled the company to be adaptive to different market and environment requirements but also established a trusting and equal relationship between top decision-makers and the senior and middle managers. This straightforward communication has greatly improved the efficiency of communication and laid the foundation for Huawei to deal with a more complex and diverse environment.

The ability to foresee development opportunities and challenges has become the most important part of Huawei's strategic capability. Without this ability, the company will find the difficulties even more challenging. Huawei's executives are always honest with the employees about the difficulties they face, especially with the core team. They always rely on collective wisdom for decision-making. Ren thinks if he is the only one who is farsighted, it is not good for the company. He calls on his senior management team to establish a long-term vision for self-development and encourages people with a strategic vision to fill in management positions. He asked Huawei's "senior generals" to lead the team forward especially in the midst of endless darkness, just like Danko, a character from the Russian folktale, who tears out his heart and sets it alight to illuminate the road for his people.

Thanks to strategic thinking and foresight, Huawei is usually correct about the future trend and can adapt in advance. "The reason that we can survive and thrive is that our responses to the anticipated problems conform to the trend. The reason that our *Basic Law* proposes to conform with the general trend of technological development, market changes, and social development is that only by conforming to these general trends can we substantially reduce risks. So, we are confident of ourselves because we have the capacity to anticipate not only success but also difficulties."[29]

[29] Ren Zhengfei: "Acting according to universal laws, giving full play to core teams, constantly improving per capita efficiency, and working together to survive hard times" at the meeting of the R&D Management Committee and the Q3 meeting of marketing & sales, 2002.

3.5 Paradox Thinking of the Leadership

Paradox thinking refers to the capacity to see that two opposites are correlated. They are not only competing with each other but also interdependent and transforming into each other. The paradox thinking prevents people from going to extremes of black or white (either/or) thinking. It helps people embrace rather than reject contradictions. Paradox thinking emphasizes that a pair of two opposites are also correlated; therefore, conflicts shall not be repressed, excluded, or dismissed. Instead, a proactive management approach should be adopted to balance the two opposites dynamically, and fully tap the potential of mutual transformation. We shall use creative ways to develop both ends while identifying ways to create and increase value between the two opposites.

Ren's paradox thinking is reflected in his dynamic grasp of the key elements of Huawei. He points out that the company's operation relies on two wheels: one is the business model, and the other is technological innovation. How to balance the two is a test for management.

Long-term goals versus short-term gains

Ren has a clear understanding of the relations between long-term goals vs short-term gains: if a company earns big money in a very short time, it will go down in no time; so, to sustain itself, Huawei needs to have long-term benefits, but rather earn big and fast. In 2001, he proposed that Huawei's incentive mechanism should not encourage short-term behavior but instead focus on sustainable development. It is important to recognize not only the short-term contributions of employees but also the long-term needs of the organization. The two do not negate each other; so, we should neither be short-sighted nor ignore short-term benefits completely.[30] There are times that we need to focus on the short-term, and other times, on the long-term. A smart strategy knows how to balance the two. If one cannot see it clearly, then they are not general material.

Then how can we balance long-term development with short-term benefits? Ren has proposed a two-pronged method: first, setting a long-term goal for the company. For Huawei, the goal is to enhance its core competitiveness. The long game is to be the most competitive network equipment supplier. With that in mind, the management will not be lost in immediate errands. Moving in this direction, the short-term and long-term development would not be in conflict. The enhancement of the core competitiveness will sustain the company and create value for it.[31] Second, making the organization a dissipative structure by absorbing new and better resources to replace existing ones. Specifically, Huawei should increase investment in good times to dissipate its existing resources and create new advantages. Therefore, Huawei should not be stingy with investment in the future. Ren used a vivid metaphor to explain how the dissipative structure works: If you eat a lot of beef and live a sedentary life, you will be a big fat guy. But if you eat a lot of beef, and you jog regularly,

---

[30] Ren Zhengfei: "Huawei's winter", *Huawei People*. 2001.

[31] Ren Zhengfei: "Survival is fundamental to an enterprise", Huawei People. 2000.

you may be very athletic. So, there is a big difference between whether you exchange energy and matter or not.

Boom and bust both have values

Ren has a dialectical view of market boom and bust and sees clearly the value of the transformation of the company. He is able to see the damage that may be brought by the market boom to the company; therefore, he warns his employees to be prepared and sets up systems to maintain continuous hard work. At the same time, he is aware of the value of the market bust to the company; therefore, he urges Huawei to be adaptive and make a dynamic adjustment when the market changes. Ren points out that there could be a crisis behind every boom. The crisis is not inevitable but could happen if people get sloppy. Hard work brings wealth; if you do not work hard anymore, you will inevitably lose wealth. Therefore, dedication and hard work are the core Huawei values to ensure that it can sustain its development. Ren believes that the market winter can be a wake-up call for the company. "Winter is lovely, not hateful. If we let success go to our heads, it will be very dangerous. Winter is not terrible. We can survive it. This year we may lose some profit, but we will not make a loss. Compared with our peers, our profitability is relatively strong. We need to pull ourselves together to face the future."[32]

Centralization versus delegation

Centralization and delegation, and unity and diversification are common paradoxes in organizational management. If there is no centralization, there will be a lot of leaks, so to speak, but too much centralization will also compromise the rapid response and flexibility of the business. Ren believes that the development of an enterprise must have its own pace and strike a balance between centralization and delegation. In the early days, the company needs to be more centralized, but when it develops to a certain stage, there should be some degree of delegation. The company should maintain sober and encourage innovation. When Huawei began to decentralize in 1997, it also enacted strict system restrictions. When the business grows, the power is constantly redistributed and delegated so that more resources can be generated and utilized. However, if no restrictions are placed on decentralized resources, corruption will incur. Centralization and delegation are a dialectical contradiction. Although power may be abused by some unscrupulous people in the decentralization process, the company still needs to be decentralized, and we must believe that most managers are good. High salaries cannot guarantee integrity, but a good system has a good chance. Although we may be lack experience in formulating the system, if we give up regulating the decentralization, we will never be able to establish an effective management system.[33] To succeed, we need to have strategic unity and consistency

[32] Ren Zhengfei: "Acting according to universal laws, giving full play to core teams, constantly improving per capita efficiency, and working together to survive hard times" at the meeting of the R&D Management Committee and the Q3 meeting of marketing & sales, 2002.

[33] Ren Zhengfei: "Resolutely implementing ISO9000". February 26, 1997.

instead of operational uniformity. Every unit in the company can use its discretion to some extent.

Centralization versus localization

In the process of globalization, Huawei is faced with the issue of how to coordinate the head office and local companies in various host countries. This is a common problem faced by many multinationals. Inspired by the leadership of CPC, Ren realizes that the recipe for success is its extensive, massive, and strict organizational system guided by the unification of thoughts and common goals. Such an organizational system regulates and administers the country to make sure that it stays on the right course. Ren's idea is to combine the company resources with local needs to create a new management model in different regions. The problems that emerged include the company interfering too much in the local affairs yet without much effect. Huawei has 30 plus offices overseas. If a senior manager visits these offices only every two years, how can he/she have a grasp of the business of these offices? So, Huawei establishes a regional joint meeting mechanism as intermediaries between the local offices and the head office. The responsibility of the regional joint meeting is to localize the use of Huawei's resources. The head office establishes a unified resource system, and the regional offices can use the resources according to the local needs.

Move up without giving up the lower-end market

In 2015, Ren pointed out that while Huawei was competing in the high-end market, it should not give up the lower-end market, because otherwise, they may give breathing space to potential competitors who may also compete in the high-end market someday. This is exactly how Huawei moved up, and its competitors may well follow its pathway.[34] To win both markets, Ren's idea is that the low-end products need to be standardized, streamlined, and require no repair during its life cycle. "We will not be engaged in a poor quality-based price war, because it will drag us. To stay ahead of the competition, we need massive streamlining." If customers want to enjoy more functions, they can buy our high-end products. This is called the "Mile-a-minute vine Spirit"[35] in Huawei.

Be flexible

In 2009, Ren first proposed the concept of "be grey" (as opposed to black or white), meaning be flexible. With its rapid globalization, Huawei gradually has become less

---

[34] See http://finance.ifeng.com/a/20150312/13548071_0.shtml accessed on March 12, 2015.

[35] The "mile-a-minute vine", also known as the bitter vine, climbing hemp vine, or American rope, is to the sub-tropical zones of North, Central, and South America. It now has widespread in tropical regions of Asia and has become one of the world's most invasive weeds in the sub-tropical zones. It is a vigorously growing perennial creeper that grows best in areas in high humidity, light, and soil fertility, though it can adapt in less fertile soils. The featherlike seeds are dispersed by wind. A single stalk can produce between 20 and 40 thousand seeds a season. Because the "mile-a-minute vine" can quickly cover the growth environment with abundant seeds, it can slow the germination and growth of a variety of plant species through competition or allelopathy. Even some large trees cannot compete. (英语根据wiki整理, 原文的 "他感作用" 应为 "化感作用").

stressed. Be flexible means striking a balance between stakeholders in the international landscape and keep a balanced mindset. Ren believes: "An important quality of leaders is to see the direction and pace themselves. They understand the importance of grayness. To stay on the right course, the leadership needs to be flexible and tolerant and knows when to compromise."[36] The grayness concept is accompanied by compromise and tolerance. It helps companies in three aspects: its strategic direction, the pace of change, and the balance of different interest groups.

In terms of strategic direction, Ren said: "Even a clear direction is stemmed from chaos. The direction can change with time and space, and it can be a blur at times. It is not white or black." The direction would not change, but the course could bend a little bit. It may not necessarily be a straight line; it could be a curve, and at some point, it could go around a circle. If we take a step back, we may find that the course leads exactly to the same goal.[37]

In terms of the tempo of change, the key is to maintain a balance between changes and stability so the change will not go to extremes. Ren pointed out: "Managers must not go to extremes, because it will lead to arguments and conflicts, and may disrupt mature processes. We need moderate approaches, not radical ones, to improve processes. When building our systems, we should build upon the past, instead of starting from scratch. Huawei does not welcome a binary view. Everyone must be realistic and seek truth from facts."[38] Ren has reflected on many radical changes in Chinese history. If they had taken a longer time to introduce the change, the results may have been different. The reason for the failure of many changes, in his eye, is the lack of flexibility.[39]

Ren believes that tolerance is essential for handling different interest groups. In his view, compromise out of tolerance should be purposeful and well-planned, and the party that makes a compromise can still take charge. Only the brave understand tolerance. The coward never does. Only with tolerance can we unite the most people for the common goal; only with compromise can we reduce confrontation while moving toward our goal. We will not compromise our goal or principle. But anything else can be negotiable. Ren tells his employees that compromise does not mean giving up principles or surrender. A wise compromise can get something in return. Making concessions on the secondary goals can help achieve the primary goal. If you have compromised your primary goal, simply because you don't know how to trade off or you hate to make concessions on the secondary goals, that would be rather stupid. Of course, the concession shall not be too costly to incur unnecessary costs. A wise compromise is an art and a virtue, the desired quality for managers. Only compromise can bring win–win results. If everyone wants to win, it may end up with a lose-lose situation. Compromises can eliminate conflicts; refusing to compromise is likely to cause confrontation. A practical person knows when and how to compromise. After

---

[36] Ren Zhengfei: "Openness, compromise and flexibility" at Huawei Global Analysis Summit. 2009.

[37] Ibid.

[38] Ibid.

[39] Ibid.

all, it is rationality instead of ego that sustains a company. Compromise is a consensus reached by two or more parties under certain conditions. It may not the best approach to solving the problem, but it is the best until a better one presents itself, because it can bring many benefits.

Innovation versus stability

In the early days toward standardization, Ren always maintained a realistic and rational understanding of innovation. He repeatedly warned his employees not to over-innovate, and not to innovate at will; instead, what Huawei needs is to maintain a stable process and properly strike a balance between management innovation and process stability. Management innovation and system innovation are of course important, yet frequent changes will disturb the internal and external order of the company. But without changes, core competitiveness and efficiency cannot be improved. What is to be changed in innovation is a serious issue, and the decision shall not be made lightly. An effective process should be maintained as long as possible and should not be changed frequently on account of a single tiny problem; because the cost of the change may well offset the benefits of improvement. Even if the efficiency is not ideal, unless the defect is fatal, otherwise we shall leave a stable process as it is. I would rather err on the conservative side.[40] Management must be both standardized and innovated. Innovation also requires management. The two should strengthen and check each other.[41]

Management by exception (MBE) versus routine management

Routine management refers to methods and processes that have proven to be effective in practice and can be reused in similar situations or regulations and policies that shall be observed and implemented in any case. The main purpose of routine management is to improve organizational efficiency and consistency. MBE, on the other hand, focuses on identifying and handling cases that deviate from the norm, and usually requires a new solution upon negotiation and exploration. If a business lacks effective routine management, then proven knowledge cannot be reused, the policies and regulations formulated cannot be enforced, and the organizational efficiency cannot be effectively improved. It will consume the business too much time to deal with unexpected situations, let alone innovation. Therefore, only with a proper balance between the two, can the company respond to unexpected events promptly and flexibly while maintaining its high efficiency. Huawei has set a good example in this regard. ISO 9000 defines the principles of routine management; *Huawei Basic Law* also defines the concepts of routine management and MEB. By routine management, it refers to matters that can be dealt with according to ISO 9000; those that cannot fall into the category of MEB. A 3:7 ratio of MEB to routine management for a company would be ideal. The 30% MEB, after being standardized, can later

[40] See Ren's speech "Why self-criticism" at the research department meeting on September 22, 2000, when he "rewarded" overstock and dead stock to researchers who had serious mistakes due to over innovation among other things.

[41] Ren Zhengfei: "Survival is fundamental to an enterprise", Huawei People. 2000.

be transformed into routine management, thus refining and improving the overall management.[42]

Internal relations versus external relations

One reason for Huawei's success in its internationalization endeavor is that it enjoys a good rapport with countries around the world, including Russia, Japan, and Canada. When Vladimir Putin was elected president, Ren Zhengfei sent a congratulatory letter. Huawei has established a large research institute in Canada. It also called on its employees to travel to New Zealand and buy New Zealand milk powder. "Since New Zealand gave us the order of the national broadband network, we will try to return the favor in some way somehow."[43]

Customers versus employees

Balancing internal and external relationships is also reflected in balancing the relationship between customers and employees, both of which are part of Huawei's core values. The interests of the two may have conflict from time to time but they also share some common interests. Therefore, in its philosophy and institutional design, Huawei has turned customers and employees into a community of shared interest.

3.6 The Power of Unity and Sharing

The dedication, learning ability, and collectivism of Huawei in the past 30 years are a telling example of the great strengths of Chinese people. The strengths stem from the sharing mechanism of the organization and self-knowledge. In the early days, Ren has realized the limitations of individuals and fully understood the power of unity. "When I look at the Great Wall, the barge haulers, and the galloping high-speed train, I see the power of the organization, the power of many. Only when one sees the insignificance of one, can they do something great together."[44] When Ren started his company when he was 46 years old, he understood that the power of individuals is limited. No matter how hard one tries, one can never catch up with the pace of the times, let alone in the era of knowledge explosion. It takes dozens, hundreds, and thousands of people working in one mind to catch up with the times. The company should respect its teams and give full play to every individual. This way something great may be achieved.[45]

The unity of organization relies on the design of multiple systems

When Ren founded Huawei, he had no idea of the option system, nor did he know that the West already had many mature incentive mechanisms in this regard. However,

[42] Ren Zhengfei: "Resolutely implementing ISO9000". February 26, 1997.

[43] The minutes of the 2012 Laboratory Seminar. July 2, 2012.

[44] Ibid.

[45] The minutes of the 2012 Laboratory Seminar. July 2, 2012.

based on his own setbacks, he was fully aware of the importance of shared responsibilities and shared interests. He talked with his father about ESOP, and he received his father's full support. Huawei's benefit-sharing mechanism includes three aspects: First, shared management power, which is mainly reflected in the CEO rotation system. Second, shared benefits, which are mainly reflected in ESOP. Third, shared learning. Please refer to the chapters regarding human resource management and learning-oriented organization in this book.

I was asked by a chairman of a high-tech company: "Why do Huawei people look so happy even they often work overtime?" This is a very good question, but it is also a difficult question. As Ren sees it, there are two levels of happiness: spiritual happiness and material happiness. Spiritual happiness comes from within and has nothing to do with money, while material happiness is in the hands of others and requires equivalent exchange. If one's goal is to achieve something, and they are willing to do so at any cost, then they will be very happy, because happiness comes from participation and dedication.

When many enterprises are troubled by how to manage the millennials, Ren finds it quite easy. The Post-80s are straightforward and always wear their heart on their sleeve. He does not see any major difference between those who were born before the 1980s and those after. Eventually, the Post-80s will be the backbone of our nation.

3.7 Self-management of Leadership

The key to achieving long-term goals is desire management

Huawei teaches people to manage their desire and aim for long-term development and not to be distracted by petty profits. Inclusion is the most important feature of the sharing mechanisms proposed by Hu Houkun, a rotating CEO. The company should be inclusive and accommodate the interests of customers, employees, capital, and various elements (such as intellectual property rights). We must adhere to the distribution system and management system guided by the sharing mechanisms, and gradually rectify and improve it.

How to evaluate success and failure

Can past success lead to future success? Not necessarily. Past success may lead to empiricism and traps too. The cases are many. Time, space, and managers are constantly changing. So, we should not attempt to copy success.[46]

Critical thinking

Ren clear-headedly and rationally sees the negative results that success may bring. He also sees that success easily leads to sloppiness. People may not bother to explore how to streamline the process or contribute more to the company. In a fast-changing

---

[46] Ren Zhengfei: "Success is not a reliable guide to future development" at a market meeting. January 17, 2011.

environment, success cannot be replicated. That is why even in the early days, Ren began to cultivate self-criticism as part of the corporate culture.

Keep calm and ignore doubts

In the course of Huawei's growth, there have been a lot of questions, speculations, and controversies at home and abroad. Huawei has adopted a low-key approach and made few comments. In 2001, Ren said that no matter how badly Huawei was attacked, they did not have to explain, because they simply did not have the time. What matters is self-development. He advised his employees to "not comment on media. We should all keep a low profile and be self-disciplined. Even if we are misunderstood, we don't have to argue with them. We should not engage in the online debate, otherwise, it will only harm the company." In terms of doubt from others, Ren encourages employees to "exercise strict self-discipline. Do your job well. If they are right, correct your mistakes accordingly. If they are not, then time will tell. We need to keep calm and move on. I hope everyone can grow and share the responsibilities of the company. This way, our company will not demise."[47]

Self-knowledge

Ren once said in his self-analysis: "My strongest suit is that I am willing to correct my mistakes. I am not worried about bruised ego. I don't think it would be much difficult to find someone like me. The most important quality I am looking for is democracy. With that, I will trust them to sign documents. We shall never put anyone on a pedestal, otherwise, it will disintegrate the whole value system of Huawei, and the company will go down. When every employee believes that they are creating value, everyone will be motivated; however, if they believe that only one person creates value, then their enthusiasm will be dampened."[48] When asked about his successor, he was very candid: "If Huawei does not exist anymore, everyone loses everything and added value means nothing. All growth involves metabolism. I myself will become a burden at a certain point. This is the law of nature. It is inevitable, so we should be cool about it."[49]

Self-discipline

A highly united leadership with criticism and self-criticism is a critical part of the company's success. The trials of the past 30 years have taken their toll on the health of many Huawei executives. But all the frustrations have only made them more determined, and they have improved their management skills. The executive team is committed to the company's success, not personal gains. They lead by working hard themselves. They are clean economically and politically. They have the courage to criticize themselves and others and impose rules to discipline themselves. They are visionary and fearless in the face of challenges. They follow the principle of *from each according to his ability and to each according to his contribution* and

---

[47] Ren Zhengfei: "Huawei's winter", *Huawei People*. 2001.

[48] Ren Zhengfei: remarks at the orientation. November 11, 1999.

[49] Ren Zhengfei: "Huawei's winter", *Huawei People*. 2001.

they care about the interests of Huawei people. That is why they are qualified to lead and capable of leading the company to success. "We shall not take advantage of the company. You may think that given my status, I must fly first class. Actually, the company policy does not allow it. It only allows reimbursement for the business class at most. If I fly first class, I have to pay the difference from my own pocket."[50]

Stress management

Ren used to have anxiety disorder and suffered from insomnia due to the mounting stress from work. "More than once, I thought that there was no point in living. So, I understand their pains, because I had been there. But luckily, I did not hide my pain. I spoke out. When I thought it was too much, I called my families and friends. You know, no one would suggest that you should kill yourself. In the beginning, I did not know that this was a kind of illness and could be cured. Fortunately, I was cured. I still remember that in the States, Guo Ping suggested that I should find something to kill time. Shoot the breeze could be good because it is distracting. If you take your mind away from the anxiety, gradually, you will be well."[51]

Openness and learning

Ren sets an example of learning for Huawei. His field of study includes history, culture, in particular military strategies, failure cases, and entrepreneurship. Every time he visits a different country, he tries his best to learn as much as possible about the successes and failures of the country and its companies; he writes down his reflections and shares them with all employees. These reflections are part of Huawei's future. On the one hand, they encourage employees to be inspired by innovation and craftsmanship; on the other hand, they warn the employees about the mistakes of the failed companies. In Fig. 3.2, we counted the number of times Ren mentioned the USA, Germany, Israel, and Japan respectively in his speeches and listed the aspects that Huawei should pay attention to.

3.8 Huawei Versus Cisco

Based on the study of Ren, we found that entrepreneurs with practical wisdom often take on multiple roles. Ren is a philosopher who can grasp the essence of things and find problems from accidentally observed phenomena. He is a strategist, who foresees changes in the environment at critical moments, and leads the organization to transform and evolve. He is a craftsman, focusing on quality, and the long-term development of the company. He is an idealist politician, who creates values for business and society and inspires people to act. He is a writer, who tells good stories with metaphors. He is a teacher, who encourages employees to learn and embrace beautiful values and principles. Leaders with practical wisdom make good use of

[50] Ren Zhengfei: remarks at the closing ceremony of the Shanghai Expo. October 2010.

[51] Ren Zhengfei: "Do not be a perfect man" at a meeting with model CPC members. May 21, 2008.

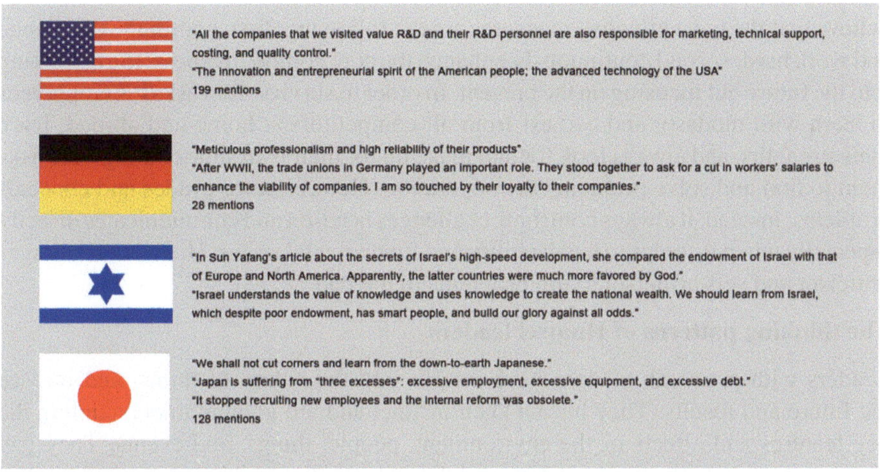

Fig. 3.2 Mentions of countries in Ren Zhengfei's speech (as of December 31, 2014)

power and wisely unite people and integrate resources towards a common goal. The leader understands when to use the carrot and when to use the stick. He knows how to motivate and take care of his employees, but he can also be "brutal" and fire the bottom 10% non-producers for the good of the company. These multiple roles prove that good leaders need to have cognitive and behavioral complexity for business development.

The qualities of Huawei leaders

Great leaders can gain experience from adversities and failures and transform these experiences into determination and perseverance. They have clear directions and goals in mind and will not yield to challenges and difficulties. They don't mind being lonely, misunderstood, neglected, and will not be daunted by setbacks. They are resilient. They can tell goodness and excellence and distinguish between short-term gains and long-term benefits. They have a great vision and a broad mind. They can translate perceptions, beliefs, experiences, and emotions into articles, the code of conduct, and corporate culture. Without corporate culture, a company is no more than a shell. A smart leader is a good communicator and understands the importance of showing care. A smart leader encourages all employees to communicate with each other formally and informally because communication and active listening bring new information and inspiration. A smart leader is good at telling stories, using metaphors, symbols, or other images to inspire the creativity of employees. They understand employees' demands, emotions, and opinions, and can resonate with them through various channels of communication.

Attention management of Huawei leaders

Leaders with practical wisdom put the viability of the company high on their agenda. They will examine the issue from the global, industrial, and corporate levels and believe that the most effective measures are the following: first, continuously change and work hard; second continuously enhance the core competitiveness; third, looking into the future but focusing on the present. In order to survive, Ren asks his employees to learn with modesty and earnest from all competitors at home and abroad, learn their strengths, and always look for and make up for their own shortcomings. He asks them to find and solve problems in cooperation. Huawei never evades and conceals problems; instead, it always confronts challenges head-on and communicates directly especially when it comes to harsh reality and fundamental issues. Huawei encourages criticism and self-criticism to nip problems in the bud.

The thinking patterns of Huawei leaders

Leaders with practical wisdom have insight into the nature of things and foresee the future and results. They have a keen instinct and are good at understanding the key features and effects of the environment, people, things, and events. They pay special attention to the time window, and they can predict and discover opportunities in the early stages of industrial and market transformation. As a result, they can always seize the critical moment to take action to guide and promote organizational change. Leaders with practical wisdom have paradox thinking. They see people as both rational and emotional, civic and brutal, optimist and pessimist, diligent and lazy. With paradox thinking, they see the correlation between the two opposites rather than see everything in binary terms; therefore, they can come up with decisions that are in the interest of their own development without harming the public interest. As Francis Scott Key Fitzgerald once said: "The test of a first-rate intelligence is the ability to hold two opposing ideas in mind at the same time and still retain the ability to function." "Tolerance, compromise, and flexibility" are Ren's expressions of paradoxical thinking.

Idealism and perfectionism of Huawei leaders

When the leaders go all out for the survival and development of the company and fly coach to markets around the world, even at their old age, even when they are already fabulously rich, you may wonder: what do they really pursue? If what they are after are just career success, recognition, and wealth, we will not be able to explain their behavior. We can only find their motivation from the spiritual level, that is, idealism, the sense of mission and responsibility, the sense of crisis, vision, and perfectionism. People who visited Huawei's showroom in Beijing and Huawei Academy in Shenzhen were all impressed by the interior decoration and perfectionism. They are a manifestation of the idealism and perfectionism of Huawei leaders.

Key characteristics and self-management of Huawei leaders

In Fig. 3.3, the author identifies some key characteristics of Huawei leaders in four aspects. 1. On the level of corporate culture and values: they demonstrate a sense of crisis, self-refection, and long-term hard work. 2. On the level of strategic leadership: with a global vision, they focus on industrial structure, the company's core strategies, and businesses. 3. They unite all forces that can be united and align the goals of key employees with the goals of the company to form synergy. 4. On the level of

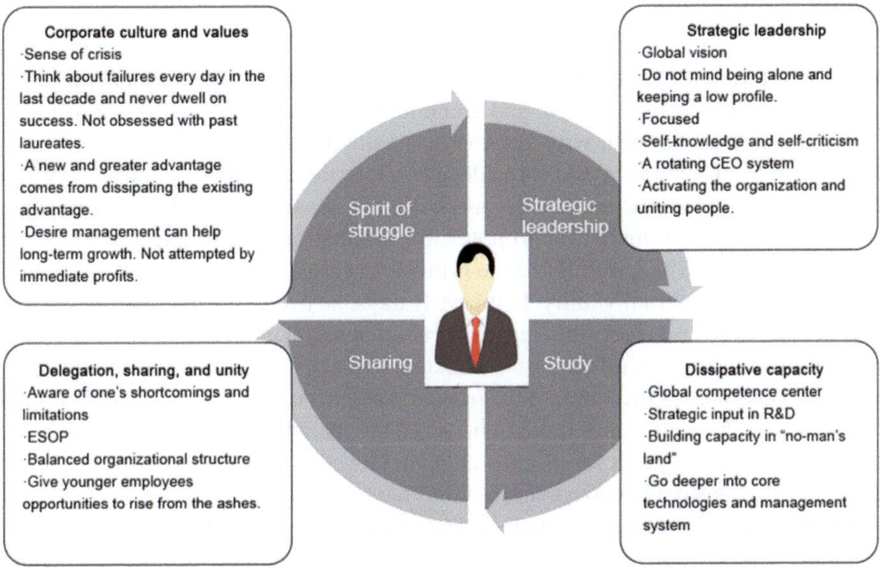

Fig. 3.3 Key characteristics of Huawei leaders

dissipative structure, they value the building of key capabilities by introducing global best practices and build core capabilities in the so-called "no man's land".

In the course of its development at home and abroad, Huawei has always been facing controversies, skeptics, and criticism, but no matter what it always keeps a low profile. Firstly, it is partly because of the leaders' self-knowledge. They are aware of the obstacles they may encounter when dealing with the media. Secondly, Huawei leaders require all employees to be self-disciplined, focusing on the survival and development of the company. Thirdly, the low profile is also a kind of self-protection, protecting the company from controversies so that it can focus on its business. Enterprises with less attention are safer, but the mystery around Huawei has attracted more attention and curiosity in society.

We find Ren and Chambers, former chairman and CEO of Cisco, have a lot in common.

Vision. Both are far-sighted. They set a clear and correct strategic vision and long-term goals for enterprise development. Even in the early days, Ren fully realized that the future would be an era of knowledge instead of bubbles. China is big but not abundant in resources. So, it must tap into its human capital and make it prosperous with science, technology, and education. In the communications equipment industry, you are either a leader or a loser. There are no other alternatives. As early as 1996 when Huawei's sales were only 10 billion yuan (approx. 142 million USD), Ren put forward his strategic goal to make Huawei a global leader; he also drew a road map to achieve the goal. When I visited Cisco, Chambers said that when he saw the Internet was changing how we work, live, play, and learn, as envisioned by Cisco, he could not help feeling the passion for his company. Every year when we visited Cisco, we found that its strategic focus changed from cloud computing to big data, from the Internet of Things to AI, the company's senior management is constantly stimulated by emerging markets and technologies, and the company is constantly evolving. They cannot bear with slackness and staying put.

A sense of crisis. In the last three decades, Ren thought about failure every day and never dwelled on success. He always harbors a sense of crisis, but never a sense of honor or pride for himself. He proposes that dissipating the existing advantage is a greater advantage. The question that he is most concerned about is Huawei's survival and activating its internal vitality. In the early days, he even suffered from an anxiety disorder, but it was precisely this sense of crisis that has made Ren pay more attention to capacity building toward the future and dare to dissipate the existing advantage to build the new one for the future development. When visiting Cisco, Chambers told us frankly that his colleagues thought he was a bit "paranoid". For every strategy, he would only give 3–5 years for its enforcement. However, it is this sense of crisis and insecurity that has made entrepreneurs continue to invest in the future.

Cultural development. For many private enterprises, entrepreneurs are the most important builders of the corporate culture. Their childhood experience, values instilled by their families, setbacks, and lessons in their life will all be reflected in the corporate culture they develop. In Ren's childhood, his family was poor; however, his father told him that being born poor was not shameful, just as born rich but lack of ideas and knowledge was not honorable. His father told him "Knowledge is power. Even if others do not study, you should; on this matter, you should never follow the crowd." Upbringing has a profound impact on Huawei's ESOP scheme and its corporate culture featured by dedication and flexibility. Chambers believes that leaders who have experienced failures are crucial to the building of the corporate culture. When he was working at Wang Laboratories founded by Wang An, he often played tennis with Wang. After witnessing the boom-to-bust of the company, he realized that the failure of Wang Laboratories is due to its self-centered culture. Wang Laboratories believed that only they understood technology, and customers did not, so the company should direct the customers no matter what. That is why Chambers vigorously promoted a "customer-centric" and "high-adaptive" culture at Cisco.

Communication skills. Both Ren and Chambers are great communicators. The difference is that Ren is a good writer and Chambers is a good speaker. Ren's writings are sincere, smooth, and emotional, with clear logic and good metaphors and analogies. He can resonate with his readers. Despite dyslexia, Chambers is good at giving poetic and inspiring speeches. He likes to walk amongst his audience when giving speeches and has posted videos on the Cisco website to communicate with his employees. They both understand how to resonate with their employees directly and effectively.

Chapter 4
From a Mom-and-Pop Operation to a World-Class Player

One of the most important capabilities for a company to survive is the capability to transform and surpass itself. When the market or technology transforms, if the leading company is constrained by its old thinking patterns and underlying organizational structure, it will miss the window of opportunity for adaptation and transformation. The old core competencies will turn into obstacles as the original system is unable to adapt to the changing environment. Different company leaders have different perceptions of the market and technological transformation, and different interpretations of the timing, the speed, and the intensity of transformation. In this regard, companies can be categorized into the following types: proactive, adaptive, reactive, and eliminative.

Adaptation and transformation are different. Adaptation refers to the adjustment of strategic positioning, development path, and competitive edge of a firm in response to changes in the external environment. Whereas transformation refers to an organization's continuous improvement of its internal organizational system, processes, and technology and management systems to effectively respond to the threats and opportunities of the external environment. Adaptation and transformation are highly industry-specific. In a relatively stable and mature market environment with a high entry threshold, the frequency of adaptation and transformation is low, and gradual improvement is the norm. Leading companies maintain their leading position by constantly reinforcing their existing competitive edge. However, in a highly competitive environment of rapidly changing technologies and market demands, new entrants are constantly breaking new ground through disruptive innovations, so the incumbents face huge pressure to make transformation and adaptation. The ICT industry is a highly dynamic industry with frequent radical technological innovations, so how to lead transformation and adaptation of the firm is inherently challenging, especially at the cognitive, behavioral, and organizational levels.

At the cognitive level, visionary and innovative leaders take the initiative to adapt and transform. They typically have a strong sense of crisis and are highly sensitive to external changes. They are ambitious, and never content with past glories. As the market environment is ever-changing, new technologies and products are emerging

X. Dong et al., *Huawei*,
https://doi.org/10.1007/978-981-19-4078-1_4

all the time. How to identify the weak signals of changes in the market, technology, policy, and consumers and how to initiate organizational change are critical for corporate leaders to take advantage of transformational opportunities. In this process, the leaders' ability to anticipate uncertainties is essential. The leader needs to adjust their strategic thinking and push forward a new strategic layout according to the anticipated changes, lead and drive the organizational transformation, and meanwhile change the mindset of all employees and encourage them to embrace adaptation and transformation.

At the behavioral level, as the strategic thinking changes, organizational leaders are not only embracing the uncertainties of the future but willing to invest in future-proof critical capacities and incubate and nurture future technologies and markets through a combination of investment strategies. They also tilt support toward personnel and divisions developing the new capabilities by personally leading the new teams, merging and acquiring, bringing in external professionals or promoting aspiring young talent within the organization, or by forming a new division in the organization. In practice, corporate adaptation and transformation can be very painful, because it must re-divide the pie and change people's mindset, the organizational system, and processes. In the process, the old experiences, skills, resources, and social relationships may become invalid, the rights and interests of many people will be affected; therefore, worries, anxieties, and fears emerge. Usually, the more people were benefited from the old system, the more they are contented with the old, and the greater the resistance. On the other hand, those who are marginalized, young and vulnerable are more responsive to changes. Therefore, when leaders advance organizational transformation, they need to analyze the underlying resistance, find a way to incentivize the employees, and make them understand the necessity and urgency of adaptation and transformation. Only when they are motivated and optimistic, can the transformation be less painful. This is the most difficult part of adaptation and transformation. Tough as they are, soft skills alone are not enough; sometimes an iron fist is needed.

At the organizational level, adaptation and transformation require changing the existing underlying structure and build a new one. The underlying structure of a firm consists of five levels.

First, strategic positioning, including the core beliefs and values of the organization and its employees. Innovative businesses require flatter organizations, blurred boundaries, and more flexibility, which inevitably have a huge impact on the inertia, the hierarchy and consistency that have formed in the stable environment.

Second, product and service positioning. Products and services can be categorized to high, medium, and low segments, or by different customer groups and market characteristics. Corporate transformations include not only moving from the low end to the high end, but also from a niche market to an integrated market and vice versa.

Third, organizational structure, including the allocation of resources and decision-making power. Strategic restructuring usually gives strategic emerging sectors more resources and will naturally dissatisfy traditional divisions.

Fourth, organizational processes and the value chain. The customer demand-driven processes and the value chain require the creation of customer-focused, end-to-end responsiveness, which is a major change for the internally focused management process.

Fifth, control system. To cope with uncertainties, companies need to empower their grassroots units to increase their responsiveness and flexibility, which constitutes a major challenge for centralized, and rigid control systems.

Large firms usually try to ensure the stability and efficiency of their underlying structures during periods of steady growth and focus on incremental innovation as a counterbalance to internal or external disruptions and changes. The company's core objective is to continually strengthen the existing underlying structures. As the alignment of the structures, systems, controls, and resources within the organization gradually improves, the organization operates more efficiently. However, the emerging new technology requires rapid disintegration and optimization of the old underlying structure, with a fundamental shift toward new strategies, power, structures, and systems.

The adaptation and transformation of Huawei are even more challenging. First, the competition in the communications equipment industry is already rather fierce with quite a few multinationals leading the market. Huawei had to keep up with the pace of transformation of these peers. Second, as a growing private company lagging far behind multinationals in terms of management, R&D, product quality, market, and branding, particularly because of the cultural gap, Huawei must constantly reform itself to be on a par with their international counterparts and look for opportunities to surpass. The private sector has extremely limited resources to cope with competition, so it must constantly evolve and improve its operation and efficiency. Adaptation and transformation must go hand in hand. Therefore, important questions include: How to adapt and transform? What are the priorities? What are the means of transformational change?

4.1 Start-up Phase: The Survival Period (1987–1996)

The Large Company Strategy

Since the late 1980s, the fast-growing China's telecommunications industry and market have given rise to China's telecommunications manufacturing industry. Manufacturers all over the world are vying for this big cake, thus resulting in large surpluses of products. Foreign products are expensive and have taken the lion's share of the Chinese market; Chinese manufacturers manage to maintain a fragmented operation, with great difficulties. Under these circumstances, Huawei realized that a large country with a population of 1.2 billion must have its own ICT industry. Therefore, it must formulate a Large Company Strategy.

As a dynamic start-up, Huawei witnessed an annual growth of over 100%. Its annual output reached 363.5 million USD in 1996 and about 870 million USD in

1997. It employed about 3,100 people, of these, 40% were engaged in R&D, 35% in marketing and technical support, 12% in administration, and 13% in manufacturing. In 1998, it employed over 5,000 people, with 1,500 newly recruited college graduates. The average age of the employees was around 26, and 60% of the employees had a master's or doctoral degree, or a senior engineer title. Many of them grasped advanced technology and had more than five years of experience in telecommunications.

It is these well-educated and competent young people who were driving the company's rapid growth. Huawei has experienced many risks and difficulties in the early phase of its development. From acting as an agent for Hong Kong-produced telecom equipment to investing all the proceeds in the R&D of PLCs, every day Huawei was faced with the test concerning its survival. Therefore, the sense of crisis has become the most obvious feature of the organization. At the same time, as a private start-up, it encountered fierce competition from multinationals at its doorstep. Therefore, to survive in the fierce competition, Huawei had to learn fast and learn it all. Initially, Huawei relied on its founders to seize opportunities despite insufficient resources. Their dedication, vision, and courage have made the company bigger and stronger. In the first ten years, Huawei had more failures than successes, but it moved forward against all odds. These failures and some unduplicable experience are valuable food for thought for its second phase. In the start-up phase, Huawei adopted different strategies in organization, R&D, marketing, and branding.

Flexible organization

The greatest advantage of a small business is its high responsiveness to the environment and customer demands. With a professional team, Huawei had a flexible and effective management system and incentive mechanism. In the early days, Huawei paid special attention to system reform, organizational reform, remuneration reform, corporate culture education, business process reengineering, and the introduction of management information systems, among others, which have laid a solid foundation for its future. To encourage all Huawei employees to always stay alert, Ren asks them to always benchmark against the international industry leaders.

In addition to benchmarking against the leading companies, each department and each link must continuously optimize itself. All those who are lazy, irresponsible, and reluctant to learn will be repositioned or even laid off. The legitimate interests of the employees even if they are laid off will be protected and guaranteed. Huawei maintains an annual elimination rate of 5% and a repositioning rate of 10% to prevent slackness. As its hallmark of corporate culture, Huawei people always toast those who succeed and offer a helping hand to those who fail.

R&D: all-time priority

Huawei has attached great importance to research and development since its early days. The proportion of R&D staff is around 40%, and three parallel R&D systems have been established: product strategy development research system, product central system planning, and integration research system, intermediate test system (see Chap. 6). Huawei's R&D headquarters is located in Shenzhen, and it has branches in Silicon Valley, Beijing, and Shanghai. Every year, the company allocates 10%

of sales for research, with additional support in good times. Huawei never stopped investing in R&D even in the hardest times, because its leaders believe that high input leads to high output and that companies should not only consider the immediate development, but also have a long-term goal. Although this high investment puts a lot of pressure on the company, Huawei knows that if the company focuses only on immediate benefits, it will hurt the consistency and scalability of the products, and thus hurting users. Huawei is always balancing between short-term performance and long-term goals which is also reflected by its allocation of R&D expenses. According to Huawei's early allocation plan, when its R&D fund reached 100 million yuan per year, 80 million yuan is spent on the support for research and development, 20 million on training and study tours at home and abroad. In other words, Huawei spends 80% of its funds on R&D and deepening of existing systems, and 20% on acquiring new vision, new projects, and new knowledge. Ren has always believed that if Huawei remains steadfast in this direction for 10 years, a world-leading enterprise will take shape.

Attracting the best knowledge workers

In 1995 when Huawei was still a long way from an industry leader, it began to prepare itself philosophically and structure-wise. Ren put forward the goal of developing a big market, conducting big research, and setting up a big structure with a well-functioning organizational system and service network. In order to achieve ambitious goals, the company needs to lay a broad and solid foundation. Huawei's human resources were highly knowledge-intensive, with more than 1,400 of its 1,750 employees having received a bachelor's degree or above, including more than 800 Ph.D. and master's degree holders. Its greatest assets were not big oil or forests, but the brains of its employees. At the very beginning, Huawei was trying to develop a set of methodologies to attract, use, retain and develop talent. In my interviews, some of the employees who joined Huawei in the early days were very much impressed. One of them was a postgraduate from Nanjing, who had been dumped by his girlfriend because of his poor salary. When he was interviewed for the job, he first found that the interview room was the only office in the whole building that was air-conditioned, but later he also found that his first month's salary was 10 times what he had earned in Nanjing. He immediately burst into tears.

Ren values talent. When he saw a resume of a Tsinghua graduate whose parents were peasants, he hired him on the spot and paid him much higher than the market average. After Ren met a mathematics graduate from Peking University (PKU), he immediately set up a scholarship of 100,000 RMB (a very large sum at the time) for the math department at PKU and offered to recruit all the math graduates to Huawei. Even in the early days, Huawei showed its care for its employees by improving the canteen food and making the office brighter, among other things, young employees were happy to stay and grow with the company.

Huawei is more than a company; it is also an academy. It encourages its employees to learn from leading companies in the developed world. MNCs are more than competitors; they are also teachers. These MNCs that bring competition to Huawei's doorstep showed Huawei what it meant to be internationally advanced in marketing, professionalism, business ethics, etc. Huawei has learned the rules of the competition and more importantly learned how to win in the competition.

Working hard before playing hard

Huawei's R&D expenditures have increased rapidly with the expansion of its market and the increase in sales. The total amount of the R&D budget was $25.47 million in 1996, and somewhere between $42.44 million and $56.59 million in 1997, and $113.18 and $141.47 million in 2000. Increasing R&D input helped Huawei to close the gap with the world's leading companies. For the same period, the living conditions of its employees were far from ideal; the homeownership increased from 1.5% to only 5.5% during that period. Many degree holders and senior executives live in rented houses and led simple life. However, Huawei people were still an optimist. Ren told them that they worked so hard, partly for the purpose that they could live a better life in the next century, but more importantly for the purpose that the motherland would have the core technology and our country would not be overshadowed by developed countries. Of course, it was also for the purpose that one day they could buy a larger house with a nice terrace. So, it is not just for the country, but also for themselves and their loved ones.[1]

Huawei's employees understand that in order to win, they first must survive. They are willing to defer their payment and focus on productivity gains. Together, they have created miracles by building consensus and working toward common goals. Huawei first achieved internal consensus before they opened up, because they know if they are in disarray, opening up does not help. During this period, Ren encouraged Huawei to learn from the spider and the bee. The spider is always tirelessly knitting its web, and the bee is always tirelessly gathering honey. Only such diligence and perseverance can guarantee sustained development of the organization.

Conquer the toughest market first

In the early days, Huawei has encountered many difficulties, embarrassment, and even humiliation in both domestic and overseas markets. For example, once a marketing executive waited for a client in the lobby after dinner until 1:30 in the morning. When the client showed up, he simply said that he had no time for Huawei. Another time, a doctor at Huawei waited for four hours in a cold winter at the capital airport to pick an important client. The client at first was happy to see that someone had come to pick him up, but when he found out that the doctor was from Huawei, an obscure company back then, he ditched the doctor. Another example is a project in Yichun city, in northeast China. The marketing team presented their proposals a dozen times during six months, but in the end, they had to give up for some reason. The men involved in this project cried bitter tears.[2] Expanding the market is the fundamental condition for the business to survive. Without a market, it cannot develop in

[1] Ren Zhengfei: "Standing against pride and complacency and being mentally dedicated" at the Market and Research Award Ceremony. April 6, 1996.

[2] Ren Zhengfei: "Huawei people refuse to fail", at Huawei's annual meeting. December 26, 1995.

scale; without scale, it would be difficult to lower the cost. Without low cost and high quality, it would be difficult to compete.

Under these difficult circumstances, Huawei had to expand its market from tough places in which multinationals had no interest. In 2000, Huawei set up many joint ventures across the country and began to use these JVs to get to clients on multiple levels. Many Huawei Project Managers were stationed in tough areas with poor conditions, but they never backed down. They not only built and defended the bunkers, i.e., the regional market, one after another, but also dug trenches for greater gains.[3] By expanding its market, Huawei has reduced its costs and its executives are fully aware that the market economy will eventually compel companies to operate at thin margins. So lower cost is not enough; to maintain the edge in the market, it is necessary to improve the quality, sophistication, functionality, and diversification of products. Only a large market can incubate a large business, and only a large business can meet the market demand. So, how to expand market share, increase its supply, and reduce the cost at the same time is a real challenge for Huawei.

Building sales platforms and moving the command closer to the market

In 1996, Huawei began to move its decision-making structure closer to the market, and build sales platforms based on regional engineering departments and offices. The main function of the platform is to sell multiple products of multiple companies (including affiliated JVs), with the aim of creating a community of shared interests and market resources. At the same time, Huawei has established payment collection teams headed by office directors. The management of payment collection is benchmarked against the management of sales. If they fail to reach the payment recovery rate, then the directors would be deemed as unqualified. Ren proposed that no matter how big Huawei grew, how many partners it had, there would always be only one unified sales platform.

In Huawei, business planning is the core function of regional offices: business personnel should have a deep understanding of products and technologies, and the management and services are benchmarked against their foreign counterparts, so are the college graduates working at sales platforms, except for their English proficiency. Huawei adopts a rotation system to nurture platform managers and junior managers. The marketing department sets up a number of working groups to effectively help, check and evaluate the sales platforms.

Meanwhile, Huawei explored a technology-for-market strategy to develop international markets and moved its market operation command closer to the market. In addition to regional offices and customer service centers across the country, Huawei set up 22 JVs with provincial telecom authorities. Huawei has also started exploring the global market. For example, it set up an office in Moscow, and JVs in a few countries, and installed equipment in more than a dozen countries in Eastern Europe.

[3] Ren Zhengfei: "Phoenix rising from the ashes" at the fourth anniversary of the collective resignation of Huawei's marketing department. January 28, 2000.

Huawei also provided business networks, smart networks, and access networks for Hong Kong SAR.[4]

Cultivating world-class marketing gurus

As early as 1996, Huawei began to build a marketing system with international standards that also meets Chinese conditions. It took Huawei only 5 years, half the time of the R&D department took, to internationalize the marketing system. The marketing department upgraded its sales strategy toward strategic marketing which aims to serve customers at all fronts. In order to achieve this strategic goal, Huawei must achieve five transformations at both the concept and organization levels: from public relations-focused to planning-focused, from sales-oriented to marketing-oriented, from segmented sales to team-based marketing, from local markets to global markets, and from product marketing to strategic marketing.

Ren required the marketing department to plan everything. In 1996, Huawei began to put market planning high on agenda and used the annual planning report to guide the company-wide work. Huawei required dynamic tracking, evaluating, revising, and summarizing the planning. A comprehensive customer service awareness has been established to enhance service to both internal and external customers and showcase the company's new image through good service. Huawei believes that international marketing is not just about building a few factories and selling products abroad; it is more about having world-class marketing gurus. It aimed to cultivate 50–60 generals to command marketing. To this end, Huawei encourages and attracts outstanding talent. In order to promote the deep integration of technology and market, Huawei has put forward the slogan of marketizing technology and technology-empowered marketing to encourage the finest marketing talent to work in the field. Huawei encourages a large number of employees with a master's degree or doctorate to work in the marketing team and they usually will make a major contribution to the development of the company in 3–5 years.

What it lacks in quality, it makes up for in service

When Huawei was founded, its product quality was not good, and it had to rely on the 33 maintenance and service centers across the country to fix it. After seven years of development, Huawei realized that to win the market, it had to rely on advanced technology, reliable quality, and good after-sales services. It began to earn the trust of the market. Today, it has a responsive three-tier support system with 200 outstanding engineers. The company later spent nearly 14.25 million USD to build a customer service building with a centralized maintenance system to provide remote support to users nationwide.

Branding as a great company

In China, many companies pay little attention to branding, or the design of their office buildings, exhibitions booths, or product packages for that matter, especially when the

---

[4] Ren Zhengfei: "Adhering to customer orientation & aligning with the world trend". December 13, 1996.

budget is tight. Poor design is always associated with poor quality, especially in the eye of foreign customers. Huawei is an exception. It paid close attention to design and branding even in the early days. For example, it hired first-rate international architect companies to design its Longgang factory, making the soul, skeleton, and heart of the company first-rate through and through.[5]

Many overseas customers only know China from movies (especially Hollywood movies), which usually produce an obsolete stereotype of China that is impoverished and backward. They don't believe that China has high-tech companies or high-quality high-tech products. It is rather difficult for Chinese companies to go global against such a backdrop. During its transition from public relations-based sales to strategic marketing, Huawei branded itself as a world-class company.[6] During its transition from small teams charging forward separately to unified marketing by large groups, Huawei gradually shifted its marketing focus from the country to the company, and often invite overseas customers to Shanghai, Beijing, and Shenzhen to build trust with the customers and change their perception of China.

4.2 Standardization Phase: From a Local Company to a Multinational Company (1997–2007)

Between 1997 and 2003, the Internet boom spread worldwide, with large amounts of capital invested in the Internet and IT startups, making a new economic wave, as President Clinton put it. The appealing Internet as an emerging industry, fueled by leverage funds, created huge bubbles and irrational behaviors. When the bubble burst, some very prominent Internet companies were wiped out overnight, and many leading multinationals began to downsize. Between 2005 and 2006, Lucent laid off more than 50,000 employees and its sales fell to $18.9 billion from $37.5 billion; Nortel laid off two-thirds of its workforce, with its market share down by more than half.

At that time, Huawei was also facing both internal and external difficulties. Competition, market crises, and declining sales compelled Huawei to consider how to improve its core competencies in this gloomy winter. During that period, Huawei encouraged its employees to start their own businesses, which risked the leak of Huawei's trade secrets and technology and created a number of potential competitors. Its internal management became shaky.[7] Huawei had anticipated such difficulties in 1999 and thought it would take place three years later; they did not see it coming so early.

What issues should the executives address to maintain growth while avoiding crises? After 10 years of rapid growth, would there be a prolonged period of low growth, and would the business be sustainable in the long term? What structural and

[5] Ren Zhengfei: "Huawei people refuse to fail", at Huawei's annual meeting. December 26, 1995.

[6] Ibid.

[7] Ren Zhengfei: talks at Huawei's acquisition of Harbor Networks. November 6, 2007.

management problems did the company have? Can employees who have experienced fast-track promotion during times of smooth development survive the cold winter? Would there be a cash flow crisis in the rapid growth? Can Huawei survive the winter?

So how did Huawei handle the challenges from domestic and international markets, the enormous pressure of management transformation, and the difficulties brought by key-employees-turned-potential competitors?

In fact, instead of being crushed, Huawei formulated a second business venture plan and a strategy to be a world-class company. This was an ambition and a challenge for Huawei, whose sales were less than 1.43 billion USD at the time. Ren suggested a three-step approach. The first step is to achieve international standards in production and management in three years; the second is achieve international standards in marketing in five years; the third is achieve international standards in R&D in 10 years. To achieve these targets, Ren took his senior executives to visit world-class companies to explore ways for a breakthrough.

Strategic rethinking: sustainability lessons learned from the rise and fall of Japanese companies

As Huawei prepares for its second venture and moves to scale, it needs to learn from international powerhouses and absorb their valuable business thinking and theory.[8] At this strategic juncture, Ren took his team to Japan and tried to figure out what problems Huawei should avoid. Huawei executives realized that Japan, as a mountainous island country, was good at making things nice and small, hence their renowned craftsmanship. Thanks to their diligence, their products were stunning in the era of the booming electromechanical industry. However, it has missed four strategic opportunities after WWII.

The first strategic opportunity that Japan missed is the high-value transfer that follows the IT applications to industries. In the 1950s, the Japanese economy relied on orders from the military and support from the United States. It became the world workshop of electromechanical products in the 1960s and 1970s with added value mainly in the manufacturing sector. However, after the Cold War, the United States quickly put military technology to civilian use, contributing to the rapid development of information technology (IT). After IT was applied to the industrial system, the main added value of the industry was quickly shifted to the R&D of core technologies and sales. The manufacturing industry became increasingly competitive with increasingly thinner margins and evolved into the contract manufacturing model. Japan with the manufacturing sector as its pillar industry was hard hit.

Second, it missed the strategic transition to a knowledge-based economy. In the 1970s, in the era of mass production, the growth rate of Japan was about 10%. In the 1980s, when mixed innovation and knowledge productivity became the norm, Japan's corporate system failed to adapt. Japan soon slipped from the center to the periphery of the world economy and its growth rate soon dropped to less than 4%. In the late 1990s when economic globalization and informatization became the

---

[8] Ren Zhengfei: "Shifting from the realm of necessity to the realm of freedom", *Huawei People*. April 6, 1998.

norm, and knowledge became more valuable, the corporate system of Japan remained unchanged. Its growth rate suddenly dropped to 2%.

Third, Japan missed out on a global talent market. The United States regarded Japan and Germany as its main opponents, so it sorts of closed its door to these two countries but opened its door to other countries. It welcomed talent and introduced advanced technology from other countries across the world. It also attracted capital from all over the world with its long-term bull market. Japan, on the other hand, is a mono-ethnic country, and lacks internal competition; its relatively even income inhibited innovation. The presence of foreign firms in Japan did not stimulate internal competition in Japan. Without fierce competition that drives innovation, Japan's original advantage became diminishing.

Fourth, Japan was slow in transforming its industrial structure. In Japan's economic take-off era, Kakuei Tanaka proposed an ambitious infrastructure plan for Japan. At the time, Japanese companies and people were very rich, and the island country has very limited land resources, so land prices and property prices skyrocketed and boomed for decades. When the financial crisis hit Japan, compounded with weak manufacturing innovation, earnings and real estate prices plummeted, dragging many property owners in negative equity and heavily indebted in a matter of days. Most local companies were funded by banks, which were dragged down too. If the companies could not repay these debts, they would not be able to turn over a new leaf.

In addition to the failure to seize the opportunities mentioned above, Japanese companies were over-staffed, over-equipped, and over-indebted, which made transformation particularly difficult. The average age of Japanese employees was increasing as Japanese companies have not taken on new employees for a long time, and the HR structure has shifted from a pyramid shape to a spindle shape. With fewer talented employees, fewer newcomers, and more older employees, Japanese companies were generally lack of vitality with higher wage costs. The flow of people was slow, positions were stagnant, and the innovation was obviously insufficient. Meanwhile, good social security and comfortable life made people content with the status quo; not many young people chose to study abroad. Such complacency is not conducive to reform. Japan, as an island country, has a strong sense of insecurity and always prefers stability, resulting in older managers and an overly cautious decision-making process, which is always protracted by the practice that important decisions must be unanimous.

What Huawei can learn from Japan?

After gaining a deep understanding of the plight of Japanese companies, Ren gave three caveats about Huawei's future development.

First, crisis awareness and self-criticism. Ren believed that in Huawei, the crisis awareness was not strong enough, especially among junior employees. Huawei was in the late autumn and early winter, so to speak, and needed to learn from others to improve work efficiency. The company needed to continuously make its process more reasonable and effective, eliminate unnecessary organizations, reduce redundant employees, and strengthen the self-training and competence of its employees.

In short, Huawei needed to prepare for the coming winter. Ren believes that as long as Huawei continues to identify problems, develop and improve, constantly engages in self-criticism, there will be a way out. As the case of Matsushita Electric showed that only Matsushita employees could save the sinking ship of the company in the icy sea, only Huawei people can save Huawei.

Second, redefined success. After visiting and reflecting on Japanese companies, Ren realized that the success of a company lied in its ability to survive the toughest time. By this definition, Huawei has not been successful yet, as it was still growing. However, if the company goes too smoothly, and promotes too many people to managers and executives during the good times, it can invite a disaster for the company. Therefore, Huawei's self-criticism and dedication culture are instrumental in keeping the company in check, humble and prudent, and critical to avoiding failure as it grows.

Third, a reasonable growth rate. The visit to Japan made Ren realize the mutually reinforcing and supportive relationship between growth, wealth, talent, and management. Therefore. Ren believes that Huawei must maintain a certain growth rate even in difficult times. If the growth rate slows down significantly, Huawei will also suffer from all the above-mentioned excesses in Japanese companies. Without early recognition and adequate preparation, Huawei will be stuck.

The importance of a reasonable growth rate is manifested in three aspects. First, to secure the position in the industry competition. Without a reasonable growth rate, the company will fall behind the competitors and eventually disappear. So, how can a company grow faster? The answer lies in management and service. Without management, there is no synergy, and without service, the company will have no direction. We have to make ourselves strong before we expand. The basis of expansion is a solid foundation. Without good management, it is difficult to maintain faster growth than your competitors. Secondly, more development opportunities should be given to employees to attract more talent. The Matthew effect is at play: good benefits and management attract more talent; more talent creates more wealth; more wealth attracts even more talent to further optimize the management. This is how the business grows sustainably. Third, a solid foundation is the only way to ensure reasonable growth. Without a solid foundation, sprawling expansion is but a suicide. If the quality of the product is not reliable, if there is no good after-sales service system, the company will die. Therefore, Huawei initiated management transformation, introducing a series of leading management systems and management methods.[9]

In the tough time, Ren and his executives conducted market research and analysis of leading multinationals, and realized that the cyclical downturn in the industry may turn out to be a good opportunity for the business. So, he encouraged the top management to be upbeat and use this window of opportunity of 5–10 years to rationalize internal relationships so that Huawei people would become forces driving the upcoming expansion rather than constraints to drag the company. For this reason,

[9] Ren Zhengfei: "Spring in the North". April 24, 2001.

the company's strategic layout did not retreat, but rather grow counter-cyclically. The strategies adopted by Huawei are:

First, entering international markets. Huawei realized that when difficulties arose in the existing markets, it had to be brave like Columbus to discover new continents: the marketing department had to march on valiantly across the Pacific Ocean and the Indian Ocean, even under the toughest conditions, to relentlessly explore and fight for new markets.

Second, improving the vitality of traditional products and gaining new shares in the existing markets. If the product quality becomes more stable, orders will increase and so will the production scale.

Thirdly, increasing the input even in financial difficulties and opening up wider. Huawei has made a point of acquiring valuable overseas small businesses that are on the verge of bankruptcy.[10] Huawei intends to try to bag them through acquisitions. Ren likes to quote Huawei's acquisition of an American small business with $4 million in the early 1990s and later it has made a significant dent in the long-range optical telecommunications market.

Fourth, increasing investment in new product development. In 1999, Huawei's budget for R&D reached USD 214.23 million. Some departments thought it was too much: what if they could not use up all the funds? In Ren's view, if that happened, it would mean two things: First, Huawei did not have enough good academic leaders. Second, the organizational structure and management are not standardized enough to accommodate more people and projects. If Huawei always fails to use up its R&D budget, it will hurt the company's core competency.[11]

Fifth, exploiting the latecomer advantage. Being behind helps avoid blindly chasing the frontier technologies, and instead focus on market and customer demand-oriented innovation.

From old thinking to creative thinking

Huawei encourages new thinking on working methods, marketing techniques, and segmentation of customer needs. When things are difficult, we need to reexamine the old ideas. A rational market is good for good companies. When the economy is difficult, users no longer put the price first, instead, they choose to buy products from the company they trust. In the case of a price war, small companies will fail, not large ones. Some small companies in the U.S. didn't know how long they can survive, so they had no choice but to sell their companies to Cisco and engaged in R&D complementary to Cisco's technology portfolio.[12]

Under the complicated market environment, Ren asked his company to further strengthen crisis awareness. Based on his understanding of the industry, competitors, technological changes, and the difficult days of Huawei's early development, Ren realized that Huawei could collapse at any moment. What is the crisis? A crisis

[10] Ren Zhengfei: "Meet the challenge and consolidate skills for the arrival of spring". 2006.

[11] Ren Zhengfei: "Entrepreneurship and innovation must be centered on improving the core competitiveness". March 5, 1999.

[12] Ren Zhengfei: "Meet the challenge and consolidate skills for the arrival of spring". 2006.

is not knowing what the crisis is, or not sensing it. If we know what the crisis is, Huawei will have no crisis and would be secure in its position. Crises could arise from internal or external. External crises are usually caused by directional errors; for high-tech companies, such crises are sometimes inevitable because there are so many uncertainties in technology selection and development. The internal crisis is usually derived from confusion and self-inflicted chaos. If employees are constantly improving, when the difficulty hits, the team can be well organized with well-trained people, and the business will be less exposed.[13]

In the period of smooth development, the company needs especially to guard against slackness. Ren believes that potential crisis always lurks in prosperity. Hard work will bring wealth, but when people no longer work hard, they are bound to lose their wealth. That is why Huawei encourages its employees to be pragmatic, persistent, and dedicated. Success can create favorable conditions, capabilities, and greater driving forces for the business, systematically overcome the weaknesses of its rapid growth; it can boost people's confidence and courage and encourage them to boldly capture strategic opportunities. Succeed or fail, Huawei should keep calm and move on.

In Ren's view, the market winter is not necessarily a bad thing; it could be a good time for the company to adjust its teams and structure properly to improve per capita efficiency and ensure that the organizational structure and strategic formation remain intact when spring comes. Therefore, in a chaotic and volatile environment, Huawei has been able to progressively strengthen its R&D team and system by strengthening information security, deliverables management. The morale of the marketing executives has been boosted after education. The company was brought back to life from the brink of collapse.

From individual decision-making to democratic decision-making

During this period, Ren repeatedly emphasized the need to downplay the influence of individuals and make the management more professional and process-based. This is manifested in the gradual development of top-level democracy. Huawei implements the principle of democratic decision-making by committees and collective management by department heads, which are important measures to bring into play collective wisdom. The Committee, composed of senior executives, senior professionals, and heads of relevant administrative functions, implements a merit-based selection process. In the decision-making process, democratic principles are fully utilized to reduce and avoid individual errors in high-level decision-making. In case that a judgment error is made, it will be corrected by many before being implemented because the issue will be thoroughly studied before implementation. The main functions of the committee include determining management objectives and measures through discussions, and selecting, evaluate and monitor managers to ensure the company always stays on the right track.

[13] Ren Zhengfei: Speech at a Meeting with New Hires. November 11, 1999.

Seizing the window of opportunity and business fundamentals

Huawei believes that in a difficult market, quality, service, and low cost are the three major issues that determine the survival of a firm. With good management and sound rules and regulations, in the event of market volatility, the chances of survival are greater. The survival of Huawei could mean that its competitors are likely to be pushed out. When that happens, Huawei is ready to absorb their outstanding employees and give them opportunities to grow. Therefore, the marketing department should be inclusive.[14]

To seize the window of opportunity is to have the courage to create direct demand, narrow the gap, and keep pace with the times. Facing the relentless international competition, Huawei must improve its foresight on future needs and technology trends, and plan accordingly. Only this way can Huawei reverse the adversities facing a late entrant. It needs to improve the accuracy of judgment of customer needs and reduce unnecessary consumption. It also needs to strengthen front-end demand management and make a rational commitment so that the back office can have enough time for delivery, reducing unnecessary haste. Huawei needs to consolidate the foundation of planning, technology, and delivery to enhance its responsiveness to a changing market. Good planning should go before every move, and lessons should be summarized and disseminated within the organization.[15]

Cash flow is the key to survival

In the difficult time, Huawei dropped its extensive sales model and shifted the offensive strategy to a defensive one, and used its cash flow as a jacket to keep the company warm in winter. In addition to securing the fundamentals of the business, Huawei also attached greater importance to establishing alliances with shared interests along the supply chain. Ren pointed out that the supply chain is the focus of future competition, as it gathers hundreds of manufacturers, distributors, and agents. Huawei should rally the whole system as an alliance. In a market recession, Huawei should actively develop allies; it should rather suffer a loss than make its allies suffer. Sometimes, it can even join hands with its competitors to reduce R&D costs.

Consolidate organizational culture with *Huawei Basic Law*

In 1997, Huawei invited professors from Renmin University of China to formulate the *Huawei Basic Law*, which incorporates and makes an explicit characterization of Huawei leaders' implicit ideas to enhance organizational consensus and alignment. *Huawei Basic Law* clarifies Huawei's missions, strategic outlook, culture, values, and guiding principles, laying the foundation for the unity of thought in the process of scaling up. *Huawei Basic Law* expresses what the company does and doesn't do, providing clear boundaries for organizational self-management and motivation, and significantly reduces communication costs in the unification process (see Sect. 5.6 for details).

---

[14] Ren Zhengfei: Meet the challenge and consolidate skills for the arrival of spring. 2006.

[15] Ren Zhengfei: "Hard work will pay off eventually". Huawei People. July 21, 2006.

While ensuring the stability of the organization's culture, Huawei also needs to continue to activate the organization's development momentum. The more difficult the market is, the more important it is to train the team. Otherwise, how can its employees march forward to new markets when opportunities arise. Cultivating a strong team during the market downturn is a big project. The key is to strengthen performance management by implementing last-place elimination and laying off laggard employees. The purpose of last-place elimination is to reduce the unnecessary burden so that Huawei can move faster. Jack Welch, the former CEO of General Electric once said that we shall never stop eliminating the last-placer. Only this way can the entire organization be activated. The secret of the century-old GE is the Vitality Curve. The Vitality Curve is a performance management practice that calls for individuals to be ranked or rated against their coworkers. It is also called stack ranking, forced ranking, and rank and yank. Welch believes that the Vitality Curve can enable a large company to stay as dynamic as a small one. The rank-and-yank system in Huawei survives much longer than five years, and Huawei implements it as patiently and responsibly as the West Point.

Introducing an international management system

Since its inception, Huawei has drawn on the managerial expertise of international companies and established a corporate system with clear property rights, clear authorities and responsibilities, and scientific management. It is a new company with standardized operations and market orientation; new product development and production are the main focuses of the company with assets as the link. As a new high-tech company, Huawei has a flexible mechanism and thus has no baggage. It exercises the principle of from each according to his ability and to each according to his contribution, the practice of which is conducive to talent retention and collective endeavor. Huawei has invested heavily in importing the management systems and practices of IBM and other multinationals to create Huawei's own management system and platform of international standard, laying a solid foundation for larger-scale operations. Ren was aware that there was still a big gap between Huawei and international industry leaders in almost every aspect, including technology development, product quality, marketing capability, branding, and management system, and the resources available to the firm were limited. He chose to prioritize the management system, because management, as a matter of life and death for the company, is the platform that can bring technology, talent, and capital to their maximum potential. Without management, talent, technology, and capital cannot form a synergy, and without service, management will have no direction. To this end, Huawei invested heavily to reverse localized management, and initiated the process of de-localization, introducing American management systems by rigidifying, solidifying, and optimizing. For more information on the topics, see Fig. 4.1 Building market capabilities with external resources.

The main goal of management transformation is to move from the flexible operation of a private firm to a process-orientated multinational. Huawei's production system was gradually moving toward ISO9001, and the reliability of its products

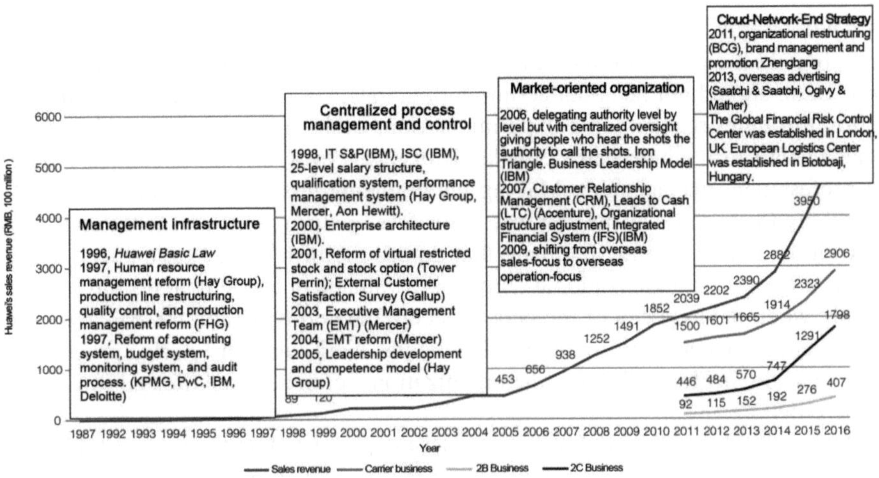

Fig. 4.1 Building market capabilities with external resources

has greatly improved, strongly supporting the front end.[16] The firm plans to execute IT-based management and end-to-end process management in 2–3 years, with every manager operating according to the process. To achieve this, Huawei needs to import a mature Western management system and combines it with its design and reform, rather than totally rely on consultants to improve the management.

Expanding international markets

When the domestic market hit the wall, Huawei adopted a strategy of aggressively expanding overseas markets. When the East goes dark, the West shines. This strategy helped expand the market for larger-scale operations. Huawei focused on Africa, because it believes that the tougher the market is, the more the faster both the people and the market will grow. Young people who bravely explore the international market at their best age will benefit a lot in their lifetime.[17] Huawei decided to take 2–3 years to increase its export value to 2 billion US dollars, laying a solid foundation for the company's survival and security. During this period, Ren and Sun Yafang visited country after country to understand the local conditions and challenges, leaving no stones unturned. They took proactive measures to solve problems, join forces at home and abroad to fight a good battle.[18]

From personal worship to professional management

An important part of Huawei's second business venture is the transformation toward standardized and professional management. The purpose of professional management is to make it difficult to put any senior executive on a pedestal so that the

[16] Ren Zhengfei: "Don't forget the heroes". January 23, 1997.

[17] Ren Zhengfei: "Meet the challenge and consolidate skills for the arrival of spring". 2006.

[18] Ren Zhengfei: "Spring in the North". April 24, 2001.

firm will be truly customer-focused. Only in this way can a large firm truly improve operational efficiency and reduce internal friction. In Huawei's view, organizational innovation should not be about certain individuals, but standardization-based innovation through organizational experimentation, evaluation, and review.[19] Huawei, once a small firm where heroes made history, was evolving into a company based on professional management. Making the company less about certain individuals, especially the founder, is the pathway to professionalism, which turns the charisma, motivation, and drive into a climate that guides the firm to stay on the right track. In this process, the organizational climate is a valuable management resource, and it is only when the majority of the people accept the corporate culture, can a team of competent managers who share the same values work together to drive progress on a larger scale. In Huawei's case, the organizational climate is manifested by *Huawei Basic Law*.

Although, Huawei's employees were less experienced and knowledgeable than their counterparts in leading companies in the developed world, they were young, ambitious, energetic, and enterprising; more importantly, they were good learners. They have made breakthroughs in certain technology frontiers. Meanwhile, the multinationals were suffering from a talent gap as their senior employees were retiring and new ones were not mature yet. Such a situation gave Huawei a window of opportunities of 3–5 years to overtake its competitors. If Huawei could establish itself as an international player through sustained efforts and improvements, it would secure its place in the international market when entering the twenty-first century. Of course, this was a huge challenge but also an opportunity for the young team. In the worst-case scenario, the young team could be blindly complacent at the slightest success, and the business could risk bankruptcy. Under these circumstances, it was also a challenge for Ren to manage thousands of energetic and ambitious young employees and ensure they stay on the right track.

Building corporate image

Corporate image is important to win customers' confidence in Huawei, especially in a difficult time. In 2004, Huawei's overseas sales were good. The CIS region and the Asia Pacific region made sizeable breakthroughs, and exports were starting to outstrip domestic sales. The swanky glass curtain wall of the Huawei Building was particularly built for the marketing department. When customers from all over the world saw Huawei's imposing building, they would have more confidence in this firm and were more likely to sign the contract.

[19] Ren Zhengfei: "The responsibility and mission of a professional manager". 2000.

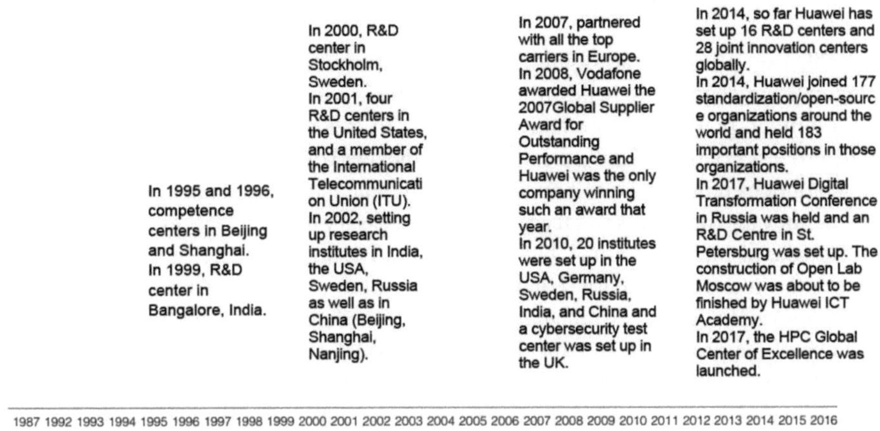

Fig. 4.2 Huawei's global capability

4.3 Marketing Phase: Toward a Multinational Company (2008–2011)

Following the success of its management transformation and internationalization strategy, Huawei entered a period of rapid growth. In 2007, its sales hit the 10 billion USD threshold for the first time. A year later, the global financial crisis unraveled. Huawei saw it as both a challenge and an opportunity, as although the crisis cripples the weak, it makes you stronger if it does not kill you. At that time, Huawei was neither weak nor strong. When analyzing Huawei's strengths and weaknesses, Ren pointed out that there were two barriers to Huawei's journey to becoming a strong player: one is end-to-end delivery; the other is financial management.[20] Thus, Huawei is constantly seeking change and improvement in both areas: it imported an LTC project from Accenture to support the end-to-end delivery system, and achieve coordination with other departments, so as to empower Huawei to become the strongest company in the world.

Global capacity building

Huawei's globalization process is capability-oriented instead of export-oriented. From the evolution reflected in Fig. 4.2, we can see that Huawei attaches great importance to establishing competence centers close to international leading enterprises, so as to obtain first-hand information and top talent from international competitors through close-range learning and observation and the use of networking resources. In this way, Huawei can quickly close the knowledge gap with leading international companies and put international talent to its use. A salient feature of a global company is that they understand the value of top talent.

[20] The minutes of the meeting between Ren Zhengfei and PMS senior project managers. March 7, 2009.

Let those who hear the shots call the shots

In 2009, Ren proposed an organizational transformation to let those who hear the shots call the shots. The head office did not have a full picture of field offices yet had too much power and too many resources. In order to manage operational risks, many process control points were set up, and the head office was reluctant to delegate. Such practices reduced overall operational efficiency, increased operating costs, bred bureaucracy and dogmatism. Of course, it is necessary to set up process control points for the sake of internal control, but the command posts should be stationed in places where the shots can be heard. Huawei's exploration in North Africa provided some food for thought. The decision-making power was delegated to the field teams, with the back office providing support. Under this model, the process should be adjusted and optimized with front-end offices as the starting point. The needs and objectives of front-end offices should be supported, and company-wide effort should be applied to effective process points, and processes and personnel should be streamlined, lay a solid foundation for survival.

Building a customer-oriented organization

The design of the organizational system has always been a challenge for a large corporation. Before 2009, Huawei had moved from decentralization to centralization through process transformation. After 2009, with customer resources becoming scarce, Huawei need to move from centralized control to customer-centric coordinated development. Through global process integration, the back office has been turned into an organizational support system. Delegation, exercise, and supervision of power are arranged along the process to avoid inefficiency and bloated organization. The purpose is to achieve the customer demand-driven process. By this time, Huawei had a clear focus, i.e., the operational needs of the front-end office with the back-office platform providing timely and accurate support. The purpose of setting up the organization is to fight to win, meaning making profits.

Managing transformation: building a front-end-centric organization

At this stage, with Huawei's diversifying global customer demands, the collaboration between its marketing teams and back offices became an important issue hampering corporate development and its ability to meet customer demands. Huawei found that less than one-third of the time of front-end employees was spent on finding leads, and turning leads into results and that a lot of time was spent on frequent communication and coordination with the back office. The coordination difficulties are generated due to the process, organization setup, mindset, and lack of mutual trust, and understanding of the main business by the non-main business departments, and so on. At this stage, Huawei needs to identify the key to improving the efficiency of the field operations and the back offices. It should be noted that the key has been found, but it was somehow jammed in the keyhole.

In order to solve this problem, Ren asked the employees to revisit IBM Business Process Manager (BPM), top management accurately understand and strictly implement BPM, and management at all levels to assume their responsibilities, so that

Huawei can get rid of the rigid centralized model. These authorization documents are continuously revised as the company changes to meet new needs.

From scale-focused to profit-focused

At this stage, Huawei's focus shifted to the profit center, which is supported by the head office. The profit center regards profit as the basis for decision-making, and the current system must be turned around. The pilot reform began with six offices.[21] Cost control is naturally an important indicator. However, excessive cost-cutting will impact quality. Therefore, cost should not be the only concern; the quality/cost ratio is even more relevant, since if something goes wrong, the cost will only be even higher. When the market was growing fast, too much emphasis was placed on sales. It was believed that more contracts would bring more profits. As the market became saturated, the chances of making profits are getting thinner. So, in order to survive, it is important to implement lean management. To ensure the profit-centric strategy, Huawei has established regional financial management systems across its global network and cultivated 200–300 CFOs to manage these systems. The CFOs role is not solely accounting; they need to understand both business and finance, and have the ability to execute planning, budgeting, and accounting.

Internationalization started in difficult markets

When Huawei began to expand its international market, it found that all the fertile markets had already been taken by Western companies, and only remote and troubled areas were left. However, Huawei people were not daunted; the employees hiked eight days on an oxygen-deprived plateau, climbed snow-capped mountains, and crossed jungles to serve customers. Some were attacked by muggers and received 30 stitches on his head in a foreign country, but immediately threw himself back to work upon recovery. Some who had survived a plane crash offered to help others while still in a state of shock, and earned the respect of the local government and people. Some were injured in terrorist attacks or contracted malaria, but continued to perform their duties upon recovery. Three talented young African employees were killed in a plane crash while on a business trip…[22]

In 2007, Ren led his team to attend the SVIAZ EXPO COMM MOSCOW2007. The Expo was attended by 600 exhibitors from more than 30 countries and regions. Apparently, they were all interested in Russia's potentially huge market. Huawei attended a small exhibition in Geneva in 2006. This was the first time it had participated in such a large international exhibition, and it prepared tens of thousands of copies of various brochures. The experts from Russia's Presidential Executive Offices Information Office visited the exhibition secretly for about an hour and found that China was not as backward as they had thought. They showed their business cards and

[21] The minutes of the meeting between Ren Zhengfei and PMS senior project managers. March 7, 2009.

[22] Ren Zhengfei: "Hard work will pay off eventually". Huawei People. July 21, 2006.

asked to meet the head of the delegation. When Ren accompanied Russian buyers on the tour, they more than once expressed their appreciation for the Chinese products.[23]

In the process of meeting international standards, Huawei realized that the most part is to improve efficiency. Since most of the international standards come from the West, so it is important for Chinese employees to use English proficiently. However, the communication barrier is not just a language issue; it also involves management style, way of expression, and cultural differences. Huawei hoped to solve the cross-cultural communication problem in 3 years by transferring a large number of employees with successful experience from overseas to the head office.[24,25]

Creating a globally unified platform that balances consistency and regional differences

After Huawei had more operations globally, more local employees joined the regional divisions. To meet the management challenges, Huawei first established a globally unified platform and made it a mandatory communication and management channel. Then it allowed each local platform to have its own unique features. Since the situation of the market is ever-changing, the platform should not be rigid. So, it is important to have a standardized central support platform, but also allow for flexible tactics at the front end.

4.4 Branding Phase: Building a Consumer-Centric Premium Brand (2012–2016)

Before 2012, Huawei was mainly a 2B business serving carriers. In 2011, the company decided to focus on the Cloud-Channel-Device model and mobile phone business, upgrading its low-end phones to high-end ones. The figures behind this change were as follows: Huawei already had 30% of the global carrier's market, the size of which was around $100 billion. The mobile phone market was about $400 billion, and if Huawei can take 20% of the market, the company's revenue can grow by $50 billion to $80 billion. In order to find new growth opportunities, companies must continue to find new growth markets.

Apple and Samsung the two smartphone giants naturally posed a daunting challenge to Huawei's transformation from a low-end smartphone maker to a high-end one. Ren picked Yu Chengdong, who had scored big in the wireless business and European market, to charge this new business. Yu is bold and aggressive, the most criticized Huawei's executive, and considered to be a braggart. Yet his personality played an important role in this job of great uncertainties and challenges. In the R&D

[23] Ren Zhengfei: Notes to Huawei's Exhibition in SVIAZ EXPO COMM MOSCOW. January 17, 2007.

[24] The minutes of the meeting between Ren Zhengfei and PMS senior project managers. March 7, 2009.

[25] Ibid.

process, Yu and his team encountered many challenges, doubts, and failures but Ren always gave him full trust, as well as time and space to explore; he even shielded Yu from many arrows so to speak. When facing a variety of conflicting views, Ren said that strategic dissent is a strategic reserve, and expression of different views should be embraced. He always gives maximum support to innovators.

Originally, Huawei was an OEM of subpar products for European carriers, excessively reliant on carriers, and had very low consumer recognition. When Huawei adopted a bold strategy to discontinue the production of low-end white-label phones for European carriers, it met fierce backlash. However, Huawei executives did not back off.

Another challenge was choosing the sales channels. At that time, Xiaomi was the most known Chinese smartphone brand, so some people in Huawei suggested going online to compete against Xiaomi. But Yu insisted on taking the high-end route, benchmarking against Apple and Samsung, using existing offline channels to promote sales. Neither side can convince the other, so in the end, Huawei decided to adopt a dual strategy: Honor phones go online, while Huawei high-end phones go offline.

The quality and technology priority strategy

Huawei's aim is to become the world's No. 1 high-end smartphone maker, rather than some short-lived phenomenon, so it does not pursue short-term profits, but rather is committed to making high-quality products and taking the high-end route. Although many people at the time were rather skeptical; especially as Huawei always focused on enterprise business, so there were many uncertainties as to whether it could succeed at the consumer level. Fortunately, Huawei's strength is its technical reserves. As early as 2004, Huawei established Hisilicon, a subsidiary to research wireless communication chips, the predecessor of Hisilicon is the Huawei Integrated Circuit Design Center, founded in 1991. Hisilicon mainly serves the system equipment business and mobile phone terminal business. In the beginning, the team of the terminal business was small, but now it has grown to several thousand people.

Changing the product development strategy

When serving enterprises, Huawei took an engineer-led approach to make the product the best it could be. However, when making mobile phones, Huawei changed its strategy to designer-led, putting the customer experience first. Huawei believes that aesthetics should be decided by professional designers, not by company leaders. While making the product better, the customer experience should be the best.

Global resources consolidation

It took Huawei 4–5 years of trial and error to develop its smartphones, eventually, great improvements have been made, and problems such as overheated chips and standby time have gradually been solved. The Kirin 950 released in 2015 was a success; it was a TSMCs 16 nm FinFET process-based chip. On the chip algorithm, design, camera functions, and other features that consumers are particularly interested in, Huawei invested profusely to combine its premium resources: the Russia-based

Research Institute, its France-based chief designer (a former BMW designer), and Germany-based Leira, to create a high-end smartphone, which turned out to be very popular around the world (see Chap. 13 for details).

Building a consumer brand

In 2018, Huawei overtook Apple as the world's second-largest smartphone vendor, according to the report by IDC released in October 2017. Also, according to Interbrand's 2016 Best Global Brands Report, Huawei ranked 72nd, up by 16 places from 2015. Huawei became the first Chinese mainland brand to make the list in 2014 and has made the leap up the rankings for the second year in a row. Focusing on consumer experience, Huawei has conducted a series of global branding activities, including sponsorship of Spain's La Liga and Italy's AC Milan, which have greatly increased Huawei's visibility.

4.5 Digitization Phase: The World's Leading Digital Company (2017–Present)

In 2017, Huawei rolled out a strategy for digital transformation, which encompasses digital collaboration, digital production, digital services, and digital assets. The key objective of digitalization is to create values through digital products and services for customers by using data and ICT systems as tools.

Huawei's digital production benchmarked against the American Joint Strike Fighter (JSF) program of the late twentieth century, which is a development and acquisition program intended to replace a wide range of existing fighter, strike, and ground-attack aircraft for the US, UK, Italy, etc. Lockheed Martin led a team of 50 companies from 30 countries to collaborate on design, manufacturing, testing, deployment, and tracking the entire project development process digitally. The results were dramatic: design time was reduced by 50%, manufacturing time by 67%, final assembly by 90%, parts count by 50%, and design, manufacturing, and maintenance costs all by 50% respectively.

Key concepts for digital transformation

Huawei believes that a digital strategy is a key for traditional enterprises to make data their core competency. To achieve the digital transformation, three main dimensions must be involved: First, asset digitization. Three types of data are critical in this process customer data, operational data, and asset data (specifically, product and service data). Of these, the asset data are unique to the industry, which is, therefore, the key to digital transformation. Second, data mobility. The firm needs to centralize the scattered data of not only their own but also of their partners, build a unified database, and achieve data consistency and sharing through good data governance, so that data can generate value in the flow. Third, product modeling. For most enterprises, piles of data are like breadcrumbs that are basically valueless. To capitalize on the data, the firm needs to build data models for their core products and to achieve two-way communication and a feedback loop between the digital and physical worlds so as to maximize the value of data.[26]

Based on the accumulated data of its 3.5 million base stations, Huawei can shorten the network service launch time, reduce costs and improve the efficiency of the entire process: in R&D and design, designers can wear VR goggles and sensor gloves for virtual installation of various scenarios to quickly and iteratively optimize designs; in engineering and installation, with just one 3D scanning instead of frequent station surveys, the survey of the base station is done; for the acceptance, it only needs to take a few photos for the backstage to go through image recognition, saving the huge cost of manual acceptance.

Main objectives of digital transformation

The ultimate goal of Huawei's digital transformation is to provide better services for the enterprise business. Huawei is a large and complex organization with 180,000 employees, over 900 branches, 15 R&D centers, and 36 joint innovation centers around the world, not to mention its millions of partners and more than 60,000 suppliers. With the increasing complexity and uncertainty of global businesses, Huawei's original approach of managing all processes in a centralized manner cannot meet the flexibility and efficiency requirements of future development. In the face of such management challenges, Huawei believes that it must align its business objectives to drive business change and achieve lean operations on a big platform, i.e., efficient decision-making in field office with full authorization. Under this distributed management model, the entire company's management structure, operational processes, and IT infrastructure will have to change. Through digital transformation, Huawei will increase its platform capacity.[27] Huawei has experienced the benefits of getting rich, first build roads, and building the Great Wall with European and American bricks; therefore, digital transformation is just a new chapter in its long-term information system development.

Three dimensions of digital transformation

Huawei believes that there are three main layers of digitalization: the first layer is ICT infrastructure, which is the foundation of the digital economy; the second is network security, including the security of both the physical and cyber worlds, which is the guarantee for development; the third is the digitization of various industries, on the basis of which information integration and integrated management from the city level to the national level can be achieved and thus forming an Intelligent Operation Center (IOC).[28]

---

[26] Xu Wenwei: "How to win in the digital transformation?". *Harvard Business Review* (Chinese Edition). October 2017.

[27] Tao Jingwen: Huawei CIOs account of digital change and IT practices. *ICT New Vision*. October 31, 2017.

[28] Guo Ping: Exploring digital transformation in the Asia Pacific at Huawei Asia-Pacific Innovation Day. November 9, 2017.

In order to build a digital production system, Huawei's vision is to build talking machines at the terminal level. Digital production requires astronomical information from terminal equipment, which requires machines to talk and continuously spit out data through sensors, so that all behavior will be recorded as data in the system. At the network level, an Internet of Things (IoT) will be created. Digital production needs to connect and manage all kinds of assets and equipment of the enterprise. Through NB-IoT, it can realize low-power and wide-area mass connectivity. At the cloud level, a multi-tier cloud platform will be created. Huawei expects that 85% of enterprise applications will be deployed in the cloud by 2025, and applications can't be developed without the platform as a service (PaaS), including modules such as big data analytics, IoT platforms, and AI platforms. The bottom layer is Infrastructure as a service (IaaS), which provides computing, storage, network, security, and other cloud services. Large and medium-sized enterprises generally use a hybrid cloud for data security considerations. For the public part of the hybrid cloud, enterprises will choose a safe and reliable provider. For example, a big part of the reason that Airbus chose Deutsche Telekom's public cloud is that Deutsche Telekom can meet the government's regulation requiring 80 years of data storage.

At the service level, the digital age has greatly reduced the time and cost of converting data into opportunities, turning what used to be high-cost, fragmented services into low-cost and large-scale, and even making formerly unavailable services available. Large-scale digital services were becoming more profitable, and industry value was beginning to shift from traditional products and services to digital ones.

Strategic advancement of digital transformation

In the view of Huawei's senior management, the future is not about new firms eliminating old ones, but about transformation and upgrading. Firms can gradually realize digital transformation through trial and error. Huawei decided to act quickly on the premise that the direction is basically correct even if its people did not see eye to eye for the moment and establish a data-based efficient feedback loop and promote the strategy while continuously adjusting it.

In the journey of digital transformation, Huawei decided to start exploring on its own first. It built its own public cloud business to work with global carriers. Together with the carriers and business partners, an industry ecosystem cloud was created, thus realizing its vision of becoming one of the five top clouds in the world. Huawei's greatest advantage over pure Internet companies lies in its partnership with carriers and ability to serve industry players offline. In the process, Huawei unites all those who can be united with shared benefits including players along the upstream and downstream industry chains, its customers, and suppliers. In the entire cloud ecosystem, Huawei takes only 1% and gives the rest to its partners.

Key applications for digital transformation

To achieve digital transformation, the IT system should be based on the solid foundation of IPD/ISC/LTC/IFS. The key for digital transformation in the next five years is ROADS. R stands for Real-time. Everything should be done with a simple click. Business provision should be done in real-time: from older generation to payment, to system configuration, business provision should only take a few seconds, so that the order should be generated before the user loses interest. Compared to the old days when business provision took hours, even days or weeks, it has greatly improved customer satisfaction. O stands for On-demand, which allows users to customize services according to their needs. A stands for All-online. Nowadays, users have become more and more accustomed to performing various operations and ordering various services online, shopping online, paying bills online, working online... In the future, based on cloud technology, more and more services can be completed online, which will bring even more convenience to users. D stands for DIY, which provides users with the opportunity to do whatever they want, or even to participate in the development and optimization of various services, thus accelerating business innovation and enhancing users' participation. S stands for social. ROADS is the manifestation of user-centricity in the information age, which requires an all-around change in the business model, marketing model, R&D model, operation model, and service model of the firm, as well as the reconstruction of the telecommunication network itself to support the above changes.

Who leads the digital transformation?

Huawei attaches great importance to management, and its information department will play an important role in the digital transformation. However, digital transformation should be led by the business department, and the business manager should know how to support business development through digital transformation and what business problems to solve; the IT department, as an enabling department, should not overstep, but instead fully communicate with the business department to build a strong IT platform to drive and support the rapid change. The core of digital transformation is customer demand. Huawei believes that digital transformation requires building a multi-ecological and fully connected digital platform for all five types of users, including enterprise business, consumers, partners, employees, and suppliers, rather than just employees. The digital architecture should include the digitization of business objects, processes, and rules, to make it an all-around digital transformation. The path of digital transformation starts with the transformation of Huawei's business platforms; the ROADS model is used to improve effectiveness, efficiency, and customer satisfaction; after successful transformation, the model and methods will be applied to other enterprises to help them achieve digital transformation with seamless and efficient services.

4.6 Huawei's Transformation Methodology

Huawei has developed a set of transformation methodology Program Management Operation Process (PMOP) in the process of transforming the organization into a process-and-information-based organization. PMOP is a process of prudent program management that treats change as an investment decision, to ensure successful program development. Program management focuses on both vertical and horizontal dimensions: the vertical transformation refers to the phased program decision-making process, and the horizontal transformation refers to the supporting processes such as revenue management, project management, and transformation management.

Decision Check Point DCP Technical Review TR Plan Decision Checkpoint PDCP Program Readiness Review PRR Technology Review TR IT.

Vertical transformation projects are controlled and evaluated through Decision Check Points (DCPs) and Technical Reviews (TRs) at each stage of the program to allow interaction between the investor and the program team to determine whether the investment shall continue, and the program shall move to the next stage. The purpose of DCPs is to ensure the return on the investment; they include the decision to establish the program, the decision to make a high-level plan, the Plan Decision Checkpoint (PDCP), the Program Readiness Review (PRR), and the Program Readiness Review (PRR), Implementation Readiness Review (IRR), and Program Closure Review (PCR). The Technology Review (TR) is defined as a review point for a technical solution, regarding feasibility, outline design, and access; TR is typically conducted by the program team or demand management teams in specific domains to ensure the rationality, feasibility, and architectural compliance of the business process and IT solution.

The horizontal transformation requires project management, transformation management, transformation value management, and other supporting processes. The project management process requires clarity and detail-orientation, including project scope, project change management, project scheduling management schemes, and rules, human resource management methods and rules, consultant procurement management, costing management, problem and risk management, communication management, overall project operations management and process compliance.

The transformation management process includes stakeholder management, transformation impact, readiness and acceptance assessment management, transformation organization design and alignment, transformation communication and advocacy, and training.

Transformation value management is about managing the transformation value and value-based transformation management. In other words, it should set the benefits target of the transformation, regularly measure and evaluate the benefits achievement progress at each milestone of the transformation in the whole cycle, and timely develop and implement the improvement action plan to ensure target attainment. Setting metrics for the target attainment will help the program to focus on its objectives and generate more benefits.

In 2012, Huawei's Transformation Management Committee set forth three requirements to maintain value management in the transformation and ensure the attainment of transformation benefits. First, the transformation should be supported by budget and generate benefits; relevant departments are required to sign off on the benefits commitment. The benefits will be reviewed upon PCR. Second, the transformation value should be measured along the business process as much as possible, using existing metrics, and considering both direct and indirect benefits as well as intangible values for strategic investment projects. Third, building an IT platform for demand management to analyze the inputs and outputs of the project; summarizing the reasons for poor benefits; giving recommendations for improvement.

For example, in the Lead to Cash (LTC) transformation, the implementation process involves 158 frontline teams around the world, with highly complex processes and IT implementation. In integrated transformation, a set of transformation methods for front-end offices, regional offices, and head office were summed up, according to the requirements of the Business Transformation Management System (BTMS), to guide the transformation and ensure that the transformation meets the basic quality requirements as well as expectations and the goal of the transformation. The approach for front-end offices is based on the 3-Stage and 16-Step Guideline, under which the front-line teams take full ownership of and drive the value-oriented transformation. The 3-Stage and 16-Step Guideline adapts and simplifies the theory and basic requirements of BTMS. Each step is supported by a corresponding guidebook, tool templates, and examples, all of which constitute a toolkit for and provide sufficient guidance to the front-line business team to implement the transformation. At the same time, the Guideline also provides unified standards and requirements for transformation; some steps are required to be enforced to the letter. For example, PRR requires the frontline business team to conduct self-assessment in four aspects before initiating LTC: organizational readiness, personnel readiness, capacity readiness, and supervisor readiness. If the self-assessment scores under 80 points, in principle, the transformation should not be initiated.

Huawei later upgraded BTMS to its 2.0 version with optimization mainly in two aspects: First, the project group management process is streamlined. Second, architecture control requirements and its support teams are added to strengthen architecture management, requiring the architecture to set rules for the entire process in accordance with the development and release mechanism. The architecture elements are integrated into the planning, requirements, and implementation to make the whole process work in an orderly environment according to the architecture rules.

4.7 Success Factors for Huawei's Transformation

Key drivers of business transformation and change

The key drivers of Huawei's transformation are threefold: First, the leadership's crisis awareness and survival pressure. Second, corporate vision and strategy. Third, the need for business growth and corporate development.

First of all, based on a profound understanding of the innovative characteristics of ICT technology and the global competition, Huawei always harbors a sense of insecurity; it never rests on its past achievement. Crisis awareness has become an integral part of its survival, development, and transformation. Such a trait drives Huawei to constantly anticipate future changes in technology, market, policy, and industry, to grasp the key needs of the market and the main contradictions of industry development, so that it can steadily and accurately enter the key areas of transformation. Huawei's transformation is not some attempt to follow the crowd due to hot-headedness or some big leap forward, but rather it is an orderly advancement guided by rational analysis and methodology after thorough discussion and debate. Facing a myriad of uncertainties, Huawei requires a basically correct direction. When many Chinese companies speculate on heated investment projects, Huawei calmly observes and acts based on its profound understanding of global industrialization and informationization development.

Second, every transformation in Huawei is driven by the corporate vision and ever-upgrading strategy, namely from becoming a world-class enterprise in 1997 to internationalization in 2008, from the Cloud-Channel-Device strategy in 2011 to the digital transformation in 2017. Huawei has driven the upgrading of its internal management and service system through its ever-upgrading strategies. The goals of transformation are clear, prioritized, well-prepared, methodologically effective, and risk-controlled.

Finally, to survive is the ultimate goal of transformation and upgrading. ESOP ties 180,000 Huawei people with the company. In order to survive, company-wide effort is required to ensure growth. Growth is realized by evolving from an industrial application with limited capacity to a large industrial platform. This is Huawei's way to generate benefits and attract and retain talent. This ingenious mechanism is designed to greatly reduce resistance and barriers to organizational change and has led to transformational success over and over again.

Strategy-led organizational transformation

From the evolution shown in Fig. 4.3, Huawei's transformational change has a very clear strategic orientation, which guides the internal change of the organization and gives the change a realistic meaning. The strategy-led organizational transformation helps the whole firm build synergy and clarify its direction; meanwhile, internal management and organizational transformation serve the strategic objectives. The two processes are complementary to each other, and the pains caused by transformation and change are alleviated by the realization of strategic objectives, thus maximizing organizational value. Figure 4.3 shows the roadmap of Huawei's transformation from a mom-and-pop operation to a global player step by step. It also shows the transformed and upgraded internal management system is the most important cornerstone to support the strategic goals.

Balancing change and stability and managing the pace

From Fig. 4.3, we can see that transformation and change takes place in Huawei every 7–10 years. Ren is well aware that many reforms failed because they were executed hastily, stretched too thin, or were too rigid. That is why Huawei has been taking a stepwise approach to improve itself over the past 30 years, with only one or two radical changes. Ren believes that during the transformation, Huawei should always focus on the most important issue and the relevant determinant factors, set the correct direction, and plan before moving forward. It should promptly identify feasible plans that are urgently needed even though they are not perfect. It should

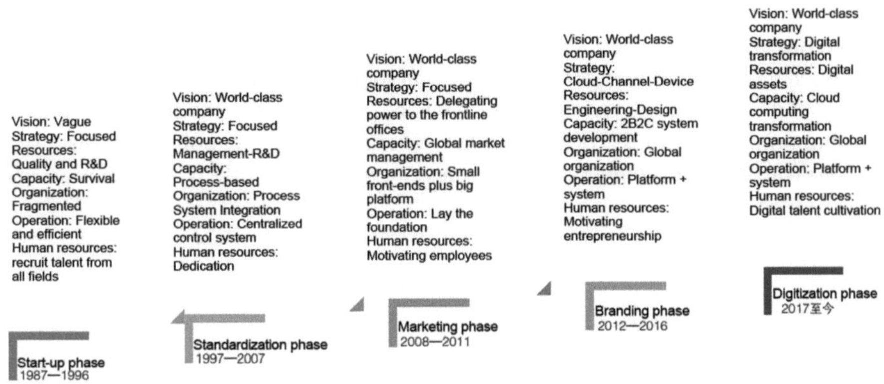

Fig. 4.3 Huawei's transformation, change, and evolution

not pursue perfection or take credit for the success of others. Perfectionism is not feasible for Huawei. What it really needs is pragmatism. To achieve the great mission, Huawei people must have a clear mind to follow the correct direction. They must take solid steps and stay focused on the core business, which will allow the company to surf the wave of this new era, progress, and reap the harvest of the transformation.[29] In the process of transformation, Huawei started with reforming the front offices, strengthening its capability, integrating the service and management of the back-office platform, and reducing the friction between the front and back offices. Huawei always keeps the adaptive change of the back-office platform in check and moves forward prudently step by step. In its view, even a one-thousandth improvement in efficiency is a welcome result.

Balancing interests in the transformation

Huawei understands that transformation means the redistribution of benefits, so it is a big thing. Only when the redistribution of benefits is carried out by a strong management structure, can the transformation take place. In the process of transformation, the old balance is gradually replaced by a new one, which will also be replaced by the next new balance: it is an endless cycle, which leads to the improvement of the core competitiveness of the firm and the growth of benefits. With the support of the IT system, the previous multi-layer administrative system becomes flatter. The disappearing middle management makes a large number of managers redundant, so all departments should transfer the redundant managers to new positions in a timely manner to avoid excessive layoffs.[30]

Balanced development in the transformation

According to the Wooden Bucket Theory, a buckets capacity is determined by its shortest stave. The original background of senior management has a big impact on

[29] Ren Zhengfei: "Do not be a perfect man" at a meeting with model CPC members. May 21, 2008.

[30] Ren Zhengfei: "Huawei's winter", *Huawei People*. 2001.

their decisions. In Huawei, senior managers were mainly promoted from R&D and Marketing and Sales. Their subconscious favoritism for their original departments prevented them from making the best decisions and developing the right value assessment system. As a result, strong departments became stronger and the weak weaker, forming bottlenecks in the organization.[31] Therefore, Huawei constantly discovers the shortest stave to achieve balanced development with timely remediation and improvement.

4.8 Huawei Versus Cisco

Self-negation is by no means easy. Transformation and change are a process of constant self-negation and self-improvement according to the changes in the market and competition. In this process, the company must never rest on its past success. It should dynamically follow the future, and tenaciously explore the emerging markets; it should, without hesitation, get rid of the shackles of the past, and courageously make self-transformation.

In my long-term study of Huawei and Cisco, I found that these two firms have a common characteristic that makes them thrive in the telecom equipment industry, that is, the courage and efforts of continuous transformation and change. In the past 30 years, Huawei has undergone four major strategic transformations: the first transformation took place in 1997 and it proposed a vision to build a world-class company and introduced IBMs IPD system to achieve the transformation toward the international practice. This transformation lasted more than twenty years. It was the transformation of the management system that has transformed Huawei from a mom-and-pop operation into a modern company, from undisciplined discrete management to integrated, digital, and standardized management with processes, information systems, supply chains, and value networks at its core.

Based on integrated management, Huawei proposed the second transformation to let those who can hear the shots, to call the shots in 2008. It transformed the frontline offices from head office-driven to market and customer-driven. The transformation enabled Huawei to effectively respond to the diverse and dynamic demands of the global market and struck a balance between the consistency of internal management and the diversity of external demands. The third transformation marks the efforts toward a global enterprise. The fourth is the transformation from 2B to 2C after putting forward the Cloud-Channel-Device strategy in 2010, and especially after realizing the shift from a low-end to a high-end mobile phone maker. Huawei's four transformations are initiated of its own accord and are accelerated with strategic focus. Cisco has undergone nine transformations: some were based on corporate development; some were from the pressure of shareholders.

Huawei and Cisco have something in common in their transformation.

---

[31] Ibid.

Obtaining new growth drive through transformation. The transformation goals of Huawei and Cisco are closely related to the growth of the companies. Cisco transformation is focused on external dynamics. By dynamically tracking the latest technological trends, Cisco gains rapid access to emerging markets and rapid growth in those markets via M&A, strategic alliances, partnerships, and internationalization. As a latecomer, Huawei's transformation adopts a gradualist strategy, moving from rural to urban, from domestic to international markets step by step. In addition, Huawei has paid great attention to strategic focus in its transformation, managing its desires to allocate limited resources. For example, *the 1997 Huawei Basic Law* clearly states that Huawei will never enter the information service industry. In 2012, it proposed the Cloud-Channel-Device strategy and continuously invest and improve its internal management with the strategic focus of transformation.

Seizing the window of opportunity for transformation. Both Huawei and Cisco promoted transformation and change at a time of rapid growth and sound corporate health. This is due to the sensitivity of the leaders of both companies to changes in markets and technologies, their acute predictive capabilities, a strong sense of crisis, and a distaste for slackness. These leaders are good at leveraging customer needs as the drive for transformation. The telecom equipment and Internet industries are known for fast technological change and frequent radical technological innovation. In the transformation process, leaders need to anticipate the new trends and dynamics of the market, technology, customer, and industry, carry out strategic layout and capability building ahead of their competitors, grasp the window of opportunities for transformation, identify capability gaps in the new competition landscape, and make great efforts to build these capabilities.

Breaking organizational inertia through transformation. Transformation is a painful process, because it needs to break down the existing underlying structure of the organization and reconstruct a new one. In a stable structure, people's thinking, skills, behaviors, and interests have matured, and the organization's processes, paths, incentives, and culture are stabilized. In the stable environment, inertia develops and intensifies; resistance to change emerges; organizational vitality is slowly disappearing. In the first transformation, Huawei sent a clear signal to those who resisted change: whoever refuses to change cannot be a manager and all managers need to rigidify, solidify and optimize new processes. Cisco, on the other hand, analyzes different approaches of resisting change based on the resistance zoo concept, and vigorously promotes organizational change through vision, communication, and the formation of transformation teams led by star employees, etc. Both companies use the resistance zoo as a metaphor for change. Both companies have four strong capabilities in promoting the transformation: strong leadership, strong will, strong executive teams, and strong support.

Leaders are key to driving organizational transformation and change. The leaders and senior management of Huawei and Cisco have a clear understanding of the key characteristics and inherent rules of the industry. For example, Ren recognizes that the telecom equipment industry is a base industry; therefore, you either become the industry leader or you are eliminated. There is no third option. So, companies must have a strong sense of crisis, because they will fall back if they do not advance.

Cisco recognizes that the Internet is constantly changing the way people learn, live, and work, so they are constantly capturing the direction and fields of novel technology penetration and quickly entering the fields through organizational changes.

Pacing the transformation. In Ren's view, the most important quality of a leader is to have a good sense of direction and pace. The leadership needs to maintain appropriate flexibility; sticking to the right direction comes from flexibility, compromise, and tolerance. The flexibility is manifested in the cognition of the strategic direction, the grasp of the transformational pace, and the handling of diverse interests. In terms of the transformational pace, an organization needs to maintain the stability of an effective process and should not change it any time when any small problem pops up, because the cost of change will offset the benefits of improvement. Managers at all levels must check on unnecessary changes and should rather err on the conservative side.

Management should not only be standardized, but also innovative, and the innovation itself should be managed. Companies need both promotion and constraint mechanisms. Transformations are always carried out to break old stability and make a new balance, so that the company can maintain its vitality.

Huawei and Cisco also differ significantly in terms of transformation and change. External change and internal transformation are two wheels that carry the organization forward. The greater the intensity of market change, the greater the demand for internal transformation. However, it takes leadership wisdom to prioritize internal transformation. When Huawei put forward its strategic vision of becoming a world-class enterprise in 1997, it also proposed three steps to achieve the goal. The first step is to achieve international standards in production and management in three years; the second is to achieve international standards in marketing in five years; the third is to achieve international standards in R&D in 10 years. Considering the gap between Huawei and the world's leading companies at that time, Ren recognized the importance of the management platform. He understood that a management platform can enable technology, talent, and capital to maximize the potential, and without it, they would not have any synergy. However, Huawei's resources were limited, and it was impossible to change all aspects of management. Therefore, Huawei adopted the strategy of staying in the right direction and moving fast in case of urgent needs to make major breakthroughs in key areas first. Cisco has a clear analytical framework for the drivers of change within the organization, and the strategic transformation of the organization must be ensured and achieved through a change in the internal operating system. The internal operating efficiency includes the following four aspects: improving the experience of employees and customers by enhancing business convenience; accelerating business growth through operational excellence; creating higher profits by improving the efficiency of the supply chain and value chain; setting the right mix of mass manufacturing and customization to balance the universal and specialized customer needs and ensure market scale and high profitability.

Chapter 5
Corporate Culture and Practice Integrated with Key Interest Groups

Culture, in its broadest sense, is cultivated behavior; it is a spiritual state other than material demands of human. From an anthropological perspective, culture is the cumulative deposit of knowledge, experience, beliefs, values, attitudes, meanings, hierarchies, customs, religion, notions of time, roles, and spatial relations, concepts of the universe, and material objects and possessions acquired by a group of people in the course of generations through individual and group striving. It is a system of values, beliefs, and knowledge shared by a large group of people. Culture can be perceived, accumulated, and transmitted through social learning, and is presented and expressed in spontaneous behaviors. Culture consists of explicit and implicit patterns. The explicit part is presented in objects, language, and communication patterns that can be perceived, while the implicit part is deeply embedded in people's subconsciousness, thinking patterns, and values.

Corporate culture in the first phase is determined by the entrepreneur's personality and values. As the enterprise develops, the entrepreneur's personality will be overshadowed by the growing wisdom of the organization, and the corporate culture, as an orientation, will become more enriched. For example, the slogan of the marketing department we will toast those who succeed and offer a helping hand to those who fail is an orientation. Here, to offer a helping hand part is much more difficult than the toast part.

To put corporate culture into practice, the company needs to achieve consistency in three aspects, namely, goals, cognition, and emotions. If employees do not embrace the corporate culture, it will be difficult for them to advance their work.

Not only do we need to understand the corporate culture, but also to practice it. Huawei is constantly refining its corporate culture: it absorbs and digests the excellent culture of others while maintaining the entrepreneur's original traits. To shape corporate culture, we need to build a platform for the unity of thought. We need to have a clear corporate culture in place before further delegating authority. If we had delegated authority before reaching a consensus on our corporate culture, Huawei might have fallen apart.

X. Dong et al., *Huawei*,
https://doi.org/10.1007/978-981-19-4078-1_5

Many people believe that corporate culture is what the boss believes and preaches, especially in the case of a private enterprise. The boss's ideals, values, beliefs, attitudes, and behavioral norms will be mapped onto the organizational culture, program the collective thinking, and leave a distinctive mark on the organization. Many business leaders and managers find themselves often encounter three difficulties in creating corporate culture.

The first difficulty is how to clarify the core meaning of corporate culture and communicate it accurately and concisely. Many enterprises hire external resources to help develop their corporate culture, but the real corporate culture comes from the innermost thoughts and values of the top leadership. The process of externalization (e.g. manifestation and conceptualization) of corporate culture is actually a process of self-exploration, self-validation, self-discovery, and self-confirmation by both entrepreneurs and enterprises.

Culture is not only expressed in the integration of body, mind, and soul, and the consistency of thought and behavior, but also in specific activities such as strategic selection and sequencing, resource allocation, and talent selection. Therefore, the tricky part is how to align the cultural expressions and the entrepreneurs' pursuit and how to use the alignment to resonate with employees.

Another barrier is when clarifying the core connotation of corporate culture, how to make it understood, and easy to be communicated and disseminated to employees in different positions. If the words are obscure, redundant, banal, or too complex, it will be difficult for the corporate concept to be accepted, let alone turned into a code of conduct for the organization. Therefore, clarity, understandability, uniqueness, and operability are essential for corporate culture.

Second, how to translate corporate culture into conscious behaviors of employees. Only when corporate culture is supported by systems, incentives, and promotion mechanisms, and other key institutions, will people accept the authenticity of the corporate culture. Furthermore, effective integration of the core propositions of the corporate culture with the operation of the company is an important way to practice the corporate culture. This way helps to translate it into organizational behaviors.

Corporate culture is reflected in how to handle customer relationships, employee relationships, relationships with oneself, and relationships with other stakeholders. To manage these relationships, the firm needs to set up the talent selection mechanism, financial incentives, and the reward and punishment mechanism. Meanwhile, to showcase corporate culture, role models are needed. As the saying goes, the power of role models is infinite. Therefore, whether the firm's operation is consistent with the corporate culture determines whether it is just a slogan on the wall or a code of conduct that is truly integrated into the DNA of employees.

Third, how to transform the corporate culture as the company grows. Huawei in the catch-up phase is known for its wolf culture. Although this has never been confirmed officially, the passion, thirsty, and toughness of the employees were quite well-known. When it grows to be a world leader, Huawei proposes a culture of inclusiveness, compromise, and grayness (flexibility). Huawei's relationships with its stakeholders vary at different stages of development, and its corporate culture gets more inclusive with its boundaries pushed further. Corporate leaders need to trade off stability and simplicity against change and complexity at different stages of development. It not only affects whether the organizational characteristics can be retained in the long term, but also the direction and methodology of transformation, adjustment, and operation of the organization.

In Huawei's more than three-decade development, it is particularly noteworthy as to how it established the core values, how it has made them deeply rooted in the company and transformed them into conscious behaviors of employees, and how it has expanded cultural inclusiveness as it grows and gets increasingly international.

5.1 Service Is at the Heart of Corporate Culture

In 1997, Ren said, Huawei is a result-driven company, and all our efforts are focused on generating business returns. Our culture is purely corporate, not political or anything else. Our corporate culture is based on service, because only good service generates business returns. There are many types of services: after-sales, research, production, and upgrades till the end of the product's life … Therefore, service should be used to be the keyword to define team building.[1]

How to translate culture into conscious behaviors of employees is a matter of great interest to every enterprise. Huawei requires all its employees to learn something about management. Ren generally will take one or two years to lay the groundwork before any major transformation. Some people are foresighted and quick to respond, and these people will be on the fast track of management. In Huawei's view, corporate culture simply sets a direction, rather than give direct and detailed instructions on specific issues; otherwise, it will only produce confusion.

Cohesion is the key strength of corporate culture

In the early days of Huawei's development, conditions were tough, and resources were scarce, but Ren never thought that Huawei had nothing. He realized that thousands of Huawei's lovely employees, bonded by the corporate culture, could be an inexhaustible source for development. Today's community of shared interests can be tomorrow's community of shared future. When Huawei has low internal friction and high vitality, it will be more resilient, and it will be able to tide over whatever storms in the international market. The key is a culture of continuous self-improvement.[2]

[1] Ren Zhengfei: "Resources can be exhausted, only culture endures" at the work report meeting of the User Service Center. March 20, 1997.

[2] Ren Zhengfei: "Resources can be exhausted, only culture endures" at the work report meeting of the User Service Center. March 20, 1997.

5.2 Core Culture I: Customer Centricity

The core of Huawei's culture is customer-centricity and dedication. It is not unique; many companies have similar slogans and Huawei also learned it from others. So, the key is how to put it into practice. In Ren's view, as long as you take it to your heart, you can do it all.[3]

The Customer instead of technology is the most important focus at Huawei

What is the force that pulls Huawei in the right direction and sustains it? Faced with the uncertainties of the future, Huawei needs continuous exploration and even the slightest deviation may cost dearly. In Huawei's view, it is Customer Centricity rather than technology-centricity that will lighten the way ahead. To be technology-centric is sort of to be self-centered, which may be justified in an era of material shortage.

There are two manifestations of technology-centricity. The first is a belief that the more sophisticated the technology, the more valuable it is. Under this belief, the company will usually impose its will on customers, by developing highly sophisticated technologies and products, and making things so complicated because the more difficult they appear, the more valuable the engineers would seem to be. However, in reality, sometimes what users need are just simple things; most of the products and services that really meet their needs are the simplest features. The second manifestation is to center on the technologies and solutions that the company can provide, rather than the real needs of the users. In other words, the company only meets the partial needs of the users based on its limited resources and capabilities, rather than go all out to come up with a total solution for the users. To provide a total solution to its customers, Huawei will use its best products or outsource, if necessary.[4]

So, what is customer-centric? First of all, the company should provide solutions based on customer needs, and it only gets the contract if it can do a good job. In order to be truly customer-centric, Huawei has initiated a customer-centric R&D transformation and set up separate departments for carrier solutions, enterprise solutions, and consumer solutions.

Make customer satisfaction, not profit, a core objective

Huawei is committed to the continuous improvement of its core competitiveness and has never taken profit maximization as its objective. Huawei understands from its own experience that a business must have two elements to survive: customers and supplies.

Therefore, first of all, the company must stay customer-oriented and continuously improve customer satisfaction. With 100% customer satisfaction, you don't have to compete, which of course will never be the case. However, companies can continuously improve their customer satisfaction. Improving customer satisfaction is a comprehensive and complex project. The firm should provide different solutions

---

[3] Ren Zhengfei: "Success is not a reliable guide to future development". January 17, 2011.

[4] Ren Zhengfei: "Customer focus, increasing platform investment, open to cooperation, & achieve win-win results" at the PSST Managers Meeting. August 2010.

for different customer groups to meet their specific business needs; based on such solutions, making corresponding quality products, and delivering good after-sales service. By providing low-cost, high-value-added solutions, customers will continue to buy Huawei products.

In practice, Huawei always puts customer needs first even if it has to take some losses. For example, unlike Japanese automotive companies that emphasize zero inventory, Huawei always keeps in stock some equipment that others think has been obsolete as a strategic reserve in case the customers need a backup, as some customers are still using the old equipment.

Secondly, enterprises must achieve low cost and high value-addition by managing the supplies. The key is to have strong R&D capabilities and to be able to provide new products in a timely and efficient manner. As the technology replacement cycle of the IT industry becomes shorter and shorter, the market share of slow-moving companies can shrink quickly, so equipment manufacturers have to be front-runners, otherwise, they will be eliminated. The IT industry shakes up every 49 days, which is brutal. To catch up with the world's leaders, Huawei must not waste any time, as it has to catch up in 10 years with those which have decades-long development.[5]

All employees should be customer-focused

In Huawei, the whole company from top to bottom, instead of just a couple of senior executives, revolves around customers. Thanks to this practice, process-based, institutionalized operations have been established to serve customers more efficiently and the governance without intervention model has been also established customers need to attain goals even in the absence of control. Huawei believes customer demand orientation is rational, equivocal, and represents the truth of the market. While meeting customer needs, the company has to distinguish between genuine needs and opportunistic needs. Opportunistic needs are like a blade of grass that has been crushed by a rock and can hardly grow. But once the rock is removed, it will surely grow straight forward. Therefore, it is always important to keep the focus on rational customer needs, of course, different strategies may be adopted at a different time according to different needs.[6]

Make the customer service wall thicker

What does it mean to make the customer service wall thicker? It means that the marketing system should establish a top-to-bottom customer relationship. It means that Huawei should not only establish rapport with the CEO and the CTO, but also with the employees and related personnel in the technology-related department. This approach facilitates familiarity with Huawei's products and services by all relevant personnel in the customer's organization; it requires long-term vision as well as patience and dedication. The VPs of the R&D Institute should establish a system

[5] Ren Zhengfei: "Innovation is the inexhaustible driving force of Huawei's development". July 20, 2000.

[6] Ren Zhengfei: "Customer demand-oriented product development, and process-oriented management at the PIRB product roadmap planning review meeting". May 26, 2003.

of meeting customers a couple of times a week, and each account manager and product manager should maintain communication with customers no less than five times a week, while paying attention to the quality of communication. In the overseas market, for production to go up, executives need to go down; therefore, each office should be equipped with sufficient cars. The marketing teams should not have to drive themselves. Huawei hires local drivers for overseas offices, who can also serve as a quasi-bodyguard.

Ren believes that an all-around customer relationship is a differentiated competitive advantage. Many companies follow the 80/20 rule, but he believes that the 20% big accounts will not be possible without the 80% small accounts. Huawei has accumulatively established over 200 regional offices overseas. At some point, some offices had no revenue or order. So, it was suggested that these offices need to be dissolved to reduce costs. However, Ren decided to adopt a different strategy from that of Western companies and small businesses. Huawei insisted on maintaining all-around customer relations even if some customer has no contract with Huawei. Every level of the company should stay close to customers to alleviate their concerns. This is the way Huawei wins customers. All the votes they earn will add up, in the end, will even outweigh the most critical one vote. Of course, Huawei will also work on the most critical vote. Small companies usually only work on the bosses, so their service wall is rather thin, so to speak. An all-around customer relationship has become a common practice in Huawei.

Take customer feedback seriously

Ren asks the heads of the marketing departments to categorize customers and recognize the value of customer criticism. According to Huawei, there are two types of customers: The first type is critical customers, who point out the shortcomings of products and give directions to product improvement; therefore, their criticism provides opportunities for improvement. If the enterprise turns its back on this kind of customer, instead of carrying out self-reflection, it will lose the opportunity for self-improvement. The second type is informed customers, who understand products and can put forward good suggestions. Ren once said, if we put the interest of the company first, we will be able to modestly accept the suggestions of the users and improve the products. Some people in Huawei do not understand how to deal with customer criticism, and even have the wrong viewpoint; they may think that it is no big deal or that only certain types of products have problems, other products are very good, and they use this excuse to stop learning and improving... That is why Huawei always proposes to be a good people first because it believes that only a good human can produce good products. To start with, one needs to heed customer needs, listen to customer suggestions with an open mind and actively improve the product. This is the key to Huawei's survival. All the progress Huawei has made so far is taught by its customers.[7]

[7] Ren Zhengfei: "Acting according to universal laws, giving full play to core teams, constantly improving per-capita efficiency, and working together to survive hard times" at the meeting of the R&D Management Committee and the Q3 meeting of Marketing & Sales. 2002.

In Huawei's view, customer criticism and opinions help the company grow. As the "Essay on learning" by Peng Duanshu aptly pointed out: Is there a difference between what's difficult and what's easy? If one is willing to do it, then the difficult things become easy; if one is not, then the easy things become difficult. Ren urges that all employees reflect on customers' criticism, respond promptly, and make continuous improvement, because otherwise if one makes excuses and procrastinates, things will only become more and more difficult.

Customer-centric assessment

The Buddha once said a finger pointing at the moon is not the moon. The finger is needed to know where to look for the moon, but if you mistake the finger for the moon itself, you will never know the real moon. So, the pointing finger isn't what matters most. It only matters because it helps you see the moon for yourself. Here the assessment indicators are like the finger: they help you see the moon customers. In 2015, Ren proposed to tilt the quality resources in favor of quality customers.

5.3 Core Culture II: Dedication

The price of success

How did Huawei, with only 20,000 RMB of startup capital, catch up with Western companies? If measured by resources, Huawei was by no means a strong player in its early days. Ren once said that Huawei could not make a difference unless it worked harder than all others. Huawei executives and its many employees did exactly that, and unfortunately, their health was hurt as a result. Nevertheless, they still cherish their time at Huawei, especially those who came from mountainous areas, villages, and small towns, and had experienced the hardships of life in their childhood and adolescence. They are happy and have a sense of mission at Huawei, as they can see a tangible improvement to themselves and their family with their honest hard work. While sharing the fruits of their work, they have greater expectations for the future and have enhanced their understanding of work itself.

What does dedication really mean?

Huawei's core value is Customer Centricity and dedication. Dedication is different from people-centricity: people-centricity is focusing on caring for employees and creating a relaxed and harmonious atmosphere. Dedication requires employees to work hard and make sacrifices before they are awarded, so dedication is more about company-centric. Employees are classified and graded according to the value they create, which reflects the utilitarian nature of the company, which is supposed to be a highly efficient machine. Huawei has established a rigorous system to assess the dedication of its employees.

Huawei's dedication value proposal is not an idealistic political slogan or romantic concept, but a rational code of conduct concerning the survival and development of the enterprise and motivating employees to contribute. It is also a contribution-based rewarding system.

Ren once said: Don't regard hard work as a sacrifice; hardworking is a traditional Chinese virtue. We understand that some people have lofty ideas and they put the interest of the nation and the community above themselves and their families. But great people are very few; we may as well start with loving our families, our colleagues, and our work.[8] Huawei regards dedication as its core value, because it understands that in the fierce international competition, there is no way out without hard work. No matter how the situation changes, there is always a way out if we stick together with honesty, hard work, and without losing our composure.

What makes a dedicated employee?

In 2012, Huawei asked all employees who regard themselves as dedicated employees to sign a Personal Business Commitment (PBC), to distinguish them from average employees. Opportunities and income packages are drastically different between dedicated employees and average employees. The more they contribute, the more they earn, and often more than expected, which creates a strong drive for employees. Dedicated employees commit to going the extra mile, which means they assume more risks and responsibilities of the company's development. They are the best and backbones of the company and played important roles at critical moments such as the IT bubble burst in 2001 and Cisco's lawsuit against Huawei in 2003. At that time, Huawei's business growth stagnated due to the global bubble burst. In order to tide over the difficulties, managers of and above the director level asked for a 10% pay cut of their own accord. Go the extra mile may mean two things. First, the employees have to put in extra effort in their work; second, the employees need to embrace the corporate culture and absolutely obey the organization. It is such a group of stalwarts with their extra hard work in the last three decades who have made today's Huawei. In Huawei, the extra mile has always been handsomely rewarded in the form of power, status, and remuneration. Through its feasible incentive system, Huawei makes it clear to its employees that their hard work and extra efforts can make a significant difference in their lives.

Dedication is more about the mindset

In Huawei people's view, dedication is more about the mindset than the material life and the environment. If you are mentally dedicated, you will always put the interests of the company at heart. Specifically, it could mean visiting customers often and communicate with them frequently. If you use your brain a lot, your working method will be constantly improved, and the processes will be enriched and yet streamlined continuously. In the repeated cycles, an advanced and practical management methodology will take shape. Each enrichment and streamlining is not a simple addition or simplification, but a qualitative leap.[9] The dedication is not just a slogan; it needs to be measured in assessment. As long as the policy-maker of each link is dedicated

[8] Ren Zhengfei: "Let people who can hear the shots call shots". January 2009.

[9] Ren Zhengfei: "Resolutely implementingISO9000". February 26, 1997.

every day to refine their decisions and actions and make sure they are contributing to the customer's value creation, it will only take three to five years for Huawei to make a difference.[10] For junior employees, any activities, no matter how small they are, as long as they create values for the customer, and any effort, as long as it enriches and improves themselves, can be regarded as dedication. For dedicated employees, they must be reasonably rewarded and remain healthy for the long game. Rationality, moderation, and long-termism are the guiding principles of human resources policy.[11] Dedicated employees with Customer Centricity at their heart, will always smile at the customer and don't have to worry about buttering up the boss.

Rats in the company

Sun Yafang once said that there were three types of rats in the company: First, people who steal the company's technical secrets and trade secrets and sell them to malicious competitors. Second, people who embezzle and take grafts. Third, people who spend a lot of time and energy on how to butter up their supervisors.[12] Huawei has a strict audit system to prevent corruption, but problems still exist. In this regard, Sun Yafang said: We acknowledge that there are loopholes in the system, so we should improve the system by strengthening the audit and management. If the line manager has already perceived a problem but did not come forward to stop it, then they should also be held accountable. Huawei believes that corruption prevention should start with little things. As early as the 1990s, the company made it a rule that if it is not a reception, no meal expenses should be reimbursed. Huawei also tests its managers with little things; those who can't pass the test of the little things will never be entrusted with big responsibilities. If one is easily tempted by small benefits, they may end up as grabbers at more important positions.

5.4 Core Culture III: Self-reflection

Reflection of traditional Chinese culture

Ren summed up the importance of self-reflection based on his deep understanding of Chinese culture. He pointed out that, throughout history, many great people have elaborated on the importance of self-reflection. For example, Zeng Zi (also known as Master Zeng), a Chinese philosopher and disciple of Confucius, said over 2000 years ago, I examine myself three times a day; Mencius of the same period said, When heaven is about to confer a great responsibility on any man, it will exercise his mind with suffering, subject his sinews and bones to hard work, expose his body to hunger, put him to poverty, place obstacles in the paths of his deeds, so as to stimulate his mind,

[10] Ren Zhengfei: "Embracing the enthusiasm of youth and living a life without regrets" at the Wireless Product Line Conference on May 31, 2008.

[11] Ren Zhengfei: "Deepening understanding of the corporate culture of Customer Centricity and dedication" at the Mid-Year General Meeting of the Marketing Department. July 15, 2008.

[12] Sun Yafang's speech at Huawei's management meeting. May 9, 2011.

harden his nature, and improve wherever he is incompetent. Chairman Mao Zedong's wrote in *On Practice*, Fully to reflect a thing in its totality, to reflect its essence, to reflect its inherent laws, it is necessary through the exercise of thought to reconstruct the rich data of sense perception, discarding the dross and selecting the essential, eliminating the false and retaining the true, proceeding from the one to the other and from the outside to the inside, in order to form a system of concepts and theories All these are good examples of self-reflection. I would say without self-reflection, they would not have scored such great achievements. Zeng Guofan, a Chinese statesman and general, in the late Qing Dynasty, was best known for self-reflection. He was known to apply self-reflection in battle plans, governance, social networking, and self-cultivation. It is suggested that that is why he seldom made major mistakes, and never made the same mistake twice. The generals of the Heavenly Kingdom, an unrecognized oppositional state in the Qing Dynasty, believed that Zeng Guofan and his self-reflection were their worst enemy.

In the fierce international competition, Ren realized that without introspection and reflection of traditional Chinese culture, it would not be possible to overcome the entrenched habits of the Chinese people or make world-class products. Without self-reflection, it would not be possible for Huawei to meet the strict standards of craftsmanship of Japanese and Germans. Without the high quality on par with international standards, Huawei would not have survived to this day. As a young company, Huawei is full of vitality and passion, but it is also sometimes naive and conceited and its management is not fully standardized. So, only with constant self-reflection, can Huawei grow faster.

Self-reflection should go beyond vanity

Ren always reminds his employees of the perils of China's to face culture. In his opinion, if for vanity's sake, or for the sake of saving the face as Chinese like to put it, it will lead the company to failure or even demise, it would be so much better to put aside your face, so to speak. The only way to survive is to surpass and first and foremost, one must surpass oneself, which entails correcting mistakes in time. To this end, we must embrace self-reflection. As Confucius put it, whenever walking in a company of three, I can always find one who has something to teach me. In the eyes of Ren, of these three, one of them is a competitor, another one is a critical customer, and if you are modest enough, you will find the third is a subordinate who dares to speak frankly, or a colleague who offers sincere criticism, or your supervisor who have strict requirements. There is no mistake that can't be corrected if you truly respect the wise, even if you outrank them.[13]

Self-reflection is the way forward for young businesses

In 1999, a recruit asked Ren what's the best lesson he had learned from the company's growth. Ren replied that a young person should always engage in self-reflection. Only by constant self-reflection can a person make continuous progress. To help Huawei

[13] Ren Zhengfei: "Why we need self-reflection" at the research department meeting. September 22, 2000.

grow faster and bigger, it needs every employee to be open-minded and be self-reflective. In the same year, Ren answered another question from a recruit about Huawei's greatest strengths and weaknesses compared to its foreign competitors: Huawei's greatest strength and weakness both lie in the fact that Huawei's a young company. Because it is young, Huawei is full of vitality; because it is young, it is sometimes nave and lacks professional management. To overcome the weakness, Huawei regularly engages in self-reflection. Being nave is not scary. From the top leaders to junior employees, everyone can be nave at a certain point, especially when they face new things and new problems. It always takes some time to get to the bottom of a new thing. Therefore, Huawei people should pay special attention to learn from others, especially, they should observe how the senior employees do. Learn and innovate. Little by little, step by step, you will grow.[14]

Top-to-bottom self-reflection

Huawei has different requirements for different levels of managers, but no one would be promoted if they are not good at self-reflection. Self-reflection starts with senior managers, who attend democratic life meetings every year. The issues raised in the democratic life meetings are very sharp; some outsiders who sat in the meetings would think that Huawei had serious internal conflicts. The truth is, sharp as the issues are, what happened at the meetings stayed at the meetings. People shake hands and fight together afterward. Ren pointed out that the company's junior employees should also attend democratic life meetings, but the atmosphere should be milder and gentler. Do not turn the meetings into crossfires. But for senior managers, they have the stomach, so they should be able to take tougher criticisms. Moderated criticism is recommended at democratic life meetings. Criticism and self-reflection are observed from the top to the bottom. Within the company, criticism of superiors and subordinates is both encouraged, otherwise, if everyone is a yea-sayer, the management would head nowhere. If you cannot criticize others, you will never be promoted either.

Self-reflection is for continuous optimization

Figure 5.1 sums up Huawei's self-reflection culture and the value it creates.

In 2001, Ren proposed to carry out organizational reform and optimization centered on self-reflection, so that employees can better learn from customers and competitors and cultivate confidence and optimism to face problems head-on. Employees can improve themselves through self-reflection and cultivate a modest and pragmatic work style; this way the organizational management system can also be continuously optimized. In addition, self-reflection should not be window-dressing; telling the truth is the most important sign of a healthy corporate culture. All in all, the ultimate goal of self-reflection is to improve the overall core competitiveness of the company. Self-reflection is more preferred than mutual criticism because criticism can be tricky. Mutual criticism is likely to hurt each other and create tension in the company. Self-reflection usually will not come too strong. But even if it is just a slap

---

[14] Ren Zhengfei: remarks at the orientation. November 11, 1999.

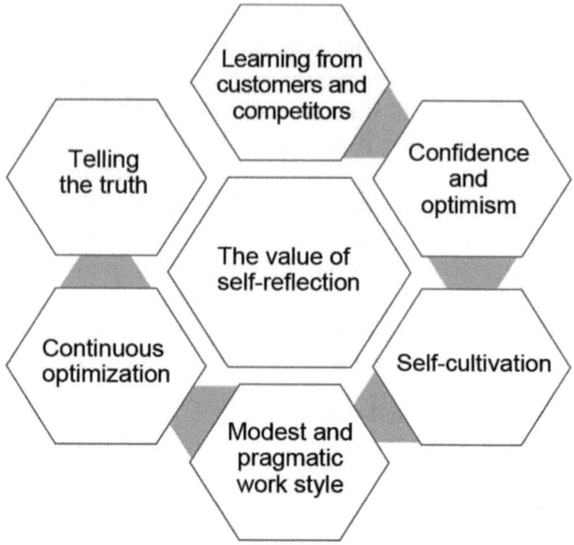

Fig. 5.1 Huawei's self-reflection culture and the value it creates

on the wrist, years later, your wrist will be stronger. It's definitely better than no slap at all. Self-reflection applies not only to individuals but also to organizations. Backbone managers should cultivate themselves through self-reflection, move towards professionalism and a better international vision. Only through serious self-reflection can we continue to absorb the advanced experience and optimize ourselves.[15]

Improving management through self-reflection

Self-reflection is of great significance to the improvement of management at Huawei. Huawei has grown from a small company, from no management whatsoever to rough management, from simple management to integrated product development (IPD), integrated supply chain (ISC), Four-pronged Harmonization (processes, systems, controls, and coding), and the preliminary IT infrastructure. If not for continuous self-reflection and substantial progress in management, how could Huawei provide lower cost and higher value-added services to its customers? Huawei continuously discloses its shortcomings and mistakes and is brave enough to engage in self-criticism in internal publications like *Huawei People* and *Huawei Management*. A group of employees who have the foresight and take the initiative to correct their mistakes and overcome their shortcomings grow up quickly.

Enhancing self-healing through self-reflection

Huawei has an internal newspaper called *Huawei Management*, which encourages people to find managerial flaws and problems. The department where the problem is found will have to explain itself but cannot defend itself. It also has to answer how to fix the problem in its next step. The person who is criticized cannot criticize

[15] Ren Zhengfei: "Huawei's winter", *Huawei People*. 2001.

the person who pointed out the problem, but should instead accept the criticism and humbly correct the mistake. In this way, Huawei can spot problems on its own initiative instead of covering problems; gradually it has developed the ability for self-healing, and continues to improve through the company-wide effort.

Salespeople need to criticize the company from the customers perspective

From the change in the name of Huawei's marketing mechanism, i.e., from an account manager system to a customer representative system, you can see that Huawei has enhanced the strength of self-reflection. An account manager works one way; it is simply about promotion, whereas the customer representative is first and foremost responsible for overseeing Huawei's operations on behalf of the customer. The responsibility of the customer representative is to criticize Huawei from the customer's standpoint. If they do not criticize, it would be a dereliction of duty, but arbitrary criticism is no good either, and the appraisal will reflect it accordingly. Only by criticizing more and being truthful, can the problem pointed out in the criticism be rectified and progress be made. This way, we are sure to hear criticism from customer representatives. Why was this system introduced? Because at a certain point we seldom heard criticism from customers, because they thought that our staff worked so hard, if they complained about some small issues, it would affect the staff's progress in the company, so they gradually dropped mentioning any of it. Over time, we would think that all was good, but if the problems accumulated without being addressed, they would eventually ruin the customer relationship. The customer representative is a different story. Their duty is to criticize the company, from the late delivery or an incomplete set, to lack of service during the Spring Festival. As long as the customer's interest is always placed first, and their problems are timely addressed, customer satisfaction will continuously improve. Without self-reflection and failing to recognize your own shortcomings, how can customer satisfaction increase?[16]

Focus on self-improvement amidst external criticism

In its growth, Huawei has been subjected to constant rumors and doubts, especially during its internationalization process, it has faced negations, contempt, and even hatred. In this process, Huawei has to endure tremendous pressure. After reading unfavorable comments about Huawei in newspapers, Ren said that the world would change eventually over time, so why should Huawei bother to explain anything? Time will tell everything. Huawei should focus on internal management by identifying its problems from other people's criticism and meanwhile strengthen self-reflection.[17] Ren also encourages his PR people to speak up, even if what they say is wrong. The company will not collapse because he or she makes an incorrect statement. If we stumble over anyone's misstatement, we don't deserve anything in this world. Huawei must tolerate criticism. As you see, I've been calling on our colleagues to

[16] Ren Zhengfei: "Why we need self-reflection" at the research department meeting. September 22, 2000.

[17] Ren Zhengfei: "Entrepreneurship and innovation must be centered on improving the core competitiveness". March 5, 1999.

speak out loud, even if they don't agree with me or other senior executives. We may not always be right, or at least I may not always be right. Therefore, I must reassure everyone in the company that no one will be punished for speaking their mind.[18]

An appropriate degree of criticism and self-criticism

In 1998, Ren proposed that managers at all levels should embrace self-reflection. To care about the subordinates, one must listen to different opinions. Many of these opinions are of good intentions. Managers should make friends with people with different opinions, analyze their problems, and give them help. First, managers can help them change their way of thinking; second, they can help them transfer to different positions to avoid head-on conflicts with their supervisors. When our managers become friends with the staff, they will pour their hearts out. This way, managers can better make up for the shortcomings in their work.[19]

Ren also admonishes employees for going too far on self-criticism. He believes that excessive self-criticism may compromise the mature and stable operation, so it is not desirable. Self-criticism should be adapted to the different stages of operation and different environments. Management should be based on facts and truth; you cannot say one thing and do another. Only through serious self-reflection can we continuously absorb the advanced experience and improve ourselves and truly shape our own future.

Case study: the value of the Blue Team

Blue Team in China originally refers to a combating unit that plays the role of a hypothetical enemy in military simulation exercises and conducts confrontation drills with the Red Team (representing the PLA, the home team). Huawei's Blue Team has a similar role. Huawei created a special organization, the Blue Team Staff, under the Strategy and Marketing Department in the earliest days, which was one of the core functional platforms for the Huawei Group. Organized by the company's EMT, debate, simulation, tactical extrapolations, and other ways are used for reverse analysis, and critical debate on current strategic thinking, and technical differentiation of disruptive technologies and products is sought after. According to Ren, the sole purpose of the Blue Team is to negate the Red Team in every way it can. In Huawei, every department must form a Blue Team, with the sole purpose of knocking down the Red Team, its own department. In this process, the Red Team will become stronger. The Red Team represents the current strategic development model, while the Blue Team represents the main competitor's models or innovative models. The main tasks of the Blue Team are to fight the Red Team by voicing confrontation, simulating possible scenarios, or maybe even by issuing alarmist warnings. Through such self-reflection, the Blue Team provides decision-making reference to the board of directors, and points out the Red Team's vulnerabilities and problems, thus ensuring that Huawei is always on the right path.

---

[18] Ren Zhengfei: "Huawei needs to improve its relationship with the media". 25 November 2010.

[19] Ren Zhengfei: "Don't be a flash-in-the-pan hero". *Huawei People*. September 28, 1998.

Main responsibilities of the Blue Team Staff

The main responsibilities of the Blue Team Staff include the following:

1. Observing and reviewing the company's strategic and technological development with a reversed mindset and simulating the competitor's strategies/products/solutions to point out the vulnerabilities and problems of Red Team in those areas.
2. Establishing the confrontation system and operation platform for the Red Team and Blue Team. Under the organization of the EMT, debate, simulation, tactical extrapolations, and other ways are used for reverse analysis, and critical debate on current strategic thinking, and technical differentiation of disruptive technologies and products is sought after.
3. Assisting the construction of the Blue Team in all Business Groups, with the responsibilities of developing and operating the processes, and platforms of the Blue Team, and organizing the sharing of experience and capacities.[20]

Dissents are a strategic reserve

At Huawei, the Blue Team is a mindset embedded within the organization. Ren said: The Blue Team exists in every aspect of Huawei. The Blue Team is not a top organization; it exists at the primary level too. We should have red versus blue in our minds too. I think red versus blue happens in people's whole life. As for me, more than often, I am critical of myself and my own decisions. I believe that the Blue Team should exist in any field, any process, anytime, anywhere. If an opposing force emerges in an organization, I'm more than happy to accept it. We should unite all the people we can to fight together, including those who disagree with us. It doesn't matter if they form an opposition coalition within, as long as they are not sowing discord or going astray. Technical opposition should always be allowed. Let a hundred flowers bloom and a hundred schools of thought really bring out the best of people's ingenuity.

The core value of the Blue Team is to identify potential crises

According to Ren, China's development has come so far and achieved so big, because it has grown amidst criticisms. Huawei is what it is, because it is committed to self-reflection, and that is why it becomes stronger. But in Ren's view, crisis always lurks around somewhere despite the company's success. If we don't disrupt our advantages, others will.[21] Don't be naive to think that we are safe in the fierce competition. Our company's strategy is all open, so competition is unavoidable. Ren said, Since it is inevitable, we might as well be on the offense. To this end, we need to hear different voices, and that's where the value of the Blue Team lies.[22]

---

[20] Tian Tao, Wu Chunbo. Will Huawei be next to fall? Beijing: CITIC Publishing House, 2012.

[21] Ma Xiaofang. "The secret of Huawei's Red Team and Blue Team: Blue Team mimics the opponent's strategy and targets Red Team's loopholes". *China Business News*. 2013.11.26.

[22] Ren Zhengfei: "The best defense is offense" at the wireless business briefing. September 5, 2013.

In 2007, Apple launched its game-changing product iPhone. Although mobile phone manufacturers including Nokia did not take it seriously at that time, the Blue Team at Huawei was keenly aware that the landscape was changing: the terminal would play an increasingly important role. In 2008, Huawei began to negotiate with Bain & Company and other private equity funds, ready to sell its terminal business. At that time, the Blue Team produced a one-page report with one conclusion: the future telecom industry would be a trinity of the terminal, network, and cloud. The terminal business determines demand, so giving up the terminal business means giving up Huawei's future. This report prevented the sale of the terminal business, leaving room for Huawei's transformation.

In 2014, Huawei's CFO Meng Wanzhou announced that Huawei's main business profit margin was at the same level as in 2013 (around 12%), a result that was due to great management changes. The Blue Team strategy was also introduced into the financial department. Huawei has set up a financial risk control center in London, the equivalence of a Blue Team.

The Blue Team is a cradle of talent

If the Blue Team fails to defeat the Red Team, then its commander will not be promoted as a commander in the Red Team because it means he/she does not know where to lead the company. Guarding success is not a way to move forward. If the managers can't be critical of the company, they will not be promoted either because they have no more to offer. Those who are capable of being critical demonstrate that they have a wide horizon and good ideas, and are thus promotable. In Ren's view, as long as you can face up to yourself, you have a future. We should not worry that criticism will bring mental pressure, instead, we should be happy to be criticized. We should also be modest, confident, and ambitious. With all these qualities, we shall certainly overtake the United States someday. I especially support the wireless product line to set up a Blue Team, Ren said at a wireless business briefing, if you wish to rise to the top, first you need to go to the Blue Team. You can never have top positions without defeating the Red Team. If the Red Team commander doesn't have Blue Team experience, they shall not be promoted either. If they don't know how to beat the competitors within the company, it only means that they have reached their ceiling.

Creating an enabling atmosphere for the Blue Team

Huawei gives a lot of tolerance to the Blue Team and the dissent voices that it represents. According to Huawei regulations, the Red Team commander shall be selected from the best of the Blue Team. In Ren's view, we have to create a protection mechanism in Huawei and grant the Blue Team status. The Blue Team may talk bullshit/shoot the breeze. There might be some crazy people, who dare to think, dare to speak up, and dare to take actions. After the battle, so to speak, we need to give them some tolerance and credit. After all, how do you know they can't come up with a solution? At the above meeting, Ren told the story of how the Maginot Line failed to deter invasion by Germany. He said that for the defense to be invincible, it must be offense-oriented. To enhance the offense, attention should be paid to the role of the

Blue Team, which tries every means to fight against the Red Team. Even if it fails, it has contributed some good food for thought.

Inviting opposition in the R&D

In Ren's view, Huawei's poor R&D planning was mainly due to the lack of democracy. So, he proposed to form a Red Team and a Blue Team in the R&D system. The two teams work in parallel; the Blue Team tries every possible way to defeat the Red Team and pick the Red Team's fault. The commander of the Red Team can be selected from the Blue Team. The soldiers of the Blue Team can be transferred to the Red Team and serve as colonels. Those who are particularly good at reverse thinking and picking holes can be trained to become the commander of the Blue Team. The commander of the Blue Team can serve long-term, but the soldiers must be mobile. Each product line should have a Blue Team. Don't be afraid of opposition. It's good to have dissented, because it will break our inertia and path dependency.

The purpose of setting up a Blue Team is to promote research and development and to solicit new ideas, especially from the top. Mistakes are nothing, and who wouldn't make them? No one is always right. People who have made mistakes can still be promoted if they can correct their mistakes. No one is perfect. What matters is we can achieve the ultimate goal. So don't have a big ego and don't care too much about your vanity. I made the most mistakes in Huawei, but I stand up every time from the mistakes. Have I ever been hot-headed or made bad decisions? God knows. Sometimes, you are just trying to maintain the leader's credibility and humor me, but I am fully aware of what is really going on. In research and development, we should encourage a variety of voices and democracy, summarize everyone's opinions to come up with the right thing, and then discuss it again. In this regard, we need to learn from Indians. Although they are slow, they repeatedly discuss solutions, and they work after the solutions have been thoroughly discussed, so as to avoid rework. We, on the other hand, work first and then change it when it is not right, thus entailing a lot of overtime and rework. It is a sheer waste.[23]

The key values of the blue team lie in three aspects: First, self-transcendence. When an organization makes a decision, it is easily affected by inertia, solidified thinking, and blind spots, and the role of the blue team is to break through these thinking barriers and achieve self-transcendence. Second, thinking out of the box. The crossfire of different opinions creates the ability to think out of the box and thus creativity and innovation. Third, the self-healing ability. Red versus blue is a process of reaching consensus from multiple perspectives. It can draw on the greatest range of information and identify vulnerabilities and risks as far as possible before making decisions. In addition, it gradually forms the common memory of the organization during the argument process. When companies encounter difficulties and obstacles in the implementation process, these two aspects can help the team quickly identify plans, collaborate, and work together effectively (see Fig. 5.2).

---

[23] Ren Zhengfei: "Understanding laws of nature, giving play to the core team, continuously improving the per capita benefits, and working together to overcome difficulties" at the Q3 marketing meeting. 2002.

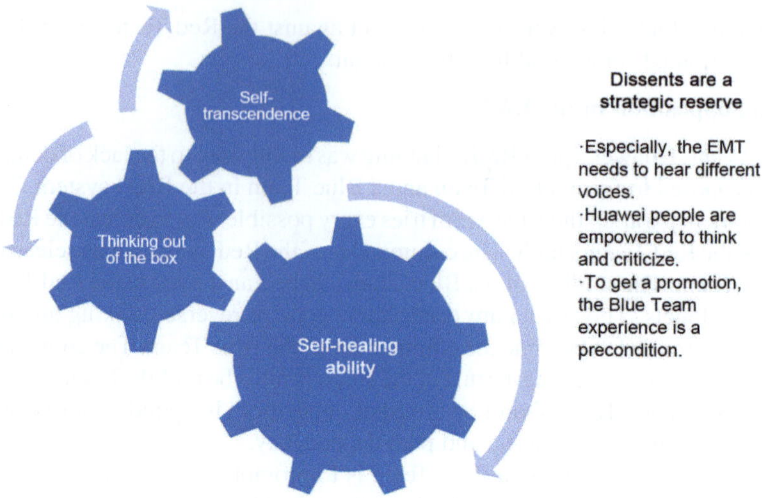

Fig. 5.2 Strategic values of the blue team

5.5 Core Culture IV: Openness, Compromise, Grayness

In December 2007, Ren met with former U.S. Secretary of State Albright and his delegation. Known as a tough, iron-fisted, hawkish Secretary, Albright said, in a rare emotional tone, to Ren: Before I meet you, I read your *My Father and Mother*, and *Huawei's Winter,* among others, I am impressed. Human feelings are similar. Albright also told a few stories about her father. It was during this meeting that Ren explained the logic of Huawei's growth and success in response to Albrights questions. For the first time, Ren put forward the three core concepts of openness, compromise, and grayness, which were considered to be the secret weapon of Huawei's rapid development from scratch. Ren said: We emphasize openness and learning from others, because this way will bring us new goals, true self-examination, and a sense of urgency of the times.[24] On January 15, 2009, Ren gave a speech entitled Openness, Compromise, and Grayness at the Global Market Working Conference. At the outset, he said: Two of Huawei's core values are openness and enterprising. A leader should be able to control the direction and tempo and maintain a certain level of grayness. To hold onto the right direction and keep an appropriate tempo is an art, not a skill or method. The key is compromise and tolerance.

Regarding the relationship between compromise and grayness, Ren Zhengfei said, To maintain a certain level of grayness, we must create a certain harmony among various factors of development within a certain period of time. This process of harmonizing is compromised, and its result is grayness. To illustrate this point, Ren Zhengfei

[24] Ren Zhengfei: "Openness, compromise, and flexibility" at the Global Market Working Conference. January 14, 2010.

said: The managers at Huawei are mostly young and passionate. They don't understand the necessity of compromise, so they meet with strong resistance. In the history of China, reforms have affected the course of social development, but most reformers had not really reached their goals. I believe that, in their own time, they had gone too far and had been too rigid with the resistance before them. If they had taken a softer approach and been more patient, they might have achieved better results. In fact, they lacked certain grayness. The direction would not change, but the course could bend a little bit. It may not necessarily be a straight line; it could be a curve, and at some point, it could go around a circle. If we take a step back, we may find that the course leads exactly to the same goal.[25]

Openness and compromise are associated with grayness. Openness ensures that the company will try its best to draw on the best of others, otherwise it will gradually be marginalized and even eliminated.[26] Openness, and cooperation are about uniting more people to achieve win–win results, instead of lose-lose results. Compromise implies tolerance and cooperation, and a strong person is usually the result of equilibrium. When we work with others, we cannot act as a black widow spider. It is a spider in Latin America known for its sexual cannibalism. After mating, the female spider eats its male partner in order to provide nutrition for its offspring. Huawei used to eat up or dump its partners one or two years after the partnership was formed. Now that we have grown stronger, we should do better. We must be more open, modest, and broad-minded. We must develop better partnerships to achieve mutual wins. We should absorb more of the different ways of thinking out there, keep brainstorming, and don't be narrow-minded.[27] These words were targeted at the predatory growth stage of Huawei. Ren once remarked, Look at Huawei's previous black widow image. how terrible it is! However, as the company grows, it begins to pay increasingly more attention to corporate social responsibility and long-term symbiotic relationships with its partners.

5.6 Consensus Building Through the *Huawei Basic Law*

In 1995, Huawei was headquartered on the sixth floor of the Shenyi Building in Nanshan District, Shenzhen. Five professors from the Renmin University of China, including Prof. Peng Jianfeng and Prof. Bao Zheng, were invited by Huawei to teach courses on the second startup and strategic transformation, marketing, and human resource management. After listening to Peng's lecture on The problems and solutions of second startups in China, Ren immediately said to him: Prof. Peng, Huawei is faced with the same problems that you talked about, and we are thinking

[25] Ibid.

[26] Ren Zhengfei: "Deepening understanding of the corporate culture of Customer Centricity and dedication" at the Mid-Year General Meeting of the Marketing Department. July 15, 2008.

[27] Ren Zhengfei: "Customer focus, increasing platform investment, open to cooperation, & achieve win-win results" at the PSST Managers Meeting. August 2010.

about the solutions too. Professors should not just talk about theories, because that would lose touch with reality. You must use the enterprise as your testing ground. You are welcome to provide consulting services, and you can use Huawei as your testing ground. If you follow an enterprise long enough, and with your consulting service, you make a small business into a big enterprise, this will be a great academic achievement as well as a practical outcome, and this would be a win–win result for us. Ren then told Zhang Jianguo, Huawei's then vice president in charge of marketing, to officially hire Prof. Peng as a consultant.[28]

In the early 1996, Prof. Peng, Prof. Bao, and Wu Chunbo began to provide consulting services for Huawei's marketing system, and the first project they worked on was the assessment scheme for marketing personnel and the regional office management model. The consulting service was gradually extended to human resources, operation management, corporate culture, and other areas; the consulting team later was expanded to nearly ten scholars, including Huang Weiwei, Yang Du, and Sun Jianmin. The Huawei Expert Advisory Group was officially established, with Prof. Peng as the head. This was the beginning of the relationship between the professors and Huawei, and the whole project lasted more than three years. The *Huawei Basic Law* was the crystallization of the corporate culture shaped with the consulting services at that time.[29]

Thus, Huawei started its second startup. However, it faced many difficulties.

Communication barriers between supervisors and subordinates

Huawei has developed a distinctive culture, and all the leaders who have inspected Huawei praised its culture. Gradually, Huawei's managers and employees also like to mention the buzzword corporate culture, but when they engaged in a discussion, they found that they had not really understood what corporate culture was. What is the function of corporate culture? No one could tell. The Publicity Department organized several debates and only found that what Ren agreed was often not accepted by most Huawei people. For example, Ren once criticized the concept of going through thick and thin together as obsolete, but many managers and employees were confused and did not understand why Ren thought so. What's more, with Huawei's rapid growth, the company is getting bigger and bigger, it is difficult for top and middle-level management to reach a consensus on the company's mission and core values. Ren is a quick-thinker and innovator, who is often struck by some novel ideas. However, with the expansion of the company, the contacts between the company's senior management, middle management, and junior employees have been greatly reduced. Ren found himself was increasingly distant from the middle management: he could not keep abreast of the work and ideas of his subordinates, and the employees were increasingly difficult to understand his intentions too. During Huawei's rapid growth, the management and employees both misunderstood the company's development prospects and values, and could not reach a consensus.

---

[28] Peng Jianfeng. *The Birth of the Huawei Basic Law*. www.docin.com/p-832186645.html.

[29] Ibid.

However, none of them, including Ren, knew what the problems were and how to solve them.

Succession of the new to the old in business transformation

In January 1996, the annual training for marketing executives came to an end with the collective resignation of all the marketing department's management. In order to prepare for the decisive battle in the market in 1996 and 1997, the management of the marketing department was ready to step down and win re-election. The courage of collective resignation raised some fundamental issues: what should we do if managers do not adapt to corporate development? What if a meritorious older employee falls behind? How do you make the best new employees stand out? How do you institutionalize the two-way mobility of management?

Adapting to the incentive mechanism

In 1995, Huawei set up a Remuneration Reform Group to redesign the company's wage distribution. The team encountered some questions: What should be the wage basis? Performance, position, or competence? Should seniority also be considered? It took the team six months to come up with a remuneration scheme based on positions. However, when it was applied, they found that some employees did not deserve the payment of the position. Should we make people fit the position, or make the system fit the people? Before 1995, the biggest problem troubling Huawei's managers was how to make money, but what bothered managers now was how to distribute the benefits and how to evaluate the employees.

Process-orientation versus flexibility

In early 1995, Huawei began to implement ISO 9001 to standardize its business processes and improve operational efficiency and customer satisfaction. However, what should be the responsibilities and authority of each department in the reorganized business process system? Would a process-based organization be rigid?[30]

Faced with the above issues, the Expert Group began its research with Huawei's historical records. To their surprise, Huawei had already accumulated a large number of materials, including Ren's speeches, documents of the company's management system, a total of 29 issues of *Huawei People*, a thick volume of *Huawei Digest*, and the records of the discussion on corporate culture, and so on. At that time, very few Chinese enterprises had so many documents to record their growth. What was even more surprising was that Ren was quite visionary. The theme of each of his speeches not only addressed a major issue in Huawei's development, but also involved a major issue in China's political and economic development or corporate management in general. At the same time, it is clear from these documents and records that Huawei has many thoughtful and insightful leaders. These historical records have formed the ideological basis of the *Huawei Basic Law*.

The birth of the *Huawei Basic Law* allowed Huawei to reach a consensus on a number of fronts, as reflected in the following.

---

[30] Peng Jianfeng. *The Birth of the Huawei Basic Law*. www.docin.com/p-832186645.html.

Creating a company philosophy and development strategy

When the group discussed the structure of the *Huawei Basic Law*, Peng believed that the core issues are the fundamental contradictions and problems in the company's second startup, as well as the rules of the game and the core value system for dealing with internal and external contradictions. Bao suggested that the *Huawei Basic Law* should address three basic propositions for the survival and development of the enterprise: First is about the future of the enterprise where is Huawei heading? What kind of company does Huawei want to be, i.e., what is Huawei's mission and vision? Second, management efficiency. What kind of regulation system should Huawei establish to avoid the loss of management control caused by rapid expansion? The Third is employee's sense of accomplishment. What kind of philosophy and HR policy should be established to establish a sense of corporate identity, and a sense of accomplishment? Prof. Huang also pointed out three fundamental issues that the *Huawei Basic Law* should address in the process of growth and development: First, what were the keys to Huawei's past success? Second, what kind of challenges and crises does Huawei face in a new competition? Third, which success factor(s) can continue to help the business and which has/have become barriers to success? What will support Huawei's future success? Based on the results of the discussions, Ren proposed that the *Huawei Basic Law* should provide the basic rules for dealing with internal and external contradictions, establish clear core values, as well as basic policies and management rules to guide Huawei's future growth and development.

Addressing the *Tao* and tactics of corporate development

The team carefully studied the mission statements and codes of conduct of world-renowned companies such as IBM, Hewlett-Packard, and Intel, and was especially inspired by the structure of *the Art of War* by *Sun Tzu*. Each chapter of *the Art of War* discusses one aspect of warfare and how it applies to military strategy and tactics. Each chapter begins with the *Tao* of warfare and continues with the major determinants and relationships of warfare, clarifying its essence and principles before moving on to strategy and tactics, which reflect the *Tao* and principles of warfare. The entire text is tightly structured and coherent. Corporate management also has its *Tao*, that is, the mission and core values. Focusing on the *Tao*, we try to provide a conceptual framework of the *Huawei Basic Law*, including the following parts: (1) purpose, (2) management philosophy, (3) basic management policy, (4) basic organizational policy, (5) basic personnel policy, (6) basic regulation policy, and (7) work ethics and discipline.

Identify the essence and cornerstones of the corporate culture

Huawei intended to build a world-class workshop in three years, which incorporated first-class management, first-class technology and equipment, and first-class buildings. Managers who do not understand *Huawei Basic Law* or use it to guide their work and those who have no field experience will not be allowed to enter the upper and middle management. At the same time, a mechanical interpretation of the provisions, or left in form but right in essence is not allowed. They are both manifestations of a lack of dedication. We hope every employee can bring a copy of the *Huawei Basic Law* back home with them for the Chinese New Year celebration. You can read it while waiting for the New Year's dinner. We hope you will understand every word and every sentence of it. I believe the two weeks study will benefit you for the rest of your life.[31]

A spiritual contract with the entire workforce

Ren pointed out that the *Huawei Basic Law* is a spiritual contract with all employees to guide the medium and long-term development of the company on a macro level. It is necessary to improve the horizon of every Huawei person, and make them more ambitious and goal-focused. Every employee should be involved in the drafting and discussion of the *Huawei Basic Law* to reach consensus, make a common commitment to Huawei's growth, and reach a convention to guide future actions. *The Huawei Basic Law* should empower every intelligent and enthusiastic employee to work hard towards a common goal and to integrate it into their behaviors.

Internal checks and balances

Huawei establishes a hierarchical management system, as well as layered power and constraints system through the *Huawei Basic Law*, which makes the company's development orderly and rule-based. However, it takes more than days to achieve it and it will not be easy. But once the orderly and rule-based power and constraints system is established, Huawei will not make the mistake made by Wanguo Securities, no matter how much personal prestige the president has, because his/her decision will always be checked.[32]

Making the management systems more standardized and international

Huawei has been stepping up its business process reengineering efforts, using ISO 9001 to standardize every operation and create the conditions for subsequent open network management. It is also using MRP II management software to program business processes and realize network and data-based management, thus strengthening the company's integrated management of business planning (budgeting), business statistics analysis, and business (economic) auditing.[33]

---

[31] Ren Zhengfei: "Don't forget the heroes". January 23, 1997.

[32] Ren Zhengfei: "Cultivating and selecting managers with field experience" at the Second Quality Management Report and Award Ceremony. 1998.

[33] Ren Zhengfei: "Revisit on refraining from complacence and no slack in the mind" at the Market and Research Award Ceremony. June 30, 1996.

5.7 Huawei Versus Cisco

For many enterprises, the corporate culture is the philosopher of the boss, what the boss has inherited from his/her family, the lessons learned in the business development, and his/her bitter-sweet life experience. Together with the characteristics of industrial development and competition, it casts the core of the corporate culture. Over time, the corporate culture of Huawei is becoming more condensed, more focused, and clearer. Ren's life experience has created Huawei's crisis awareness and foresight. In the face of global industrial and technological development, Huawei constantly makes strategic layout and investment; in the face of obstacles and temptations, Huawei maintains perseverance, steadfastness, and concentration; in the face of fierce global competition and difficult catch-up, Huawei always remains rational and calm, always confronts its own problems head-on, and is open to change and learning.

With the development and growth of the enterprise, the corporate culture itself also faces the issue of transformation. Corporate culture is associated with the corporate strategy, and the needs of different stages of development. Different enterprises have different scales, face different obstacles, so they naturally have different cultural characteristics. In Huawei, the corporate culture has two layers: the first layer is the core values known as Customer Centricity, dedication, and perseverance, which remain unchanged under any circumstances and is the root culture of the company. The second layer is the situational culture formed according to the enterprise scale. As shown in Fig. 5.3, Huawei has undergone three stages and two major cultural transformations. The first stage is at the startup period, and the corporate culture of that time is referred to as a simple philosophy of farmers where the company relied on flexibility, passion, and tenacity to fight. At this stage, the company worshiped heroism and needed daring heroes who were organized, but undisciplined and tough. The second stage is process-focused. After Huawei declared its goal to become a world-class company in 1997, to support the development expansion, Huawei must build strong processes to manage information systems and platforms. At this stage, Huawei began to systematically introduce Western management systems and methods to strengthen centralized management and control capabilities in order to enhance the core competitiveness and its capacities to scale up. At the third stage, as Huawei is increasingly international, its business is covering much wider fields, and the number of stakeholders is also increasing, the grayness culture becomes an important principle and guide for handling complex relationships. Dealing with dynamic and complex relationships requires a broader perspective and mindset, and openness, compromise, and inclusiveness have become the main criteria for survival in a diversified international environment.

The transformation from heroism to standardization is a painful process for Huawei, which means it had to abandon its previous ways of thinking and behavior and introduce a new code of conduct. In this process, there is usually great resistance, but in order to survive and develop, it must overcome it, and press ahead toward its

Fig. 5.3 Huawei's two-layer culture

vision and goals at full steam and transform employees' philosophy and behavior through cultural reshaping. This is the toughest issue for the catching-up company.

Culturally, the most striking commonality between Huawei and Cisco is the focus on Customer Centricity. It does not just at the conceptual level, but more importantly, it is integrated into the incentive mechanism and employee's behavior. Huawei's core values are customer centricity and dedication. These two words tie Huawei's two main stakeholders, customers, and employees, closely together: satisfying customers is the ultimate goal and dedication is the only way and means to ensure that this goal is achieved. Huawei's incentive mechanism and talent selection mechanism are all designed around this ultimate goal, and whoever is dedicated to satisfying customer needs will be promoted and receive extraordinary rewards in material terms. Binding customers and employees together not only creates a comprehensive cohesive organizational atmosphere and a system with customers at the core, but also allows employees to devote themselves to serve customers without distractions, saving them the non-productive effort on office politics and interpersonal relationships. Huawei's corporate culture effectively manages the attention and energy of its employees, making them focus on the core goals of the organization. It is the high alignment between the interests of customers and employees that simplifies, equalizes, and institutionalizes the complex and obscure cultural orientation, permeates the essence of organizational culture into the cognition and behavior of all employees, and deeply integrates corporate culture with the incentive system, which translates well into the conscientious actions of employees and achieves unity of knowledge and action.

In Huawei's culture, the institution and practice of self-reflection ensure that the company always looks at itself rationally and confronts problems honestly. This methodology constantly corrects self-overestimation and self-contentment brought about by previous achievements, breaks slackness in the thinking, and makes weak link discovery a key driving force for its growth. Among the nearly 100 Huawei employees I interviewed, exposing shortcomings and confronting problems seem to have become a norm and, a group thinking pattern; they even have the same attitude to the senior leadership. Some interviewees even showed benchmarking figures to reveal the gap with leading companies. In the communication with Huawei people, we did not hear any self-praise, disguised glorification, nor any false modesty; what we saw is sincerity and pragmatism. For such a brave enterprise that always faces the truth, its focus is all rest on how to do better, because in their minds, Huawei could well be the next company to fall down.

Cisco's former CEO Chambers himself experienced the painful bankruptcy of Wang Laboratories and realized that technology companies should not just be technology-based, and should also be customer-oriented. Enterprises are expanded in pursuit of customer needs. Customers-orientation instead of technology orientation certainly gives companies opportunities and space to survive. Therefore, Cisco's customer-oriented code of conduct and incentives are deeply embedded in the thinking and behavior of Cisco people at all levels. In the face of fierce competition, Cisco has further developed a highly adaptive culture within the organization, driven by a culture that focuses on customers rather than technology. This culture focuses on decision-making mechanisms and communication processes, by establishing a common language within the organization, and by using collaborative techniques to allow a variety of opinions (especially those from junior employees and other countries) to be heard, to increase the efficiency and effectiveness of consensus building, and decrease delays and errors caused by suspicion and hearsay within the organization. At the same time, leaders at all levels need to be accountable to their staff for their decision-making, be consistent and straightforward in their actions, increase the efficiency of consensus-building, and improve the organization's execution and responsiveness to the external environment.

In Huawei and Cisco, the customer-centric culture is integrated into employees' DNA and shown in their behaviors. It is continuously strengthened through cognitive, institutional, motivational, and behavioral feedback, and becomes people's conscientious actions.

Cisco culture encourages its employees to bring their whole selves to work while Huawei emphasizes dedication. In my opinion, there are some subtle differences between the two.

Firstly, they demonstrate different relationships with the company. In Cisco the employees who bring their whole selves to work still demonstrate a contractual and employment relationship with the employer. On the other hand, in Huawei, dedication implies a sense of ownership, and alignment of the personal ideals, goals, and interests with those of the organization.

Secondly, they show different degrees of effort. To bring their whole selves to work means conscientious and meticulous work at their posts in the working hours. While dedicated employees always go the extra mile to give full play to their potential in order to exceed the goals and requirements; they strive to learn and grow without fear of hardship and suffering. In Huawei, dedication is manifested in two ways: dedication with your heart and dedication with your strength. The former refers to those who constantly seek personal and career development in their thinking and take the initiative to seek breakthroughs in the face of various challenges and pressures.

Thirdly, the motivation is different: the motivation of those who bring their whole selves to work comes more from job descriptions and incentive mechanisms, while dedicated employees are more driven by themselves. Huawei asks its top management to have a sense of mission, the middle management a sense of responsibility, and junior employees a sense of hunger, which stimulates the underlying needs from material to spiritual in accordance with the different stages of the employees.

Chapter 6
Rational and Controlled R&D Innovation System

By the time Huawei entered the telecom industry, leading international companies had already been in the industry for decades, if not longer, and had accumulated a wealth of technical and intellectual capital. For example, Ericsson, founded in 1876, accounted for 30–40% of the global market share for mobile phone systems in the 1990s. Cisco, founded in 1984, dominated the market of networking equipment such as routers and switches. It is a worthy research topic that how a catching-up company like Huawei established its innovation strategy and allocated R&D resources when its technological base was weak, its technological resources were limited and its technological capabilities were lagging behind.

First of all, how should the company prioritize for survival? In the early days of Chinese enterprises, most of them had extremely poor resources, and their strategic priorities varied greatly. However, many of them had to earn their first bucket of gold from low-threshold activities (such as trading, manufacturing, agency marketing, sales, etc.) and technological innovation was simply out of reach. Despite powerful international competitors and a lack of resources, Huawei still saw that in the field of information technology, small companies had opportunities to compete with big ones in a technological revolution, especially disruptive innovation: every company was in the process of trial and error. Therefore, in the early stage, Huawei did not adopt an all-around catching-up strategy; instead, it focused on the software and hardware of core network technologies and invested all its resources to build its core technologies, strengthening its leading capabilities through long term investment.[1]

Second, how to choose the innovation roadmap. According to a study on Korean and Japanese firms, catching-up firms usually take two paths of technology absorption. First, a gradual transition from an original equipment manufacturer (OEM)[2]

[1] From Ren's internal speech "Innovation is the inexhaustible driving force of Huawei's development" on July 20, 2000.

[2] OEM is a company that manufactures and sells products or parts of a product that their buyer, another company, sells to its own customers while putting the products under its own branding.

X. Dong et al., *Huawei*,
https://doi.org/10.1007/978-981-19-4078-1_6

to an original design manufacturer (ODM)[3] and an original brand manufacturer (OBM).[4] OEM usually refers to catch-up firms providing assembly services; ODM refers to those having their own design capabilities which have gradually transformed from simple processing to complex tasks and processes; OBMs are usually multinationals, focusing on high-value-added segments, that usually work with ODMs to scale up at lower costs and achieve win–win results for both parties. Second, reverse engineering. The innovation process in developed countries is usually an R&D approach, that is, starting from basic research, and then moving to development. But catching-up firms usually adopt a D&R approach, that is, directly using, assembling, and integrating existing technologies. Through rapid learning, imitation, reverse engineering, talent introduction, and other means, they directly enter the engineering development process (D&E). With the lower-cost advantage, they reduce the cost of applying new technologies, and enter the low-end market with higher efficiency.

In 1998, Ren set a goal for Huawei: We shall extensively absorb the latest technology in electronic information, open-mindedly learn from the best at home and abroad, develop leading-edge core technologies on the basis of independence and open cooperation. With our superior products, we shall join the ranks of the world's leading telecommunications companies. It is worth studying how Huawei chose its innovation path and how it overcame the obstacles of resource shortage.

Third, how to balance radical innovation against incremental innovation. As an enterprise grows, it needs to engage in both radical and incremental innovation. Radical innovation is an invention that destroys or supplants an existing business model. It blows up the existing system or process and replaces it with something entirely new. Despite a high failure rate, radical innovation contributes to long-term growth, helps entry into growing markets, and ensures greater room for growth. Incremental innovation involves a series of small improvements or upgrades made to a company's existing products, services, processes, or methods. The changes implemented through incremental innovation are usually focused on improving an existing products efficiency, productivity, differentiation and thereby increasing short-term profitability.

The two types of innovation are mutually reinforcing, complementary and interdependent under certain conditions: the proceeds of incremental innovation can be

---

[3] ODM is a manufacturer that designs a product based on its knowledge of the international market, which is eventually rebranded by another firm for sale and makes it available to buyers. This type of company has the system design capability to increase its added value through design, but avoids the risks involved in launching its own brand. This allows the buying firm to reduce the time required for development on its own.

[4] OBM refers to an OEM that has its own brand. As OBM requires an extensive marketing network, and the cost of channel development is very high, the effort required is much higher than OEM and ODM. Also, the products often have to compete with their OEM/ODM customers. So, to ensure the interests of their customers, OEMs rarely engage in OBM on a large scale. (OBMwikiOBMwikiwiki).

OBM is typically a company that sells an entire product made by a second company or including a component from a second company source as its own branded product. Selling the product of the second company under its own brand just adds a virtual extrinsic value to the product.

invested in radical innovation and the accumulated knowledge and capabilities from the former can serve as a basis for the latter. Successful radical innovation may in turn expand the scale of incremental innovation and discover the needs of growth markets. However, the co-existence of the two types of innovation within an organization will bring about tension from competition for the limited resources of the organization, distinctly different requirements on the organization's structure, culture, leadership, and other elements, and from diverging self-reinforcing tendencies. The key issue that the firm needs to address is how to allocate resources between radical innovation and incremental innovation at different stages of development, and how to create synergy between them to develop new businesses while ensuring the profitability of existing ones.

Finally, how to improve the return on investment in innovation. Innovations are trials and discoveries of potential future technologies and new markets with unclear business models and unpredictable returns on investment. The process requires firms to change or break away from their existing paths and capabilities, and it is quite risky. Therefore, firms are very cautious about radical innovation. The greater the uncertainty, the more cautious the firm will be. Lack of resources is a constant constraint for catching up with companies. Due to the constraint, firms are unable to fully explore potential opportunities, or experiment with new technology through portfolio strategies, or bear the cost of failure in radical innovation. In order to survive, companies need R&D and innovation investments to bring positive returns. How to do this effectively, and what methodologies Huawei has adopted, are of great interest to us.

6.1 The Status and Inputs of R&D

Over the past 30 years, Huawei has continued to invest more than 10% of its sales revenue in R&D, even under very difficult circumstances. Huawei believes that leading technology can bring a window of opportunity to make profits, and that the accumulated profits should be invested in the R&D to upgrade products. Such virtuous cycles of continuous improvement and innovation are thus repeated. Although Huawei's strength has been greatly enhanced, it still adheres to the principle of staying focused, and concentrates its efforts on the R&D of core technologies, enabling it to advance step by step to today's world-leading position.

In its early years, Huawei was struggling to win orders and capture rural markets bit by bit, while generously investing its revenue in R&D. At that time, the difference in scale between Huawei and the world's telecom giants was about 200 times. With perseverance and hard work, over a decade later, finally, in 2005, Huawei's sales revenue exceeded $5 billion for the first time, but the gap with the communications giant was still several folds. 2006 witnessed some major mergers in the industry: Ericsson acquired Marconi, Alcatel merged with Lucent, and Nokia and Siemens merged their telecom networks, which suddenly widened the gap that had been narrowed. Just when Huawei expected to get some respite, all of a sudden, it had to start an even longer uphill trek.[5]

Huawei was granted licenses for its full range of equipment in 1998, but eight years later, it still did not have much share in the domestic wireless market and could not even recover its costs. With the lost opportunities in the 2G era, Huawei did not stop, and launched a larger-scale R&D and market development on 3G. Every year, Huawei invested nearly 1 billion yuan in R&D, which has lasted for seven or eight years. As it was unable to recover its costs, Huawei had to look overseas for a chance to survive.

In 2000, Huawei allocated more than 15% of its annual sales revenue for R&D, sending the most talented people to the market and the service front line. With technology leadership, it gained a window of opportunity to make a profit, which in turn was used for R&D, in the hope of making more breakthroughs.[6] Huawei made its share of mistakes in R&D and missed some opportunities too. However, it firmly believes that the key to R&D is to create market value, not to innovate for the sake of innovation. Many technology companies failed because they deviated from this principle, such as Nortel and CNC.

In 2005, Huawei had more than 25,000 employees engaged in R&D and capital investment remained at 7–8 billion yuan or more per year. After 18 years of hard work, Huawei has not invented a single original product, but has made some improvements in functions, features, and integration capabilities mainly on the achievements of Western companies, which was reflected by progress in engineering design and product realization. Compared with the decades-long or even century-long accumulation of foreign competitors, Huawei still faced a big gap to catch up.

In 2007, Ren said, In practice, we have learned that the biggest risk for an enterprise is not to take any risks or not to innovate. In retrospect, if we had not taken risks and simply followed others, we would be a second-tier or even a third-tier company for a long time, and we wouldn't stand any chance to compete with multinationals, and we wouldn't even survive. If we had always followed the old ways, we would not have achieved such rapid growth.[7] Huawei grew up by learning the hard way, and after many hardships, it finally becomes a world leader in SDH optical transmission, access networks, smart networks, signaling networks, carrier-grade Internet access servers, 112 test heads. It is also a technology leader in dense wavelength division multiplexing (DWDM), C&C08iNET, routers, mobile communication, and other system products.

In 2017, Huawei invested 90 billion USD in R&D, about 14.9% of its sales revenue (see Fig. 6.1). Of the nearly 170,000 Huawei employees, more than 45% were engaged in innovation, research, and development. Huawei held core positions in over 170 standards organizations and open source organizations and held over 36,000 patents, one of the highest in the world.

---

[5] Ren Zhengfei: "Hard work pays back". *Huawei People*. July 21, 2006.

[6] Ren Zhengfei: "Innovation is the inexhaustible driving force of Huawei's development". July 20, 2000.

[7] Ibid.

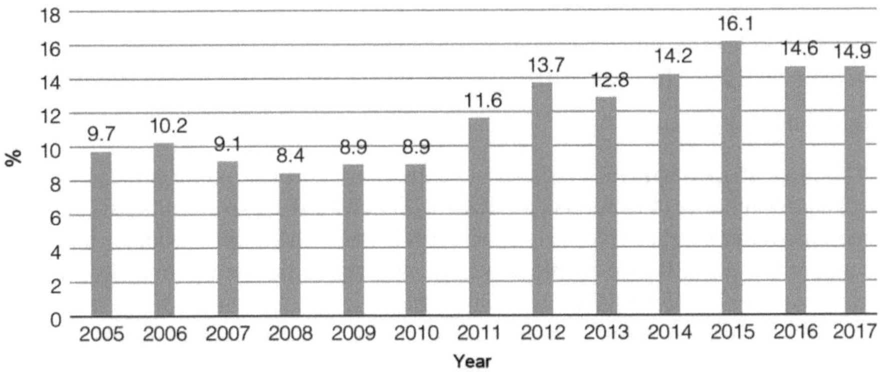

Fig. 6.1 Huawei's R&D input as a percentage of sales revenue (2005–2016)

6.2 The R&D System Development

In 1999, in order to reach international standards, Huawei developed three major R&D systems in line with the company's overall strategy. They are: (1) the strategic research system centered on long-term development goals, which is undertaken by the Central Research Department (CRD); (2) the Central Product Planning and Integration Research Department (CPRD) centered on short- and medium-term goals; (3) the Intermediate Pilot Department (IPD) with the main objective of near-term commercialization. These three systems are positioned differently with different focuses, while at the same time they complement each other.

The strategic research system

The CRD while focusing on the long-term strategy, is also down-to-earth: it also focuses on bold and yet precise and systematic research on basic research, the research and management of public resources, the strategic training of talent, the pre-research support to doctoral and master's supervisors, the acquisition of creative but immature semi-finished research results and the introduction of advanced products and technologies. CRD has cultivated a large number of outstanding employees. They are far-sighted and keen-minded, not afraid of failure, and never interested in any project that they are absolutely sure of success. They dare to think out of the box. They are science maniacs and tech geeks, who lead Huawei from technological creation to idea creation. CRD employs a large number of experts in a certain field, and a large number of young people, who are bold, creative, and keen to find breakthroughs in parameter design.

Product-based studies

The central product planning and integration research system (CPRS) centered on short-and medium-term goals. Its functions include applying technical products in a broader market, accelerating the development of a hierarchical structure and target assessment management, benchmarking against the world's leading enterprises led by academic leaders, to close the gap in the product, research, scale, and quality of personnel. CRD is always a battlefield, and always for creative young people.[8]

Market-based research

IPD is more aligned with the market around the goals and positioning of the CRD. IPD hires a large number of experts in all fields with rich knowledge and extensive experience, who make a large sieve, so to speak, that can test all kinds of products and helps commercialization. It also employs a large number of talented young people. IPD is well equipped, offering extensive staff training, and known for its indefatigable work style. Through years of design tests, process improvements, quality demonstration, IPD reduces product costs, improves product reliability, performance, and engineering indicators. Through continuous device and process experiments and accumulation, IPD shortens the Time-to-Market (TTM) and thus seizing the first opportunity in the market. IPD is best described as liberating development, guiding production, and supporting the market. IPD, as the cradle of backbone managers of Huawei, is also responsible for providing key personnel to CRD, the Marketing Department, and the Production Quality Management System.

Positioning of the three systems

Ren attaches great importance to professionalism and knowledge accumulation. He believes that the defining feature of an expert is the depth of knowledge in a specific field. That is why he calls the CRD a narrowband with a high amplitude strategy: by narrowband, it means specific targeted research field; by high amplitude, it means cutting-edge knowledge way beyond the average level in the highly technical field. Huawei requires basic research personnel to be dedicated and patient and take all the time needed to reach the frontier of the discipline. Ren believes that Huawei needs to go deeper in R&D like multinationals such as Microsoft.[9] Ren calls the IPD broadband with a low amplitude strategy. In other words, the product platforms, the links between products and markets, the product framework systems should all be wide with good adaptability.

In the early days, Huawei placed great emphasis on product seriation and quality optimization for the purpose of survival and achieve commercial and market success. Applied technology innovation and integrated innovation became Huawei's focus. It is commercial success-oriented, and its investment and management improvements are market and innovation-based. Therefore, technology-oriented rather than market-oriented innovation will not be supported, because Huawei understood that technology that did not create commercial value, and blind innovation were suicide for new startups without financial resources.

---

[8] Ren Zhengfei: "Huawei people refuse to fail", at Huawei's annual meeting. December 26, 1995.

[9] Ren Zhengfei: "Entrepreneurship and innovation must be centered on improving the core competitiveness". March 5, 1999.

Case study: Successful breakthrough in Europe with distributed base stations

Communication base stations are important network nodes for mobile communications, through which operators achieve network coverage of urban and rural areas, thus enabling mobile communications. The cost of renting and maintaining the base stations is a huge investment for operators. Before 2008, operators around the world used macro base stations.

Communication base stations are the main products of equipment manufacturers. Huawei began to expand into the European market in 2001, and until 2003, Huawei has not sold any 3G products in Europe. During the expansion in the Netherlands, Telfort, a local mobile operator, said that although Huawei's technology was good, it still could not buy Huawei's products, because Telfort assessed that the equipment cost in the network TCO only accounted for 14%, so even if Huawei gave away the equipment as a gift, it could only reduce the total cost by 14%, yet penalties from breach of the contract with Ericsson would offset all the benefits brought by Huawei. Therefore, European operators were unlikely to choose Huawei just because their equipment was cheaper, unless Huawei could bring more.

So, what should Huawei do? Huawei's mobile products had not yet entered the European market, so the company took this opportunity very seriously and the R&D director personally supervised the project. During the field visits, Huawei found that the operator's biggest expense came from the rental of station sites, amounting to 43% (plus 15% for electricity, 14% for equipment, 10% for installation, and 18% for other items and services). There are two types of station sites: outdoor and indoor. The indoor station sites require the rental of equipment rooms and cost a lot more. Even the outdoor station sites need to spend hugely on the rental of equipment rooms. With more than 3,000 station sites, Telfort spent tens of millions of euros per year.

Macro base stations and antennas are connected by feeders; the two must be located in close proximity, because the feeder attenuation is so high. Macro base stations are generally very large, so expansion requires the addition of new outdoor base stations, which adds even more cost. Huawei, therefore, proposed a new solution: to develop distributed base stations, which are divided into two parts: RRU (the RF part) and BBU (the baseband part). The RRU will be installed near the antenna, while the BBU will be installed in the cabinet. In other words, there is no need to rent a new outdoor cabinet, thus expansion can be achieved without incurring new rental expenses. In the end, 90% of Telfort's station sites were retrofitted this way, saving 30% over conventional solutions. Based on the customers' new needs, Huawei creatively proposed a distributed base station solution to help the customer solve the pain points.

With the unique weapon of distributed base stations, later on, Huawei's mobile products were invincible in the European market. By 2016, the distributed base station shipment had accounted for more than 80% of its total shipment.

6.3 Early R&D Principles

In the early days when resources were scarce, in order to survive, Huawei focused on commercial value-oriented innovations. To avoid wasting limited R&D resources and to prevent R&D staff from being detached from customer needs, Huawei specifically developed six principles of controlled innovation.

1. Avoid hasty innovation, which simply pursues the speed of technology launch without considering the market need. It does not give the innovation sufficient time for stable application, and always keeps on innovating and upgrading. It may satisfy the creative desire of technical personnel but is uneconomical.
2. Avoid premature innovation, which usually finds itself in the difficult songs find few singers situation. As the saying goes One step ahead the customers need is a leader; three steps ahead, a martyr.
3. Avoiding over-innovation: both hasty innovation and premature innovation are examined from a technology and product perspective. Falling into these two traps may be due to competition but are usually closely related to the firm's over-emphasis on technological orientation. Over-innovation refers to another type of undesired innovation, which means firms innovate too aggressively and rapidly in terms of organizational or managerial change.
4. Continuity. Continuity can help prevent a vacuum in decision-making and responsibility in the process of change, to ensure that the old decision-making model does not completely disappear before the new organization is completely established, and to ensure that business changes are carried out in an orderly manner.
5. Inheritance and development. Huawei opposes "every new sovereign brings his own courtiers" which means every new CEO replace all key managers by his own team. Huawei does not allow new managers to change whatever their predecessors accomplished as soon as they assume their positions. It opposes arbitrarily destroying the original rational elements in culture and management.
6. Evaluation and demonstration. During the period of stable development, bold exploration of management is not encouraged. Any management improvement must be evaluated against the bigger picture, and any major change must not be approved until fully justified.

During the catching-up period, Huawei has long been in the phase of practical R&D, setting limits for the scope of innovation, limiting it to only those areas that are most critical to the survival of the company, in other words, areas relevant to Huawei's core competencies.

In response to some of the behaviors and preferences in the pursuit of technological leadership, Ren suggested: Some people are very confused. They thought that they had made something that obviously was the latest technology. They did not understand why the innovation award was given to someone who simply used a very common technology. The reason is that I don't think their innovation has any commercial value.[10]

In 1999, in response to a question from an R&D staff as to whether Huawei intended to train academic engineers, Ren replied that Huawei's main aim was to train a large number of business engineers. It is always necessary to train people with high theoretical accomplishment. Without theoretical foresight, there can be no technological breakthroughs, and no windows of opportunity to make profits. However, it was very difficult for Huawei to do that at this stage. Huawei was not going to cultivate academicians at this stage; Huawei would only further cultivate those who had already made some achievements.[11]

The principle of staying focused and making a breakthrough. In the early days, Huawei almost had nothing except knowledge, enthusiasm, and motivation. Since its inception, Huawei has always been focusing on just one thing: the R&D of core network technologies and has never been tempted by other opportunities. Under the conditions of limited resources, Huawei dared to put all its eggs in that one basket. Huawei almost used all of its profits from agency sales on R&D of small switches, and eventually made local breakthroughs and gradually achieved technological leadership and bigger profit margins. Ren used CPCs siege strategy as an example: the troops were deployed vertically. The attacking troops concentrate on break one weak link, then two main forces would get inside and expand the attack from both sides, and then four more divisions would go in to expand their presence.

Guided by the principle of staying focused, Huawei attaches great importance to dedication and craftsmanship. Ren wrote a special article to sing Sun Yongfang's praise, who had worked at Huawei for 13 years, commenting that she lived a history of Huawei. Huawei has been doing only one thing for more than 20 years adhering to the pipeline strategy. Your path and Huawei's overlaps. Why you are so successful? Because you never deviate from this path. People just need to put their strength, no matter how small it seems, to good use. If they keep going, step by step, they will reach their destination.

Big rewards for small improvements principle. In 1998, Huawei asked its employees to follow the principle of Big rewards for small improvements; encouragement only for big suggestions, to encourage employees to make incremental changes to short-term, local, and small problems, instead of being obsessed with big but empty issues. Small incremental improvement aiming at improving the core competitiveness of the company, will lead to optimization, standardization, and rationalization of the work. Big rewards for small improvements is a long-term policy at Huawei.[12] Huawei evaluates these improvements to see if they align with the company's major processes, and if they can integrate with relevant processes and then streamlines and solidifies these processes. Whether a process is advanced or not depends on the value

---

[10] Ren Zhengfei: "Entrepreneurship and innovation must be centered on improving the core competitiveness". March 5, 1999.

[11] Ren Zhengfei: remarks at the orientation. November 11, 1999.

[12] Ren Zhengfei: "Cultivating and selecting managers with field experience" at the Second Quality Management Report and Award Ceremony. 1998.

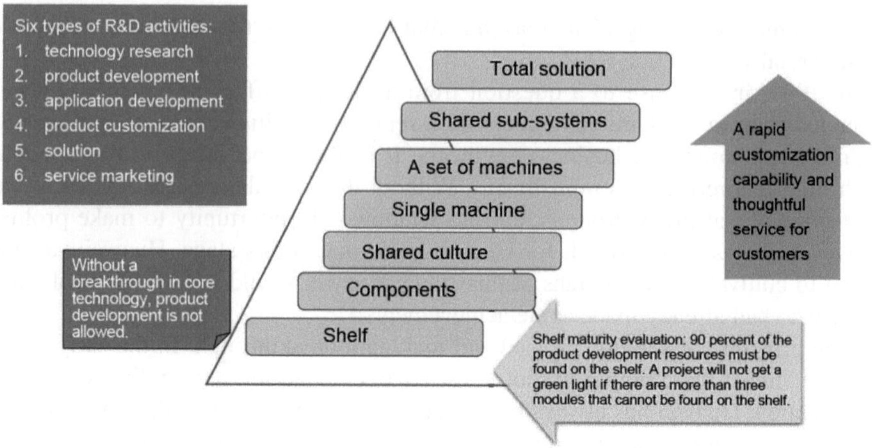

Fig. 6.2 Huawei knowledge product shelf system

it contributes to the company. This is also the criterion Huawei is using to evaluate transformation projects.

Knowledge reuse principle in R&D. In the early stage of R&D, in order to improve efficiency and ensure the continuity of R&D, a knowledge product shelf system was established (see Fig. 6.2). Knowledge product shelf emphasizes reuse of existing outcomes and resources, in particular, in the following six types of R&D activities: technology research, product development, application development, product customization, solution, and service and marketing. Only when the development involves 90% of existing resources in the early period (the 1990s) or 70% in the recent period (last 10 years), can it get a green light. The R&D personnel is also evaluated on their use of the knowledge product shelf. Meanwhile, the company's R&D accumulation is also reflected in the maturity of the knowledge product shelf. In this way, the knowledge product shelf is gradually upgraded to serialization of components, which are combined into a single machine and a whole set of machines through a shared culture, and then a systemic solution is formed through shared subsystems, which ultimately results in a rapid customization capability and a thoughtful service for customers. This is how Huawei greatly enhances its efficiency and ability to serve customers and reducing costs. As Ren said, in new product development, we should try to use mature technologies that we already have and technologies that can be purchased in the market. Technology with a reuse rate below 70% is regarded as a waste rather than an innovation in Huawei, as it only increases development costs and instability of the product. Although Huawei does not adopt Cisco's massive acquisition approach to achieve rapid product line expansion, it has always been emphasizing reuse in its indigenous R&D management.[13]

[13] Ren Zhengfei: "Entrepreneurship and innovation must be centered on improving the core competitiveness". March 5, 1999.

6.4 R&D Organization Design and Management

Prioritize the establishment of an R&D management system

In 1995, Huawei started to learn software management from the West and India, and has since then been practicing and optimizing it in joint projects with many world-class software companies. Huawei has been practicing software process improvement for many years by observing the standard requirements of SEI-CMM, such as quantitative assessment, defect management, quality control, project process, and configuration management.

Adjusting R&D system according to market changes

The strategic formation and organizational structure of Huawei's R&D system are constantly adjusted with the changing environment, and the evaluation system of R&D achieves equilibrium. Huawei is deeply aware that in war, the formation of an army changes from time to time. In its early development, due to the lack of resources, Huawei's R&D was highly focused, and resulted in rapid technological progress, but its adaptability to market needs was weak. With the diversification of the market and customer needs, Huawei's R&D system should become flattered. In other words, the formation of the R&D team should be adjusted according to the environment, corporate needs, and technical characteristics. For example, when working on new technology breaking through, the formation should be highly focused, but when the guiding effect of the new technology is weakened, the team should become flatter and work more on products that customers have real needs but are not necessarily technically challenging.[14] In short, the organizational structure of Huawei's R&D team is aligned with its focus. Its structural adjustment is always business-oriented instead of technology-oriented. So should the evaluation system.

Introduction of advanced R&D process and management system

Huawei has a huge R&D team and an ambitious R&D plan. Without good organization management and process optimization, it will not be able to achieve the preset targets, and lead to a waste of R&D resources, products, and market disconnection, ultimately even dragging the company's development. Based on the above considerations, in 1997, Huawei retained IBM for consulting services. After a long period of research, and modeling, Huawei established the Integrated Product Development (IPD) framework, covering pre-market research, planning, formal development, product validation, and product release. IPD ensures that the purpose and timeliness of product development can be effectively monitored. Meanwhile, IPD also takes into account the dynamic matching between the management of market segments and performance and the product development process to ensure that the development process is aligned with market needs. More importantly, IPD, as an

[14] Ren Zhengfei: "Understanding laws of nature, giving play to the core team, continuously improving the per capita benefits, and working together to overcome difficulties" at the Q3 marketing meeting. 2002.

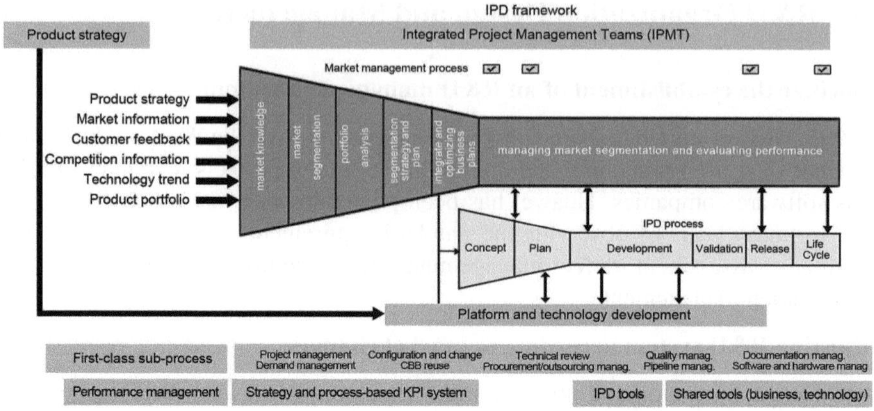

Fig. 6.3 IPD system and framework flowchart

R&D platform, can store and accumulate a large amount of information and knowledge in the process (such as project management, requirements management, change management, quality management, etc.), and quantifiably manage the performance of the R&D process (see Fig. 6.3). Huawei's product innovation is not disruptive, but continuous innovation based on evolving customer needs. Huawei firmly believes that meaningful innovation is based on a deep understanding of customer needs and the satisfaction of those needs.

Building cross-departmental teams by integrating processes

Huawei continuously restructures and reforms, with its entire system configured and operating in accordance with the IPD.

Because IPD processes take advantage of cross-functional teams, they are characterized by integrated team structures. Team members from sourcing, maintenance, and other services participate in early design phases alongside the R&D, development, engineering, and marketing departments. The cross-departmental teams have the power of decision on behalf of the company and oversee all processes.

R&D assessment taking into account both long-term and short-term objectives

Huawei's R&D system takes special attention to prevent short-and medium-term efficiency-oriented internal competition and conflicts from going too far, and excessive silo operations within the R&D team. Unlike its competitors, Huawei does not conduct the evaluation solely based on the project, but rather on the potential growth, and the contribution to the company. Potential growth implies the contribution to future growth, while the current contribution is related to the revenue. The assessment mechanism for the large R&D team is based on long-term and short-term objectives alternatively, which means for a certain period of time, the focus on the assessment of the team is on short-term earnings, yet for another period of time, the focus will be shifted to growth potential. To this end, Huawei has designed a virtual profit system, encouraging the team to focus on medium-and long-term gains while evaluating current gains, and to dynamically adjust the R&D team according to changes in the external situation.

6.5 Innovative Use of Internal and External Resources

Fully sharing internal resources for innovation

Huawei's early product development was totally based on personal experience, and when problems arose, they were solved one by one. Ren advocated that all departments should be fully open and make full use of internal resources, and that no department or individual should hide their technological innovations, successes, or even failures. Huawei mobilized all employees to contribute their insights, which proved to have saved a lot of time and resources. In 2000, Ren said at a Quality Control Circle (QCC) event, Huawei's products are unstable, and when project managers take office, they are afraid that others will take their credit, so they say that the whole products are developed by themselves. Then I will tell CRD that people like this shall not be given the Entrepreneurship and Innovation Award, and they shall not be given a promotion simply based on the innovation, and they shall certainly not be made project managers. At Huawei, innovation is only allowed when it is built upon at least 70% of current existing resources. Every new project is like a lego project: most of the base pieces are the same; only a few bricks are different.[15] In response to the repetitive work caused by some employees' reluctance to share knowledge and resources, Huawei has made adjustments in the team building and reward and punishment mechanisms. In terms of team building, Huawei organized discussions on what innovation was. Each group shared what small improvements it had made. Reinventing the wheel is certainly discouraged in Huawei, because the costs will be too high. And it is not regarded as an innovation but a waste of the company's valuable resources. As for the reward mechanism, people who have used the knowledge of others and are willing to share their knowledge with others will be promoted. Huawei's R&D staff understands that for a large company the most effective way to reduce costs is to share resources: what has been developed can be reused, because within the company technical confidentiality and patents are not a problem. Existing technology plus some optimization is the real deal. Those who are obsessed with big innovations are nave and hopeless. Through discussion and publicity of typical cases, CRD developed new forms of resource sharing, not only the company's resources, but also external resources, including knowledge and skills learned from the competitors (see Chap. 11).

[15] Ren Zhengfei: a speech at the Second Quality Control Circle Event. 2010.

Old knowledge to new knowledge is like a heap of dung to flowers

On the matter of inheritance and development, Huawei's principle is that new technologies and products should be based on the existing market and product system. It shall never turn a blind eye to the company's tradition and blindly innovate. Hence the flowers on the dung strategy. When flowers wither, they become the new dung; so the company shall always innovate on the basis of its existing technologies.

Making good use of external resources for integrated innovation

In the early days, CRD widely promoted the following ideas among the R&D teams: opposing blind innovation; rational selection, borrowing, copying, and assembling are all be regarded as innovation. The pace of technological progress and market changes is breathtaking. Product technology is like capital and other resources that can be developed or assembled. Technology can be developed by CRD itself through in-house R&D activities, or it can be acquired in a variety of ways. For example, for many non-core technologies, the cost will be high if the company develops them all on its own, so it can learn from Microsoft, Cisco, Dell, Intel, etc. It can also obtain licensing or procure technological innovations. Meanwhile, Huawei can acquire small companies in the USA, engage customer demand research, and tailor-make products to improve the accuracy of R&D planning. It can also recruit local employees in the chip team in the USA.

The importance of innovation integration

Today, it is becoming less and less likely to achieve business success by monopolizing a technology, because technology is easily available to everyone. Therefore, the most important thing for the enterprise is the integration ability, rather than how strong it is in technology. Business success depends on the ability to integrate technology, resources, and channels to form the competitive edge, which is the key to enterprise management. This is true for Microsoft and Cisco. Cisco's most important ability is that it integrates advanced technology into its own products and pushes them to the market. So, Huawei believes that whether the technology is obtained through licensing, or in-house development, or M&A, the key lies in whether the product is competitive and accepted by customers.

Procuring external resources to secure market capacity

For the core technologies that Huawei lacks, it will have to buy them or pay the patent licensing fees so as to get in the international market and survive the market competition. This is actually much cheaper than bypassing the patents. By paying the licensing fees Huawei has made peace with Western companies.[16] Huawei often encounters bottlenecks in product engineering, including algorithms, heat dissipation, processes, energy efficiency, which are often obstacles to gaining a competitive edge. In order to overcome these obstacles, Huawei did not rely entirely on in-house R&D, because by the time the R&D is accomplished, the market opportunity

[16] Ren Zhengfei: "Practical research and 20 years of hard work" at a national demonstration meeting of an in-service project. December 2006.

would be long gone, or the competitors would have already dominated the market, preventing Huawei from profiting in the competitive market. Therefore, Huawei directly procured the technologies to narrow the gap and build up its leading capabilities. For example, a key technology of Huawei's was acquired from a foreign company and it is that technology that has helped Huawei to produce the world's leading products and has the largest market share. This company is a leading company of ultra-long-haul (ULH) transmission technology and solutions. The company has invested more than US$70 million in this technology. Huawei's analysis concluded that its products and technology had a high market value, so the decision was made to purchase the technology. After the technology transfer and secondary development, and of course necessary legal formalities, Huawei completed the integration development in just nine months, successfully launching the product that applied the new key technology to achieve large-capacity, long-haul (4,600 km) repeaterless optical transmission turning it from an obscure company to the number one company in the global long-haul transmission market in 2005. Huawei has ever since maintained its position.

Building an open innovation system

Ren always insists that Huawei needs to create an open innovation system, using high-end chips from foreign competitors as much as possible and understand how it works. Only when foreign companies refuse to sell their products, then Huawei will use its own, and its own stuff should not be bad. He believes: Huawei should not have a narrow sense of pride, for it will kill us. Our purpose is to make money.[17] Today's creativity and invention are less based on self-reliance than an open system. Countries around the world gain tremendous capabilities through the Internet, which in turn gives Huawei a solid foundation. Technical systems should not be closed. Huawei also believes that it should not only choose its subsidiaries or affiliated companies as suppliers, otherwise, it would be a closed system, which will eventually deplete its energy and demise. A closed system, be it of human resources or technology, will only end up exhausting the system resources.

The importance of an open innovation system is reflected by the opposite: if you totally innovate on your own, the ultimate result is entropy death. Why do we reject others? Can we do everything better than anyone else? Why do we have to be self-reliant? Self-reliance means parochialism, which we don't think is a good idea. During the innovation process, Huawei's in-house R&D only engages in where it has advantages; where it is not, we welcome open cooperation. Only this way can we build a true strategic power. We are very supportive of innovation, but only if it revolves around the company's main business. We must avoid building closed systems. We must build an open system, especially with hardware systems. If we are not open, we are dead.[18]

Closed innovation is dangerous. Huawei is facing a complex and changing world. A company that does not innovate is bound to perish, while adopting a narrow and

---

[17] Ren Zhengfei: a speech at the 2012 Noah's Ark Lab Symposium. September 2012.

[18] Ibid.

closed innovation model, and one-sidedly emphasizing fully independent innovation is also perilous. Closed innovation leads to repetitive labor and low efficiency; refusing to use other people's ideas and technologies means giving up the opportunity to gain extra profits by using mature and advanced ideas and technologies. Huawei has learned a hard lesson from Japan's closed innovation. Japan developed its own set of technology standards, PDC, in the era of 2G mobile communications, and it was precise because of this completely independent innovation that its 2G network became a narrowband incompatible with other networks around the world. The disintegration of Bell Labs and the subsequent acquisition of Lucent also prove that closed innovation is obsolete. After years of hard work, Huawei's technological innovation has evolved from following the trend to open R&D synchronized with mainstream technology. Globalization is inevitable. Huawei should be courageously open, instead of being closed, and actively compete with the West and learn to manage itself in competition. If we close the door and survive by protectionism, we will collapse once the door is open; therefore, Huawei should embrace globalization with better products.[19]

Joint innovation

Huawei has established more than 20 joint innovation centers with the world's leading operators to translate leading technologies into competitive advantages and commercial success. Huawei has established competition relations with its partners: competition impels everyone to innovate, while collaboration makes innovation faster and more effective. Huawei not only learns from its domestic competitors, but also partners with Lucent, Motorola, IBM, TI, and more than a dozen other companies in future chip design, and work together to build future solutions that serve customers.

Huawei's customers are also instrumental to its growth. In the development of China's communication networks, in the negotiations, biddings, and evaluations of bids with Western companies, they have helped Huawei to be more professional and in line with international practice. Thanks to the vigorous standard, Huawei has grown from a small and informal operation to an international company. Because Huawei would not be shortlisted to compete with western companies in technology maturity, rationality, cost, value creation, service, and especially solutions, if it cannot produce the best it can offer.

6.6 Innovation Climate

Value innovative talent

Huawei's attitude toward R&D staff is demonstrated in the following four aspects.

- Managers should respect R&D staff, sing praises to them, give them honor and awards first.

[19] Guan Liang: *Ren Zhengfei on Management*. Shenzhen: Haitian Publishing House, 2009.

- Managers should know how to poach the talent, whether they work at Huawei or other companies. Huawei has a whole set of mechanisms to get outstanding talent, and has set up an internal Talent Recommendation Award. Huawei certainly has great appeal to talent.
- Managers should know how to nurture employees. For example, they can adopt a positive incentive policy, keep failed project team members around, and emphasize that the key for young people is that they are willing to learn. Huawei has set up a Scholarship for Financially Challenged Students to encourage them to change their fate with diligence.
- Managers should build a community of a shared future and benefits. Huawei attracts and retains talent by offering high compensations, much higher than the second-highest level in the industry of the same region. Meanwhile, it encourages internal competition and creates equal opportunities. In Huawei, honest work always pays off. It is also important to create a good leadership and culture to retain talent.

R&D culture building

First of all, the R&D team should be clear about the vision and mission of the company: to become a world-leading company by realizing the customer's dreams. Huawei's R&D team believes in the vision and mission of developing world-leading core technologies and products independently and creatively on the basis of open cooperation and taking it as our responsibility to serve the country and revitalize the communications industry. Huawei people know that in the communications industry, lagging behind means that it will be eliminated, so they encourage the wolf spirit in R&D, which is reflected in learning, innovation, benefit-seeking, and unity. Learning and innovation represent a keen sense of smell, benefit-seeking represents the aggressive spirit, and unity represents the spirit of group struggle. The employee's sense of belonging and identity encourage Huawei people to take the initiative to engage in innovation activities and it goes deep into their mindset.

Customer-focused innovation

Ren criticized the CRD for not being willing to participate in the quality control circle activities. In his view, good R&D must focus on customers' needs, ideas, and satisfaction. If the R&D team makes products without systematically sorting out and summarizing customers' needs, and ignores customers' needs, the products will naturally be undesirable. Blind innovation is not real innovation.

How to face failure in innovation

Huawei believes that the company should be more tolerant toward failure. But tolerance should be based on a specific evaluation mechanism; not all fields allow large-scale failure. In the field of high-end research, there are more fuzzy areas, and when you enter a fuzzy area, you don't know what it will look like in the future. Therefore, it is important to be open-minded. You can go have coffee, talk to people, brainstorm, write down your thoughts, post them online, and inspire younger employees to think about it. But some R&D fields are not fuzzy. For example, engineering contracting should be clearly quantified, so if you have done it poorly, it only indicates poor management.[20] The key elements of successful innovation are efficiency and synergy of the management platform.

Patient with basic research

Huawei people believe that even if the basic research is useless for the moment, they should not give it up. If an individual is gloomy about the future of the research, he or she can be transferred to other posts. Some technologies may not be useful for decades, but they still have to be done. Because a slip of strategic significance would cost hundreds of billions of dollars, making the accumulated wealth go down the drain. For basic research, Huawei should be tolerant of whimsies. The company must be patient with basic research, even it means that it will be of no use for a decade. Do not cut corners or seek the number of papers published. What matters is down-to-earth research.

From technical breakthrough to theoretical breakthrough

Huawei should not only focus on customer-centric products and services, but also increase investment in the core of the platform for future-proof technologies. It should command the strategic high and take the risk in cutting-edge technologies such as chips and platform software. Therefore, it is necessary to understand and appreciate the mavericks. Huawei should make the leap from technical breakthrough to theoretical breakthrough. So said Ren.[21]

Value applied research and nurture business engineers

In Ren's view, Huawei is an integrator of technology and products, and applied research is important to keep the company alive. Taking material science as an example, Huawei focuses research on material applications rather than inventions. For example, Japan is zooming in from the whole machine to components and to materials, which presents a great opportunity for Huawei. While Japan is doing material science research, Huawei is studying how to use these materials to make better products than the U.S. does. That's take the advantage of others ingenuity.[22] Japanese and German machines are recognizably reliable, so why not let the Japanese and Germans do our intermediate tests to assure the quality of our products.[23]

---

[20] Ren Zhengfei: "Open up or die". *Business Review*. 2012.

[21] Ren Zhengfei: "Success is not a reliable guide to future development" at a market meeting. January 17, 2011.

[22] Ibid.

[23] Zhao Renzhe Zhao, Chief Scientist, Electronic Material at Huawei. Meeting minutes of 2012 Lab Symposium. July 2, 2012.

6.7 A Two-Wheel-Drive: Basic Research and Applied Research

Engaging in disruptive innovation within boundaries

After 2012, as Huawei had greater international competitiveness and fewer competitors to catch up with, Huawei increased its investment in basic research of strategic significance and established the 2012 Laboratory. In 2015 Ren pointed out that Huawei's innovation needs to focus on the main business with incremental innovation while allowing a small team to engage in disruptive innovation within boundaries. The Internet always shouts disruptive innovation, but we must insist on creating value for the world and innovating for value creation. Our innovation should focus on the needs of the next 5–10 years, and most people don't have to look too far ahead. Most products should focus on incremental innovation. Meanwhile, we allow a small number of people to engage in disruptive innovation and talk nonsense. Within the boundaries, they can be as disruptive as they wish. Disruptive innovation should be open. Incremental innovation can continuously absorb energy from disruptive innovation and vice versa when the disruptive innovation is mature.

2012 Laboratory

The 2012 Laboratory refers to Huawei's research institutes, which include Central Hardware & Engineering Institute, Hisilicon, Competence Centers, and Central Software Institute. It is said that Ren came up with the name from the movie 2012. He believed that future information would be like a digital flood, and Huawei need to construct its Noah's Ark if it hoped to survive. 2012 Laboratory's research focuses on the next 5–10 years, including next-generation communications, cloud computing, audio, and video analytics, data mining, machine learning, etc. Huawei's official data shows that in 2015, Huawei invested 59.6 billion RMB (about 8.65 billion USD) in R&D, accounting for 15.11% of its sales revenue in 2015. In the past 10 years, Huawei has invested more than 240 billion RMB (about 34.83 billion USD) in R&D.

Noah's Ark Lab

Headquartered in the Hong Kong Science Park, and headed by Professor Yang Qiang at the Hong Kong University of Science and Technology, Huawei's Noah's Ark Lab focuses on AI, and employs researchers from around the world for basic research. It consists of five divisions.

- The division of natural language processing and information retrieval, which focuses on seamless machine communication with people in natural language, and text and social data mining.
- The division of large-scale data mining and machine learning, which focuses on the development of highly scalable and effective data mining and machine learning algorithms, as well as the development of the data mining system.
- The division of social media and mobile intelligence, which focuses on the development of state-of-the-art algorithms, self-learning systems that leverage social

media, social networks, and mobile data, and gaining insights from social network data.

- The division of human–computer interaction systems, which focuses on making human–computer communication more natural and easier, as well as developing large-scale intelligent systems.
- The division of machine learning, which focuses on human–machine learning and adaptive capabilities with the help of modeling and mathematical theory.

Scientist's labs

Currently, the 2012 Laboratory has set up a number of labs named after world-renowned scientists, such as the Shannon Lab, the Gauss Lab, the Sheard Lab, the Euler Lab, and the Turing Lab. The Shannon Lab has invested early in the research of High Throughput Computing (HTC) and has developed a great technical accumulation in big data hardware and software architecture, operating systems, new programming methods, and business application benchmarks. It reserves cognitive-related key technologies and algorithms for intelligent ICT development and provides intelligent services for related products and keeps abreast of the leading research in the industry in information storage, distributed computing, and software-defined devices. The Gauss Lab mainly creates the industry-leading database management system. The Sheard Lab mainly focuses on network security, endpoint security, virtualization security, and cryptographic algorithms. The Euler Lab is a proprietary operating system R&D center. The Turing Lab is Huawei's embedded processor core architecture Research Department.

Overseas Research Institute

The 2012 Laboratory has set up eight research institutes overseas; they are located in Europe, India, the USA, Russia, Canada, and Japan. The European Institute is extremely important because it is one of Huawei's two mathematics centers and has a heavyweight team for 5G research. Ren once attributed Huawei's success in Europe to its algorithms. Huawei has two disruptive architectural innovations in Europe: the distributed base station and Single RAN, which is a radio access network (RAN) technology offered by Huawei that allows mobile telecommunications operators to support multiple mobile communications standards (2G, 3G, and 4G) and wireless telephone services on a single network. Theoretically, it can help customers save half the construction cost. Huawei's competitors have tried to imitate it, but have so far failed, because the technology relies on highly complex algorisms behind the convergence of the communication standards. The core research focus of the Russian and French institutes is mathematics, as they are respectively ranked first and second in the world in mathematics. As early as 2012, in an article The future of Huawei's innovation: Ren Zhengfei's reply to 16 questions from the 2012 Laboratory Scientists published by Lei Feng.com, Ren said, Huawei's strength lies in mathematics, not in physics.

- The France Research Center. In 2016, Huawei set up a mathematics research institute in France, aiming to tap the basic mathematical resources in France, focusing

on basic algorithm research such as communication physical layer, network layer, distributed and parallel computing, data compression, and storage, as well as 5G and other long-term strategic projects and short-term products like the global architecture design of distributed algorithms. Huawei has also established four R&D centers in Paris for mathematics, aesthetics, home devices, and wireless standards. On the day of its inception, Huawei Managing Director Xu Wenwei said, Huawei has entered no man's land: there are no guides or followers, and there are a lot of uncertainties.
- The Russia Research Center. Huawei's Russian Institute is independent from the European Institute, which has made great breakthroughs in the 3G and 2G algorithms. The Russian Institute consists of seven Competence Centers that pools local talent of fundamental algorithms. They are Nonlinear Competence Center, Algorithm Engineering Competence Center, Optimization Competence Center, Channel Encoding and Decoding Competence Center, Source Coding and Decoding Competence Center, Big Data Analysis Competence Center, and Parallel Programming Competence Center.
- The Canada Research Center. Established in late 2008, the Canada Research Center is a Core Competitiveness Research Centre for 5G with more than 400 researchers located in four cities: Ottawa, Toronto, Montreal, and Waterloo.
- The Japan Research Center. It is mainly engaged in materials research.
- The India Research Center. It focuses on software delivery.

The 2012 Lab, Huawei's research base, is not the only top-class in China, but also has global clout. However, Ren still has his concerns. In May 2016, Ren said that Huawei was still a business engineer by nature and its innovation went only to engineering deep rather than at the theoretical level. Huawei should work harder on basic research. Later at the National Conference on Science and Technology Innovation, Ren again said: Huawei's innovation is still at the engineering level, for example, engineering mathematics, and physics algorithms. It has not yet gone into basic research. As we are approaching the limit of Shannon's theorem, and Moore's Law, the high-flow, low-latency theory has not yet been created. Huawei was at a loss.[24]

The CRD is mainly responsible for the technology system development, which currently has very few disruptive technologies and mainly focuses on hardware R&D. The CRD focuses on the mainstream of industrial development. Through heavy input (ranging from a few hundred to thousands of people) of global resources, it achieves company-level and department-level innovation. Depending on the value and significance of the innovation, the company's attention varies, as does to whom it reports. For example, the investment for 5G is US$600 million, and its R&D personnel accounts for 10% of the entire R&D staff. The funding is so abundant that its annual budget will always have some surplus every year. Its assessment cycle (3–5 years) is relatively longer too. Innovation is focused on the main business and aims to produce high-end products in the European and American markets. In this

[24] Ren Zhengfei: a speech at the National Conference on Science and Technology Innovation. May 30, 2016.

process, money and resources are invested in product R&D; failure is allowed by the organization; freedom is nurtured in the corporate culture. Huawei has invested in three research centers in Europe, with tens of millions of euros investment on each, focusing on patents, high-caliber talent, and discovering valuable markets.

6.8 Huawei Versus Cisco

According to Huawei's rotating CEO Xu Zhijun's report at Huawei Global Analysts Summit, Huawei's global sales revenue in 2016 was RMB 521.6 billion (USD 76.23 billion), up by 32% year-on-year, and its net profit was RMB 37.1 billion (USD 5.42 billion), up by 0.4%. Huawei's R&D input reached about 15% of its sales revenue, amounting to RMB76.4 billion (USD 11.17 billion), second only to Google in terms of the ratio. The cumulative R&D investment over the past 10 years has amounted to RMB 310 billion (USD 45.31 billion), and the number of employees in the R&D division has exceeded 80,000. According to the 2016 EU Industrial R&D Investment Scoreboard, Huawei ranked first in China and eighth in the world with 8.358 billion euros of R&D investment. Compared to Samsung's 12.5 billion euros and Apples 7.4 billion euros, Xu said Huawei's R&D input was still inadequate, especially the R&D investment in intelligent terminals are pitiful compared to Apple and Samsung; the investment in the wireless field is less than Ericsson, and the router field is way less than Cisco. Therefore, Huawei decided to invest $10 billion to $20 billion in R&D every year in the coming years to maintain its R&D intensity and strength.

Since Huawei's inception, R&D has been high on its agenda as the core competitiveness of the company. In the early days, Ren has already seen trends at three levels that affect the company's development. At the global level, the future world is knowledge-based, not bubble-based. At the domestic level, with limited per capita natural resources, China's development has to be driven by science and education, which means its development will only be sustainable the potential of humans is fully tapped into. At the industrial level, the company is either a leader or a loser; there is no alternative in between. Guided by this understanding, Huawei makes sure that in the incentive system design, the value of the intellectual property and know-how is always prioritized than capital, as capital can only retain and increase its value if it is attached to knowledge. The development and utilization of intellectual capital are placed in a more important strategic position, making capital to serve the acquisition of knowledge and talent, thus forming a virtuous circle in which knowledge and capital support and enhance each other.

Throughout its history, Huawei has been always investing more than 10% of its sales revenue in R&D, no matter how difficult it is. R&D goes before smelling the flower; building capabilities goes before chasing profits. Explore in no man's land and delay gratification. This long-term aggregation of key corporate resources and core interests provides a solid foundation for sustainable growth. With focused input, key breakthroughs have been made in products, engineering, technology, and research, strength has been accumulated, and core competencies built.

In terms of the innovation path, Huawei has evolved from imitative innovation, to controlled innovation, and from incremental innovation to basic innovation (see Fig. 6.4). In the first stage, in order to survive, Huawei mainly adopted imitative innovation to reduce innovation costs, quickly learn from and follow up the technical standards and product features of leading companies. It started with low-end products, and marginal markets, and succeed in markets dismissed by MNCs. In the second stage, Huawei focuses on the main business on the basis of accumulating certain resources, promoting rational, controlled, and incremental innovation. Based on customers' needs, Huawei entered the market with a low-cost strategy with technology and product combination and integration and gained customer trust with quality service. Huawei positions itself as a business engineer and it is wary of overreaching or overdeveloping to ensure that the company can survive in the market. This rational principle reduces the risk of innovation, increases the market return on innovation, and closely aligns innovation with market demand. Its product technology content has been increased incrementally through continuous improvement and upgrading. This is a very distinctive feature of Huawei. As of the end of 2014, Ren has made 212 references to be wary of over-innovation, because over-innovation implies risk and disruption. Companies need to strike a balance between innovation and order, which can be very tricky. Huawei rationally chooses the path and method of innovation according to its resources and capabilities. Especially in the early stages, Huawei regarded innovation as patches, and gave big rewards to small innovations. It aligned innovation and R&D tightly with customer needs, market needs, and capital management to avoid risks and failures, and ensured that the company survived and gained sustainability.

In the third phase, Huawei independently developed unique products to meet the differentiated customer needs of the global market. As Huawei has transformed itself from a technology follower to a market leader, it has intensified its effort into more cutting-edge basic science and disruptive technologies. Huawei's 2012 Lab recruits

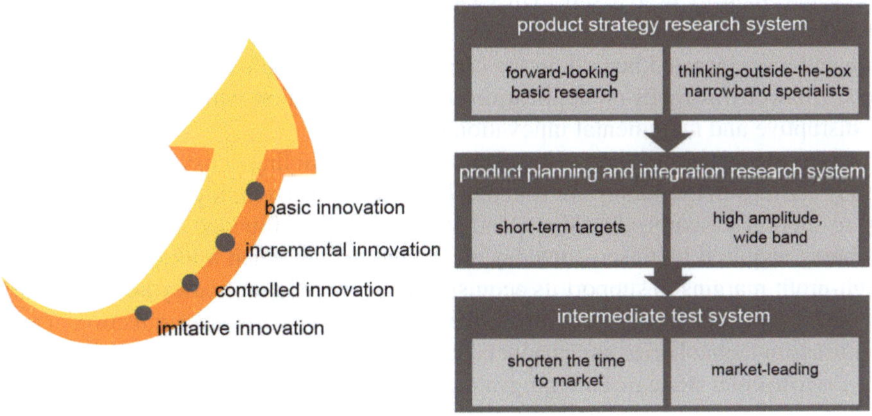

Fig. 6.4 Huawei's R&D and innovation system design

the world's best talent and it invests heavily in fundamental research. It has created a solution platform for all Huawei products. Meanwhile, Huawei increases R&D on basic and disruptive technologies, especially cutting-edge technologies in the next 3–7 years, which mainly takes place in CRD. Huawei culture values diversity, singularity, and uniqueness. It recruits top specialists or cross-disciplinary talent in natural sciences, gives them more freedom, and supports them with a more flexible incentive mechanism. For example, the usual 5% elimination rate does not apply. It also collaborates with top global research institutions. At this stage, as Ren said, in the next 20–30 years, human society will evolve into an intelligent society, the depth and breadth of which is unimaginable. Huawei needs to make breakthroughs in the basic theory research so as to eliminate the confusion in the no man's land.

To sum up, in the early days, Huawei was highly focused on incremental innovation, and its R&D was restrained by the company's knowledge resources, customer demand and market returns to avoid unnecessary risks and uncertainties and ensure market returns on R&D input. This was a very rational choice under the historical conditions of the time to ensure the survival of the company. As Huawei's strength grew and its competitive position improved, Huawei began to prudently and gradually increase the proportion of radical innovation, Huawei's vision, its courage to Van Fleet load-like[25] investment and its focus on capability building made it an awe-inspiring competitor in any area that it set its heart.

Huawei has always been closely aligning its R&D and innovation with marketing and management to ensure that innovation pays off. Through a two-pronged strategy driven by technology and business, Huawei has evolved from an operator-oriented network-focused strategy to a smartphone consumer-oriented end-focused strategy and a business-oriented cloud-focused strategy. Huawei aims to be a top-three player in each segment globally. This market demand-driven R&D strategy is essential to its commercial success.

Cisco and Huawei are both R&D-focused companies. In addition to technology and product innovation, they both focus on leveraging complementary IT, process, and value chain-focused assets to turn technology products into market benefits, and excellence centers into core competence. Both companies value incremental innovation and have invested heavily in the continuous optimization of their mature products. Huawei was focus on application-oriented innovation while Cisco investment in disruptive and incremental innovation is.

Cisco is located in Silicon Valley, known as an enabling ecosystem for startups. Many startups in the Valley are founded by former Cisco employees: some were set up to support Cisco product lines, and some were even founded with the intention of being acquired by Cisco someday. Cisco has accumulated a lot of cash through high-profit margins to support its acquisitions not only in the Valley and other parts of the U.S., but also in other countries like Israel and India. So, the acquisition of non-mainstream technologies and products has become an important innovation strategy for Cisco to enter strategic emerging markets rapidly. Cisco's strategy is two-pronged.

[25] Van Fleet load means a large amount of ammunition bombing the enemy regardless of cost—noted by the Chinese editor.

It focuses on incremental innovation in the existing R&D system, while acquiring new technologies from external resources. Then based on its integration capabilities and complementary assets, it will quickly integrate new technologies with existing technologies and products and market them.

Huawei is not located in Silicon Valley and does not have access to acquiring a large number of startups, so it is difficult for Huawei to use M&A as a key strategy for innovation. Therefore, Huawei's innovation was not open enough. Meanwhile, Huawei has always been benchmarking against leading international companies, whether in the field of communications equipment, mobile phones, or cloud computing. This catch-up approach has delivered commercial success, but in the foreseeable future, it is difficult to make breakthroughs in innovation.

Another characteristic of Cisco is that it avoids mistakes in innovation investment with a horizontal portfolio model. In contrast, Huawei's innovation ecosystem is very different. It is difficult for Huawei to leverage a large number of startups and an innovation ecosystem that enable it to internalize external technologies. Simply put, Huawei cannot just buy the best startups in the US. Under these circumstances, Huawei can only rely on its own R&D strength. To conclude, Huawei always focuses its innovation on incremental innovation, and only after entering the no man's land does it begin to invest in the R&D of basic and disruptive technology.

Chapter 7
A Cobweb Organizational Structure

As market conditions and stages of development change, companies will take on different organizational forms. Small startups need a flat and flexible organizational structure to solve simple problems quickly, with little need for standardization and specialization. As the organization grows in size and business processes become more complex, it is important to define the responsibilities, rights, and benefits of employees, and a hierarchy emerges. The hierarchy system requires that employees, no matter at which level, must strictly comply with corporate rules and regulations to ensure the overall efficiency of the organization. Strict hierarchical management leads to an ultra-stable structure, resulting in organizational inertia and rigidity, and when the external environment changes and market volatility increases, it will be difficult for the organization to adapt. At this point, the organization needs to break through the original strictly defined hierarchy and achieve cross-departmental and cross-process collaboration through total quality management, culture management, and matrix management.

In order to improve efficiency and specialization, the organization gradually establishes a management system based on the specialized divisions of R&D, production, and marketing; functional departments have become an important organizational form. The mega-enterprise develops a business unit system based on product and market segmentation. The advantage of the business unit is that it adopts independent accounting, which can greatly incentivize the employees; at the same time, the internal communication and collaboration of the business unit is smoother, which greatly improves the operational efficiency. However, the competition between business units leads to information and resource silos, resulting in the duplication of construction.

In order to solve this problem, achieve mass production and reduce product costs, the matrix organization was created. The matrix reinforces the dual leadership of the profit center (production departments) and the cost center (functional departments), which has the advantage of enhancing synergy and avoiding silo operations. However, due to the dual leadership, employees are often confused as to which leader they should follow, and leaders are distracted by issues like employee loyalty. With

X. Dong et al., *Huawei*,
https://doi.org/10.1007/978-981-19-4078-1_7

the widespread application of communication technology, the flat organization, the networked organization, the hypertext organization, the community-based organization, and the virtual organization have emerged one after another. The departmental boundaries are getting blurred, and organizations are getting flattening. Customer and market-oriented professional collaboration are increasingly convenient, and organizational systems continue to innovate.

In order to support the realization of corporate strategic objectives, in addition to the design and adjustment of the organizational system, the distribution, coordination, and management of tasks are also important for the efficiency, flexibility, innovation, and continuous optimization of the organization. Organizational systems need to maintain high responsiveness and interaction with the external environment, as well as efficient information sharing, cross-departmental cooperation, and overall coordination within the organization. The first capability of an organization system is process capability. In the industrialization era, in order to improve the overall operational efficiency of the organization, it must have standardized operational processes, procedures, and paths, so that it can disseminate and reuse proven processes, and reduce unnecessary discussion, consultation, and communication. IT application further strengthens and optimizes the value and efficiency of the processes, making business activities digital, visual, and measurable.

The second capability of an organizational system is the capability of group decision-making. Decisions involving a small number of people are fast and efficient, but the participation is low, and the information gathered is limited. It may lead to errors or blind spots in decision making, and the lack of participation makes it difficult to form effective consensus and make employees take responsibility, so many problems can occur in the execution. Therefore, how to balance between efficiency and participation in decision-making is an important issue for managers.

The third capability of an organizational system is the ability to achieve internal stability against environmental volatility. To ensure efficiency, an organization's overall structure and system must be stable, but stable organizations tend to develop organizational rigidity and inertia and gradually lose their vitality. Huawei's rapid growth from a small local company to a global giant and its unique approach to organizational structure and systems are of particular interest to us, especially in the following aspects:

First, how Huawei does understand organizational capabilities? How does it design its organizational system according to its company scale and strength (from the strength in flexibility to the holistic strength)? What core elements does it focus on in the process? How does it address the relationships between flexibility and stability, individuals and the organization, and the individual capabilities and the organizational capabilities?

Second, what is Huawei's methodology for organizational change? Huawei's transformation over the past 30 years has been very successful, with improved capacities, expanding market, and a solid organizational system. What methodology has Huawei adopted to drive its organizational change? What role did management play in the process?

Thirdly, Huawei has created many famous organizational structures, such as the Regional Joint Committee, the Iron Triangle, and the Elite Team. What exactly are these structures? What are their unique roles in enhancing organizational capabilities and improving organizational efficiency?

7.1 Principles and Methodology of Organizational Design

Four elements of organizational capacity building

Organizational structure, talent, process and IT are the four elements of Huawei's organizational model. The organizational structure establishes the position of each department in the organization, determines the responsibilities of the organization, and defines the organizational strategy. Talent is the greatest asset of the organization, and the talent team is crucial to building organizational capacity. Processes ensure that the organization rids its dependence on individuals and achieves effective end-to-end connectivity, and that the demand of the customers will be timely and accurately met, which is the lifeline of Huawei. IT solidifies processes, improves organizational efficiency, reduces management fatigue, and makes knowledge management possible, maximizes application through case sharing and experience transfer. Huawei's organizational design philosophy and logic revitalize organizations and demonstrate unparalleled organizational capabilities, which are not reliant on certain people and therefore are sustainable. Ren often proudly states that Huawei can run smoothly no matter who leaves the company. This is a distinguishing feature that sets Huawei apart from other Chinese companies.

Organizational design methodology

In addition to the above four elements, the organizational design also involves aspects such as strategic objectives, cost management, and incentive mechanisms. Huawei adopts a top-down design approach, in which the organizational system implements the leaders' will and strategic intent; executives are the main driving force for organizational innovation and development. Specifically, Huawei's organizational system design consists of the following nine steps (as shown in Fig. 7.1).

Step 1: understand the corporate strategy. When Huawei designs the organizational system, the first thing to think about is the corporate strategy. Strategy, the departure of the organizational system design, can be implemented throughout the organization. Different strategic positioning leads to different organizational structure. Huawei's organizational system is constantly changing with the changes in the environment and its strategies. For example, in order to adapt to the burgeoning demand of the consumer market, share Internet dividends, and expand and strengthen the mobile phone and network markets, Huawei adjusted its business structure in 2011 by making the network department independent and improving the strategic position of the mobile phone business in the Group. Since then, the network business has developed rapidly, with smartphone shipment reaching 139 million units in 2016

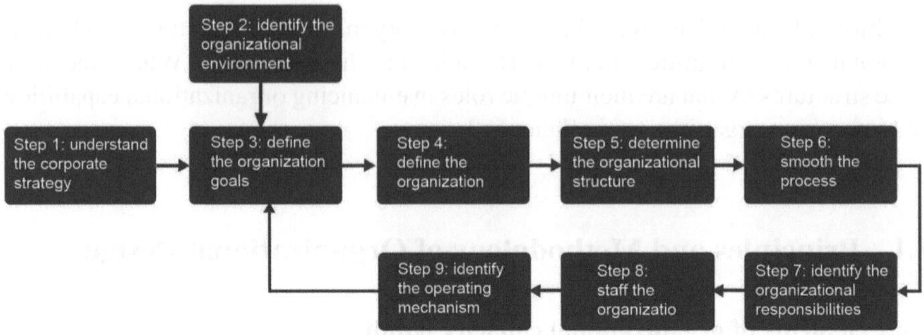

Fig. 7.1 Huawei's design methodology of the organizational system

and sales revenue of 179.8 billion yuan (26.48 billion USD), up by 44% year-on-year. Prior to 2011, Huawei's network business was but a marginal supporting service for communications equipment, and was even considered for sale in 2009.

Step 2: identify the organizational environment. Any organization has to form a development system that is dynamically adapted to the environment. In its organizational design, Huawei pays special attention to the satisfaction of customer needs and the perception of the external environment. For example, Huawei's regional matrix structure and the "Iron Triangle" organization are essentially cross-departmental teams in which each member has a dual role: each has his own responsibilities, but also checks and balances with one another. Such a system helps Huawei identify and seize all possible leads and opportunities in the market; it also helps the management and decision-makers have access to accurate information of customers, markets, and specific projects.

Huawei's organizational structure and staffing have always been highly aligned with the business ecosystem, and when the market environment changes, so does its organization. When the mobile and telecom business at the central level split in 1999, Huawei correspondingly split its System Department into a Telecom System Department and a Mobile System Department, with a centralized carrier procurement strategy. In 2017, with the development of cloud computing technology, Huawei elevated its cloud business to a level-1 department. Ever since then, its ICT business organizations have been made up of the Carrier BG, the Enterprise BG, the Network Products and Solutions BG, and the Cloud BG, which are independent of Huawei's existing IPD and management system and can build new business models and management processes of their own.

Step 3: define the organization's goals. According to James D. Mooney, an early leader in managerial theory, organization is the form of every human association for the attainment of a common purpose." So, an organization is but a tool to attain its goals and without goals, the organization loses its purpose of existence. Organizational goals need to be consistent and synergistic with the company's strategies.

When setting organizational goals, Huawei usually involves two-way communication so that it ensures that the message is received at every level and employees can have a good understanding of the company's strategic intent.

Step 4: define the organization. In principle, an organization needs to be defined in the following four aspects: the organization's distinctive values; the organization's authority framework; the rules of authorization; and the organization's boundaries and scope of activities.

Step 5: determine the organizational structure. Huawei designs the division of labor within the organization according to the organization's strategy, objectives, work content, and development stage, structuring and modularizing the organization and rationalizing the relationship between all divisions.

Huawei is a flexible organization, and its flexibility is not only reflected by its perception of the external business environment, but also in the company's internal environment. In the design of the organization, senior leaders tend to focus only on the framework of responsibilities and the boundaries of the system, the organization's commitment to the company's strategy. Specific organizational responsibilities are handled by the organizational designers by fully tapping into the motivation, imagination, and execution capacity of employees. In the regional organization, the regional directors can make one part of the organization bigger and stronger, or cut another part, according to their market and competition conditions, and design different organizations. The autonomy is entirely in the hands of regional directors. In Huawei, there is a saying that "Whoever reaps the harvest is the owner", which fully illustrates the flexibility of its organization. By virtue of its flexible organizational design, Huawei is both aggressive and resilient. The people in the organization can decide what actions to take according to their abilities and the information they have. They fill in the missing gaps in the organization design, and achieve self-renewal and growth. Organizational flexibility gives Huawei employees more responsibilities and creates conditions for autonomy. As Huawei's business booms, both the organization and its people grow rapidly.

Step 6: smooth the process. Starting from the organizational strategy and goals, "customer-centricity, and survival-orientation"[1] is the hallmark of Huawei's organization, and process-based organization building is Huawei's management goal. Huawei regards people as a molecule of the organization, a node in the process. It aims to help the company rid of the dependence on any individual. However, meanwhile, people understand that their contribution and value matters, understand their relationship with the organization from the perspective of the part and the whole. It empowers everyone in the organization with "holistic thinking", so as to form the synergy of the organization. By smoothing the process, it integrates the organization and every individual in the value creation process, to ensure alignment of the individual behavior and the overall strategy and goal. In other words, it makes "a pack of wolves" fight as a group. The process of the organization makes it possible that the organizations can both cooperate with each other, and check, balance, and monitor each other.

---

[1] Ren Zhengfei: "Living with peace of mind". *Improvement*. August 30, 2003.

Step 7: identify the organizational responsibilities. According to the organization's objectives and the requirements of business activities specified by the process, the organization's responsibilities are clearly defined; then the job responsibilities and evaluation criteria are established according to the organizational responsibilities. The design of organizational responsibilities and job responsibilities follows three principles: first, the principle of a smooth process, second, the principle of value creation, and third, the principle of efficiency improvement. The organizational responsibilities and job responsibilities are embedded in the activities of the process.

Step 8: staff the organization. Staffing is in strict accordance with the job responsibilities, which are of course set up before staffing and not set up for certain employees. The selection of supervisors is based on both competence and willingness. The competence is based on demonstrated ability and future potential. In principle, a team is led by two supervisors, one director, and one deputy. The organization should be staffed according to its output. Meanwhile, the output per staff is expected to increase by 10–20% every year.

Step 9: identify the operating mechanism. Huawei has established a well-designed operating mechanism for the organization.

- Separating the evaluation of business and personnel. In 1996, Huawei started to experiment with the separation of administrative management and business management and enhanced the compatibility of hierarchical management and business information matrix management. Each management level has two organizations, led by ST (staff team) and AT (administration team). ST is responsible for business decisions, whose members are the heads of regional departments of the Business Group (BG). AT members are selected from ST, and its responsibilities are all human resource-related, including management selection, performance appraisal, salary adjustment, and equity issuance. The two organizations adopt different decision-making mechanisms, The decision of the ST is made mainly by the head of ST instead of a majority vote and the decision is result-oriented. AT follows the principle of democratic centralism. Because the evaluation of human resources is relatively complicated, so collective decision-making is required. Meanwhile, it can avoid nepotism and cliques. Huawei also records the whole meeting of AT, and if necessary, conducts a post-inspection to check whether there are any irregularities.
- A combination of centralization and decentralization. The power structure of Huawei is both centralized and decentralized. The financial and personnel power is centralized, while the business decision-making power is decentralized, thus forming a power system with the business unit playing the major role and the financial unit a supervisory role. This organizational design makes Huawei's business operations flexible enough to seize market opportunities timely; meanwhile the conservative financial management ensures the stable development of the company. The two strikes a good balance.
- Efficient horizontal and vertical collaboration. Top-down vertical operations and strategic execution can be led by specific targets to ensure vertical synergy

in the organization. Operating through cross-functional teams can enable horizontal synergy in the organization. For example, the Strategy and Development Committee analyzes customer needs and industry trends at the corporate level to determine how Huawei can meet and guide customer needs; the ST teams at the middle and lower levels are horizontal virtual organizations, composed of directors and experts from various departments, responsible for cross-departmental business collaboration, focusing on discussing and resolving issues around products, services, processes, and resource provisioning. The virtual organization operates by breaking down departmental silos and expanding organizational boundaries. Through the vertical command and horizontal collaboration, organizational responsibilities can be aligned, processes can be optimized, and the organization can become more resilient and be continuously improved and upgraded in practice.

7.2 Business Leadership Model for Organizational Change

Huawei has adopted IBM's Business Leadership Model (BLM, see Fig. 7.2) for its organizational change and transformation. In the consulting industry, BLM, comparable to Boston Matrix, SWOT, and Porter's Five Forces, is a platform for corporate strategy formulation and execution. The model developed by IBM and Harvard University is a theoretical model and methodology of strategy formulation and execution based on the summary of IBM's business management and customer service experience, and has become a unified strategic planning method for IBM from the top management to each business unit. The goal of this method is to solve a common problem faced by many enterprises, the dichotomy between the enterprise strategy and the execution of the strategy. An enterprise needs more than a good strategic design; it needs strong execution too, because, without the execution, even the best strategy is useless. BLM can assist enterprises to diagnose the weak link from strategic intent to strategic execution.

BLM advocates that the strategy development and execution process should be structured and disciplined, and driven and led by business leaders, and it should be

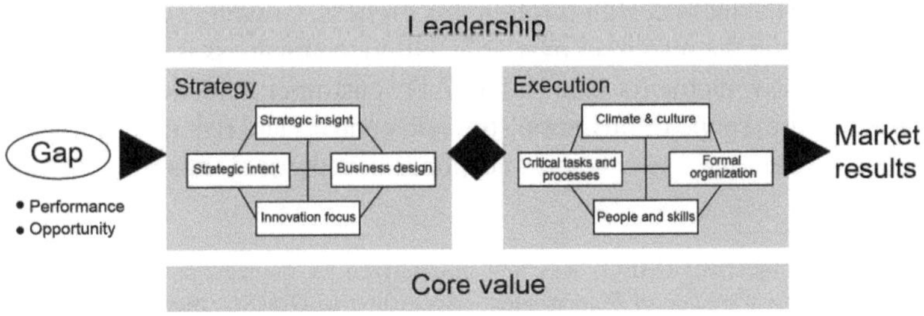

Fig. 7.2 Business leadership model

a fact-based dialogue and collaboration. **Leadership is a prerequisite for strategy and execution.** At Huawei, strategic thinking is considered a must for top management. Executive leadership is developed through opportunity insights, strategic design, and project execution. As executives are accountable for business results, they must personally lead the design and execution of strategy. This is achieved through continuous market insights, identifying new opportunities, developing business designs with a focus on innovation, and ensuring that the designs are realistic. **Values are the foundation of strategy and execution.** Huawei's values are "value creation for customers, diligence, self-criticism, openness, enterprise, honesty, trustworthiness, and teamwork". The Managing Director ensures that Huawei's values are reflected in the company's strategy. Managers at all levels ensure that Huawei's values are translated into the routine operation of the company and that Huawei's values are implemented on a daily basis as a basic guideline for decision-making and actions.

The BLM has eight golden guidelines that follow the business logic from strategic intent to strategic execution and they are eight interdependent and interacting key elements in the sequence.

First, market insight determines the depth of strategic thinking. Market insight means to understand customer needs, competitor moves, technological development, and market conditions, understand and interpret what is happening in the market, and its impact on the company's prospect, as well as the corresponding opportunities, challenges, and risks. IBM's strategic transformation in the 1990s was built around Gerstner's insight into two market opportunities: first, the service business has great promise in the IT industry, and consolidation of resources is important to IBM; second, the new opportunities of e-commerce make it possible for IBM to overtake Microsoft and Intel and return to the center of the IT industry.

Second, strategic intent determines strategic thinking. Strategic intent is the departure for strategic thinking, and clear strategic planning begins with the statement of the strategic intent and the expression of strategic objectives, and it is subject to the SMART principle.[2] Strategic intent is embodied in the formulation of organizational goals, including strategic and business objectives. In defining the goals, the benchmarking approach is used to compare business processes and performance metrics to the industry best practices.

Third, the business design charts the path to the objectives. Strategic thinking is embedded in the business design through this process. Creating sustainable strategic control points using the resources available within the business is essential. Business design involves six elements (see Table 7.1): customer selection, value proposition, value capture, scope of business, strategic control, and risk management. Good business design answers two basic questions: can the new business design build

[2] Management by objectives (MBO) was first popularized by management guru Peter Drucker in his 1954 book *The Practice of Management*. According to Drucker, managers must avoid the "activity trap." You can't just simply work while keeping your head down without looking up and end up forgetting your main goal. Objective set must be specific, measurable, attainable, attainable, relevant, and time-bound.

Table 7.1 Elements of business design

Customer selection	Who are your customers? Criteria for customer selection: value-driven, competition-driven plus effectiveness-driven Identifying valuable customers and potential customers
Value proposition	Why do the customers select me? How do you achieve a competitive edge (differentiation)? Customer needs How to make a profit (profit model)
Capturing value	How do I make a profit? Is there an alternative profit model? How to make money? How to make a profit (profit model)?
Scope of business	What are the role and the scope (time and space) of the business activity? Position in the value chain Partnerships
Strategic control	How do you achieve sustained profitable growth? Shifting trends in client demand Strategic control points
Risk management	What are the potential risks? How do you manage them? Uncertainty Potential risks: market, competitors, and technology Comprehensive perspective: external, internal

on existing capabilities? If not, how do you build and acquire the new capabilities needed?

Fourth, focus on innovation is the key to building a competitive edge for the organization. Companies need to develop a business strategy portfolio that differentiates them from their competitors and builds core competencies, taking into account market characteristics and product features. This is the key to win. Making innovation the focus of strategic thinking is to capture more ideas and experiences. A good innovation system is one that enables companies to explore and experiment with the market in tandem, rather than companies working behind closed doors.

Fifth, set critical tasks and coordinate the execution. According to the requirements of business design, rethink and adjust all the elements that affect the execution, and through strategic decoding, transform the strategy into understandable and executable targets for employees, so that the strategy is not just something on paper, but can effectively ensure the long-term and short-term gains and sustainable and stable development of the organization. The key is to link the strategy and its execution, stipulating the critical tasks and timeline for the execution, and putting forward specific requirements for process transformation, which constitute the basis for other parts of execution. Focus on these five main areas: products, sales, service and delivery, capability building, and platform support: what are the actions necessary to meet the business design requirements? Which tasks are performed by the company? Which can be outsourced to partners in the value network?

Sixth, Organizational culture is the basis for strategic execution. Different strategies target different markets, serve different customers, and have different decision-making models and processes, so it is important to establish an organizational culture that is compatible with the strategy, and to identify whether there are cultural factors that impede the strategic execution. In a knowledge-intensive economy, most companies that have successfully transformed themselves eventually develop a culture of openness, empowerment, and sharing. Huawei emphasizes that "every leader should learn how to lead and create an environment where others can be dedicated to the work; leaders need to understand that the success of the deployment is their greatest success".[3] For example, Huawei's enterprise business is a new business, so there is a need for an atmosphere that encourages innovation and tolerance for failure, which is different from the traditional carrier business.

Seventh, people are the key to strategic execution. Competent, motivated doers are needed to carry out critical tasks for effective strategic execution. It requires identifying the personnel gap and challenges in the strategic execution and what critical personnel needs to be acquired and how. Only people with the right skills can ensure strategic execution, and the people elements include skill descriptions, measures to acquire, develop, motivate, and retain talent, etc.

Eighth, the formal organization guarantees strategic execution. To ensure the effective execution of critical tasks and processes, a reasonable organizational structure, management systems, and assessment criteria need to be established, including (i) the organizational form: structure and efficiency, decision-making mechanisms, collaboration mechanisms, knowledge management, and sharing; (ii) the organizational size: whether the staff, hierarchy and regional layout, etc., can support organizational capacity; and (iii) the organizational performance: how to evaluate and motivate the organization and individuals to continuously improve. The objective of this task is to make it easier for managers to direct, monitor, and motivate individuals and groups to accomplish important team tasks.

The organization's strategic execution has always been a real problem for top management. Business strategic plans made by various departments are often shelved, as the plans for how to execute them were not even made. BLM is a connection between the strategy and the organization and creates synergy; it establishes a common language, clarifies the strategic direction, and realizes the synergy between groups. By following the BLM's logic and setup, the strategy will be clear, specific, and executable. The introduction of BLM has greatly improved Huawei's strategic planning and strategic plans are longer shelved. Therefore, it was fully recognized by the entire company. At present, BLM has become an essential tool for every Huawei senior manager. Huawei uses BLM twice a year for strategic planning. The beginning of the year planning is pragmatic, mainly focusing on debriefing the company's strategic and organizational goals. This is where the management makes annual commitments, and it marks the beginning of the organizational assessment. The mid-year planning focuses more on the macro situation instead of the immediate tasks, mainly including the market, trends, changes, competition, free discussion of

[3] Ren Zhengfei: "Living with peace of mind". *Improvement*. August 30, 2003.

future business development and how Huawei should respond, and the layout for the upcoming year or two.

7.3 Huawei's Organizational Change Process

In 2012, Huawei launched a new round of strategic transformation, shifting from a carrier-based business to a "Cloud-Network-End" multi-business model to provide end-to-end ICT business solutions. Along with this strategic shift, Huawei's organizational structure has also changed from a matrix to a process-centric model (see Table 7.2).

Horizontally, Huawei has divided its carrier business into three BGs: carrier BG, enterprise BG and consumer BG, which assume the functions of major operation centers and profit centers. Each BG is independently operated and accounted for to ensure sustainable development. Vertically, Huawei establishes market organizations such as regional departments and representative offices, led by Regional

Table 7.2 Huawei's organizational structure and its functions before and after the change

	Before	After
Organizational structure	Matrix management, personnel-oriented logic	Process management, business-oriented logic
Market unit	Carrier market-focused	Telecom carrier equipment and services Enterprise equipment and applications Terminal equipment
Business unit	CT-related products such as networks	Full range of ICT products, IT products such as servers, and storage rise to a strategic level
R&D unit	Carrier's mainstream communications products	Mainstream ICT products for different customer segments Creation of 2012 Lab
Management center	Two-level management: company and regional department	Three-level management: company, regional department, and representative office The representative office starting to call company resources
Competence center	Unified planning and construction by the company	Three-level system: company, regional department, and representative office
Profit center	Two-level profit centers: company and regional department	Three-level profit center: company, regional department, and representative office

Joint Committee (RJC), with the regional department as the competence center, the resource center, and the profit center, and the representative office as the operation unit, the profit center, and the executing center for the company's strategy. The management model has shifted from unified management by the company to decentralized management with the regional department as the center, the representative office as the operating unit. Each representative office is required to achieve profitability and ensure the sustainable development of the market and business. Each regional department establishes its own competence center to adapt to the development needs of the regional market and support the representative office with the operational resources it needs.

Huawei's strategic adjustment is due to the low growth of the global communications equipment manufacturing industry. The overall scale of the industry has remained largely unchanged for several years, and the development of the top six communications equipment suppliers has almost all stagnated or even regressed. At the same time, the booming development of software and hardware technologies in the IT industry has comprehensively penetrated and impacted the traditional communication equipment industry, and new Internet vendors have begun to enter the traditional market of communication carriers. The company's strategic adjustment is to make the optimal choice according to the current development stage, and synergize the advantages of each system's resources to maintain long-term growth momentum. Over the past 20 years, Huawei has been an opportunity-driven company, which has enabled the company to grow to its present scale; in the next 20 years, Huawei will become an efficiency- and scale-driven company, which will not blindly pursue the maximization of scale, but will pursue efficiency and stable growth, signifying a shift in the company's growth model. This is another major strategic adjustment following the promulgation of *Huawei Basic Law*: it seeks the future main business development from a technology perspective and an industry perspective, seizes opportunities through focused strategies, pursues effective growth and long-term profits, and sets out the development goal of reaching US$100 billion in sales revenue by 2019. Huawei's organizational change process is illustrated in Fig. 7.3.

Fig. 7.3 Huawei's organizational change process

Table 7.3 Strategy decoding before and after the change

	Before	After
Business change decoding	Scale-oriented Multiple focuses	Equal emphasis on profit and scale Business focus
Organization change decoding	Management center Full matrix management Centralized control	Competence center, resource center, profit center Consolidation of identical departments and organizational flattening Extension of authority to representative offices Sound risk management and control
Market strategy decoding	Opportunity-driven, pursuing growth at scale Organization-based performance evaluation Two-level authority: company and regional department	Benefit-driven, pursuing strategic business growth and return on opportunity projects Highlighting performance evaluation of critical positions Authorization to the representative office

Step 1: strategic decoding

Huawei has a clear strategic execution for its regional departments: to maintain growth and sustainability. Without deviating from the company's main strategic course and the overall organizational structure, the regional department can adjust its organizational structure and business strategies according to the situation. Strategy decoding includes business change decoding, organization change decoding, and market strategy decoding (see Table 7.3).

- Business change decoding. The regional department needs to adjust and focus its business priorities in accordance with the company's overall strategy. Firstly, the business units at all levels sort out the business scope they are involved in to determine which are the main businesses, which are relevant businesses, and which are unrelated businesses. Secondly, all businesses need to be analyzed systematically to draw a clear market map, and they need to understand which parts of Huawei have established a competitive edge, and which parts are weak links or even a vacuum. Finally, clear growth targets are set up and put critical businesses as the next-step focus for all relevant departments, so as to "maintain unwavering focus and receive maximum income". Through business focus and resource matching, Huawei has made its mark in the strategic market, occupying the strategic high ground.

For example, in the process of business decoding, the Northern Latin America Region has made it clear that in its original carrier business, it would shift from the single pursuit of scale and profit growth, to the focus on the breakthrough of strategic objectives of the main business on condition of maintaining the scale and profit growth. In the consumer business, it has shifted from relying solely on carrier resale to placing equal emphasis on carrier resale and distribution to build the Huawei brand and further expand sales. In the enterprise business, Huawei is learning business models from industry benchmarks such as Cisco and IBM. With reference to the development experience of enterprise networks in China, Huawei's development strategy in the North Latin American Region is sort out with rapid deployment, rapid increase in sales, and early profitability.

- Decoding organization change. First, the regional department transforms its positions and functions. Secondly, implement a greater department system, and reduce process nodes by merging the same units, focusing on the main business, and simplify management. For example, the regional headquarters of the Northern Latin America Region is the competence center, resource center, and profit center of the entire organization in the region. Organizational flattening and increasing the autonomy of the field office, so that it can call more resources. Improving the norms and efficiency of process operation by reducing the organizational hierarchy. Efforts are made to build a service platform to support the integration and efficiency of the main processes. Lastly, while increasing the authorization, the risk management and control system has also been improved. Through the establishment and improvement of the board of directors, the supervisory board, and the internal control department, process risks are controlled and continuously mitigated. The regional headquarters set up subsidiaries according to the business needs of each country, and the board of directors and supervisory board at all levels are established in the subsidiaries: the board of directors takes the pulse of, so to speak, the subsidiary's development strategy and major decisions, while the supervisory board supervises the organization and operation of the subsidiary. The newly established internal control department monitors and supervises the operations of the subsidiary and the regional department in four areas: environmental policy, assessment and early warning, control communication, and monitor and discipline.
- Market strategy decoding. After business positioning and strategic objectives are identified, the market strategy is refined to guide subsequent deployment and resource distribution, so that organizations at all levels can better execute the strategy on the ground. When executing operational tactics, organizations at all levels of the regional department should improve their people's "combat" capability, increase the number of people in the field, enhance the motivation through a combination of long-term and short-term incentives, improve operations through comprehensive support and combining training with competition, and enhancing the standardization and freedom of the teams in the field through increased authorization.

Step 2: organizational restructuring

At the macro level, the organizational restructuring focuses on the matching of structures, value creation for customers by the organization, reviewing the organizational structure top-down along the process, qualitatively analyzing the organization-level issues that lead to lack of responsibilities, overlapping responsibilities, and unclear responsibilities, and identifying the corresponding improvement measures.

At the micro-level, the organizational restructuring focuses on the matching of organizational roles, process roles, and individual positions, examining from the bottom-up whether the process roles and responsibilities are effectively executed through the organization's position settings, qualitatively analyzing from all dimensions the position-level issues that lead to the lack of responsibilities, overlapping responsibilities, and unclear responsibilities and identifying the corresponding improvement measures.

Ren once said: "There are no bad soldiers, only bad officers. The key is to grasp the main contradiction and the main aspect of the contradiction, make reasonable arrangements, and give full play to the collective role."[4] Specific elements of organizational restructuring include establishing a project team to lead the organizational change, establishing the principles, and nurturing the golden seeds of change.

- Establishing a project team to lead the organizational change. The project team is responsible for the concrete work of the organizational change that addresses the "last-mile" of organizational change. The main task of the team is to take full responsibility for the achievement of the project objectives, in terms of the process and quality. In addition, it should also take responsibility for the business objectives of the change, because all changes should ultimately serve the business. The project team must ensure that the results of the change achieve the expected business results. It also must ensure that risks and problems arising from the change are addressed as the project progresses, minimizing the impact of the change on the company's current business development. For example, in order to better unify understanding, the CEO of the Northern Latin America company organized a project team to lead the organizational change, which was staffed by all the departmental heads, as well as related personnel responsible for the company's strategy and organizational change, and thus achieved orderly coordination between the regional company and the headquarters. The project team is made up of the leadership group, the execution group, and the support group, jointly responsible for the organizational change goals of the Norther Latin America company. The leadership team is responsible for grasping the overall direction and pace of change, reviewing, and making decisions on the change program and key issues in execution; the execution team is responsible for the design, execution, follow up, and solution of critical issues; the support team provides professional support, and on-site support, if necessary, according to the needs.
- Establishing the principles of change. This means that the project team must hammer out a consensus to clarify the purpose, basis, and focus of the organizational restructuring in light of the characteristics of the original structure and the upcoming critical business areas. For example, when formulating the operating mechanism of the project team, the execution group and the support group

[4] Ren Zhengfei: "Customer focus, increasing platform investment, open to cooperation, & achieve win-win results" at the PSST Managers' Meeting. August 2010.

shall hold bi-weekly meetings to review and examine the change plan, discuss, and optimize relevant solutions, clarify the next priorities, and expose problems, and promote problem-solving. The leadership group shall hold monthly meetings to provide routine progress reports, discuss critical issues, and evaluate and make decisions on key points to ensure smooth organizational change. After the understanding has been unified, the project team shall take action with great enthusiasm.

- Cultivating "Golden Seeds" of change. "Golden Seeds" are usually department heads and backbone employees who will become critical change agents through practice and training in organizational optimization at the secondary level of the regional company. As a role model for change, the Golden Seeds will positively influence and motivate people around them to participate in the change. The Golden Seeds must be able to devote more than 50% of their time and energy to the execution of the change, be responsible for the execution of the change in the regional company, guide the organization optimization and staffing of the subordinate departments, and participate in the optimization process of the corresponding department in the representative office to ensure that the organization optimization in the lower-level units.

Step 3: Process optimization

- Process management division. According to Huawei's process management principles, there is a strict division of responsibilities between the first-level and the second-level process owners. The company-level process owner has the following responsibilities.

  1. Define process architecture, including the boundaries, interfaces (process input and output), and process control requirements.
  2. Plan, develop/release, execute and operate global standard processes.
  3. Collect best practices in process operation and adaptation in each region and representative office, continuously optimize the global standard process and expand the scenarios and scope of effective applications of the global standard process.
  4. Audit localized processes that do not meet the process control requirements.
  5. Regularly review the compliance of process architecture, control requirements, and authorization by the subordinate process owners. Hold the process owner accountable should there be serious in compliance issues in the process management and execution at all levels.
  6. In the absence of a global standard process, develop locally applicable processes and release, execute and operate them.

- Process Optimization Methodology. Process optimization is led by the CEO of the regional company, with all the major business departments participating in the process change team. It links the whole command chain from the headquarters to the regional company and the lower-level business units, with an integrated process view, integrated IT system, and integrated data pipeline management.

The workflow and integration system is solidified with IT tools to ensure that the process is ramped up and the follow-up is organized.
- Organizational support. First, change needs to take place top down. The first-level change involves most of the company's departments, with the company's top decision-maker chairing the team. The heads of all relevant departments sit in the project team in charge of each module, and assign the people in charge of specific operations, thus forming a linkage system. All changes must be approved by all functional modules of the team and should be effectively executed in all functional systems and market systems. Therefore, any organizational change must include all relevant departments and result in an effective and well-executed project team. The change shall not just be a grand slogan at the top, but instead, a gradual optimization that ensures business continuity, starting at the regional company and disseminated to the representative offices and the operational units. Second, all project teams must operate in accordance with the organization's charter, and the role of each module leader in the change is clarified in the charter, and specific operating methods and the roadmap for the change are formulated in the beginning. In other words, all the operations of the project team should be traceable and replicable; the change process at the top generates effective experience and documentation that can be replicated at lower levels of the organization.

7.4 RJC: A Regional Commissioner Agency

RJC means Regional Joint Committee. It is not a department, but a stand-alone organization. In Huawei's official terminology, it is a special commissioner agency that coordinates and oversees managers on behalf of the company, an organizer of regional strategy formulation, a supervisor of strategy execution, as well as a manager of regional platform development and organization operation.

The primary responsibilities of RJC include supervising regional managers, selecting, appointing, and transferring people to critical positions, and assessing and supervising managers in critical positions. It represents the authority of the company but does not directly interfere in business decision-making. RJC supervises managers and drives improvements in critical regional operations through personal influence and process procedures, rather than making direct decisions.[5] RJC is staffed with people with seniority and prestige, the vast majority of whom have been regional company CEOs.

Accelerated mobility of managers

One of the roles of RJC is to promote the mobility of managers and strengthen the zigzag growth system for managers. The Human Resources Department is a department that formulates the corporate HR policy; the RJC is the Corporate Leadership Management Department, responsible for the flexible examination and use of

[5] Huawei EMT Resolution No. [2011]044.

managers in sales, products, R&D, finance, administration, and other systems. Previously, Huawei's managers were promoted vertically in the same system, so they had little idea about the business in other departments. In 2009, Ren proposed to speed up the zigzag development of managers like the way U.S. aircraft carrier captain is trained, so that the managers can take on all-around coordination responsibilities.[6] We need to break localism and sectoral interests that get in the way, enhance the mobility of managers, and form a strong team that selects the best talent in an all-around manner. Huawei makes the best people stand out through performance-oriented evaluations and brings good experience and methods to areas where the business has yet to be developed through dynamic rotation.

Appraisal and selection of managers

The most important task for RJC is to appraise managers. Huawei had 150,000 employees. Previously, it was the executive board that was responsible for the selection of managers. The executive board often selected and promoted people based on the materials they submitted. So, if you could write beautifully, you would have a better chance to get promoted. Naturally, it resulted in an over-focus on making fancy PowerPoints slides.

Ren, therefore pointed out that the old way to select managers was no good, and that more face time with the candidates and field investigation is necessary. The selection of talent should pay attention to the people's personality; those who are enterprising and tough and will not settle for less should be promoted. When selecting managers, we need to think long. Don't just focus on their shortcomings. Give them opportunities to improve themselves. We need put shortcomings and achievements into perspective. When someone makes achievements, it does not mean that their shortcomings disappear. Everyone has shortcomings, so we should not pass someone in promotion simply because they have flaws. Meanwhile, managers should know how to control their desires and look at the long game, instead of being tempted by petty profits.[7]

Optimizing the administrative system

Huawei spent 20 billion RMB (2.85 billion USD) in admin annually. We all know that unqualified personnel will cause great waste. Huawei did not streamline to improve administrative efficiency, but transferred competent managers who were trusted with handling large sums of money to the admin posts. The existing admin personnel who have years of experience and are capable can also be promoted. Thanks to the examples set by RJC members, Huawei began to pay equal attention to admin as it has always paid to customer relations, and R&D, and achieved an all-around and balanced development.

[6] Ren Zhengfei: "Managers should not only try their best, but also do their best".

[7] Ren Zhengfei: "RJC is an important department of the company". July 19, 2013.

7.5 Iron Triangle: Customer-Facing Field Operational Units

"Let the people who hear the shots call the shots." "Form a customer-facing 'Iron Triangle' of an Account Responsibility (AR), a Solution Responsibility (SR), and a Fulfill Responsibility (FR)." "The field operation should be transformed from the operation of a single AR to a small team." This is Ren's elaboration on the "Iron Triangle".

The Iron Triangle, Huawei's most basic customer-facing organization and field operational unit, is a customer/project-based organization consisting of AR, SR, and FR as the core management team (see Fig. 7.4). The Iron Triangle came into being because Huawei found that employees in African field offices spent only one-third of their time looking for opportunities and working on leads, and a lot of their time was spent on coordinating and communicating with the back office. Problems that should be solved at the back office are told to be solved at the front office; the non-business executives did not understand the main business, and the back office had too many resources and authority and set up too many process control points. In order to shorten the process between the front office employees and the management platform, improve efficiency, reduce unnecessary coordination, and ensure effective growth, and self-circulation, Huawei proposed to put the command in places where the "gunfire" can be heard. Decision-making is authorized to the front office and the back office supports with resources. The organizational mechanism has been transformed from being pushed and driven by the back office to being pushed and driven both by the back office and the front office, and mainly by the front office.

The Iron Triangle is Huawei's unified interface with its customers. It takes on end-to-end responsibilities from lead management to contract fulfillment to enhance the full-cycle customer experience and customer satisfaction and thus to achieve project

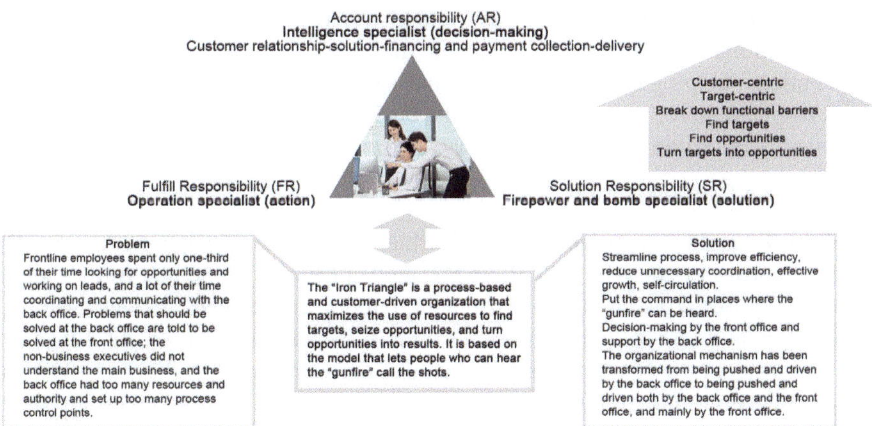

Fig. 7.4 Iron triangle operation module

efficiency and profitability. An effective Iron Triangle requires two capabilities: First, customer-centric capabilities, including customer insight, lead discovery, opportunity exploitation, comprehensive solution response, customer expectation and satisfaction management, project delivery, and service capabilities. Second, company-centric capabilities, including role recognition, business management, internal resource acquisition, and integration and resource allocation optimization, etc.

The essence of the Iron Triangle is to break down functional barriers and form a project-centric operating model with the customer as the core. The triangle is just a metaphor; it could be a quadrilateral or a pentagon. These frontline iron triangles form an internally efficient mechanism, leverage company resources, and are calling shots at the frontline. The company's back offices are equipped with advanced equipment and quality resources that will be put into use as soon as targets and opportunities are identified by the front office, rather than hold back the resources themselves.

Teamwork

The front-line operation should be changed from the AR's one-man show to small-scale teamwork, and the AR should strengthen its comprehensive marketing capacities, namely, customer relationship, solution, financing, and payment collection and delivery. In short, it needs to improve its ability to do business. SR should be multi-tasking. If it is not familiar with any professional field, it needs to know who to turn to. FR should have the ability to communicate engineering and delivery clearly with the customer and have a clear picture of the deliverables of the back office and every link of the delivery process. This cross-functional team helps to break down departmental barriers and ensures smooth communication within the team, thus enables rapid response to customer needs.

Clear division of responsibilities

AR is the first responsible person for the project, with objectives and values-aligned SR and FR working in unison. AR is the first responsible person for the operation, planning, client platform development, client satisfaction, attainment of business metrics, and market competition. SR is the first responsible person for the product and solutions, helping clients achieve business success from a solution perspective, and is responsible for the attainment of the business objectives of the solutions. FR is the first responsible person for delivery and service.

Project-based authorization

The Iron Triangle is a project-based flexible organization facing customers. By building a project team with an AR, an SR, and an FR at the core, the Iron Triangle can better meet the needs of the customers, build a thicker and broader customer relationship, and achieve win–win results with its customers. Huawei has also introduced a project-based authorization system in conjunction with the Iron Triangle to move decision-making forward, enhance frontline decision making, ensure rapid response to customer needs, and stay ahead of the market competition. In addition to the basic authorization (contract profitability, contract cash flow, customer credit line, contract terms, and conditions, etc.), project-based authorization gives the authorization in project setup decision, bidding decision, contract signing decision, contract change decision, contract closure decision according to the project level. If it is not within the scope of authorization, an application for approval according to the procedure is required. The project-based authorization enhances the flexibility of frontline decision-making and aligns the interest of the decision-maker and those whose performance will be evaluated and affected by the decision, so it encourages the enthusiasm and creativity of the frontline team.

Stand-alone business unit

Within the authority and budget granted by the company, the Iron Triangle has the authority over operation management, bonus distribution, resource allocation, decision making on major issues, and setting key performance indicators, etc. to ensure the effectiveness of the Iron Triangle system. As the smallest operational unit, the Iron Triangle has corresponding authority and resources and is an independent accounting unit, which is good for the unity of the purpose and pace, as well as team enthusiasm and creativity.

Specialized back-office support

The key to the Iron Triangle model is that the front-line team must form synergy (rather than being divided by function) toward the needs of the customer. Through the company's long-established and heavily invested platforms, the company provides full support and service to the Iron Triangle units to meet the needs of customers. Since the 1990s, Huawei has invested heavily in the management system and IT solutions by learning from leading international enterprises, and has built 10 platforms, including a technology development platform, an intermediate testing platform, a product manufacturing platform, a global sourcing platform, a marketing platform, a human resources platform, a financial and financing platform, an administrative service platform, a knowledge management platform, and a public data platform. The platform support, standardization, and integration capabilities of the back office are an important basis for customized and efficient front-line services. If the front office did not get professional support from the backend, the more power it gets, the further astray it may end up.

Case study: How the "Iron Triangle" was made[8]

In August 2006, the temperature in Khartoum, the capital of Sudan, was approaching 50 degrees Celsius, and it made people dizzy with oxygen deprivation. In a small, box-like room gathered over a dozen red-eyed men. Rao Xiaobo, an account manager, buried his head deep in his arms and groan with clenched teeth, "Why? Why did we lose?"

In June, Sudan Telecom was awarded a license to operate telecommunications in Mauritania, where it intends to invest in a mobile communications network. Huawei was one of the two vendors that received an invitation to tender. The representative

[8] *Huawei People*, Vol 5, 2009.

office immediately sprang into action, braving the heat, water, and power outages, and worked for two whole months, only to found that another company had won the tender exclusively, and Huawei was completely rejected!

"We had no idea what had happened," recalled Xiaobo, "The moment when the client announced the result of the tender, we were blindsided! This was a huge blow! The client did not even give us a tiny share! We're completely out!" We kept asking ourselves: why did we lose so badly? What was our problem? How to solve it?

In 2004, Peng Zhongyang was sent to Sudan to set up a representative office. It only took Huawei, a latecomer, one year to make its mark. By the end of 2005, its sales revenue reached 100 million yuan. Although everything seemed to be going in the right direction, some problems began to emerge. As business increased, the issue of departmental silos becomes increasingly acute. The management of several departments became one big mess, and internal friction increased. Huawei became slow, passive, and even passed the buck when facing the customer's needs.

All these problems became clearly visible in the 2006 project. The customer was very disappointed with the inconsistent and negative responses from various departments in Huawei. They even said that Huawei only talked the talk. Someone who was once involved in the project said that they not only lost the project, but also their dignity.

The heat in Khartoum continued to come in waves, as did the discussions in the Representative Office. During the discussion, some issues caught the Representative Office's particular attention.

In a network analysis meeting held by the client, seven or eight people with Huawei attended, yet each only explained the issues in their respective areas. The client's CTO was disappointed and complained about the spot: "We don't want a digital network, we don't want a core network, and we certainly don't want a TK network. We want an operational telecom network!" There was this thing that everyone remembered. The competitor designed a "solar-gasoline" dual-powered TK site, but Huawei still used a large conventional gasoline generator.

This is a clear failure resulting from not pay sufficient attention to the cost of operations. The customer relationship personnel had obtained the information from their interactions with the customer but failed to pass it on to the production personnel. Influenced by the traditional bidding process, the product people had assumed that the customer would give a standard bid document. Voila, opportunities lost.

"Little details like those are being overlooked. On the surface, it seems that it is because of rapid business growth, new staff, and the exhaustion of staff due to logistical inadequacy," said Peng, "but the root cause is that our organization was not well aligned with the customer. We're still following the traditional operation model: the customer line doesn't understand delivery; the delivery line doesn't understand the customer; the product line only focuses on the offer; every line only focuses narrowly on its own scope of business. We are passive to customers' needs, and even when we responded, we focused only on what we could offer instead of what the customer needed. So, how could we not fail?"

Break the silos

The more they debated, the clearer they saw. The Representative Office recognized that to get back on its feet in the Sudanese market, it had to adapt its organization to be well aligned with the customer, and that building a "thick" interface with the client was the key. "First of all, the Representative Office should see the business as a whole." Peng, who came from a technical service background, came up with this idea when he was a director in the Yemen Representative Office. He said, "When our account managers visited customers, they used to ask them when the contract could be signed, and easily neglected to listen to their needs. But when we add perspectives such as delivery, product, and even financing and payment collection, our focus shifts from 'what do I have to do' to 'what can I offer', meaning we shift from being passive to proactive and we are better equipped to help our customer to succeed."

At the end of 2006, the Representative Office appointed Rao Xiaobo together with Wang E and Wang Haiqing to form the core management team of the Customer System Department. Xiaobo was in charge of the customer relationship, E, delivery, and Haiqing, product and solution.

In a country with tough conditions like Sudan, people have long been bonded from building up the office from scratch. Now with the new system, the roles of the account manager, the product manager, and the delivery manager have been quickly integrated. They see customers together, deliver together, work together, and even live together. When facing the customer, they no longer tell their own separate stories. What's more, through integration, they also gained more knowledge and acquired new skills in each other's field.

After six months, Peng saw big changes in the Representative Office. He said, "The most typical example is the core management team made up of Xiaobo, E, and Haiqing. When Xiaobo was away, E and Haiqing could still maintain good customer relations, and Xiaobo and E could also guarantee good product quality in Haiqing's absence. The Representative Office began to see big smiles on the face of the customers and gradually gained upper hand on some projects."

The story of the Iron Triangle

In 2007, Peng reviewed business development in Sudan in the last three years in his work report. The previous customer complaints, internal barriers, and expansion pains experienced by the representative office all flashed back in his mind, and it was the tripartite model that closely integrated customers, products, and delivery that solved these problems. "Those three people are of the same mind, and their edge can cut through metal." Peng said, "let's call it the 'iron Triangle'."

From then on, the story of the Iron Triangle was known in the Sudan Representative Office, and the operation mechanism became clearer and clearer. In the Iron Triangle made up of Xiaobo, E, and Haiqing: Xiaobo was the account manager, in charge of nuances of customer relationships, when to make what moves, and how to spot opportunities at critical moments. After identifying critical opportunities, Haiqing would be responsible for designing a solution that met the customer's value. When it came to delivery, E would play a key role.

Peng said, "Not just for the customer's leadership, we have Iron Triangle teams for every layer in the customer's organization. Our relationship with the customer has transformed from the initial point-to-point passive response to face-to-face proactive interaction."

As the Iron Triangle model gets maturer in practice and development, the Representative Office reaped its rewards. In 2007, Sudan Telecom decided to build a mobile communications network in Senegal. "Now it's time to test the effectiveness of our Iron Triangle!" Xiaobo recalled excitedly, "In June, the Representative Office invited the customer to Shenzhen for the final solution discussion. After the presentation, the CEO, the CTO, and other chief officers and managers present, stood up and applauded with nodding and smiling for a long time. At that moment, I knew we hadn't suffered in vain! The Iron Triangle really rocks! We're back on our feet!"

7.6 The Elite Team: A Pool of Resources to Assist the Front Line

In 2014, Huawei established three strategic reserve teams—the Solution Elite Team, the Major Project Department, and the Project Management Resource Pool—to support the three core roles of the Iron Triangle. The name "Elite Team" suggests global quality resources and rapid mobility.

Assisting the frontline representative offices

The Strategic Reserves are the "special forces" that connect the resource platform with the operational platform, which understands both equipment and operations. Representative offices are conventional armies, so to speak, and they are sufficient in routine operations. When the Representative office encounters a strategic point of opportunity, the Elite Team is needed to fill in, but it is a call made by the front office, not the back office. The operational command remains with the Representative Office, with the Elite Team assisting technically and providing operational resources based on the needs of the Representative Office.

On-the-job training for empowerment

The Elite Team is part of the RJC Leadership Management Department, which empowers, operates, and evaluates managers in a circular manner, and completes the strategic global talent cycle of the entire company, allowing the talent to participate directly in operation and local manager appointments. The Elite Team is an operation unit, not a training unit. Through a combination of on-the-job training in a variety of scenarios, excellent solution managers and experts are cultivated. They summarize and pass on relevant experience and help enhance the company's overall solution and sales capability. Basically, six months is a training cycle. 15-day case studies and sharing sessions are arranged at the beginning and the end of the training. The beginning sharing sessions take place at the headquarters training camp. The training includes standardized skills training, and scenario-based simulation exercises. It follows business processes, and standard actions, scenarios, and tools and templates for front-line operations. The training chooses key solution-based modules to continuously simulate the front-line operation with lectures, case sharing, project review, competition, etc., The immersive repeated reinforcement training helps improve the trainees' shortcomings, and core capabilities for the team.

Another sharing takes place at the end of the 6-month training, possibly with new trainees of another group. The training is based on simulation of real situations. Positions are not configured based on personal positions or seniority, but rather according to the difficulty of the project and future strategy. The people of the Elite Team may work anywhere they are needed. Whoever is the best fit will work wherever he is needed most. The flexibility enhances Huawei's effectiveness.

According to Ding Yun, 30% of his Elite Team employees were of 13–14 level and 50% had no overseas experience. When these people flew to Latin America, first, they did not know what to do because they were not technically capable; second, they could not even communicate with the locals because their English was poor. These workers brought high costs to the company. We need to step up our efforts to get the green hands to the front lines and pull back the veterans to teach and train recruits and to revitalize the human resources. All those that are selected in the Elite Team are excellent seedlings. We grow the seedlings on the front line, in two or three years, they will grow into small trees.[9]

Strategic opportunity points

The Elite Team can also participate in the company's 68 strategic plans as the general staff does. For example, the Russia Representative Office failed to make a deal in Moscow for years. So, the company needs to find out what kind of organizational plan is needed to get this strategic high ground? What measures should be taken? The Elite Team needs to make a strategic sandbox, and bring it to the training, and then go back to put it into practice. Recruits need to study and optimize this sandbox year after year following the footsteps of their predecessors. If each country plans one or two leads, then the company has more than two hundred leads. The regional department and the Elite Team then need to plan how to deploy people, how the back office can support the front. It's a systematic project, not a matter of sending a few brave soldiers to dump grenades, so to speak. The purpose of Huawei's Elite Teams is to seize strategic opportunities.

Case study: building a cobweb organization[10]

Back in 1996, Ren said: "Spider is my most admired warrior. Because no matter how stormy the weather is, how hard it is, how many times it takes, the spider

[9] Ren Zhengfei: "The company expects to see three people doing the work of five and earning the salary of four". 2013.

[10] Wu Chunbo. "How was Huawei's Strategy Created". www.360doc.com/content/15/031808/22413410456082924.shtml

will tirelessly weave its web." Now, it may strike you that Huawei's organizational strategy and structure have so many similarities with the cobweb: the operation forces in the strategic front are similar to the sticky capture-spiral silk, once it gets close to its prey, it sticks around until it captures it. The major-ampullate (dragline) silk resembles the effective back-office support system that includes the Strategic Command, Staff, Logistics, Human Resources, and other departments. In Huawei's new round of organizational change, the R&D department, which accounts for nearly half of the company's employees, is also included in the back-office support system.

The support system provides support of people, capital, products, technologies, and solutions as well as strategic directives from the "Command Department": Strike or not? Where to strike? When to strike? However, questions like how to strike are tactical issues, and should be the call of the divisional commanders of the field offices. Another function of the support system is to guide; the core functions are institutional support, the dissemination of values, checks, and balances of power, responsibility, and interests, etc.

7.7 Huawei Versus Cisco

Huawei, a fast-growing organization, has grown into a market leader from a technology follower thanks to the following four main reasons: First, its leaders' thinking and plan for the organizational system is ahead of the current development, so it can always see the future trend and achieve self-improvement. Second, its leaders' knowledge of organizational innovation transcends the boundaries of Chinese culture, and they are keen on absorbing the fine elements of the world's leading companies. Third, its leaders have clear methodologies for key transformations and changes. Fourth, on the issue of centralization and decentralization, with an innovative establishment of the organizational structure, Huawei lets those who know the people best to find and select talent, so that it can avoid blind spots and loss of control of its peripheral nerves, so to speak; such problems are commonly found in the large firm. Through a systematic review, we have the following findings.

First, Huawei has built a comprehensive model for integrating organizational capabilities, which is composed of four elements: organizational structure, people, processes, and IT system. Its greatest value is that, based on the global best business practices, it builds an organizational system that is not reliant on "individual capabilities", meaning "Whoever leaves the company, Huawei can still run smoothly". Therefore, Huawei's organizational system development is closely integrated with its management system and platform. These four elements are embedded and integrated with one another, forming a stable, networked "cobweb" organization that is adaptive to the changing environment, resilient enough to withstand external pressure and challenges, and flexible enough to handle internal reconstruction and corrections.

Second, Huawei has absorbed the methodologies proposed by consulting firms most effectively and is adept at summarizing and refining them to form a new set of methodologies to guide organizational change and development. These methodologies enabled Huawei to realize orderly top-down transformation and change from pilot projects to full participation through a series of organizational analysis tools and means, such as systematic thinking and strategic decoding, organizational restructuring, and process optimization. They make the organizational change more targeted, orderly, and predictable. This paramilitary-style approach greatly improves organizational efficiency and reduces risks in organizational development. The Business Leadership Model has helped Huawei develop a set of methodologies for environmental analysis, strategy formulation and execution, and talent analysis. Although BLM is not unique to Huawei, it has been well executed in Huawei and proven to be effective.

Third, Huawei has done in-depth research on the history of the Communist Party of China (CPC), its military ideology and establishment, and cases, and has drawn a lot of valuable nutrients. Meanwhile, based on its own practical needs, it has been continuously summarizing the development experience of advanced regions and exploring the methods and paths of organizational strategy execution. In all these processes, Huawei's core focus is on the "people". The purpose of RJC is to make sure that the people who have the clearest picture select talent. The Elite Team is about the organic integration of talent development and use, so that the empowerment of talent is closely linked to talent growth. The Iron Triangle emphasizes true customer-centric cross-departmental teamwork.

Of course, Huawei's organizational innovation goes far beyond the above-mentioned. It has learned from the U.S. military, the world's leading Internet companies, and the most efficient and competitive innovative organizations. It never stops exploring the development patterns, dynamics, and value-creation processes of cobweb organizations according to its own needs to ensure that the organization is always relevant.

Huawei and Cisco both place great emphasis on organizational capability and continuous optimization. Unlike the cobweb-like Huawei, which focuses on the overall organizational efficiency and execution, Cisco focuses on a highly adaptive organization. Cisco focuses on improving the transparency and effectiveness of its decision-making and communication processes by building a culture of adaptability. The five attributes of an adaptive organization are transparent decision-making, a common language, authentic leadership, clear accountability, and horizontal allocation of resources. The first four are designed to ensure that the organization communicates and makes decisions without unnecessary suspicion, confusion, under-the-table deals, and ambiguous accountability, so that internal consensus building is as cost-effective and efficient as possible. Such an organization can adapt and respond quickly to external market and customer changes. The last item is a strategic investment approach. As an Internet company, in an environment where technological innovation is fast-changing, it is important to increase the breadth of technology investment to avoid strategic mistakes and strategic blind spots.

Chapter 8
Management Transformation and System Building in Line with International Standards

The earliest management theory in China can be traced back to *The Art of War* by Sun Tzu of over 2000 years ago which explains the core elements of management in a systematic way. If we translate Sun Tzu's military thought into modern corporate management, then *Tao* can be understood as the company's vision and mission. "Success comes to those who share in one purpose" can be interpreted as "if the top leadership can establish a common vision espoused by all employees, a tremendous synergy will be formed". "Heaven" can be interpreted as the external environment. "Timing" is related to the intensity of market competition and boom-and-bust conditions. "Earth" can be interpreted as the evaluation of the strength and threats of the enterprise in the competitive environment, as well as the strategic choice and positioning based on the analysis of the competitive strategy. "General" represents the enterprise's management. According to Sun Tzu, the general's selection criteria in descending order are wisdom, integrity, benevolence, courage, and rigor; wisdom and integrity are considered the two most important qualities. The "law" stands for organizational management, such as organizational structure, incentives, logistics and supply chain systems. One can only win the war if one has a thorough understanding of these five elements.

However, China and Western countries are so different in management thinking. Traditional Chinese thinking evaluates the value of the individual in the bigger picture; it emphasizes the intrinsic and implicit correlation and cause-and-effect relationships between myriads of things. It pays attention to the opposing yet transformative and accommodating relationship in contradictions. China's agricultural civilization has been in existence for millennia. For that reason, the understanding and measurement of time, processes, indicators, and methodologies under the influence of the agricultural civilization are much less precise and quantified than that under the influence of industrial civilization in the West.

Western thinking originates from ancient Greece, which values freedom and individuality, focuses on static and linear thinking, and emphasizes analysis, the discovery of rules and the understanding of nature. With the development of the industrial revolution, the West has summarized and refined a set of management theories,

X. Dong et al., *Huawei*,
https://doi.org/10.1007/978-981-19-4078-1_8

systems, methods, and tools based on production and supply chain processes. For example, Henri Fayol (1841–1925), a founder of the modern management method, identified six primary functions of management: to manage is to forecast, to plan, to organize, to command, to coordinate and to control. Frederick Taylor, Father of Scientific Management, believes that management is to look at each job or task scientifically to determine the "one best way" to perform the job. Herbert Simon believes that to manage is to make decisions. According to Peter Drucker, management is work, and as such it has its own skills, its own tools, its own techniques. Management is the organ, the life-giving, acting, dynamic organ of the institution. Management is a discipline—that is, an organized body of knowledge and as such applicable everywhere—it is also 'culture'. In recent years, as information technology has been increasingly integrated into the industrial management process, Western management has started to shift from philosophical, humanistic and behavioral-focus to scientific, rational and quantitative-focus, and developed many management methodologies and tools from the digitization, standardization and visualization of the enterprise operation, such as Management by Objectives (MBO), Business Process Reengineering, Six Sigma, Agile Software Development and Integrated Performance Management (IPM). The Industry 4.0 Initiative proposed by the German government and the Industrial Internet of Things (IIoT) proposed by the United States are both derivatives and extensions of the above-mentioned management ideas. The differences between Chinese and Western cultures and thinking patterns have led to many conflicts and contradictions in the integration of Chinese and Western management systems. How did Huawei handle these conflicts in the process of growing from a local company to a world-class enterprise? We are particularly interested in the following issues.

First, what is the role of management in corporate development? For catch-up firms whose resources are usually stretched thin, there is an urgent need to upgrade and improve every element and link of the firm. The leader of the catch-up firm should make judgment calls and concentrate the attention and resources on one place, to expand the market and increase your profitability, or to improve your management system. The former will pay off quickly; the latter, however, will be costly with a slower pay-off. Meanwhile, management will always involve a lot of pain, risks, and dilemmas in the process. So, how does Huawei solve these problems?

Second, how to resolve the conflicts between Chinese and Western management approaches. Chinese-style management emphasizes the holistic approach and the people, and is usually flexible, emotional, and fuzzy; while Western management emphasizes the analysis, systems, norms, and is basically rational and quantitative. Many Chinese companies feel uncomfortable when introducing Western management tools and methods and suffer from frequent conflicts. However, to become a world-class enterprise, world-class management is required. The question is should we explore the Chinese management path, or introduce Western management systems? In the latter case, how should we resolve culture clashes, implement change, and effectively integrate advanced management systems into our business? What is Huawei's experience in this area?

Third, how to promote organizational change. In corporate development, stability and change are the two aspects of the contradiction. Stability can help improve efficiency, but on the other hand, the more stable the management system is, the stronger the organizational inertia will be. Therefore, it is helpful to promote the change in the management system timely to break the organizational inertia. The organizational change affects every aspect, including employees' thinking patterns and competency requirements, work styles and methods, departmental relationships, process structures and benefit distribution. How should we drive the organizational change to continuously improve management systems?

8.1 The Strategic Value of the Management System for Catch-up Firms

Why there was no business giant in China's history?

When Ren was exploring the development of Huawei, he was wondering why China had not produced such large enterprises as IBM, Lucent, HP, and Microsoft in the past 5,000 years. He realized that China's management systems, rules, as well as managers who adapt to such management were not sufficient to produce a large enterprise. Chinese are free-spirited, imaginative, restless, ambiguous; they dabble in innovation, but lack quantitative training and capabilities. Most are unwilling to engage in tedious and repetitive work or be bound by processes and regulations. It is hard for those people to treat the process and quality in a truly professional manner. In Ren's view, "one of the vices of Chinese people is that they are never willing to comply; they are always obsessed with blind innovation. Chinese people are always thinking about this and then messing with that. To put it nicely, curiosity is a defining characteristic of Chinese people".[1]

Small companies are strong in creativity and flexibility, while large ones in the management platform

Huawei has grown from a small company to a conglomerate, the process of which is full of challenges and self-negation. Small companies are different from large ones in many aspects. Small companies usually leverage their creativity and discovery of market segments to achieve rapid growth, but they often struggle to survive. They are flexible, passionate, and the leaders' attention is focused on product development and market expansion, instead of the management system. Or they do not have the energy to tend to manage themselves. As the scale of the enterprise expands, the management system becomes increasingly complex, and its difficulty and depth are increasing, so management optimization becomes an urgent matter.[2]

Ren is well aware that to become a world-class company, Huawei needs to drop the habits of a small company, think and operate in a more professional manner, and

[1] Ren Zhengfei: "Entrepreneurship and innovation must be centered on improving the core competitiveness". March 5, 1999.

[2] Ren Zhengfei: a speech at a Secretaries Workshop. February 22, 1997.

be ready for management optimization. Compared to Western companies, Huawei lacks management knowledge and capabilities. Its operation and delivery are disconnected, repetitive and inefficient. The whole process has quite a few serious hiccups. Ren is aware that small companies are strong in creativity, and large ones, the platform. With a strong platform, the company can go all out and invest in the targeted area to catch up. Therefore, Huawei must invest in its management system and build a strong platform, which will be the core competitive edge to ensure the sustainable development of the company. To this end, Ren proposed that Huawei should be more forward-looking in platform building and that is necessary to increase investment in the platform to build a solid foundation for long-term success. The reason for insufficient investment in the platform is due to poor management. Huawei's management platform must surpass its competitors and strive to be the most flexible and the most cost-effective platform in the world.[3]

Ren's determination to promote standardized management and process was reinforced after he had visited a famous Indian software company. He found that the Indian company's IT research staff alone had 5,000 people, its software annual output value was $500 million, annual profit growth was 68%. These companies are long-term suppliers to many leading international companies and have very strict standards. Software is of no good if it is not standardized. In 1999, that company's software engineering was rated at SE IV, and the following year it was rated at SE V. There are only two or three SE V companies and a dozen SE IV companies in the world. The visited Indian companies were all SE IV companies, indicating a high level of management in Indian software enterprises.[4] The visit to India made Huawei more aware of the importance of management and management capability in software enterprises, providing an important impetus for Huawei's management transformation.

Why management outweighs technology

Ren's view of the importance of management stems from a basic perception of the resources and capabilities of Western companies. In Western companies, management outweighs technology, but in many enterprises in China, it is the other way around. In his view, the core competitiveness of an enterprise is multifaceted; technology and products are only two aspects of many, and management and service are far more important than technology. Because, without management, talent, technology, and capital will not form a synergy; without service, management will have no direction. Compared with leading multinationals, Huawei did not have a strong foundation, so without good management, it will have nothing in case of a breakdown and can never be resurrected.[5]

Ren pointed out that for high-tech enterprises, management innovation is more important than technological innovation. In 1996, Huawei decided to benchmark

---

[3] Ren Zhengfei: "Customer focus, increasing platform investment, open to cooperation, & achieve win-win results" at the PSST Managers' Meeting. August 2010.

[4] Ren Zhengfei: "An essay on India".

[5] Ren Zhengfei: "Huawei's winter", *Huawei People*. 2001.

against international standards, and hired Western consultants to provide services in R&D, production, finance, human resources, among others. As a result, it has made progress in professional and institutionalized development, improved the core competitiveness, and the management started to be more standardized. In the process of transforming into a world-class enterprise, Huawei was facing fierce competition and was once lagging in all aspects. So how can it "make a good meal out of chicken ribs"? Ren suggests a three-element combo for the success recipe.

Management and service are life-and-death issues for businesses

Of the three elements, Ren believes that management is the most critical one. For many high-tech enterprises, the management's focus is usually on technological innovation, product development and market expansion. However, when the company reaches the plateau, it will be difficult to continue to expand and make breakthroughs. Why? In 1996, Huawei put forward the strategic vision of becoming a world-class enterprise. Although the company's R&D, technology, products, market, and management were all lagging far behind those of the world's leading companies, Huawei's leadership still made a big commitment. The future is bright, yet the reality is harsh, so how should Huawei proceed to achieve its ambitious goal? Ren said: "Talent, capital and technology are not a matter of life and death for Huawei, as they can all be imported; however, management and service cannot be copied and imported, we can only rely on the joint efforts of all staff to form our own effective service and management system: the system should be based on advanced management and service theories, and integrated with our own practices, and applied to the whole company and all the processes."[6]

Ren clearly stated in his article "How long will Huawei's red flag stand?" that Huawei will become a great multinational. We are all prepared mentally and at the organization level, yet the management methods and means are not ready. Management progress is only possible when there are good management practices. Otherwise, the efficiency will suffer, and the company may eventually go down. Huawei's per capita output is about one-third of that of the Western company, so what caused the gap? It is a waste of resources and time caused by ineffective management. That is why we are importing all kinds of advanced management systems from the West and apply them with adaptation to a certain extent.

Competitiveness loss due to management deficiency

Huawei found that ineffective management hampered its growth and development in three ways.

First, it causes serious waste. IBM and many Western companies that visited Huawei joked about Huawei's waste: "You have no time to do things right at one go, yet you have time to redo them repeatedly." Even if you developed some good stuff, if it is not needed by the market, you cannot sell it; so, this is a waste of resources. Therefore, it is important to focus on the entire management system.

---

[6] Ren Zhengfei: "Don't be a flash-in-the-pan hero". *Huawei People.* September 28, 1998.

Second, it limits the scale-up of the company. A bigger scale does not automatically lead to lower costs, which is usually the result of good management. Blind scaling-up leads nowhere.[7] In 1996, Ren proposed that Huawei should first formalize its management. When measuring management, the cost is a major indicator of the competitiveness of an enterprise, and it is also the most difficult part of management. Without scientific and reasonable costing, the enterprise will always strive to survive. Therefore, Ren said to the financial department that a financial system that fails to control cost is deemed unqualified. Therefore, the enterprise should first establish a complete cost accounting, analysis, and control system, to provide credible and reliable information basis for decision-making. The enterprise also needs to establish an organizational structure for payment collection covering all levels of the network. An effective management structure for payment collection needs to be set up to support the overall objectives and the marketing functions of the enterprise. To sum up, payment collection needs to be treated as a matter of life and death for the company.

Third, it directly affects the market capacity. Even a small company can create world-class inventions, but once this invention is detected by a large Western company, it will make a better product in a very short period of time and quickly market to the whole world, making it impossible for small companies to sell their products. Therefore, Huawei is determined to build a management and service system so that if a new opportunity arises, the company may capitalize on it and grow bigger. Right now, Huawei at best wins a small victory in the marginalized Chinese market, but lost a large chunk of the international market to Western companies. As a result, the new technologies cannot be effectively translated into huge benefits. To realize the transformation, Huawei needs excellent management and good service.[8] As Ren once said, "A good company should have the ability to operate a large company like a small business." In order to continually improve Huawei's management, Ren proposed to rename its internal magazine *Huawei Briefing* as *Improvement* on November 18, 1997.[9] The *Improvement* was mainly used to reveal problems in management, so that Huawei can confront them head-on, and deal with them without getting personal. Through criticism and self-criticism, the problems are exposed and disposed of with the focus on the right and wrong of the work rather than people.

8.2 Objectives and Focus of the Management System

In 1994, Ren talked about the importance of management when commenting on the crisis management by Korean Air and China Northwest Airlines respectively. In the first case, when it landed, the plane of Korean Air was expected to explode in a few

---

[7] Ibid.

[8] Ren Zhengfei: "Huawei's winter", *Huawei People*. 2001.

[9] Ren Zhengfei: "Focus on lower-level management and all levels need to do a solid job". November 15, 1996.

minutes. With the guidance of the flight attendants, the plane was evacuated within two minutes. After the last flight attendant jumped out of the cabin, the plane was in flames. Fortunately, there were no casualties caused by the explosion. In the second case, it appeared that the autopilot yaw-channel had been connected to the bank control and the bank-channel to the yaw control. If a rigorous pre-flight inspection had been carried out, or if the pilot had handled the situation more decisively under the guidance of the tower, the 160 people on board could have been saved. Ren believed that this disaster was due to a lack of rigorous management, especially that of junior staff. For this reason, Huawei decided to increase the intensity of employee training and management, so that its work on site can be on par with international standards.[10]

The key to management improvement is to focus on the lower levels

The management of the lower levels reflects the overall management level of an enterprise. Huawei's management is not about building a fancy framework, but more about the solid work of every employee. In 1996, Huawei started the campaign of awarding outstanding employees in all links and departments, including kitchen workers, janitors, welders, warehousemen, parts managers, housekeepers, typists, operators, drivers, secretaries, installation engineers, editors, translators/interpreters, accountants, auditors, sourcing specialists, marketers, planners, business managers, and salespeople. Take drivers, for example, Huawei drivers have to follow very specific requirements regarding time management, communication etiquette, dress code, etc., and the Huawei drivers I met were all doing a good job. Huawei organized many competitions to hone the grassroots employees' professional proficiency and abilities. Ren said, "Do not dismiss competitions. Maybe you cannot see the immediate results, but in two or three years, Huawei will be the best". The competitions can enhance employees' awareness of professionalism at the grassroots level. From industrial competitions, one can find out the advantages of others and shortcomings of their own. Competitions can bring out outstanding talent, resulting in a strong sense of honor and responsibility, thus playing a self-promoting role for each employee. Huawei's competition did not aim to achieve everything. What matters is learning by doing. It is always better to compete than not to compete. The more you compete, the more experienced you will be. This way, Huawei can keep discovering and promoting talent, and maintains the vitality of the company. In Ren's view, "As long as we dare to criticize ourselves, and always struggle hard in our thinking, we will never fail."[11]

Building a process-oriented organization

At this stage, Huawei became more standardized, institutionalized and science-based. This is a painstaking process. However, when the enterprise grows, it has

[10] Ren Zhengfei: "The Importance of staff training: a case analysis of the two air crashes" on December 25, 1994.

[11] Ren Zhengfei: "Revisit on refraining from complacence and no slack in the mind" at the Market and Research Award Ceremony. June 30, 1996.

to improve its efficiency through continuous optimization of the process and streamlining non-value-creation processes, standardizing repetitive work, simplifying non-critical communication and day-to-day operations, automating repetitive labor. When the organizational system and process system are built up, the company won't need so many senior managers. The purpose of process building is to improve per capita productivity; when the number of managers is reduced, human costs drop significantly.

Huawei-defined "process" includes process architecture and process description documents, operating instructions, templates, checklists, specifications, and other types of process documents. The Organization and the process are most relevant to the business. The organization is the business executor, and the process embodies the rules of and path to business execution. If organizations are the cell, then processes are the blood vessels and nerves that allow the business to run smoothly. Process optimization is an important part of the reform and is crucial to the attainment of the reform goals, so that the optimized organization can better support the business. During its development, Huawei has introduced 14 primary processes based on functional needs and practical experience, forming a set of a process management system. The process architecture includes backbone processes and end processes, with backbone processes managed by the global process owner and end processes by regional owners to maintain the flexibility of each business unit on the basis of overall unity. Huawei's process management system is shown in Table 8.1.

In Huawei's internationalization process, the company has 10 first-level processes that need to be localized in various regions around the world, including MTL (market to lead), LTC (lead to cash), IPD (integrated process development), ITR (issue to resolution), SD (service delivery), Supply (supply chain), HR (human resources), MBS (management base support), BT and IT (business transformation and IT), and MPR (managing partner relationship). These are the 10 first-level processes at the company level, and the owner of each process is the decision-maker of the first-level department at the company level across the entire organization, covering R&D, production, sales, delivery, human resources, finance, etc., as well as all organizational departments in their regions.

Promoting template-based standardization

At Huawei, in order to promote professionalism, standardization, spreadsheet and template-based data to reduce duplication of effort and improve efficiency[12]; standardization is the key. The key to standardization is to develop templates for day-to-day work. Three months is sufficient for recruits to understand the templates as they are all well-educated. Being able to use templates at work means they art global and professional. The templates are the summing up of decades of experience. There is no need for recruits to reinvent the wheel. Monitoring is part of standardized management; its purpose is to serve business units effectively and efficiently. Standardization is like a sieve; supervision is completed in the service process. Huawei implements a reverse audit system to implement accountability. During the process,

[12] Ren Zhengfei: "Spring in the North". April 24, 2001.

Table 8.1 Huawei process management system

Item	Content
Process architecture (generally, L1–L4)	Boundaries of the process architecture
	Interface (input and output) of the process architecture
	Process control requirements (business rules, data quality requirements, critical control points, etc.)
Global standard process document (general description L4–L6)	管理体系手册 Management system manual
	流程说明文件 Process description document
	规范&标准 Specifications/norms and standards
	操作指导 (含流程视图) Operational guidance (with process view)
	Templates
	Checklists
Localization process documentation (general description L4–L6)	管理体系手册 Management system manual
	流程说明文件 Process description document
	规范&标准 Specifications/norms and standards
	操作指导 (含流程视图) Operational guidance (with process view)
	Templates
	Checklists

outstanding managers are identified and those who slack off are demoted. In the process of standardization, a business-led, accounting-monitoring management mode has been established, preparing for regional, national and even global unified financial services management.[13] By using templates, the employee can achieve the same performance with less labor and time. Only when templates are created and integrated with processes can IT systems achieve their intended purposes. So, more attention should be paid to template development. Standardized format and language expand the management scope and content of each manager. As data become more and more developed, there will be fewer layers of management, and thus fewer managers, and lower costs. The stability of processes and information systems must be maintained, and blind innovation will only undermine the efficiency gained.

[13] Ren Zhengfei: "Huawei's winter", *Huawei People*. 2001.

8.3 The Principle of Balance in the Management System

From the rule of man to institution-building

Huawei aims to evolve from the rule of man to the rule of law, from chaos to order, from the realm of necessity to the realm of freedom, so that all management systems will be in line with international standards. We cannot simply rely on a few "heroes", but instead, we should rely on the entire management team to bring the enterprise onto the right track. Ren once said to a HAY consultant that in two or three years, when the company's management became standardized, Huawei would bring in talented professionals who aim high but might be poor. They would not accept the status quo, nor would they confine themselves to existing conventions. Huawei would not allow people to simply get by after they have achieved fame and success.[14]

Establishing problem-centric and people-centric systems of accountability

According to Ren, the reason for the poor efficiency of an enterprise is that it fails to distinguish problem-centric and people-centric systems of accountability: the two are fundamentally different. The people-centric system of accountability is convergent while the problem-centric system is a divergent one: it empowers the most capable people under effective monitoring to solve problems in accordance with the process and authorization. Huawei's senior and middle managers were consciously or unconsciously accustomed to being accountable to people, which hindered the implementation of process-oriented IT management. Simply put, the process-centric system is problem-solving-oriented. Asking for permission for everything is about being accountable to people. Business efficiency comes from simplifying the cumbersome process of validation and reducing unnecessary and unimportant aspects of management. Many complex or even unnecessary reports, documents, and procedures are artificially created to make redundant admins seemingly essential. Therefore, Huawei needs to make the organization thinner under effective monitoring.

Distinguishing between routine and exception management

Routine management is a process-based approach; when a window of opportunity arises or a routine approach is not applicable and creativity is needed for the solution, exception management becomes necessary.[15] The secretary has authority over the routine management work, and the manager mainly deals with exceptions and important routine matters that cause confusion. The more routine matters are, the fewer managers are needed, and the lower the cost; therefore, an efficient business must have relatively smaller staffing. Under the same conditions, the smaller the admin the better. Redundant admins should be assigned to positions that directly create value. The appraisal of the admins should be scored by those they serve directly and should

[14] Ren Zhengfei: "Governance by inaction". *Huawei People*. March 20, 2000.

[15] Ren Zhengfei: "Focus on lower-level management and all levels need to do a solid job". November 15, 1996.

be linked to their salaries and bonuses. This is also a customer-oriented approach: after all internal customers are also customers.[16]

The management system and the dissipative structure

Management and dissipation are a paradox: management is about collecting, through which the resources and strengths of the enterprise can be concentrated; the potential energy can be maximized through centralized management. Without the management system, the enterprise will be like a sheet of loose sand. Dissipation is about releasing, through which the old potential energy is transformed into the new one; when the vitality of the enterprise, the ability to expand the market, and the ability of its employees are fully released through dissipation, and the enterprise will thus be developed. The ability to build the capacities for collecting and releasing and balance between the two determine whether the enterprise has both the integration advantage and control ability like a large enterprise, and the flexibility and vitality like a small one. Only when an enterprise has both qualities, can it survive and thrive in the fierce competition. Or in Ren's words, if you jog every day, you are in a dissipative structure. You are dissipating your energy and turning it into muscle and improving blood flow. If you dissipate all redundant energy, you will not get diabetes or obesity. In the same vein, employees need to dissipate their commitment to the company and turn it into the effort to make the company stronger and better.[17]

A balance between decentralization and centralization

With years of development, Huawei has established a matrix-based hierarchical, flexible, forward management system and a limited authorization system that are both reasonable and effective. In Huawei, separation of powers is adopted: bottom level managers are responsible for the daily operation; department managers, managing, restricting and balancing the right to use; top management, major decision-making.[18] At this stage, Huawei has established a hierarchical, graded and segmented work system to refine the management and division of labor; meanwhile, a company-wide network has been established to set up an attendance system and a unified evaluation system and remuneration management system. The improvement of the entire management system is carried out step by step.

Improving shortcomings and promoting overall balance

In its drive for management improvement in 2001, Huawei focused on improving shortcomings, especially in the supporting processes that are linked to its core business, which were often overlooked in its work. Why prioritize addressing shortcomings? Say if the company from top to bottom are focused on research and development, marketing, but does not pay much attention to the tally system, central transceiver system, cashier system, order system, etc. These undervalued systems

[16] Ren Zhengfei: "Huawei's winter", *Huawei People*. 2001.

[17] Ren Zhengfei: "Success is not a reliable guide to future development" at a market meeting. January 17, 2011.

[18] Ren Zhengfei: "Huawei people refuse to fail", at Huawei's annual meeting. December 26, 1995.

are the shortest staves, which will eventually hinder or delay the main business. No matter how efficient your other links are, if you cannot deliver, it is no good. Similarly, no matter how amazing the innovation is, if it cannot be transformed into a commodity, the value is lost. Usually, corporate executives attach great importance to R&D, but not so much to customer service, but in fact, customer service engineers usually have stronger overall capacity than the R&D engineers of the same level. If the company does not recognize the after-sales service system, then the system will never be staffed with outstanding talent. A team of underperformers will cost hugely. For example, a mediocre technical support engineer flew somewhere to fix a system, and he took several flights and yet could not get it fixed. How much cost could the company have saved if the engineer had fixed it in a single shot or even better if he could fix it via remote guidance without showing up at all! Therefore, enterprises should value balanced development instead of one-sided development.[19] Under the guidance of balanced development, Huawei's top management askes all departments, sections, and process leaders to focus on their weak links, and meanwhile, the company has established a unified evaluation system, so that employees can be fully mobile internally.

The balance between short-term and long-term interests

In 1997, Ren made it clear that benefits were to be improved with better management efficiency. Through the continuous execution of strict, scientific and effective management, overtime was gradually reduced, and the health of employees was better protected. A healthy worker can work harder and better. Huawei cannot and should not take any action because of short-term emergencies or short-term gains that it will regret in the long term. There is no point in extinguishing a fire today while planting landmines that may blow tomorrow. Management reform should be practical and feasible. Since 2001, Huawei has taken three years to focus on management to improve per capita output. In evaluation, Huawei emphasizes not only the current per capita contribution to financial indicators, but also the future growth potential. What the company pursues is not size, profit, or short-term profit, but sustainability.[20]

Establishing a greater quality system architecture

In 2015, Ren proposed that in the era of high traffic data when traffic management was changing, network stability would have a greater impact on the brand, so it was essential for Huawei to establish a greater quality system architecture. Previously, Huawei's quality system focused on the "tactic" level, i.e., the operation, products, and engineering. The quality system of tomorrow should focus more on the "strategy" level, such as culture and philosophy. Therefore, Huawei aims to establish quality competence centers with its partners in China, Germany, and Japan.[21]

---

[19] Ren Zhengfei: "Huawei's winter", *Huawei People*. 2001.

[20] Ibid.

[21] "The Story of Huawei". ifeng Finance. http://finance.ifeng.com/a/20150312/13548071_0.shtml. (页面已不存在-译者注).

8.4 Principles and Objectives of Management Change

Starting with small improvements

Ren was once asked when Huawei could take a break, and he said not until we saw the final nail in the coffin.[22] Change is the only constant in the world, and management improvement should be constantly implemented. Huawei is facing a strategic turning point in management and service. Without this, there will be no market expansion, or moving forward organization-wise. "Huawei aims to take three to five years to complete this strategic shift. If we can accomplish this strategic shift, we can at least narrow the gap with Western companies in terms of profitability. That could account for something."[23] "Huawei is establishing various process management and gradually achieve management automation. Huawei is learning foreign advanced technology management massively and applying it to our own practice. When the new IT system is in place in three to five years, and when the employees who have experienced three to five years of management standardization are familiar with international norms, the core competitiveness of the enterprise will be greatly strengthened, and the per capita profitability and efficiency will be greatly enhanced."[24]

"Seven Nos" in Management

Huawei has put forward the principle of "Seven Nos" in continuous management improvement: No perfectionism. No red tape. No blind innovation. No partial optimization without overall efficiency improvement. No transformative leadership without a panoramic outlook. No transformations involving employees with no business experience. No deployments of premature or untested processes. The seven Nos set the boundary for management improvement, and the main idea is that management improvement must be rational, pragmatic, and timely to avoid damage by improper improvement. Huawei's senior management believes that management improvement and transformation should be gradual rather than radical. As Ren said, "We have never advocated a drastic change, but rather a continuous improvement. We have to be patient and plan first." For a developing enterprise, management change may be a double-edged sword, while bringing changes to the enterprise may also hurt its stability and order. Many developing enterprises cannot bear this price in the face of enormous survival pressure; therefore, set principles for management change is self-protection and an act of restraint: the change should be controllable, predictable and applicable.

Absorption of foreign management expertise

In 1999, Huawei proposed to innovate to enhance core competencies. How? A company has limited resources, so it is essential to stay focused. During this period

---

[22] Cheng Dongsheng, Liu Lili: Ren Zhengfei on International Business [M]. Hangzhou: Zhejiang People's Publishing House, 2007.

[23] Ren Zhengfei: "Don't be a flash-in-the-pan hero". *Huawei People*. September 28, 1998.

[24] Ibid.

of time, Huawei implemented the competency & qualification (C&Q) assessment system introduced from the UK, and organized personnel to attend training and study in the UK. The standardized management of the UK is very clear, but Huawei was thinking: why did the UK gradually decline? The answer, Huawei believes lies in the lack of innovation. Therefore, Huawei not only introduced the British C&Q system but also the remuneration evaluation system from the Hay Company from the US, to combine standardization with innovation. So, Huawei absorbed the British process-based and standardized management, while avoided its stiffness and rigidity.[25]

Take off the "straw sandals" and put on the "American shoes"

In the process of management change, Huawei focused on introducing foreign expertise. Huawei was a small company not long ago, and its external resources were not as abundant as companies in the States had. Its decisions were more based on hunches, and not exactly rational, or science-based. Therefore, we need to draw on the expertise and methods of the companies in the States. The American shoes may not fit Chinese feet, but in order to learn the advanced management system, we need to wear them anyway, even if it means to force to fit. So, let's take off the straw sandals and put on American shoes. However, wearing new shoes is not enough, we also need to walk on the new path, the path trod by the world's leading enterprises. These companies have been around for a long time, and the path they have taken must be a well-trodden one.

The United States is successful in HR management, which nurtures the innovation spirit and facilitates the innovation mechanism. First, we introduce a Western management system to establish our company's systems and standards. When the HR management system is standardized and our corporate operations are mature, we will move away from the system initiated by Hay Group and begin innovating our own. We will bring in talented professionals who aim high but might be poor. They will not accept the status quo, nor will they confine themselves to existing conventions. They will drive a new round of transformation in our HR management system, and stimulate another round of growth for the company.

The principles of rigidity, optimization, solidification, and innovation

Rigidity is an important link of acquiring external experience. To fully replicate the learning target is to comprehensively and systematically imitate it in every detail. Even it is a forced fit and even it means huge pains, it is a learning experience standing on the shoulders of giants. This approach sometimes has conflicts with the original business, management, and cultural systems in the organization, but failure to imitate steadfastly often leads to the abortion of the entire learning process. Ren recognizes that judging the best and worst of a leading company from the perspective of a learner is like judging the right and wrong of an adult from the perspective of a child, which is likely to result in taking things out of context and putting the cart before the horse.

---

[25] Ren Zhengfei: "Entrepreneurship and innovation must be centered on improving the core competitiveness". March 5, 1999.

In learning human resource management from Hay, Ren stressed, "We are now buying a pair of 'American shoes' from Hay, which may not fit Chinese feet. However, we need to wear them anyway, even it means huge pains. We need to rigidize the system first and optimize and then solidify it at later stages." "We must understand the compensation ideas of Western companies provided by Hay in a comprehensive, full and realistic way, rather than simply and mechanically introduce one-sided or fragmented part. In Huawei, what we need most now is not innovation but standardization, which is a very painful process... Therefore, we must not let our imagination take control, otherwise it is impossible to learn the truth of management."

In learning the IPD process from IBM, Ren expressed a similar view: "We should learn how IBM does it, learn from its advanced experience, and listen to the consultants. First, senior and middle management should be trained and understand IPD. They shall not mislead consultants, otherwise the mistakes will catch up. Right now, we only understand the technical concept of IT, but not what it implies. Before we do, we shall not try to assume that we know better." At the IPD Phase I conclusion briefing, Ren summarized the company's principle for introducing the IT management system as "rigidifying, optimizing and solidifying". He said, "We must not have the illusion of making a Chinese version or a Huawei version. The introduction should first rigidify, then optimize, and we should also pay attention to solidify. Right now, in two or three years, our focus should be to understand and digest. After that, we can try some improvements." Rigidity can certainly prevent companies from taking shortcuts or playing smart. However, Ren also pointed out that "rigidity" is a phase. It does not mean we undervalue ourselves or we will always remain unchanged.

Optimization needs to be based on true understanding, and it can be applied to external resources and the organization itself. When optimizing external resources, in addition to not playing smart, one should also be refrained from overturning everything. Reformism should be an important principle of optimization. Self-optimization is to prevent oneself from being stuck in the old ways, or refusing to acknowledge new ideas. The ultimate goal of learning advanced external management ideas and tools is to solve problems. Therefore, the learning should take the company's history and status quo into account. IPD implementation started in 1998, and after two years of rigidity, Huawei initiated optimization as a top ten management priorities in 2001. Optimization does not mean to overturn the old system on its head, but to improve it and adapt it based on the understanding. The purpose of optimization is to make management more effective and practical, rather than simply creating some Chinese style management or Huawei style management.

The learning and optimization of management need to find inspiration from the enterprise's own practice. Only through the reflection and summary of each employee can knowledge and wisdom be generated, and this knowledge and wisdom cannot be replicated by other enterprises. Huawei encourages its employees to look for optimization areas in every ordinary job and continuously optimize seemingly simple tasks. The result? A production scheduler continuously improved the inventory turnover rate of SDH from 15 to 26 times/year. In the optimization process, if one can ask five whys, it shows that they are trying their best; if they can ask "can we do better?" five times, it shows that they are dedicated.[26]

Solidifying is the process of routinization (institutionalization, proceduralization) and standardization (templatization, specification). The solidifying phase is an important step of management progress. Its purpose is to solidify the learning outcomes of the organization in stages and to consolidate the management platform. Solidifying is the process of institutionalizing, proceduralizing, templatizing and standardizing the optimized results in the previous steps, which is an important step of management progress and innovation. In Ren's view, innovation needs to be bounded by a standardized system and also needs to be consolidated in phases, otherwise it will become disorganized and disorderly. Like rammed earth, compacted layer by layer, Huawei should solidify innovation and improvement results step by step. On the surface, it seems that the company's operation is characterized by optimization and change, but in essence, it is constantly solidified and standardized. Ren has repeatedly emphasized the role of solidifying management processes in his internal speeches, arguing that process solidifying can help the organization quickly cultivate talent. "A large amount of hardware for our end products will be standardized, universalized, and simplified, which can and should be solidified so that at least a few thousand skilled engineers who design circuits in our R&D team can be saved and they can be put into chip development." In addition, solidifying can form an enabling working atmosphere in the organization, so that good work habits become part of the organizational culture, allowing employees to naturally improve efficiency.

Innovation is the ultimate goal of learning. Solidifying is not the end but the beginning of learning and knowledge creation. On the basis of mastering external knowledge thoroughly and systematically, integrating reflection and optimization of the company's practice, and then making good work habits and good management tools become a work norm, the organization at this time has developed the basic conditions for knowledge creation, and can freely consolidate and integrate knowledge to create novel, practical and valuable knowledge. Ren said, "When our HR management system is standardized and the company is mature and stable, we will break the Hay system and innovate. We will then bring in a group of talented people who will are ambitious but not yet rich and will not settle for the status quo or be bound by the old norms, thus enabling our HR management system to innovate again to promote renewed growth."

These four steps reflect dialectical thinking. Management must be both standardized and innovated, and innovation itself must be managed to form a mutual promotion and constraint mechanism. In the initial period, there must be a strict management and control system, while when the enterprise has reached a certain stage of development, it must be decentralized to a certain extent. It shall not be arrogant or impatient; it shall always be hungry for innovation. It shall have its own pace and strike a balance between centralization and delegation.

[26] Ren Zhengfei: "Can we do better?". *Improvement*. October 31, 2000.

Case: IPD-enabled Management Transformation

Background

Huawei's IPD started with President Ren's trip to IBM in 1997.

IBM encountered serious financial difficulties in 1991 and 1992: the company's sales revenue stopped growing and profits dropped sharply. After analysis, IBM found that they lagged far behind the industrial leader in several areas such as R&D expenses, R&D loss, and time to market. For example, IBM's R&D expenses were 12% of its sales revenue, while the industrial leader was 6%; R&D loss was 25% of the total R&D expenses, while the industrial leader was only 3.3%. In terms of time-to-market, 36.5% of IBM's projects took 1.25 times longer than the industry leader, and 27% took twice as long. In order to regain a competitive edge in the marketplace, IBM set a goal of reducing time-to-market by 50% and reducing R&D expenses by 50% without compromising product development results. Driven by these goals and guided by a framework that integrates industry best practices, IBM applied the Integrated Product Development (IPD) approach to achieving shorter time to market (both in terms of process reengineering and product reengineering), higher margins, more effective product development, and greater value for customers and shareholders.

After three years of implementation, IBM's operations improved dramatically: time to market was significantly reduced from 70 to 20 months, and R&D expenses dropped from 12 to 6%. More importantly, the amount spent on obsolete projects dropped from 26 to 6%. Meanwhile, sales revenues continued to rise, profits rallied, and the ratio of R&D expenses to total revenues decreased. The company's competitiveness has greatly improved, and it has shown that IPD plays an important role in shortening product development and design cycles, reducing product costs, and improving product quality.

Ren was impressed by how IPD played off on IBM. At that time, after ten years of development, Huawei had grown from a switch distributor to an innovative company with the ability to develop its own digital switch with a capacity of 10,000 lines. On the one hand, the company has grown to a scale that the existing operation mode could not keep up with the expansion and has brought a series of problems. Ren felt that he was so overwhelmed that "five fingers could not hold down the grasshopper", so to speak. Therefore, he has been thinking hard about how Huawei can transform from guerrilla to a "regular army". At that time, product development in Huawei was very chaotic. When they received market demand, a bunch of R&D personnel swarmed in without a reasonable division of labor, or coordination. So, in the end, they always found out that what had been made was not at all what the customer wanted, or the product was repeatedly reworked, driving up the costs. On the other hand, the competition in China's telecom market has become more and more intense, and the market has changed from a high-margin, high-growth market to a general-purpose market with little product differentiation and fierce price competition. In order to enable Huawei to continue its rapid and stable development, the internal and external difficulties compelled Huawei to adjust and change its product development model and corporate strategy. It was also in this context that Ren set out on the road to learning from IBM.

In 1997, IBM made a comprehensive diagnosis of Huawei's management status: First, due to lack of accurate and forward-looking customer demand focus, it has repeatedly done useless work, wasted resources, and entailed high costs. Second, there was no cross-departmental process (although each department has its own process); the cross-departmental processes were manually connected, and the operational processes were fragmented. Third, organizational fragmentation and departmental silos caused internal frictions. Fourth, insufficient professional skills, irregular operations, and reliance on "heroes" whose success is difficult to replicate. Fifth, ineffective project plans, chaotic project implementation, no change control, and proliferation of versions. From the initial improvement of IT strategy and procurement, to the later reorganization of R&D management processes and supply chain processes, to key IT projects such as system integration, data centers and network research, IBM guided Huawei to reform its internal processes and explore efficient process-based operations.[27]

A year later, Huawei forcefully implemented IPD, "first rigidify, then solidify, and then optimize", Ren said. Just like this, IPD nudged Huawei on the fast track of management. In the next five years, it achieved the evolution from "a hyena" to "a lion" in a difficult and gradual manner.

The core concept and structure of IPD

As an advanced product development concept and management system, the core ideas of IPD include the following aspects.

First, treat new product development as an investment decision and manage the project with a budget. For a high-tech company like Huawei, new product development is not just an investment decision; it is the most important one. For any company, resources are always limited. An improper decision on new product development costs not only resources, but also market opportunities. IPD emphasizes effective portfolio analysis of product development, phased investment in new product development, periodic checkpoints in the development process (to decide whether the project should continue, suspend, terminate or redirect), so as to reduce investment mistakes and minimize the loss of mistakes.

Second, market-based new product development. IPD is market-driven, so product innovation must be based on market demand and competitive analysis. Therefore, the first step of IPD is to define product concept and market demand, focusing on doing things right from the beginning. Also, throughout the product life cycle, customer-centered plans are developed.

Third, cross-department and cross-system collaboration. In the traditional product development model, the departments of marketing, R&D, finance and manufacturing are divided by discipline functions. They mostly work in silos. However, in IPD, the

[27] http://www.huawei.com/cn/industry-insights/digital-transformation/ecosystem?ic_source=fhc17 (页面不存在-译者注).

development team takes into account the cost, development, testability and maintainability of the product throughout its lifecycle from the very beginning, thus avoiding working in silos to the greatest extent. IPD involves the participation of different functional departments at the very beginning of the project. There are two types of cross-functional teams in IPD: one is Integrated Portfolio Management Team (IPMT), which is a cross functional executive team; the other is the Product Development Team (PDT), which is a cross functional execution team reporting to IPMT). PDT works in the structured development process. IPD achieves the goal of cutting time to market as much as possible through effective communication, coordination and decision making by cross-departmental teams.

Fourth, asynchronous development, also known as parallel engineering, is used extensively. Asynchronous development is used to cut the time to market through detailed planning and accurate interface design, so that many follow-up activities can be conducted in advance. Parallel engineering is more than parallel product design; it applies to other activities as well.

Fifth, reusability. It refers to the use of common building blocks (also known as common base modules) to improve the efficiency of product development.

Sixth, a reasonable balance between the structured and unstructured. The uncertainty of product development requires a balance between structured and unstructured in the development process. The IPD process is structured to a certain extent.

Seventh, the customer's needs are the starting point of the process. With management tools and processes, valid market needs are analyzed, translated to the business plan, and formed into product roadmaps. The business plan ensures that the business does the right thing, while integrated development ensures that the organization does it the right way. The final IPD output goes to market, creating negative feedback on customer requirements and closing up the loop.

Implementation difficulties and preparation

IPD projects are divided into three phases: plan, develop, and launch. In the planning phase, much "tilling and ploughing" is needed. Based on research and diagnosis of the status quo and characteristics of the company, the "tilling and ploughing" work involves multiple sessions of training and seminars, and sufficient communication to make the relevant departments and personnel truly understand the ideas and methods of IPD. The main task of the invention phase is to design the program and select several pilot PDTs (i.e., Product Development Teams) and coach the pilot PDTs to operate according to IPD. The rollout phase was a gradual progress, starting with 50% of the projects, then expanding to 80%, and finally to all projects.

The difficulty of IPD project implementation is firstly the change of mindset, and secondly the change of organization and process. The organizational model, roles and responsibilities of each department involved in product development had to be transformed, and the evaluation and incentive mechanism needed to be changed accordingly. The company had to gradually transition to the new process without affecting the existing operation and business as much as possible, which was like changing the engine of an aircraft while it is flying. Lastly, Huawei has to face daunting challenges to transform from a peasant operation to a coffee-drinking, rules-based international company, especially in terms of the corporate culture and management system; in fact, this is a process of regeneration on the basis of self-denial. Many people do not understand Huawei's choice, and many chose to leave. Although Huawei arranged training sessions for all employees, and made it clear that middle managers would not be promoted without engaging in the organizational change, it is still difficult to make everyone understand the value of IPD, and ISC (i.e. Integrated Supply Chain), especially when the old and new systems are converted, it requires a lot of coordination. Some employees, especially some experts who are not good at coordination, left because they could not adapt to the new system.

Against the backdrop of management change, Ren thought about the value of IPD and ISC. Looking back at the mistakes Huawei has made, the most fundamental impact IPD has had on Huawei is a change in marketing approach. Before the change, Huawei used to make products by just burying their heads in the sand and try to sell them to customers, claiming how good they were. This model maybe feasible when the demand is strong, but when the situation changes, if companies still bury their heads in making the "good stuff" they unilaterally decided so, that stuff will not sell. It is essential to be customer-orientated for an enterprise to survive and thrive. In essence, IPD is a change of research, adaptation and strategic decision-making, and this is a correct path.[28]

In the process of introducing IPD, Huawei gave trainings to all employees, and explicitly asked them "to learn from the consultants with an open mind, and not to fight with the consultants". To the senior management who have difficulties and resist the change, Huawei asked them to force themselves "to wear the American shoes even if they don't seem to fit". The message is clear and loud: "If you don't change, you will not be promoted; if you change, you will get a raise."

As Huawei's core managers have become tough "heroes" in some regions, the change process was very painful. In the end, the company replaced 90% of its management.[29] In the process of implementing IPD, the main obstacle came from within the company, from senior and middle-level management who suffered from the loss of power and a drastic behavior change due to information flow management. It is a process of power redistribution. Ren reiterates that the survival of the company must come from the progress of the management system, which should be fast, accurate, end-to-end, and point-to-point, removing intermediate links as many as possible. Therefore, Huawei was prepared that a large number of senior and middle managers would lose their "hats and scepters". Ren said, we would not stop, not until our competitors decided to stop. Clearly this would not happen. "A thousand ships pass by the wrecked vessel". If we do not move forward, we will be done.

---

[28] Ren Zhengfei: "Customer demand orientation is the roadmap for product development, and the goal of corporate management is process-oriented organization building" at the PERB product roadmap planning and review meeting. May 26, 2003.

[29] Ren Zhengfei: "Spring in the North". April 24, 2001.

Knowledge transfer in IPD implementation

1. The knowledge acquisition phase (see Fig. 8.1). Huawei's knowledge transfer process originated from two starting steps: demand generation and knowledge screening.

   Huawei's demand mainly stemmed from Ren's sense of crisis and strategic vision. Ren's sense of crisis came from two aspects: first, his forward-looking thinking made him realize that the telecom industry winter would eventually come; second, he worried about company expansion. He worried that the existing management system would not be able to support the expansion, but he would also hate to split the company. In addition, at that time, Huawei already had a strategic plan for international development. To materialize the vision, Ren realized that Huawei needed to be in line with international standards in all aspects, and management was a particularly important part of it. Huawei was therefore motivated to learn from the world-leading companies.

   To screen knowledge, Huawei interviewed IBM consultants one by one. The IBM consultants working at Huawei were not ranked and paid according to their original rankings, but their interview results. This shows that Huawei knew what it truly needed. In a sense, the knowledge transfer from IBM to Huawei began with Huawei developing a demand framework and then it was filled with screened IBM knowledge. In the process, Huawei showed full "initiative", and it has won the respect of IBM. Meanwhile, the insight of IBM consultants who helped Ren sort out the current state of affairs was impressive and they have won Ren's trust too. Huawei strengthened its determination to change its processes under IBM's guidance, laying a good foundation for the knowledge transfer phase.
2. The knowledge implementation phase. This phase involved frequent communication between IBM consultants and Huawei employees, who held seminars and training on IPD-related knowledge. Like most consulting projects, at the beginning of the IPD project, IBM consultants conducted a lot of interviews and research with Huawei employees from various departments to make a diagnosis, which coincided with the process of knowledge transfer from Huawei to IBM. Based on the diagnosis, IBM consultants designed an IPD process applicable to Huawei based on their professional knowledge and experience and conducted numerous training and frequent communication within Huawei through various forms, such as small-scale meetings, all-staff meetings, and brochures. To better learn IPD knowledge, Huawei specially deployed key personnel from R&D, marketing, service, production, finance departments, and set up a close-knit working group with IBM consultants. Through such horizontal and vertical communication and training, key personnel from all departments in Huawei have been familiar with the main concepts of IPD.
3. The knowledge solidifying phase. In this phase, Huawei implemented a "pilot" project for four product lines, and under the hand-holding guidance of nearly 200 IBM consultants, the IPD process was put into full operation. For example, in the project investment meeting, each senior manager was equipped with an IBM "coach", making decisions at each decision point on behalf of the senior

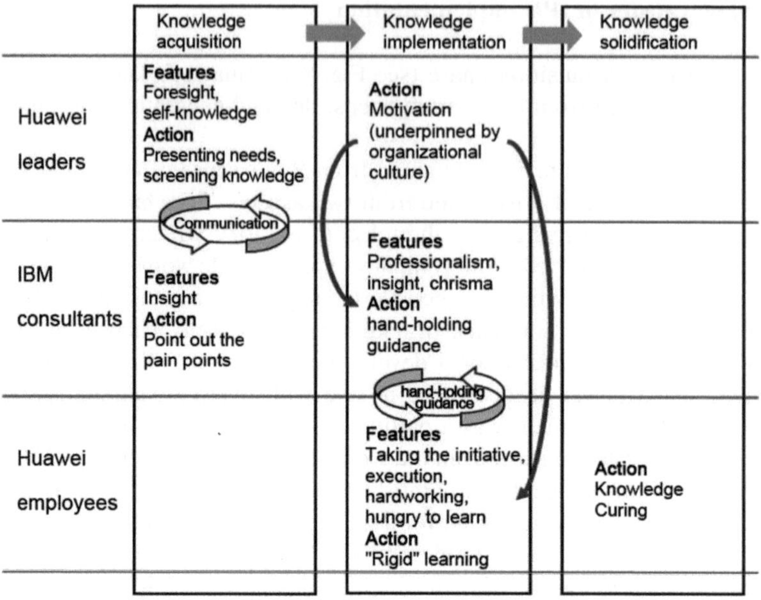

Fig. 8.1 Knowledge transfer in Huawei's IPD process. *Source* Fang Fei. Research on Knowledge Transfer Mechanism between Consulting Firms and Clients: The Case of Huawei. Master's thesis, Peking University, 2011

managers, who sat aside watching and learning, including tacit knowledge of IBM consultants.

Since Huawei's original R&D process was based on its corporate culture, it encountered a lot of pain caused by cultural conflicts when making changes to IPD. Huawei's wolf culture emphasizes swiftness, and the original R&D mechanism is like a group of elites forming a team to "take over the mountain", with no boundaries in responsibilities, each giving full play to their initiative and enjoying a sense of accomplishment brought by new R&D results together. However, the IPD process is more rigid, with specific processes and boundaries of responsibilities, and requires the participation of people from various departments, such as marketing, purchasing, production, and quality. Although the pace has slowed down, this is to "get things done at one go", rather than "do it over and over again".

This process was painful for Huawei people. First, the original comfortable way of working was completely changed with a variety of new rules and regulations. Second, the power and interests of some employees may be compromised and coordination is needed between departments. So, a small number of Huawei people either did not take it seriously, or questioned it a lot, fighting back and forth. In a nutshell, unwilling to accept it, they caused a lot of obstacles to knowledge transfer.

Faced with such a situation, Ren put forward the iron-clad slogan of "accept IPD or leave". Some Huawei managers were demoted for not being actively participating in the IPD project. In fact, the concept of "rigidity, solidification, and optimization" proposed clearly reflects his attitude toward knowledge transfer. The above slogan together with the one "wear the American shoes even if they are not fit" demonstrates Ren's determination to comprehensively and unconditionally transform Huawei's processes according to IPD concepts. Ren asked his employees not to change or selectively accept IPD concepts before fully absorbing the essence of the concepts. It is the determination of the leader and the organizational culture that helped Huawei effectively overcome the obstacles to knowledge transfer.

4. The knowledge solidification phase. In this phase, Huawei can ore comfortably use the knowledge transferred from IBM, and finally solidify it in its daily activities, and the whole process of knowledge transfer is thus completed. After the "pilot" project was accomplished, the next step was to independently extend the IPD process to all the projects of the company. After practicing it under IBM's "coaching-style" guidance, Huawei people have understood the essence of the knowledge and can apply it comfortably themselves. The IPD process has now been solidified in Huawei's daily work and has enabled Huawei to survive the industry winter and become a key to achieving its globalization strategy and becoming a world-leading company.[30]

The "four fast and three deliberately slow" in the project implementation

During the IPD process introduction, many middle and senior managers left, and some even took away the entire team of certain departments, but Ren was determined to see it through, and fired those who refused to embrace IPD. At that time, Huawei even encouraged some employees to start up their business by selling Huawei's enterprise network (data communications) equipment. If you do not understand or accept the reform, you can leave and do something else. The company can lend you equipment to sell, and you can repay the company after you have sold it. This is a win–win situation. Imagine, if due to various obstacles, Ren had kept silent, or could not handle the opposition, then the voice of opposition would have increased, and some swing managers would have changed their attitude and the project would have been half-baked. Therefore, when there is a stumbling block to change, we must show our position, firm up the belief, and at least contain the voice of opposition within a certain range. The key to Huawei's transformation success lies in the "four fast and three slow" approach. The specifics are as follows.

First, it is important to confirm the person responsible for the process fast. Change implies the adjustment of external and internal interests, and such adjustment may have different impacts on different people. In particular, the adjustment of internal interests will disturb the existing interests and power, which may cause strong opposition from vested interests. In such cases, it is difficult to succeed with the informal

[30] Fang Fei. Research on knowledge transfer mechanism between consulting firms and clients: the case of Huawei. Master's thesis, Peking University, 2011.

efforts of the entrepreneur or a small group of people alone. Therefore, it is necessary to mobilize company-wide efforts to allocate resources effectively to achieve the desired purpose of the change. This requires a dedicated organization to steer the change and ensure a strong momentum and alignment of interests. People responsible for the organizational change should work full time to stay focused.

Second, the unification of ideas should be fast. Generally speaking, managers at higher levels can sense the changes in the external environment earlier and more accurately, and recognize the need for change earlier than others in the company. So, the junior employees usually have not realized the significance and importance of change when the company leader hires an external professional consultant to manage the change. So, the timing of the change is very important. If the change is carried out when the employees or even the management does not have enough sense of urgency or crisis, it may not get strong support or may even meet opposition, even if the leader forces the change, and the probability of success will be greatly reduced. Therefore, when the leader senses the potential crisis of the company and the need for change, in-depth communication is essential to create a consensus throughout the organization and among the majority of the managers.

Third, fast implementation after the timeline is set. The change will never be 100% smooth as it will always encounter resistance, whether it is a conflict of interest, organizational inertia or risk aversion. First of all, change is the adjustment and redistribution of benefits, which will naturally lead to conflicts of interest, and the vested interests will try every possible means to obstruct the change. Second, is organization inertia. Just like when the locomotive tries to stop, the inertia will force the train to continue to move forward. Inertia is the Counteracting force of change and is inevitable. Finally, because change itself is uncertain and companies' aversion to uncertainty can also hinder change.

Fourth, course development and training should catch up fast. What is the most important thing after a new product is successfully launched? In Huawei, it is the development of two guidebooks, namely the product specification guidebook and the sales guidebook. The product specification guidebook is an important product document that outlines key requirements for building a new product. The sales guidebook is the key information for sales, the value of the product to customers, sales price and sales strategy, etc. To make the two guidebooks truly useful, training is essential. In the implementation of the IPD process, to eliminate concerns over changes in the position, job description, processes, and the organization, training is needed. The supporting training includes much more than the introduction of the significance and benefits of the processes; it needs to touch each link of the organization, which shall, together with the training department, develop the curriculum, and constantly explore and optimize the processes in the practice, and finalize new training courses. There are no data about documents and training materials used in the process of Huawei IPD reform. As far as the author knows, there are hundreds of officially released versions of training materials, CDs and PPTs for training in various categories, and they vary in technicality according to the target.

Fifth, be deliberate about identifying the direction and strength of the reform. The direction of process reform is essential. The reason to reform is that the current system of the company is problematic, or without reform, it will hinder the longer-term development of the company in the near future, or it is not adequate to help the company to seize the window of opportunity and achieve strategic goals. Therefore, the direction is critical and requires scientific assessment, comparison and weighing. The strength of the reform is also important. The internal situation of the company should be taken into consideration; the pace should be measured, which requires the wisdom and art of leadership. Different companies in different times have different demands; therefore, the reform should have a suitable pace. For example, Huawei burned its bridges. With the help of IBM coaches, a thorough and vigorous reform has been carried out and helped Huawei, this giant elephant, to dance. The reform of growing SMEs may not involve a complete change of the corporate culture, so the strength of reform is naturally different.

Huawei's vigorous IPD reform is well-known, but many do not know that in 2008 and 2009 Huawei successively executed quite a few minor reforms. For example, during this period, the management of Huawei did not have an in-depth understanding of the current positions and had encountered market-oriented time allocation issues. Huawei, therefore, adopted a reform led by the senior leadership team. As a result, the understanding has been improved substantially in a short period of time. Meanwhile, to support the reform of moving the command to the front office, the head office was transformed from an administrative authority to a supporting agency, and the whole process was quite gentle.

Sixth, be deliberate about selecting partners. By partners, here we refer to consulting firms. Every year, consulting firms will be ranked. McKinsey, Accenture, Roland Berger, BCG, Bain Capital, General Consulting, AC Nielsen are often ranked among the tops. Next, we'll compare a few top consulting firms to shed some light on how to choose a partner. First, multinationals are more likely to convince executives and employees. This is what it is. So, when it comes to change, large companies are more likely to see multinationals as their first choice. However, a common problem of these multinationals is that they may not fit local conditions. How to overcome it? Different firms have different strategies. For example, McKinsey is known as a "religious" consultant holding non-interference with internal affairs as its precept and always restrains itself from involving too much. It is so neutral that sometimes the client may feel that it doesn't give any conclusions or direction. It focuses on quantifiable improvements, such as financial indicators. BCG focuses on knowledge transfer and requires that the client's internal team take more action, and it only acts as the brain. Bain Capital, on the other hand, generally involves itself deeper, and will submit proposals about the unquantifiable, such as strategy and management systems.

Seventh, be deliberate about setting the timetable for the change. Before the process change, a timeline must be set for each node with corresponding monitoring measures. For example, process change is bound to bring about corresponding changes in the organization, which will bring about a redefinition of roles. So, the timeline and monitoring measures are established to guarantee the completion of the process on time. Otherwise, without a guaranteed direction, the desired results are not guaranteed, let alone implementation.

Execution evaluation

In 1998, Huawei had 8,000 employees, including 4,000 R&D staff. Inspired by Ren's the slogan of "If the shoes won't fit, fix the feet", Huawei has finally worn the "American shoes" customized by IBM. The previously independent and sort of isolated R&D department became a market-driven segment. After taking the five-year course designed by IBM, Huawei gradually put itself into American shoes. It combined with learning Huawei's specific conditions to design corresponding processes, and deployed from small-scale trials to large-scale execution. By 2003, IPD had been updated from 1.0 to 3.0. The initial discomfort and pain gradually disappeared and new corporate culture has been developed; the impact of IPD on Huawei was obvious.

After nearly two years of hard work, Huawei finally developed more effective coordination and the continuous impact of IPD becomes increasingly visible. After a period of execution, Huawei people have not only accepted the change, but also changed their guiding ideology and worldview. In the process, Huawei gradually transformed its head office from a centralized management center to a support and service center with a monitoring function. The idea is not only building the command office in the place where the "shots" can be heard, but also making the resources allocated to the project in a timely, accurate and effective manner, so that the project owner can take charge, make informed decisions with IT support and has the power to rationally and effectively schedule and allocate resources. After three years' execution, no one will be allowed to remotely control the project. Within the three years, the heads in charge of support and services should be staffed by managers with successful field experience.

The organization has shifted from technology-driven to market-driven. For example, maintainability should be taken into consideration in the R&D process, corresponding technical support staff should be available at all times. In other words, on the first day of product development, every department should be involved to ensure functionality, quality, and maintainability with the market demand serving as the compass for technology development.

In terms of organizational structure, the change birthed an entirely new department. In 1999, in line with the market-driven shift, many technical experts and chief engineers left their former technical department. Meanwhile, marketing personnel introduced from overseas and people with "technical sense" from the former marketing department formed a strong department—Marketing and Engineering Division, which is directly under the Market Department. This organizational orientation solved the "technical complex" of tens of thousands of R&D personnel and made sure that each project was market-oriented.

Any advanced management and process systems are based on tools and methods. The ultimate goal of IPD is to help maximize the benefits and value of the enterprise. The effectiveness of IPD is generally measured through both short-term and long-term indicators.

The short-term indicators are generally qualitative, which are shown in the following aspects.

(1) Change of R&D concept. The company's R&D philosophy has been changed through training, co-creation of system design, and IPD implementation. For example, market-oriented product development, cross-departmental cooperation, process-based business activities, asynchronous technology development and product development, project management, etc.
(2) Establishing/optimizing product development process and related templates. Based on the integration/optimization of existing processes, an IPD-based product development process is established.
(3) Rationalizing the structure of the R&D system and R&D team and improving the responsibilities of functional departments.
(4) Managing the development process as a project and developing project managers' capabilities and skills.
(5) Improving the quality management system and establishing processes and systems from the perspective of a process audit, technical review, and product testing.
(6) Providing the company with a set of process assets for R&D management through co-designing the consulting project.

Long-term indicators are quantitative indicators measured after 1–2 years of implementation, which are shown in the following aspects.

(1) Improving product quality. Through system identification and setting technical review points and testing activities in the structured process, and process management, product yield rate and customer satisfaction are improved.
(2) Shortening product development cycle. Through a standardized product development process, rework and waiting time in development is reduced and the company can beat its competitors to seize market opportunities.
(3) Reducing product development costs. Product development costs are reduced through the shortened development cycle and reduced rework brought by reviews, testing, etc.
(4) New employees are learning faster with better knowledge management and accumulation of experience. The management documents, process documents, development documents and lessons learned generated in the process of product development are important contents for knowledge management and orientation training, which can effectively shorten the growth cycle of new employees.

8.5 Huawei's IT Capacity Building

The evolution of Huawei's information system is roughly divided into six stages, as shown in Fig. 8.2.

Decentralized and customized IT application phase (1993–1998)

Before 1993, Huawei mainly focused on the domestic market and expanded its business from rural areas to cities. At that time, Huawei did not have a clear IT strategy,

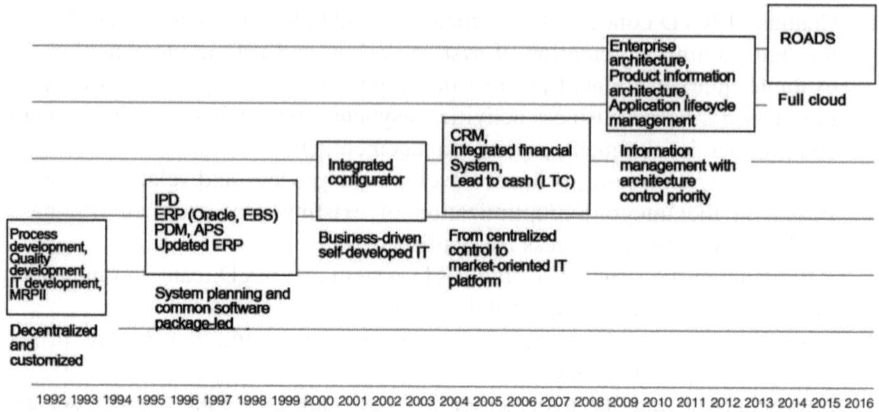

Fig. 8.2 Huawei's information system evolution. *Source* Su Wei. A case study of process and it integrated change in enterprise informatization process. MBA Master's thesis, Guanghua School of Management, Peking University, 2017

and the IT systems were developed in a rather disorderly manner. From 1993 to 1996, Huawei started its IT development with the external help featured by the introduction of the Oracle-based MRPII system. At this stage, only a few business representatives participated in Huawei's IT projects, which was a far cry from its slogan of "business first, and IT on the ground". The forced push of IT and passiveness of businesses have led to a mismatch between software packages and businesses, which of course could not fit the needs of businesses.

Huawei ERP system went online in 1997 and was the first application of Oracle *E-Business Suite* (EBS) in China. Due to legacy reasons, Huawei required customizations from ERP vendors to support the special needs of the company's growing business. These customizations broke the logic of the software package to varying degrees, which not only made it difficult to meet the needs of continuous business development, but also brought great problems and risks to system upgrades and maintenance. As the business scale and area continue to expand, the ERP platform's ability to support the business is increasingly challenged, and many problems are exposed.

System planning and common software package phase (1998–2002)

In 1998, Huawei started to enter the international market, and based on the demand for business strategy development, the company began to formulate a clear strategic plan for IT application. Huawei initiated large-scale process change projects such as IPD and ISC with the support of IBM.

Given the problems in the first phase, Huawei's IT department, together with the supply chain, procurement, finance and other departments, set up a joint ERP "de-customization" team to clean up the ERP customization function points and return to ERP standard functions. The joint team regularly reviewed the package standard features and the existing customization list; cleansed up unused customization, analyzed the customization in use, and reviewed with the business units to support business needs with the package standard features. In 2000, Huawei put forward the slogan of "If the shoes won't fit, fix the feet", "wear American shoes", "rigidify, solidify, and optimizing", and established "software package-driven" as the basic strategy for the company's business change and IT development.

Business-driven self-developed IT phase (2003–2006)

Starting from 2003, Huawei truly launched its globalization strategy. By then, it had completed the implementation of IPD and ISC, and successfully upgraded its ERP system and implemented the Advanced Planning and Scheduling System (APS) to manage the supply chain, starting to implement its IT system to all its businesses worldwide and provide the IT platform for more businesses. At this point, Huawei needed a support platform to connect CRM and ERP and harmonize data such as quotes, orders, configurations and shipments. This platform is called a configurator and is no less important than CRM and ERP for product delivery. Huawei started the selection of the Configurator software package in 2001, and finally decided to develop it in-house, because there were no mature software packages available in the industry.

The Configurator is a platform that by using the product configuration rules and algorithms in the system, automatically generates product configurations, quotations, and production and shipping data based on the input configuration requirements. It is a core IT system that supports Huawei's sales configuration, order management, and shipping management. Huawei's self-developed Configurator includes three modules: 1. The configuration algorithm module for the Bill of Material (BOM). 2. The quotation module. With the module, quotation personnel only need to enter quotation parameters, such as the number of users, the number of links, software configuration, etc., a quotation will be generated automatically. 3. Delivery module, which can automatically match the BOM with the ERP order system, and generate a complete set of equipment shipping lists based on the configuration algorithm module.

The Configurator has gradually become the main IT platform supporting Huawei's quotation and delivery. With the Configurator, the public data used by the marketing, R&D, supply chain, and service teams are managed and published in a unified manner. On this platform, the R&D team maintains the configuration algorithm, the marketing team uses it to quote, the supply chain uses it to process orders, and engineering services, training, maintenance, and commercial expenses are also configured via the platform.

After two years of online implementation, the following figures demonstrate the efficiency boost in all aspects: quotation efficiency increased by over 30%, the contract processing cycle shortened by 25–30%, the contract fulfillment accuracy rate increased by 35–40%, and the contract change rate has dropped from 32 to 10.7%. More importantly, this milestone in-house IT system has brought optimization confidence to Huawei's IT methodology, thus gradually forming an IT strategy that combines software package and in-house R&D to support its core competitive businesses. In the subsequent process optimization and IT development, Huawei identified core competitive business processes such as R&D of devices of high-reliability and security, and carried out successful process optimization and IT development based on the practice of the Configurator development.

From centralized control to market-oriented IT platform phase (2006–2011)

In 2005, Huawei had 30,000 employees. It launched a large-scale R&D and global marketing of 3G communication technologies, and generated 3.4 billion USD in overseas sales. As a late-comer, Huawei had to demonstrate a competitive edge in flexibility and efficiency in sales, orders, and shipments. So, it built flexible processes and IT systems on the architecture of the original software packages, and rapidly iterated and innovated the processes and systems to support the rapid and massive development of the company's global business. 2006 saw Huawei's overseas sales reaching 7.2 billion USD, surpassing the domestic market for the first time. Facing the increasingly large organization and complex businesses, Huawei proposed to establish a strict, orderly and simple management system that would support the company to stay ahead of its competitors. To this end, the company began to reshape its information management capabilities. Based on the existing management platform, it connects processes, streamlines management, and optimizes resource allocation. Huawei has been successfully applied Business Transform Management System (BTMS) in large-scale management transformation projects such as Integrated Financial System (IFS) and Lead to Cash (LTC).

An information management model that prioritizes architecture control (2011–2016)

In 2011, Huawei had 146,000 employees in more than 140 countries and regions, of which foreign employees accounted for 20.19%. There were three business groups (BGs) in Huawei: the carrier BG, the enterprise BG and the consumer BG, with over 100 representative offices worldwide, so standardized IT management was particularly important. In 2011, Huawei's investment in process and IT accounted for more than 1% of sales revenue (2.5% in 2016). Every employee in the process and IT team can support 100 employees in the company. The integrated transformation of process and IT plays an important role in supporting Huawei's globalization. Such a large organization is bound to have complex businesses and rules; methodology transformation and project management alone are inadequate for process management. Huawei found that by holding on to the management of the core architecture of the processes and IT systems, it can more effectively implement the change. In this phase of the process and IT change, Huawei gradually explored and summarized the Enterprise Architecture (EA) methodology, and implemented the principle of planning architecture and standards before building and optimizing enterprise processes and IT.

Full cloud and digital transformation strategy (2016–present)

We are moving into an intelligent society, where everything is sensed, connected and intelligent, and where cloud and cloud services, big data and AI are the core of enterprise information development. In 2016, Huawei put forward the strategy of full cloud-based service, driving Huawei's IT development through ROADS, i.e., Real-time, On-demand, All-online, DIY and Social, to support efficient business operations.

8.6 Risk Management

Internal control system

Huawei has a very wide range of businesses and supports many business units. Although there are matching organizations and processes to support these businesses, systemic risks still exist. So, how can we ensure the long-term stability of the company, make the businesses run effectively, and eliminate systematic corruption? Huawei hopes to establish an internal control system to provide the necessary review and supervision of business processes. Through the application of tools such as proactive testing, proactive review, and semi-annual internal control assessment, process owners/business managers at all levels will conduct self-assessment, improve process management and business control, identify business risks, effectively prevent, and reduce business risks and internal control risks, and enable business goals to be achieved.

Huawei requires all processes to be implemented in accordance with the principle of segregation of duties. When building a process, a corresponding internal control process system should be considered, and the internal control management should be constantly improved. The internal control process system should be developed in parallel with the business process system, and the board of directors and supervisors of the company are responsible for supervising the first-level business process and internal control process respectively. The board of directors and supervisors of the regional company or the BG are responsible for supervising the second-level processes. The responsible persons are responsible for the development, implementation, and optimization of the internal control process system from end to end.

In terms of responsibility, like business processes, the internal control system also needs to identify process owners and their responsibilities, who should be appointed by the company with clarified responsibilities. Internal control work meetings should be held regularly to discuss and solve the problems related to routine internal control, track key issues, and facilitate the implementation of improvement measures.

The three-tier risk control architecture

Huawei has established an effective three-layer monitoring system through the integrity environment nurturing, business process monitoring, independent audit deterrence, covering all the points, lines, surfaces, and fields of internal control. By point, it refers to the business pain point. By line, it refers to the internal control responsibilities of managers at all levels. By surface, it refers to high-risk points revealed by auditing. By field, it refers to a benign atmosphere for internal control.

The first line of defense is the business manager. They are responsible for the effective implementation of internal control and risk management in the day-to-day operations and assume the responsibility for identifying, assessing, controlling and handling risks, supervising the implementation of internal policies and processes, and ensuring that measures effectively support the business or organization's operational objectives.

The second line of defense deals with cross-process and cross-business risks and internal control challenges that cannot be addressed by the first line of defense. Its specific functions include enterprise risk management and establishing various cross-departmental, cross-business, and cross-process risk management committees, which hold roundtables of senior executives from relevant business units, to regularly address important issues not dealt with by the first line of defense. The goal is twofold: first, to monitor the results of the first line of defense and examine whether its design is reasonable, its implementation is effective, and whether its operation works; second, to solve the issues that the first line of defense cannot solve due to departmental isolation, the limitation of scope, status, and influence.

The third line of defense refers to internal audits. It should be independent and reasonable. A professional and efficient internal audit is critical for effective corporate governance, and it should provide the company with comprehensive, objective, and independent forensic opinions. First, through continuous auditing of the results of the first and second line of defense to keep them toe the line and put in place the control results. Second, an efficient audit team itself is a deterrent to the front-end business, ensuring that the risk management and control of the organization are always effective.

Risk management is most effective when there are three separate and clearly defined lines of defense in an organization. The three-tier system has the following characteristics: first, the center of responsibility is at the front; second, the hierarchy is always maintained; third, efficiency is prioritized to maintain effectiveness. Examining Huawei's internal control and risk management framework from these three dimensions, we will find that there is still a lot of room for integration, synergy, and efficiency gains. For example, the center of responsibility is tilted more backward than it is supposed to be. Risk management and business execution have not yet formed real synergy. Although various risk management activities are carried out frequently, some outstanding cross-business and cross-process problems have not been solved by the platform. Whether an optimized proportion of inspection and development is set in the organization also needs further examination.

Internal control tools

Internal control has a major role in overseeing the safety of company operations and must have clear operational standards. Internal control tools can provide standardized templates to make internal control more standardized and reasonable. The Semi-Annual Control Assessment (SACA) is a self-assessment mechanism for internal control that is conducted by business management/process owners with the assistance of the organization at all levels, with the goal that managers at all levels proactively expose internal control issues by themselves. If the SACA result is "unsatisfactory", usually a 12-month improvement period will be given, during which time no other audit will be scheduled until the SACA result is "acceptable" or "satisfactory".

Management platform and mesh networking

The linear administrative system will make full use of the multi-level business management platform and mesh networking formed by the secretary management system hand in hand to effectively manage the business objectives and benefit distribution. If we use the fishing net metaphor—"if you lift the headrope, the net spreads open", then the administrative system is the headrope, and the business management is the mesh. "If you take care of the big things, the small things will take care of themselves." The management system innovation fundamentally overcomes bottlenecks and failures of the previous management processes due to poor and distorted information. Moreover, it will clarify responsibilities and the division of labor, which is conducive to the objective and fair evaluation of each organization and each employee, and to form a strong constraint mechanism, thus further opening up the management system and greatly improving the effectiveness of work.[31]

Ren's fishing net metaphor is quite apt. He believes that business management is the "net", which is made of many meshes (power centers). If one mesh is broken, the fish will probably get out of the net. If you do not pay attention to each mesh, you are likely to end up with nothing. The headrope itself cannot catch any fish. To implement the business, the business management should have the highest authority, instead of powerless due to its low status, because you see, only the net can catch fish. If the net is not big enough to catch a big fish, we must fully mobilize the resources, knit more meshes. The supervisors are the net rope, and the role of the rope is to assess, check, supervise, and plan so that the net can spread as wide as possible. You see, if the net is not spread, it cannot catch fish either. Goal management means whoever knows the goal best, shall become the center of responsibility for solving the problem, and mobilize and use all resources available. Project managers should learn to track the process, and fully mobilize all resources and they must understand how resources are utilized to achieve goals. If they do not know how to mobilize resources, they can only catch a few small fish and miss the big fish. Mobilization of resources should be done in the easiest and most efficient way possible by following the ISO 9000 process. This is the de facto highest authority granted to project managers. The way to fully mobilize resources is matrix management.[32]

[31] Ren Zhengfei: "Revisit on refraining from complacence and no slack in the mind" at the Market and Research Award Ceremony. June 30, 1996.

[32] Ren Zhengfei: "Resolutely implementing ISO 9000". February 26, 1997.

8.7 Huawei Versus Cisco

Both Huawei and Cisco place great emphasis on the operation. Cisco ranked fifth in the USA in supply chain management. Large companies usually rely on one or two strategies for success, and one of Cisco's most important strategies is operational excellence, involving its processes, supply chain, and value chain. Cisco's operation system supports it in scaling up and reaching global markets quickly. In Cisco's view, the biggest difference between a large tech company and a small one is that the operating system of the large company helps it continuously and quickly bring new technologies and products to the global market, while the small one, albeit producing new technologies and products, does not have matching operation system to support its globalization. That is why Cisco keeps acquiring new technologies and products through M&A and maintains a leading position in the market through its efficient end-to-end value chain system.

After Huawei's top management has learned the key secrets of Western companies' success, it strategically prioritized the development of management systems. In 1996, Huawei first put forward its strategic vision of becoming a world-class enterprise with a three-step roadmap: align production and management with international standards in three years, align marketing with international standards in five years, and achieve international standards in R&D in ten years. It puts management improvement high on the agenda, as it has realized the importance of management platform, and recognized that management ability represents system integration ability, without which talent, technology and capital cannot form a synergy. Based on such understanding, Huawei has invested hugely in the past 30 years to purchase management and information system solutions from IBM, Accenture, and other international consulting firms, and applied them to Huawei's management system. Many enterprises encounter bottlenecks in development, mainly because they put too much effort and too many resources into market expansion while paying insufficient attention to management improvement. Blindly expanding without a solid management foundation will result in a significant increase in costs, serious operational problems, and a severe lag in responsiveness to the market.

Huawei encountered a culture clash in the management change. The standardization of Western management systems has placed great constraints on the flexibility of Chinese companies. Given the fact that China has not produced a single world-class company in the past 100 years, when Huawei introduced Western management systems, it has to first overcome the old mindset and management style. It endured the pain of self-denial, and other pain caused by change and self-correction, and realized the strategic goal of transforming from a local company to a multinational by rigidifying, solidifying, optimizing and innovating and by "wearing American shoes." Huawei's persistence on management change, its investment in management systems, and its continuous optimization of the management platform have laid a solid foundation for its long-term goals and its core competitiveness.

The balanced thinking in Huawei's management change has enabled it to intermittently change its management system on the basis of stable development. The process of management system change involves many deep structural changes, including thinking patterns, behavior patterns, work patterns and interest patterns.

The first principle Huawei adopts in the process of management change is the principle of staying focused: if the situation is urgent, Huawei will move fast without being obsessed with perfection. It uses the management process as a system integration force. In the process of management change, Huawei has spared no effort. It uses modern methods to do modern things and to seize the high ground. The second principle is that those who do not embrace change will not be promoted. To prepare for the profound change, Huawei organized company-wide training to create an atmosphere for organizational change, and through the incentive mechanism, it encourages employees to participate in the change and promotes those who do so to management positions; it demonstrates the organization's strategic intent by sending a clear signal to those who may hinder the organizational change. The third principle is "If the shoes won't fit, fix the feet". People who find it challenging to accept the new management methods and processes, need to adjust, and change to adapt to the \ new environment.

The difference between Cisco and Huawei is that many of Cisco's management systems are self-developed, while Huawei, in order to rapidly catch up, introduced mature global management systems to build its management system and platform.

Chapter 9
A Dynamic and Empowering Organizational Learning System

Organizational learning is a process by which members of an organization modify or reshape organizational behavior with the help of knowledge. A highly computerized enterprise is itself a learning institution that needs to absorb the latest knowledge about environmental changes, disseminate the new knowledge to each employee and empower them. So, the efficiency of learning determines the efficiency of work and organization. C. Argyris and D. Schon, pointed out in *Organization Learning: A Theory of Action Perspective* in 1978 that organizational learning is an adjustment of pre-existing beliefs, attitudes, behaviors, and structures in practice as a response to environmental change in order to promote long-term effectiveness, as well as the survival and development of the organization.

In terms of the learning process, organizational learning includes four segments: knowledge acquisition, knowledge dissemination, knowledge interpretation, and organizational memory. Knowledge acquisition sources include the practical experience of employees or teams internally (direct learning) and lessons learned from external organizations. Direction and efficiency are two key elements of knowledge dissemination. It includes both top-down and bottom-up dissemination, and also includes horizontal dissemination across departments and organizations. Knowledge interpretation is about the knowledge transformation process by which the organizational leader's strategic intentions become organizational consensus. Organizational memory is the common experience of all members of the organization, which affects the process of knowledge reuse and institutionalization. Organizational memory is the basis of organizational knowledge, and influences the organization's judgment on the type, dissemination direction and value of new knowledge.

For catch-up companies, efficient organizational learning is especially important. In the words of Ren, "We ran into international competition at our own doorstep from day one when Huawei was established. As communication products are monopolized by the industry giants, our survival was threatened since the day the company was born. So, we will be broken to pieces if we are not tough. Without self-reliance,

X. Dong et al., *Huawei*,
https://doi.org/10.1007/978-981-19-4078-1_9

there is no way out."[1] In Ren's view, only when all employees, especially managers, proactively solve problems through learning, can the company survive in the fierce competition, quickly close the gap with the world's leading companies, and maintain its competitive edge. In our collection of 80 plus internal speeches by Ren, the word "learning" appears 220 times. We are paying special attention to the following issues concerning Huawei's organizational learning.

First, how does Huawei inspire employees to learn? Employee's willingness to learn is affected by leaders' willingness to learn, personal career development, competitive pressure, and growth needs. Organizational learning can only be truly transformed into motivation when it is based on the intrinsic needs and motivation of personal development and becomes an indispensable part of their lives and work. The interaction and integration of learning and career development can become the true driving force for personal growth, thinking reconstruction and skill development. How does Huawei inspire employees to learn? How does Huawei set up different learning targets, priorities and methods in different stages of corporate development? How has its learning system evolved?

Second, the development of knowledge processes and knowledge systems in Huawei's organizational learning. For example, how does Huawei University set up its learning system, mechanism and methods? How to promote the formation of organizational memory? Many enterprises have corporate universities and/or training departments. What are Huawei's experiences and practices on how to design efficient learning methods and systems to enable managers to achieve dynamic empowerment, quickly learn the knowledge needed in their work, and improve their capabilities?

Third, how does Huawei learn thoroughly and quickly? In the process of catching up, Huawei's R&D, management and marketing capabilities were lagging far from those of leading companies. The only way to catch up is to improve the density and efficiency of learning. In this process, Huawei has internalized and strengthened its capabilities by drawing a lot of new external knowledge. What are the specific principles and methods that Huawei has used in learning that can provide reference to other companies?

9.1 Organizational Learning Builds Key Competencies

The most important goal of organizational learning is continuous self-renewal. In Ren's view, "learning" means proactively renewing oneself. One way of self-renewal is to bring in first-class management ideas and tools from international competitors and strategic partners. For example, Huawei has hired IBM as a consultant to implement IPD, Hay as a consultant to implement its tenure system, and adopted Ericsson's end-to-end LTC process. Another important approach to self-renewal is to keep exploring and summarizing. For example, Huawei summarized its corporate culture during the wild growth period into the Huawei Basic Law, developed the "Iron

[1] Ren Zhengfei: "Huawei people refuse to fail", at Huawei's annual meeting. December 26, 1995.

Triangle" model in its globalization, and launched a number of internal publications such as *Huawei People* and *Improvement*. In the early stage of Huawei's development, only employees with a strong sense of self-renewal were promoted to management positions, constituting the backbones of the company, leading the company to continuously learn from leading international competitors and strategic partners, while summarizing their experience, and eventually achieving rapid catch-up.

Depending on the degree of self-renewal, learning in Huawei is categorized into strategic learning and operational learning. Operational learning follows the organization's existing learning track, continuously optimizes and consolidates established rules, continuously refines practical knowledge related to specific tasks, and helps the organization improve efficiency and reduce costs by following, repeating, extending, and reinforcing existing rules and experiences.

Strategic learning requires companies to step outside of their original trajectory and rethink organizational strategy and repositioning themselves in the face of changing circumstances. Breaking the mold and questioning the fundamental assumptions of the organization is a critical step to innovate and achieve breakthrough growth. However, due to a number of reasons, such as organizational inertia, behavioral rigidity, short-termism and risk aversion, strategic learning tends to remain only as slogans in most companies. But not Huawei! Huawei always challenges itself. In 1996, the resignation of several thousand people in Huawei's marketing department broke the seniority-based promotion system in the wild growth stage and institutionalized job mobility within the company, laying the foundation for the rapid implementation of the subsequent tenure system. In 1998, Huawei re-evaluated the R&D process and efficiency of the enterprise and introduced the IPD system. This has enabled the company to have first-class R&D management capacity and finally be on a par with the top companies. In 2001, when Huawei's international business was expanding and its domestic business was booming, Ren wrote an article entitled "Huawei's Winter" and inspired the company to think about the potential management crisis behind the prosperity and find room for improvement in efficiency. In 2007, more than 7,000 Huawei employees resigned a masse and overturned the existing workplace hierarchy. In 2008, when Huawei's management platforms have been built and the management system gradually matured, Huawei once again challenged the top-down standardized management, and proposed to reverse the organizational process, transforming from being "technology-centered" to "customer-centered". In 2017, Huawei dispatched many senior R&D staff to overseas markets. This measure together with a series of other initiatives is all part of Huawei's self-renewal.

We are not suggesting that the more radical reforms the better, and certainly they should not be launched at the whim of the company. Any change while brings vitality to the company, also poses a great risk of failure. Therefore, many companies have a hard time weighing between stability and change, and deciding when and how to conduct strategic learning.

Ren noticed the dialectical relationship between strategic and operational learning quite early. In 1995, Ren mentioned in his acknowledgment speech at the Shanghai Telephone Information Technology and Business Management Seminar, "if we focus on immediate benefits and ignore long-term investment, we will hurt users in terms of product succession and expansion. At present, we are torn by how to trade-off today's low prices against tomorrow's ambitious goals. If we go with the low prices of today, we will lose tomorrow, but if we go with tomorrow, we may not even survive today." In advancing strategic learning, he encouraged employees to be boldly self-reflective, while cautiously defending the results of the change. In his internal speeches, he repeatedly stressed the importance of avoiding blind innovation. Some of his frequent remarks include "Staying half a step ahead is advanced, but staying three steps ahead is doomed",[2] "We need to stand on the shoulders of giants to move forward, rather than pursue blind innovation",[3] "Technology innovation without boundaries may be misleading",[4] "We should evolve and be prepared, but not blindly pursue disruptive innovation; innovation should create value."[5] These seemingly contradictory statements that encourage change but curb innovation have led to Huawei's unique approaches and principles for acquiring, disseminating, and interpreting knowledge and forming organizational memory; it has improved the company's ability to adapt in an uncertain market and competitive environment.

9.2 Approach and Evolution of Organizational Learning

Knowledge acquisition is the first step for an organization to initiate the learning process. In the knowledge acquisition process, Huawei's learning is reflected in extensive sources, independent learning and learning from failed experiences. It focuses on raising the awareness of active learning among all employees, establishing a culture of continuous optimization and progressive learning, stimulating employees' intrinsic drive to learn, and encouraging them to explore appropriate learning methods.

Vigorously promoting independent learning

At Huawei, Ren asks all employees, including new employees, especially all managers and outstanding employees, to engage in independent learning. Ren told management that independent learning was the only way to expand their knowledge and capabilities and meet the challenges of the new era. "Read more books, improve your skills, expand your scope of knowledge and ability, so that you can better embrace the new era and become an executive yourself in the future."[6]

He told Huawei's top ten outstanding employees that only independent learning can create outstanding talent. "Knowledge, methods, and achievements all come

[2] Ren Zhengfei: "Huawei's Core Values" (revised version). 2007.

[3] Huawei EMT Resolution No. [2011]044.

[4] Ren Zhengfei: "A cup of coffee absorbs the energy of the universe" at the seminar with experts from Shanghai Research Institute. April 23, 2014.

[5] Ren Zhengfei: Speech at the 2013 Carrier Network BG Strategy Retreat. December 28, 2013.

[6] Ren Zhengfei: "Revisit on refraining from complacence and no slack in the mind" at the Market and Research Award Ceremony. June 30, 1996.

from accumulation bit by bit. As long as you keep learning and thinking, a few years later when you look at yourself, you will be a little surprised how far you have come. Huawei is also a university; it transforms and cultivates people."[7]

He told the marketing staff that independent learning can help them understand rules and laws from the practice and improve themselves faster." Each marketing personnel should use some time to learn. In fact, every day, when you are dealing with others, you are trained in a certain way, except that you may not be aware. We encourage active learning, especially learning by doing. You will improve yourself faster by actively reflecting and summarizing your experience."[8]

He told new employees that independent learning is a contribution to the enterprise. "It is imperative for employees in the high-tech industry to learn. You can read books in your spare time, summarize what you have learned, and accumulate knowledge and practical methods to continuously improve yourself and contribute to the development of the company."[9] In his remarks at the orientation in 1999, Ren said, "Technical training depends on your own, rather than listening lectures. In fact, every position is receiving training every day, everywhere and any time. No Nobel laureate is trained. Let me ask you who trained Mao Zedong, and Deng Xiaoping? Successful people are made by active learning, so become effective learners, rather than passive learners, and continue to improve yourself."

Leaders should be exemplary learners

Ren's knowledge comes from a wide range of sources. He often captures knowledge signals no matter how weak they seem to be from trips, visits, lectures, and news, and generates inspirations, understanding, and judgments about the corporate environment, market, change, and future development. He shares his learning experiences in reports to all employees, which play an important role in the formation of employees' global vision, knowledge dissemination, and organizational memory. His Confucius practice that "Even when walking in a party of no more than three I can always be certain of learning from those I am with" has left a deep imprint on knowledge acquisition at the organizational level, and become an important knowledge acquisition principle for Huawei. In 1998, Ren learned the importance of corporate culture from his study tour in the United Arab Emirates, and proposed: "Resources can be exhausted, only culture endures. Our company has nothing but knowledge, technology, and management to unearth wealth in the minds of people. This is what I learned from my visit to the UAE. The UAE, as a small country in the desert, is as great as Israel. It transforms the money from oil into national cultural wealth, encourages the whole nation to go to UK, USA and other advanced countries to receive good education. With repeated cycles, within a hundred years, UAE has become a developed country."[10]

---

[7] Ibid.

[8] Ren Zhengfei: "Don't forget the heroes". January 23, 1997.

[9] Ren Zhengfei: Speech at a Meeting with New Hires. December 25, 1994.

[10] Ren Zhengfei: "How long can Huawei's flag stand" at a seminar at Unicom headquarters. 1998.

Learning from failures

Ren's sense of crisis makes the organization highly value and good at drawing lessons from failures. Unlike the crisis management approaches of other enterprises, Huawei usually goes beyond the resolution of the crisis, and focuses more on the reasons behind, so as to prevent similar problems in the future. At the end of 1995, Huawei's marketing department suffered a huge failure and lost all the biddings for communication equipment in five western provinces. Recognizing the dangers of "individualism" and "fractions", Huawei resolutely launched a collective resignation of more than 1,000 people and eventually introduced a competitive mechanism to eliminate underperformers, which to a certain extent has ensured organizational vitality. In 1998, In order to make quality switch products, Huawei's R&D department and Intermediate Pilot Department explored product and service improvement plans by repeatedly listening to recordings of customer complaints. In 2000, Huawei's Central Research Department "rewarded" the backbone of the R&D department with overstock and dead stock, so that they could keep in mind the lessons of R&D mistakes. In 2007, Huawei lost a Sudan Telecom mobile communication network bidding. This led Huawei to reflect on how to match the organizational structure with the "customer-centric" approach. Again in 2017, users complained about the flash memory performance of Huawei's P10 cell phone. Huawei quickly launched a "Listening to Consumer Task Force" to investigate work processes and services.

Learning by doing

Learning by doing is important for both employees and the company. Many of Huawei's managerial expertise is accumulated and optimized in practice. Ren told new employees: "Practice, practice and practice. It is especially important for new employees. Only by practicing first and then using theory to summarize will you improve by leaps and bounds." As a private enterprise, a late-comer, with limited resources, Huawei has to rely on itself in many aspects. In the decades of efforts, dynamic empowerment is a typical practice of Huawei to obtain practical knowledge.

The importance of dynamic empowerment

Dynamic empowerment refers to the practice of timely acquiring new knowledge, fast learning and iterating knowledge and skills to adjust one's decisions and behaviors according to competitors' strategies and demands from practices. For each "battle", "Huawei will conduct a cross-departmental collaboration, including strategic management department (to analyze customer needs), marketing department (to analyze competitors and their advantages), solution department, business department, IT department, and other related departments. We summarize specific situations, similar to Lenovo's review practice." The interviewees shared two stories with us. One is about how Huawei learns from interviewees and uses the knowledge for talent selection, and the other is about how Huawei learns from its competitors in the bidder's offer to find opportunities.

Case Study: Huawei's interview methodology and learning methods

Interviews are also an important source for Huawei to acquire knowledge. Huawei always interviews people of the same level from different companies. When doing the first interview, interviewers usually spend 10% of the time to ask questions, listen carefully to the responses, quickly absorb and obtain information, and thus gain basic knowledge and understanding of the new subject; during the process, the interviewers only interrupt occasionally. In the interview with the second person, based on the knowledge acquired from the first interview, interviewers usually spend 30% of the time asking more professional questions. In the interview with the third person, interviewers will ask more in-depth and specialized questions.

Huawei attaches great importance to communicating with top talent and improving the speed and efficiency of knowledge acquisition through the interview methodology. Every time Huawei hires talent, the company will provide training on interview techniques and summarize the experiences to improve comprehensive interviewing skills. During the interview, interviewers actually ask only three to five questions to judge the interviewee's response, ideas, abilities, and stability. At the same time, it will consciously compare with the strengths and weaknesses of competitive companies and products to quickly obtain valuable information. Huawei treats interviews as good learning opportunities. In the second round of interviews, it is possible for Huawei to communicate with the interviewee on an equal footing, because by then Huawei has a clearer understanding of their respective strengths and weaknesses. The knowledge accumulated in the interviews will later be summarized, and HR will translate this knowledge into training courses and materials in a compelling manner, including how to conduct an interview and make judgments.

Case Study: Researching competitors to get orders

Huawei and Ericsson bid against each other a lot. The technique Ericsson used for quotation was that the price of the product was set relatively low, but the equipment maintenance cost would increase year by year. For example, its maintenance cost was 100 million yuan in the first year, 300 million in the second, and 1 billion in the fifth. Initially, Huawei directly copied this quotation scheme, but customers were quite unhappy with the high maintenance costs. One customer questioned Huawei, "Why do you need 100 million yuan a year for maintenance? Does it mean that your product is shabby? Will the equipment still work in 3 years?"

In response to the customer's question, Huawei reanalyzed Ericsson's offer and concluded that its product offer was close to or even below its cost, and that its main source of revenue was from the maintenance fees. So, Huawei adjusted its quotation scheme to slightly increase the price of its products while greatly reducing maintenance costs, and even promised to repair the equipment for free in the third year. After adopting the new quotation, Huawei has won the trust of its customers while ensuring its profits.

Learning from leading international companies and customers

Huawei has a wide range of learning targets. This is especially evident in the company's start-up phase. Ren encourages his employees to learn from not only developed countries but also the best among themselves, especially learn from their professionalism and dedication. In the internal speeches, such as "A letter to new employees", "Revisit on refraining from complacence and no slack in the mind", "What to learn from the Americans?", "Training and selecting managers in practice", Ren has repeatedly asked the employees to learn from the down-to-earth style and responsibility of Japanese and Germans, and the innovative spirit of Americans.

Ren asks his employees to be open-minded and learn leading technologies and expertise from famous international companies. Well-known western companies such as IBM, Hay, Accenture, and Ericsson have all served as Huawei's teachers. In the early stage of development, Huawei learned a lot from its competitors including R&D operation and quotation strategies. A vice president of Huawei once shared an example of Huawei learning from Ericsson: Huawei spent hugely on R&D to follow Ericsson's R&D footsteps: from selling products to selling networks, and from selling solutions to turnkey projects, to make up for the shortcomings of its R&D capability and market experience.

Ren asks his employees to learn from domestic competitors too. Huawei's executives have repeatedly mentioned in interviews that Huawei respects ZTE and Lenovo a lot. ZTE has unique experience in internal management, incentive mechanism and follow-through strategy. Lenovo's transparent cost is also something worth learning. Lenovo is not a company that stands out due to its core technology; it focuses on production and sales, and has developed its unique core competencies.

Customers are also one of Huawei's most important sources of knowledge, because feedback from customers can not only provide suggestions for optimizing current products, but also insights into future development. Ren once said that customers are the reason for Huawei to survive, and they are the soul of Huawei. He asks all vice president-level staff in the R&D department to regularly meet customers several times a week, to remember the names and phone numbers of marketers and customers, and to integrate the value of "customer-centricity" into the process and system.

Around 2009, Huawei's development strategy shifted from a technology-centricity to a customer-centricity. Ren believes that it is important to fully consider the needs of users and user orientation. Huawei's product development and solution should be based on customer needs and continuous innovation. No matter for management or processes, blind innovation should be avoided; continuous improvement and optimization should be based on the existing conditions. Therefore, learning from users has also become a key focus at Huawei. In addition, Ren is good at capturing learning signals no matter how weak they appear from visits and news reports to shape the organization's management concept and planning. Table 9.1 summarizes the learning targets and contents involved in Ren's speeches from 1988 to 1997.

Table 9.1 Huawei's methods for learning from external sources

Learning target	Learning content	Ren's words in his speech/interview
Developed countries and outstanding employees	Professionalism and dedication	"Drop the illusion of quick success and learn from the down-to-earth Japanese and the meticulous Germans" ("A letter to new employees", 1994)
		"Learn from the meticulous and pragmatic work of Germans" ("Revisit on refraining from complacence and no slack in the mind", 1996)
		"We must learn from the loyalty of Japanese, and the meticulous and down-to-earth spirit of Germans." ("Training and selecting managers in practice", 1999)
		"I congratulate those who have been fighting on all fronts and working hard for this achievement. They are all examples of hard work. We need to learn from their down-to-earth ethics, determination and focus on R&D achievement" ("Revisit on refraining from complacence and no slack in the mind", 1996)
		"Heroes are around us every day, and we can all learn something from them." (speech "Don't forget the heroes", 1997)
Leading foreign companies	Advanced international management experience	"Huawei is not really comparable with famous international companies ... Huawei is young, bold and courageous. It has made a breakthrough in some technologies and earned the qualification to compete in the international market. However, in the face of the current situation of complex networks and multi-network integration, the young Huawei still needs to continuously learn from the international leaders, find out the gaps, accumulate experience, and work a hundred times harder." ("Revisit on refraining from complacence and no slack in the mind", 1996)
		"Now the company has to benchmark against the best in the industry in terms of product development and management, and we should not just emulate them, but surpass them eventually. For example, in the intelligent network business and some new businesses and new functions, our switches are already ahead of Siemens, but there is still a gap between us and Siemens in terms of product stability and reliability. Only by benchmarking with the industrial leaders, can we survive ...... It is imperative to learn attentively from the big names" ("How long can Huawei's flag stand", 1998)
		"In the ten years since Huawei was established, it has been following closely with all outstanding competitors and partners and gradually developed its product lines ...... All decent manufacturers are good examples to learn from ...... Huawei still has a huge gap in management with world-famous companies, and we must learn from Lucent, Ericsson, Nokia, Siemens, Alcatel and so on to keep narrowing the gap." (Progress in self-criticism—Ren's thank-you speech at the GSM appraisal meeting, 1998)

(continued)

Table 9.1 (continued)

Learning target	Learning content	Ren's words in his speech/interview
Domestic competitors	Industry and market experience	"Our competitors and partners, such as 04 Switchboard, Datang and ZTE have made visible progress. 04 has a larger market coverage, and stronger support from the central government; Datang has a foundation of 10 years of research as a national institute, and its research depth and breadth are exceptional, and has the support from ministries too. They have a deeper understanding of the telecom system than we do. ZTE is located in Shenzhen, just like us, and has a similar culture to ours. We should learn from ZTE's solid work. Huawei is good at hyping up, but not as effective as ZTE in doing the groundwork. ("Revisit on refraining from complacence and no slack in the mind", 1996)
		"While learning from our competitors, we must find ways to discover their strengths and weaknesses and identify what exactly we need to learn and how to learn it" (Staff interview notes, 2015)
Customer complaints and criticism	Product and service improvement direction	"The names of the VPs of R&D Department should be reported to the Customer Group Management Department, which submits the assessment of the VPs to the R&D Personnel Division. They have to meet with customers several times a week, and it is up to the Customer Group Management Department to decide the exact number. If we continue to communicate with customers and listen to them, we will understand them better. All the progress we have made is taught by our customers." (Ren's speech at Huawei's Research Committee meeting and the Q3 market meeting, 2014)
International news	Work Ethics	"Ren can often spot things to learn from various trips abroad and current events for him and Huawei" (Employee interview notes, 2015)

9.3 Organizational Learning and Knowledge Dissemination

Knowledge dissemination is a key step in transforming individual learning outcomes into knowledge assets at the organizational level. In the process of transforming external knowledge into internal knowledge of the organization, Huawei takes "rigidity, solidification, optimization, and innovation" as the principle; in the process of knowledge dissemination within the organization, Huawei values cross-departmental and informal knowledge dissemination, but for top-down knowledge dissemination, Huawei relies more on formal and standardized channels. Huawei pays special attention to learning from failures, and giving employees channels to air their grievances. Huawei is never afraid of exposing problems, and even believes that exposing problems is the only way to transform the enterprise and create knowledge that truly belongs to the enterprise.

Cross-department learning

In order to better optimize and create knowledge, Huawei has opened a series of cross-department and hierarchy-breaking knowledge dissemination channels, including cross-department communication and collaboration teams, *Huawei Voice Community*, democratic life meetings, and debriefing conferences. These channels are informal ways to air grievances of individuals, teams and the organization, to prevent inertia and path dependence in the organization, and to discover organizational diseases from acute conflicts, thus stimulating the vitality of the organization.

Cross-department communication and collaboration take various forms and play an important role in management reform, contract negotiation, market development, and talent recruitment. In the process of optimizing the IPD system, to establish seamless processes in the organization, Ren suggested using cross-department teams involving marketing, services, and R&D first, and production and procurement later to jointly rectify the process chokepoints and simplify procedures. The cross-department teams represent the company, have the right to make decisions and oversee all processes. However, these teams are mainly responsible for rationalizing the whole processes of product lines; they are not an additional management layer.

Cross-department teams are also organized to compete for market orders with the Strategic Management Department analyzing customer needs, the Marketing Department analyzing competitors and their strengths and proposing solutions, and the Business Department, IT Support Department and other relevant departments providing technical support. In response to customer needs, the Marketing Department has formed an iron triangle model, with an Account Responsibility (AR), a Solution Responsibility (SR), and a Fulfill Responsibility (FR), to take care of customer needs. The AR is responsible for listening to customer needs and maintaining customer relationships, the SR, for product and solution-related work, and the FR, for delivery-related work from financing and payment collection. The three work together, meet customers together, and share knowledge of customers, products and delivery, forming a flexible and integrated team with their respective strengths.

Huawei often organizes internal seminars to share, summarize and review experiences, some of which are jointly organized by a number of departments: the strategic department analyzes customer needs, the market department analyzes competitors, the solution department proposes solutions and plans, the commerce department proposes business solutions, the IT department proposes how to provide technical support, and so on. When the seminar is concluded, the joint requirements of different product lines and different departments have been sorted out. Based on the discussion and consultation, senior and major project sponsors will collaborate to advance the whole project.

Huawei Voice Community is an online forum that encourages employees to share their experiences and thoughts, and even offers rewards for some of the best work. Employees can post their articles either in real names or anonymously, criticize unreasonable processes and systems, air grievances, and expose organizational ills. Many organizations may choose not to make their internal BBS public, but Ren insists that Huawei Voice Community should remain open. Many people refer to it as a "transparent community", because non-Huawei employees although cannot post on their comments, can browse most of the content and learn about the imperfect but real Huawei. Since its inception on June 29, 2008, Huawei Voice Community has been visited by more than 98% of its Chinese employees. In fact, many organizational problems have been exposed here, which has served as a wake-up call for management.

One of the executives in the interview said, "When the company decided to make the community public, I was stressed out; so were many people. However, we eventually decided to make it public, and it remains public till today. I don't believe that we should keep the skeleton, if any, in the closet. As long as we seek the truth, even if we have done something wrong, why should we be afraid of making it known? We have recently removed a clause regarding maintaining the company's reputation from the Severance Agreement. Because we don't think a tainted reputation can be artificially maintained spotless unless we make it right. We should allow people to speak. In fact, the vast majority of employees will not distort the truth. After the launching of Huawei Voice Community, we are actually in a much better shape."

The democratic life meeting is a communication method that Ren borrowed from Mao Zedong's method of leading the Communist Party of China (CPC), which has been practiced in Huawei for 25 years. Its main purpose is to solve teamwork problems in a timely manner so as to avoid corrosion of team cohesion due to estrangement and misunderstanding. According to the recollections of senior employees, in the democratic life meetings in the early days, everyone, regardless of their positions, was asked to criticize themselves and one another frankly, and give solutions and suggestions where possible. Everyone expressed their views and problems were exposed, and then corrected courageously. If the problem was embarrassing, the person in question would be asked to leave the room. The issue would be discussed in the group, and after the meeting, the supervisor would convey the message privately to the person, and urge him/her to make it right. Participants in the meeting can point out any problems without being afraid of retaliation or personal grudges. Some seek help from team members by talking about their difficulties in life and work at the democratic life meeting, which in turn nurtures team camaraderie.

Huawei's senior management attends democratic life meetings every three months or six months. Self-discipline declarations, rectification meetings and integrity oaths in response to organizational ills such as related party transactions, deviation from customer-centric values are different forms of democratic life meetings. A vice president told us, "In the democratic life meeting, self-criticism should be 'strict' while criticism of others should be 'gentle and mild'. A tacit agreement seems to have reached in Huawei that at celebration meetings, one should always say that others are doing great while at criticism meetings, one should always first say where he/she is inadequate before they point fingers at others."

The debriefing conference and the strategy formulation process

A debriefing conference is an important form of organizational learning in Huawei. It incorporates elements of strategic decision making, strategy alignment, strategy implementation, self-criticism, organizational consensus building, organizational memory, cross-departmental collaboration, and self-healing capabilities. When the top management sets strategic goals for the following year, these goals are assigned to the heads of each region and major business segments worldwide. At the top management debriefing meetings, the person in charge of each strategic unit will first make a self-critique of the past year's development, and then give his or her opinion on the feasibility of the goals for the next year. If they believe that the goals are too high or the resources to achieve them are not enough, they can present their case at the debriefing conferences and the top management will adjust them as appropriate. Such discussions are extremely important for key management to understand the self-evaluation and strategic intent of each strategic unit. This process of bargaining and information exchange between the top and bottom management helps reach strategic consensus, and make the information known on key issues such as whether the strategy can be practically implemented and what are the difficulties in implementation. After the top management debriefing meeting, similar meetings will be held at the middle level, where tasks are further decomposed, information dissemination is further carried out, and feasibility issues are further clarified in the process. After that, the project leader will directly assign tasks at the next debriefing meetings, and the strategic goals are broken down to each team and person, and the strategy implementation process at the cognitive level is basically completed (see Fig. 9.1). The debriefing meeting is a formal channel for Huawei's middle and senior managers to disseminate knowledge to the decision-makers, with the main purpose of optimizing management processes and achieving results-oriented management. In many companies, debriefing is seen as an ordinary work report; however, in Huawei, debriefing is a powerful tool to energize the organization, combining the performance commitment system for middle and senior managers, the last-place elimination system, and the automatic salary reduction mechanism. In Huawei, debriefing meetings have a strong flavor of criticism and self-criticism. Many employees find the debriefing meeting uncomfortable. Even crueler is that Huawei enforces a 5% last-place elimination among managers. Ren pointed out that in Huawei no manager has a tenure. At the end of their term, managers, including senior managers, need to give debriefing reports to be reviewed by the organization and other employees; they also need to re-apply for the position with their compensation renegotiated and reset.

Improvement by facing problems head-on

Huawei constantly discloses its shortcomings, and mistakes in *Huawei People*, *Improvement* and various company documents and conferences. It is not afraid of self-criticism and revealing its shortcomings and problems. Many employees who take the lead to correct their mistakes grow quickly. Huawei encourages its employees to learn and improve through self-reflection. Huawei's internal newspapers, documents and conferences become institutionalized channels and knowledge bases for organizational learning. This mode of organizational learning turns individual knowledge into organizational knowledge and tacit knowledge into explicit knowledge, which is conducive to Huawei's organizational learning throughout the enterprise. In order to adapt to the development of the Internet, the editorial department of *Huawei People* and *Improvement* also launched a "Huawei Journal" App for internal users.

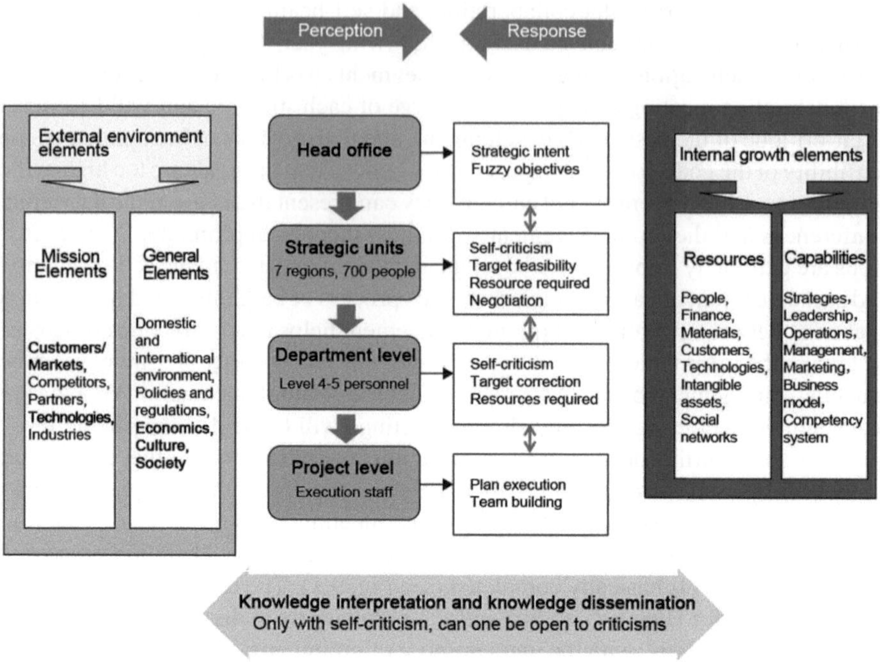

Fig. 9.1 Huawei's debriefing meetings and organizational learning

Improvement is dedicated to self-reflection, i.e., exposing the "ugly Huawei people" to help employees discover their shortcomings and reasons for failure, so they can better improve themselves and support future work. For example, when Tianjin Telecommunications Administration came to visit Huawei, they made some comments. All employees of CRD and IPD were organized to listen to the recording and write their reflections. The editors of *Improvement* compiled these reflections in a book entitled "Purgatory" to help R&D staff understand how to evolve from being responsible for research results to be responsible for products."[11]

With the rapid development of information technology, Huawei also moved online and began to use mobile channels to disseminate knowledge on top of the previous paper versions. The i-Learning platform developed by the in-house team plays an important role in the sharing and updating of knowledge within the company. i-Learning platform consists of learning zones for the market system, with special briefs, job standards, and audio learning materials.

Take the application of i-Learning in the marketing and sales system as an example. i-Learning platform designs separate learning zones for regional marketing managers, overseas high-caliber experts, and strategy and marketing qualification; it also has a "2010 Customer Strategy Pain Points Analysis Audiovisual Materials Zone". Through the learning zones, the i-Learning platform collects best practices

[11] Ren Zhengfei: "How long can Huawei's flag stand" at a seminar at Unicom headquarters. 1998.

and disseminates them to key personnel to improve the marketing capacities of the front offices, and to improve the overall marketing capacities of the company.

On top of building learning resources, i-learning also supports the dissemination of learning resources through various means. First, it integrates and publishes corporate strategies and marketing briefings and disseminates them to the whole organization. Second, it integrates position requirements into learning resources, so that employees can enhance their abilities and learn the corresponding knowledge. Based on optimized position requirements, learning resources are sorted out and categorized, so that employees can better recognize the gap in their abilities and learn from benchmarks and improve accordingly.

9.4 Openness and Diversity of Learning

Huawei's knowledge dissemination process determines the diversity and richness of knowledge interpretation, which brings both abundant materials for knowledge creation, and resistance to organizational collaboration. So how can we improve the efficiency of knowledge use and reach consensus at the team and organizational levels while maintaining knowledge diversity? Ren first proposed the idea of "openness, compromise and flexibility" at the 2009 Global Marketing Conference.

Openness

When an organization does not have adequate knowledge, it is important to learn external knowledge to quickly fill in the gaps and keep up with the changes of the times. As knowledge gradually accumulates, it is more important to maintain humility and openness with a thirsty to learn. In his speech "Openness, compromise and flexibility", Ren emphasized the importance of openness to learning, absorption and keeping up with the times." In fact, because Huawei has achieved a certain level of success, we are now becoming more and more confident, proud, and complacent, and are becoming more and more self-absorbed. We need to be open and learn more from others so that we can have fresher goals, we can truly examine ourselves, and have a sense of urgency."

When it comes to meeting customer needs, an open mind can avoid myopia and help truly practice customer-centric values. In 2008, in his article "What is happiness?", Ren said, "To better meet customer needs and build a century-long business, the platform must be open and innovation-oriented. A narrow-minded culture will not learn from the strengths of others, and there will be no way out. A narrow-minded organization is like a pool of stagnant water, and it will be stinky. In product development, we need be open to absorb the finest achievements of others, and we need to fully reuse the achievements of the company and other organizations."

Redundant Learning

Redundant learning, also known as multi-team learning in Huawei, is heavily influenced by Huawei's early horse-racing culture, or internal competition culture. The competition between teams and projects within Huawei is likened to horse racing. Ren has emphasized that the selection of business backbones in regional departments and expert teams in representative offices should be based on a horse racing mechanism. Multi-team learning, or redundant learning is to learn from different perspectives. Redundancy leads to a variety of different solutions and enhances multi-faceted thinking and exploration of problems. This "redundancy + competition" multi-team learning helps Huawei to achieve breakthroughs with a targeted focus. "5–6 teams may simultaneously study competitors, create a learning redundancy, but through the internal competition mechanism, the team's potential can be maximized and the best solutions can be identified."[12]

9.5 Formation and Accumulation of Organizational Memory

Organizational memory is the process of accumulating knowledge, solidifying experience, and creating culture. Ren has always been attaching great importance to summarizing experiences and lessons learned, hoping that all employees can summarize Huawei's values, ideas, and management principles in organizational learning from both successes and setbacks Huawei has achieved in the past 30 years. The purpose is to identify those key elements that can support Huawei's long-term success, as well as potential risks that may lead Huawei to failure. Through knowledge accumulation, Huawei expects its leadership successors to understand, learn, and pass on the company's management ideas to guide and help the company to sustain and achieve long-term stability. At the same time, open seminars within the company can help these management philosophies that guide Huawei's success achieve wide understanding and consensus within the company and with its partners.

The accumulation and value of organizational memory

Organizational learning can be traced back to the *Huawei Basic Law*, various internal newspapers and magazines, and the Huawei Voice Community. So, how does organizational learning turn into organizational knowledge and be used to guide the organization's development? Since day one, Huawei has been exploring and summarizing the training methods for employees, including new employees, and after Huawei joined the ranks of leading enterprises, it has increasingly been focusing on the training of professional teams and managers.

As early as 1994, Ren learned about the importance of training from an air crash accident. In 1998 when the *Huawei Basic Law* was published, the employee training system has taken shape. Subsequently, Huawei continued to invest hugely in training. The *Huawei Basic Law* clearly states that "In Huawei, the appreciation of human capital shall always be greater than that of financial capital." Even in the early days, Huawei has allocated huge resources for training. For the annual recruit of

[12] From the authors' interviews with Huawei employees.

3,000 employees, Huawei sets up a new employee training brigade, which is divided into several squadrons, with quite a few senior managers, including vice presidents, serving as squad leaders. In 2005, Huawei University was set up, aiming to be the Whampoa Military Academy in China's business community. It has launched more diversified and more professional training programs for a learning organization.

In 1997, Ren proudly mentioned in his speech that Huawei had a professional and standardized division of labor thanks to the introduction of advanced management systems and processes, and that the "lower level-focus" employee training initiative had brought a large number of technical and business experts to the company." QC and 5S systems were fully implemented in Huawei's manufacturing system in 1996; ISO 9000 and MRPII were pressed ahead toward just-in-time production. Huawei has also implemented Quality Statistical Process Control and the PDCA cycle for quality improvement. It has improved the Performance Measurement and Evaluation System for production workers, implemented the training for junior managers and workers, and made great efforts in doing solid work. Through competitions, a large number of technical and business experts have emerged, and a large number of production managers, who had no professional training before1996, have taken up modern management positions. They are the foundation of our business."[13]

In order to make the new employees, especially the freshly minted graduates, better integrate into the company, Huawei implements systematic training for them, such as development process training, basic programming training, business knowledge training, marketing knowledge training, and defense and assessment of the new recruits. After six months of systematic training, most of the new recruits are able to master the professional knowledge required for their respective positions, and more importantly, have developed a life-long learning and improvement habit.

Mentor System

In addition to business skills, Huawei also focuses on the morale of the new employee. It has established an effective mentor system to help new employees fit in the organization as soon as possible. Every new employee will be assigned a mentor to clear their doubts and solve problems at work and in life. For example, the mentor will introduce the living environment around the company and help them overcome difficulties they may encounter. During the three months before a new recruit becomes a formal employee, the mentor is responsible for the new employee's performance, and it will factor in the mentor's performance. In addition to the mentoring system, there is a team of senior experts in each department to provide advisory support for employees. Most of the team members are professors from prestigious universities, and some retired experts from R&D centers. They use their extensive work and life experience to give solid advice and consultation.

"We have established a mentoring system, which started with party members in CRD. The company is making it a rule that employees who have not served as mentors cannot be promoted to management posts, those who can no longer serve

[13] Ren Zhengfei: speech at a meeting of representatives of share-holding employees. May 2001.

as mentors shall not be promoted. The good system for training successors should be solidified."[14]

9.6 Construction and Development of Huawei University

Huawei University must be different from regular universities because our trainees have already received formal education. Huawei University is about on-the-job training. Huawei first needs to work hard and second to learn how. If you don't know how, simply working hard is not good enough.

— Ren Zhengfei

In 1996, Huawei's self-developed C&C08 switch was very popular in the market, and that year its contract sales reached 2.6 billion yuan (about 401 million USD), which marked the end of Huawei's start-up phase with agency sales as the main profit model, and Huawei officially entered the adjustment and development phase. However, with the rapid expansion of production scale and workforce, and the increasing number of managers, and the efficiency was not improving (the R&D efficiency of Huawei's engineers was only one-fifth of that of Cisco).

Huawei found that lack of professionalism was one of the main reasons for the gap between Huawei and leading international companies. Therefore, Huawei started internal training in 1997 and initially mainly provided training for new employees and customer management. At that time, the training system was not professional, and lacked an overall understanding of the training industry. It was not improved until 2000, when manager centers were established in each business unit. However, the silo management mode made it more difficult for vertical management and resources sharing, which drove further reform of the training system. In early 2003, the Huawei Training Center was established, with unified objectives, curriculums and teachers and its training capabilities reached the top of the ranks in China. In 2005, Huawei University was officially established to provide internal and external training. It offers joint programs with internationally renowned management schools and has become a first-class corporate university. Based on a sound qualification management system, employees have a clear understanding of abilities required for promotion, and the training has become more targeted. So, guided by qualification standards, with the support of the training system and focus on the development function, Huawei University has truly addressed the issue of employees' career development. Thus, Huawei put all six training centers under the Qualification Management Department, and later under Huawei University.

Huawei University is located in Shenzhen, covering a total area of 275,000 m^2. The campus is divided into the teaching area and the accommodation area. The teaching area covers 155,000 m^2 and has a floor area of over 90,000 m^2, and a green coverage of over 85%. The campus has nearly 9,000 m^2 of computer rooms, 100 plus

[14] Ren Zhengfei: "How long can Hawei's flag stand" at a seminar at Unicom headquarters. 1998.

classrooms, 500 plus cubicles, and can accommodate over 2,000 trainees. Huawei University has more than 300 full-time staff trainers and over 1,000 part-time trainers either located at its head office in Shenzhen or branches/representative offices in other parts of China or other countries.

Huawei university was explicitly positioned by Ren as an independently operating unit, a cradle of capable managers and a booster for Huawei's strategic development. Huawei University aims to train professional managers and develop international leadership with the managerial wisdom of East and West and Huawei's corporate practical experience.

The missions and organization of Huawei University

Huawei training focuses on cultivating innovation-minded technical talent and international management talent, serving both external customers and Huawei employees. The following are the four missions of Huawei University:

(1) To become the base for manager training and a booster for the globalization strategy of the company.
(2) To build a unified corporate culture and code of conduct, as well as shared values, forming coherence, and maintaining Huawei's overall image and competitive edge.
(3) To improve employees' capacity and business skills, promote employees' professional development, attract and cultivate talent, and support the company's business development and human capital appreciation.
(4) To introduce advanced management concepts in line with the company's sustainable development strategy and promote corporate change and internal management progress.

Based on the above four missions, Huawei University's system is set up to support the human resources strategy. For example, the university president/executive vice president is a member of the company's Human Resources (HR) Committee, participating in the company's HR strategic planning; the university president concurrently serves as the vice director of the HR Department of the company, the department director concurrently serves the vice president of the university; the head of the internal training management department of the university sits in the regular meetings of the HR Department, is assessed both by Huawei University and the HR Department. The annual training performance assessment of heads of business units is conducted by the university and the business department's satisfaction rate of the university services also factors in the annual performance assessment for university leaders. The setting of major positions at Huawei University is closely aligned with Huawei's HR strategy, and most positions are subject to dual assessment to ensure that the university stays on track to cultivating talent with practical skills. The university also has strict requirements for and controls on the output results. Its organizational structure is shown in Fig. 9.2.

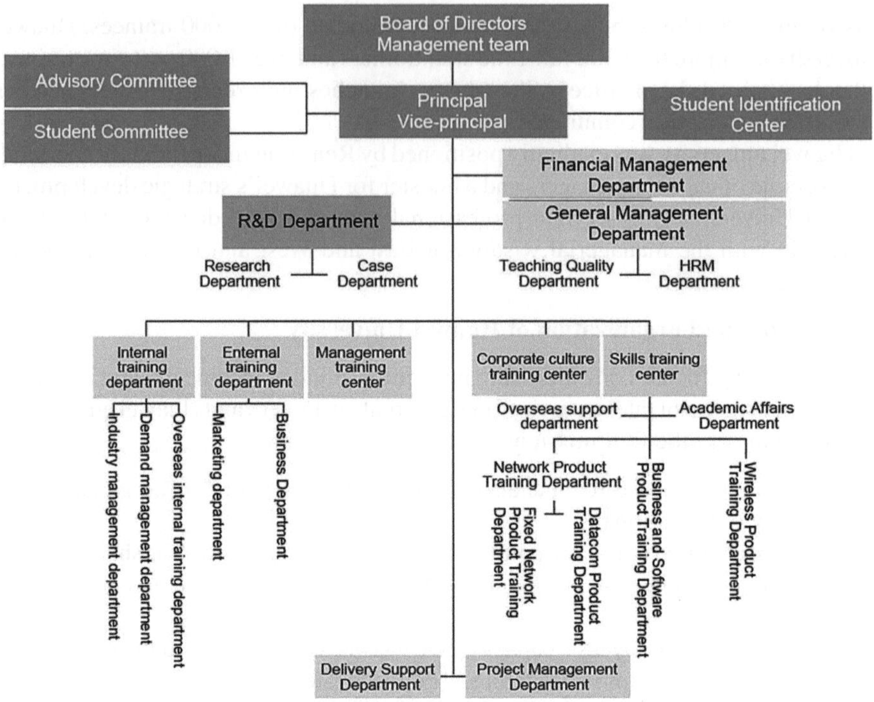

Fig. 9.2 The organization of Huawei University

The operation mode and training system of Huawei University

Huawei University serves both internal and external customers as a training service provider. After internal or external customer puts forward its training needs, it will prepare a targeted training curriculum, and implement the training plan. Meanwhile, Huawei University has a good course database, and the sources are twofold. First, Huawei has an annual budget for the introduction of external resources, i.e., proven, and effective courses in the market. After the courses are bought, they will be adapted by in-house trainers, incorporated in the database and used for training. Secondly, the company continuously delivers business and management cases to the university by extracting key events, interviewing key people, and inviting executives or outstanding performers to share their experiences. In this way, with professional training tools, the practical experience can be translated into training courses. Under this operational mode (see Fig. 9.3), its training courses have been continuously polished and become even more pragmatic.

The training by Huawei University must meet the company's requirements to improve the trainees' competence, and even the internal training planning must be based on the needs of employees, so that the training can be integrated with the business as much as possible. After years of research and practice, Huawei University

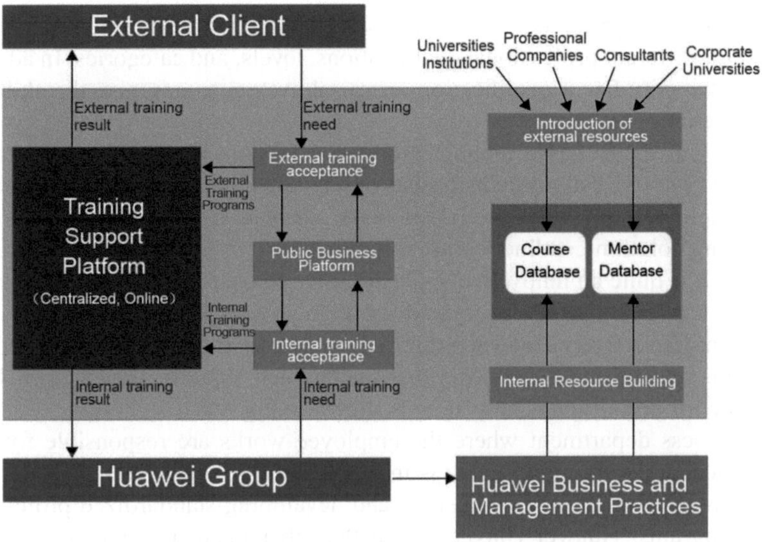

Fig. 9.3 The operation mode of Huawei University

has developed a professional competence model and based on the model it has established a series of courses and training programs. Built on this, Huawei also provides training courses to external customers with diverse training models (see Fig. 9.4).

Huawei University provides orientation training courses for Huawei's new employees on-the-job training for all employees as well as customized training for external customers. The orientation training can take one to six months based on the jobs and positions, covering various aspects such as corporate culture, product knowledge, marketing skills and product development standards. On-the-job training

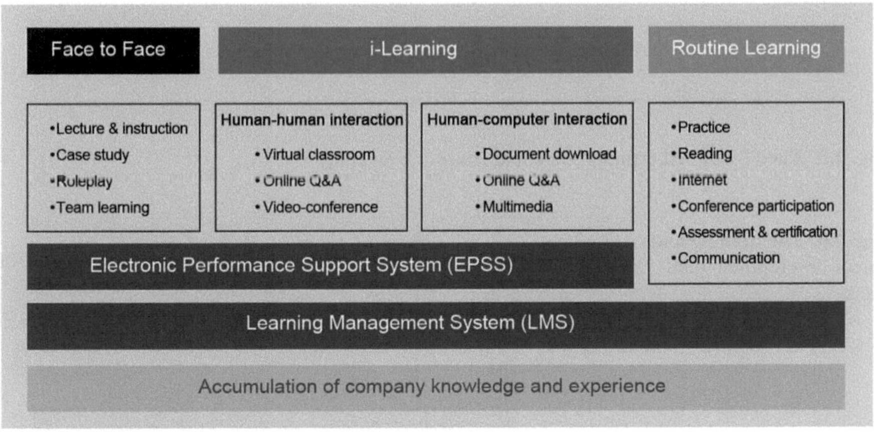

Fig. 9.4 Diverse training models of Huawei University

includes both managerial and technical aspects, and different training programs are designed for different professional qualifications, levels, and categories. In addition, Huawei University has a qualification appraisal system to appraise the skills and abilities of employees.

Huawei University has a unique information system in its employee training system (see Fig. 9.5). This system consists of separate modules, each for one trainee, allowing them to complete a series of tasks, such as training demand formulation, learning solutions, online learning, training system management and training evaluation. It is quite an innovative application-based training system in China.

Huawei University's training system is aligned with Huawei's internal career development track. Every Huawei employee needs to participate in training courses or programs as well as assessments that match each stage of their career. It is a prerequisite for promotion. The system is shown in Fig. 9.6.

The business department where the employee works are responsible for business/technical skills training, which is more of an on-the-job training model, with the business department assessing skills and developing standardized professional training programs. Huawei University, on the other hand, is responsible for the management and general skills training, leadership training, and other training programs to help employees use effective management tools to help the organization create business value more efficiently (see Fig. 9.7).

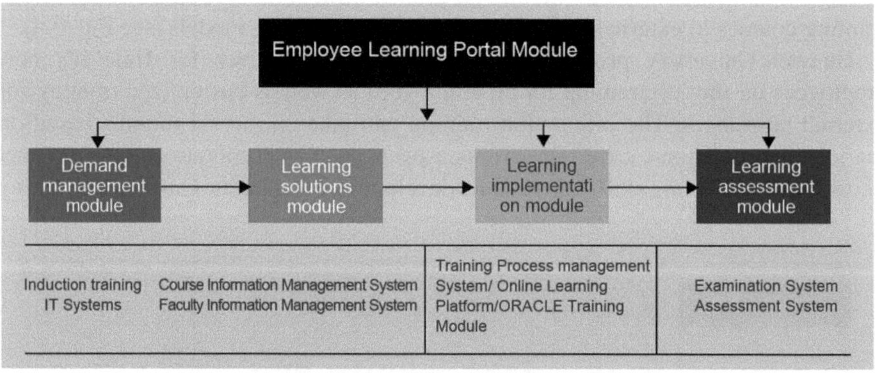

Fig. 9.5 The IT-enabled training system at Huawei University

Fig. 9.6 The training and career development dual track

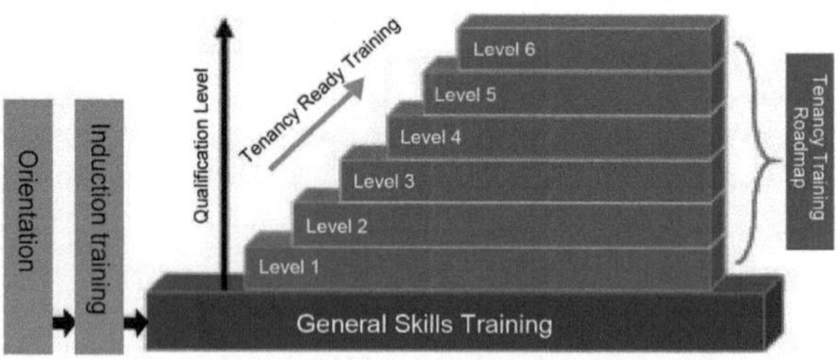

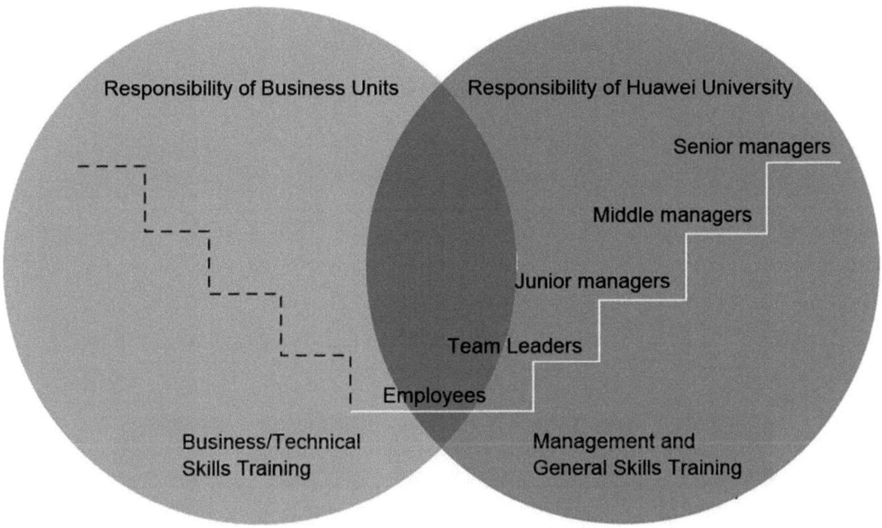

Fig. 9.7 The division of responsibilities of training and career development dual track

Huawei University's training approach emphasizes the combination of training and practice. According to Ren, training should be as real as practice. All the forms, codes and identifiers used in the training should be exactly the same as the real ones. Ren also asked Huawei University to simplify the empowerment when designing training courses, use actual tasks for the course scenarios, so that participating employees can truly understand the principles behind.

The training and examinations are all centered on the sandbox. For example, in Germany, Huawei set up a training team to ensure consistency of inventory accounts and goods, LTC, and other comprehensive management. Some staff responsible for organizational change in the representative office also joined the training and they brought the real-life "sandbox". Emphasis is placed on proceeding from reality and finding solutions in the training and then applying the solutions to work scenarios.

Huawei does not hold many exams in the company, because it believes that exams will waste time for real work. But Huawei University organizes quite a few exams, at least three times a week, so as to constantly help trainees to consolidate their knowledge and skills acquired in the training, and make the trainees recognize the problems they encounter. Before the training is concluded, each trainee is required to know their sandboxes from the inside out. When they graduate, they will bring their sandboxes back and modify them in practice, and finally output the results.

Huawei University faculty system

Huawei University's trainers are mainly in-house from the following three channels: managers at all levels, professional and technical backbones, and some employees who are interested in training (see Fig. 9.8). The first two channels are the main sources of the trainers: they have rich knowledge and coaching experience; they can

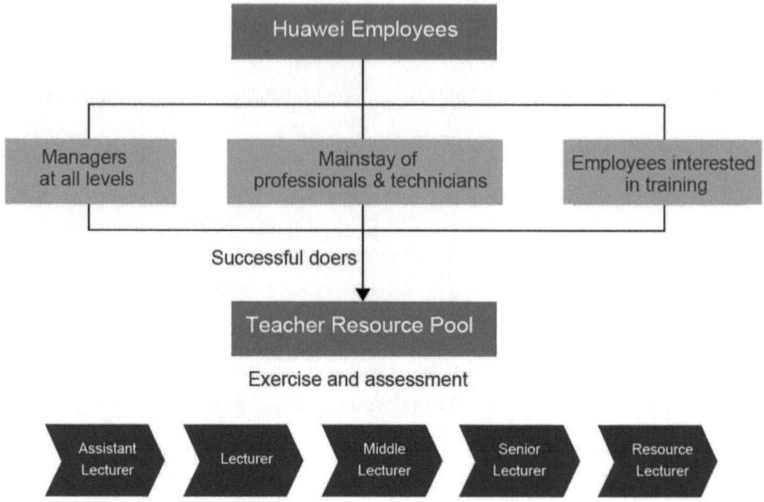

Fig. 9.8 Huawei University faculty system

both teach and consult, especially in software maturity certification, performance improvement, Six Sigma and quality management. Their experience comes from their years of management and technical experience in Huawei. Their advantage is that they know both technology and management, and they are themselves the doers. Some consultants are multi-talented, with expertise in teaching, practice, and research. They have been academic leaders and project leaders, and many of them are still holding senior positions in different fields.

Selection mechanism

The trainees of Huawei University are either selected or accepted upon paying the tuition out of their own pockets. The purpose is to stimulate employees' willingness to learn and cultivate their awareness of self-development and self-responsibility.

Unlike other training systems which usually involve passive learning, the selection system requires the trainees to learn proactively. It only selects outstanding employees who have met the company's screening standards. In Huawei, excellent learning resources and growth opportunities are not for everyone. The selection system is not designed to merely save resources, but rather to stimulate the intrinsic drive of employees to learn so that resources can be effectively allocated to the 20% promising employees. "One difference between us and Western companies is that we will not be kind to the laggards; the mercy you show to laggards is a blow to the go-getters."[15]

The voluntary paid training system is another stimulation of enthusiasm for learning. It requires Huawei University to provide truly valuable educational services. In the words of Ren, Huawei University should use various methods, both monetary

[15] Ren Zhengfei: minutes of the meeting with staff from Institute of Education of Huawei University, 2013.

and non-monetary incentives to revitalize education methods, spice up professional education and create a new education model.

9.7 Evolution of Organizational Learning

Since its establishment in 1988, Huawei has gone through three stages of development: "technology-centric", "management-centric" and "customer-centric". From 1988 to 1997, Huawei was technology-centric, and its organizational learning only stayed at the strategic level, focusing on establishing awareness, creating a learning atmosphere, and encouraging independent learning. From 1998 to 2007, Huawei was management-centric. In addition to strategic learning, it added business learning. Especially by introducing a series of advanced western management systems such as the IPD system, the qualification system, and the financial management system, Huawei has improved its business capabilities, formulated a set of standardized, professional, and transparent business learning methods, and institutionalized business learning. From 2008 till today, Huawei has been customer-centered, focusing on how to balance strategic learning and business learning in the organization, harmonizing the contradictions and conflicts between the two. The evolution of Huawei's organizational learning is shown in Fig. 9.9.

Phase 1: the budding organizational learning concept

The period from 1988 to 1997 was the start-up phase of Huawei. Huawei's strategy at this phase focused on R&D and market development. Judging from the leaders' understanding of organizational learning and Huawei's learning behavior, at this phase Huawei's learning objects were diversified and broad in content. The form

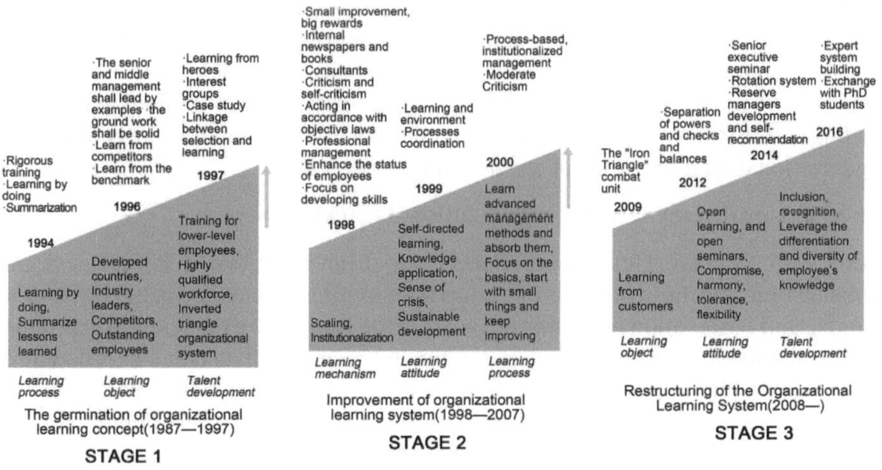

Fig. 9.9 The evolution of Huawei's organizational learning

of learning is mainly independent learning. Through learning, Huawei accumulated fragmented and unsystematic operational and practical knowledge, completed the accumulation of primitive capital, and survived in the fierce market competition. At the same time, in the process of learning from customers, developed countries, multinationals, and domestic competitors, Huawei constantly discovered its gap and developed a strong desire for change. It was at this stage that based on its strategic learning methods, Huawei questioned its existing management processes, and established a belief in continuous optimization and progressive learning. The perception and vision of leaders, as well as role models for knowledge sharing are essential.

Huawei adopted many organizational learning methods at this phase, demonstrating its eagerness to survive. These methods include learning by benchmarking, summarizing lessons learned, encouraging independent learning, and exploring and refining oneself in practice. Ren stressed that Huawei's team was too young. They were daring but lacked international experience. "Look at the world leaders and examine ourselves. We still need to work a hundred times harder." Therefore, the drive for learning was very strong.

However, while the organization was enthusiastic to learn, it lacked systematic methods, and some learning methods remained at the conceptual stage, difficult to achieve practical results. For example, on the one hand, Ren emphasized the hierarchy of training, which should be tough and rigorous, and the linkage between learning and promotion; on the other hand, he also proposed to allow people with similar interests to voluntarily form learning study groups. It clearly shows a conceptual conflict, but the organization did not discuss how to combine the two concepts in practice. Ren himself acknowledged that the company was "crossing the river by feeling the stones" at this stage. In addition, hierarchy poses some constraints on employee empowerment. The hierarchy is reflected in the different learning methods and goals between senior managers and junior staff. For example, Ren proposed that "the senior and middle management shall lead by examples, and the groundwork shall be solid". The slogan emphasizes that junior employees should work hard, learn basic skills, constantly think about how to improve their work; while the senior managers should focus more on public relations, marketing and management. Hierarchy is also reflected in the way that employees participate in training, newspaper reading and other learning activities. The methods and processes of Huawei's budding organizational learning concept are shown in Table 9.2.

Phase 2: Improvement of the organizational learning system

From 1998 to 2008, Huawei experienced rapid development of its business and globalization, and during this period, it has built its internal management system. The struggle and observation in the first ten years made Ren realize that the gap in product quality and the market experience was ultimately a gap in management. Therefore, in the second phase, Huawei's organizational learning is management-centered. At this phase, Ren still advocated learning from developed countries, famous foreign companies, and domestic competitors, but the learning was more focused on the management systems and tools. At this phase, Huawei took IBM's IPD System as an entry point and pilot project, and used the management experience of leading

Table 9.2 The methods and processes of Huawei's budding organizational learning concept are shown in

Method	Source
Staff training shall be organized by level and be tough and rigorous	"The Importance of Employee Training Reflected from Two Air Crashes", 1994
Learning by doing, summarizing with theory	"A Letter to New Employees", 1994
The senior and middle management shall lead by examples, and the groundwork shall be solid	"Revisit on refraining from complacence and no slack in the mind" at the Top Ten Outstanding Employee Recognition Ceremony, 1996
Learn from competitors and internationally renowned companies	"Revisit on refraining from complacence and no slack in the mind" at the Top Ten Outstanding Employee Recognition Ceremony, 1996
Learning from heroes (outstanding employees of the company) Interests-based learning groups are encouraged, and organizational learning is not mandatory	"Don't forget the heroes" at a briefing of the market front, 1997
Case Study Learning is linked to the talent selection system	"On Study", 1997

international consulting firms to change the management of R&D, HR, and finance in the company. As a result of the changes in the external environment, significant adjustments in corporate strategy and changes in the leader's style, organizational learning became institutionalized and systematically improved, and restrictions on employees' thinking were reduced.

Compared with phase one, Huawei's learning behavior in phase two is characterized by three features. First, Huawei gradually formed a learning system that combines internal knowledge development and utilization with external knowledge introduction and absorption, and the way of learning is more process-oriented and explicit. For example, Ren encouraged employees to publish articles in internal journals such as *Improvement* and *Huawei People*, express their views in Huawei Voice Community, and write self-reflection reports in democratic life meetings. Secondly, the organizational culture also began to focus on regularity and sound strategy rather than pure passion and struggle. "Small improvements, big rewards" is a learning strategy that emphasizes robust institutionalization. By encouraging employees to make suggestions for small improvements through learning, it emphasizes the need for steady, continuous progress. The reading of internal newspapers and books was also institutionalized as a mechanism for knowledge building and utilization. Knowledge production and application have been facilitated by combining a forward learning stream from practice to system and a feedback learning stream from system to practice. Third, unlike organizational learning that focuses on strategic learning in the initial phase, Huawei conducted both strategic and operational learning in this phase. At the cognitive level, organizational learning is reflected in continuous self-reflection and arming oneself with mature management ideas; at the practical level, it is reflected in continuous improvement of process standardization, transparency, and controllability, emphasizing "continuous optimization". Ren began to have more dialectical thinking on strategic learning. He encourages Huawei people to think things through and criticizes over-ambitious reforms. At the business learning level, Huawei has created more organizational mechanisms and a better environment conducive to knowledge manifestation.

The main challenge Huawei encountered during this phase was how to integrate the introduced management processes with the existing practices and make the two compatible. The new management and process system is still quite strict under the principle of "rigidity, optimization, solidification and innovation". "New employees need to learn the corporate culture behind closed doors for two weeks to achieve a unified understanding". The mechanism of spreading ideas from level to level is also more obvious. The method of criticism and self-criticism is sometimes too strict, even causing some employees' mental problems and sometimes even leading to extreme behaviors. The methods and processes of improving Huawei's organizational learning system are shown in Table 9.3.

Phase 3: Restructuring of the Organizational Learning System

From 2008 to 2017, Huawei reinitiated the change in organizational learning, with the goal of building a future-oriented open learning system. Over the past 20 years, Huawei had implemented a high degree of centralization in management, which resulted in a variety of problems, such as bloated organization, inefficiency, and increased customer complaints. Senior management, including Ren, recognized that the future success of Huawei depended on the organization's capacity and dynamism, as well as the company's ability to improve the business ecosystem. Such strategic positioning guided the further evolution of Huawei's organizational learning. In this phase, Huawei's development strategy is shifting from technology-centric to customer-centric, and the company is evolving from centralization to decentralization with checks and balances, inclusiveness, democracy, coordination, and sustainability, with more focus on global benefits, balanced capabilities and sustainability. Through global process integration, the back office is turned into a supporting force for the system. To get rid of the inefficiency and bloated organization and build a customer demand-driven and process-oriented organization, power is delegated, exercised, and supervised along the process.

Guided by the principles of "openness, compromise and flexibility", the company's learning behavior is reflected in the following three aspects: First, Huawei has initiated a restructuring of its learning organization, changing it from a strict, centralized hierarchy to a more flexible, flatter, and inverted triangle structure. Second, a decentralized check-and-balance design was adopted to enhance the interconnection and checks between departments while retaining departmental division of responsibilities and independence. The "Iron Triangle", CEO rotation system, and cross-departmental teams are all manifestations of this mechanism. Third, the company attaches more importance to suggestions from employees, and systematically integrates the diverse intellectual capital of employees through benefit sharing.

Table 9.3 The methods and processes of improving Huawei's organizational learning system

Method	Source
Small improvement, big rewards Study internal newspapers and read books Spread ideas level by level in employee training Hire management consultants to improve the learning organization	Ren Zhengfei: "Cultivating and selecting managers with field experience" at the Second Quality Management Report and Award Ceremony, 1998
Criticism and self-criticism Leaders listen to criticisms from staff, top-down study Digest and assimilate knowledge after learning the introduced methods and integrate them	Ren Zhengfei: "Don't be a flash-in-the-pan hero", 1998
Sustainable development, professional management	Ren Zhengfei: "Shifting from the realm of necessity to the realm of freedom", 1998
Lower level-focused, professional training	Ren Zhengfei: "Small Improvement, Big Rewards" at the Quality Control Circle (QCC) Results Report and Award Ceremony, 1998
Mentoring system	Ren Zhengfei: "How long can Huawei's flag stand", 1998
Learning and progress should be better coordinated with the environment and processes	Ren Zhengfei: "Professionals are the valuable assets of our enterprise", 1999
Establish a process ownership system, implement a committee system at the top, and transform exception management into routine management through monitoring and control	Ren Zhengfei: "The responsibility and mission of a professional manager", 2000
Moderate criticism	Ren Zhengfei: "Why we need self-criticism" Ren's speech at the research department meeting when he "rewarded" overstock and dead stock to backbone researchers, 2000

Huawei has introduced initiatives such as the self-nomination system, exceptional promotion, and Huawei University to motivate knowledgeable employees, enhance the diversity, differentiation, and dynamism of the organizational structure, so that the organization can respond more quickly to environmental changes. The methods and processes of Huawei's organizational learning system reorganization are shown in Table 9.4.

9.8 Huawei Versus Cisco

Both Huawei and Cisco are fast learners. During my study at Cisco, I repeatedly heard its senior executive talk about the importance of rapid learning, and its senior managers also repeatedly talked about the importance of learning from young people.

Table 9.4 The methods and processes of reorganization of Huawei's learning system

Method	Source
The "Iron Triangle" combat unit	Ren Zhengfei: "Let people who can hear the shots call shots" at the awarding conference of Huawei's sales and service system, 2009
Separation of powers and checks and balances in the learning organizations	Ren Zhengfei: "Openness, compromise and flexibility" at the Global Market Working Conference, 2010
Benefit Sharing Senior management seminar Rotating CEO system Streamlining the administrative process of the learning organization, with practical work as the focus Training and self-nomination of the reserve team	Ren Zhengfei: "The river flows eastward in spring", 2011 Ren Zhengfei: "Success is not a reliable guide to future development", 2011
Expert system development	Ren Zhengfei: "Don't expand blindly; don't think you're already strong" at the market work conference", 2012
Debriefing conference	Ren Zhengfei: "The responsibility and mission of a professional manager", 2000
Diversified training (skills, management methods, management ideas, grassroots training, performance appraisal and training, senior training)	Ren's speech at the Symposium for Huawei University and Party Leaders, 2006

We need to look at the value of the future with the futuristic vision. In order to understand the ideas of young people, Cisco even invited twenty young employees to participate in the board meeting many times to share their ideas.

Huawei's willingness and drive to learn are even stronger than Cisco and works even harder. As a catch-up enterprise, benchmarking with the world's top enterprises is the only way to narrow the gap in a short period of time. In 2015, when I received a group of senior managers from Ericsson, I talked about Huawei's learning ability, which is a factor often neglected. The Western media often attribute Huawei's success to external factors.

Huawei's learning is motivated by a variety of factors: a strong sense of crisis, a clear understanding of its shortcomings, rational analysis, the enormous pressure to achieve short-term and long-term goals, the ESOP-boosted development momentum and the organizational atmosphere that does not dare to slacken in the slightest. In an environment turbocharged with opportunities and challenges, slackness even in thinking is destructive and could be fatal. When people around you are sharing learning experiences, a person who has no one to share is very lonely. In the interview, some Huawei people talked on and on. Some could talk about Huawei stories for eight straight hours and could still go on. I was amazed by the energy and knowledge that a good company can give to its employees.

Huawei people are fast learners because organizational learning continuously breaks path dependency, overcomes organizational inertia, and maintains a balance between radical and incremental innovation. In the process of knowledge acquisition, Huawei learns from extensive sources, including from failed experiences, and constantly engages in self-directed learning which allows for the enhancement of personal vision and capabilities. It makes an extra effort to learn from leading enterprises and renowned consulting firms and benchmark against the most advanced knowledge system to enable the company to quickly grasp the operating methods of the international leaders and narrow the gap. In addition to the competitive pressure of the industry, the reasons that Huawei succeeds also include its strategic vision, its passion, its determination to be a first-class enterprise, as well as the alignment between personal goals and organizational goals. Every employee understands that the only way to catch up is through rapid learning and growth. This atmosphere motivates every employee to learn.

Huawei is a good learner. First of all, the leaders' strategic thinking is effectively disseminated and implemented in the senior management team and the entire organization. The top leader's instructions can reach the bottom of the enterprise, which demonstrates a strong execution capacity. In this process, the highest decision-makers make their thinking and requirements in the form of documents (such as speeches, and the *Huawei Basic Law*) and publicly disseminate within the organization, which helps reduce speculation and ambiguity, and improves the consensus on the company's goals. Second, the debriefing conferences at all levels discuss and decompose the company's strategy, which reinforces the information and deepens employees' understanding of the issues. Finally, various sharing mechanisms such as Huawei's information platform, Huawei Voice Community, and informal study groups have created redundant learning that helps employees understand the company's strategic intent and ideas from multiple dimensions.

Huawei is an extensive learner, because Ren is good at reflecting and summarizing failed cases in the industry, knowing that a strategic investment mistake may cost hugely, and that a wrong idea will lead to a wrong direction. Therefore, Huawei needs to draw on a wide range of knowledge and nutrition from all over the world, including from Chinese history. Huawei needs to constantly remind itself to avoid taking detours and making mistakes. In other words, Huawei's sources of learning are very extensive. Chinese history, international cases, industry failures, observations and inspirations from overseas visits, and problems discovered by employees can all serve as constant alerts and reminders. Only a humble and prudent enterprise can truly learn and see the revelations and wake-up calls; only the company that is good at self-criticism and self-denial can maintain true humility and try its best to draw and absorb the wisdom of all mankind, thus avoiding the arrogance that usually quietly grows after one succeeds; the arrogance will block the spark of ideas, hurt the momentum, and impede the rapid pace forward.

Chapter 10
Human Resource Development System to Unlock Potential

The most challenging issues for a team leader include how to improve employees' sense of belonging, loyalty and dedication and avoid slackness. To address these issues, the company must be attractive to ambitious talent, especially young talent and be cohesive so that employees are willing to invest their emotional and intellectual input in the process of accomplishing the organization's vision and mission. Therefore, the company must have a good reputation and its values must resonate with the young talent; meanwhile it must meet young people's diversified needs and provide a platform for them to fulfill themselves. To achieve this, the company's strategy, culture, business development and incentive mechanism need to meet a high bar. With more and more "post-90s" joining the workforce, how to fully motivate them gives many executives a headache. In this chapter, we focus on Huawei's practices in the following three areas.

First, how does Huawei continuously train talent and managerial candidates? Huawei people are courageous, passionate, and hardworking. How to cultivate such talent? How do Huawei's values and culture fit with talent development? What innovative initiatives are used to retain key managers?

Second, what are Huawei's criteria and methods for selecting and assessing managers? The process of manager selection truly reflects the corporate culture. Only by rewarding dedicated employees can encourage more to be dedicated. Which organizations have inspired Huawei in the selection and use of people? Does Huawei have any unique criteria? What is Huawei's mechanism for talent selection? What key qualities and characters are especially valued? How to make the process fair, transparent and standardized, so that employees are convinced and can solely focus on business development and core corporate goals without being distracted?

Third, how to fully stimulate the potential of employees and their fighting spirit? In order to grow and expand, Huawei, as a technology follower, has overcome all kinds of difficulties and obstacles through tenacious struggle in the highly competitive market environment. In this process, how did Huawei build a team of passion and vigor, a team that can bear hardships, dare to challenge, and is full of strength and wisdom? What incentives did Huawei offer on the spiritual and material levels? What

X. Dong et al., *Huawei*,
https://doi.org/10.1007/978-981-19-4078-1_10

kind of organizational atmosphere has been created so that employees who are eager to succeed work hard and grow into the backbone of the company? We draw special attention to the management and motivation of the "post-80s" and "post-90s", an issue that many companies find particularly challenging.

10.1 Organizational Talent System

As Huawei was increasingly international, Ren cited the example of Israel to illustrate the importance of bringing in external professionals. He pointed out that the largest wealth transfer after World War II was the immigration of three million Jews from Poland and the former Soviet Union to Israel. He hoped that hundreds of thousands of talented people would join Huawei's team. He opened up management positions and introduced foreign experts to work with Huawei's outstanding young people in the same teams, especially the following professionals.

Senior experts

These experts use their expertise to lead the organization to improve and take responsibility for decision-making in their respective fields of expertise. They also serve as coaches and help the new generation grow with their guidance, education, training, evaluation and supervision.

Senior management

Decisiveness is critical for executives, as strategic mistakes can endanger the survival of the company. Executives do not need to be overly technically savvy, but they need to find the right direction, have clear business goals and have the ability to think strategically.[1] Senior managers should inspire all employees with their passion and belief.[2] The more difficult it is, the more passion the senior management must demonstrate. They must take the initiative to inspire the team to win, and lead the team to victory.[3] The job of the first-in-command is alignment, deployment and customer engagement. Alignment refers to building organizations. Deployment refers to effectively resolving issues in manager selection, appointment, appraisal, incentives, and replacement. Customer engagement means fully understanding the needs of both internal and external customers.

Ren once commented: "The health of most members of Huawei's leadership was undermined, but they have become tougher through a thousand times of refinement, and their management has also become more mature. This is a team that does not seek personal gains, a team that leads by example, a team that is economically clean

[1] Ren Zhengfei: remarks at Huawei Shanghai Research Center in 2007.

[2] Ren Zhengfei: "We must inspire all employees with passion and belief". 2002.

[3] Ren Zhengfei: "Understanding laws of nature, giving play to the core team, continuously improving the per capita benefits, and working together to overcome difficulties" at the Q3 marketing meeting. 2002.

and politically untainted, a team that is courageous to criticize others and themselves, a team with a self-restraint mechanism, a team that is far-sighted and not afraid of hardship, a team that adheres to the socialist principle of "from each according to his ability and to each according to his contribution" and cares for the interests of employees. Therefore, this team is qualified to lead the company and can lead the company to success."[4] These well-tested managers study hard and have a strong sense of self-renewal; they form the basic platform of Huawei's management and are the powerful leaders of Huawei towards success.

Mid-level managers

The most important quality for mid-level managers is the ability to comprehend, as they are responsible for conveying the strategy from the top and execute it on the ground. They are doers. Their primary responsibility is to lead their teams to conquer the market. They should not only focus on a specific business, but also team management: training the team and helping it grow.[5] Managers need to be strict as well as caring, and help their team members grow, so that everyone is on the same page.[6] Mid-level managers also have to develop the comprehensive business ability, and flexible response to complex business scenarios.

Junior managers

The most important quality for junior managers is the execution ability, because if execution is not in place, all strategies are nothing but a mirage. Huawei expects its junior managers and employees to love what they do and excel in their respective field. In Huawei, the transfer of positions is strictly controlled, and the application must be strictly reviewed before approval. Ren told new employees that Huawei would never promote a person without any groundwork experience to the management position. As a new employee, you must first be nobody. Do your job well, then, you may be somebody. Practice is the basis for improvement."[7]

Secretaries and operators

Secretaries and operators do not require a high rate of elimination and mobility, and do not have an age limit, but there are restrictions on wages. A team of secretaries has been built to reduce the overall cost of the company. Secretaries take on a lot of transactional and repetitive work to reduce the workload on managers and ensure that their energy and time are spent on more important things. If the R&D personnel and senior managers have to mop the floor and bind documents by themselves, it will undoubtedly slow down their work and hurt the efficiency. A good secretary needs to have a good understanding of people and take the initiative to reduce the workload of R&D personnel and senior managers. If the workload is too much, you

---

[4] Ren Zhengfei: "Huawei people refuse to fail", at Huawei's annual meeting. December 26, 1995.

[5] Huawei EMT Resolution No. [2006] 016.

[6] Ren Zhengfei: "Customer Centricity and Dedication" at the Mid-Year General Meeting of the Marketing Department. 2008.

[7] Ren Zhengfei: "A letter to new employees" (Revised Version). 2015.

can add another secretary, or two till the workload is reasonable. This way the overall productivity is enhanced.[8]

Huawei never discriminates against female employees, who account for about 25% of the company's total workforce. Female employees enjoy the same pensions and have equal treatment as male employees. Many companies are reluctant to hire females because they think females are inefficient, and some of them like to gossip, thus disrupting unity. Huawei sees female employees as a lubricant to the management. Ren said that female employees should know that it is not managers or male employees, but themselves, who can uplift them. If secretaries want to have better salaries, they have to learn more; self-improvement is essential. Secretaries are not necessarily always secretaries. Some have extensive knowledge, are quite capable, and even more convincing than professionals. Huawei encourages excellent secretaries to work in the front office, and the representative office, to increase their understanding of the market, to be tested by the market, and to strengthen their market awareness. It will be conducive to the company's development.

10.2 The Value of the Rotating CEO System

The emergence of the Rotating CEO system

In 2002, Huawei experienced the first negative growth in its history. At that time, the dot-com bubble just burst and the global telecom market was very gloomy. The domestic market share of Huawei's leading products exceeded 30%, and the 2G wireless market was dominated by international giants such as Ericsson and Nokia, so Huawei encountered the ceiling of growth. At that time, Huawei adopted a highly centralized management model, and Ren was basically the only one who made the major strategic and operational decisions. However, with Huawei's increasing international expansion and global market share, its strategy became less and less visible, and it became increasingly more difficult to solely rely on Ren's personal ability to judge and predict. In order to avoid risks, Huawei created the Executive Management Team (EMT) in 2004 as a collective decision-making mechanism, and the eight members rotated to serve as the chair, each for six months. After two cycles, at the end of 2011, Huawei started a Rotating CEO system under the board of directors, with three rotating Chairmen serving for six months each. Ren said that the Rotating CEO focused more on the company's strategy and system building, and the authority of daily operation decisions is further delegated to BGs and regional companies to promote rational expansion. Each rotating CEO will try their best to drive the company forward during the rotation. If some Chairman goes off course, the next Chairman will correct it in time to avoid accumulating too many problems without solutions. In Ren's view, the Rotating CEO system is about empowering a group of smart people to make decisions within certain boundaries.

[8] Ren Zhengfei: a speech at the meeting with secretaries. February 22, 1997.

Guo Ping joined Huawei in 1988 and has served as R&D Project Manager, General Manager of Supply Chain, Director of Huawei Executive Office, Chief Legal Officer, President of the Business Process & IT Management Dept, President of the Corporate Development Dept, Chairman and President of Huawei Device, and Chairman of the Finance Committee. Currently, Mr. Guo serves as Deputy Chairman of the Board and Rotating CEO of Huawei.

Hu Houkun joined Huawei in 1990 and has served as President of the Marketing & Sales Dept in China, President of the Latin America Region, President of the Global Sales Dept, Chief Sales & Service Officer, Chief Strategy & Marketing Officer, Chairman of the Global Cyber Security and User Privacy Protection Committee (GSPC), Chairman of the BOD of Huawei USA, Deputy Chairman of the Board, and Chairman of the Human Resource Committee. Currently, Mr. Hu serves as Deputy Chairman of the Board and Rotating CEO of Huawei.

Xu Zhijun joined Huawei in 1993 and has served as President of the Wireless Network Product Line, Chief Strategy & Marketing Officer, Chief Products & Solutions Officer, Chairman of the Investment Review Board, Rotating CEO of Huawei, and Chairman of the SDC. Currently, Mr. Xu serves as Deputy Chairman of the Board and Rotating CEO of Huawei.

Responsibilities of the Rotating CEO

The four main responsibilities of the Rotating CEO are as follows:

First, evaluation. It directly affects the organization's strategic focus, resource allocation and incentive mechanism, as well as the investment in R&D and the recognition of IPRs; therefore, it directly affects the development direction of the whole enterprise. Second, business ecology. The cultivation and development of the business ecosystem are related to the security and sustainability of the long-term development; it is a matter of overall layout. Huawei requires the middle and senior management to focus on project management and business, while the rotating CEO must focus on the construction and optimization of the business ecology. Third, technology development. The ICT industry is technology-intensive, with frequent radical technological innovations, meanwhile incremental innovations are also important. So, the top management needs to anticipate and evaluate new technologies to avoid technological miscalculations or missing development opportunities due to strategic blind spots. Fourth, streamline management. As Huawei's scale grows and the number of employees increases, the problems of a bloated organization are inevitable. Therefore, how to streamline the organizational system and operation mechanism is the departure of the management innovation.[9]

Cultivating top leaders

The Rotating CEO system establishes a dynamic balance in the leadership team: the team members agree to disagree, making it adaptive to changes in the environment. As the decisions are made collectively, it can avoid rigidity brought about by individual stubbornness and uncertainties brought about by unexpected risks.

[9] Ren Zhengfei: "the Regional Joint Committee is an important organization". July 19, 2013.

In most companies, the burden of corporate decision-making is often placed on one person, who must manage the company day-to-day, be sharp-minded, never lose direction or make any mistakes, meanwhile he/she should be able to build cohesion in the team. This concentration of power is risky; the one who leads to success often leads to failure too. In order to live up to the expectations of shareholders, the chairman usually has a tunnel vision for quarterly and annual business results and has little time to learn new knowledge. They spend a lot of time handling various affairs, without time for self-reflection. Unless they are supermen, it would be difficult for them to keep their companies stay ahead. With the Rotating CEO system, the ability of the management team can be enhanced, inter-departmental communication costs reduced, cross-departmental coordination improved, and prospect senior leaders cultivated.

Ensuring policy consistency

Democratic decision-making can make up for the deficiency of one person. The Rotating CEO System allows the Chairman to fully understand the status and operation of the company under the leadership of his predecessor, reducing the systemic changes and attrition caused by the change of leadership, and ensuring the continuity and consistency of management. At the same time, the retired Chairman does not leave the core leadership entirely, which avoids reshuffling in the company and enables outstanding employees to continue working under a different chairman. Meanwhile, the company must answer to investors and the board of directors, so it will not develop blindly.

10.3 Cultivate Talent with Practice-Based Training

The experience of many companies proves that "airborne troops" can be good, but how to make the right proportion and how to use the airborne talent are critical issues. In Ren's view, the scale of "airborne troops" should not be too large, and the integration of the airborne troops depends on the existing capability of the company. At the end of the 1990s, Huawei was a developing company, so its ability to absorb the "airborne troops" was weak. At that time, a few PhDs from Harvard University tried to introduce some practices to Huawei, only to find that it was so difficult for the company to adapt, and their talent and experience were wasted. If they had been forced to take charge, the entire chain of command may have become a mess. In this particular period, Huawei made a clear policy: "backbone managers at the turn of the century must come from Huawei, and they will be cultivated according to the company's system and policies.[10]

---

[10] Ren Zhengfei: "Cultivating and selecting managers with field experience" at the Second Quality Management Report and Award Ceremony. 1998.

Fig. 10.1 Huawei University executive training outline

"A cradle of generals"

An important mission of Huawei University is to make it a "cradle of generals". By "generals", it refers to the backbone of the enterprise's management at all levels. Huawei University selects a group of outstanding managers for training. They study cases instead of theories so that these "home-grown soldiers" can drive tanks and cruisers, so to speak. The cases are either from Huawei or other real-life sources; all trainers have practical experience. All the forms, codes and identifiers used in the training should be exactly the same as the real ones.[11] To ensure the direction of Huawei University, Huawei set up a steering committee, with Ren as the chair and three rotating Chairmen as members; the committee meets once every six months. The university also has an administrative organization. The sales and service systems of Regional Joint Committees (RJCs) represent the demand; Huawei University is the supply, which is managed according to the talent demand of RJCs. Ren stressed that Huawei University must be different from regular universities, because our trainees have already received formal education. Huawei University is about on-the-job training to empower trainees to fight.

A pool of managerial candidates

Huawei has created a strategic pool of managerial candidates to continuously identify and use talent, and to meet the needs of the company's functional systems, service support system and business processes; simply put, the pool is built to meet the company's development needs. The executive training outline developed by Huawei University shown in Fig. 10.1, includes three parts: HR management, financial management and business management, and the training methods include self-study of theories, group discussion, case presentation, major issue discussion, thematic exchange, debate, executive-led exchange, and thesis defense. The participants come from different positions and regions, and the diversified background increased the richness of information. The training method was designed to encourage everyone to share their experience as much as possible, and because the training topics are practice-based, the participation and enthusiasm of trainees are very high.

[11] Ren Zhengfei: a speech at Party leaders meeting at Huawei University. 2006.

The pool of managerial candidates adopts a combination of training and practice. During the process, everyone has a fair chance to achieve progress through practice, transformation and tests. After the training, those who still cannot keep up with the development of the company will be eliminated, and those who can be promoted. The best talent is thus selected through rounds of screening. Major Generals, Lieutenant Colonels and Privates are selected, and these people will be air-dropped to the front lines. The Private and the Admiral will fight side by side, and the Private may become the Admiral's assistant, and their ability can be improved in the field. This is how knowledge is passed on, and this is mentoring. The pool can accelerate the selection of people with practical experience and comprehensive capabilities to the front line, so that employees can grow from "screws" to "engines". The candidates learn by doing; during the process an obscure teacher can grow into a famous professor, and a private can be promoted to a general."[12]

The pool is like a constantly shaking sieve: people are either promoted or eliminated; there is no other outcome. Getting into the system is relatively easy, but to graduate is not. You can apply to it by yourself or be recommended by the management team. However, to get in you must pass the review on certain key conditions. Once you get in, you will go through more difficult challenges and be subject to more stringent inspection and discipline. This is the training process. This is an open system. If you are eliminated at a certain point, after improving yourself, you can re-enter the system. However, you will have to face the possibility of being eliminated again. So, the university is a melting pot rather than a safe; only those who have passed the most stringent tests can take the management positions.

The following are the sources for the strategic reserve team. First, top 25% of the best employees. Second, layoffs due to risks in the host country. Third, laid-off talents due to structural reform.[13] Huawei also clearly stipulates that three types of people cannot be part of the pool, i.e., the last-place eliminated employees, employees during the probationary period and hourly employees. Ren believes: "While attracting high-caliber talent from outside, we should pay more attention to the growth of our own managers and experts. Tolerate their shortcomings. Give full play to those who have made great contributions. We should accept flawed perfection. Flawless perfection is a delusion."

Huawei implements dynamic management of the pool. Once a vacancy arises, candidates can compete for the position and the winner will receive induction training. Those who fail can stay in the pool for the next opportunities. At the same time, an elimination system has been established. The following three types of candidates will be eliminated, namely those who have failed two examinations during the training, those who have failed to compete for the vacancy during the training (up to six months) and those who have failed the probationary assessment after reinstatement.

[12] Ren Zhengfei: "Be the first to know that spring is coming and the last to leave the post" at the "Marching—Honing—Winning the Future" R&D Conference. October 28, 2016.

[13] Ren Zhengfei: speech at the debriefing of the team-building of the pool of managerial candidates. August 15, 2016.

10.4 The Qualities of Managers

Integrity is the most valued quality in selecting managers at Huawei. In Ren's view, "We need to avoid a one-sided understanding of meritocracy. Meritocracy should not be based on technical skills but rather on virtues."[14] It is managers of great character that lead Huawei to forge ahead in difficult times. They will not let success go to their head, and stay focused on strategic businesses even in a complex environment. They stay open-minded and continue to grow in a rapidly changing environment. To sum up, Huawei's requirements for managers involve the following three aspects: on the spiritual level, a sense of mission, dedication and sacrifice; on the cognitive level, a broad mind, global vision and structured thinking; and on the behavioral level, pragmatism, self-discipline, self-reflection and balanced management ability.

Sense of Mission

What is a sense of mission? With a sense of mission, we work out of passion regardless of the payment.[15] Huawei's managers certainly have a sense of mission, that is why they can maintain a lasting enthusiasm and are highly responsible. A manager with a sense of mission will actively create vitality for the organization, much like cells that produce blood for the body. By attempting every means of achieving a goal, managers produce the vitality that is the lifeblood of a vigorous company.[16] People with a sense of mission are self-motivated and inspirational. In adversity, the sense of mission supports them to lead the team to success without ever giving up, no matter how slim the chance seems to be. In good times, the sense of mission can support them to lead the team to continuously challenge themselves and strive for excellence, instead of being complacent with what they have and giving up the opportunity for greater success.

Dedication

Do you take your job seriously? Have you tried every means to improve? Will you continue to improve? If your answers to the above questions are all positive, you are dedicated. Only with a high degree of commitment and dedication can one see through a myriad of things, find opportunities for improvement and achieve development. In Ren's speeches, he mentioned the importance of dedication nearly 30 times. He visited many factories in different countries, and he was impressed by the dedication he saw, not just the dedication of individuals, but also the dedication of the leadership. People without drive cannot make their way to the top, and senior managers without dedication will certainly be repositioned. In Huawei, to become a senior manager, you need to be dedicated. Hard work alone does not make a good manager.[17]

---

[14] From the minutes of Huawei's president's office meeting in 1997.

[15] Ren Zhengfei: "A simple interpretations of 'three principles for success" in 2010.

[16] Ren Zhengfei: "It's not always easy to enjoy the shade under a big tree" at a seminar on management. 1999.

[17] Ren Zhengfei: "Building the Intermediate Pilot Department as a sieve". 1996.

The success of Huawei today is not the story of one dedicated individual, but the stories of selfless leadership and teams with an unyielding spirit. We will not compromise on dedication. Those who are not dedicated and those who play it safe will be dismissed. This is necessary to ensure the company's long-term stability.[18]

A spirit of sacrifice

A spirit of sacrifice is a very important factor in manager assessment. Huawei believes: "The evaluation system cannot ensure absolute fairness. If managers haggle over minor details, they are not good managers. Employees without a spirit of sacrifice shall not be promoted to managerial positions."[19] "Managers should have a firm will and a spirit of sacrifice, which means one is ready to compromise when necessary."[20] In Huawei, managers should not be complacent with personal achievement; anyone who has not shown social responsibility cannot be a senior manager or a middle manager. A dedicated manager will be understanding even if they feel wronged. Huawei requires departments at all levels to be as fair and just as possible, but also requires managers to be understanding even if they are demoted or their wages are cut. Managers should treat themselves properly, but also can bear with it even if they feel wronged. The business is bound to fail, if it does not have such managers. Huawei requires the management and leadership to have a spirit of sacrifice, not ordinary employees, who shall receive reasonable compensation for their work. Dedicated employees will be cultivated and promoted to managerial positions. The more senior the position, the tougher the requirements.[21]

Broad-mindedness

Probably no one will admit that he or she is not broad-minded, but in fact not everyone is. To be selfish is human, and broad-mindedness is an acquired quality. To be broad-minded means one can see the bigger picture: they can seek common ground, while putting aside small differences, and deal with different opinions and even conflicts tolerantly. Being tolerant does not mean one is not principled. In fact, a broad-minded person should be principled, otherwise they will be confused, and narrow-minded. For those who we don't like or who don't like us, we should know what their strengths are. For those who we like, we should know their shortcomings. Only a broad-minded manager can unite people and put their strengths to good use. Huawei also requires managers to cultivate successors who can surpass themselves, which is seemingly a mission impossible. However, this is how Huawei can sustain itself. Without predecessors paving the way, there will be no successors to speak of, not to mention the lasting prosperity of the business. Everyone must be open-minded and embrace Huawei's culture. For the survival and development of the enterprise, it is

[18] Ren Zhengfei: "CFO should be process-oriented and professional". 2009.

[19] Ren Zhengfei: "Guidance on HR Management Change". 2005.

[20] Ren Zhengfei: "Customer focus, increasing platform investment, open to cooperation, & achieve win–win results" at the PSST Managers' Meeting. August 2010.

[21] Ren Zhengfei: "Huawei's winter", *Huawei People*. 2001.

important to be philosophical about the change of one's rankings. Only those who can bend and stretch will have great success.

Global vision

Huawei's managers should have the foresight and the ability to navigate the business ecosystem, as well as insights into the global market landscape.[22] The rapid globalization of Huawei makes it necessary to update the company's philosophy and managerial skills, managers need to face the unknown with a more open and positive mind. Prospect managers are expected to have a deep understanding of the markets and a broad knowledge base.[23]

We cannot simply rely on resources in China to become a global industry leader. Instead, we must leverage capabilities and resources from all over the world to become a leader.[24] We need to learn from Western companies and follow the global pattern closely.[25] Team leaders with an open mind can see both the forest and the trees, but managers with a narrow mind are likely to ignore strategic opportunities, or lead the team to do the wrong thing even if the methods are right; local victory may cause difficulty at the global level, and ultimately to failure.

The integrity, talent, and aggressiveness of managers

Ren requires that senior managers of Huawei have integrity, talent, and prestige (see Fig. 10.2). Integrity refers to the quality of being honest and morally upright, seeing the big picture, keeping the strategy in mind and not playing politics. Talent refers to sharp intuition, foresight, tact, and affinity. Talent starts from the endowment, and is strengthened through learning from books and others including peers. Aggressiveness shows self-confidence, determination, willpower, and a special charm that brings security to the team. Only spineless leaders always compromise, and over-aggressive leaders are usually not confident. The central role of senior managers in the organization is to guide their teams, especially in the midst of endless darkness. Huawei requires that senior managers have a sense of mission: only those who have a long-term goal can aim beyond fame and fortune. Middle managers shall have a sense of urgency: they should never slack off, otherwise opportunities will be missed. Junior managers shall have a sense of hunger. The hunger for success, growth, and wealth is the main motivation for young employees to work hard. Different positions have different requirements for the leaders: senior managers should have visionary insight, and be capable of seeing the whole picture like high-flying eagles; strategy executors should be decisive and capable of leading a strong team like fierce tigers; marketing and sales personnel should be sensitive and tenacious like predatory wolves; risk managers should be loyal to their duties like watchdogs.

---

[22] Ren Zhengfei: a speech at the share-holding employee representative meeting on March 30, 2013.

[23] Ren Zhengfei: a speech at the Farewell Meeting for R&D Staff and Managers Sent to Field Offices in May 2001.

[24] Ren Zhengfei: a speech at the Workshop on the Business Environment in Europe in 2012.

[25] Ren Zhengfei: a speech at EMT Meeting Minutes in 2013.

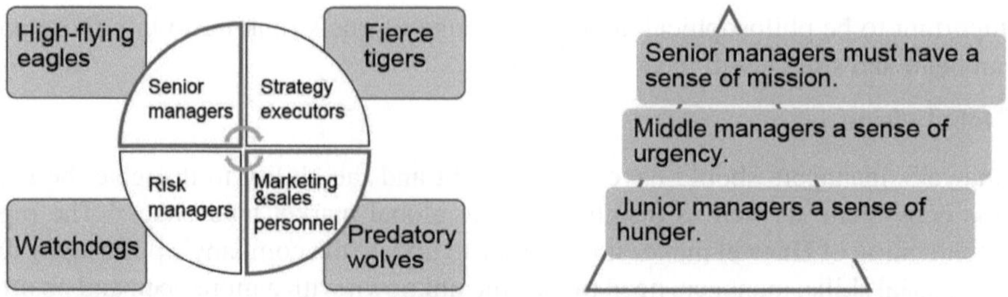

The central role of senior managers in the organization is to guide their teams, especially in the midst of endless darkness.		
Integrity	Talent	Aggressiveness
Integrity refers to the quality of being honest and morally upright, seeing the big picture, keeping the strategy in mind but not playing politics.	Talent refers to sharp intuition, foresight, tact, and affinity. Talent starts from the endowment, and is strengthened through learning from books, or others including peers.	Aggressiveness shows self-confidence, determination, willpower, and a special charm that brings security to the team. Only spineless leaders always compromise, and over-aggressive leaders are usually not confident.

Fig. 10.2 Different requirements for different position leaders at Huawei

Structured thinking

Managers with structured thinking can clearly see the essence of the problem and grasp the focus of work. The managers should not just focus on the "short stave" to solve immediate problems. Instead, they should have the ability to establish mechanisms, prevent problems and improve management efficiency, so as to be proactive rather than reactive. Structured thinking comes from learning and sharing. Learning is an important means to improve management. Only when the managers are good learners themselves can they cultivate learning organizations and only learning organizations are adaptive to the highly uncertain business environment. There are many ways to learn. Books can inspire us to solve problems, but just like "replay" is the best way for chess players to improve, every success and failure (including their own and competitors') are the best learning cases, so we must learn to summarize from the real cases. People have memory, but the organization does not automatically have memory. In the current situation where new managers are promoted quickly and the training system cannot keep up with the needs of organizational expansion, how to take effective measures to ensure the dissemination and sharing of individual experience in the organization is an issue that every team leader needs to take seriously. It is very important to summarize cases, but cases alone are not enough. A system needs to be established to ensure that the experience and lessons contained in the cases are effectively replicated in the organization, which will directly affect the efficiency of HR and the entire organization.[26] The author is impressed by Huawei people for their passion for learning, especially by the self-driven outstanding managers. In addition

[26] Ren Zhengfei: "What kind of managers do we need". 1997.

to reading, Huawei people always actively engage in open discussions on a very wide range of topics.[27]

Truthfulness

In Ren Zhengfei's speeches, he mentioned over 100 times that managers should always seek truth from facts and dare to tell the truth. They should never cover-up, reporting good news and bad. They must be even-handed with their subordinates; they must have the courage to call out problems with the company and with their supervisors. Huawei values managers with different opinions, because it believes that they are well-intended. They put the interests of the company before their personal interests, and take responsibility. Yes-Sayers are not good managers.[28] As long as managers are in management positions, they should show no favoritism. Rather, they must adhere to the company's principles, and completely implement the value assessment system while putting personal feelings aside and keeping the company's interests at heart.[29]

Self-discipline

Huawei requires its managers to be the first to endure hardship and the last to enjoy relaxation and comfort, just like a general must be the first to charge forward and the last to withdraw. Managers must place strict requirements on themselves and set a good example for their subordinates.[30] All managers must be clean and honest, and take work seriously. Not only should they be strict with themselves, but also with their subordinates. Only when the team is a good team, can we say the team leader is a good leader. Huawei persistently requires its middle and senior managers to adhere to principles, and oppose corruption, waste, theft, cronyism and attaining private ends by abusing public position.

Self-reflection

Huawei promotes managers who dare to speak the truth, are self-critical, and listen to others' criticism. Generals grow from self-reflection. Soldiers will never become generals if they don't know where they've gone wrong. If they know when, where, and how they made mistakes, they will learn valuable lessons.[31] Self-refection is essential to developing a good character and an open mind, which in turn makes it possible to tolerate all that must be tolerated.[32] Self-reflection helps managers refresh their

---

[27] Ren Zhengfei: "Catch up with the dragon spaceship with the spirit of the tortoise". December 30, 2013.

[28] Ren Zhengfei: a speech at the Huawei Corporate Committee's Management Law Review. 1997.

[29] The minutes of Huawei's president's office meeting. 1998.

[30] Ren Zhengfei: "Changing the assessment mechanism for managers to adapt to the difficult industry transformation". 2006.

[31] Ren Zhengfei: "Soldiers will never become generals if they don't know where they've gone wrong". 2007.

[32] Ren Zhengfei: "Famous battles do not automatically produce generals, but all generals were once heroes". 2006.

thinking and open their minds so they can endure criticism from others.[33] Ren once said, "Without self-reflection, Huawei would not go this far. Without self-reflection, we would not have listened to our customers so attentively or understood their needs so well. We also would not have noticed the merits of our peers or learned from them. In short, we would have become egocentric, and would not have survived in this volatile and competitive market. without self-reflection, we would not have been able to introspect, motivate ourselves, and boost team morale in the face of crisis. Without self-reflection, we would have isolated ourselves from the outside world, ignored our weakness as an inexperienced local company, and missed out on the new ideas that have been essential for us to become a world-class company. Without self-reflection, we would have been blinded by pride in our achievements and easily fallen into the abyss. Without self-reflection, we would not have streamlined our organization or processes, improved our management system, or reduced our operating costs. Without self-reflection, our managers would not have spoken the truth, listen to critical voices, studied the best ideas, or made progress. As a result, they would not have formulated and implemented the right decisions. In other words, only people that reflect on themselves can be truly open-minded, and only companies that reflect on themselves will have a bright future. Self-reflection has helped us get where we are. How far can we go depends on our ability to maintain our tradition of self-refection.[34]

Balanced development of management capabilities

Huawei's development has created a very good opportunity for managers to continuously improve themselves; however, many managers are good at "fire fighting" but not at "fire prevention" so to speak. They have courage and experience but lack a systematic method. At present, most of Huawei's managers used to be business backbones, and it is not uncommon that they tend to be business-oriented and ignore management; therefore, there is an urgent need to improve their comprehensive management capabilities. The increasingly complex business environment requires managers at all levels to be professional and have systematic knowledge and skills including financial, HR, operation, so as to continuously improve the quality and efficiency of organizational management.

10.5 Selecting Managers

Huawei's management system is the locomotive of the company. The transparency and fairness of the selection criteria allow all employees to focus on their work rather than on office politics, which helps truly outstanding people stand out and are willing to stay in Huawei.

---

[33] Ren Zhengfei: a speech at the Communication Meeting with the Steering Committee on Self-Reflection. 2006.

[34] Ren Zhengfei: "Anyone who climbed out the pit of setbacks is a saint". 2008.

Selecting managers from those with successful field experience

Huawei does not focus on developing managers. Instead, it selects outstanding employees for managerial positions and demotes incompetent ones. Unlike many companies that adopt the process of "select–nurture–use–retain", Huawei's process is "select–use–nurture–retain". The difference in sequence reflects the different understanding of what makes a good manager. The former believes the key is to nurture, but Huawei thinks the key is practice. Huawei insists on selecting managers from among those who have successful field experience. As a Chinese saying goes, "a valiant general always starts as a soldier, just as a prime minister from a local official".[35] All those who do not have successful field experience will not be appointed as managers or promoted.[36] Why Huawei values field experience? Because no matter how small a project is, they can succeed because they have developed their own methodology and they are able to put their knowledge into practice. After they are trained, they can improve further and contribute more to the company as they are skilled at self-reflection.[37] Without successful field experience, they will not know which issue is the most important for their success. They work hard but go nowhere and incur high costs. But people with successful field experience will be able to identify and focus on the most important issue and know how to address it to ensure success with the best efficiency and lowest costs.[38]

Huawei spares no effort to cultivate the selected managers. Personalized development plans will be formulated for supervisors and experts at all positions to help them grow rapidly, which include coaching from the following five aspects: challenges, key experience assessment, key competency assessment, career development interests, and study plans. This selection mechanism provides a constant stream of managers for Huawei's development and organizational vitality. The success recipe for Huawei's long-standing success is dedicated employees who are always available at any time and on any occasion.

Huawei encourages employees to learn by doing and make progress by learning, and it selects managers from field offices. Ren said, "Knowledge acquisition is a process of preparing for work, and this process is something employees should take care of and invest in on their own.". Huawei only selects people who meet the requirements of the position. To acquire the required skills, managers must learn and pay the tuition out of their own pocket. Huawei only selects and cultivates people who have successful field experience.

Fast-track promotion

Huawei dares to fast-track outstanding managers and young managers, because it believes that this is the way to win them over and retain outstanding talents. We should choose department heads that have obvious strengths and are capable of leading

[35] Ren Zhengfei: The New Year Message. 2010.

[36] Ren Zhengfei: "Building a professional financial team with strong morality, responsibility, and principle". 2006.

[37] Ren Zhengfei: "Guidelines for Human Resources Management Transformation", 2005.

[38] Ren Zhengfei: Speech at the EMT ST Meeting. July 27, 2012.

teams. People with obvious strengths also tend to have obvious weaknesses, which may prevent them from becoming competent managers. We should not expect people to be perfect. We should focus on our employees' strengths rather than weaknesses.[39] But if a person has moral or ethical problems, we will not promote them no matter how capable they are.

Fast-track promotion is applicable to the following five groups:

1. Employees who have achieved outstanding performance over a long period and are role models for employees at the same job level;
2. Employees who take the initiative to work long-term in hardship regions or take challenging positions, and make outstanding contributions;
3. Key employees who assume great responsibilities and produce outstanding performance in key projects, competition projects, or corporate transformation projects;
4. Managers who are bold enough to undertake risks and meet challenges head-on in new business areas and achieve outstanding results;
5. Managers and key employees who assume responsibilities at critical moments, overcome difficulties, and achieve complete or nearly complete turnarounds in operations or management.[40]

Walk the walk versus talk the talk

Huawei believes that manager development is mainly about being down to earth. We will tamp our management team like you tamp the earth: driving out the airy parts and leaving a solid foundation for development.[41] Managers at all levels should not only learn how to be a decent person, but also learn how to do things right in a down-to-earth manner. Those who only talk the talk, or just do some window dressing work, and those who only have theoretical knowledge of management but do not get their hands dirty, shall never be promoted or assigned with important responsibilities. We shall promote those who walk the walk and do a good job in a down-to-earth manner.

Ren used to explain his "Lotus Theory" when Huawei was a small company with only several employees. Hard workers are like the lotus roots that maintain a strong grip deep in the ground. By taking nourishment from these roots, lotus leaves and flowers have the strength to sway in the air. Like these leaves and flowers, our senior managers lead the way forward; like the roots, our dedicated employees remain down to earth and get things done. At Huawei, there must be more doers than big talkers.[42] He believes that senior managers can talk the talk to some extent, but the middle and junior managers should get things done. The key to the success of an enterprise lies in low-centered management; managers at all levels and all the employees should be down to earth, as talk is cheap. Groundwork involves three levels. First, management.

[39] EMT Meeting Minutes No. [2007] 025.

[40] EMT Meeting Minutes No. [2012] 034.

[41] Ren Zhengfei: "Focusing on a down-to-earth approach to seize opportunities for development", 1998.

[42] Ren Zhengfei: Speech at the CEO's Staff Team Meeting, July 24, 1996.

Without excellent management, it would be difficult to stay ahead of competitors; only a solid internal management system can support the expansion of the company. Therefore, solid management is the foundation of corporate development. Second, the HQ support system, rendering strong support to the field offices.[43] Third, financing.

Only very few senior managers mainly do the talk; all lower-level managers must walk the walk and get things done. The four main responsibilities of those who talk the talk are as follows: clarifying the objectives, formulating measures, assessing and selecting managers, and supervision. The doers should implement the strategies, mobilize resources, and assess and grade managers, turning human resources into material wealth. Everyone is welcome to join the talk and express their opinions freely and these opinions will be summarized later. The whole process will follow the democratic decision-making principle. The doers will implement the authoritative management system of the department head meeting.

Indicators and methods of selecting managers

Manager's selection is based on three key indicators: integrity, values and performance. Integrity is the most important quality when it comes to promoting managers.[44] When selecting middle and senior managers, Huawei put integrity first. Loyalty to the company, and advocacy for collective interests are more important standards than abilities. Integrity is an umbrella term that covers not only honesty, but also the willingness to work in hardship regions, the courage to bear hardships, and the boldness to take on responsibilities.[45]

At the same time, Huawei focuses on the assessment of employees' values, including whether they identify with Huawei's vision, mission, strategy, and values, and whether they are willing to work hard and make a sacrifice with passion and motivation, etc.

High performance is a prerequisite for managers. The manager selection process is applicable only to those who have achieved high performance and rank among the top 25%.[46] Only those with outstanding performance and who meet Huawei's requirements for managers in terms of integrity and values can be promoted.

As you can see, Huawei's promotion channel is very clear, and the whole system is based on performance (or contribution); such institutional arrangements make fast-track promotion for young people possible. Once they are selected as management candidates or managers, follow-up measures are also in place, such as "the zigzag development path", "the 180-day turnaround plan", "the personal development plan", and "the succession plan." These distinctive systems are designed to be operational for the rapid growth of young employees. Huawei's ability to find "thoroughbreds" has built its competitive edge, with generations of young people dedicated to Huawei.

---

[43] Ren Zhengfei: "Don't forget the heroes". January 23, 1997.

[44] Ren Zhengfei: Speech at the Third Quarter Meeting Regarding Marketing in China, 2004.

[45] Ren Zhengfei: Remarks at a meeting with staff of the United Arab Emirates Representative Office, 2004.

[46] EMT Meeting Minutes No. [2005] 053.

PBC: a strategic performance management system

Personal Business Commitment or more famous with PBC, designed by IBM, is a performance management system linking employees' activities to corporate goals. PBC is divided into three parts. The first part is Personal Business Goals (80%) include KPI and key tasks. KPIs are regular indicators, including indicators of revenue, development, quality, safety, etc., which are reflected in the breakdown of the result-oriented objectives. The key tasks are dynamic indicators, which complement the KPI system. The second part is Developmental Goals (20%). If the PBC agreement is signed by a team, the team leader must set the management objectives of the team. However, before setting the objectives, it is necessary to think about the following three aspects: first, the requirements of the objectives for the organization and staff management; second, the seven effective management behaviors (target-setting, teamwork, performance management, encouraging innovation, subordinates nurturing, contribution recognition and atmosphere creation); third, the competency system that needs to be built urgently. Based on the above, the manager should clarify the key points and pain points of departmental management in order to further clarify the objectives. The third part is people development goals (reference indicators). The goals should be set with the assistance of the manager, and the total number of indicators is between two and four. These goals are only used as a reference, but all employees are required to set their goals.

Compared with other performance management tools, PBC has the following five unique features: 1. PBC is based on the decomposition of corporate goals and key tasks, and facilitates the attainment of goals through process management and coaching; 2. PBC is a comprehensive assessment system integrating KPI, target results, project management, competency assessment and career development; 3. PBC increases the manager's role of the corrective function in performance evaluation, which empowers managers and ensures the fairness and objectivity of evaluation; 4. PBC better aligns job performance with organizational performance, and establishes a community of interest, which is conducive to teamwork; 5. PBC reduces the weight of KPI scores and increases the weight of other elements such as key tasks and competency on evaluation.

Four qualities of managers

Huawei uses four qualities of managers as core standards: decisiveness, execution, comprehension, and interpersonal connection. Decisiveness refers to the ability to grasp the main contradiction and the main aspect of the contradiction, and the courage to make decisions and take responsibility. Execution refers to a results-oriented approach to achieving goals and completing tasks with excellence with given resources and time constraints. Comprehension refers to understanding the business, culture and environment. Interpersonal connection refers to openness, willingness to engage with customers, compromise and flexibility. Different levels of managers and business areas have different requirements. Generally speaking, decisiveness is the most valued quality of senior managers and executives, middle managers. PBC is used to assess performance and key events, so Huawei's managers are nurtured in practice, promoted from junior employees according to their assessment results.

Huawei clearly specifies manager assessment items, indicators, standards and methods, and the selection of manager candidates is jointly organized by the HR Department and Huawei University. The management team of each business unit is collectively responsible for the selection of manager candidates of the unit, and the head of the management team is the first responsible person for the selection of manager candidates. The HR Department and Huawei University provide training support for the selection. As part of their duties in the company, managers at all levels should actively participate in the selection and recommendation of manager candidates. Manager assessment also requires an archival information system to support decision making and ensure the assessment is evidence-based, objective and fair. For example, for integrity assessment, the information includes the integrity files, the key events database, managers' major decisions, typical behaviors, non-supervised performance, exclusive behavior, etc., and departmental notification of criticism, if any. The manager management department/division of the recommending unit can also adopt a survey on the candidate if necessary. When examining the performance-related indicators, reference information includes the results of quarterly and annual performance assessment, qualification records, SAP records, company appointment document, and the results of the workplace survey. For such reference indicators as organizational team building and cross-departmental work, the results of the organizational team building survey and the cross-departmental work records serve as a reference.

Promoting and demoting managers based on their performance and dismissing underperformers

Huawei assigns roles based on performance. Through hands-on practice, Huawei identifies people who have done their jobs well and promotes them to managerial positions, regardless of their seniority. At the same time, it is also resolute in demoting unqualified managers.[47] Huawei borrowed the system of demoting underperformers from West Point. The aim of this system is to streamline and motivate the organization, encourage employees to overachieve, and spur on the underachievers, and ultimately form a mechanism conducive to HR development. Huawei's polity of demoting underperformers is primarily targeted at managers, rather than ordinary employees.[48] The policy applies to not just junior managers but also to middle and senior managers. The bottom 10% of managers at each level will be demoted, and the figure is higher for departments or teams that have failed to achieve their annual target.[49] Unqualified managers can be transferred to non-managerial positions that are more suitable for them. When they are ready, they still have the opportunity to be promoted again. "From the ashes the phoenix is reborn"—this is how Huaweiers think and act when they are wronged or feel frustrated. It is also the principal Huawei

[47] Ren Zhengfei: Speech at the Mobilization Meeting on Asset Cleanup and Verification, 1997.

[48] EMT Meeting Minutes No. [2009] 016.

[49] EMT Meeting Minutes No. [2007] 022.

uses to select managers. Decreasing pay or adjusting positions is also an opportunity to test the managers. If they stay positive and work hard after being demoted or receiving a pay cut, they still have the opportunity to be promoted again.

10.6 A Comprehensive Incentive Mechanism for Continuous Motivation

A dedication-oriented value distribution system

Huawei's value distribution system values dedicated employees, employees with successful track records, and employees who have made contributions. Differences generate driving forces. For instance, differences in temperatures result in the wind, and differences in altitude make water flow. To motivate our best employees is just like making the car go further, it needs to be fueled.[50]

Huawei divides employees into three categories: the first category is average employees at level 12 and below. These employees will be paid in accordance with relevant compensation provisions of the law, or slightly better if the company's finance allows. The second category is average dedicated employees. Huawei understands not everyone can be a high-performer. As long as employees work hard in their positions, and contribute more than they are paid, their jobs are safe, and their compensation may be even a little higher than the market average. The third category is productive high-performers. These people are the backbones of the company. Huawei always shares the surplus-value of the company with high-performers. According to Ren, "(The success of Huawei owes to) the 130,000 smart employees, and the tolerance and guidance of our customers. I simply use benefit sharing to pool their talent together."[51]

A comprehensive incentive mechanism

Huawei aligns employees' personal goals with the company's with a comprehensive incentive mechanism and thus creates synergy. The company aims for long-term interests, i.e., how to continuously improve the long-term competitiveness of the company while employees mainly consider short-term interests, because they do not know whether they will stay in Huawei in the future. To solve this conflict, we need to find a balance between the long-term interests and the immediate interests. Huawei adopts a comprehensive incentive mechanism combining long-term incentives and short-term incentives, and material incentives and non-material incentives to continuously tap into employees' potential and encourage them to hard work. Huawei's material incentives mainly include bonuses, equity and welfare. The position determines the salary, the performance determines the bonus, and the contribution, especially the prospect contribution determines the equity income. The income

---

[50] Ren Zhengfei: "From 'Philosophy' to Practice", 2011.

[51] Ren Zhengfei: "The river flows eastward in spring". December 2011.

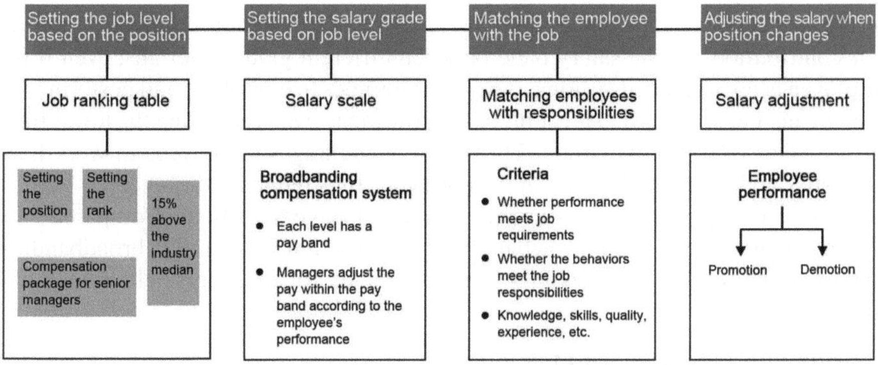

Fig. 10.3 Huawei's salary administration system

composition of employees at different levels is completely different: for employees below level 16, salary constitutes the main income; for middle and senior managers, it is the equity income, which may account for over 70%. Non-material incentives include development opportunities, organizational power, etc.

Huawei's position and remuneration management can be summarized as setting the job level based on the position and salary based on job levels, matching the employee with the job and adjusting the salary when the position changes. Salary-setting of each level and each position needs to consider not only competitiveness in the industry but also affordability and fairness. Later we will explain in detail Huawei's systematic approach in Fig. 10.3.

Setting the job level based on the position

Each position has a corresponding level, which is the evaluation of the position's contribution to the enterprise, including the evaluation of the organizational performance, the position and the employee.

Here, Huawei has done two things: First, each type of position has corresponding job series, such as R&D job series, marketing job series, etc. R&D job series include assistant engineers, engineers, senior engineers. Second, all the job series are assessed, focus on the responsibilities, the resources involved, the output, as well as the complexity of the customers and environment it faces; the knowledge, skills and experience of the people at the position are also taken into consideration. Responsibilities and output are the two major measuring indicators, and the result of the measurement is its corresponding grade. Huawei uses the Hay rank sequence. Based on the two steps, position-based job levels are determined.

Setting the salary grade based on job level

Setting the salary grade based on the job level is essentially a salary scale. Huawei uses a broadbanding compensation system, and the manager of each department can adjust the salary of the employees according to their performance within the band. Salary adjustments within the same grade can be requested based on the employee's performance, during the annual salary review, or when the employee makes a particular contribution. As the salary band between different grades overlaps, even if the employee is not upgraded, as long as he/she continues to contribute and perform well enough, his/her salary still has room for improvement, even exceeding the lower limit of the salary of the above grade. This setting encourages employees to work hard and better and helps retain them in the company, thus reducing turnover.

Each company can set its own compensation management mode. Compared with a salary point system or a narrowbanding compensation system, this broadbanding compensation system requires higher requirements for managers' ability for pay adjustment.

Matching the employee with the job

Matching the employee with the job means matching employees with the required responsibilities of the job to ensure the compatibility between the employee's grade and the job requirement. The core is to determine whether the employee's performance meets job requirements and responsibilities. Fundamental elements like knowledge, skills, quality, experience, etc. are also considered.

In the case of transfer, generally speaking, the matching is based on the new job requirements. The grading is often done in three or six months after the transfer, not immediately after the transfer, and it is based on the employee's qualification and compatibility with the new position.

Adjusting the salary when the position changes

After the transfer, the salary adjustment plan needs to be formulated. The transfer usually involves either promotion or demotion. In the case of promotion, if the compensation of the employee in question has already reached or exceeded the lowest limit of the band, his/her salary can be unchanged or increased, depending on the performance; if not, his/her salary should be adjusted to at least the lowest limit of the new band, or higher; the specific amount depends on the employee's performance. In the case of demotion, the new salary is also set according to the employee's performance, within the corresponding salary band of the new grade. If the salary before demotion is higher than the upper limit of the grade after demotion, it needs to be immediately reduced to the upper limit of the corresponding grade or below.

Bonus incentive

The salary of Huawei employees is mainly determined by their positions and duties, and the allowance is based on the working environment: the tougher the environment, the higher the allowance. The salary is set at 15% higher than the median level of the industry to maintain the competitiveness of the salary. In addition to setting the salary grade by the position and the job level, high-caliber professionals can also negotiate with Huawei for their compensation packages. Bonuses are determined by both the employee's level and performance. Bonuses for employees at the same position with different appraisal results can differ greatly. For example, if performance B is set as the benchmark of 1, the appraisal result A is more than 2 times B, B+ is 1.2–1.5 times

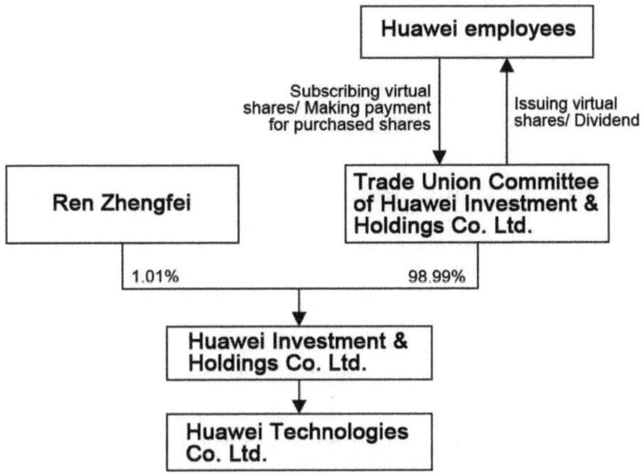

Fig. 10.4 Huawei's ESOP

B, C is 0.5 of B, and D is zero. For the lower-level employees who mainly rely on bonuses and salaries as their source of income, their income can be vastly different if their performance is different. Huawei purposefully uses the bonus to widen the income gap, and motivate lower-level employees to work hard.

Equity incentive

Huawei implements an employee stock ownership plan (ESOP), so that the cumulative contributions of labor, knowledge and entrepreneurial expertise can be reflected and rewarded. The equity arrangement creates the backbone of the company and maintains effective control over the company, so that Huawei can continue to grow. All exemplary employees in Huawei will be rewarded with equities, which enhances their sense of ownership and forms a community of common interest between the company and the employees.[52]

ESOP

Ren said, "Who owns Huawei? I have no idea. I only have a bit more than 1% of the shares." Legally speaking, Huawei has two major shareholders: one is Huawei's labor union, which holds 98.99% of the shares on behalf of all employees, and the other is Ren, who holds 1.01% of the shares. These shareholding employees are different from shareholders under corporate law, because since 2001, their shareholding has been changed to virtual restricted stock. In short, the employees are not direct shareholders of the company, but enjoy the right to dividends and stock appreciation. The large-scale employee shareholding contributes to the success of Huawei's corporate governance. In addition to serving as incentives, the arrangement serves as an internal financing practice. Figure 10.4 shows the structure and distribution of Huawei's ESOP.

Huawei was founded in 1987 with a registered capital of 20,000 yuan (about 3100 USD). Back then, Ren only had a bit more than 3,000 yuan, so he had to raise capital

[52] *Huawei Basic Law.*

from several friends to get business approval. Later, through legal proceedings, these people obtained handsome compensation. In the article "The river flows eastward in spring", Ren explained how he had come up with the idea of ESOP. "My idea is to unite employees through benefit sharing. At that time, I had no idea of the option system, let alone that it is already a mature system in the West ... The idea was born out of my past frustrations; I understand the importance of responsibility sharing and benefit sharing."

Huawei started ESOP in 1990. During the start-up phase, Huawei needed a lot of capital for market expansion and R&D; however, it was very difficult for a private company to get a bank loan. Against such a backdrop, Huawei put forward the concept of "financing by employee stock ownership" for the first time. Internal financing does not need to pay interest; its risk of financial distress is much lower, and it does not need to pay a high rate of return to external shareholders. Meanwhile, it can motivate employees to work hard. At that time, the price per stock was 10 yuan, and 15% of after-tax profits were distributed as dividends. At that time, Huawei employees' remuneration consisted of salary, bonus, and dividends, each taking around one-third of the total. The basic practice is as follows: all employees who have worked for more than one year are entitled to buy the company stock; the amount depends on the employee's level (13–23 levels), performance, contributions, etc. Generally, the company informs employees at the end of the year how much they can buy; employees then buy stocks with their salaries and year-end bonuses. The company also provides assisted loans to those who did not have sufficient funds. The stock is one yuan per share, which is not linked to the net assets of the company, and the main income of the stocks comes from dividends, which are linked to the company's profits. When the employee leaves the company, the company buys back the shares at the original price of one yuan/share. The company does not issue certificates of shareholding except in the years 1995 and 1996, but the employee can check the amount of his shareholding in the company's system. The labor union (which has a shareholding committee) manages the stocks held by the employees on their behalf and is the real shareholder of the company. The employees themselves do not have the full rights of shareholders under company law.

This approach can reduce the cash flow risk, and can enhance the sense of ownership of employees, thus retaining senior employees. It was at this stage that Huawei completed the strategic task of "making inroads into urban areas after establishing a presence in rural areas". However, Huawei's ESOP is different from the international practice mainly in two aspects: first, employees only have the right to dividends, but no other rights under the company law; second, when the stocks held by employees are bought back, they will be bought at h the original price, which means employees can not enjoy the premium price of the shares.

At the end of 2001, due to the dot-com bubble, the IT industry experienced unprecedented financial distress, and Huawei experienced its first winter in history. So, Huawei replaced the original ESOP with "virtual restricted stocks", a profit-sharing model based on human capital.

With the strong push of Ren, Huawei implemented a reform: the one-yuan stocks are no longer issued to new employees, while old employees' stocks are gradually converted into virtual restricted stocks, a special type of stocks issued to employees by the Huawei Investment & Holding Co. Ltd. Each year, the company determines the amount of stocks the employee receives based on his or her performance and contribution to the company. Employees buy the stocks at the price of the company's net assets in that year. Employees who own virtual stocks can receive dividends, as well as a portion of the appreciation of the company's net assets corresponding to the virtual shares, but they have no ownership rights or voting rights, and cannot transfer or sell these stocks. When an employee leaves the company, the stocks will be bought back by the trade union.

The issuance of virtual stocks helps Huawei's management maintains control over the company and does not lead to a series of management problems. The reform reflects the shift in Huawei's incentive mechanism from a "universal" benefit to "targeted" incentives.

In 2008, due to the impact of the global economic crisis, Huawei introduced a new equity incentive scheme—"saturation allotment", that is, different job levels are allotted with a different upper limit of stocks. For example, for employees at level 13, the upper limit is 20,000 shares; for level 14, 50,000 shares. Most of the old employees at Huawei HQ did not participate in the allotment because their shareholdings had already reached the upper limit of their levels. This is a major transformation. Subsequently, the scheme was further optimized with the introduction of the allotment reward system, which has made the distribution mechanism more reasonable and balanced. With the new system, all employees are entitled to receive rewarding stocks, regardless of whether their stocks hit the upper limit or not.

Huawei believes that the virtual stock scheme is more reasonable. The company stipulates that employees can cash in one-quarter of their virtual shares per year, at the latest net asset price per share, but middle and senior managers can only cash in one-tenth, except when they leave the company. When they leave, they have to wait for six months to cash in their stocks if the company confirms that there is no violation of the non-compete clause and other clauses. Each shareholding employee has the right to vote and be elected as a shareholder representative. A total of 51 representatives are elected to represent the shareholding employees. Of these 51 representatives, 13 are elected on a rotating basis as members of the Board of Directors and five as members of the Supervisory Board.

Huawei maintains the vitality of the entire organization by constantly adjusting the distribution of shares. This mechanism has attracted, united and bonded a large number of talents, including international employees. In Ren's words, it is this mechanism that has shaped the company's "benefit-sharing, and dedication-centered culture".

Huawei's equity allocation is based on contributions, talent, character and risks, and is assessed in three main areas: First, demonstrated ability, performance and especially ability to handle critical events; second, dedication; third, prospect contributions to the company. The allocation of equity is tilted toward key employees, and the equity structure always remains dynamic and rational. People of the same position may have different shares. Some employees have good performance and high bonuses but may not have many shares because they do not show much potential for further contribution to the company. It does not necessarily mean that "smart" people or competent people will get more stock; how much stock one gets depends on whether their intelligence has created or will create value for the company, and whether they identify themselves with the company's culture. How much stock one gets is strictly confidential and it is not allowed to exchange such information among employees, which largely prevents conflict among employees due to perceived unfair distribution or comparison of salaries.

It is important to note that Huawei's virtual restricted stocks are not gifted; employees have to pay for them. So, apparently, the appreciation of the stocks is in the best interest of the shareholders. For new employees, in their first five years of service, their main income will be put into the company's stock, so that the bonding between the employee and the company is constantly strengthened. Huawei always awards progressive employees with more stock than their year-end bonus. With continuous capital investment, the value of the stock snowballs, and the sense of ownership is getting stronger, and ultimately aligning the interests of the company with those of employees. By 2016, nearly 90,000 of Huawei's 150,000 employees have held virtual restricted stocks, with a total ratio of 98.99%, and Ren only owned 1.01%. From 2000 to 2010, Huawei's virtual restricted stocks have increased in value 15 times, and in recent years, the rate of return has been over 20%. Table 10.1 summarizes the differences between virtual stocks and regular stocks.

Welfare System

To ensure that its employees can live and work safely around the world, starting in 2005, Huawei has transformed its insurance and benefits system and enacted a series of policies on employee protection, medical insurance, medical aid, and

Table 10.1 Differences between Huawei's virtual restricted shares and regular shares

	Regular stocks	Huawei's virtual restricted stocks
Legality	Protected by law	Different from shares in the legal sense
Stock price	Market price	Net asset value per share
Right to dividends	Yes	Yes
Voting rights	Yes	No
Transfer and trade	Free to transfer and trade	Cannot be transferred and traded; can only be repurchased by the company
Transparency	Open and transparent	Strictly confidential
Incentivizing effect	Benefit a few people, strong for founders and executives, weak for ordinary employees	Relatively universal, strong for both ordinary employees and middle and senior managers
Motivational factor	Current contribution	Future potential
Motivation time	2–3 years	Annual assessment, sustainable
Effect	Motivate only a few to work hard	Motivate many to work hard

personal insurance. Huawei also purchases commercial insurance for its employees, including personal accident insurance, life insurance, critical illness insurance, and business travel insurance. For employees assigned to countries with poor public medical systems, Huawei purchases commercial medical insurance for them and their families. It has also established close relationships with global medical service organizations (e.g., ISOS) to ensure that its employees assigned overseas, and their families can receive timely medical assistance and care.[53]

For overseas employees, the company takes care of the canteen, accommodation, medical insurance and life insurance as well as assistance to their families. Canteens are high on the agenda of overseas companies, especially for canteens in tough regions and field canteens. Field canteens include and are not limited to resident canteens, mobile canteens, certified catering services and so on. Each region, representative office and project team can develop their own solutions to field canteens according to the local conditions. In principle, where there are over five people, a field canteen can be constructed, and where there are two or three people, it should be guaranteed that employees can have delicious meals. Family members living with the team can either dine in the resident canteen, or receive food subsidies.[54]

In terms of working environment, Huawei has sent its infrastructure department to Silicon Valley, and Huawei's industrial parks and office sites are modeled on high-tech companies in Silicon Valley. Whether it is the Longgang head office, or Nanjing Institute and other research institutions, they all have a quiet, elegant, beautiful and unique environment, which is one of Huawei's strengths to attract and retain outstanding talents.

Non-material incentives

Huawei's non-material incentives are also an important aspect of compensation. They are not only a supplement to material incentives, but more importantly, they meet the needs of employees at multiple levels. Huawei's rewards for employees include not only monetary value, but also opportunities, status, assignment of duties and responsibilities. Huawei regards development opportunities and organizational power as assignable value resources, and prioritizes them in the value allocation. The company not only provides growth and development opportunities for employees by continuously opening up new businesses; through a fair competition mechanism, it also allocates opportunity resources reasonably, creating a good environment and conditions for the growth of talent.

In Huawei, work is not just a means to earn a living. Huawei is more like a school or an army, which provides many learning opportunities. You can rub shoulders with the world's best talent, ask them for advice, dialogue with them, or compete with them on the same stage. As long as you have a dream, work hard, and study hard, within a few years, this platform can shape you to be a better self than before, standing out among your peers. Ren often says that Huawei will take seven or eight

---

[53] Ren Zhengfei: "Notification on the Status of Human Management Transformation", 2007.

[54] Ren Zhengfei: "Improving the Protection Measures for Employees in Hardship Regions", *Huawei People*, 2007.

years to cultivate a president. In Huawei, as long as you are willing to work hard, you can certainly achieve something. Once you make it, there will be more opportunities and in Huawei, fast-track promotion is often out of most people's expectations. Nowadays, the presidents of regional companies are basically the "post-70s"; some are even "post-80s". Here, nepotism does not work, nor does buttering up. The only passport needed to succeed is performance, and that makes young people, especially those with ambitions, willing to fight for the company.

10.7 Huawei Versus Cisco

I am impressed by the simplicity, diligence, self-discipline, toughness, thirst for knowledge, and intrinsic drive for success of Huawei people. As we found these traits are quite common among Huawei people, we can see the corporate culture has made a visible imprint. Most of them came from small towns or rural families, without rich or powerful parents. They have changed their fate with their education. In Huawei, the family background or even the education background is not important; performance is the most important indicator, followed by competence, values and character. If you share with the corporate values of hard work, dedication, passion and drive, and if you have integrity, you will have a good chance of becoming the future leader of the company.

There are three reasons that Huawei can fully stimulate the potential of its employees: First, Huawei leaders' strong sense of crisis, foresight and idealistic sentiments have continuously drive Huawei people forward who have also been staying alert and sharp to keep up with the development of the enterprise. Especially after Huawei became bigger, the leaders have always been focused on the continuous motivation of the organization, to avoid inertia and other ailments of big companies, which puts most Huawei people always on alert, and encourages them to learn, explore and develop themselves constantly. Therefore, their potential is constantly developed. Secondly, at the strategic level, Huawei guides its employees to aim longer and put their materialistic cravings in check. It focuses on dynamic empowerment. Both the enterprise and employees are always running, so to speak. So, if you stop moving forward, you will lag behind. Finally, at the system level, Huawei has designed the "benefit-sharing system". Through ESOP, the personal and corporate goals and interests are closely aligned. When employees fight for the company, they are also fighting for themselves and their families. Huaweiers are self-motivated. They are driven to work hard with great passion. In summarizing the advantages of the benefit-sharing system, Hu Houkun noted that this mechanism was inclusive rather than oppressive; it takes into account the interests of customers, employees, capital and other stakeholders, such as intellectual property. This mechanism, which embraces multiple interest groups, is critical for the long-term permanence of the business.

At Huawei, selecting managers is like a horse race, which always picks the best. It helps avoid cronyism and the practice of greasing palms for promotion. Huawei always gives priority to promoting managers from successful teams, from strategic markets, from field offices, from tough areas and markets. It pays special attention to key events that affect the long-term development of the company, and promotes managers based on their work in those events. This mechanism allows employees to focus on work and business development, rather than on interpersonal relationships. At the same time, Huawei never hesitates to reward those who work in the toughest places, who contribute the most to the company, and who perform the best. This fair and just organizational system helps simplify interpersonal relationships in the organization, reduces unnecessary loss of attention, uncertainty in personnel growth and development; it compensates employees who deserve it, and encourages employees to work hard, so that dedicated employees have the opportunity to taste the fruits of their effort.

Both Huawei and Cisco are passionate and mission-driven companies with a strong drive for success and innovation. Cisco believes that passionate people are even more valuable and scarce than capable people. Executives' sense of mission is an important part of their character, and a major source for sustainable development and success of the company. Cisco's leaders see it their mission to change people's work, life and learning with Internet, and achieves fulfillment of positive feedback from the mission and customer satisfaction. Huawei's leaders constantly seek breakthroughs and strive to become a world-class enterprise. Both companies attach great importance to the global vision of their executives, and require executives to be promoted to have overseas working experience (especially in less developed regions). It is this high standard and strict requirement for the leadership that ensures that both companies survive in the exceptionally competitive market. Like Huawei, Cisco has a very standardized performance evaluation for senior leaders: it has a special talent evaluation process and a comprehensive performance evaluation card, with evaluation dimensions including leadership, future development, personality and career development paths.

Employees of both companies are dedicated and hardworking. When I studied at Cisco from 2010 to 2014, the teaching team usually discussed late into the night to evaluate the quality of teaching, and the head of the team paid close attention to the grading of lectures and the questions and feedback from the trainees. Both companies are customer-oriented. Whether it is the receptionist or the engineer in the back office, every employee knows clearly that their income is correlated with customer satisfaction. Although they have different slogans, customer-centricity and dedication are the true corporate culture put into practice by these two companies.

Unlike Huawei's Rotating CEO System, Cisco is led collaboratively by a leadership team of ten people, each in charge of a different business area. In order to reach better consensus and collaboration, the ten executives need to fully share information with each other. Even in cases where consensus cannot be reached, they need to communicate openly, and straightforwardly. If the executive cannot be persuaded, then he or she needs to be accountable for his or her decision. In addition, Cisco is a listed company. According to the incentive mechanism of Cisco, the biggest proportion of income for base employees is salary and the equity is relatively small; however, for the senior managers, the base salary only accounts for about 15% of their total income, and the equity is the most important part. The amount of equity is based on their leadership behavior and future market conditions, with a lot of uncertainties. The purpose is to make the top management accept challenges and strive to create the best results.

Chapter 11
Knowledge Management Integrating Organizational Knowledge

In business management, knowledge management (KM) emerged as a scientific discipline in the early 1990s. In 1999, the first Chief Knowledge Officer (CKO) position was created by Skandia, a Swedish insurance company. The core responsibility of the CKO is to manage the knowledge assets within an organization and maximize their value (knowledge assets are also called intellectual capital, intangible assets or light assets). In 1995, Oxford University Press published the book *The Knowledge-Creating Company* by professor Ikujiro Nonaka of Hitotsubashi University. In the book, based on case studies of many enterprises, professor Nonaka proposed the well-known knowledge creation model, which pioneered the study of KM and creation. In 2001, Thomas A. Stewart, the editor of *Fortune* magazine, pointed out that intellectual capital was becoming corporate America's most valuable asset in his article "Brain Power".

According to IAS 38 of International Financial Reporting Standards (IFRS), knowledge asset, also known as intangible asset, is an identifiable non-monetary asset without physical substance. An asset is a source that is controlled by the entity as a result of past events and from which future economic benefits are expected. Knowledge assets have a significant impact on the capitalization of high-tech companies. Among the companies with the highest capitalization in 2017, the vast majority had knowledge assets as their core assets.[1] Intellectual capital includes human capital, social capital, market capital, structural capital, and intellectual property capital. Human capital consists of knowledge, know-how and skills. Integrating human capital with other capital helps companies solve complex problems and develop proprietary intellectual property. However, with brain drain knowledge also flows, companies can develop and utilize human capital but take no possession of it. Therefore, how to attract and retain human resources, give them full play and unlock their

[1] According to Bloomberg, the most valuable companies in 2017 were Apple, Alphabet (Google's parent company), Microsoft, Amazon, Berkshire Hathaway, Facebook, ExxonMobil, Johnson & Johnson, JPMorgan Chase and Tencent.

X. Dong et al., *Huawei*,
https://doi.org/10.1007/978-981-19-4078-1_11

potential becomes the key to human capital management. Social capital is the sum of customer relationships, supplier relationships, and government relationships and relationships with other stakeholders. It not only helps companies build their business ecosystem but also facilitates the sound development of the company. Market capital refers to the assets a company has accumulated from serving customers, including reputation, impression, recognition, brand and channels. Structural capital refers to the company's knowledge assets excluding human capital, including management information systems and processes, databases, value chains, management platforms, corporate culture, rules and regulations, etc. Structural capital helps maximize the value of human capital. People come and go, but structural capital stays in the company. Intellectual property capital is closely related to a company's capability to innovate and upgrade. Its achievements include patents, technical secrets, standards, trademarks, goodwill and the franchise system, etc.

For high-tech companies, the accumulation, development and use of intellectual capital are closely related to their KM capability which depends on whether managers regard knowledge as their most important strategic resources and know-how to take a strategic and tactical approach to KM. Unlike fixed assets (i.e., finance, equipment, materials and plants), knowledge, as an intangible asset, exists both in people's minds and organizational processes, systems, methods, as well as its learning, innovation and cultural activities. Knowledge influences the way people think, make choices, judgments and decisions, solve problems and take actions; likewise, organizational knowledge affects the organization's creativity, efficiency and ability to generate added value. To leverage knowledge as a strategic resource, KM is essential. It involves collecting, analyzing, integrating, creating and applying organizational and individual knowledge and information systematically and purposefully to facilitate knowledge sharing among individuals and teams, within and outside the organization. Since in many cases knowledge is intangible, tacit and unmeasurable, managing knowledge requires the integration of strategic leadership, culture, human resources, information technology, incentives, and other skill sets. So, what should we pay special attention to Huawei's KM practices?

First, how Huawei handles the relationship between knowledge assets and financial assets. Many entrepreneurs understand that wealth shared can attract talent, who then can generate knowledge and wealth. However, to understand it is one thing, to put it into practice is another. Huawei, as a private enterprise, had neither favorable conditions nor rare resources in the startup stage, not to mention reliable connections. The senior managers of Huawei realized early that against such a backdrop the company needed to adopt inspiring measures like setting visions, incentives and building corporate culture so that the employees would be motivated, open-minded, self-reliant, and ingenious in learning new things. In this way, knowledge capital created and accumulated can soon close the gap with competitors, driving financial capital to serve the company's knowledge capital. So, how did Huawei put these ideas into practice?

Second, how to effectively absorb external knowledge. Huawei's development has confronted many competitors from developed countries. With a rich business history, those competitors have decades or even centuries of knowledge accumulation, a stable industrial structure and environment, copious human and social capital, world-class R&D systems, abundant funds and globally recognized brands and reputation solid customer bases, and efficient management systems and operational expertise. Facing such competition and technical and market barriers, how can Huawei acquire and absorb knowledge faster, maximize the value of knowledge, and use external knowledge and experience to its utmost?

Third, how to improve the reuse and sharing of internal knowledge. Corporate KM involves many aspects: collecting and absorbing external knowledge and best practices to extensively share and utilize the knowledge required for business development; accumulating experience and know-how from dealing with customers, suppliers and business partners to lay a solid foundation for future business; identifying, sharing and implementing best practices based on a refined working methodology to enable peers and younger employees to improve efficiency with fewer detours and mistakes; accumulating existing knowledge with more efficient knowledge sharing and reuse to improve R&D efficiency and reduce costs; establishing a KM platform to support cross-department and cross-region business collaboration and knowledge sharing; ensuring the accuracy, integrity and reliability of organizational data, information and knowledge and improving their timeliness and security and confidentiality, etc. These are the major concerns of high-tech enterprises.

11.1 Strategic Awareness of Knowledge Assets

At the early stage of Huawei's development, Ren was keenly aware that this is the era of knowledge economy which fundamentally changes the way people create wealth. Wealth creation is no longer solely capital-driven, but more importantly, driven by knowledge held in people's hands. With the changes in information networks, many changes have also taken place in the space for innovation, unleashing human creativity like never before. Therefore, human should be the first and foremost factor for corporate strategy.

Ren believes that resources, be it oil, coal, forest and iron ore, will be exhausted, but knowledge, on the other hand, will increase. China, "a large land with limited resources", has the least per capita resources in the world, so the only way out is "invigorating China with science, technology and education". The smart way to create national wealth is to make all Chinese people better educated, and improve social and organizational management systems, nurture talent and generate more values from knowledge. If China sees people as a resource and develops it, the disadvantage of a big population will be transformed into an enormous advantage, which will play a great role in China's peaceful rise.

Huawei models itself on Israel in developing knowledge capital. The Jews were scattered in over 100 countries by the dispersion more than 2,000 years ago. However, with just over 10 million people, Jews have produced nearly 25% of Nobel prize winners along with many great thinkers and scholars. Jews are more likely than other peoples to become engineers and scientists and more likely to innovate and start up new businesses. Israel, extremely lacking in natural resources and a stable environment, respects knowledge and creativity, values education, and champions the spirit of challenging, questioning and exploring, so it has created many miracles in the desert through systematic management of human resources.

Ren came to understand that the best resource at Huawei's disposal is the knowledge created by the human brain, and that the knowledge and knowledge capital is the best strategic resource to support the sustainable development of Huawei. In order to quickly acquire, accumulate and use knowledge capital, the company must design a package of incentives to reward those who have committed their "smart brains" to the company. This is the logic behind the ESOP.

Therefore, Huawei has long been committed to copious investment in R&D and "staying focused" to make breakthroughs in patents, standards and key technologies. It has been wholeheartedly introducing the world's most advanced management methodologies and systems from international consulting firms. It has been establishing "competence centers" in proximity to its competitors and encouraging its employees to work frenetically. It never hesitated to replace inadequate employees no matter how much they had contributed historically. Back in the time of working fingers to the bone, in order to accumulate more working capital for production, many employees with a doctorate or master's degree and even senior managers had no house to their name.[2] These are just a few examples showing how self-reliant Huaweiers bridged the knowledge gaps with leading companies.[3]

11.2 Institutionalized Respect for Knowledge

In 1997, the *Huawei Basic Law* explicitly institutionalized the value of knowledge, the recognition of intellectuals and the incentive mechanism, with a clarified relationship between people and capital. It begins by stating, "Huawei's philosophy of putting knowledge first emphasizes the special status and role of knowledge, intellectual work and people. At Huawei, we believe that value is created through labor, knowledge, entrepreneurship and capital." As the company's guiding document, *Huawei Basic Law* not only takes knowledge and the carrier of knowledge, i.e., people as the greatest assets of Huawei, but also sees knowledge as an independent factor driving the company's value creation. It acknowledges that knowledge is also a form of capital and the source of a company's value creation and prioritizes human capital before other forms of capital. Both the concept and practice were very pioneering in China at that time. "Huawei's greatest asset is its conscientious, responsible and savvy employees. Respect for knowledge and individuality, collective hard work and not giving special treatment to anyone even if they have made special contributions (Article 2) are intrinsic to the sustainable growth of our business."

---

[2] Ren Zhengfei: "Resources can be exhausted, only culture endures" at the work report meeting of the User Service Center, March 20, 1997.

[3] Ibid.

Human capital appreciation outweighs financial capital appreciation

Huawei prioritizes human capital appreciation over financial capital appreciation. Its philosophy of putting knowledge first is also embodied in distributing benefits and profits. Huawei was founded by Ren in 1988 with a capital investment of RMB 20,000. Now, Ren's stake has been diluted to 1.01%; the rest 98.99% is held by other employees. In addition, the idea of giving a reasonable return to the intellectual work that creates value is stipulated in *Huawei Basic Law*: "Huawei advocates that a community of shared interest should be established among customers, employees and partners. We are exploring an internal incentive mechanism where benefits are distributed according to factors of production. Dedicated employees will be rewarded (Article 5)." Huawei's knowledge-based business philosophy acknowledges residual values of intellectual work, so knowledge workers, together with investors, are rewarded, because like capital, knowledge also contributes to the company's value creation.

Huawei has invented a path for capitalizing on knowledge. At Huawei, those who are "100% mentally dedicated" are rewarded even more. Those people have the following three traits: first, they are results-oriented constant overachievers. Second, they are innovation-minded nonconformists. They have original ideas and can make their voices heard; they can spot problems and make suggestions; they can think in customers' shoes; they know flexibility helps get their jobs done and they do their work effectively. Third, they are value-creators for customers. They, together with the leaders of the company, constitute the core force driving the growth of the company. Meanwhile, the incentive mechanism contiguously attracts young and outstanding employees.

Knowledge capital-based stock allocation

At Huawei, knowledge is concerted into capital so that it can be awarded along with labor, entrepreneurship and other forms of capital. The ESOP is adopted to develop the nucleus of the company, effectively control the company, and achieve sustained growth. Huawei continuous to explore how to transform knowledge into capital and how to develop a dynamic stock ownership system that adapts to technological and social changes. Exemplary employees who identify with the corporate culture will benefit from the plan. As a result, a group with a vested interest within the company will be created. The most responsible and talented employees will be selected to be part of this nucleus.[4] The ESOP allocates shares according to knowledge capital rather than financial capital. The annual stock dividends materialize the return on knowledge as capital.

In 2007, when questioned about ESOP, Ren refuted, "We're not real estate guys; we deal with technology. Technology is not just something coming out of my head; it has to come from all of us." Nearly 80,000 employees in Huawei jointly hold the virtual restricted shares and they decide the future of the company. So, how can one person decide where the company should go? "I didn't do this when I had a much

---

[4] *Huawei Basic Law.*

larger share. Now with less than 1.5% share, is it possible for me to do that? Or do I really want to do this?".[5]

11.3 Key Paths to Closing the Knowledge Gap

Strategic patience

Ren knows that rushing it cannot narrow the knowledge gap with developed countries. Huawei must understand that it takes time to obtain basic patents. Haste only needs to waste. It usually takes at least 7–8 years to obtain even the utility patent. It is only natural to take time to discover something that was regarded as non-existent, to develop a theory about it and material the value of it.

IPR is the entry ticket to international markets.

In today's competitive market, due to the openness and transparency of technology standards, it will be difficult for one company or one country to dominate basic patents. This decentralization of key patents has laid the foundation for cross-licensing patents, so granting patent licenses to each other will become more common. The Internet has also made creativity and invention more popular and easier. So, IPRs hold the key to the international market, without them, it would be impossible to produce high-tech products and compete in the international market. In Ren's view, China's failure to create value is largely caused by its barren ground for IPR protection. Huawei invests more than 15% of its annual sales revenue in R&D, and more than 45% of its nearly 170,000 employees engage in innovation, research and development. It is a key member of more than 170 standards organizations and open source organizations. Its 2016 financial report shows that Huawei applied for 62,519 patents (57,613 in China and 39,613 abroad), of which more than 90% are invention patents, ranking first in the world in terms of the number of patents applied.[6]

IPR protection

To compete with high-tech giants, Huawei would not survive without world-leading technologies. Developing cutting-edge technologies should be accompanied by protecting IPRs, so every employee should do so as if they were protecting their eyes. Trade secrets are the results of the two-decade effort of tens of thousands of employees, and even every software is the result of the brain product of hundreds or even thousands of employees. Do not disclose any trade secrets to competitors is the

[5] Ren Zhengfei: Speech at the Shanghai Research Center, November 8, 2010.

[6] According to the 2016 Report Detailing Global Intellectual Property Activity released by the World Intellectual Property Organization (WIPO), Huawei ranked second in the world with 3,692 PCT applications, surpassing Qualcomm and Mitsubishi. At Huawei 2017 Global Analyst Conference, Xu Zhijun, vice chairman and rotating CEO of Huawei, said that Huawei's accumulated R&D investment reached 310 billion RMB (about 48 billion USD) and would maintain an annual investment of 20 billion RMB (about 3.1 billion USD) in the coming years.

basic code of conduct for Huawei's employees. The shares of ESOP are the pledge of employees to do no harm to the company's business interests. Any employee who steals the company's technical secrets, trade secrets and bidding information, will pay for the loss first with their shares and will face disciplinary actions too. Without IPR protection or rewarding IPR holders, no one would devote themselves to the hard work of invention. Without abundant inventions and innovations, China would not become a member of the "Powerhouse Club". If that is the case, China will always be at the mercy of other countries, which will hurt the most promising Chinese companies.[7]

Value truth seekers

Huawei has a unique way to select talent. In 1996, Ren asked his employees who graduated from the School of Mathematical Sciences, Peking University (PKU) to set up a scholarship at PKU and recruit all the job-seeking graduates from the School of Mathematical Sciences. In 2016, when I visited Huawei and asked about its recruit criteria, the person in charge answered that Huawei looked for talents who excel exceptionally in their fields, even if they are no good in other areas as well as those who have the exceptional interdisciplinary ability in the field of natural sciences. Huawei has a soft spot for mavericks.

"Truth always rests with the minority. They are painfully far-sighted, and they are devout believers in their findings, but only to find few that recognize the truth. Their theories may receive no feedback after being published. Maybe it would take decades or even a century for someone to see the value of their theories. It is only then that their researches become invaluable. Some die before that ever happens. We, at Huawei, shall not allow it. We need to establish incentive measures to recognize them, otherwise, no one will work tirelessly and unremittingly to explore, innovate and create."[8] Ren always encourages tolerance for pioneering entrepreneurs, scientists and professionals, "They are doing no harm, why can't we let them be?"

External knowledge acquisition

When Huawei started up, the leading companies in the international market had already accumulated a large amount of knowledge and expertise. For a catch-up company like Huawei, if it had started from scratch, and done everything all by itself, it would have had no advantage at all. As a catch-up company, the right approach is to learn from the leading companies, avoid their mistakes, buy and leverage their expertise, so as to stand on the shoulders of giants. Therefore, when Huawei sought management solutions, it always aimed at globally successful solutions. It would never pinch a penny to import and absorb them efficiently. In Ren's eyes, Huawei has benefited hugely from what it has bought.

---

[7] Ren Zhengfei: "Practical scientific research and twenty years of hard work" at a major national project validation conference, December 2006.

[8] Sun Yafang: "Basic Education for All May Empower China with the Richest Resources in the World", the National Science Conference, 2006.

Organizational knowledge reuse and sharing

As a catch-up company, Huawei had limited resources at the early stage, so it is impossible to squander resources on R&D and innovation. To explore the unknown may produce great talents and great achievements. However, Huawei realized that in the process of catching up, in order to survive, Huawei needed to focus on making products in the early days, and invention for invention's sake was unnecessary and even impossible.[9] Therefore, Huawei attaches great importance to the use and reuse of existing knowledge, and solidifies it as part of the corporate institutions and assessment and promotion criteria.

Huawei has developed a "knowledge shelf" in its R&D process. When launching a new product, it would first check the shelf to see what "knowledge" can be reused for the new products. It stipulates that the development of new products should use as much as possible the company's mature technologies or technologies that can be procured from the market. Technology reuse below 70%, i.e., new development above 30%, is regarded as a waste rather than an innovation in Huawei, as it only increases development costs and instability of the product.[10] The reuse of existing knowledge is also a major indicator to be considered in promoting R&D personnel. At HW, every new project is like a Lego project: most of the base pieces are the same; only a few bricks are different. If people do not share resources for innovation, it will only lead to duplication and delay, and the production, if it takes place eventually, is likely to be unstable. So, knowledge sharing is vital. At Huawei, everyone is encouraged to share what small improvements they have made in innovation brainstorming.[11]

In a large company, the most significant cost-cutting measure is resource sharing. For a large company the most effective way to reduce costs is to share resources: what has been developed can be reused, because technical confidentiality and patents impose no problem on the company. Existing technology plus some optimization is the real deal. Those who are obsessed with big innovations are naive and hopeless. In Ren's view, old knowledge to new knowledge is like "a heap of dung" to "flowers". Any new product is a combination of old and new products. When flowers wither, they become the new dung; every new product will eventually become part of the company's knowledge and the company will always innovate on the basis of its existing know-how.

[9] Ren Zhengfei: "Entrepreneurship and innovation must be centered on improving the core competitiveness", March 5, 1999.

[10] Ibid.

[11] Ren Zhengfei: "Cultivating and Selecting Managers with Field Experience", the Second Quality Management Report and Award Ceremony, 1998.

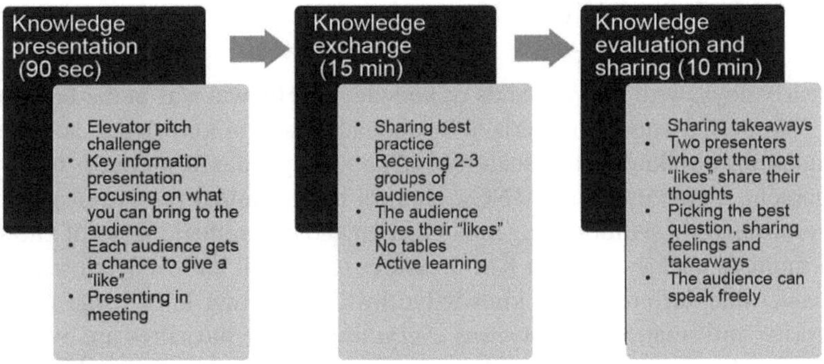

Fig. 11.1 Knowledge fair

Case: Huawei's Knowledge Fair

The staff of Huawei's various product lines regularly share best practices at the knowledge fair. The fair is efficient and effective, and I have participated three times. It consists of three major parts (see Fig. 11.1).

First, knowledge presentation. Knowledge presenters have to pitch the key knowledge information within 90 s, they must be concise and yet impressive. PowerPoint is allowed as a visual aid. This kind of knowledge presentation, as an elevator pitch challenge, is a good test and practice for the presenter. The 90-s timeframe improves the efficiency of communication by avoiding unnecessary introductions and pleasantries.

Second, knowledge exchange. After the brief introduction by about 6 presenters, the fair is open for business. Each audience gets a chance to give a "like". At this point, presenters unfold their roll-up banners to introduce the details and process of their business to the audience. With colored pictures and flow charts, roll-up banners provide the details of the KM. Participants are free to talk to the stand they are interested in. Even by listening to the questions and answers, other participants also can acquire some knowledge. The audience will in the end stick a "like" on the banner that he/she likes. During these 30 min, each presenter will receive 2–3 groups of audience. There will be no tables standing between them. During this process, the audience is learning by asking questions and the presenters can also identify valuable comments and questions from the audience.

Third, knowledge feedback. After 30 min of sharing, the organizer will invite two presenters who get the most "likes" to share their thoughts the two stand owners with the most "likes" to share their thoughts. The best question raisers will also be invited to share their feelings and takeaways. In the end, both the best presenters and best question raisers will receive books as rewards. In just two hours, information on ten topics will be shared with presentations and QAs. Everything proceeds in an efficient manner. Everyone can obtain enormous information in a short time. Therefore, it is fair to say the knowledge fair is quite knowledge intensive.

11.4 Evolution of KM at Huawei

In the early days, with many islands of knowledge, Huawei was at the fast-growing stage. This period was characterized by the emphasis on knowledge shortage and accumulation, with knowledge security and knowledge manifestation as the focus of management. Compared with MNCs, Huawei had a limited reserve of proprietary IPs. The company's senior management recognized the strategic value of knowledge and formulated a series of strict KM measures to prevent knowledge loss and theft. As Huawei had suffered from knowledge loss, preventing knowledge loss was a top priority; information security was everything. Some measures are even stricter than those taken by the military. For example, office computers in Huawei have no ports for external devices. Meanwhile, Huawei invested tremendous resources in acquiring management solutions from international consulting firms, as it determined to understand, absorb, utilize and share the knowledge efficiently within the company in a very short time. To this end, tacit knowledge must be made explicit. Also, Huawei must effectively accumulate and form its own knowledge system and reduce the risks of making mistakes in fierce competition. In order to achieve all these goals, Huawei took various measures to establish knowledge libraries. However, at this time, Huawei's KM still lacked top-level planning and arrangement. In addition, the company did not have full-time KM personnel for coordination and planning, so all the knowledge libraries were silos, creating information islands in the company.

Before 2005, Huawei's KM focused on knowledge and information security. Knowledge could only be shared within the department, or even only among specified positions of the department. Self-built file servers with complex permission groups were the main carriers for knowledge storage, making knowledge sharing highly difficult. Yet meanwhile, employees were hunger for knowledge sharing.

After 2005, Huawei's KM began to pay more attention to supporting marketing. The Marketing Material Management System, known as 3MS, a company-wide integrated system for marketing materials sharing became the most visited platform. In 2010, the focus of KM shifted to R&D. The same year witnessed the official launch of the knowledge sharing community (hi3ms) with distinctive characteristics of Web 2.0, marking the start of KM in R&D. Meanwhile, in order to analyze the company's knowledge more comprehensively and enable the employees working at field offices and new employees at entry-level to acquire such knowledge faster, the company-level i-Learning platform for online training and test was launched. As the concept of knowledge sharing was accepted by R&D employees, Ernst & Young was hired by the software BG to produce a KM solution involving personnel, process, content, culture, metrics, and technology. When the president of the software BG reported to the senior management about the program, the latter believed that the KM project should be launched company-wide. In November 2010, with the approval of the company's Business Change Steering Committee, the company initiated a project group for KM reform.

2008 to 2010 was a period of knowledge connection and sharing. During this period, Huawei accumulated strong knowledge assets in China with a competitive edge. At the same time, with accelerated internationalization, Huawei realized the importance of KM more than ever, so it began to connect the knowledge islands to make knowledge output and sharing more efficient. At this stage, R&D and marketing teams were the focus of Huawei's KM. The R&D team not only designated a full-time KM team but also began to collect experience and lessons learned from R&D projects. Through effective knowledge sharing, the efficiency of the R&D team was improved, and the R&D error rate was reduced. To facilitate the exchange of experience within R&D teams and improve employees' problem-solving ability, Huawei's KM team established all kinds of communities on the company's platform. These communities provided better communication through Q&As, blogs, and topic discussions, which accelerated knowledge flow and sharing in wider areas. For marketing teams, Huawei established the 3MS platform to enable Huawei's representative offices around the world to expand markets more efficiently and effectively. This platform aims to integrate and share relevant marketing knowledge and experience in different countries, regions, and businesses to avoid duplication of efforts and reduce the time wasted in information searching. At the same time, with Huawei's rapid expansion, there was a need to find a more effective way of learning. To this end, Huawei University leveraged i-Learning to train new employees.

In October 2011, Huawei invited the former CKO of the U.S. Army and the senior KM consultant of BP to introduce KM in their respective organizations and piloted project-centric KM and knowledge harvesting in a product development department. At the end of 2012, the pilot project was reported to and recognized by the senior management. The senior management instructed, "We should expand the pilot project in R&D in 2013. We should also find appropriate project pilot in delivery and solution sales". As for setting performance assessment indexes for KM, the senior management made it clear, "We should not assess the value of KM in isolation but assess it according to business results". KM, as an enabling system and method, plays a key role in supporting business.

From 2011 to 2013, the knowledge platform was strengthened. Built on the previous effort, Huawei further developed its KM system and designated a position for KM at the company level. The position is also responsible for developing competence centers, designing KM policies, processes and rules, studying and absorbing KM methodology, and building and operating KM platforms. The company's Quality and BP Department was a business partner for KM, responsible for promoting and implementing KM methods, and coaching business departments to conduct KM activities. At this stage, Huawei's 3MS platform was enriched and developed with newly-added functions like company-level search, multidimensional classification of knowledge systems and real-time communication, so that Huawei people around the world could use this platform more effectively. In addition, R&D teams became more mature in project-based KM and knowledge acquisition, which was widely adopted by various project development teams. In this way, experience and lessons learned can be used in new projects. Knowledge sharing has become a consensus.

In April 2012, Huawei established a dedicated KM team at the company level to more effectively support the project group. The KM team has solved the information security issue. At the end of 2012, with the barriers between R&D and non-R&D

departments broken, R&D and non-R&D knowledge communities were merged into a company-level Hi community, thus achieving “One Huawei, One Community”.

In 2013, when the Carrier BG put KM at the top of its agenda, KM started to advance from R&D to marketing and delivery and expanded pilot projects in R&D. At the institutional level, in January 2013, the company released its KM architecture and related guidance documents, which was a landmark for KM formally elevated to the company’s management system. Meanwhile, it clearly stipulated that the Quality and BP Department was the owner of KM responsible for its implementation in various fields.

Huawei’s vision for KM is to actively share and quickly acquire knowledge to outperform itself in every project. Its mission is to plan and deploy an efficient KM system benchmarked against the best practices, provide KM solutions for business teams in typical scenarios to support businesses, improve efficiency, product/service quality, and create a sustained competitive edge. According to MIT’s KM curriculum, the value of KM is less about knowledge or IT, but rather about the application of knowledge by organization members.

In order to promote KM in the company and share the best practices, Huawei awards teams and individuals for their outstanding contributions. The KM Department organized the first Huawei KM Conference and invited senior managers who render support to KM. At the conference, the rotating CEO Xu Zhijun gave a keynote speech “Create Value for Huawei with Knowledge and Expertise” and called on managers at all levels to master KM concepts, methodologies and tools and use KM to continuously strengthen employees’ capacities and improve business efficiency. After the conference, Xu posted his speech in his blog in Hi Community, creating an enabling atmosphere for KM in the company. Subsequently, more and more business teams began to understand the importance of KM and actively practice KM. In R&D, more than 20% of product development departments take systematic approaches before and after the project is executed, and throughout the whole project. Eighty per cent of product development departments used the “After Action Review” (AAR) method. Competency-centers in marketing/sales and delivery began to take on the role of knowledge owners to identify, harvest, integrate and refine knowledge and experience to provide higher-quality knowledge products for employees of field offices. They also bring together business peers, respond to requests for help, and disseminate best practices. Huawei’s KM teams have taken the lead to update and release KM job descriptions, opened up channels for the career development for full-time and part-time knowledge managers, and integrated KM activities with main business processes.

Case: KM practices in the Huawei Dragon Project

In 2015, Huawei started the Dragon Project in Japan. Huawei was determined to make it a flagship project. Huawei had projects in Germany, but the Japanese customers were arguably most critical. In the end, Huawei made customers truly satisfied through KM (see Fig. 11.2).

Project Background. Japanese customers are a high-end customer group for Huawei. Before the Dragon Project, Huawei failed to enter the Japanese market

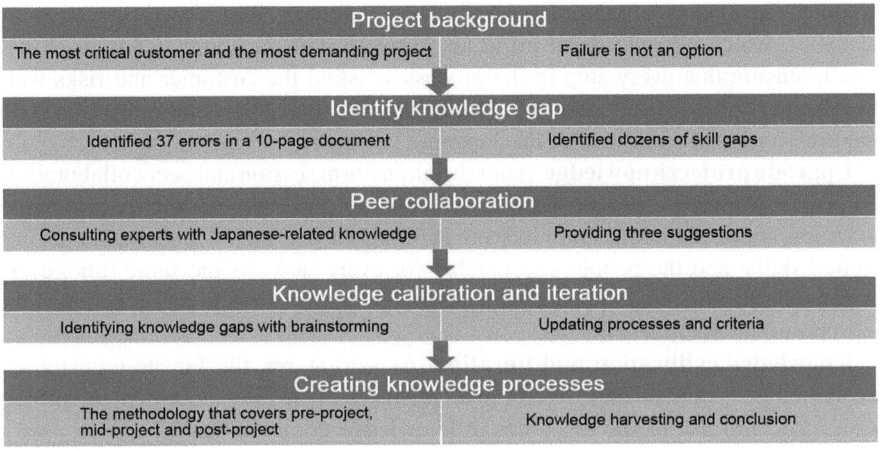

Fig. 11.2 KM process in the Huawei Dragon Project

despite years of efforts, due to Japan's extremely stringent quality standards. In 2015, Huawei was fortunate to win a bid in Japan, which was the first bid for EPC network, so Huawei's senior management demanded that the project must be made into a flagship project with a lighthouse effect. Failure was not an option.

Identify Knowledge Gap. Because it was the first cooperation with a Japanese customer, at the beginning of the project, Huawei had no idea about the quality standards of the Japanese customer. Once the Japanese customer picked out 37 errors in a 10-page document submitted by Huawei, including spelling errors, structural errors and punctuation errors. Japanese believe that if you cannot even do small things right, your product quality is at great risk. This is how the Japanese make great products. In addition, the Japanese are well-planned and detail-oriented, and they record everything. Therefore, Huawei set the goal of "three zeros"—zero delay, zero complaint, and zero accident.

To this end, the project team first held a brainstorming session to identify what gaps they had in knowledge, processes, and methods. At the session, the team identified dozens of skills gaps, including a dozen key knowledge gaps. Afterwards, based on each gap, the team made a detailed KM plan. For example, the Japanese are meticulous about data and documentation, so the team took the initiative to reexamine materials submitted to the customer. In short, the team examined the whole process from end to end and every activity to spot all the gaps in knowledge activities.

Peer collaboration. Based on the identified knowledge gaps, the project team started knowledge collaboration on Huawei's KM platform. The collaboration mainly took the form of seeking advice from Huawei's experts who had dealt with Japanese customers to find ways to bridge the knowledge gaps. The project team first consulted with the wireless department because its staff had successful projects in Japan. They made dozens of valuable suggestions. First, the team must dispatch its best people to deal with Japanese customers, because the Japanese are very demanding and highly technical. Second, a laboratory needed to be established jointly with the Japanese customer, which allowed the team to keep in line with Japanese standards in real time to ensure that every step in the process satisfied the customer and risks were dissolved even before they emerged. Third, they also shared the communication skills and preferences and customs of the Japanese customers.

Upgrade project knowledge. After the brainstorm session and peer collaboration, the project team reviewed the system again and proposed new quality requirements and a new action plan. Many details were included such as major concerns for testing, needed skills, and the people accountable for every task. At the same time, every responsible person is equipped with a seasoned mentor, so that they could develop appropriate interaction skills.

Knowledge calibration and iteration. As said above, the Japanese customers are meticulous about details. To eliminate mistakes in the files submitted, the project team made full use of the resources in knowledge communities. The team used a very popular online game "Carrot Defense" to promote knowledge calibration in knowledge communities. A total of 4 groups of more than 20 "post-90s" joined the "data defense". If a team spotted a mistake in the document, it would be awarded a carrot. If another team found another mistake, the carrot would be transferred to the new team. The game was very successful and productive. A "post-90s" was responsible for the entire planning and operating of the project. Finally, the quality of the project documents was improved by 30%.

In the process of knowledge iteration, the project team continuously dovetailed with the customer's requirements and quality standards. Especially in specific testing, the team identified new problems and correcting them in real time. In this process, the team kept upgrading the processes and standards through continuous improvement and timely review. As a result, the success rate of delivery increased over time. The team also drew on lessons learned to iterate quality standards through AAR. The team also learned a lot from the Japanese customer. For example, in the process of equipment cutover, the Japanese customer is very strict on mounting on the insulation pad. There are always two employees responsible: one standing at the front of the pad to operate, and the other at the back to protect. The former will report that he/she is going to mount on the pad three times to notify the latter. By contrast, Huawei employees did not have to engage in such procedures and simply pressed the start button. However, these few steps can greatly reduce human error, which is worth learning, so the team added these steps to Huawei's processes too.

Creating knowledge processes. By learning before and during the project and reviewing, the team continuously summarized experience and lessons and improved, and in the end, solidified the results in the processes. Before the cutover with the Japanese customer, the team made a lot of run-throughs to improve the quality according to the customer's requirements. Many steps that had not been identified were identified during the run-throughs. There were two levels of the run-throughs: one took place in the lab by the team alone, and the other was done jointly with the customer. The Japanese customer recognized Huawei's team for their preparedness. All four sets of equipment in the Dragon project were successfully launched with a single cutover with basically zero mistake, which had never happened before, not even with Ericsson. So, even by Japanese standard, what Huawei achieved was quite amazing.

11.5 KM Platform

Knowledge integration is the core competence of a company. For an MNC with 170,000 employees and businesses in over 200 countries, knowledge integration capability (KIC) can be measured in terms of the breadth, depth and speed of knowledge acquisition. If the lessons learned by individuals, project teams, business units and regional companies can be integrated and shared quickly, organizational efficiency will be improved significantly and the cost of trial and error reduced. This will bring about differentiated knowledge assets that can be easily integrated.

Huawei's KM platform was launched in 2005. It began with marketing-oriented knowledge integration and gradually covered all its businesses. 3MS was originally used to release standard marketing materials and other department-level documents for market-facing products. Later, it added channels for cases, videos, pictures, terminology, market information, etc. In 2012, it created the company-level Hi community by integrating with the previous R&D community. In 2013, with the knowledge asset library launched, the largest knowledge-sharing platform of Huawei took shape. The platform now brings together company-level resources, refined knowledge libraries and video sharing function, the Hi community, and carrier and BG-related marketing materials.

The four-layer architecture of the KM platform

The 3MS platform architecture is divided into four layers: the access layer, the application layer, the service layer, and the content layer. In the access layer, a mobile version of 3MS was launched in 2014 for users to access knowledge anytime and anywhere in a secured manner. In addition, several business departments have also developed their specific mobile apps based on 3MS. These apps have business scenario-oriented interfaces and operation modes but their contents are all taken from 3MS. In the application layer, the most visited apps are Team, Blog and Document. Currently, there are more than 8,000 teams in 3MS; visits to the Team account for 85% of the total visits. The contribution/visit ratio of the Team channel is 1.5 times higher than that of the Blog channel. This may tell us that most of the users are more interested in the work of peers and colleagues in the department. So, the next challenge for 3MS is to enrich the circle-based applications while respecting users' preferences and to make the information from different circles connected. The service layer builds key functions needed by the application layer. The service layer is more demanding than the application layer: the latter makes the platform "useful" to users, and the former makes it "sticky" to users. At present, 27 services are provided on Huawei's KM platform, including search, multidimensional classification, report statistics, smart recommendation, online editing, online reading and online comment. The quality of the service layer directly affects the user experience. For example,

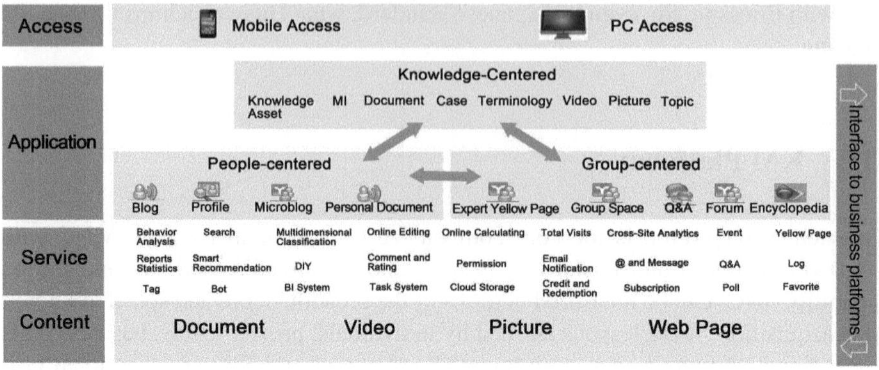

Fig. 11.3 The architecture of 3MS

to improve the accuracy of the "search" service, a lot of efforts have been made, such as optimizing the search engine, sorting out the frequent searches in key business areas, organizing the standard names and corresponding synonyms, designing multiple models with different weight of search ranking, sorting out the recommended frequently searched keywords, configuring Bestbets, improving search UI experience, and so on. The high cost brings about a great value. It is estimated that for every second saved in search, 380,000 RMB will be saved per year. The content layer offers multiple types of content, including documents, videos, images and web pages. Usually, certain types of content can only be found in certain applications, but in the future content will be decoupled from applications to enable cross-application content transfer (see Fig. 11.3).

Business demand drives the development of KM platform

New products on the platform are managed by the 3MS "idea factory" and the product planning and demand management teams of the product developer; they jointly discuss product planning, user requirements and determine version requirements. The budget for products developed by 3MS mainly comes from the department with the business demands, so the demands for KM products and services are sort of like investment projects of business departments.

The 3MS operation organization has three levels. Platform operation is undertaken by the company's KM Department, the departmental operation often by knowledge managers (KMers), and team managers are usually business personnel. In practice, platform managers and department managers have the closest relationship and provide solid support to each other. Department managers are usually KMers, and the VIP users of the platform. They are the channel to receive users' opinions, an important target group to consult on demand planning and operation policy formulation, and the key partners in organizing major operating activities. The team is the most important "cell" of the platform, so it is especially important to cover the team managers. When it comes to collect opinions on major changes, promote new features, hold major operating activities, direct and clear communication with the

8,000 team managers is required. In addition to the three levels, platform fans also play an important role in the operation. They will give constructive comments on platform optimization, participate in internal testing for new features and respond to the platform's operating activities. They help create positive public opinions.

11.6 Community of Practice

The Community of Practice is an informal, unstructured network group that consists of a group of participants (members of an organization, external experts, or even consumers) who come together for a shared purpose, topic, interest, or other presumed relations. The fundamental function of the community is to communicate and share knowledge and experience. Due to a large number of information islands, people's tacit knowledge cannot be effectively shared and exchanged, and an organization's creativity and innovation potential cannot be easily tapped. The loss of employees usually takes away a large amount of valuable experience, resulting in huge knowledge loss. Therefore, the community provides a smooth channel for people to exchange knowledge and skills. In the workplace, people usually gather in the same department, but in the community, the departmental boundaries and even company boundaries are broken, as are the barriers of space and time. People can talk to people within the company or to experts outside the company. They may come from the same geographic location or not. People don't have to "meet" at the same time to discuss a topic; they can communicate anytime and anywhere. The virtual Community of Practice plays an important role in promoting knowledge flow across organizations and national boundaries for MNCs.

In Huawei, there are three types of Community of Practice. First, a community of peers, i.e., people of similar professional backgrounds and have similar knowledge demand. They can create common ground and have a shared identity. The more professionals a community attracts, the greater value the community has. Second, a community formed by mutual trust and help. People in such a community influence each other, learn from each other, and exchange skills, knowledge, information and feelings. There is a strong sense of identity and belonging among the community members. Third, the virtual Community of Practice, where people analyze cases, stories, experience, ideas, solutions, etc.

Huawei's Community of Practice has two major functions: First, it helps to improve employees' ability to solve practical problems in an efficient and cost-effective fashion and enables employees to have dynamic communication and share high-value experience. The orientation can help transfer information or knowledge to new employees, but it is not easy for them to become business backbones quickly, because knowledge is not automatically transformed into capabilities, which are often gained by applying knowledge in practice. What companies need is that people can use their knowledge to solve problems, but the problems are usually scenario-based, and they change over time. If they learn as they go, it will take several years for them to become a good problem solver. To shorten the time frame, in Huawei's

Community of Practice, people can ask questions when meeting problems, peers with similar experiences will provide solutions which the questioner can immediately apply to solve the problem. Such a process greatly cuts the time by transforming one person's ability into another's. Second, it promotes synergy. People in the community get to know and understand each other through multi-level and multi-dimensional exchanges. This is a mechanism that creates reciprocity-based trust among community members, and this trust will evolve from business knowledge and information dimension cut to emotion dimension later. Based on the weak connection, cross-organizational collaboration is more efficient. Also, interpersonal relationship based on the professional level is more stable, which will not be affected much by organizational restructuring. This stability helps enhance the sense of belonging and reduce the turnover rate.

Huawei's KM teams have made a lot of efforts to lay the groundwork to build, operate and maintain communities of practice, such as identifying key knowledge domains in the company, establishing community operation organization and mechanisms (including setting up community development and operation teams consisting of supporters, community leaders and community facilitators), and building community IT platforms. All of these promote online communication among community members. Huawei takes each community of practice as a new project, so the management focuses on formulating community planning at the initial phase and illuminating community goals, expected outcomes, development roadmaps, etc. The community platform should be tailored to the target group and content in the community. Established communities of practice need to be marketed so as to reach the target group. The marketing draws on the practices of social networking sites, such as theme operation, content operation, user operation, section operation, event operation, etc. This phase focuses on the number of visits, the growth of target users, etc. and the community is regularly measured. After a community is established, it is necessary to make the community more adhesive so as to guide the community users to form different circles. Typical practices include sub-domain community operation, community crowdfunding, etc. This stage focuses on aligning the development of the community with that of the organization and the community is expected to undertake part of the organization's work and exert its influence on the company. The KM department needs to periodically measure how active the community is and whether the community has reached its goals. If the goals or the businesses covered by the community have changed, the community needs to make adjustments accordingly, including redefining goals, replanning the community, and remarketing. Similar to the development of organizations, communities may be also dissolved if the company canceled the business that the community used to serve. The Community of Practice is a huge mobile knowledge library, where a large amount of tacit knowledge is stored. This is a new KM form which emerges from the company's failure to apply knowledge library and it is the best way to store and disseminate knowledge, adapted for tacit and dynamic knowledge. It is fair to say that the Community of Practice itself is a knowledge-based networking circle, which roots in people, knowledge and knowledge exchange between people. A good community is meant to promote orderly knowledge exchange, and the Community of Practice needs to integrate with organization business for its long-term development.

11.7 Project-Based KM

With project management at the core of Huawei's business practice, Huawei's management has changed from "function-centric" to "project-centric". The project-centric KM aims to make the new version better than the old ones by taking the knowledge system of product development as its core and collecting experience of previous projects. It is a process of knowledge collection and reuse, which can greatly improve the efficiency and reduce costs. In October 2011, Huawei introduced two KM consultants from the U.S. Army and BP to introduce advanced concepts and methods. The most important thing of all is the U.S. Army's AAR,[12] which has brought the best practices in KM to Huawei and help it explore tailored KM solutions.

On the basis of the industry's KM practice, the KM system framework based on the Product Development Department was systematically constructed. This framework, through AAR, Knowledge Exchange, Retrospect (project review),[13] peer assistance, knowledge visits and other professional KM methods, can enhance the capability of organizational personnel and summarize the lessons learned in the project process for continuous improvement and optimization, and ultimately supports the continuous improvement of delivery quality. Project-centric KM mainly works in the product development department. Based on the company's process-oriented operation, KM requires recording all the process-oriented and structured development actions, making tacit knowledge explicit and then turning it into a guide for the development of new versions. Knowledge reuse improves the efficiency and quality of the development of new versions. Meanwhile, Huawei accumulates a large amount of explicit knowledge in project development and with KM, a large amount of tacit knowledge in team members' brains can also be made explicit through the project-centric KM. Finally, effective project KM enables rapid response to the fast-paced changes in the market and new product development.

The details of project KM include making effective knowledge planning at the early version design stage to identify the steps of low-level testing (LLT) needed in this version. The steps specify the automated testing operations. At that time, without sufficient relevant experience, the project team couldn't implement these steps effectively. So, the department made a knowledge planning and knowledge visit. They went to the Beijing Research Center (BRC) because it started LLT earlier. They found that the use cases of BRC's LLT could be automated. Using KM methods

[12] AAR is a lightweight, systematic method of instant review and reflection. It is commonly used by the U.S. Army after each training or mission to help the army reflect and learn during operations.

[13] Retrospect is a heavyweight project review method; it is mostly applied after the project is concluded.

to plan and learn in advance, with the help of the pilot project team, the visit has been made more systematic, more efficient, and more focused. Greatly inspired by a team at the BRC, they developed a set of automated LLT use case generation platform suitable for equipment-level products for the J Product Department. Eventually, the time of use case generation dropped from 90 min to 10.

Project-centric KM process

Project-centric KM brings the following benefits to product development:

1. Transforming previous experience into a systematic knowledge system. Through three agile iterations, actions, paths, methods and experience are systematically summarized to transform individual knowledge into team and organizational knowledge, which is more effective than previous spontaneous behaviors. Thanks to it, the quality is greatly improved and the design by the product department is passed in one go without redo.
2. Taking full advantage of IT tools to support the product development process.
3. Getting the value of project KM more widely recognized. Through a course of pilot, Huawei's R&D teams came to accept project process learning, Community of Practice, and knowledge asset accumulation. In particular, they agree that the application of KM should shift its focus from on asset accumulation to application in practice. The concept of integrating KM into the business development site is implemented in process, IT, and organizational settings.
4. Recognizing the principle that KM always revolves around business. The pilot courses of KM always aim at business delivery targets and revolving around business. The pilot team works hard to win support from managers at all levels and makes each KM activity achieve desired results with the well-designed arrangement. It does not engage in a one-size-fits-all approach and always provides the most appropriate KM solution well-adapted for the pain points of the team.

Huawei has formed a set of systematic processes and methods for its project KM, as shown in Fig. 11.4.

At the early phase, project-related KM activities include the following steps:

1. Confirming customer. It involves systematically investigating the customer's needs and get confirmation.
2. Benchmarking against leading standards. It involves the search for reference materials from existing materials, experts, knowledge libraries and hardware equipment.
3. Customer benchmarking. It focuses on collecting service processes and standards from similar customers.
4. Maturity assessment. It involves identifying the resources, personnel and services that the company should match based on the above materials and data.
5. Formulating strategies. It refers to formulating strategies and methods to meet customer needs on the basis of sufficient knowledge.

In mid-project, it's time for the implementation and advancement of the project, which requires rapid capacity enhancement. By effectively transferring the

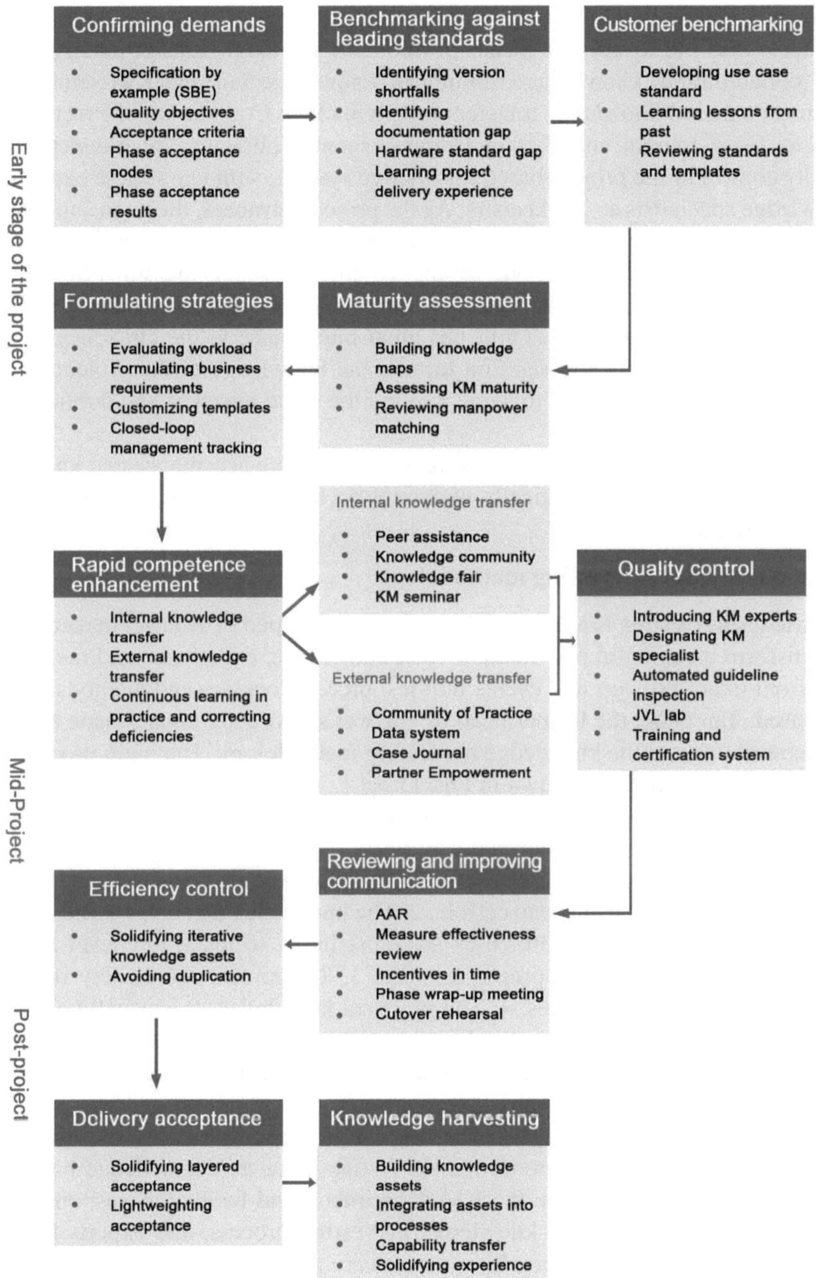

Fig. 11.4 KM process of Huawei Project

company's internal and external knowledge to the project team, the quality of the project is thus improved. The means of internal knowledge transfer mainly include peer collaboration, knowledge community, knowledge fair and KM seminar; the means of external knowledge transfers mainly include Community of Practice, data system, Case Journal and Partner Empowerment. Following the transfers is the quality control of the project-based knowledge system, with knowledge experts and knowledge specialists as gatekeepers. As the project advances, the team summarizes good experience by reviewing and improving communication (incentives in time) and correcting what has been done wrong in a timely manner (measure effectiveness review). In this process, AAR, the most commonly used method by the U.S. Army, is of vital importance. Huawei attaches great importance to the efficiency of KM, and its efficiency control focuses on turning the knowledge of the project into the company's knowledge assets to avoid making the same mistakes and duplication in knowledge effort.

In the closing phase, the priority of KM is knowledge acceptance and knowledge harvesting. We will systematically elaborate on how to harvest knowledge in the project case analysis.

Case: Knowledge harvesting methodology

Knowledge harvesting is an important KM tool developed by Huawei in recent years to transform meaningful and valuable tacit knowledge, experience and methodologies from major projects and events into resources, processes and methods that can be reused. Tan Qide, the former head of Huawei's KM department, made a significant contribution to the knowledge harvesting methodology. The main processes of knowledge harvesting are shown in Fig. 11.5.

Defining the target of knowledge harvesting. Usually, for new projects (known as the zero-to-one project) and major projects, Huawei's KM team would initiate knowledge harvesting. There are five major types of knowledge that Huawei values most: 1. The knowledge that can cash in. 2. The knowledge that helps avoid repeated mistakes. New employees (30–70%) are most likely to make low-level mistakes which can be reduced after proper training. 3. The knowledge closely related to work, especially best practices. 4. The practical knowledge. It is usually generated from delivery results. 5. The methodologies that can especially benefit new recruits. Such knowledge can help them learn much faster by identifying key success factors and replicable methods and paths.

The process of knowledge harvesting. The process focuses on the target, participants and output of knowledge harvesting. Huawei's knowledge harvesting team includes personnel from the KM department, and facilitators responsible for designing and managing the knowledge harvesting process, and experts from the company's competence centers. Interviewees are mainly core members involved in the project and field office team members. Huawei has trained KM facilitators responsible for agenda arrangement and issued more than 1,000 facilitator certificates. The project team leverages interviews and meetings to understand the methodology, key processes, members' feelings, and major difficulties and problems and solutions during the project implementation. The output of knowledge harvesting comes in

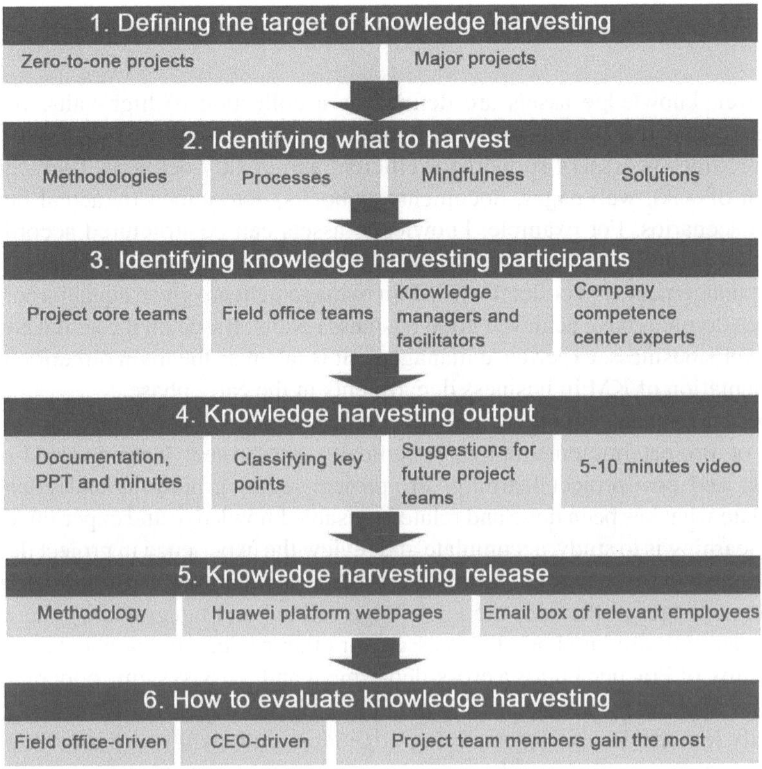

Fig. 11.5 Knowledge harvesting process

different forms, such as documentation, PPTs, minutes, key points classification, success stories, feedback and suggestions for future project teams, and 5–10-min videos.

Knowledge harvesting output. The output will be sent to the company's proprietary and well-categorized KM platform. Meanwhile, the KM team will forward the output to relevant business teams for their reference. Some of the output is open for all employees; some is only open for specific teams and individuals. The average hit of the output is about 15 or 16 times, the most read output exceeded 3,000 hits. The methodology of knowledge harvesting will greatly reduce the cost of exploration and trial and error for other teams and improve the efficiency of doing businesses. For the project team, the process of knowledge harvesting is also a process of AAR and refinement.

11.8 Management of Knowledge Content and Assets

In Huawei, knowledge assets are defined as a collection of high-value reusable knowledge that has been organized, refined and recognized by the organization, which provides necessary support for efficient and quality delivery. They can take the form of wiki, web pages, documents or books, determined by actual business demand scenarios. For example, knowledge assets can be structured according to workflows or topics. In the KM framework, explicit knowledge management, experience management, and collective wisdom management are given equal importance. The three domains have achieved good business results. Based on the actual situation of Huawei's business, experience management is taken as the main direction for the implementation of KM in business departments in the early phase.

Experience management includes the management of knowledge at different phases of project implementation, specifically, pre-project learning, mid-project learning, and post-project learning. Pre-project learning aims to understand and investigate what has been done and related reusable knowledge and experience. Mid-project learning is to study, accumulate and review the experience in project development on the basis of existing knowledge. Post-project learning is to summarize and refine knowledge. In the end, the knowledge refined and integrated by the knowledge owner will turn into knowledge assets for other projects to learn and apply. The Community of Practice builds a cross-department and cross-system cooperation and exchange platform for people of the same field. In the Community of Practice, people can easily join the discussion on cutting-edge ideas with their peers, receive prompt answers to thorny questions, share experience and lessons, and reduce the risks of making mistakes and taking a wrong path. In the post-project learning, through effective KM, many processes, specifications, guidelines, checklists/inventories, contacts, communities, FAQs and other knowledge assets are accumulated from practice. Knowledge is divided into primary knowledge, secondary knowledge, tertiary knowledge and knowledge refinement. Some knowledge is discarded according to their use efficiency and life cycle to ensure its recycling. On the platform, employees have easy access to knowledge through search engines and Baidu Wenku-style knowledge libraries.

Building professional knowledge maps

The knowledge asset management of Huawei Finance & Accounting Center (FAC) is a typical domain-level knowledge asset repository. The center is responsible for Huawei's procurement and payment and handles about 5.3 million invoices per year. Its employees work in seven sharing centers around the world, with a high turnover rate. Many of them are from outside China or newly enrolled. The business of the center involves a large number of different business scenarios, countries, interface departments, etc., so employees need to work with many complex scenario combinations. The explicit knowledge such as operation guidelines and scenario descriptions, great in number and poorly organized, updates quickly.

In the process of managing professional knowledge, the customized knowledge map is adopted to screen important instructions, classify knowledge according to demands and structure knowledge systems so as to make knowledge easy to find, convenient to use and update. As FAC was dealing with a large amount of informal knowledge, had very little integrated official guidance and had to face rapid knowledge updates, it worked with the KM team to analyze the problems and the needs in KM. They have thus formulated targeted measures and plans. Specifically, they have designed a full cycle of explicit knowledge flow, covering the stages of knowledge acquisition, knowledge sharing, knowledge reengineering/refinement, knowledge recycling and knowledge application and appointed knowledge owners. As the keeper of each subdomain and knowledge point, the knowledge owner is responsible for refining and integrating and maintaining the knowledge assets in the domain to create the latest, credible and authoritative knowledge collection. The O&M of the finance and accounting knowledge library is led by the KM team with the knowledge owners of each sub-domain to delegate the duties downward, so minimum manpower input can obtain maximum benefit. For example, in the knowledge system of finance and accounting, according to work demand, it includes work scenarios, regions, processes, product solutions, tags and specialized domains. When dealing with complex business scenarios, users can combine different keywords, such as country, process and business type, for their search. Each combination will lead to different operation guidance and knowledge. The knowledge library adopts "search + multi-dimensional classification filtering" to facilitate knowledge access and meet users' inquiry scenarios as much as possible. It has solved the problems of poor access and conflict versions of guidelines, and thus improved accounting efficiency and helped the center achieve expedited payment.

11.9 Huawei Versus Cisco

Even in the earliest days, Huawei already prioritized knowledge assets over financial assets. Huawei realized that it had no natural resources to depend upon, but what it did have was the brainpower of its employees. This is its oil, its forest, and its coal. Human ingenuity is the creator of all wealth. Therefore, responsible and effective employees are Huawei's greatest assets. So, Huawei respects knowledge and individuality, and advocates collective hard work. I met some young employees working at Huawei after leaving their previous companies, where they were often neglected and had no decent payment. However, in Huawei, they not only received good working conditions and decent renumerations but also were assigned important tasks and given good opportunities. Young people working at Huawei today are willing to stay despite high work pressure because in addition to above the average payment, they can work with amazing teams, have fair opportunities and room for growth. Huawei's institutional design is based on the understanding that intellectual property and technical know-how have greater value and weight than financial capital because capital needs to rely on knowledge to retain and increase its value.

Second, Huawei's rapid growth is a journey of absorbing external knowledge, including absorbing the world's latest research achievements and humbly learning from outstanding companies at home and abroad. In order to learn from global leading companies including consulting companies, Huawei has invested tens of billions of RMB since 1995 in purchasing knowledge systems and solutions. From IPD to integrated supply chain, from human resources to quality management, from financial management, to LTC, it spares no effort to learn from the best. Taking KM as an example, in order to understand the best practices, Huawei invited U.S. Army's CKO and professors from the Community of Practice to offer consultancy services or give lectures. At the micro-level, Huawei conducts in-depth and detailed research on competitors through simulations. Huawei calls this method a dissipative structure theory which is about quickly absorbing and acquiring external knowledge to invest in building its future capacity. Through excellent R&D and management, Huawei gains returns which are later used to invest in better knowledge systems to pave the way for future development. According to Ren, Huawei should never be penny wise when it comes to investment in the future; if you are true leaders or generals, or you have a future-oriented strategy, you would not behave like this. Huawei requires that its senior managers and employees should not only communicate with Ph.D. supervisors but also with Ph.D. candidates to take in everything useful from the universe, so to speak. Huawei believes the ability and vision to apply knowledge are more important than simply have it. When many foreigners try to interpret Huawei's success, they tend to focus on their perceived Ren's military background and alleged support from the state. What they fail to see is Huawei's learning capacity and its courage and ambition to catch up.

Finally, Huawei's KM platform and system are unique. This uniqueness lies in its close integration with business, user-orientation, and emphasis on content management. Based on these methods, Huawei distills the organization's best practices and lessons and effectively integrates and utilizes them to improve the reusability and transferability of knowledge. User-orientation means that Huawei never uses administrative ordinance to force users to export knowledge but takes user needs as guidance to build the KM platform. To this end, Huawei's KM team conducts user research regularly to understand users' demands and expectations. It also analyses the data and behavior of platform users to discover and determine what functions need to be optimized and prioritized. For the management of the internal platform, it is necessary to constantly balance the conflicts, preferences and demands of all parties.

Compared with Huawei's KM platform and knowledge harvesting method, Cisco places more emphasis on cross-departmental collaboration in the organization. By leveraging its advantages as a communication technology company, Cisco has developed a cross-country, cross-culture and cross-department KM collaboration platform, which has brought about barriers-free knowledge flow and sharing and created a new work ecosystem for employees. This ecosystem has integrated technologies and applications such as video and audio, documents and archives, social media, expert maps, and expert collaboration platforms and carved out a smooth channel for communication and collaboration within the company and especially between the sales team and other teams. Such a KM platform is well-designed for global office work, reducing knowledge search and communication costs, attracting expert resources, and for remote working.

Part III
Research Papers

Chapter 12
How Huawei Broke Through the Triple Dilemmas to Build Dual Capability?

12.1 Triple Dilemmas to Build Dual Capability

Dual capability refers to the capability to sustain intense exploration and application activities in parallel; it is a core dynamic capability that enables Huawei to survive and thrive as the world's leading ICT solutions provider. Through intense exploration activities, Huawei is able to perceive cutting-edge technologies, gain insight into the potential needs of customers, and quickly launch new products and features to adapt to the rapidly changing environment. Through intense application activities, Huawei is able to continuously optimize existing products and technologies, consolidate its position in the market, and solidify and expand the application of existing knowledge and experience, thereby improving the efficiency and reducing operating costs.

However, high-intensity exploration and application activities not only promote each other but also interfere with each other from time to time. The two are mutually reinforcing in that the knowledge summarized from high-intensity utilization activities can be used to scan, discover and predict the direction of exploration activities and evaluate the value of new technologies, thus reducing the risk of exploration; at the same time, high-intensity exploration activities can provide new ideas for knowledge refinement and application, avoiding application from falling into the trap of local optimality. This is because both exploration activities and application activities are essentially learning processes of firms, and they can both generate new knowledge, but the learning methods and the degree of novelty of knowledge are different: exploration activities deviate from the original learning track and create new knowledge that differs greatly from the original knowledge, while application activities follow the original learning track and refine and abstract new knowledge on the basis of the original knowledge.

The competing relationship between the two is the key dilemma in the construction of ambidexterity, which is manifested in the following three main aspects. First, **the competition for resources**. Both high-intensity exploration and application activities consume a large amount of resources, and there is tension between the two in

X. Dong et al., *Huawei*,
https://doi.org/10.1007/978-981-19-4078-1_12

resource allocation. Second, **mode conflict**. High-intensity exploration and application activities have very different requirements in terms of organizational structure, value orientation, management system, and performance indicators, and the opposing and conflicting elements cause distress to employees and confusion to the overall management of the company. Generally speaking, exploration activities require a flexible and organic organizational structure, a loosely coupled management system, and an evaluation system that encourages trial and error and tolerates failure, while application activities require a strict mechanical organizational structure, a tightly coupled management system, and an elimination-based evaluation system to avoid mistakes. Finally, **a closed loop**. Both high-intensity exploration and application activities tend to form their own reinforcing cycles, which are mutually exclusive, and it is difficult to form a mutually reinforcing relationship. High-intensity application activities pursue short-term efficiency improvement and cost reduction, but risky and uncertain exploration activities cannot meet this requirement; similarly, high-intensity exploration activities focus on future-oriented values, but conservative and rigorous application activities cannot meet these requirements either. When exploration and application activities are repeated in their respective modes, they tend to form rigid, inertial, and closed cognitive systems.

In order to avoid interference between the two activities, while giving full play to their respective roles as much as possible to achieve mutual promotion, companies often use a separation-integration strategy of to build dual capability. The separation strategy refers to the establishment of separate organizational units within the firm to implement exploration and application activities separately. These organizational units are independently configured with their own organizational elements so that the two cannot interfere with each other in space and time. The separation strategy is based on the firm's strong capital and relies on its experience in resource allocation and distribution capabilities. The integration strategy refers to a firm's ability to create active links between the two activities with the help of specific organizational structures, contextual design, leadership and team design so that the results of exploration and application can build on each other and create positive interactions. The coordination and reconciliation of the dual capability ae more challenging and thus more valuable for the firm.

The purpose of this paper is to identify the separation and integration strategies used by Huawei in building the ambidexterity, and to answer the question "as a catch-up firm with scarce resources, backward management, and immature market knowledge in the early stage of growth, what difficulties did Huawei encounter in building the ambidexterity and what effective solutions did it adopt? The key research questions focus on the following three areas.

(1) How did Huawei conduct exploration and application activities when it lagged behind in terms of capital, talent, management knowledge, and market knowledge? What is its strategy for allocating resources to exploration and application activities (separation strategy)?
(2) In order to solve the problems of conflicting exploration and application activities, what approaches does Huawei use to establish positive links between

the two so that exploration and application can mutually promote each other (integration strategy)?

(3) How do Huawei's separation and integration strategies help resolve the dilemmas of building dual capability, and what role does each integration strategy play?

To answer these questions, and systematically study the separation-integration strategy adopted by Huawei, we have studied first-hand interview information with senior and middle managers, middle and junior employees, and Huawei consultants, 166 internal speeches of Huawei's top management team (including 136 internal speeches by Ren from 1994 to 2016), relevant information from Huawei's official website, annual reports, internal journals and forums, and secondary data such as academic studies home and abroad, authoritative media reports and research reports from third-party research institutions on Huawei.

12.2 Huawei's Dual Capability Model

The separation-integration strategy of Huawei's ambidexterity building is systematically presented in Fig. 12.1. The purpose of the strategy is to focus on the differences between exploration and application. The advantage of the separation strategy is that the exploration and application activities can be separated in terms of time or space to avoid the two interfering with each other, and the organization can mobilize its resources to keep the two activities independent and consistent within their respective business unit. Huawei's separation strategy is executed as follows according to the way it works (temporal or spatial separation) and the level to which it belongs (senior management or organization level). First, at the senior management level, the temporal and spatial separation is reflected in the "focus principle", which means that the executive team sets strategic priorities for organizational goals and commits resources at high density in the right direction to achieve local breakthroughs. Second, the time separation strategy at the organizational level is reflected in "job rotation", including the Rotating CEO System for the senior managers, the "job rotation" for middle managers and the "business rotation" for junior employees. Finally, the spatial separation strategy at the organizational level is reflected in the creation of different "business units" to focus on exploration and application activities separately.

Huawei's exploration activities are mainly in three forms: First, using external consultants for management introduction and change. Second, building a future-oriented basic R&D system (Huawei's 2012 Lab). Third, establishing joint innovation centers and labs mainly based on external resources (such as universities, research institutions, and R&D teams from partners). The first exploration activity is to explore management concepts and models, while the latter two are mainly to explore technologies and products.

Huawei's application activities are mainly in the following four forms: first, management optimization activities, including internal publications and forums that

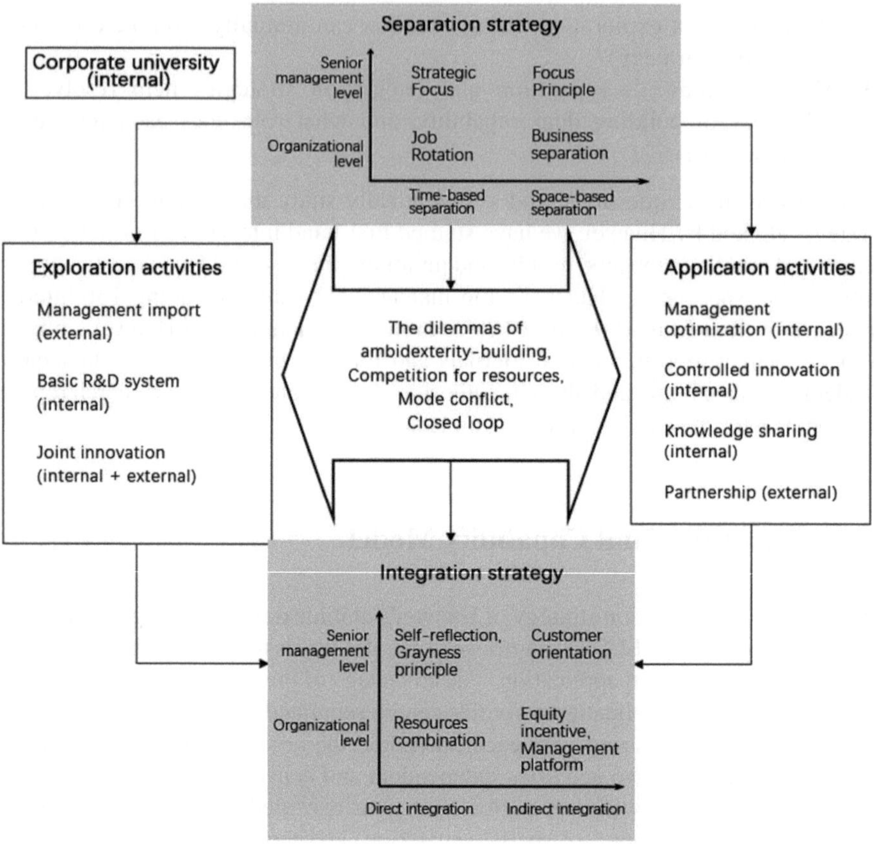

Fig. 12.1 Huawei's separation-integration strategy for building the dual capability

summarize and disseminate best practices, such as *Huawei People*, *Improvement* and Huawei Voice Community; second, innovation control activities, with "controlled innovation" as the orientation; third, Huawei University to solidify and refine internal and external tacit knowledge; fourth, regular partner conferences to consolidate and tap into existing customer markets.

The disadvantage of the separation strategy is that separate exploration and business units will consume a large number of organizational resources. Moreover, the separation strategy will intensify the closed cycles of exploration and application activities, and the organization will face obstacles in knowledge sharing. For this reason, the organization also needs to build integration strategies that enable exploration and application to promote each other.

The purpose of the integration strategy is to find the connection between two seemingly opposite "elements" and to build ambidexterity by making connections between them. Increasingly, scholars are recognizing that exploration and application activities can build a complementary relationship, with exploration activities providing material for optimization and expansion of application activities, and application activities providing the knowledge base for the next-round exploration activities. The integration strategy plays a key role in the mutual enhancement and transformation of the two activities.

Huawei's integration strategy can be classified into four forms according to the mode of action (direct or indirect integration) and the level to which the integration strategy belongs (senior management or organization level). Direct integration refers to directly combine exploration and application and set up a new organizational practice accepted by all the members, while indirect integration refers to converge the results of exploration and application activities so that the results of exploration activities are be used as input of application activities, and vice versa.

The direct integration strategy at the senior management level is reflected in "self-reflection" and "grayness principle", which help Huawei achieve the coexistence and integration of exploration and application activities. The direct integration strategy at the organizational level is reflected in "resources combination", which means to set up a hybrid team of members who are good at both exploration and application activities. The indirect integration strategy at the senior management level is reflected in the "customer-centric" corporate culture. Finally, the indirect integration strategy at the organizational level is reflected in Huawei's "dedication-oriented" equity incentive system and its continuously optimized management system and platform. These indirect integration strategies enable rapid commercialization of exploration activities and make application activities more creative.

12.3 The Separation Strategy

The separation strategy enables the organization to focus its superior resources on completing exploration or application activities within a specific time frame and avoid mutual interference between the two. In terms of space, Huawei has set up different business units for exploration or application activities separately. In terms of time, Huawei has set up rotation mechanisms to enable exploration and application activities to be carried out alternately. The separation of time and space depends on Huawei's senior management's prioritization, which is known as Huawei's "focus principle".

12.3.1 Exploration Activities

Exploration activities refer to activities such as trial and error, experimentation, and daring conjecture by the firm that deviate from their original learning tracks. Exploration activities are mainly, but not limited to, research and development of products and technologies. For example, the firm's bold attempts and changes in management models are also considered as exploration activities.

Huawei values exploration. Take its R&D input for example, in 2007, Huawei mentioned in its first public annual report, "Huawei will continue to invest at least 10% of its sales revenue in R&D and allocate 10% of its R&D investment to research on cutting-edge technologies, core technologies and basic technologies." Over the past 12 years, despite fluctuations in the market and fierce competition, Huawei's cumulative R&D input reached RMB 321.7 billion (equivalent to about US$46.32 billion), and its R&D input as a percentage of sales revenue has never been less than 8.4%, with a 12-year average of 10.78%. Huawei has three main models of exploration activities: management introduction, basic R&D system and joint innovation.

Management Introduction

Ren once said, "As far as high-tech companies are concerned, management innovation is more important than technological innovation. Huawei still has many problems to solve, and the biggest gap between us and Western companies lies in management."[1] Since 1997, Huawei has initiated a series of management changes. Huawei has paid a lot to hire IBM, Hay, Accenture, TowersPerrin, the German National Institute of Applied Research (FhG) and other well-known companies as consultants to provide guidance and help for Huawei's management changes.[2] Huawei has invested nearly RMB 2 billion for the IBM consulting project alone.

An IBM consultant who spent 23 years at IBM and was responsible for the Huawei project from 1998 to 2003 recalled, "The collaboration started with a small project known as ITS&P (i.e., IT strategy and planning), and a procurement project that lasted for three or four months. In 1999, Huawei launched two key management change projects: in March 1999, Huawei started to reorganize R&D management and processes with IPD, and at the end of the year, Huawei launched ISC to improve the efficiency of the supply chain. Between 2000 and 2002, we also helped Huawei with key projects in IT such as system integration centers, data centers, and network research. In 2002, we started to focus on organization and talent training, and cooperated with Meizhi Corporation on organization research and with Huawei University on leadership development projects. From 2000 to 2003, Project Office was established to manage and coordinate all these projects until they were completed. From 1998 to 2003, I was the leader of all IBM projects at Huawei. I maintained daily communication with Huawei executives, listened to their requirements to improve service quality and satisfaction. I also managed all IBM consultants, and served as a consultant myself in Huawei's IPD/ISC program."[3]

In 1997, Huawei started to cooperate with Hay Group for HR management reform. It established a positioning system, a compensation system, a qualification system,

---

[1] Ren Zhengfei: "Innovation is the inexhaustible driving force of Huawei's development". July 20, 2000.

[2] http://www.360doc.com/content/16/1004/10/27935442_595670328.shtml.

[3] *Huawei People*, vol 199, April 30, 2008.

a performance management system, and competence models for positions and roles. On this basis, Huawei set up the principles for hiring, selecting, nurturing and retaining employees and the principles of selecting, training, appointing and assessing managers. Since 1998, Hay has conducted annual audits of Huawei's HR management to identify problems and then handed them over to Huawei for final resolution. In 2005, Huawei started to collaborate with Hay on leadership training, development and the establishment of a leadership competence model to train managers for the firm's global development.

> We introduced Hay's compensation and performance management, because we found that following the old path, although we are alive today, we might not be in the future. Now we need to take off our straw sandals and put on a pair of American shoes ...... When our HR management system is standardized and the company is mature and stable, we will break the Hay system and innovate. We will then bring in a group of talented people who are ambitious but not yet rich and will not settle for the status quo or be bound by the old norms, thus enabling our HR management system to innovate again to promote renewed growth.[4]

In 1997, Huawei started to work with FhG in terms of quality control and production management, to transform the entire production system and set up AS/RS, and the entire production lines, and successfully completed the process and quality control reorganization of 21 production lines.

In terms of changes in the accounting system, budget system, monitoring system and auditing system, Huawei has worked with PwC, KPMG, Deloitte and IBM, achieved "Four Harmonizations" (processes, systems, controls, and coding), set up a flexible closed-loop budgeting system that involves planning, budgeting, accounting, analyzing, monitoring and assessment. It has realized the sharing of domestic accounts, and the global unification of accounting codes and online financial management. The flexible and efficient budgeting system and the concept of whole-process cost management introduced by the consulting firm have enabled Huawei to establish an independent audit system and build a three-tier monitoring system of external audit, internal control and business audit, thus reducing the company's fiscal risk and financial risk.

In 2007, Huawei hired Accenture[5] to launch Customer Relationship Management (CRM) to strengthen the lead-order-cash process management. In 2008, Huawei and Accenture reorganized the CRM system and opened up a new lead-to-cash (LTC) process to improve the company's operational efficiency. In October 2014, Huawei and Accenture signed a strategic alliance agreement to jointly develop and promote innovative solutions for ICT customers of carriers and enterprises.

Huawei Rotating CEO Xu Zhijun said, "In an era of accelerated integration between the real world and the digital world, it is difficult for any single company to meet all the needs of its customers. Companies therefore need to be open and collaborative, integrate resources and capabilities to help their customers succeed. The partnership with Accenture will further strengthen Huawei's capabilities in the enterprise ICT market, enabling us to provide more innovative software and service

---

[4] Ren Zhengfei: "Viability is everything". *Huawei People*. 2000.

[5] http://www.360doc.com/content/15/1228/05/10348693_523596377.shtml.

solutions, based on our rich product portfolio, to enterprise and carrier customers and help them improve efficiency and increase revenue."

In addition, Huawei hired Mercer and Boston Consulting Group (BCG) as consultants for strategic management and human resource management, Zhengbang and Ogilvy & Mather for brand management, Gallup for customer satisfaction, TowersPerrin for equity incentive. It also worked with professors at the Business School of Renmin University to develop *Huawei Basic Law*. As of 2015, Huawei's 18-year reform costed about RMB 30 billion.

Basic R&D System[6]

Huawei established the Pre-Research Department (PRD) in the second half of 1988, and Ren made a clear statement about its function: "The department is to find the strategic direction in the chaos, seize strategic opportunities, and quickly establish pre-research projects." Since then, Huawei began to systematically research and develop forward-looking products and technologies, while establishing a pre-research system with a clear division of labor.

The predecessor of PRD goes back to the three major R&D systems set up in 1996, namely, the Product Strategic Research and Planning Office (PSRPO), the Central Research Department (CRD) and the Intermediate Pilot Department (IPD). The PSRPO was responsible for guiding the product development and projects of CRD, that is to answer the question of "what product to produce" so as to avoid "producing the wrong product"; the CRD was responsible for organizing the product development, with the goal of "in-time delivery"; the IPD was responsible for small batch production, testing and verification, production process, and product maturity research, with the goal of "producing good products", spotting possible quality problems and solving them in the early stage of R&D. PSRPO, CRD and IPD are responsible for the planning, management and control of R&D respectively, and the Pre-research system is developed on the basis of PSRPO.

In Huawei's pre-research system, in addition to the PRD under the CRD, each business department, say the Wireless BU, and Transmission BU, all has its own PRD. PRD is responsible for the latest and more challenging core technologies and forward-looking product development. Huawei stipulates that pre-research funding should account for 10% of the total R&D funding, and accordingly, the personnel should also account for 10% of the total R&D personnel, and the competence requirement of pre-research personnel is generally higher. Since 1998, PRD has done nearly 100 pre-research projects. Up to 2009, more than 80% of personnel in the R&D department have worked on projects developed by PRD. The quality of pre-research work is very difficult to evaluate. PRD's target is to maintain a 70–80% pre-research results conversion rate (based on inputs). A low conversion rate means that the product is not marketable, while a high conversion rate means that the pre-research work is too conservative, and it is likely to miss market opportunities.

The 2012 Laboratories (2012 Labs) is Huawei's research organization dedicated to basic R&D innovation. The 2012 Labs invested nearly US$2 billion in basic

[6] http://blog.sina.com.cn/s/blog_53bbdb8c0101rnli.html.

science in 2016. In the future, Huawei's investment in basic science research will gradually increase to 20–30% of R&D expenses. The organization has 18 research institutes, including eight in China and 8 overseas. Local employees at the overseas institutes account for more than 70% of the total number of employees at these institutes. The 2012 Labs is positioned to earn small profits for long term by Ren. The research of the 2012 Labs is oriented towards the long-term development goals and core competencies instead of quick money. Specifically, 2012 Labs focus on the R&D and testing needs in the next 5–10 years. Huawei's labs under each business unit focus on needs for the next 1–3 years. So, the mission of 2012 Labs is to make Huawei thrive rather than just survive. The 2012 Labs have no profitability target. A lab staff said, "This is a pure R&D department, and the income of the staff is the average of Huawei's overall income; the income beyond the salary of average employees is about half of the level of the Wireless BG. However, if you work your way up and become a fellow, the compensation is much higher.

Joint Innovation

Joint innovation is Huawei's strategy to integrate external resources for innovation. Based on the cooperation partner, Huawei's joint innovation takes three forms: Joint Labs, Joint Innovation Centers and OpenLab.

The **Joint Labs** are partnerships between Huawei and universities/research institutions, with the aim of developing cutting-edge technologies and entering foreign markets. Huawei's narrowband CDMA technology, SDH optical network technology, and intelligent network technology have benefited from the cooperation with universities such as Tsinghua University, Peking University, University of Science and Technology, Beijing University of Posts and Telecommunications, and University of Electronic Science and Technology. Currently, Huawei has established a joint laboratory for electromagnetic technology innovation with Zhejiang University and the Laboratory for Optical Interconnection Network and Advanced Computing System with the Hong Kong Polytechnic University. In addition, Huawei also invests heavily in cooperative R&D with overseas universities, and almost all its overseas R&D centers are sited close to well-known universities. In the UK, Huawei invested £10 million in 2017 to form a cooperative alliance with UK universities, for example, it conducted research on big data with Imperial College London, and on 5G technology with the University of Surrey.

> We must engage in basic research, without which it is impossible to create opportunities and guide consumption. Our basic research is conducted by joint laboratories with domestic universities. Our Pre-Research Department will be massively engaged only when there is an opportunity for basic research to be transformed into a commodity.[7]

In 1999, when Ren visited a company and its large joint laboratory in Bangalore, India, he was impressed by the strong innovative strength of the joint lab not only in terms of the hardware but also its technical strength. He said, "In order to make up for the lack of talent and tap into the complementary advantages of talent, we

[7] *Huawei Basic Law.*

decide to set up a joint laboratory at IIT University[8] to fund research projects, and grant scholarships and fellowships. We can also invite some talent to work in China so that they can establish branches in India in the future."[9]

The Joint Labs Huawei has built with leading companies not only help promote technology development but also help improve the R&D capabilities of Huawei's personnel. In 1997, Huawei and Texas Instruments established a joint lab for digital signal processing (DSP) hardware and software development. This cooperation has led to a new technology platform department set up by DSP-related personnel. Through the cooperation with Texas Instruments, Huawei achieved a rapid technological breakthrough and built a technology platform, which not only improved the ability of Huawei's engineers to develop and apply DSP chips, but also rapidly spawned new technology applications in the multimedia field. In April 2000, Huawei and Intel established a joint development center in Shenzhen to jointly design communication solutions Internet Exchange(IX). In the CDMA and 3G fields, Huawei has achieved rapid technological breakthroughs with the purchase of Qualcomm's protocol patents. In addition, Huawei has established joint labs with tech giants such as Motorola, Agere, Altera, Sun Microsystems, Microsoft, and NEC.[10]

The **Joint Innovation Centers** are mainly partnerships between Huawei and telecom carriers, with the aim of providing innovative solutions to meet the needs and strategies of carriers. Huawei and the carrier both dispatch their excellent experts to the centers, where the carrier's strategies, ideas and needs and Huawei's technologies, and concepts meet, and result in leading solutions. At the same time, these solutions can be quickly executive in the joint innovation center and launched into the market in time to achieve a win–win result for consumers, carriers and Huawei. In October 2006, Huawei and Vodafone officially established their first joint innovation center, the Mobile Innovation Center (MIC), in Spain. As of September 2016, Huawei has established 36 joint innovation centers with its global customers and partners.

The Joint Innovation Centers have incubated many influential innovations, such as SingleRAN, IP microwave, and convergent billing platform (CBP), which have become the mainstream deployment models in the industry, for which carriers have saved a lot of network costs and subscribers have enjoyed better and cheaper communication services. Each innovation center has its own focus area to help carriers address technology challenges, explore business models and achieve efficient operations.

> In the mobile sector alone, Huawei and Vodafone's joint innovation center incubates more than 40 innovations every year. For example, the jointly innovated SingleRAN solution was the first in the world to be tested and commercialized in the field, improving coverage for Vodafone's wireless network by 25 percent, reducing the number of sites by 40 percent, and saving 33.6 percent of TCO.[11]

---

[8] Indian Institute of Technology.

[9] Ren Zhengfei: "An essay on India", September 26, 1999.

[10] http://blog.sina.com.cn/s/blog_53bbdb8c0101rnlb.html.

[11] http://www.huawei.com/cn/publications/communicate/61/HW_141516.

The **OpenLab** is a program where Huawei, industry organizations, customers and other partners in various fields and industries can "create customer-centric and innovative industry solutions and achieve win–win digital transformation of the industry".[12] Huawei and its partners can also achieve mutual certification and authorization in OpenLab.

As of 2016, Huawei has built 13 OpenLabs. By the end of 2019, Huawei has invested $200 million to build a total of 20 OpenLabs. These OpenLabs form a network that leverages global resources and capabilities to capture opportunities for ICT needs across industries in response to digital transformation and serve the development of the local ICT industry ecology. OpenLabs have been established in Suzhou, Munich, Mexico City, Singapore, Dubai, Johannesburg, Bangkok, Paris, Cairo, and Moscow, covering a wide range of industries and sectors, with the aim of identifying innovation opportunities beyond the telecom industry and exploring digital transformation solutions with partners. In the area of smart cities, OpenLabs have now served 800 million people of more than 200 cities in more than 80 countries or regions around the world, including Europe, Africa and Asia–Pacific. In the financial sector, Huawei OpenLabs have conducted joint innovation with more than a dozen top financial institutions and independent software developers to help financial institutions accelerate digital transformation at three levels: platform transformation, product innovation, and channel services. It has helped ICBC complete infrastructure cloudization. Huawei has served more than 300 financial institutions worldwide, including six of the Top ten global banks. In the fields of digital city and rail, manufacturing, education, Internet, energy, and public safety, Huawei also cooperates with many partners to build joint solutions for digital transformation.

12.3.2 Application Activities

Application activities refer to activities that optimize, expand, solidify, and improve the firm's knowledge on its original learning track. Application activities focus on cost reduction and efficiency improvement to secure short-term profits and revenues. Application activities are essential for all firms, as they are necessary for them to "survive". In contrast to exploration activities, application activities do not require risky activities but are part of the firm's routine work.

Huawei has been successful in its application activities. From 2005 to 2016, some firms were crippled by the financial crisis and restructuring and mergers in the telecom industry; some left the stage forever. So why can Huawei still achieve year-on-year growth in sales revenue and profit? The following section outlines Huawe's initiatives in its application activities. At Huawei, typical application activities include management optimization, controlled innovation, knowledge sharing, and partnerships.

---

[12] http://www.huawei.com/cn/industry-insights/digital-transformation/ecosystem?ic_source=fhc17.

Management Optimization

Huawei's management optimization activities are guided by the strategy of "controlled innovation"; its internal publications and employee communities are used as a platform to expose problems and to solidify and disseminate best practices. Huawei has a variety of publications. *Improvement* is the one that focuses on management optimization. Launched in 1997 and originally called *Huawei Brief*, it is considered as a self-reflection tool for management improvement. *Improvement* focuses on problems and best practices in various departments and business units, but mainly problems. The editor asks employees to present problems and solutions. Cases are most welcome, especially those with good details and data. Even theoretical articles are not just about theories, but rather the application of theories in actual work. As for the topic, the editor requires that it "must go beyond the circle of the department, and it should look at the bigger picture and refrain from getting personal or radical."[13]

> The company has a publication called Improvement, dedicated to self-reflection. It is joked that the magazine is to expose the "ugly Huawei people". When Tianjin Telecommunications Administration came to visit Huawei, they made some comments. All employees of CRD and IPD were organized to listen to the recording and write their reflections. The editors of Improvement compiled these reflections in a book entitled "Purgatory" to help R&D staff understand how to evolve from being responsible for research results to being responsible for products.[14]

In order to further open up, expose problems and solve them, Huawei officially launched the Huawei Voice Community on June 29, 2008, with the slogan: "You make Huawei wonderful". The community has the following sections: "Huawei Core Values ", "Huawei Family Matters", "Colorful Life", "Administrative Services Window" and "Video Zone". At this online forum, employees can share their experiences and ideas, criticize unreasonable processes and systems, vent their grievances, and expose organizational ills. Many people refer to Huawei Voice Community as a transparent community because even non-Huawei employees can browse most of the content in the community and learn about an imperfect and real Huawei.

When introducing Huawei's openness, Huawei consultant Wu Chunbo said, "Since December 2008 when the company launched a discussion on Huawei's core values called 'One Huawei, One Vision', as of today (April 5, 2011), 244,660 comments with 959 replies have posted, twice the total number of Huawei employees. The most famous article was written by Wudoumi, entitled "Huawei, who abandoned you: an analysis of Huawei's ten internal frictions" published on December 15, 2010, which received 86,600 views and 599 replies. This article was also republished in *Improvement*.

Since its launch, the Huawei Voice Community has been visited by more than 98% of the employees in China. In fact, many organizational problems have been

---

[13] http://xinsheng.huawei.com/cn/index.php?app=forum&mod=Detail&act=index&id=1472721&search_result=8.

[14] Ren Zhengfei: "Hong Long Can Huawei Survive" at a meeting with managers above the division level at Unicom headquarters. 1998.

first exposed in the Huawei Voice Community, giving the management a wake-up call and pointing a direction for continuous management improvement.

Controlled Innovation

Although Huawei does care about future-oriented and radical innovation (exploration activities) that deviate from the original learning track, the "innovation" Ren talks about is mainly incremental and continuous improvement. At Huawei, it is also known as "controlled innovation". The "control" is reflected in the emphasis on the continuity, commerciality and collective nature of the application activities as opposed to disruptive, blind and individualized application activities. "Controlled innovation" is the strategic orientation of Huawei's innovation activities.

Continuity refers to existing knowledge-based continuous optimization, without breaking the rhythm of management, or hindering accumulation and maturity of knowledge. To this end, *Huawei Basic Law* points out that "major business decisions should be stable in stages, and we should not keep making suggestions at every stage."

In 1998, Ren proposed the system of "providing big rewards for small improvements but only encouragement for 'big' suggestions". He believes that in the early stage of development, due to the lack of management experience, if the firm cannot accumulate management skills through "small improvements", but rather always wavers on "big suggestions" and "big strategies", it would not be able to grow quickly but instead fail in no time. By making small improvements, we can optimize, standardize and rationalize our work. In 1999, Ren summarized the achievements of Huawei's "small improvements": "This year, thanks to the 'big rewards for small improvements' strategy, we have improved the quality of our products, improved our work efficiency and reduced our costs."[15]

In 1999, Ren introduced the knowledge shelf system. "For large companies, resource-sharing can make the biggest dent in costs… At Huawei, to innovate, you have to use at least 70% of the existing technology.[16] At HW, every new project is like a Lego project: most of the base pieces are the same; only a few bricks are different. If people do not share resources for innovation, it will only lead to duplication and delay, and the production, if it takes place eventually, is likely to be unstable. True innovation is always based on resource-sharing.

In 2001, Ren described the dialectical relationship between management change and stability in "Huawei's Winter", that is, organizational stability instead of change should be the norm. Otherwise, the cost of reform and innovation would be too high, and the cost of change will offset the benefits of improvement. For this reason, managers at Huawei must have a strong sense of mission and responsibility; they need to be passionate yet calm, intense yet organized. As a Taoist saying goes, "the governance of a state must be carefully done in the same way a cook fries a small

[15] Ren Zhengfei: "Cultivating and selecting managers with field experience", the Second Quality Management Report and Award Ceremony.1998.

[16] Ibid.

fish", we must be cautious with everything we do to avoid damage to our workflows, which may trigger off a chain of errors.[17]

In 2009, Ren reaffirmed the company's approach to innovation. "In the management improvement, we will continue to adhere to the principle of "Seven Nos": No perfectionism. No red tape. No blind innovation. No partial optimization without overall efficiency improvement. No transformative leadership without a panoramic outlook. No transformations involving employees with no business experience. No deployments of premature or untested processes."[18]

In 2010, Ren talked about Huawei's cloud platform innovation efforts and again emphasized the application activities. "Huawei's long-term strategy is based on the "flowers and cow dung" strategy, meaning Huawei will never blindly innovate; it will never "grow flowers" without using "the dung"—the old knowledge. All innovation must be based on existing knowledge. When flowers grow, they will eventually become new dung, providing the nutrients for more flowers. In the process of cloud platform construction, we always emphasize the "flowers and cow dung" strategy; we have to leverage the telecom carrier to innovate, otherwise our cloud will be groundless."[19]

Commerciality means that innovation needs to revolve around the core competitiveness of the firm, especially the application activities, which need to be assessed based on the management contribution rate and target achievement cost. Innovation should always be oriented toward commercial success; we oppose the idea of innovating for the sake of innovation. Because arrogant technology-centered innovation is tantamount to suicide."[20] Ren believes that Huawei will remain in the stage of technological utility research and development for a long time, which means innovation should be assessed by its commercial value. Huawei's corporate motto of "evolving from being responsible for research results to being responsible for products" proposed by Ren in 1998, has always been the guidance to its customer service.

Collectivity means that Huawei's application activities emphasize innovation at the organizational level rather than at the individual level. "We need organizational innovation, and the most important feature of it is that it is not some individual behavior; instead, it should go through testing, assessment, and review by the organization. Anyone who simply aims to gain recognition will certainly become an obstacle. We must remove these obstacles."[21]

[17] Ren Zhengfei: "Huawei's Winter", *Huawei People,* 2001.

[18] Ren Zhengfei: "Digging in and Widening out", Operation and Delivery System Recognition Conference. 2009.

[19] Ren Zhengfei: "Huawei to be a leader in the world's communications industry", Seminar on Decomputation. 2010.

[20] Ren Zhengfei: "Practical scientific research and 20 years of hard work", speech at the demonstration meeting of a major national project. December 2006.

[21] Ren Zhengfei: "Governance without Intervention". 2000.

Knowledge Sharing

In order to cope with the problems revealed in Huawei's internationalization, such as insufficient cohesion, huge differences in values and service concepts, and inadequate professionalism, Huawei University was established in Shenzhen in 2005 to provide the best platform for knowledge sharing within the company. It aims to be the best corporate university in China and build Huawei into a learning organization. It provides numerous training courses for Huawei employees and customers, including orientation training, induction training and customer-specific training.

Huawei University has three missions: inheriting the corporate culture, cultivating talent and consolidating best practices. Huawei University trains more than 20,000 new employees every year; "the orientation training is a cultural education". The purpose is to help new employees identify themselves with Huawei's basic values, i.e., customer-centricity and dedication. Huawei University, hailed as "a cradle of generals" by Ren, pays particular attention to manager training. As of 2013, Huawei University has offered more than 20,000 courses, 60% of which were offered online.

In addition to the strict selection mechanism for trainees and instructors, Huawei University is known for its practice and competition-based training mode. Some staff will be asked to leave their posts temporarily and be trained in the university for a short period and then go back to their posts. They bring real problems to the classroom and have a strong thirst for learning; later they will bring back what they have learnt and put it into practice, bringing new drive and methods to their work. Through this cycle, the ability of employees will be rapidly improved and soldiers will be cultivated into generals.

> We should summarize our success stories over the past 20 years: why we are successful and how we can continue to be successful. Then we will standardize and baseline these management ideas with western methods so that they can be widely disseminated and mastered and used to train managers at all levels. This way we will not be some rigid Western model, but an effective firm with a living soul.[22]

Partnerships

Since 2011, Huawei's Enterprise BG has been holding Huawei Partner Conference every year,[23] with the aim of better aligning with partners in business and processes, better complementing each other in technology and resources, and continuously improving Huawei's service capabilities and service solutions, while building industry ecosystems. In the seven years of partner conferences, Huawei has always adhered to the "integration" strategy and "focus" strategy in channel cooperation. "Integration" means that Huawei, as an ICT infrastructure provider, aims to embed itself in the business of its partners and catalyze their success, rather than compete with them. Facing the massive enterprise business market (40 million enterprises in

---

[22] Ren Zhengfei: "Digging in and Widening out", Operation and Delivery System Recognition Conference. 2009.

[23] For the first three years from 2011–2013, the Huawei Partner Conference was organized and hosted by its subsidiary Ansys, responsible for the enterprise business.

China alone), Huawei cannot rely solely on its own project managers. Actually, of the enterprise business, more than 80% of sales revenue comes from channel partners, and 60% of the delivery and services are provided by its partners. Hence the slogan of "Put the customer at the center; work with the partner in the field; Huawei provides the best support". The purpose of "integration" is to help partners build and cultivate a good operating environment. Sun Maolu, Vice President (Delivery and Service) of Huawei Enterprise BG China, said:

> In the era of big data, the 6.8 billion mobile phone subscribers and 2.7 billion Internet users worldwide are driving the transformation of firms from the traditional sales model to a user experience-centered new model. The ICT service ecosystem is facing transformation too. End-to-end "big service" is essential for the reorganization of the ICT service market. This is a partnership-based and customer-centric integrated business model.

The "focus" strategy means to focus on ICT infrastructure and related fields, with continuous investment in R&D in telecom infrastructure networks, cloud data centers and smart terminals. It means the firm has to be selective in what it does. Based on its "focus" strategy, Huawei has also optimized and adjusted its sales organization, reducing the number of customers from 4,000–5,000 in 2011 to more than 2,000 in 2014, and then to about 1,000 in 2016. After the adjustment, Huawei, on the one hand, can devote more resources to the industry and dive deeper, and, on the other hand, can give partners more market opportunities.

> We will be committed to the "integration" strategy; we will transform from sales-centered to giving equal emphasis to both sales and marketing and build an industrial ecosystem with streamlined processes, efficient cooperation, and complementary strengths. Facing the massive ICT market, we are ready to strengthen cooperation with partners such as channels, value-added system integrators and independent software vendors, to expand the scope of cooperation, and actively explore new cooperation models.[24]

12.3.3 Separation Strategy 1: Job Rotation

To avoid the long-term stability of individual positions causing organizational preference or path dependence on exploration or application activities, Huawei has designed a series of job rotation systems to enable the firm to maintain a dynamic balance between the two activities. The job rotation system includes the "rotating CEO", "job rotation" (for middle managers) and "business rotation" (for junior employees). These rotations allow the firm to switch flexibly between exploration and application without head-on conflicts between the two while enhance employee mobility and improve their adaptability.

The Rotating CEO System is an important practice to promote balanced development at the strategic level. In 2004, Huawei transformed the Executive Management Team (EMT) system from the U.S. into the "Rotating CEO System": the CEO is not a permanent position but will be rotated among eight senior managers. Ren explained

[24] Ma Yue, Vice President of Huawei Enterprise Business Group, at the Partner Conference. 2013.

the benefits of the system: Firstly, the ability of senior managers to handle routine work and make strategic decisions will be enhanced. Second, it can naturally get rid of cliques in the firm and form a global balance of interests; the rotating CEO can be given bigger play of their personal strengths, while avoiding the rigidity that may be caused by excessive individual paranoia. Third, it allows individual mistakes to be mitigated by group efforts, avoiding excessive accumulation of problems. After the system was implemented for two rounds later in 2006, Huawei officially launched the Rotating CEO System under the leadership of the board of directors: the three vice chairmen take turns to be the CEO for a six-month period. CEO is the highest executive head of the firm, responsible for the company's strategy and system development, while the decision-making power of routine operation is delegated to each business group and region company.

The new rotation system reduces the number of rotating CEOs, allowing the organizational system and direction to maintain stability and continuity within a certain range, better balancing between stability and change. The vice chairmen who are not the incumbent rotating CEO will still participate in collective decision-making and get ready for the next rotation.

> Huawei's rotating CEO system is composed of a small team, which can steer the firm to be adapted to changes constantly and quickly. The decisions are made collectively, which avoids the rigidity brought by excessive individual paranoia; it can reduce the uncertainties of operation brought about by unexpected risks.[25]

Job rotation and business rotation

> Huawei implements two kinds of rotation. First, business rotation. For example, R&D personnel are rotated to pilot testing, production, service, so that they really understand what it takes to produce a good product, then they can become senior technical staff; otherwise, there is nothing senior about it. Therefore, to be worthy of the title "senior", they must work hard. Second, job rotation. Changing the positions of senior and middle managers is conducive to the spread of managerial expertise and balanced development and helps the rapid growth of outstanding managers. They have practical experience and progress quickly in various positions, which in turn drives new employees into this virtuous cycle. The cycles of technology, business, and management bring fine knowledge all the way to the bottom.[26]

The purpose of the business rotation is "practical", specifically, it is to familiarize managers and employees with the connections between related businesses, help them accumulate working experience in a business field, and increase the depth of knowledge. The purpose of job rotation is mainly to cultivate the management skills of employees, accumulate experience in collaboration in different business areas, and expand the breadth of knowledge.

---

[25] Ren Zhengfei: "Clarifying the Rotating CEO System under the leadership of the Board of Directors". 2012.

[26] Ren Zhengfei: "Hong Long Can Huawei Survive" at a seminar with managers above the division level at Unicom headquarters. 1998.

12.3.4 Separation Strategy 2: Focus Principle

In terms of product development, technology development and management change, Huawei emphasizes prioritizing, staying focused, and working towards the same goal in strategic identification and resource allocation according to the strategic focus of different stages. In the past 30 years, Huawei has been highly focused on the main business, concentrating its limited resources on the most urgent and important areas to make breakthroughs, building its core capabilities step by step by grasping the main contradictions.

The principle of focus is an important principle that has guided Huawei to break through R&D and market bottlenecks in the early days when it had very limited resources. Article 23 of the *Huawei Basic Law*: "We adhere to the principle of focus and allocate resources to the key success factors and selected strategic growth points with an intensity greater than our major competitors. We either don't do it at all, but when we decide to do it, we need to concentrate our human, material and financial resources to achieve a key breakthrough."

In 1991, Huawei concentrated all its capital and manpower, and within a few months, developed and produced three BH-03 (24/224), Huawei-branded program-controlled switches, completing the transformation from an agent to a manufacturer. In 1995, when Huawei launched its own R&D, many R&D backbone staff jumped ship. Ren said, "Huawei's unwavering spirit and the principle of focus mean that we will concentrate all the available resources, make breakthroughs at a certain point, and take the lead in a certain area so that Huawei can survive start-up hardships." "In the early stage, except for knowledge, enthusiasm and drive, we had almost nothing. From its creation till today, Huawei has done only one thing, the research and development of core communication network technology. It has never been tempted by other opportunities. We dare to put all the eggs in a basket."[27]

The principle of focus has also worked wonders for Huawei when expanding its market. When competing for a local market, Huawei can gather thousands of salespeople and technicians from around the world with the ratio of customers to employees reaching 1:100, so that it can respond to the needs of customers as quickly and effectively as possible. In order to gain market share and survive in the fierce market competition, Huawei intensively allocates resources in marketing and sales. Some veteran employees described Huawei's focus principle in the market as "human sea tactics" or "a pack of wolf tactics," i.e., spare no human resources to seize every potential customer, meet the need of customers at any time and as much as possible, leave no stone unturned, and no opportunity to the competitors. Thanks to its "a pack of wolf" tactics, Huawei has defeated Ericsson, Nokia and other top-ranking equipment manufacturers, and has won one market after another in China and beyond. Under the principle of focus, Huawei concentrates a large number of organizational resources in a short period of time and maximizes the value of internal resources, to quickly bridge the gap with its competitors, thus making success possible.

[27] Ren Zhengfei: "Innovation is the inexhaustible driving force of Huawei's development". July 20, 2000.

The principle of focus is also applied to the exploration of radical technologies. In 2013, in the face of all possibilities brought about by big data, Ren emphasized focus and pointed out that to compete with leading foreign companies with limited resources, the focus is the only answer for Huawei to succeed. "We can only beat American companies in the area as big as the tip of a pin so to speak, if we expand to the area to the tip of a match or a small stick, we will never be able to surpass."[28]

> When a strategic opportunity is identified, we should go all out to catch up. We must be bold enough to pile up resources and invest hugely, not just input more manpower, and that's where Huawei and other smaller companies innovate differently. People are the most valuable assets. We shall not be conservative, but rather dare to catch up with the leaders. Huawei people who are open-minded and enterprising are our most valuable assets. With them, we have a good chance to catch up with "Tesla".[29]

12.4 Integration Strategy

The integration strategy, as a supplement to the separation strategy, aims to create links between exploration and application activities. If the organization does not intervene temporally and spatially in the separated exploration and application business units, the two will be permanently separated in their respective closed loop, making it difficult to create synergy. Therefore, the integration strategy determines, to some extent, the effectiveness of the separation strategy. Many scholars have pointed out that the integration of exploration and application activities includes both cognitive-level change and organizational mechanism design.

There is direct and indirect integration. Direct integration refers to the direct combination of exploration and application activities into a new organizational practice accepted by members of the organization, which is reflected in Huawei's "self-refection" and "grayness principle" at the cognitive level and internal and external resource combination at the organizational level. Indirect integration refers to the mutual transformation between exploration and application activities via the organization's culture, mechanism and management platform so that the results of exploration activities become the input of application activities, and vice versa. In terms of cognition, it is reflected in Huawei's "customer centricity" corporate culture, and in terms of organizational mechanism, it is reflected in Huawei's "dedication"-oriented incentive mechanism and constantly optimized management system.

[28] Ren Zhengfei: "Catch up with the dragon spaceship with the spirit of the tortoise". December 30, 2013.
[29] Ibid.

12.4.1 Self-reflection and the Grayness Principle

Self-reflection is adopted by Huawei employees, especially executives, who take the initiative to reflect on their behavior and that of the company, expose problems, change their thinking, and look for possibilities for continuous improvement. Self-reflection is a manifestation of crisis awareness at the behavioral level. Ren has repeatedly stressed that self-reflection is an important weapon to loosen the soil of the company's culture. Managers who are not good at self-reflection will find it difficult to get a promotion at Huawei.

For example, in R&D planning, Huawei's self-reflection is manifested in the "Red Team" and "Blue Team" confrontation system. The Red Team is responsible for proposing R&D programs. The Blue Team's job is to do everything possible to beat the Red Team by identifying their vulnerabilities and mistakes. Ren said: "Some people are good at reverse thinking and picking faults. These people can be trained to serve as the commander of the Blue Team... Do not be afraid of opposition. Opposition is a good thing instead of a bad thing; it can change our inertial thinking and break our path dependence."[30] Democratic life meeting is another manifestation of self-reflection. Since its inception, Huawei's executives have been required to participate in three-monthly or semi-annual democratic life meetings. At the meetings, executives would ask pointed questions about management methods, the company's strategic planning and the strategic goals of their departments and find solutions to problems in heated arguments.

Since 1995, Huawei has conducted two internal collective resignations involving over 1000 people each, two R&D "negative reward" events, and numerous "customer-centric" reflections. At the end of 1995, Huawei's marketing department suffered a huge failure and lost all the biddings for communication equipment in five western provinces. Recognizing the dangers of "individualism" and "fractions", Huawei resolutely launched a collective resignation of more than 1,000 people and eventually introduced a competitive mechanism to eliminate underperformers, which to a certain extent has ensured organizational vitality. In 2007, Huawei launched a mass resignation of more than 7,000 employees to address the problems of hierarchy bias and the lack of competitiveness among senior employees. All employees who had worked at Huawei for eight years, including Ren, were required to resign before January 1, 2008. After they went through the competitive recruitment process, they signed a 1–3-year employment contract with the company. So, the second mass resignation metabolized and activated the company and kept it competitive. In 2000, Huawei's Central Research Department "rewarded" hundreds of the backbone staff of the R&D department with overstock and dead stock, due to sloppy work, confusing BOM filling, lax testing, or blind innovation so that they would never forget these mistakes. In 2010, Huawei awarded the "Trap Award", "Worst CBB Award", and "Architecture Tight Coupling Award" to teams and individuals of the network product line at

---

[30] Ren Zhengfei: "Understanding laws of nature, giving play to the core team, continuously improving the per capita benefits, and working together to overcome difficulties" at the Q3 marketing meeting. 2002.

the Network Product Line Quality Conference to warn R&D personnel of the losses caused to customers and the company due to "childishness". Appendix I summarizes 13 representative self-reflection events that Huawei has experienced since 1996.

The goal of self-reflection is to improve the core competitiveness of the company. To this end, it is essential to align the understanding and interests of employees. "Huawei is still a young company, and although it is full of energy and passion, it is also naive and sort of full of itself, and our management is not yet standardized. Only constant self-reflection can make us grow faster. We are not doing self-criticism for the sake of criticism, or negating everything, but for optimization and development."[31] At the same time, self-reflection should not stop at the cognitive level but should be combined with practice. Ren said, "The purpose of self-reflection is not to ask people to retreat and cultivate themselves behind closed doors, or to engage in some soul-searching activities, but to constantly look for a broader and more meaningful goal to strive for, and to put it into action."[32]

Being flexible is a dialectical way of thinking, which refers to the tolerance of different elements that affect the development of the organization. It means not to take an either-or, black-or-white evaluation for a period of time, but to make a compromise when necessary so that all elements co-exist harmoniously rather than be in conflict with each other. Being flexible means shifting from a local perspective to a global perspective. Leaders must move from absolute, demanding leadership to an appropriate degree, should no longer relying only on their individual abilities, but more on optimizing the overall structure, with the focus on long-term development, stability, understanding, tolerance, and following the rules. Around 2009, when Huawei realized that the hierarchical management structure was pulling the company from its customers, Ren Zhengfei proposed a management change to reverse the organizational process starting from the sales line and called on the organization to take a long-term view to understand the need for change.

> Today, we propose a change toward positive cash flow, positive profit flow, positive efficiency growth, and delegation of power to field offices by way of separation of powers and checks and balances. In the process, there may be conflicts with the decisions made in the past twenty years, and it may also affect the interests of many employees. I think we all need to have understanding and tolerance with each other.[33]

Being flexible also means respecting and tolerating unconventional talent. Effective organizational learning requires diversity. An inclusive manager knows to unite people of different personalities, different strengths, and different preferences with unified organizational goals and visions, and maximize the value of internal and external resources of the organization. Ren said, "The company should be tolerant of the whimsies of mavericks. They may look strange for the moment, but they are of strategic importance to the company.

---

[31] Ren Zhengfei: "Why we need self-reflection". September 22, 2000.

[32] Ren Zhengfei: "Anyone who climbed out the pit of setbacks is a saint". 2008.

[33] Ren Zhengfei: "Successful leaders are tolerant leaders", at Huawei Global Marketing Conference.2009.

For basic research, Huawei should be tolerant of Wang Guowei and Li Hongzhang, in fact, they were both once regarded as mavericks, so were Van Gogh, Beethoven and Google.[34]

In 2016, Ren mentioned again at the IPD Top Ten Blue Blood Award Conference: "Will everyone here recruit Beethoven to Huawei? Who would know that even a deaf person could become an artist? Huawei should tolerate mavericks, or some people who don't quite fit in and allow their ideas to ferment in the company." In addition, Ren Zhengfei has repeatedly opposed perfectionism and the idea of being a perfect person and highlighted the importance of "tolerating failure". He hopes to reduce the stress of employees and avoid the evaluation system from going to extremes, to maintain a balance between exploration and application.

Being flexible means "harmony" and "compromise". The principles and direction will not be compromised, but the methods and means can be flexible. When Huawei launched its smartphone business, there was an internal debate over whether go with "low-end" or "high-end" and whether to use "online" or "offline" channels. "In the end, Ren and Yu adopted a dual-brand and dual-channel strategy, which eventually led to a rapid rise in Huawei's brand awareness and sales in the global market. Some may think that compromise is a sign of weakness and indecision, and they may believe that the true hero is always uncompromising. However, this either-or way of thinking can cost a larger goal. In fact, compromise is a commitment to the unwavering direction, and it creates conditions for "win–win" results. Compromise is pragmatic wisdom of the jungle. Giving up principles is not a compromise; compromise involves a wise exchange and consensus under certain conditions. In the cruel competition, after all, it is the reason, not emotion, that will help us win. "During the transformation, Huawei should always focus on the most important issue and the relevant determinant factors, set the correct direction and plan ahead before moving forward. It should promptly identify feasible plans that are urgently needed even though they are not perfect. It should not pursue perfection or take credit for the success of others."[35]

"We have to seize the main contradiction and the main aspect of the contradiction in the change, to grasp the direction, to plan and move later, to use urgently first, not to seek perfection, to do the work in depth and meticulously, and not to covet the work of heaven for their own blind action."

Under the principle of flexibility, Huawei avoids focusing too much on the conflicts and differences between exploration and application activities, and instead devotes more energy to identifying and giving full play to their respective strengths. It avoids business units from fighting each other for organizational status, and instead encourages them to think about how they can make the best use of the outcome of the other side. When members of the organization encounter resistance to change, the principle of flexibility encourages them to interpret the value and meaning of change in a positive light, thus avoiding a negative response to the organizational change. The

[34] Ren Zhengfei: "Huawei aspires to a world communications industry leader" at a de-computing seminar. 2010.

[35] Ren Zhengfei: "Let people who can hear the shots call shots" at the awarding conference of Huawei's sales and service system. January 2009.

principle also encourages organizational members to tolerate different perspectives and talents, increasing the possibilities for future growth of the organization.

12.4.2 Resource Integration

Whether for exploration or application activities, Huawei has heavily leveraged external resources and integrate them with internal resources. For example, the 2012 Laboratories gather global R&D resources, and the Joint Innovation Centers integrate outstanding innovation-minded talent from universities and upstream and downstream enterprises. Huawei has also made use of "external brains" for every management change. In terms of application activities, Huawei maintains close partnerships with customers via "partner conferences" and other activities.

Internal resource integration and coordination. In order to fully stimulate and release the vitality of internal resources, Huawei breaks down the communication and collaboration barriers of internal functional departments and builds cross-departmental teams with decision-making authority. This allows employees and business units that were previously focused on either exploration or application activities to share information and complement each other's strengths. In 1999, Huawei set up a cross-departmental team including personnel from marketing, R&D, customer service, sourcing, production, and other departments with the help of external consultants, with the aim of smoothing out the entire processes, overhauling and streamlining workflows from a holistic perspective. The purpose is to avoid tunnel vision so that the R&D department will not just care about technology exploration, or production and sourcing departments not just about low cost, or marketing and customer service departments not just about the needs of existing customers. "We will first link the market, service and R&D departments, and then include production and sourcing departments to rectify the processes and streamline the procedures together. This inter-departmental team we set up can make decisions on behalf of the company and manage all the relevant processes. Of course, this team is mainly to rationalize the whole process of the product line; it does not mean to add an additional layer organization."[36]

In 2009, Huawei's team in North Africa tried to establish a customer-centric "Iron Triangle Operation Unit" (see Sect. 7.5) to effectively enhance customer trust, deepen understanding of customer needs and collaborate across departments. The AR is responsible for maintaining close relationships with customers and exploring their explicit and potential needs; the SR is responsible for finding matching solutions from the company's technology and product solution pool; the FR is responsible for the delivery and payment collection. The integration of internal resources can effectively solve the internal barriers that the marketing personnel does not know about technology and technical personnel does not know about the market, and it

[36] Ren Zhengfei: Speech at the Third Quarter Meeting Regarding Marketing in China. 2004.

helps respond to market demand quickly and accurately and commercialize R&D results quickly.

The resource reorganization of the "Iron Triangle" model first tried overseas inspired Huawei to carry out an organization-wide change toward "customer-centric" structures and processes. "The essence of the Iron Triangle is to break down functional barriers and form a project-oriented operation mode. The triangle is just a figure of speech; it can be a quadrangle or a pentagon. This gives a good idea and reference for the next stage of organizational change. The main resources of the company should be spent on finding leads and opportunities and transforming them into results. The head office is equipped with advanced equipment and quality resources and should provide effective support in a timely manner when leads and opportunities are found in the market, instead of directly commanding the operation. We should let those who can hear the shots in the field to call the shots."[37]

12.4.3 Customer Centricity

In 1996, Ren visited Dubai, and he was impressed by the "Hong Kong in the desert". He thought that Huawei was also a small company with nothing but a poor living environment, and it needed to create an enabling environment itself with its cultural resources. He said, "Resources can be exhausted, only culture endures. "Today Huawei's corporate culture consists of six core values, namely enabling customer, dedication, self-reflection, openness, integrity and teamwork, among which "enabling customer " is the ultimate strategic orientation, while the other five are organizational qualities that must be upheld to ensure the strategic orientation. Ren once said, "Customers provide Huawei's bread and butter. One of the key reasons that Huawei can survive is that it is customer-centric, and only by adhering to this principle can Huawei sustain longer." Compared with other companies that also emphasize customer-centricity, Huawei pays particular attention to "vulnerable and small customers".

At the early stage of Huawei's development, Ren emphasized that Huawei should not be like some large companies that only care about large and important customers and ignore small customers. In fact, small customers can also find defects in the company's products and services and can also bring profits to the company, so paying attention to their voices can enable Huawei to find problems, identify needs, and open up the market earlier. In 1997, markets in Europe and the United States were occupied by overseas well-known telecommunication giants, and it was difficult for the then-obscure Huawei to open up the market. Huawei's overseas market development started from serving the "disadvantaged" customers in poor and backward countries. In fact, Africa and the Middle East and Southeast Asia have later become important markets for Huawei. Since Huawei started its internationalization path in 1997, numerous employees have been sent to Africa, where they were not only at risk of

[37] Ren Zhengfei: Speech outline at the Honor Awards Ceremony of Sales and Services. 2009.

contracting diseases but also of wars and conflicts. In 2007, Huawei built the world's highest base station for China Mobile at an altitude of 6,500 m on Mount Everest. During the rainy season in Brazil, Huawei used ground tents and built over 1000 base stations in a month. When the war broke out in Libya in 2011, many well-known mobile equipment providers in Europe and the United States evacuated at the earliest time, and the Chinese government also arranged a chartered plane to evacuate Chinese nationals in Libya, but Huawei employees chose to stay with its customers. In 2011, after the nuclear crisis in Fukushima, Japan, Chairwoman Sun Yafang led Huawei's Japanese team stayed and sent additional staff to Japan to assist Softbank, E-mobile and other customers; hundreds of base stations were rescued within a day. The dedication has earned Huawei respect and trust and has brought a steady stream of orders for Huawei.

In addition to focusing on "vulnerable and small" customers, Huawei also takes "customer-centricity" as a technical roadmap, direction of change and a yardstick for value evaluation. "The company is moving to a new level of management. How can we determine the development direction of our organization, processes and managers? How can we measure the work performance? The yardstick should be effective services for customers, which of course includes direct and indirect values. The department, the process and the employee that cannot create value for the customer are redundant, no matter how hard they work—perhaps some have spent a lot of time on internal relations—they will be redundant." At the company's inception, Huawei had inadvertently established the customer-centricity value which aims to provide comprehensive and thoughtful services to make up for technical shortcomings, but at that time Huawei didn't really recognize its importance. As the company matured, Huawei learned the importance of this core value from the many failures that resulted from not being customer-centric. Ren recalled, "In the late 1990s, when the company was out of the woods, success began to go to some Huawei people's heads, and they became self-centered. They used to tell customers then what they should do and what they should not. They also told customers what good Huawei products were and how they should just use it. For example, during the NGN rollout, our people had repeatedly tried to convince carriers with our own technology roadmap, without listening to their needs, which eventually led to the failure of the bid."

12.4.4 Equity Incentive

Huawei's value distribution system is based on the principle of "to each according to the contribution, not seniority". Huawei's incentive system evolved from Full Employee Ownership to ESOP, and then to the principle of rewarding dedicated employees; eventually, a value distribution system that is based on dedicated employees and value contributors is established. In Ren's view, Huawei's employees are roughly divided into three categories: the first category is ordinary workers, the second category is average dedicated employees, and the third category is productive high performers; they are people with a sense of mission. High performers are the backbone of Huawei and are eligible to share the company's surplus value, i.e., stocks and bonuses. Huawei's incentive system is featured by "a large number of employees holding shares" and "tilting toward dedicated employees".

Huawei's incentive system has evolved with the company's development. In the early days of the company, based on his early frustrations, Ren realized that sharing responsibilities and benefits with employees was the most effective and fastest way to gather talent for a small company. In the early days, the backbone of the company is usually a small but very hard-working technical team. The company usually cannot come up with a lot of money to reward key employees, so it set up an incentive system whose main purpose is to raise capital and gather talent. "When I founded the company, I designed an employee stock ownership system to unite employees with benefit sharing, and at that time I didn't know about the option system, let alone the fact that there were multiple mature forms of incentives in the West already."[38] Ren said, "Huawei has been paying dividend and expanding its shares every year. This model involves the following two implications. First, the company must grow every year, otherwise additional float would dilute the old shares or depreciate the value of the shares. Second, the shares are held by tens of thousands of employees, and they are not tradable on the market. The risk is huge; once the company incurred losses, the consequences are unimaginable."

Thanks to the incentive system, most of the dedicated employees become part of the community with shared interests with the company. For their own long-term interests, they must support the company, adapt to changes, push R&D and market exploration activities even when the results are uncertain, and reduce the resistance to exploration activities within the organization. At the same time, the shareholding system enables companies to share the risk with employees so that decision-makers must do everything possible to reduce the risk and avoid hurting the interests of the majority of company shareholders, including themselves. In addition, when the company continues to lead in the market, this incentive system allows the employees to make collective decisions and take responsibility for the direction of the company, which to some extent makes up for the shortcomings of the uncertain direction of exploration activities.

As the company matures, the employees who received equity shares in the early years have accumulated a large number of dividends and gradually lost their momentum and motivation for change. In order to avoid slackness and to create a fair working environment for new employees, Huawei's equity incentive system is increasingly tilted toward dedicated employees, successful teams and high performers. Employees are rewarded according to their contributions instead of seniority. This means that employees must continue to strive and make contributions to the company in order to share the rewards of growth. This incentive system is consistent with the traditional Chinese value of "changing your destiny with hard work" and can stimulate employees' productivity and enthusiasm from within, aligning their self-fulfillment with the company's goals.

---

[38] Ren Zhengfei: "The river flows eastward in spring". December 2011.

Since its inception, Huawei has adopted a labor-oriented ownership structure that unites as many employees as possible into a group with shared interests. As Huawei continues to expand, we have struck a balance between labor-based and capital-based distributions. This balance has created a new environment where both new and veteran employees are dedicated. Using this distribution model, we ensure that veterans will not slack off, and new employees will feel fairly rewarded. As a result, talented professionals will continue to join us. Some 80 percent of our employees hold company shares. This increases our company's resistance to corruption. We also use high salaries to keep people incorruptible. Through this, our company has created a dynamic operating control mechanism with strong constraints. For a high-tech company that is not heavily reliant on resources, an employee shareholding mechanism is significant as it helps stabilize the company and avoids the loss of information assets.[39]

12.4.5 Management Platform

For high-tech companies, exploration and application are their core activities, while processes, systems, and value chains are the supporting activities; the assets supporting the supporting activities are called complementary assets. The successful commercialization of core technologies requires complementary assets, which will raise the barriers to entry for followers to expand their markets and enhance the commercial value of the new technologies. By sharing the organization's existing assets (e.g., manufacturing, channels, services, complementary technologies, outsourcing, marketing, finance, etc.), exploration and application activities can reduce the risk of exploration activities. As early as 1995, when Ren established the strategic vision to make Huawei a world-class company, he keenly recognized the strategic value of complementary assets, and that the gap between Huawei and world leaders was not talent or technology, but managerial expertise.

The continuously optimized management system and platform make up for the high uncertainties and risks of exploration activities by implementing scientific design and necessary control of exploration activities. Most of these management systems and platforms are introduced from advanced foreign companies, they were the brainchild of those companies, and they are also the brainchild of Huawei as they have been adapted and optimized by Huawei. Companies can reduce the uncertainties of exploration activities to a certain extent and evaluate the company's existing experience through these processes, systems and evaluation of exploration activities. Take IPD implementation as an example, Huawei has learned new R&D concepts and processes in the IPD project, increased its long-term product R&D capabilities, shifted from the original impulsive R&D to customer-oriented, and expanded R&D processes to the whole organization. In addition, these processes are not be set in stone after being introduced, but instead are constantly optimized and updated to adapt to new business needs.

[39] Huang Weiwei: *Dedication: the Huawei Philosophy of Human Resources Management*. LID Publishing Limited. 2016.

The support of continuously optimized management systems and platforms for application activities is reflected in accelerated knowledge reuse and diffusion. The management system and platform enable the dissemination of corporate knowledge beyond geographical, temporal and personal limitations, accelerates the dissemination and sharing of excellent experiences, and encourages the exchange of exploration and application results. Take the "Iron Triangle" model of the North Africa market as an example. Thanks to the discussions in the Huawei Voice Community and proliferation of internal publications, the best practice in the North Africa market was later applied to other overseas markets and eventually inspired Huawei's senior leaders to initiate organizational structure changes.

In addition, the continuous optimization of the management system and platform can accelerate the encoding, dissemination, sharing and application of knowledge by employees, promote the exchange of knowledge to the greatest extent, form a channel of knowledge exchange between exploration and application activities, and promote synergy between the two. Through flexible process combination and convenient knowledge flow and sharing, the results of exploration and application activities can be disseminated in a timely, efficient and larger scale.

12.5 How Huawei Overcame the Triple Dilemma of Dual-Capability Building

We saw that Huawei used a combination of separation-integration strategies to overcome the triple dilemma of building dual-capability, namely, resource competition, paradigm conflict, and closed loop. These separation-integration strategies require the company to both make cognitive-level adjustments and develop corresponding organizational mechanisms.

12.5.1 Getting out of the Resource Contention Dilemma

Resource contention stems from uneven distribution of resources and highly constrained resources; there are two approaches to this dilemma. First, apply the separation strategy to stay focused to cope with uneven resource distribution. Second, apply the integration strategy to solve resource shortages by combining internal and external resources.

When exploration and application compete for organizational resources, application activities often prevail. This is because application activities are less challenging and can generate stable cash flow for the organization in the short term, which is especially important for the early stage of business development. However, what is exceptionally difficult is to persevere with continued investment with already stretched capital in exploration activities that require enormous investment, and are high in risk, and uncertain in return. To maintain continuous investment in exploration activities, Huawei has written the "focus principle" into the *Huawei Basic Law* to push it to complete R&D, market, and management breakthroughs. As a result, Huawei has advanced from an OEM to a brand manufacturer, from a latecomer to a well-known brand in the market, from a company with little management to a well-managed one.

As a company grows and financial and material constraints are no longer the major limitation of the organization, managers begin to pay attention to more scarce resources, and the principle of focus takes on new meaning. In the early stage of development, when capital and resources were scarce, the focus principle helps the organization set a lower limit on exploration activities, ensuring that certain share of resources would be allocated to exploration activities. In the later stages of development, when capital and materials are abundant, the focus principle helps the organization set the upper limit and boundary for exploration activities. In Ren's view, Huawei's exploration activities should not cover everywhere, nor should it chase investment frenzy; instead, it should focus on its "main business", i.e., the "Cloud-Network-End" business of the telecom industry, and accomplish breakthroughs in the segmented field in a specific period.

The principle of focus could be risky, and Huawei has learned a painful lesson. Huawei has made two mistakes in the field of mobile communications: one is the PHS-based handset and the other is 3G technology on which Huawei betted almost everything. Huawei spent hugely on the above two technologies but did not reap the expected results. To avoid bet on the wrong horse, the key is to select the correct success factor and strategic growth point. In Ren's view, the key success factor is "customer-centricity", that is, customer needs should be the direction and roadmap of the exploration activities.

In short, the focus principle requires Huawei to prioritize exploration and application activities according to strategic needs, maintain a dynamic balance between the two, and to ensure investment in exploration activities when organizational resources are scarce, to limit the boundary of exploration activities when organizational resources are abundant. Ren said, "We used to focus too much on the core technology; as a result, our technology progressed fast, but the market was a bit weaker. Now that the market has changed and customer needs have changed, we can flatten out a bit. When developing new technology, we should be more focused to get a bigger market share. When the leading role of the new technology is weakened, we will expand the focus and make more products that meet customer needs, but the technology is not necessarily difficult."

In response to resource shortages, the organization can adopt a series of measures to internalize external resources and maximize the value of internal resources by reorganizing them. As mentioned earlier, in terms of internalizing R&D resources, Huawei has integrated excellent internal and external R&D resources by establishing joint laboratories with universities and research institutions around the world, joint innovation centers with major customers such as carriers and partners in other industries, to push Huawei's R&D level to a world-leading level. In terms of market development, Huawei encourages local employees to join the company. In some regions, the localization level of employees exceeds 75%. In terms of management change, Huawei has also introduced a large number of leading consultants to help Huawei complete the implementation of management change. These external resources made up for Huawei's early development shortcomings and ensured the quality of Huawei's exploration and application activities.

When introducing external resources, Huawei highly recognizes and respects their value. For example, when hiring IBM consultants to implement management changes in the company, Ren proposed the principle of "rigidity, solidification and optimization," which specifically refers to the full importation of the knowledge system of external consultants, without interfering with the introduction of the new system. In this process, "rigidity" is to avoid bargaining and procrastination by business departments.

> As a senior manager, I think the IPD project is the biggest thing right now for the company, which has made a great determination to do it. Everyone here has to be highly committed to it, and we must accomplish the purpose. How to do it well? Follow the consultant, even if you think the consultant is wrong. If the consultant finds that he/she is wrong later, then they will correct themselves. If the consultant does not correct it, when we find out later, we can all come back to discuss and correct it. However, right now we are certainly inexperienced, so we definitely need to learn from the consultant, follow them and change our mentality. There are many good things in the world, and there are companies better than IBM, but now we only learn from IBM not every company in the world.[40]

The full exploitation and use of internal resources can also help the company to alleviate the shortage of organizational resources. In the early days, Huawei lacked professional talent, and many Huawei employees wore several hats, and the company encouraged employees to improve their abilities through active learning in their spare time. Ren has repeatedly emphasized in his speeches that Huawei should "stand on the shoulders of giants" and take outstanding individuals and companies as learning examples to continuously optimize its processes and products. In Ren's speech, he mentioned a dozen companies that Huawei could learn from: SMIC, Datang, Lenovo, Haier, Xiaomi, IBM, Bell Labs Shanghai, Lucent, Motorola, Alcatel, Nokia, Cisco and Ericsson. Learning is encouraged across all functional departments and all disciplines. This important idea permeates all Huawei employees, especially senior management. With the continuous development of the company, the mining and utilization of internal resources has been standardized, and internal publications, Huawei Voice Community, Huawei University have all become the platform for Huawei people to learn. Business rotation, job rotation, cross-functional team building, and project-based work mechanism have become organizational mechanisms for Huawei to restructure internal resources. This full exploration and flow of internal resources have enabled Huawei employees to engage in both exploration and application activities, and the results of the two activities can thus be easily integrated and transformed in the organization, complementing each other, and stimulating efficient and flexible dual innovation.

---

[40] Ren Zhengfei: speech at the pilot PDT inaugural ceremony. May 17, 2000.

12.5.2 Get out of the Paradigm Conflict

Exploration and application have very different models in terms of organizational structure, leadership, performance orientation, and culture. In terms of organizational structure, exploration activities tend to require flat, and flexible organizational structures, while application activities tend to require hierarchical, prescriptive organizational structures. In terms of leadership, charismatic, transformational leaders are the best fit for exploration activities, while disciplined, transactional leaders are better for application activities. In terms of performance orientation, exploration activities emphasize future growth, appreciate differences, and tolerate failures, while application activities emphasize immediate performance returns, efficiency and cost and hate differences and failures. In terms of culture, exploration activities highlight improvisation and dynamism, while application activities highlight controlled efficiency. The paradigm conflict between exploration and application will always exist. This is both because of the nature of exploration and application activities and the cognitive limitations of the human cognitive pursuit of consistency and uniformity.

The paradigm conflict can also be solved by a separation-integration strategy. From the separation strategy perspective, the paradigm conflict can be avoided if exploration and application activities are separated in time and space (including the focus principle, job rotation, and separated business units). However, the separation strategy can only solve the conflict temporarily and cannot make the two activities reinforcing each other. In the long run, the separation strategy not only cannot solve the paradigm conflict but also may amplify the difference and lead to the mutual exclusion of exploration and application activities. Therefore, after adopting the separation strategy, the organization needs to adopt a series of integration strategies.

First, managers need to adjust their perceptions of the exploration-application tension so that the long-term coexistence of exploration and application becomes the norm in the organization and is accepted. This requires managers to perceive the complex relationship between the two with a paradoxical thinking of coexistence rather than an either/or mindset. The cognitive premise of the paradoxical thinking is to accept the persistence of paradox and conflict, rather than to prefer or repress one or the other. Under such thinking, it is possible to build an effective paradox management strategy. Huawei's "grayness principle" and "self-reflection" embody this paradoxical cognition. The "grayness principle" means that the organization keeps an open mind to both exploration and application activities: it does not rush to deny or support one or the other, and keeps possibilities open in the organization. "Self-reflection" helps the organization to identify the shortcomings and flaws in the exploration or application business unit, and provides possibilities for optimization and integration.

Second, managers should try to align the ultimate goal of exploration and application so that the two can be transformed into each other. Huawei's "customer-centric" corporate culture facilitates this mutual transformation.

A "customer-centric" culture shortens the commercialization path from exploration to application, because, under such culture, the company is able to develop technology and manage change according to the needs of the customers, rather than blindly chasing the cutting-edge technology, which may result in unmarketable products. It is found that organizations that are truly customer-centric often have a superb ability to connect to dynamic markets, i.e., a superb market perception, and the ability to quickly connect and combine customers and quickly build networks so that the results of corporate exploration can be tried and tested, improved, and brought to market rapidly. This capability enables the company to select optimal resources or combine resources in the optimal manner with customer in mind, rather than limiting itself to either exploration or application activities to make best decisions, thus shortening the commercialization path from exploration to application. At the same time, a "customer-centric" corporate culture reduces the difficulty of creative transformation from exploitation to application. Sincere and considerate service wins customer trust and support for the next-stage market expansion and technology development, enabling the company to complete a new round of exploration activities with less cost and effort on the basis of consolidating the mature market and entering a virtuous cycle of mutual transformation of exploration and application.

To sum up, Huawei's "customer-centric" corporate culture (1) blurs the line between exploration and application activities, combines the two activities with the common goal of customer-centricity, strengthens the common end results between the two, weakens the differences and competition between them, and continuously strengthens the synergy between the two through the customer-centric performance assessment mechanism. (2) By focusing on "vulnerable and small" customers, the company can overcome overconfidence, which is found in application activities. (3) By focusing on customer services, the company can overcome ambiguity in exploration activities. Based on the above, the "customer-centric" culture can act as a "catalyst" to promote synergy between exploration and application activities.

After the cognitive adjustment, a series of mechanisms at the organizational level, including the combination of resources, the "dedication-oriented" incentive mechanism and the continuous optimization of the platform, put the cognitive adjustment into organizational mechanisms. By combining and reorganizing internal and external resources, the organization can put individuals, some are good at exploration and others, application, into one project team, thus balancing exploration and application in the project.

"The dedication-oriented" incentive system unifies the long-term value of exploration activities and the short-term value of application activities in the broad concept of "contributions truly valuable to the company". This broad concept recognizes the positive contribution of both exploration and application activities to the company, while providing some ambiguity to reconcile the conflict between the two. Under the equity incentive system, employees are not only interested in the smooth implementation of exploration and application activities, but also in the subsequent commercialization and innovation, because only when the two interact and synergize well will shareholders get the highest returns. When the two activities are at conflict, shareholding employees will take the initiative to find creative solutions or attempt to get the best of both worlds. Therefore, the dedication-oriented" incentive system is crucial to mitigate the conflicts between exploration and application in the following aspects: (1) It brings a consensus among employees for future growth and sustainable development. When the long-term interests of employees are highly aligned with the strategic goals of the company, the resistance to exploration activities is significantly reduced. When the company engages in risky, high-investment, and uncertain exploration activities, the efficiency of change will be greatly enhanced by reaching a consensus on corporate development and growth at the top. (2) It helps ensure the realization of short-term benefits and the achievement of business goals. When personal gains are aligned with organizational gains, employees have a strong incentive to maximize the existing business value, avoiding sloppiness in application activities and the drawbacks of declining motivation for continuous optimization and overly conservative decision-making in large companies. (3) It aligns between short-term and long-term goals. The community of shared interests between employees and the company directs shareholding employees to focus on the synergistic possibilities between exploration and application activities and increases their enthusiasm to combine exploration and application activities.

The continuously optimized management platform was initially imported directly from leading foreign companies, with their best practices and management concepts. Subsequently, Huawei has continuously optimized the platform by integrating its own practices, so that the platform can connect exploration processes with application processes, establishing a link between the two activities with highly smooth and standardized processes, and facilitating the exchange and transformation of results between the two. For example, the lead-to-cash process (an end-to-end, integrated process flow) is an example of a process that transforms market opportunities (exploration-based activities) into cash flow (application-based activities).

12.5.3 Getting out of the Closed Loop Dilemma

Both exploration and application can create closed loops. Too much focus on application activities may cause the organization to be blinded by past successes, clinging to past experience and rejecting new things, which will lead the organization to further invest in the same application activities, forming a closed loop. Too much focus on exploration activities may cause the organization to be overly risk-averse, exaggerate future returns, and reject incremental improvement efforts, which will lead the organization to further invest in the same exploration activities, creating an exploratory closed loop. To break this loop, the organization needs to proactively bring in external resources and fresh knowledge into the day-to-day operations of the company.

At the cognitive level, the aforementioned "customer-centric" culture and the principle of grayness can both help introduce new knowledge into the existing model and help the organization break the self-reinforcing cycle of the existing model. But in breaking the closed loop, what is more noteworthy is Huawei's "self-critical" thinking. Sometimes just introducing new perspectives does not help the organization break the closed loop because as the organization matures and becomes standardized, the separate exploration and application activities will generate organizational inertia in their respective systems, gradually losing the momentum for change and becoming irresponsive to changes in the external environment. "Self-reflection" helps the organization to proactively tear down the "walls" of inertia, re-examine the laws of organizational development and success, and bring new vitality and opportunities to the organization. Thanks to the proactive self-examination and critique, Huawei can expose the problems of the existing systems, pick up weak signals in the environment, and initiate management optimization and change again and again. Even in the time of crisis, it can turn the crisis into opportunities and achieve leapfrog development.

Self-reflection at the organizational level allows Huawei's business units to heed to the voices of "onlookers" and look at their activities and decisions from a different perspective, thus creating opportunities to break the closed cycle of exploration and application activities. Self-reflection also demonstrates Huawei's openness and tolerance to mistakes: making mistakes is regarded as the norm in Huawei, what is more important is to get to the root of the problem and learn from them. In Ren's view, self-reflection is an integral part of the company's dissipative structure. "The management structure of Huawei is a dissipative structure: when we have energy, we need to dissipate it, and through dissipation, we give ourselves a new life… Therefore, we always alternate this change between stability and instability, between balance and imbalance, so that the company will maintain its rigor."[41]

At the organizational level, job rotation in the separation strategy is also a good way to break the closed cycle. On the one hand, it allows exploration and application business units to take turns to realize their value with the interference of the other side; on the other hand, it allows the company's talent, especially senior managers become more versatile with a broad vision. Since the executives and their teams are responsible for the allocation of the organization's key resources and key strategic decision-making, the ambidexterity of executives helps the organization make resource allocation decisions and other strategic decisions that keep exploration and application relatively balanced in the long run.

Resource integration in the integration strategy breaks the closed loop by introducing external resources (such as partners, consultants, etc.) or changing the use of existing resources (such as reinterpretation, team restructuring, organizational reorganization, etc.). The "dedication-oriented" equity incentive mechanism can stimulate employees' active learning and introspection, thus promoting the accumulation, dissemination and reflection of corporate knowledge, which can amplify the value of knowledge and avoid traps. Unlike the equity incentives of many other companies, Huawei's dedication-oriented incentives can effectively avoid inertia in a mature company and enable the organization to take the initiative to stimulate and maintain the vitality of continuous optimization.

---

[41] Ren Zhengfei: "Success is not a reliable guide to future development" at a market meeting. January 17, 2011.

When the dedication-oriented equity incentive system is combined with separate exploration activities, it will encourage employees to actively adapt to changes in the environment without rejecting changes because of short-term interests, thus reducing the resistance to change within a mature company. At the same time, the risk and value of exploration activities are evaluated from the perspective of their contribution to the company so that it will not fall into a self-reinforcing cycle of exploration activities and unilaterally pursue risk. When the dedication-oriented equity incentive system is combined with separate application activities, it will encourage employees to forget their past achievements and contributions and continue to optimize the management; at the same time, it prevents complacency and inertia caused by overconfidence. Under such an incentive system, employees can acquire shares in the company, thus forming a real community of shared interest with the company and stimulating their work enthusiasm and potential. It also helps them to strike a delicate balance between exploration and utilization at the individual level, without taking too much risk by being too aggressive or missing opportunities by being too conservative.

12.6 Conclusion

This chapter summarizes the separation and integration strategies in Huawei's ambidexterity building. According to the hierarchy at which separation and integration strategies occur (executive level or organizational level) and the way they work (temporal or spatial, direct or indirect), we classify them into four types to examine how these strategies help Huawei alleviate the triple dilemmas between exploration and application activities.

To overcome each dilemma requires the organization to use the separation-integration strategy and make adjustments at executive and organizational levels. To overcome the resource dilemma, Huawei uses the principle of focus in cognition and the resource integration strategy in organizational behavior. To overcome paradigm conflict dilemma, in addition to using the separation strategy to avoid mutual interference between the activities, it is more important to use the integration strategy to establish the connection between the two. This includes the use of the principles of grayness and self-reflection at the cognitive level to accept the coexistence of exploration and application, and the use of "customer-centric" corporate culture and "dedication-oriented" equity incentive system to align the goals of both. At the organizational level, internal and external resources can be combined to form project teams that engage in both exploration and application, or internal resources can be reorganized to make managers equally competent in both exploration and application. The organizational management platform can be leveraged to make the results of exploration and application activities easily exchanged with and transformed into each other in the process. In response to the closed-loop dilemma, Huawei breaks down the cognitive barriers of the organization mainly through self-reflection at the cognition level and job rotation and resource integration at the organizational behavior level. In the following section, we will introduce how Huawei gets out of the triple dilemma in building its ambidexterity with the help of integration capabilities.

Specifically, in terms of executive perception, **the principle of focus** helps the organization to prioritize exploration and application activities when funding, talent, management knowledge, and market knowledge are lagging behind. In particular, it ensures that the organization invests in exploration activities in the early stage of development, so as to achieve breakthroughs in R&D, marketing and management levels. In the later stage of organizational development, the focus principle helps the organization focus on its core business for exploration and achieve a dynamic balance of exploration and application with dynamic adjustment of strategic priorities. The **principle of grayness** helps the organization take a macro, long-term, holistic, and big-picture view of the differences between exploration and application, allowing different ideas, talent, and programs to coexist in the organization. This principle of grayness encourages exploration and application business units to interpret differences in a positive way, creating a cognitive environment for both to coexist harmoniously. Unlike the principle of grayness, **self-reflection** focuses not on the business unit's positive interpretation of external differences but on the business unit's reflection on itself. Self-reflection keeps the organization responsive to changes in the organization's external environment and adjusts its behavior upon reflection. It forces business units to look beyond what they are good at and familiar with (exploration or exploitation) and examine whether their current business is in crisis, thus breaking the closed cycle of exploration or application. In addition, the **"customer-centric" culture** helps overcome blind application activities by focusing on "vulnerable and small" customers, and the uncertainties of exploration activities. It also compensates for the ambiguity in the direction of exploration activities by "making customer service the direction of work.

The former prepares the market for the commercialization of exploration results and shortens the commercialization cycle; the latter lays the knowledge foundation for the creative use of application results and reduces the difficulty of its creative transformation. Moreover, the "customer-centric" culture unifies the ultimate goals of exploration and application activities, and helps them exchange customer insights, market information and cutting-edge technologies around customer needs, creating fluid knowledge and breaking the self-reinforcement cycle of each activity. With the fourfold cognitive alignment of the principle of focus, the principle of grayness, self-reflection and "customer-centric" corporate culture, Huawei has developed paradoxical thinking about exploration and application.

In terms of organizational mechanism, the **job rotation system** can avoid conflicts between exploration and application activities and improve the sophistication of managers' decision-making by cultivating versatile managers who are familiar with both exploration and utilization activities, thereby maintaining a relative balance between the two types of activities in the organization and in its long-term development. **Resource integration** expands the scope of available resources by searching for external resources, while improving the efficiency of internal resources by reorganizing them, thus alleviating the resources dilemma. The **"dedication-oriented" equity incentive system** forms a community of shared interest between dedicated employees and the company so that they will not blindly venture into exploration activities because of personal preference, nor refuse to change or take risks because of short-term interests. The synergy between exploration and utilization has ignited the enthusiasm of the key players in the company to commercialize exploration activities and make application activities creative. Finally, **the continuously optimized management system and platform** can on the one hand make up for the shortcomings of high uncertainty and high risk of exploration activities by implementing scientific design and necessary control of exploration activities, and on the other hand accelerate the reuse and proliferation of application results by providing an efficient platform and tools. In addition, the continuously optimized management system and platform can accelerate employees' encoding, dissemination, sharing and application of knowledge, maximize the exchange of knowledge, form a channel of knowledge exchange between exploration and utilization activities, and promote synergy between the two. Under the fourfold organizational mechanisms mentioned above, Huawei has formed a series of organizational practices to expand resources, reconcile conflicts, and break the closed cycle.

Chapter 13
Huawei Phones: From Low-End to High-End

Huawei is a leading global provider of information and communications technology (ICT) solutions with five strategic businesses, carrier business, enterprise business and consumer business. With more than 170,000 employees, Huawei operates in more than 170 countries and regions worldwide, serving more than one-third of the world's population. The case study in this chapter focuses on the consumer business, i.e., Huawei mobile phones. The development of Huawei's mobile phone business has gone through three phases marked by milestone events: the first phase is the old equilibrium phase. Huawei's consumer business, initiated in 2003, ranked third in the world in terms of mobile phone shipments in 2009. However, these phones were simply white-label low-end handsets. The second phase is the reform phase. Around 2008, radical innovations characterized by smartphone operating systems disrupted the competition in the mobile phone industry. In 2011, Huawei began to transform from B2B to B2C. Since then, the strategic focus of the Consumer BG has shifted from focusing on low-end white-label phones to high-end smartphones. As a result, Huawei saw its mobile phone sales fall to eighth place in the world. In 2014, Huawei's smartphone sales returned to the ranks of top three again. In 2017, Huawei surpassed Apple for the first time and joined the ranks of high-end phone manufacturers.

13.1 Initiating Products Upgrading (2003–2010)

In March 2003, Huawei established its handset department to provide mobile device support services. At that time, with carriers as its major customers, the department specialized in producing low-end white-label mobile phones which were used by the carriers as giveaways, so it was a marginalized department in Huawei. In 2009, Huawei even considered selling the whole mobile phone business.

X. Dong et al., *Huawei*,
https://doi.org/10.1007/978-981-19-4078-1_13

In the product area, Huawei set up an R&D team in October 2004 to initiate independent R&D of the HiSilicon chip based on its existing IPD process and architecture, with the hope of offending its dependence on American chips. In 2009, Huawei launched its first smartphone chip, K3V1; however, it failed to be marketable because Huawei did not understand users' real needs. For example, to reduce costs, an overseas carrier asked Huawei to remove the flash function, but the region where the carrier operated often blacked out and users there often used the mobile phone as a flashlight, so the phone without the flash function was not popular.

To produce customized phones for carriers, Huawei simply had to engineer it, as everything else, the appearance, the interface, etc. were all the carrier's call. Customized handsets updated rapidly and did not have to consider users' needs in function design; however, they were very price sensitive. To make those products, Huawei would first set a target overall cost and then broke it down into different parts: the screen, the battery, the exterior structural parts, and the RF processor, etc. This approach was apparently cost-oriented, without considering user experience. At that time, Huawei was unquestionably weak in mobile phone design.

Huawei sold network equipment to carriers with mobile phones as bundles. By doing so, Huawei maintained high sales growth which contributed nearly half of the company's profits in 2006. In 2009, Huawei shipped more than 60 million CDMA phones, making it the third-largest supplier in the world. However, as the carriers kept lowering the ex-factory price of customized phones, the profit margin kept being squeezed to even a single-digit profit margin. Despite its enormous users worldwide, as a white-label phone producer, Huawei's logo could hardly be seen on the phone, except that under the battery, you could find a small print "Huawei-made"; there was no promotion or advertising to speak of back then.

13.2 Upgrading Phase (2011–2013)

Since 2010, Huawei has been looking for wider growth areas in the global market: At that time, Huawei already accounted for 30% of the $100 billion-worth carrier business market but its growth rate was declining. So, how to ensure sustainable growth? Huawei began to set its sight on the phone business. As the consumer business had a market size of $400 billion per year, Huawei could achieve $50–80 billion in revenue if it could take 20% of the market. In December 2010, Ren talked with the key employees of the device business and proposed a new strategic focus for the phone business: shifting from making white-label phones to building its own brand. At that time, Huawei wasn't bold enough to touch the high-end market, because it had never sold a phone above 2,000 yuan before. Huawei was afraid that a wrong move would ruin its reputation. In 2011, Huawei put forward the "Cloud-Network-End" integration strategy to adjust its business structure and established the Huawei Consumer Business Group (BG), which put the mobile phone business high on Huawei's agenda. In November that year, Huawei Network Products & Solutions BG held a meeting in Sanya, Hainan, to launch its B2C transformation and made it clear that end consumers rather than carriers should be the company's real customers. This decision transformed the R&D and sales model of Huawei phones. Another important decision was the appointment of Yu Chengdong as the head of the device business. Joining Huawei in 1993, Yu once led the wireless business to the world's No. 1 by beating Ericsson. When Yu took on the new task, he was determined that Huawei must make high-end phones priced above 4,000 yuan. He acted fast and built a strong management team with talent from Nokia and Samsung as well as other business departments in Huawei. Since then, Huawei's phone business began to move from low-end to high-end and transform from white-label phones to consumer brand ones.

Huawei faced many difficulties in the transformation to B2C. First, mindset conflict. After throwing away the crutch of the carrier, Huawei has to directly face the market, which requires a huge change in mindset. In the past, Huawei's device department only needed to follow customer requirements, stay cost-oriented, rely on engineers to design the products, and sell the products to hundreds of carriers around the world. It naturally had almost zero experience in dealing with end consumers, so it did not know much about consumer insight or making rapid responses to the market. Second, internal inertia. To many employees, the established business of customized phones guaranteed stable shipment, so there was no need or reason for any change. So, when Yu slashed the proportion of customized handsets and made the decision to produce high-end phones, he was opposed by two-thirds of employees in his department. Third, external pressure. Carriers also put enormous pressure on the transformation. In 2012, in order to break free from the dependence on carrier channels, Yu, with the full support of Ren, cut the business of producing 30 million low-end smartphones and feature phones, which accounted for more than half of the previous year's total shipments. As a result, 15 carriers in Europe including Vodafone, France Telecom began to terminate their cooperation with Huawei one after another, except for one. Huawei subsequently saw a significant decline in its device business.

So, what were Huawei's advantages in high-end smartphones? Huawei made a thorough benchmark analysis. Apple has advantages in software, brand, product design, and ecosystem; Samsung in hardware and supply chain; Xiaomi and other Internet companies, online marketing. In contrast, Huawei's advantages are as follows: First, technical advantage based on its long-term R&D input. Huawei has a strong independent chip design capability, a large pool of patented ICT technologies, as well as the "2012 Labs" for advanced researches on photography technology, video technology, data mining, etc. Second, resources advantage. In 2010, Huawei achieved a net profit of 24.7 billion yuan, so it had a deep pocket for its strategic focus. Ren once said, "For any strategic opportunity, we should go all out to catch up. We must have the courage to invest hugely not just in manpower, but also in monetary terms. This is what makes our innovation different from small companies." Third, management advantage. Effective management can fully unlock the potentials of technology, talent, and capital. Huawei's "customers centricity and dedication" culture inspires employees to work hard. At the same time, Huawei paid very good money to hire top international consulting firms. With their guidance, Huawei has changed its management in R&D, supply chain, human resources, financial system, and other aspects to promote the business process standardization. With all these efforts, the team is getting stronger with great execution and flexibility.

In 2012, Huawei began to apply its chip technology to its products. That year, Huawei for the first time used the HiSilicon chip in its P1 phones. However, due to technical flaws, some P1phones easily got overheated along with high-power consumption. At the time, consumers even joked that Huawei's outdated chip K3V2 could be used as a hand warmer in winter. The subsequent Ascend D1, P2 and others built with HiSilicon chips were not received well, either. However, Huawei continued to improve its chip technology and kept developing a chip a year, along with R&D in peripheral chip technology, communication technology, image, operating system, and a number of other device-related technologies. The forward-looking basic research conducted by the 2012 Labs coordinated chip development with other departments and promoted mobile phone architecture innovation, which led to better quality control.

In product design, Huawei shifted from cost-centric to user-centric and invested a lot of resources in exploration. Huawei's design teams, with no experience in designing high-end phones, bought back all similar models from the market for teardown analysis to summarize the merits of each product in terms of structural design, performance design, and exterior design. Yu encouraged engineers to learn by trial and error and was willing to write big checks. "He is even willing to spend five times the record high money on a flagship product and allocate the company's resources as many as possible to support it." Yu also hired Hagen Fendler, former Head of Product Concepts of Siemens and former Chief Designer of BMW, as chief design director of Huawei handsets. He also set up the Dream Lab, an innovative design team, dedicated to user experience-oriented development and design.

Dual-channel strategy. In order to achieve the transformation from B2B to B2C and from low-end to high-end, Yu drastically cut off half of the customized phone businesses, which dealt a heavy blow to the carrier channel. As the channel became much less dominant year by year, Huawei had a fierce debate over the next main sales channel: one side believed that Huawei should be benchmarked against Xiaomi to develop an online e-commerce channel and cut a piece of the pie of the online market; the other side thought that the e-commerce market accounted for less than 10%, so Huawei should keep using distributors and other offline channels. As neither side would budge, in the end, Yu decided to adopt a dual-channel strategy to let the "two horses" race, "It would be a success for us no matter which horse wins."

Building a high-end brand image. In order to win the consumer market, Huawei has gradually changed its long-standing "low-profile" style by moving from behind the scenes to the front stage to convey a posh and high-end brand image so that the product can have a good premium. Since 2012, Huawei has launched a series of brand marketing campaigns worldwide, including sponsoring top leagues and national soccer teams as well as partnering with top clubs such as AC Milan and Arsenal. These moves have greatly increased the brand awareness of Huawei phones. In 2013, Huawei's smartphone shipments reached 52 million units, the third largest in the world. Also, its global brand awareness grew from less than 3% in 2011 to

52%, an indicator of its initial branding success. In 2014, Huawei entered a period of rapid development.

13.3 Upmarket Brand Phase (2014–Present)

In 2014, the rapid development of 4G LTE network presented an unprecedented historical opportunity for Huawei phones. The hot-selling flagship phone Mate 7 marked the success of Huawei's high-end phone strategy. and the Board of Directors began to incorporate the consumer business into the main businesses of the company. 2015 saw global smartphone sales growth falling below 10% for the first time; the phone market entered the replacement market from the first-time buyer market. The replacement market was characterized by demand for upmarket products. In 2016, despite the decline in Samsung and Apple shipments, Huawei achieved a strong growth of 30%, taking 9.5% of the global smartphone market share and making it a top three brand.[1] It secured its leading positions in four aspects in China's smartphone market: first in market share, first in brand awareness, first in net promoter score, and first in service satisfaction.

At this stage, Huawei shifted from technology-oriented to value-oriented, with a focus on internal key technologies while integrating external superior resources to launch strategic products for commercial success. Huawei continued to improve the HiSilicon chip and created Kirin 910, its first System on a Chip (SoC), in 2014. Huawei P7 powered by this chip was a hot-selling phone that year. In 2015, it launched Kirin 950, which was on a par with Qualcomm and MediaTek. At the same time, guided by value creation, Huawei focused on R&D in key technologies that meet consumers' needs. Across the world, Huawei integrated global resources, (including 15 research institutes and 36 joint innovation centers, such as the Algorithm Center in Moscow, the Communications R&D Center in Japan, and the UI Design Center in San Francisco), to incorporate innovations into its latest products and provide better user experience. For example, Huawei-developed Image Signal Processor (ISP) was applied to Mate 8, bringing users faster focusing speed, better definition, and more accurate colors and brightness. Huawei Mate S revolutionized touch technology by introducing the Press Touch, ushering in a new era for human–machine interaction. In addition, the much more accurate Fingerprint Sense 2.0 which improves recognition speed by 100% and the Knuckle Sense 2.0 have also become leading technologies in the industry. Huawei has also been cooperating with leading companies in multiple sectors for open innovation: the joint establishment of the Max Berek Innovation Lab with Leica Camera AG for the imaging technology of mobile devices; the partnership with Harman Kardon for better sound quality; the Huawei Google Nexus 6P, a gamechanger in North America, and so on. Furthermore, with more than a dozen open labs in China, Europe and the rest of the world, Huawei has invited more

[1] IDC Report, https://www.idc.com/promo/smartphone-market-share/vendor.

than 600 partners for collaborative research, funded by Huawei's $1 billion "Developer Enablement Program". Ren once said, "We need to leverage not only our own strength but also others'. You see, say our car runs out of gas, if we can get a hitch, we can still get to the destination."

Aesthetics in product design. The replacement market emerged with a shift in users' demands from function-oriented to improvement-oriented. Huawei sensed the emerging aesthetic needs of consumers and positioned its smartphone as a chic tech product. Huawei opened the world's first aesthetics research center in Paris and hunted ten French and Chinese designers from different fields including luxury goods, automobiles, and 3D design to apply the research results to smartphones and other smart devices. Yu Chengdong hired Joonsuh Kim, former Creative Director at Samsung Mobile, and Abigail Sarah Brody, former Creative Director at Apple, to lead Huawei's design. The challenge for Huawei at this stage was how to express the accumulated technologies.

Dual-brand strategy. The dual-channel strategy opened up the B2C market for Huawei; however, it also created conflicting prices between online and offline channels, as online distributors always undercut offline retailers, even for debut products. To address the problem, in December 2013, Huawei made the Honor brand an independent unit and proposed the dual-brand strategy: Huawei, mostly sold via offline channels, is benchmarked against Apple and Samsung in the high-end market; Honor, mostly sold online, targets young consumers in the mid-and low-end "economic moat". The strategy has significantly increased Huawei's market share, making it in the first echelon in many countries. At this stage, Huawei was not stingy with marketing. It invited Lionel Messi to be its global brand ambassador and Hollywood superstars to endorse Huawei P9. With all these efforts, Huawei's global brand awareness jumped from less than 3% in 2011 to 65% in 2014 and even 81% in 2016.[2] In 2014, Huawei became the first Chinese (excluding Hong Kong, Macao, and Taiwan) brand to rank in Interbrand's Top-100 Best Global Brands of 2014, at No. 94; the ranking rose to No. 72 in 2016 with a value increase of 18%. In 2013, Huawei's NPS was −24%, which meant that more people gave Huawei phones negative reviews than positive ones. According to internal analysis, such a bad score was brought about mainly by its low-end phones of 60 dollars. In 2014, this score, which spurred Huawei executives, jumped from −24 to 43%, ranking third in the industry.

Market channel integration. The dual-brand strategy made Huawei and Honor compete against each other in the domestic market. In January 2015, Huawei Device decided to restructure itself and strategically take Honor in to coordinate the marketing of the two brands. After Honor explored the online channel, Huawei started to expand offline channels and launched the "1000-county plan" at the end of 2015 to sell its phones at lower-tiers. As a result, 2016 saw the number of Huawei's offline service franchises grow to more than 460 in China, and the retailers worldwide over 70,000; that year, the proportion of the revenues from open channels was 71%.

---

[2] IPSOS Research Results.

13.4 Recipe to Success

Based on case studies, this chapter summarizes the following ambidexterity model-based five principles guiding the upgrade of Huawei phones.

The sequence of exploration and application: Difficult tasks first

The functional and capacity focuses of Huawei phones vary in each phase, but, in general, Huawei chooses to tackle the most difficult and time-consuming task first, i.e., chip R&D. Later, Huawei shifted its refocus gradually from product to market, with product design, channel and brand building developed in parallel. At the same time, Huawei explored and identified new opportunities in the market to guide the innovative application of core technologies in products.

The pathway of exploration and application: field-specific priorities and breakthroughs

Thanks to the principle of "staying focused", in just three years, Huawei successfully built a high-end brand as a late-comer by rapidly integrating quality resources internally and externally. In terms of product exploration, Huawei organized its joint innovation centers (JICs) and research institutes to cooperate with top companies around the world. They jointly created the "Global Innovation Hive", enabling employees to work together like bees in chip technologies, materials, user experience and aesthetics, etc. In market exploration, Yu has pooled top talent from different fields.

The methodology of exploration and application: trial and error

Huawei believes in the strategic importance of independent technological innovation, so it has been committed to chip R&D. Although, its first generations of chip technology suffered from CPU overheating and jeopardized its phone selling. It did not give up. Huawei was resolute to use Hisilicon chips in almost all its high-end phones. Huawei keeps improving the chips through trial and error, launches a new chip every year and continuously closes the gap with the industry leader. Thanks to its increasingly prominent advantage in chip technology, Huawei phones can set the pace for its product launches without being held back by core patent holders. After over a decade of development, Huawei's Hisilicon chips are finally on a par with Qualcomm, MediaTek and other leading brands.

Exploration of market channels: separation before integration

In the process of getting rid of the dependence on supplier channels to build B2C open channels, Huawei first separated online and offline channels and adopted a dual-channel strategy. At the same time, Huawei made Honor an independent unit to explore online marketing from product planning to channel strategy, and from pricing to promotion. With just one-year of development, Honor's revenues surged from 100 million yuan to 2.4 billion yuan. The online channel has taken shape and later Huawei integrated Honor's online channel with the traditional offline channel.

Exploration of branding: the dual-brand strategy

Huawei adopted a dual-brand strategy: Huawei targets high-end business people, and Honor at young people, each benchmarking against the best in the segment. The Huawei brand focuses on shaping the company's high-end brand image, which serves as a good endorsement to Honor; Honor improves brand awareness via the online channel. This has created a virtuous circle for the two brands to support each other and yield win–win results.

13.4.1 The Core Role of the Leaders in Product Upgrading

The reason that Huawei phones could break free from the old model and strike a new balance between cross-functional ambidexterity lies in its two leaders, Ren Zhengfei, CEO of Huawei, and Yu Chengdong, CEO of Huawei Device. So, what are the key roles they have played?

Ren Zhengfei

Selecting the right people. After identifying the strategic position of the device business, Ren selected Yu Chengdong, a "hero" of Huawei's wireless business, to lead the device business. Yu has tons of successful experience and worked in the fields. Meanwhile, Yu is a hopeless perfectionist, but he is also optimistic and inspirational. In short, he is a perfect match for Huawei's new device business.

Trust and delegation. Developing the device business is Huawei's exploration of transitioning from B2B to B2C. Yu's bold moves have drawn skepticism and criticism from the company and beyond. Employees didn't understand why they should give up the easy business of customized devices and they were not sure if picky consumers would buy their high-end products. Carriers didn't support the transformation either and even threatened to stop working with Huawei if the company stopped making white-label devices. Fortunately, Ren had Yu's back. "Before 2015, there were a lot of noises. He (Ren Zhengfei), ignored those noises, trusted me, and supported me. Ren is a great person with a big heart. He would not mind mishaps, because he sees the big picture."

Encouraging exploration. Ren believes that different voices inspire solutions. Facing the heated debate on whether to go with online Honor or offline Huawei, Ren decided to do both: may the best win.

Strategic patience. Ren often stresses that "in the era of great opportunities, we shall be patient instead of opportunists". "Huawei is running a marathon rather than a sprint; what matters is sustained profitability". When Xiaomi was riding the wave of the Internet, Ren told his employees that Huawei must "stick to its own path" and "not be gripped by the Internet fever". In 2014, Huawei even launched an advertising slogan of "we are not a carnival fever" for GO Honor World Carnival. Following the strategy of producing quality products, Huawei phones fully leverage their accumulated technologies, so that the phones can win the market with good quality and user experience. "If we can make quality phones that meet consumers' demand, I see no reason that they will not sell well online. Different from e-malls like JD and Taobao, we can control our product quality and we have a large umbrella of IPRs covering the global market."

Yu Chengdong

Daring to make a difference. In Huawei, Yu is known for his toughness and earned the nickname "Crazy Yu", who always makes his dream come true no matter how crazy it seems. Before he became the Chairman of Huawei Device, he worked in the telecom network equipment business for 18 years. He also served as the President of the Wireless Network Product Line and made it the second in the world in terms of sales and first in terms of shipments. As the leader of the device business, Yu constantly breaks limits. His dream is not only to catch up with Apple and Samsung but also to stand on top of the world to lead the smartphone industry. He often encourages his team, "We must improve faster. We must have a stronger sense of urgency and crisis. We must be a proactive learner to pursue excellence and make our strengths speak for ourselves. We must have the courage and determination to become the world's best." As a high-profile and outspoken man, Yu frequently interacts with his fans on Weibo and often compares Huawei with Apple. His remarks concerning other brands include, "Xiaomi is never Huawei's competitor", "I don't think Samsung is very competitive", and "the future world will only have two mobile vendors." Ren once joked, "Yu is undoubtedly Huawei's biggest bragger." Such an audacious Yu is a far cry from the traditional conservative Huawei people, but he has earned understanding from his people because the device business in dire need of transformation needs a general who has the guts to think big and act fast.

Integrating global resources. To upgrade the mobile phone business, Yu recruited global talent. He even interviewed dozens of senior managers in his office. In his eye, real talent has to be "a revolutionary thinker or a meticulous doer, or both". Yu successfully recruited Hagen Fendler, a German who was the Head of Product Concepts of Siemens and Chief Designer of BMW, to be the Chief Design Director for handsets in Huawei. Fendler even moved with his families to Shenzhen. Yu's R&D team also brings together the best innovation forces in the world. Huawei has established a UI Design Center in San Francisco, a Design Center near the West End of London, an Aesthetics Research Center in Paris (focusing on the trends and materials), an Algorithm Center in Moscow, a Communications R&D Center in Japan, a Software Center in India, and a 5G R&D Center in Europe. It has also gathered a group of excellent partners from different sectors, such as Google, Microsoft, Swarovski, Leica, etc.

Changing the exploration principles. With the transformation, Yu put forward new requirements for the exploration principles of mobile devices. In the past, when Huawei was cost-oriented, engineers had to downgrade product specifications, so obviously they were not able to design top-notch products. Yu proposed to get rid of the cost-orientation mentality and constantly break limits, so as to secure the "world-class level". He changed the design process, which required that once a new ID design is done, hardware engineers must complete hardware design under the existing framework, and in the case of conflict, the hardware engineers must comply with the design. Yu encourages his engineers to try and fail and supports them with the company's best resources.

13.4.2 The Relationship Between Product Innovation and Complementary Assets in Large Companies

Another key element for the successful transformation of Huawei's mobile phones is complementary assets. When the external environment changes, an organization's complementary assets may be depreciated, or retain their values, or be appreciated. The outcome depends on the degree of the compatibility between the complementary assets and new core technologies. The optimization and renewal of the complementary assets play an important role in improving an organization's resilience during the technological transition. Based on case studies, we classify Huawei's complementary assets for mobile phones into three categories. Huawei's complementary assets in the process of new product development include:

Management system

Ren's visit to IBM in 1997 initiated the reform and development of Huawei's management system. At that time, IPD was introduced into Huawei and enabled its product development to move from a mom-and-pop operation to a large-scale manageable and replicable process. Since then, Huawei has spent hugely hiring top international consulting firms to reform the supply chain, human resources, the financial system, etc., and Huawei's management innovation, organizational innovation and management capabilities have been thus greatly improved. Yu can directly use these mature systems and processes to set up new teams in a more efficient and orderly manner.

Corporate culture

During the transformation, the core philosophy of Huawei Consumer BG did not change, and the device business stayed committed to the core value of "customer-centricity and dedication". To realize the evolution, Yu visited many people in the mobile phone industry and solicited their opinions so that he could have a more comprehensive understanding of the 2C business. The managers of the mobile phone business must work as salespeople for one day a year, and engineers as after-service receptionists so that they can listen to consumers. Those who refuse to do so cannot have a raise or promotion. This is the real demonstration of customer-centricity. The device business also observes self-criticism to help Huawei's product system stay open and innovative to absorb from the rest of the world. For Huawei, the pace is everything: it learned pricing from the D1 model, marketing from the Maimang model, delivery from the P1 model, etc. Through continuous practice and self-reflection, Huawei finally reaped from all the experience and launched the P6 model.

Technology system

Before producing phones, Huawei has been a network equipment manufacturer for a long time, so its familiarity with 4G networks surpassed all other mobile vendors. Huawei has been investing at least 10% of its annual sales in R&D since 1992 and has grown strong muscles in communications, algorithms and some basic fields. "Other vendors cannot properly use the chip the way we use it. To avoid phone-specific problems, Huawei knows to look for solutions from platforms rather than chips only. Chip application relies on a platform instead of on the chip itself." It is Huawei's accumulated technical strengths in communications, algorithms and some basic areas that have supported it to break through the most difficult technical barriers and create a core competency by making truly differentiated products.

Funding

Trial and error require a lot of resources, and capital is undoubtedly one of the core elements. Huawei, as the company with the highest revenue and profit in global communication equipment, can provide sufficient financial support to open up the smart device market. Ren once said, "Should the device business fail, we still have seventy to eighty billion dollars from the network business to back it, so it can rise again… (we) encourage the device business to be bold."

Complementary assets for adaptive modification:

Organizational structure

With the transformation from B2B to B2C, Huawei's organizational structure has also changed accordingly, from "technology-centered" to "customer-centered", from centralized to de-centralized, i.e., "let those who can hear the 'gunfire' call the shots". The frontline (field employees) is a combat system, and the back office (managers) is a streamlined system to provide resources, service, and support. The management and decision-making are separated to some extent. The back office evaluates the feedback from the frontline to form a "heavy brigade", including technical experts, product experts, financial experts, negotiation experts, supply chain experts, etc., which can help the organization find desired solutions and respond promptly to the market. In terms of human resources, Yu built a team with veterans in the wireless business and hired experts from the company and outside in various fields such as R&D, supply chain management, product design, and marketing. In terms of sales and marketing, Ren mobilized outstanding managers from the company to supplement device business teams.

Carrier network

Huawei phones initially focused on the carrier customization business; the built-in value network was both a resource and a constraint. To maintain a close relationship with carriers, Huawei had to deliver ultra-high benefits, as a result, the early-stage product development had to be extremely cost-sensitive and inevitably at the cost of user experience. During Huawei's transition from an ODM to an OBM, only one out of the original 15 carriers in Europe stayed. They did not come back until the Huawei brand was increasingly recognized by the market. "Behind you are the suppliers, manufacturers and technology vendors you work with, who work with you, explore with you, and constantly drive you to innovate like an engine." Now, the value network has transformed from a stressor to a partner. Based on this model, Huawei and suppliers have established long-term strategic cooperation, and a number of technologies are the results of joint research and development.

Complementary assets newly built by Huawei in the development of new products include.

Brand

For the device business transformation, Yu Chengdong's idea is: "The first thing we can do better than others is the product. We can make a difference in a year. The second is the channel, which requires two years of effort. The third is the brand. It will take at least three years because it needs to influence and change people's minds, which is the most difficult part." Targeting the consumer market, Huawei phones began to build its brand from scratch and implement the dual-brand strategy. Through a series of effective brand promotion campaigns, both its brand awareness and reputation among global consumers have been greatly enhanced. In addition to globalized marketing, Huawei's marketing strategy is also highly localized. For example, as football is the most popular sport in Europe, Huawei has carried out a series of football marketing strategies including sponsorship and cooperation in Europe, which quickly earned Huawei brand a good image in the European consumer market. Huawei also pays great attention to building offline stores, as they can display the brand and serve consumers face to face in the pre-sales and after-sales process. Huawei invited the top international designers from the Aesthetics Research Center in France to lead the design, and top architectural design firms implemented the ideas and created a shop image that is posh, cultural, and artistic. All these efforts have enhanced Huawei's perceptibility to consumers. At the same time, Huawei signed up Hollywood stars Henry Cavill and Scarlett Johansson as its brand ambassadors, placing the brand in the spotlight across the world.

Service system

To respond faster to the market, Huawei has set up 16 plants and directly managed customer service centers (including two regional centers and one reverse logistics center) around the world. Of the 16 plants, two are wholly owned and the rest are joint ventures or outsourced. According to Ren, the service system is like "the horseshoe to Genghis Khan's warhorse", otherwise the hooves would be too soft to run fast. Therefore, Huawei must build up its service system for the consumer business. Providing service is not for profit. It requires bold investment to promote sales and market dominance. Ren directed that Huawei should set up at least one customer service center constructed and operated itself in each country or region with a multilevel service team. The head of the team should be fully authorized so that they can solve problems on-site.

The three types of complementary assets play an important role in configuring cross-functional ambidexterity in different phases. By reducing the uncertainty and reform risks of new technologies and the market, they have helped Huawei overcome barriers in the reform phase to a new equilibrium phase and thus achieve successful transformation.

13.5 From Low-End to High-End: Huawei Stories

The transformation process provides a perspective for radical innovation, that is, to build different combinations of cross-functional ambidexterity in the old and new equilibrium and the reform phase. At the cognitive level, companies, with a focus on building cross-functional ambidexterity at different stages of development, should observe the principle of tackling difficult tasks first, be technologically prepared and patient. At the operational level, managers need to configure different portfolios of products and market strategies for different stages of development. When the external environment is stable, product exploration should be carried out pre-emptively to stay ahead of the industry trends and get ready for the changes that may come at any time. Therefore, once impacted by radical innovation, the organization can quickly bolster exploration in the product area, and the market area according to the needs for new technologies to facilitate the organization's transformation. When entering the new equilibrium phase, the new technology will be applied to further expand the market and improve business performance.

Organizational reform is a trajectory full of ups and downs. At the early stage, a significant decline in performance may be caused by the break of the old business. At this stage, the leader should be steadfast to the strategic positioning, appoint the right person, trust them and give them full delegation, so that organization members' confidence and resolution can be boosted to tide over the painful phase of transition. Complementary assets are vital for a firm to stay competitive in radical innovation. The intangible complementary assets are of strategic value to the firm. During the reform process, the firm should fully leverage the assets that still have value and build new assets in accordance with the characteristics of new technologies and technological needs.

Appendix A
Representative Self-reflection Events of Huawei

Time and event	Description
1996, a collective resignation of the marketing department	At the end of 1995, Huawei's marketing department suffered a huge failure and lost all the biddings for communication equipment in five western provinces. Recognizing the dangers of "individualism" and "fractions", Huawei resolutely launched a collective resignation of more than 1,000 people and eventually introduced a competitive mechanism to eliminate underperformers
1998, repeatedly listened to the recording of customer complaints to improve R&D	"All departments should learn from the R&D and IPD departments, who take customer criticism very seriously. All the members in these departments listened to recordings, discussed customer criticism and rectified accordingly. Listening to criticism, constantly self-reflecting, and improving can make you better" (Ren Zhengfei: "Small improvement, big rewards". 1998)
2000, overstock and dead stock "awarding" conference	The Central Research Department "rewarded" hundreds of the backbone staff of the R&D department with overstock and dead stock, due to sloppy work, confusing BOM filling, lax testing, or blind innovation
2001, democratic life meetings	"Senior managers have democratic life meetings every year; the issues raised in those meetings are very pointed… I hope this practice will be implemented at lower management too. Managers should give each other comments and suggestions, but the atmosphere should be milder and gentler" (Ren Zhengfei: "Huawei's Winter". 2001.)

(continued)

X. Dong et al., *Huawei*,
https://doi.org/10.1007/978-981-19-4078-1

(continued)

Time and event	Description
2002–2003, Mobile Softswitch Division, self-reflection	Since the launch of the mobile core network switch in 1995, Huawei's market share had not grown much, and seven years later it even came to the point of imminent elimination by the industry. In the summer of 2002, the Mobile Softswitch Division started continuous reflection and improvement in both management and technology. Managers at all levels reviewed their processes, project management, product technology, personnel organization, staff skills, and many other problems, in particular the sense of responsibility and service
2005–2007, EMT democratic life meetings	In December 2005, Huawei held an EMT democratic life meeting. Starting with Ren Zhengfei, all companies owned by relatives and friends of Huawei's executives that had related transactions with Huawei were cleaned up. The meeting adopted the "EMT Integrity Oath", which required the completion of the declaration and cleaning up of suppliers that had related transactions with Huawei and are related to EMT members or middle and senior managers in the following two years. The Oath was later institutionalized to cover managers at all levels who are subject to the supervision of all employees
2007, a mass resignation of 7,000 managers	Previously, Huawei employees were assigned work numbers according to the time of recruit, which led to hierarchy bias in the company and compromised office efficiency. At the same time, some older employees began slack off and lose their competitiveness, even though they had high salaries. For this reason, Huawei required all employees who had worked for 8 years, including Ren Zhengfei, to resign voluntarily before January 1, 2008, and sign a 1–3-year labor contract with the company if they were successfully rehired. The second mass resignation abolished the work number system and accelerated the metabolism of the company
2010, Network Product Line Quality Conference	Huawei awarded the "Trap Award", "Worst CBB Award", and "Architecture Tight Coupling Award" to teams and individuals of the network product line at the Network Product Line Quality Conference to warn R&D personnel of the losses caused to customers and the company due to "childishness"

(continued)

(continued)

Time and event	Description
2011, review of the TM case	The TM case refers to the complaint made by the CEO of Telekom Malaysia (TM) to Huawei Chairman Sun Yafang about the failure of Huawei's team in contract performance and project management. After that, the Huawei University case team took the lead in summarizing the failure of the TM project. The case highlights the two main themes of "customer centricity" and "integration and collaboration", while taking into account specific aspects of management improvement such as project clusters, processes, and version management
2012, experiencing Haidilao Hotpot service	Ren Zhengfei invited some company leaders and representatives of TM case to experience the service of Haidilao Hotpot Restaurant, to learn from their customer-centric service
2013, Enterprise BG and Consumer BG held internal meetings to straighten out priorities	Huawei's Enterprise BG and Consumer BG failed to achieve the growth targets promised by core management at the beginning of the year. As a result, the two BGs held several internal meetings to deepen the understanding of business success orientation, emphasizing prioritizing profitability and service-oriented business success while putting "the vanity pursuit of so-called global brands" in second place
2014, Huawei Anti-corruption Conference	In 2014, Huawei disclosed at the anti-corruption conference that a total of 116 Huawei employees were investigated and punished for corruption, of which 83 confessed their misdemeanors to the company and 29 declared voluntarily, all of which were punished internally with mitigated penalties, while the remaining 4 who were found guilty were transferred to the judicial agencies
2017, Integrity Oath-Swearing Conference	Huawei held an Integrity Oath-Swearing Conference in Bantian Base, Shenzhen

Appendix B
Huawei Joint Innovation Centers (JICs)

Name	Time of establishment	Partner	Strategic positioning
Mobile Innovation Center (The first JIC)	2006	Vodafone	To create and commercialize a variety of new technologies and products and collaborate on all strategic wireless areas
Application Innovation Center	2006	Vodafone	To focus on business and operations to ensure that software innovations can be fully applied across different subnets
Wireless Innovation Center	2007	China Mobile	To jointly discuss solutions to major problems of the existing network; to follow and study new trends and technologies in mobile network development; to jointly study communication technologies for enterprise applications
Core Innovation Center	2008	Vodafone	To focus on IT and telecom convergence to support the evolution of its network architecture

(continued)

X. Dong et al., *Huawei*,
https://doi.org/10.1007/978-981-19-4078-1

(continued)

Name	Time of establishment	Partner	Strategic positioning
Fixed-Mobile Convergence Center	2010	Vodafone	To promote E2E solutions and end-to-end technology solutions
JIC	2010	China Telecom	To focus on key technology research, new technology standards and patent cooperation, and the establishment of joint laboratories based on the technical innovation of IPv6
Transmission Innovation Center	2011	Vodafone	To increase transmission capacity and effectively reduce transmission costs
JIC	Jan. 2011	Bell Canada	To collaborate on the development of broadband wireless network technologies, products, and services
JIC	Jan. 2011	TELUS	To collaborate on the development of broadband technologies for wired and wireless areas
Enterprise Cloud Business JIC	Jun. 2011	TELUS, Carleton University	To establish a cloud computing lab dedicated to the research of enterprise cloud applications
Huaqin Energy Saving and Emission Reduction JIC	Feb. 2012	TISCO, Shanxi Huaqin Information Technology Co	To improve the serialization and process of the home inverter
JIC	Mar. 2012	Tencent	To collaborate in Openflow, SDN, simplified routing networks, vSwitch applications, etc.

(continued)

(continued)

Name	Time of establishment	Partner	Strategic positioning
E-government Innovation Center	Aug. 2012	The State Information Center of China	To cooperate in e-government cloud computing standard development, IPV6 innovative application research and validation, e-government theory innovation, etc.
Digital Healthcare Innovation Center	Mar. 2013	Neusoft	Huawei provides ICT products and platforms, and Neusoft provides medical business and applications, forming an industry-leading, well-functioning and high-performing digital hospital solution, with integrated verification of the overall solution
CRSCD-Huawei Innovation Center	Apr. 2013	CRSC Research & Design Institute Group	To provide total solutions and services covering communications and information technology for global customers in the rail transit industry and jointly promote innovation in railroad communication technology, products and solutions
Zain-Huawei Innovation Center	Jun. 2014	Zain	As the first JIC in the Middle East, it helps Zain develop its network service business in Kuwait, especially providing an integrated platform for 4G LTE applications

(continued)

(continued)

Name	Time of establishment	Partner	Strategic positioning
China Unicom-Huawei Big Data Innovation Center	Jun. 2014	China Unicom	With big data as the driving engine, the traffic operation is transformed to an accurate, agile and open Internet operation mode
Backbone Networks 400G/IT Innovation Center	Aug. 2014	China Unicom	To focus on 400G/1T core router platform validation, study smooth evolution of 40G/100G networks and leverage the advanced 400G/1T platform to improve backbone network construction efficiency
Business Innovation Center	Nov. 2014	Telecom Italia	To provide diverse new services and solutions for customers in the fixed and mobile networks sectors
Open Cloud JIC	2015	Telecom Italia	To cooperate in end-to-end services of infrastructure, cloud operating system, ICT-O network automation management, cloud applications, and cloud integration services
JIC	Jan. 2015	Yusys Technologies	To develop solutions for the cloud data center for financial services and one-stop banking
NFV Industrial JIC	Feb. 2015	Tencent	To accelerate the application innovation of Internet in mobile broadband network in terms of technological innovation, product R&D, solutions, and marketing

(continued)

(continued)

Name	Time of establishment	Partner	Strategic positioning
JIC	Mar. 2015	SAP	To cooperate in HANA, all-in-one machine, cloud computing, Internet of Things, Industry4.0, and telecommunication services
Intelligent Transportation and IoT JIC	Mar. 2015	Chongqing China Transport Telecommunication & Information Center (CCTTIC)	To provide innovative industry solutions for the Internet of Vehicles
SDN/ NFV JIC	Apr. 2015	China Unicom Institute of Network Technology	To focus on the research of next-generation network architecture, SDN/NFV R&D environment construction, and business application innovation
Telemedicine and Medical Big Data JIC	May. 2015	The First Affiliated Hospital of Zhengzhou University	To jointly promote solution upgrade and business innovation in various aspects such as telemedicine system, big data application, and mobile health
Intelligent Photovoltaic JIC	Aug. 2015	Yellow River Hydroelectric Engineering Construction Co., Ltd.	To promote the construction of intelligent PV technology platforms, integrating digital information technology, Internet technology, and PV power generation technology in order to improve power generation and the operational efficiency of PV plants

(continued)

(continued)

Name	Time of establishment	Partner	Strategic positioning
JIC	Dec. 2015	The Government of India	To provide ICT solution testing and training support for Indian customers and industry channel partners to integrate multiple vertical solutions
Smart Clean Energy JIC	Dec. 2015	CMIG New Energy	Huawei plans to help CMIG New Energy build industry-leading smart PV power plants with an installed capacity of 15 GW and above within 5 years
Small Cell JIC	Dec. 2015	Telkomsel, University of Indonesia	To promote the digital upgrade of indoor network and smart service innovation and accelerate the development of small cell industry
PSNC-Huawei Innovation Center	Jan. 2016	Poznan Supercomputing and Networking Center (PSNC)	To conduct joint research in the area of high-performance computing (HPC), cloud storage, and big data
ICT Innovation Center	Jan. 2016	Indonesian Ministry of Communication	To provide creative platforms and resources to cultivate ICT talents for Indonesia
SUMEC-HUAWEI Energy IoT Innovation Center	Feb. 2016	SUMEC Energy	To cooperate in R&D and application of key components of Huawei Solar Power Stations, solutions in the Stations and technical R&D cooperation in power IoT
JIC	Mar. 2016	The Government of Malta	To develop HUAWEI Safe City solutions for public administrations in coping with safety threats

(continued)

(continued)

Name	Time of establishment	Partner	Strategic positioning
Power Innovation Center	Jun. 2016	Thailand PEA	To help upgrade the high-speed and secure power grid of PEA
Business Joint Innovation Center (BJIC)	Feb. 2018	ChinaTelecom	To jointly develop differential, innovative products and solutions that will offer users information and communication services

Source Huawei's annual reports

MIX
Papier aus verantwortungsvollen Quellen
Paper from responsible sources
FSC® C105338

If you have any concerns about our products,
you can contact us on
ProductSafety@springernature.com

In case Publisher is established outside the EU,
the EU authorized representative is:
Springer Nature Customer Service Center GmbH
Europaplatz 3, 69115 Heidelberg, Germany

Printed by Libri Plureos GmbH
in Hamburg, Germany

For EU product safety concerns:
IN TECH d.o.o., Prolaz Marije Krucifikse Kozulić 3, 51000 Rijeka, Croatia,
info@intechopen.com or visit our website at intechopen.com.

Meet the editors

Dr. Alesandra Araújo de Souza has a master's degree and a Ph.D. in Physical Education. She is an adjunct professor at the Federal University of Northern Tocantins, Brazil, where she leads the Laboratory for Interdisciplinary Studies in Sleep and Health. Her research interests include the relationship between movement behaviors and the health of preschoolers.

Dr. Sanderson Soares da Silva has a master's degree and a Ph..D in Physical Education. He is an adjunct professor at the Federal University of Northern Tocantins, Brazil, where he leads the Learning, Behavior and Motor Control Laboratory. His research interests include learning, behavior, and motor control of children with neurodevelopmental disorders.

Dr. Thaynã Alves Bezerra has a Ph.D. in Physical Education. Full Degree in Physical Education. She is a professor and research coordinator at the Regional University of Cariri, Brazil. She is a member of the Study Group on Physical Activity and Health Outcomes. Her research interests include the relationship between movement behaviors and the health of preschoolers, and health inequities.

Dr. Anastácio Neco de Souza-Filho has a Ph.D. in Physical Education. She is a professor at the Regional University of Cariri, Brazil. She is a member of the Study Group on Physical Activity and Health Outcomes. Her research interests include the relationship between movement behaviors and the health of preschoolers, and health inequities.

Contents

Preface **IX**

Section 1
Relation of Physical Fitness and Health in Children **1**

Chapter 1 **3**
Association of Occupations Usually Performed by Mexican Adolescents, with the Level of Cardiorespiratory Fitness and Body Mass Index
by Eduardo Gómez-Gómez, Ana Lilia Pérez-Huitimea and Isela Guadalupe Torres-Ruelas

Chapter 2 25
Physical Fitness in Children during Growth: Associations with Body Composition, Physical Activity, and Cognitive Skills
by Kirkke Reisberg, Eva-Maria Riso and Jaak Jürimäe

Section 2
Practical Applications to Develop Physical Fitness in Children **41**

Chapter 3 **43**
Field-Based Measurement of Cardiorespiratory Fitness for Children and the Youth in Low and Middle Income Settings
by Lenora Canizares Fernandez and Anna Czarina L. Chavez

Chapter 4 **61**
Motor Games for Learning Fundamental Motor Skills
by Valentina Biino

Chapter 5 75
Making Physical Activities a Part of a Child's Life
by Endang Ernandini and Jonathan Alvin Wiryaputra

Preface

In an era when technology advances by leaps and bounds and sedentary lifestyle habits become increasingly common, we must focus on future generations' health and well-being. Therefore, this work is an indispensable source of updated and practical knowledge on a highly relevant topic.

Physical fitness is a fundamental component of health, not only in adulthood but also during childhood and adolescence. In childhood, it is a fundamental pillar for the holistic development of children. This book presents an in-depth and comprehensive analysis of the latest scientific discoveries, practical guidance, and valuable insights from internationally renowned experts.

This book responds to the urgent need to understand the updated aspects and best practices related to physical fitness in children, aiming to promote their physical, mental, and social development integrally. In this volume, we bring together renowned experts and leading researchers in their fields to provide a comprehensive, up-to-date analysis of the latest scientific findings, best practices, and emerging trends related to physical fitness in children. Additionally, this work discusses scientific questions on several essential topics, from measurements of the components of physical fitness and the benefits of physical activity for cognitive development to strategies for promoting an active lifestyle from a young age.

Through a multidisciplinary approach, this book offers a comprehensive overview of the current state of knowledge about physical fitness in children and practical and applicable insights that can guide parents, educators, healthcare professionals, and policymakers in promoting an active and healthy lifestyle for future generations.

I hope this work is not only a source of information but also an inspiration for all those committed to children's well-being and full development. May the following pages spark reflections, encourage actions, and contribute to a future where our children can flourish to their full potential.

Finally, I would like to express my sincere gratitude to all the authors and collaborators involved in this project, whose commitment and expertise were essential in making this book a reality. May this work serve as a beacon of knowledge, guiding us on the ongoing journey toward a world where all children have the opportunity to reach their full physical and emotional potential.

Alesandra Araújo de Souza and Sanderson Soares da Silva
Federal University of Northern Tocantins,
Tocantinópolis, Tocantins, Brazil

Anastácio Souza-Filho and Thaynã Alves Bezerra
Regional University of Cariri and Paraiso Faculty,
Iguatu, Araripina, Brazil

Section 1

Relation of Physical Fitness and Health in Children

Chapter 1

Association of Occupations Usually Performed by Mexican Adolescents, with the Level of Cardiorespiratory Fitness and Body Mass Index

Eduardo Gómez-Gómez, Ana Lilia Pérez-Huitimea and Isela Guadalupe Torres-Ruelas

Abstract

This chapter shows the way in which Mexican adolescents distribute their time during the week and the possible effect on body mass index (BMI) and cardiorespiratory fitness (ACR). Using The Habitual Activities and Occupations Recall (HAOR), the percentage of time habitually devoted to seven types of activities was estimated, and the value of total energy expenditure (GET) and the ratio of total energy expenditure/basal energy expenditure (GET/GEB) on each day of the week in 63 adolescents of 17.0 (1.9) years of age. Both sexes sleep longer at the weekend. From Monday to Friday, school activities covered the largest part of the day. On the contrary, domestic activities reached higher time values on the weekend. Time spent on transportation is associated with school attendance. Sports activities were lower than recommended by the World Health Organization (WHO), and work activities registered very low values. In men, the GET/GEB ratio was significantly lower during the weekend ($p < 0.05$). Women did not show significant differences between these two periods, and their values were significantly lower than men. The value of the GET/GEB ratio showed a significant positive effect on the ACR but not on the BMI value.

Keywords: adolescents, physical activity, sedentary lifestyle, school education, physical education, economic factors, time distribution, non-competitive programs, gender perspective, healthy lifestyle, cardiorespiratory fitness, physical exercise, health promotion, Mexico

1. Introduction

Currently, large social sectors have lost or never acquired the habit of physical activity, even when its health benefits are well known [1, 2]. Studies of large populations have evidenced a notable decline in physical activity and sports practice among adolescents, observing a more pronounced decrease in women [3].

Communication and training through the use of screens (television, cell phone, and computer) are increasingly present in all aspects of children's and young people's lives [4].

In Mexico, national health and nutrition surveys have detected since 2006 that the time of physical activity in the adolescent population does not reach the minimum values recommended by the WHO. It was estimated that 64.8% of adolescents were classified as sedentary [5].

The 2012 [6] and 2016 [7] surveys estimated that between these years, the proportion of adolescents who added a minimum of 240 minutes per week of moderate-vigorous physical activity went from 56.7 to 60.5%, estimating that about 40% of adolescents fall into the classification of sedentary. In addition, the 2016 report showed that the proportion of women aged 15–19 who spend more than 2 hours in front of a screen (tablets, computer, television, and cell phone) increased substantially from 71.4% in 2012 to 82.6% in 2016, which is associated with sedentary behavior [7].

On the other hand, the results of the national health and nutrition surveys (ENSANUT) from 2006 to 2018 show a sustained increase in the prevalence of overweight and obesity, which is a consequence of poor eating habits and reduced physical activity [5, 8, 9].

Although many programs have been implemented at the governmental level to promote physical activity in the school population, the problems of sedentarism, overweight, and obesity seem unable to be reversed.

Regaining the interest of children and adolescents in sports practice and movement is a priority for the acquisition of active and healthy life habits. For this, it is necessary to develop descriptive studies that allow us to know the time and frequency that children and adolescents dedicate to performing their school, work, and domestic duties; the activities they carry out in their free time, as well as rest and sleep, to begin to elucidate the reasons for the abandonment or disinterest in exercise. From this, develop suitable educational and social strategies that can reverse this trend.

There are already previous studies that have shown a considerable deterioration of cardiorespiratory fitness (CRF) in samples of high school student adolescents from North America [10, 11], Latin América [12, 13], and México [14]. Based on this evidence, it is necessary to characterize the activities that young people perform and thereby establish whether the activities they usually carry out are the factor that explains their deterioration.

To guide any action in addressing obesity and sedentarism, it is of great importance to conduct studies that describe the occupations or activities that adolescents perform in the different contexts in which they operate: home, school, work, transport, and free time.

2. Problem statement

Recent epidemiological studies show that most adolescents are not attracted to sports practice or recreational physical activities, in addition to the fact that in Mexico, the physical education class or some subject aimed at the acquisition of habits by exercise is absent from the high school curriculum [15].

Each individual develops their own lifestyle, so their activities or occupations are not exactly the same. However, a population tends to present similar habits among its members, a consequence of the fact that, in general, everyone operates within the same context. Therefore, it is possible to identify activities and occupations that characterize them and influence their level of physical activity.

From a health perspective, lifestyle is a determinant for the prevention of diseases. The decrease in physical fitness and high prevalence of sedentary behaviors in the population aged 15 to 19 years is well documented. Sedentary behavior is linked to the development of overweight and obesity; moreover, poor development of physical fitness is a risk factor for cardiovascular disease in adulthood.

There are several tools and techniques to determine total and resting energy expenditure: direct and indirect calorimetry, predictive equations, bioelectrical impedance, doubly labeled water [16], as well as the level of physical activity that people perform in their daily life, considering objective methods such as the use of accelerometers, pedometers, and heart rate monitoring; as well as subjective methods: questionnaires like the International Physical Activity Questionnaire (IPAQ) or the Global Physical Activity Questionnaire (GPAQ) [17]. However, these tools are aimed at categorizing the level of physical activity and offer imprecise information about the purpose of physical activity and the context in which energy expenditure is carried out; in other words, these studies are reduced to a mechanistic vision of the individual without considering the utilitarian and motivational sense of physical activity.

Knowing the activities that adolescents develop would allow a better understanding of their behavior habits to be able to establish strategies that influence more effectively toward the change to a physically active lifestyle. On the other hand, although it is well identified that sedentarism is inversely linked to the level of physical fitness and directly to body adiposity, it is necessary to deepen the relationship between the time and frequency with which the different activities are classified as school, domestic, transportation, work, sports, recreational, as well as sleep time as it is a determinant factor of health. It is also important to establish the correspondence of some health indicators with the degree of energy expenditure required by the set of activities they usually perform during the day.

This chapter offers the evidence to determine in a sample of Mexican adolescents high school students in the city of Colima, if the configuration of the time allocated to each of the different types of activities and habitual occupations performed by adolescents is a condition of the level of ACR and the classification of BMI.

3. Theoretical framework

The WHO considers physical activity to be any movement produced by the skeletal muscle that results in a substantial increase in the energy expenditure needed to maintain vital functions such as respiration, digestion, blood circulation. It also states that physical inactivity is the primary cause of between 21 and 25% of breast and colon cancers, 27% of diabetes cases, and around 30% of ischemic heart disease; as well as a key determinant of energy expenditure and fundamental for caloric balance and weight control [18].

The conventional unit of energy measurement is the calorie; in biological terms, heat is primarily a manifestation of energy released during the oxidation of glucose and fatty acids [19].

Different types of activities or occupations have a utilitarian sense with a contextual social meaning, and it is important to identify them to obtain precise qualitative appraisals of the habits and behaviors that characterize a group.

Activities classified as domestic refer to all services related to home care or home maintenance. Butlers, housekeepers, drivers, cooks, janitors, caretakers, gardeners, nurses, assistants, launderers, and tutors represent domestic occupations [20].

School activities are those involved in formal teaching and learning processes. They can be carried out indoors or outdoors, with defined intentions or objectives. They also seek to provide students with opportunities to develop social attitudes, integrate a scheme of values and ideals, and acquire certain specific skills and abilities [21].

Another type of activity is work-related, which is all situations or elements linked in one way or another to work, understood as any physical or intellectual activity that receives some type of support or economic remuneration for manufacturing, sales, or professional service [22].

The definition established by the European Sports Charter was considered for sports activities: "*... any form of physical activity that, through organized participation or not, aims to improve physical and psychic condition, develop social relations or achieve results in competitions at any level ...*" [23], to complement this definition it also corresponds to the systematic practice of physical exercise, which is carried out according to the rules of each discipline and is performed to reach a goal or to overcome the adversary [24].

On the other hand, recreational activities are characterized by being carried out during free time and represent spaces for enjoyment, catharsis, and fun for the individual, promoting the integral development of people through meaningful experiences of non-formal education. They are of personal choice and voluntary participation [25].

Transportation activities cover displacement needs that the individual regularly carries out to different places to carry out other types of activities [26]. The relevance of transportation activities is to identify the degree of physical activity that the person performs for the displacement. When activities are carried out as crew personnel in a medium, then it is considered a work activity.

Energy expenditure (EE) corresponds to the amount of energy consumed per unit of time (minute, hour, day) measured in kilocalories and adjusted for body weight (kilocalories/hour/kg) [19]. The higher the energy demand, the higher the EE value.

The total value of EE depends on three factors: the basal energy expenditure (BEE), which corresponds to the energy necessary for all the metabolic chemical reactions, transportation, heat production, synthesis, and degradation of compounds required for vital functions: cardiac output, pulmonary ventilation, renal filtration, vasoconstriction and vasodilation, activity of the central nervous system and endocrine secretions, protein synthesis, ionic balance, hepatic biochemical processes [27]. The BEE represents between 60 and 70% of the daily energy requirement for most sedentary individuals and about 50% for those who are physically active [28].

BEE can be calculated using equations that consider body weight and height as proposed by Kleiber. BEE (Kcal/day) Men = 71.2 * Weight (Kg)0.75 * [1 + 0.004 * (30 – age (years) +0.010 * (height(cm)/weight(Kg) – 43.4))]. BEE (Kcal/day) Women = 65.8 * Weight(Kg)0.75 * [1 + 0.004 * (30-age(years) + 0.010 (height (cm)/weight(Kg) – 42.1))] [19].

The second determinant of EE corresponds to the thermal effect of food (TEF) that uses energy in the form of ATP to perform digestion after ingestion. Depending on the energy composition of the food, the amount of energy required for its digestion will vary. Proteins need between 15 and 30% of the energy they provide to be digested, carbohydrates between 10 and 15%, while lipids need between 3 and 4%;

this includes the storage of macronutrients through glycogen synthesis at the muscular and hepatic level or synthesis of triacylglycerols in adipose tissue [19].

During the digestive process, heat is released, and it is the only involuntary energy that is not included in basal metabolism; it is estimated that between 8 and 10% of the total energy expenditure (TEE) corresponds to the TEF [29].

Energy expenditure through physical activity (EEPA) is the third factor; this includes the energy used by skeletal muscle contraction as a result of performing daily activities such as personal grooming, walking, running, performing a job, or practicing a sport [29].

The level of physical activity is estimated through questionnaires. Currently, determining the level of physical activity in studies that seek to evaluate health risk factors in delimited populations is a priority. The International Physical Activity Questionnaire (IPAQ) is one of the most widely used self-response instruments in epidemiological studies. The review by Mantilla-Tolosa & Gómez Conesa concluded that the IPAQ survey is a reliable instrument for adults aged 18 to 65 [30], as well as those over 65 [31] in terms of its psychometric properties, the long version has a reliability of 0.8 (r = 0.81; CI 95%: 0.79–0.82) and the short version of 0.65 (r = 0.76, CI 95%: 0.73–0.77). The short version is a good instrument for studying regional and national physical activity prevalence, while the long version is suggested for more specific studies that require detailed information on physical activity.

Adolescence period. It is during adolescence when the person consolidates the values and behavior norms that will mark their identity and serve as a compass in their social behavior. For this to happen, their successes and achievements need to be recognized as part of the maturation process. The adolescent must know who they are and who they want to become. Otherwise, their decisions will not be firm and permanent [32].

As the adolescent develops, they begin to consider new conditions when choosing a friend, such as having the same concerns, ideals, and sometimes even economic conditions [33]. Adolescents also become more independent, reject family meetings, and seek to meet with their friends to carry out activities together [33].

4. Methodology

This study is approached from a quantitative perspective because the variables are quantifiable and interpreted through statistical measures [34]. It follows a hypothetical-deductive approach as it seeks to test or reject a tentative response to the situation that drives this study [34]. It corresponds to a cross-sectional and descriptive-relational study [34], as it aims to characterize the variables of caloric expenditure, type and time devoted to activities, level of cardiorespiratory fitness (ACR), and BMI, and then examine the association between the first variable and the latter two.

The protocols to assess the variables were approved by the research academy of the Faculty of Education Sciences, and the biosafety committee of the University of Colima; considering them safe, appropriate, and non-invasive.

Population and sample. The population consisted of 15,512 adolescents aged 15 to 18 years who attended high school in the 37 high schools affiliated with the University of Colima [35]. The sample was composed of adolescent students from high school number 34 in the municipality of Cuauhtémoc, Colima, as it was the school that presented the best conditions and availability of students for the study.

The project was presented to the students and their parents in a plenary meeting to communicate the objectives and evaluations that would be obtained from the young participants. Only students who presented both signed letters, voluntary participation and informed consent, were included in the study.

After learning about the project, interested students and parents signed the voluntary participation letter and the informed consent letter, respectively.

Assessment of Cardiorespiratory Fitness (CRF). The assessment of CRF is carried out using the Tecumseh step test protocol [36], which is based on the speed at which heart rate returns to resting values after a specified physical exertion. To properly administer the test, the subject should not have engaged in vigorous physical activity for at least 1 hour prior. Each participant rested for 5 minutes while seated in a chair at a constant temperature of 22°C. The heart rate was recorded using a heart rate monitor (POLAR mod. A300) and a heart rate sensor (POLAR mod. H7) placed on the skin in the midline of the chest at the distal portion of the sternum. For 3 minutes, the participant stepped up and down a 20-cm wooden step at a pace of 96 beats per minute, marked by a metronome, following this sequence: right foot up, left foot up, right foot down, left foot down, completing 72 cycles. The heart rate (HR) was recorded at rest in a seated position immediately after the exercise and 1 minute after exercise in a seated position at rest.

To classify the level of CRF in the evaluated adolescents, reference ranges established in a previous population study with Mexican adolescents were considered [37].

To calculate and classify the body mass index (BMI), height (m) was measured using a portable stadiometer (SECA mod. 213), and body weight (Kg) was measured using a clinical diagnostic scale (Beurer Wellbeing. Model BF 105, manufactured in Germany), following the protocol established by the International Society for the Advancement of Kinanthropometry (ISAK) [38]. The BMI value was obtained by dividing body weight by the squared height. The obtained value was then classified according to the standards established by the World Health Organization [18].

Methodological Foundations of the Habitual Activities and Occupations Recall (HAOR). The Habitual Activities and Occupations Recall (HAOR) is an instrument designed and applied in the adolescent population of Colima since 2016, and it has been gradually modified to adjust to the behaviors of high school students. The purposes of the HAOR are to establish the time that adolescents devote to each of the activities or occupations in their daily life, which are grouped into six categories: domestic, transportation/travel, work-related, school-related, sports, and recreational activities. Secondly, it aims to estimate the energy expenditure (Kcal) that an adolescent engages in throughout each day of the week.

The HAOR consists of 5 pages containing a matrix with 7 columns corresponding to each day of the week, arranged in a sequence from Monday to Sunday, with enough rows to record 24 hours of activities in 15-minute intervals from 00:00 hrs to 23:45. On the right side of the registration matrix, there is a menu with 81 options of activities and occupations, each assigned a number. The activities and occupations are grouped into domestic, school-related, work-related, sports, recreational, and transportation activities.

Based on the premise that the students should record what they usually do each day of the week at the corresponding time, they choose the number corresponding to the activity and record it in the space for the designated time and day.

If the activity they perform is not listed in the menu, there is a space on the last page of the recall where the adolescent can write the name of the activity and provide a brief description of it. They assign the next progressive number after 81 and record it in the time and day spaces of the recall. When reviewing their responses, the evaluator determines the classification corresponding to the activity and identifies an equivalent activity in the menu to calculate its energy cost.

To estimate the energy expenditure involved in performing habitual activities and occupations, the standardized value per minute and per kilogram of body weight for these activities published by Katch et al. [39] was considered.

HAOR Application Process. A classroom within the high school facilities was assigned for the HAOR application. In groups of 20 participants, the purpose and manner of data registration in the registration matrix were explained and exemplified, with an emphasis on recording the activities or occupations they regularly engage in. No maximum or minimum time was set for responding to the HAOR. During the application, the students were assisted by six support personnel who had received prior training to address their doubts.

Data Analysis Procedure. The data from the HAOR were entered into individual records in an automated spreadsheet (Quattro-Pro 10 for Windows) to calculate the percentage of time devoted to each type of activity, as well as the estimated total energy expenditure and energy expenditure per day of the week, in addition to the total energy expenditure (GET) to basal energy expenditure (BEE) ratio for each day of the week.

To assess the normality of the distributions obtained for each variable, the Shapiro-Wilk test was used. For comparing means with normal distributions, the one-way analysis of variance (ANOVA) test and the Tamhane contrast test were conducted. For comparing means between different groups in the sample with non-normal distributions, the Kruskal-Wallis test was used. The analysis of variance of two-way Friedman test was used for comparing means of repeated measures. Significance was set at $p < 0.05$.

5. Results

Sixty-five students fully and appropriately completed the RAOH, with 38 females (F) and 27 males (M), with an average age of 17 (±1.9) years [F: 17.1 (±1.1), M: 16.8 (±1.5)]; height: 163.4 (±9.0) cm, [F: 157.5 (±5.0) cm, M: 171.8 (±6.0) cm]; body weight: 64.0 (±15.9) kg, [F: 58.1 (±13.1) kg, M: 71.3 (±16.4) kg]; and BMI: 23.8 (±5.1) [M: 24.0 (±5.1), F: 23.8 (±5.7)]. Four of these participants declined to participate in the measurements of body weight and height, so their BMI was not obtained, and two other participants declined to undergo the CRF assessment.

Based on the records obtained from this sample, the percentage distribution of adolescents' time within a 24-hour period was as follows, from highest to lowest: sleep 37.3% (±9.1); domestic activities 24.7% (±13.2); school activities 19.1% (±12.6); transportation 10.6% (±8.1); sports activities 3.4% (±5.3); leisure activities 3.6% (±6.8); and work-related activities 1.5% (±5.9). These values include both males and females (**Table 1**).

According to the National Heart, Lung, and Blood Institute [40], a person requires 8 hours of sleep per day for healthy rest, which corresponds to 33.3% of a 24-hour day. The sample of adolescents showed average sleep times higher than the recommended amount on weekdays and weekends. It should be noted that these adolescents attend school in the afternoon.

Type	Mo	Tu	We	Th	Fr	Sa	Su
Sleep	34.8 ± 6.1	34.7 ± 6.4	35.0 ± 6.8	34.7 ± 6.5	35.7 ± 6.4	**42.1 ± 9.7‡**	**43.2 ± 11.5‡**
Domestic	21.6 ± 8.3	20.9 ± 8.7	21.9 ± 8.7	20.8 ± 8.4	20.8 ± 7.7	**34.3 ± 14.7‡**	**36.3 ± 16.6‡**
Work-related	0.7 ± 3.9	0.8 ± 4.0	0.7 ± 3.9	0.9 ± 4.0	0.8 ± 3.9	1.8 ± 8.0	1.3 ± 7.4
Transportation	11.4 ± 5.3	11.8 ± 5.5	11.2 ± 5.2	11.7 ± 5.2	11.1 ± 5.1	**7.3 ± 8.0‡**	**6.6 ± 9.5‡**
School	26.3 ± 6.6	26.0 ± 6.8	26.0 ± 6.6	26.0 ± 7.0	26.2 ± 6.9	**6.4 ± 9.5‡**	**4.9 ± 9.1‡**
Sports	3.7 ± 5.4	4.0 ± 5.1	3.7 ± 5.5	4.0 ± 5.0	3.5 ± 5.6	4.0 ± 6.4	2.9 ± 5.4
Leisure	1.4 ± 2.9	1.8 ± 3.2	1.4 ± 2.8	1.8 ± 3.5	1.7 ± 3.7	3.3 ± 6.1	**5.4 ± 8.7†**
n	65	65	65	65	65	65	65

Mo: Monday; Tu: Tuesday; We: Wednesday; Th: Thursday; Fr: Friday; Sa: Saturday; Su: Sunday.
ANOVA test, significance: $p < 0.05$. Tamhane's contrast test for heterogeneous variances.‡: different from Monday, Tuesday, Wednesday, Thursday, and Friday. ($p < 0.001$).
†: different from Wednesday and Thursday. ($p = 0.028$).

Table 1.
Percentage values of time allocated to sleep and different types of activities performed by evaluated adolescents (males and females) on each day of the week.

Domestic activities occupied more time during the weekend compared to the Monday to Friday period, whereas the time devoted to transportation activities was significantly lower on weekends compared to weekdays. School-related activities were allocated time throughout the week, but they took up more time on weekdays compared to weekends, while the time spent on school activities during the weekend focused on homework. It can be established that the time allocated to domestic activities depends on the need to attend to school activities, which are predominant in adolescents' occupations (**Table 1**).

In descending order, sports, leisure, and work-related activities received the least amount of time and did not show significant variations on any of the weekdays (**Table 1**).

To distinguish the distribution of time per activity type between women and men, the percentage of time allocated by each gender was calculated by separating the sample by sex (**Tables 2** and **3**).

The percentage of time dedicated to sleep in women varied significantly between weekends and weekdays; according to the results, women spend more time sleeping on Saturdays and Sundays compared to the rest of the week. **Table 2** shows that sleep time during the week does not exceed 36%, while it reaches 41% on weekends.

During weekdays, school activities occupy the most time for women, followed by domestic activities, and transportation in third place. On weekends, domestic activities take up the most time, displacing school activities to second place with a similar percentage value as transportation activities (**Table 2**).

Women are characterized by sleeping more on weekends and taking care of domestic activities. On weekdays, they sleep less and allocate more time to school-related and transportation activities. They also spend little time on sports and leisure activities on any given day of the week, and work activities account for barely a percentage point on average (**Table 2**).

Like women, men allocate more time to sleep on Saturday and Sunday, surpassing 43% compared to the period from Monday to Friday, which does not exceed 36% of total time (**Table 3**).

Type	Mo	Tu	We	Th	Fr	Sa	Su
Sleep	35.3 ± 6.0	34.2 ± 6.3	35.6 ± 6.9	33.9 ± 6.4	35.1 ± 6.4	**41.4 ± 9.9**†	**41.0 ± 8.4**‡
Domestic	23.5 ± 7.8	23.1 ± 8.3	24.3 ± 8.2	23.1 ± 7.9	23.2 ± 7.2	**37.7 ± 13.8**†	**39.7 ± 15.8**†
Transportation	10.9 ± 5.0	11.8 ± 5.8	10.6 ± 5.0	11.7 ± 5.3	10.8 ± 4.9	**6.6 ± 7.5**†	**6.1 ± 7.8**†
Work	1.0 ± 4.0	1.0 ± 3.9	1.0 ± 3.9	1.0 ± 3.9	1.0 ± 3.9	0.0 ± 0.2	0.0 ± 0.0
School	25.5 ± 7.0	24.6 ± 6.4	24.4 ± 6.2	24.7 ± 6.6	25.6 ± 6.8	**6.2 ± 7.6**†	**6.0 ± 9.2**†
Sports	2.4 ± 4.6	3.6 ± 4.7	2.7 ± 5.1	3.6 ± 4.6	2.8 ± 5.5	3.8 ± 6.8	2.5 ± 4.6
Leisure	1.6 ± 3.4	2.1 ± 3.8	1.6 ± 3.0	2.4 ± 4.1	1.8 ± 3.8	3.6 ± 5.7	**5.6 ± 8.5**†
N	38	38	38	38	38	38	38

Mo: Monday; Tu: Tuesday; We: Wednesday; Th: Thursday; Fr: Friday; Sa: Saturday; Su: Sunday.
ANOVA test, significance: $p < 0.05$. Tamhane's contrast test for non-homogeneous variances.†different from Monday, Tuesday, Wednesday, Thursday, and Friday ($p < 0.05$).
‡different from Tuesday and Thursday ($p < 0.05$).

Table 2.
Percentage values of time allocated to sleep and different types of activities carried out by female adolescents on each day of the week.

Type	Mo	Tu	We	Th	Fr	Sa	Su
Sleep	34.1 ± 6.3	34.5 ± 6.7	34.2 ± 6.9	35.7 ± 6.7	36.5 ± 6.4	**43.2 ± 9.5**†	**46.3 ± 14.4**†
Domestic	18.8 ± 8.3	17.7 ± 8.2	18.4 ± 8.2	17.6 ± 8.1	17.5 ± 7.1	**29.7 ± 15.0**‡	**31.4 ± 17.0**‡
Transportation	12.2 ± 5.8	11.8 ± 5.0	12.0 ± 5.4	11.8 ± 5.1	11.5 ± 5.5	8.4 ± 8.9	7.3 ± 11.6
Work	1.0 ± 3.8	1.0 ± 4.0	1.0 ± 3.8	1.2 ± 4.1	1.1 ± 4.0	4.2 ± 12.1	3.0 ± 11.3
School	27.4 ± 8.0	28.0 ± 6.9	28.2 ± 6.5	27.8 ± 7.2	27.1 ± 7.1	**6.7 ± 11.8**‡	**3.5 ± 8.9**‡
Sports	5.6 ± 6.0	4.6 ± 5.7	5.0 ± 5.9	4.8 ± 5.6	4.4 ± 5.7	4.3 ± 6.0	3.3 ± 6.3
Leisure	1.0 ± 2.0	1.4 ± 2.2	1.2 ± 2.5	1.0 ± 2.0	1.7 ± 3.6	3.0 ± 6.7	5.0 ± 9.1
N	27	27	27	27	27	27	27

Mo: Monday; Tu: Tuesday; We: Wednesday; Th: Thursday; Fr: Friday; Sa: Saturday; Su: Sunday.
ANOVA test, significance: $p < 0.05$. Tamhane's contrast test for non-homogeneous variances.†different from Monday, Tuesday, Wednesday, and Thursday ($p < 0.05$).
‡different from Thursday and Friday ($p < 0.05$).
‡different from Friday ($p < 0.05$).
‡different from Monday, Tuesday, Wednesday, Thursday, and Friday ($p < 0.05$).

Table 3.
Percentage values of time devoted to sleep and different types of activities performed by male adolescents on each day of the week.

Men showed the same behavior as women regarding domestic and school activities. They spend more time on domestic activities during the weekend, while school activities occupy more time during the weekdays. However, unlike women, the time spent on transportation is not significantly different between weekdays and weekends (**Table 3**). This could indicate that men engage in more activities outside the home during the weekend than women.

Although the average time devoted to sports activities is slightly higher in men than in women, it does not exceed 6% of the total daily time. Men allocate the least amount of time to work and leisure activities. The results show that although the time spent on work activities increases during the weekend, it is not significantly different from weekdays (Monday to Friday) (**Table 3**).

The results obtained from the estimation of Total Energy Expenditure (TEE) showed that men had significantly lower values on Saturdays and Sundays compared to Mondays and Wednesdays. This corresponds to the previous mention that men sleep more on Saturdays and Sundays. On the other hand, women did not show significant variations in TEE throughout the week. This indicates that although women also sleep more on weekends, unlike men, the activities they engage in over the weekend require the same energy expenditure as any other day from Monday to Friday (**Table 4**).

The values obtained for the TEE/Basal Energy Expenditure (BEE) ratio showed a significant decrease on Sundays in men, confirming that the decrease in TEE is due to less physical activity. In women, the TEE/BEE ratio does not show significant variations, confirming that women maintain the same level of energy expenditure through physical activity throughout the week (**Table 4**).

The average values of the TEE/BEE ratio for each BMI category and day of the week did not show significant differences. Additionally, there were no significant differences between the different days of the week within each BMI category (**Table 5**).

No significant differences were detected with respect to the percentage of time spent performing domestic activities between the BMI categories on any of the days of the week ($p > 0.05$); although there are significant differences within all BMI categories. Showing that regardless of the BMI value, domestic activities take up more time on Saturday and Sunday (**Table 6**).

Similarly, the average values of time allocated to transportation activities for each BMI category did not show significant differences on any day of the week. Only within the "Normal Weight" category, the time allocated to transportation during the weekend was significantly lower than on other days ($p < 0.001$).

The time allocated to school activities was also similar across BMI categories on each day of the week, but within the categories, except for "Underweight," there was a significant decrease in time during the weekend ($p < 0.001$).

Regarding the time allocated to sleep among BMI categories, no differences were detected. However, within all categories, adolescents slept more on Saturdays and Sundays than on any day from Monday to Friday (**Table 7**).

Regarding sports activities, statistical analyses between BMI categories, as well as within each category, did not show significant differences ($p > 0.05$). This means that the time allocated to sports activities did not have a significant effect on BMI.

Women	**Mo**	**Tu**	**We**	**Th**	**Fr**	**Sa**	**Su**
TEE	1549 ± 324	1592 ± 307	1564 ± 406	1587 ± 305	1582 ± 371	1516 ± 385	1463 ± 339
TEE/BEE	1.09 ± 0.16	1.13 ± 0.17	1.10 ± 0.22	1.12 ± 0.17	1.12 ± 0.22	1.07 ± 0.22	1.03 ± 0.18
N	38	38	38	38	38	38	38
Men							
TEE	2384 ± 699	2287 ± 609	2386 ± 724	2293 ± 631	2292 ± 640	2059 ± 672	**1952 ± 771**†
TEE/BEE	1.31 ± 0.31	1.26 ± 0.27	1.31 ± 0.33	1.26 ± 0.28	1.24 ± 0.30	1.14 ± 0.37	**1.11 ± 0.38**†
N	27	27	27	27	27	27	27

Mo: Monday; Tu: Tuesday; We: Wednesday; Th: Thursday; Fr: Friday; Sa: Saturday; Su: Sunday.
One-way ANOVA test. Significance: $p < 0.05$. †different from Monday and Wednesday ($p = 0.003$).

Table 4.
Estimated values of Total energy expenditure (TEE) and the ratio of Total energy expenditure to basal energy expenditure (TEE / BEE) in male and female adolescents.

	BMI Categories				
Days	**Underweight**	**Normal**	**Overweight**	**Obesity**	**p⁺**
Monday	1.1 ± 0.12	1.2 ± 0.27	1.3 ± 0.35	1.1 ± 0.15	*0.632*
Tuesday	1.1 ± 0.14	1.2 ± 0.21	1.3 ± 0.32	1.1 ± 0.18	*0.788*
Wednesday	1.1. ± 0.14	1.2 ± 0.26	1.4 ± 0.44	1.1 ± 0.17	*0.659*
Thursday	1.1 ± 0.13	1.2 ± 0.21	1.2 ± 0.34	1.1 ± 0.20	*0.668*
Friday	1.1 ± 0.06	1.2 ± 0.23	1.3 ± 0.43	1.1 ± 0.11	*0.440*
Saturday	1.0 ± 0.16	1.1 ± 0.30	1.0 ± 0.18	1.1 ± 0.24	*0.418*
Sunday	1.0 ± 0.17	1.0 ± 0.29	0.9 ± 0.16	1.0 ± 0.18	*0.273*
N	*8*	*30*	*12*	*11*	
p ⁺⁺	*0.244*	*0.098*	*0.085*	*0.319*	

Four participants did not undergo weight and height assessment significance: $p < 0.05$.⁺Kruskal-Wallis test for independent samples.
⁺⁺Two-way Friedman analysis of variance.
On the other hand, the values of time allocated to domestic activities, grouped according to BMI categories, did not show significant differences between the groups on any of the days of the week ($p > 0.05$). However, significant differences were observed within all BMI categories. Regardless of BMI value, domestic activities occupy more time on Saturdays and Sundays.

Table 5.
Values of the TEE/BEE ratio grouped according to BMI categories for men and women.

	BMI Categories				
Days	**Underweight**	**Normal**	**Overweight**	**Obesity**	**p⁺**
Monday	**20.0 ± 5.6†**	21.8 ± 8.2	19.5 ± 5.2	25.9 ± 12.1	*0.58*
Tuesday	21.3 ± 8.2	20.8 ± 8.1	18.4 ± 6.7	24.6 ± 12.7	*0.713*
Wednesday	21.7 ± 7.8	21.9 ± 8.3	17.7 ± 6.6	27.5 ± 11.3	*0.101*
Thursday	20.0 ± 5.3	20.8 ± 8.4	19.7 ± 7.4	23.9 ± 11.6	*0.944*
Friday	20.4 ± 6.2	21.0 ± 7.3	18.9 ± 6.7	**24.0 ± 10.9†**	*0.618*
Saturday	37.6 ± 17.5	**36.6 ± 14.9‡**	**31.9 ± 12.7‡**	**34.0 ± 10.2‡**	*0.771*
Sunday	44.1 ± 18.0	**36.7 ± 16.9‡**	**36.1 ± 13.0†,‡**	**37.1 ± 12.8‡**	*0.661*
N	*8*	*30*	*12*	*11*	
p⁺⁺	**0.015**	**0.001**	**0.001**	**0.001**	

Four participants did not undergo weight and height assessment.
Significance: $p < 0.05$.†, $p = 0.037$; Different from Tuesday;
‡$p < 0.001$, different from Monday, Tuesday, Wednesday, Thursday, and Friday;
‡$p < 0.01$, different from Tuesday, Wednesday, Thursday, and Friday.
‡$p < 0.05$, different from Wednesday;
‡$p < 0.05$, different from Thursday and Friday.
⁺Kruskal-Wallis test for independent samples.
⁺⁺Two-way Friedman analysis of variance.

Table 6.
Values of the percentage of time allocated to performing **domestic** *activities grouped by BMI categories.*

	BMI categories				
Days	**Underweight**	**Normal**	**Overweight**	**Obesity**	**p⁺**
Monday	34.7 ± 3.2	34.8 ± 5.5	34.6 ± 7.1	35.3 ± 9.3	*0.803*
Tuesday	34.7 ± 2.9	35.2 ± 6.3	34.3 ± 8.2	34.2 ± 8.2	*0.968*
Wednesday	35.6 ± 2.3	35.5 ± 5.8	33.2 ± 9.6	35.2 ± 9.3	*0.860*
Thursday	34.3 ± 3.7	35.1 ± 6.6	35.5 ± 7.2	33.0 ± 8.2	*0.833*
Friday	35.3 ± 2.7	36.3 ± 5.6	35.0 ± 8.7	35.7 ± 4.5	*0.937*
Saturday	**40.9 ± 6.9‡**	**41.3 ± 10.7†**	45.3 ± 10.0	**42.2 ± 10.3†**	*0.670*
Sunday	**39.6 ± 4.8‡**	**42.7 ± 14.0†**	**49.1 ± 12.0†**	**42.3 ± 6.0‡**	*0.299*
N	*8*	*30*	*12*	*11*	
p⁺⁺	**0.004**	**0.001**	**0.026**	**0.001**	

Four participants did not undergo weight and height assessment.
Significance: $p < 0.05$. ‡$p < 0.05$; different from Monday, Tuesday, Wednesday, Thursday, and Friday.
†$p < 0.05$; different from Monday, Tuesday, Wednesday, and Thursday.
⁺Kruskal-Wallis test for independent samples.
⁺⁺Two-way Friedman analysis of variance.

Table 7.
Values of the percentage of time allocated to sleep, grouped according to BMI categories.

No significant differences were detected between BMI categories in leisure and work activities ($p > 0.05$), nor within these categories ($p > 0.05$). The time allocated to these types of activities was minimal in the entire sample studied.

On the other hand, when comparing the average values of the TEE/BEE ratio grouped according to the level of cardiorespiratory fitness (CRF) categories, a significantly higher energy expenditure value was observed in the "Very Good" category compared to the "Regular" category on Mondays, Thursdays, and Fridays, and compared to the "Low" category on Tuesdays, Thursdays, and Fridays. Additionally, the TEE/BEE ratio value in the "Good" category was significantly higher than in the "Regular" category on Wednesdays. These findings indicate that an increase in energy expenditure for daily activities and occupations benefits the level of CRF (**Table 8**).

Only two participants showed a CRF level classified as "Excellent," which affected the statistical calculations to determine if this category also exhibits the same trend of increased CRF with increasing values of the TEE/BEE ratio observed in the "Good" and "Very Good" categories.

In all CRF level categories, Sunday had the lowest energy expenditure, although the average TEE/BEE ratio value on this day was not always significantly different from the other days of the week within the same CRF category (**Table 8**).

The statistical analysis indicated that Mondays and Wednesdays had significantly higher TEE/BEE values than Sundays within the "Low" category. On the other hand, within the "Very Good" category, Thursdays had a significantly higher value than Sundays (**Table 8**).

The time allocated to household activities was significantly higher on Wednesdays in the "Low" category compared to the same day in the "Regular," "Good," and "Very Good" categories ($p = 0.022$). Mondays, Tuesdays, Thursdays, and Fridays also showed higher values in the "Poor" and "Low" categories compared to the other categories, but they did not reach statistical significance. These trends may indicate that higher time spent on household activities is associated with lower CRF levels (**Table 9**).

Days	Poor	Low	Regular	Good	Very good	Excellent	p⁺
Monday	1.1 ± .2	**1.1Ł ± .1**	**1.1 * ± .3**	1.4 ± .2	1.4 ± .3	1.2 ± .4	**.008**
Tuesday	1.2 ± .2	**1.1* ± .1**	1.1 ± .2	1.4 ± .4	1.4 ± .2	1.2 ± .3	**.018**
Wednesday	1.1 ± .2	**1.1Ł ± .1**	**1.1 ± .3** ‡	1.5 ± .4	1.4 ± .4	1.2 ± .4	**.026**
Thursday	1.2 ± .3	**1.1* ± .1**	**1.1* ± .2**	1.4 ± .4	**1.4 ± .2**‡	1.2 ± .3	**.006**
Friday	1.1 ± .1	**1.1 ± .2***	**1.1 ± .1***	1.5 ± .4	1.4 ± .3	1.2 ± .4	**.012**
Saturday	1.1 ± .2	1.1 ± .3	1.1 ± .3	1.2 ± .5	1.1 ± .3	1.1 ± .1	.956
Sunday	1.0 ± .2	1.0 ± .2	1.1 ± .3	1.2 ± .5	1.1 ± .3	1.0 ± .1	*.871*
N	7	24	13	7	10	2	
p ⁺⁺	*.763*	**.009**	*.745*	*.863*	**.009**	*.558*	

Two participants did not undergo CRF assessment.
Significance: $p < 0.05$.⁺Kruskal-Wallis test for independent samples.
⁺⁺Two-way Friedman analysis of variance.
‡different from the Good category.
**different from the Very Good category.*
‡different from Sunday.

Table 8.
Values of the TEE/BEE ratio grouped according to CRF categories.

On the other hand, within each CRF category, except for "Very Good" and "Excellent" significantly more time was allocated to household activities on Saturdays and Sundays ($p < 0.05$) (**Table 9**).

The average time allocated to transportation was not significantly different among the CRF categories ($p > 0.05$), although the "Poor" category had the highest average

Days	Poor	Low	Regular	Good	Very good	Excellent	p⁺
Monday	21.8 ± 11.7	25.5 ± 8.8	19.6 ± 6.1	18.5 ± 6.2	17.9 ± 6.4	16.1 ± 4.2	*0.062*
Tuesday	21.5 ± 11.6	24.2 ± 8.9	19.1 ± 8.2	17.5 ± 7.0	17.1 ± 6.6	21.3 ± 9.0	*0.086*
Wednesday	23.2 ± 10.3	25.9 ± 9.0	**19.9* ± 7.9**	**16.7* ± 6.7**	**18.1* ± 7.4**	17.0 ± 3.0	**0.022**
Thursday	23.1 ± 10.3	23.7 ± 8.7	18.7 ± 6.5	18.9 ± 8.3	16.4 ± 7.4	21.3 ± 9.0	*0.185*
Friday	20.5 ± 10.3	24.4 ± 7.2	19.5 ± 6.5	17.4 ± 7.2	17.4 ± 7.8	17.0 ± 3.0	*0.086*
Saturday	**36.7‡ ± 10.7**	**38.9† ± 13.2**	**30.2† ± 13.4**	**31.8 ± 16.8**‡	30.1 ± 17.1	49.3 ± 18.2	*0.417*
Sunday	**37.2‡ ± 15.0**	**41.6† ± 13.0**	**36.0†1 ± 6.7**	**32.6 ± 18.6**‡	27.3 ± 15.7	59.3 ± 16.0	*0.098*
N	7	24	13	7	*10*	*2*	
p ⁺⁺	**0.004**	**0.001**	**0.001**	**0.025**	*0.408*	*0.086*	

Two participants did not undergo CRF assessment.
*Significance: $p < 0.05$. *different from the Low category ($p < 0.05$).*
‡different from Monday, Tuesday, and Friday ($p < 0.05$).
†different from Monday, Tuesday, Wednesday, Thursday, and Friday ($p < 0.05$).
†different from Monday, Tuesday, Wednesday, and Friday ($p < 0.05$).
†different from Wednesday ($p = 0.030$).
⁺Kruskal-Wallis test for independent samples.
⁺⁺Two-way Friedman analysis of variance.

Table 9.
Percentage of time allocated to household activities in women and men, grouped according to CRF categories.

Days	Poor	Low	Regular	Good	Very good	Excellent	p+
Monday	1.5 ± 2.6	2.5 ± 3.5	2.4 ± 5.2	7.8 ± 8.0	7.5 ± 6.5	5.3 ± 7.5	*0.051*
Tuesday	3.0 ± 4.2	2.6 ± 3.1	2.7 ± 3.7	7.8 ± 8.8	7.1 ± 6.5	5.3 ± 7.5	*0.324*
Wednesday	1.4 ± 2.4	2.1 ± 2.9	2.2 ± 5.0	**11.0*±7.7**	6.4 ± 6.7	5.3 ± 7.5	**0.012**
Thursday	2.2 ± 3.9	3.1 ± 3.1	1.7 ± 2.3	7.9 ± 8.8	8.0 ± 5.9	5.3 ± 7.5	*0.056*
Friday	0 0	2.2 ± 4.1	1.6 ± 2.4	**10.2*±8.6**	**7.1* ± 6.8**	5.3 ± 7.5	**0.006**
Saturday	9.1 ± 12.7	2.2 ± 3.4	4.3 ± 5.3	1.8 ± 3.3	5.3 ± 7.3	9.1 ± 12.9	*0.503*
Sunday	3.2 ± 5.9	1.2 ± 3.0	4.4 ± 6.9	1.8 ± 2.6	3.4 ± 6.9	5.3 ± 7.6	*0.631*
N	*7*	*24*	*13*	*7*	*10*	*2*	
p++	*0.333*	*0.310*	*0.351*	*0.094*	*0.113*	*0.999*	

Two participants did not undergo CRF assessment.
*Significance: $p < 0.05$. *different from poor, low, and regular ($p < 0.05$).*
+Kruskal-Wallis test for independent samples.
++Two-way Friedman analysis of variance.

Table 10.
Values of the percentage of time allocated to sports activities, grouped according to CRF categories.

values from Monday to Friday. Sundays and Saturdays showed lower values in transportation activities across all CRF categories.

Regarding the time allocated to school activities, no significant differences were found among the CRF categories. Within each CRF category, less time was allocated to school activities on Saturdays and Sundays compared to the weekdays ($p < 0.05$) (**Table 10**).

Although the time dedicated to sports activities was low in the adolescent sample, a significantly higher value was observed in the "Good" category compared to the "Poor," "Low," and "Regular" categories on Wednesdays and Fridays. The "Very Good" category also showed a higher value than the "Poor," "Low," and "Regular" categories on Fridays (**Table 10**).

This indicates that adolescents who dedicate some weekly time to sports activities during the week show better CRF levels. It should be noted that the differences in time between CRF categories on Mondays and Thursdays did not reach statistical significance marginally, but there is a clear trend that higher time allocated to sports activities is associated with higher CRF levels.

No significant differences were found within each category across the days of the week (**Table 10**).

Finally, the time allocated to sleep was not different among the CRF categories, although Saturdays and Sundays showed significantly higher values ($p < 0.01$) compared to the weekdays in the Low, Regular, and Very Good categories.

The time allocated to work and leisure activities did not show significant differences among the categories or within each category across the weekdays.

6. Discussion

The first point to highlight from this study is that in this sample of adolescents, both men and women sleep the appropriate amount of time, which corresponds to 8 hours a day. Furthermore, this time significantly increased on Saturdays and

Sundays compared to the weekdays. Even though their school schedule corresponds to the afternoon shift, this increase in sleep hours aligns with non-school days.

There is interesting evidence regarding sleep duration in other populations. A study conducted by Sun et al. [41] in Chinese children and adolescents evaluated the effects of the difference in sleep duration between weekends and weekdays (Monday to Friday). The results showed that a greater difference in bedtime and sleep duration between these two periods was significantly associated with poor academic performance, depressive symptoms, overweight and obesity, as well as an increased risk of using psychotropic substances.

Extreme differences in sleep duration during these two periods increase the risk of behavioral problems and suicide. This opens up new possibilities for research to determine if the findings by Sun's team are replicated among adolescents in Colima.

After sleep, school and domestic activities were the ones that adolescents in this sample allocated the most time to, regardless of gender. School-related activities ranked second after sleep, and domestic activities ranked slightly below school activities from Monday to Friday.

In contrast, on Saturdays and Sundays, domestic activities moved to the second position, while school-related activities decreased substantially. These results indicate behavior in line with the demands of academic activities, which are the ones that make a difference in how adolescents allocate their time during the school period. On the other hand, adolescents take care of household maintenance and cleaning during the weekend.

Transportation activities represented a group that received a relatively large amount of time allocation during the weekdays, which would be related to the need to attend school and other related activities. During the weekend, this type of activity decreased significantly, which, combined with the increase in domestic activities, suggests that adolescents spend a prolonged amount of time at home.

In the studied sample, both males and females allocated little time to work, sports, and leisure activities. This indicates that they do not need to work to obtain economic resources and can dedicate a significant portion of their time to school and home. Specifically, males showed a tendency to increase the time spent on work, sports, and leisure activities during the weekend, although it did not reach statistical significance compared to the weekdays. Women also showed the same trend, but only in sports and leisure activities, as work-related activities recorded average values of zero.

It is necessary to consider that in Mexico, sports activities are regularly practiced by a very small segment of the population. In their report, García and Fonseca [42] found that although public and private universities in Mexico offer a wide range of options for sports practice, with increasingly well-trained coaches, and some institutions even provide free medical, nutritional, and psychological services, only a small proportion of adolescent and young students permanently join sports clubs. The evidence from our study and the results from other reports show that sports practice is not among the preferences of the majority of adolescents.

Regarding energy expenditure, the TEE/BEE ratio allows us to observe energy expenditure in units of basal energy expenditure, enabling comparisons between groups and weekdays. This value remained unchanged throughout the weekdays in females, while in males, Mondays and Wednesdays had the highest energy expenditure due to physical activity, meaning that on at least 2 days of the week, energy expenditure increased significantly.

This corresponds to reports from Mexican national health and nutrition surveys (ENSANUT) from 2006 [5], 2012 [8], and 2018 [9], as well as a study conducted on the Spanish population by Oviedo et al. [43], which have shown more pronounced sedentary behaviors in females. However, even so, males still fail to meet the minimum recommended levels of physical activity by the World Health Organization (WHO).

The TEE/BEE ratio did not show a significant association with BMI, but it did with CRF. A higher value of the TEE/BEE ratio was associated with a higher level of CRF. The reduced sample size in the highest CRF category had a determining influence on not detecting statistically significant differences with the lower categories. However, there is evidence that engaging in physical activities, even if they are not predominantly sports-related, will have beneficial effects on the cardiovascular and respiratory systems.

BMI is an indicator widely used in epidemiological studies to assess overweight and obesity. However, it does not discriminate between adipose and lean mass. During adolescence, there is a noticeable increase in muscle mass, which is a factor that could affect the representativeness of BMI in adolescents.

In Mexico, adolescents aged 15 to 18 years enter high school after completing basic education. The 2017 reform of the high school curriculum (RIEMS) is based on a competency-based model that includes the development of knowledge, skills, and attitudes that promote decision-making by students [44]. The high school curriculum is structured around generic competencies, disciplinary competencies, and professional competencies. Within the generic competencies, there is a section on self-determination and self-care, which states that adolescents should acquire the ability to choose and practice a healthy lifestyle in their daily lives. The first attribute established for this lifestyle is that adolescents accept physical activity as a means for their physical, mental, and social development, while the second attribute mentions that adolescents should be able to recognize harmful habits and risky behaviors to avoid them [45].

Unfortunately, these two attributes do not seem to have been realized in the habitual behaviors of adolescents to date. We believe that a major impediment is that the current general curriculum did not include a specific curricular space for the didactic approach to the development of healthy lifestyle habits, including physical exercise and nutrition.

It is very necessary to establish a dynamic physical activity education system that can motivate the majority of the adolescent population to engage in various options of physical activity, whether they are sports-related, artistic, or recreational. This would represent substantial support in reducing the sedentary lifestyle that young people experience and that shapes their habits throughout their lives.

In our opinion, a physical activity system goes beyond sports promotion or the organization of tournaments or sports events, which are often already carried out in schools or by government sports institutes or state universities. These actions largely focus on sports performance and the identification of sports talents, which have an exclusive nature toward the majority of the population.

The results of this study indicate that in adolescents, the distribution of time is subject to the demands of school activities. We believe that this is evidence that Mexican society and adolescents value formal education. This space can be the starting point for the establishment of a tentative physical education system that gradually extends to different aspects of young people's daily lives, beyond school, such as the home, which is the second place where young people spend time engaging in various activities.

To achieve this goal, it is crucial that the curriculum explicitly includes a specific space for physical education with at least three weekly sessions since frequency develops habits. Secondly, it is necessary to structure programmatic content that provides knowledge and skills to students to implement their own strategies for individual and collective physical exercise. Additionally, adolescents should learn motor games, dances, circuits of motor skills, proper warm-up exercises, stretching exercises, how to interpret their heart rate, and which exercises should be avoided due to hygiene reasons.

Unfortunately, the government programs implemented to promote physical activity in the entire population are focused either on the clinical-functional vision of fitness or on formal sports practice, which, as discussed, no longer attract young people.

García Cantó, Rodríguez García, Valverde Pujante, Sánchez López, & López Miñarro in their research report argue that sports activity programs exclude young people and children who are not attracted to competitive sports, favoring the gradual adoption of passive activities during their free time [46].

Furthermore, from a gender perspective, It is necessary to consider the preferences of women regarding the promotion of physical and sports activities, as they are the ones most affected by sedentary behavior [46].

Focusing on the adolescent population, it has been observed that during the economic crisis period experienced in Argentina at the beginning of the twenty-first century, the majority of adolescents extended their school life due to the lack of employment opportunities. On the other hand, those who already had paid employment when the crisis period began tended to increase their working hours up to 35 hours per week [47].

Conversely, during the period of economic prosperity or recovery that Argentina experienced at the beginning of the second decade of the twenty-first century, adolescents preferred to engage in work activities, especially in the middle and upper classes. Although working hours decreased, jobs with up to 15 hours per week increased by 45.4% during this period.

This demonstrates that the economic situation is a determining factor that significantly modifies the distribution of time concerning the types of activities and occupations.

In future analyses of activities and habits, it is worth considering the consumption of tobacco and alcohol to assess their influence on the time devoted to sports, work, household chores, school, leisure, and sleep.

7. Conclusions

Adolescents attending high school in Colima are not affected by a reduction in sleep hours, which is favorable for maintaining good physical and mental health. On the other hand, they allocate few hours to paid work, while school and household activities receive the most time in their daily lives.

It is noteworthy that little time is dedicated to sports activities, and it is observed that those who spend more time on these activities maintain better cardiorespiratory fitness, which is a crucial factor in preventing coronary and metabolic diseases.

The high school curriculum needs to be revised as it does not present a clear didactic pedagogical approach to the development of healthy lifestyles among adolescents. Additionally, ludic and non-competitive programs should be implemented by institutes and universities to attract adolescents to engage in physical exercise.

Acknowledgements

We extend our gratitude to all academic and administrative staff of the Technical High School No. 34 of the University of Colima for the facilities and support for the development of the project as well as all the students and parents participating in this study for their trust and support.

Conflict of interest

The authors declare no conflict of interest.

Notes/thanks/other declarations

We acknowledge the valuable support provided by Karelly Monserrat Hernández Messina, Netzi María Romero Hernández, Héctor David Araujo Beltrán, and Luis Fernando Muñiz Ramirez for the correct application of the Habitual Activities and Occupations Recall.

Author details

Eduardo Gómez-Gómez[1*], Ana Lilia Pérez-Huitimea[2]
and Isela Guadalupe Torres-Ruelas[1]

1 Colima University, Colima, Mexico

2 Autonomous University of Chihuahua, Chihuahua, Mexico

*Address all correspondence to: egomez0@ucol.mx

References

[1] Burnham JM. Exercise is medicine: Health benefits of regular physical activity. The Journal of the Louisiana State Medical Society. 1998;**150**(7):319-323

[2] Warburton DE, Nicol CW, Bredin SS. Health benefits of physical activity: The evidence. CMAJ. 2006;**174**(6):801-809

[3] Ramos P, Rivera F, Moreno C, Jiménez-Iglesias A. Análisis de clúster de la actividad física y las conductas sedentarias de los adolescentes españoles, correlación con la salud biopsicosocial. Revista de Psicología del Deporte. 2012;**21**(1):99-106

[4] Barnett TA, Kelly AS, Young DR, Perry CK, Pratt CA, Edwards NM, et al. Sedentary behaviors in today's youth: Approaches to the prevention and management of childhood obesity. Circulation. 2018;**138**(11):e142-e159

[5] Olaíz-Fernández G, Rivera-Dommarco J, Shamah-Levy T, Rojas R, Villalpando-Hernández S, Hernández-Ávila M, et al. Encuesta Nacional de Salud y Nutrición 2006. Cuernavaca: Instituto Nacional de Salud Pública; 2006. Available from: https://ensanut.insp.mx/encuestas/ensanut2006/doctos/informes/ensanut2006.pdf

[6] Gutiérrez JP, Rivera-D ommarco J, Shamah-Levy T, Villalpando-Hernández S, Franco A, Cuevas-Nasu L, et al. Encuesta Nacional de Salud y Nutrición 2012. Resultados Nacionales. Cuernavaca: Instituto Nacional de Salud Pública; 2012. Available from: https://ensanut.insp.mx/encuestas/ensanut2012/doctos/informes/ENSANUT2012ResultadosNacionales.pdf

[7] Shamah-Levy T, Cuevas-Nasu L, Rivera-Dommarco J, Hernández-Avila M. Encuesta Nacional de Salud y Nutrición de Medio Camino 2016. Cuernavaca: Encuesta Nacional, Instituto Nacional de Salud Pública; 2016. Available from: https://ensanut.insp.mx/encuestas/ensanut2016/doctos/informes/ENSANUT2016ResultadosNacionales.pdf

[8] Gutiérrez JP, Rivera-Dommarco J, Shamah-Levy T, Villalpando-Hernández S, Franco A, Cuevas-Nasu L, et al. Encuesta Nacional de Salud y Nutrición 2012. Resultados Nacionales. Cuernavaca, México: Instituto Nacional de Salud Pública (MX); 2012. Available from: https://ensanut.insp.mx/encuestas/ensanut2012/doctos/informes/ENSANUT2012ResultadosNacionales.pdf

[9] Shamah-Levy T, Vielma-Orozco E, Heredia-Hernández O, Romero-Martínez M, Mojica-Cuevas J, Cuevas-Nasu L, et al. Encuesta Nacional de Salud y Nutrición 2018-19: Resultados Nacionales. Cuernavaca, México: Instituto Nacional de Salud Pública; 2020. Available from: https://ensanut.insp.mx/encuestas/ensanut2018/doctos/informes/ensanut_2018_informe_final.pdf

[10] Carnethon MR, Gulati M, Greenland P. Prevalence and cardiovascular disease correlates of low cardiorespiratory fitness in adolescents and adults. JAMA. 2005;**294**(23):2981-2988

[11] Pate RR, Wang C-Y, Dowda M. Cardiorespiratory fitness level among US youth 12 to 14 years of age. JAMA. 2016;**160**(10):1005-1012

[12] Secchi JD, García GC. Aptitud física cardiorrespiratoria y riesgo cardiometabólico en personas adultas jóvenes. Revista Española de Salud Pública. 2013;**87**(1):35-48

[13] Bustamante A, Maia J. Estatus ponderal y aptitud cardiorrespiratoria en escolares de la región central del Perú. Revista Peruana de Medicina Experimental y Salud Pública. 2013;**30**(3):399-407

[14] Gómez-Gómez E, Sandoval-Ávalos ES, Guillén-Valdez N. Aptitud cardiorrespiratoria y tiempo destinado a la realización de ocupaciones escolares, hogareñas, laborales, deportivas y recreativas en adolescentes colimenses. In: Arago IDH, Romero EC, Pineda LTB, Salazar CM, editors. La juventud en el deporte y en la cultura física. Diálogos, travesías y desafíos. México: Universidad de Colima; 2022. pp. 117-138

[15] SEMS. Nuevo curriculo de la educación media superior: Subsecretaría de Educación Media Superior; 2019. Available from: https://www.gob.mx/cms/uploads/attachment/file/241519/planes-estudio-sems.pdf [Accessed: March 4, 2020]

[16] Vargas M, Lancheros L, Barrera MD. Gasto energético en reposo y composición corporal en adultos. Revista de la Facultad de Medicina. 2011;**59**(1):S43-S58. Available from: http://www.scielo.org.co/pdf/rfmun/v59s1/v59s1a06.pdf

[17] Echavarría-Rodríguez AM, Botero_Restrepo, S. Métodos de evaluación del nivel de actividad física: Revisión de literatura. Revista de educación física. 2015;**4**(2):86-98. Available from: file:///C:/Users/Eduardo/Downloads/24403-Texto%20del%20art_culo-93896-1-10-20150923.pdf

[18] WHO. Estrategia mundial sobre régimen alimentario, actividad física y salud. WHO; 2020. Available from: https://apps.who.int/gb/archive/pdf_files/WHA57/A57_9-sp.pdf

[19] Espinosa T. Aspectos básicos de calorimetría. In: Casanueva E, Kaufer-Horwitz M, Pérez-Lizaur AB, Arroyo P, editors. Nutriología Médica. 2da ed. Atizapán, México, México: Médica Panamericana; 2001. pp. 516-527

[20] Secretary of Labor and Social Welfare. 2016. Available from: https://idwfed.org/es/recursos/el-trabajo-domestico-en-mexico-la-gran-deuda-social/@@display-file/attachment_1

[21] Duarte Duarte J. Ambientes de aprendizaje. Una aproximación conceptual. Revista iberoamericana de educación. 2003;**33**(1):1-18. Available from: https://rieoei.org/historico/deloslectores/524Duarte.PDF

[22] Temkin B, Cruz Ibarra J. Las dimensiones de la actividad laboral. Estudios sociológicos. 2018;**108**:507-538. DOI: 10.24201/es.2018v36n108.1608

[23] Council of Europe. Federación de asociaciones para la prevención del maltrato infantil. Council of Europe; 1992. Available from: https://docplayer.net/147215-The-european-sports-charter.html

[24] Pontifical Javeriana University. Actividades deportivas. Colombia: Pontificia Universidad Javeriana Bogotá; 2010. Available from: https://fear.javeriana.edu.co/facultad/medio-universitario/actividades-deportivas

[25] Salazar Salas CG. Actividades recreativas y sus beneficios para personas nicaragüenses residentes en Costa Rica. Actualidades Investigativas en

Recreación. 2010;**1**(1):1-40. Available from: https://www.redalyc.org/pdf/447/44713068004.pdf

[26] Islas-Rivera VM, Lelis-Zaragoza M. Análisis de los sistemas de transporte. Querétaro: Secretaría de Comunicaciones y Transportes; 2007. Available from: https://www.imt.mx/archivos/Publicaciones/PublicacionTecnica/pt307.pdf

[27] McArdle WD, Katch FI, Katch VL. Human energy expenditure during rest and physical activity. In: McArdle WD, Katch FI, Katch VL, editors. Exercise Physiology. Nutrition, Energy, and Human Performance. 7th ed. Baltimore - Philadelphia: Lippincott Williams & Wilkins; 2010. pp. 192-205

[28] McArdle WD, Katch FI, Katch VL. Measurement of human energy expenditure. In: McArdle WD, Katch FI, Katch VL, editors. Exercise Physiology. Nutrition, Energy and Human Performance. 7th ed. Baltimore - Phyladelphya, USA: Lippincot, Williams & Wilkins; 2010. pp. 178-191

[29] Williams MH, Anderson DE, Rawson ES. Nutrición para la salud, la condición física y el deporte. 2da ed. Barcelona: Paidotribo; 2015

[30] Mantilla-Tolosa SC, Gómez-Conesa A. El cuestionario internacional de actividad física. Un instrumento adecuado en el seguimiento de la actividad física poblacional. Revista Iberoamericana de Fisioterapia y Kinesiología. 2007;**10**(1):48-52. Available from: file:///C:/Users/Eduardo/Downloads/13107139.pdf

[31] Rubio-Castañeda FJ, Tomás-Aznar C, Muro-Baquero C. Medición de la actividad física en personas mayores de 65 años mediante IPAQ-E: validez de contenido, fiabilidad y factores asociados. Revista Española de Salud Pública. 2017;**91**:1-13. Available from: https://www.redalyc.org/pdf/170/17049838010.pdf

[32] Lillo Espinosa JL. Crecimiento y comportamiento en la adolescencia. Revista de la Asociación Española de Neuropsiquiatría. 2004;**90**:57-71. Available from: https://www.redalyc.org/pdf/2650/265019660005.pdf

[33] Gaete V. Desarrollo psicosocial del adolescente. Revista Chilena de Pediatría. 2015;**86**(6):436-443. DOI: 10.1016/j.rchipe.2015.07.005

[34] Bisquerra Alzina R. Métodos de investigación educativa. Barcelona: CEAC; 1998

[35] DGEMS-UdeC. Universidad de Colima. Dirección General de Educación Media Superior. 2019. Available from: https://portal.ucol.mx/dgems/informe.htm#2019 [Accessed: Abril 2020]

[36] Mackenzie B. In: Mackenzie B, editor. 101 Performance Evaluation Tests. Electric Word; 2005. Available from: https://docplayer.net/16085806-Performance-evaluation-tests.html

[37] Gómez-Gómez E, Del Río Valdivia JE, Flores Moreno PJ, Barajas Pineda LT. Nivel de aptitud cardiorrespiratoria en adolescentes del estado de Colima. In: Torres-Acuña GM, Toledo Dominguez ID, García Vázquez FI, Lozoya Villegas JF, editors. Bienestar físico y psicosocial en contextos escolares. México: Fontamara; 2018. pp. 29-39

[38] Stewart A, Marfell-Jones M, Olds T, De Ridder H. Protocolo internacional para la valoración antropométrica. Esparza-Ros F, AlaciF, Sancho A, Calvo MD, Trans.) Guadalupe, Murcia, España: Biblioteca Nacional de Australia; 2011

[39] Katch FI, Katch VL, McArdle WD. Energy expenditure in household, occupational, recreational, and sport activities. Appendix C. In: McArdle WD, Katch FI, Katch VL. Exercise Physiology. Energy, Nutrition, and Human Performance. 5th ed. Lippincott, Williams & Wilkins; 2001. Available from: https://is.muni.cz/el/1451/podzim2015/bp1805/um/McArdle_Katch_2006_Exercise_physiology_energy_expenditure.pdf

[40] National Heart, Lung and Blood Institute. Sueño saludable. National Heart, Lung and Blood Institute; 2013. Available from: https://www.nhlbi.nih.gov/files/docs/public/sleep/Healthy_Sleep_At-A-Glance_SPANISH_Final.pdf

[41] Sun W, Ling J, Zhu X, Mei-Chun Lee T, Xin Li S. Associations of weekday-to-weekend sleep differences with academic performance and health-related outcomes in school-age children and youths. Sleep Medicine Reviews. 2019;**46**:27-53

[42] Garcia Rodriguez J, Hernandez F. La actividad física en los y las jóvenes mexicanos y mexicanas: un análisis comparativo entre las universidades públicas y privadas. MHSalud. 2012;**9**(2):1-29

[43] Oviedo G, Sánchez J, Castro R, Calvo M, Sevilla JC, Iglesias A, et al. Niveles de actividad física en población adolescente: estudio de caso. Retos. Nuevas tendencias en Educación Física, Deporte y Recreación. 2013;**23**:43-47. Available from: file:///C:/Users/Eduardo/Downloads/Dialnet-NivelesDeActividadFisicaEnPoblacionAdolescente-4135239.pdf

[44] SEP-SEMS. Subsecretaría de Educación Media Superior. Sistema Nacional de Bachillerato; 2017. Available from: https://educacionmediasuperior.sep.gob.mx/es/sems/sistema_nacional_bachillerato

[45] SEP. DOF. ACUERDO número 444 por el que se establecen las competencias que constitiyen el marco curricular común del Sistema Nacional de Bachillerato: 2008. Available from: http://educacionmediasuperior.sep.gob.mx/work/models/sems/Resource/10905/1/images/Acuerdo_444_marco_curricular_comun_SNB.pdf

[46] García Cantó E, Rodríguez García PL, Valverde Pujante J, Sánchez López C, López Miñarro PA. Actividades físico deportivas realizadas durante el tiempo de ocio por adolescentes escolarizados de la región de Murcia (España). REXE: Revista de estudios y experiencias en educación. 2011;**10**(19):13-32

[47] Miranda A, Corica A. Las actividades laborales y extraescolares de jóvenes de la escuela secundaria en Argentina de principios del siglo XXI. Perfiles Educativos. 2015;**37**(148):100-118

Chapter 2

Physical Fitness in Children during Growth: Associations with Body Composition, Physical Activity, and Cognitive Skills

Kirkke Reisberg, Eva-Maria Riso and Jaak Jürimäe

Abstract

Fostering childhood physical activity and fitness levels could have important implications for public health, given growing concerns about high obesity rates, the amount of time spent being sedentary and not getting enough physical activity already at early childhood. World Health Organization states that from 1975 to 2016, the prevalence of children and adolescents with overweight or obesity increased more than four-fold from 4% to 18% globally. Obesity prevention is critical in controlling obesity-related noncommunicable diseases, psychological, and social problems, as well as inferior academic achievement mediated by others attitude and diminished executive cognitive function. A decline of physical activity from early childhood into middle childhood and further to adolescence has been reported. Accompanying health risks from low activity and high sedentariness are comparable to those arising from obesity, and the impact extends into adulthood. Wide range of physical, mental, and cognitive health benefits related to high physical fitness levels in children have been reported. This chapter aims to summarize current evidence clarifying whether higher physical activity is associated with higher physical fitness, and whether higher physical fitness predicts healthier body composition and better cognitive functions in children.

Keywords: children, physical fitness, body composition, physical activity, cognitive skills

1. Introduction

Physical fitness, as the capacity to perform physical activity, determines a full range of physiological and psychological qualities [1]. Besides an epidemic of obesity, accumulating evidence suggests that young children spend excessive time being sedentary, and they frequently fail to achieve physical activity guidelines [2]. While excessive sedentary time has been linked with a number of health concerns [3], wide range of physical, mental, and cognitive health benefits related to the engagement in physical activity and greater physical fitness in children have been reported, including improved motor and cognitive development [1], higher academic performance [1] and bone mineral density [1], better cardiometabolic health indicators [1, 4, 5], greater psychological well-being [1, 6], and health-related quality of life [1, 7], as well as prevention of overweight/obesity [1, 4, 8] and psychological ill-being [1, 6].

Regarding many health benefits arising from being fit, it is important to monitor physical fitness parameters during growth and maturation in children. Cardiorespiratory fitness represents the overall capacity of the cardiovascular and respiratory systems and the ability to perform prolonged strenuous exercise [1]. Peak oxygen consumption ($\dot{V}O_2$peak), the highest rate at which oxygen can be consumed during exercise, is widely recognized as the best single measure of young people's cardiorespiratory condition [9]. In epidemiological studies involving children and adolescents, cardiorespiratory fitness is most frequently assessed by 20 m shuttle run test or modified versions of that [1, 10–14]. Higher cardiorespiratory fitness is beneficially associated with multiple health indicators among children [15]. On the other hand, low levels of cardiorespiratory fitness at young age have been attributed to a higher risk of developing cardiovascular disease risk in adulthood [16].

Speed/agility fitness includes the ability to move the body or its parts as fast as possible (speed) and the ability to move quickly and change direction while maintaining control and balance (agility) [1]. The 30 m sprint test and the 4 × 10 m shuttle run test are widely used tests for assessing speed and/or agility at young age [10–14]. Several other tests such as 10 × 5 m shuttle run and 20–100 m dash have also been proposed [1, 17–20]. Better performance in 4 × 10 m shuttle run test has been associated with lower fatness [12] and stronger bones [21] at young age.

Balance denotes the ability to maintain equilibrium while stationary (static balance) or moving (dynamic balance) [20]. The one-leg stance test is widely used to assess static balance [10, 11, 20] and for dynamic balance assessment, lower quarter Y balance test [22] or balance beam [23] is applied. A well-developed postural control system is a prerequisite to manage successfully with daily (e.g., climbing stairs) and or recreational/sports-related (e.g., fundamental movement skills such as kicking, jumping, or advanced skills, such as balancing on a beam) activities [22, 24]. Deficits in postural control because of ongoing growth and maturation processes of the postural control system [25] might be responsible for the high prevalence of sustaining a fall, particularly in children [26]. Furthermore, postural control deficit is a risk factor for musculoskeletal injuries [27, 28].

Muscular fitness is the ability to perform work against a resistance [1]. Maximal (isometric and dynamic) strength, explosive strength, endurance strength, and isokinetic strength have been proposed for the prime health-related muscular fitness components [1]. The handgrip test is one of the most frequently applied tests for investigating muscular fitness in epidemiological studies [1, 10–14, 29]. Handgrip strength correlates positively with body mass index (BMI) and fat-free mass, meanwhile, handgrip strength associates inversely with body fat percentage in children [30]. Accordingly, grip strength serves as an indicator of muscle mass and healthy body composition. Handgrip strength-to-BMI ratio in children aged 5–10 yrs was positively related to different physical fitness parameters such as absolute handgrip strength, vertical jump, $\dot{V}O_2$peak, and 20 m shuttle run test results [31], suggesting that strong grip expresses general fitness of a young person. There are inconsistent findings about the associations between grip strength and cardiometabolic risk factors. Some studies have shown that higher handgrip strength at young age is associated with lower cardiometabolic risk [29]. Meanwhile Rioux et al. [32] reported inverse association between handgrip strength and cardiometabolic risk score specifically in girls, but not in boys. But it has been also stated that handgrip strength is not suitable as a predictor for cardiometabolic risk factors in children of both sexes [33].

Among jump tests, standing long jump test has been widely used in young population for assessing explosive strength [1, 10–14]. Since standing long jump test is strongly correlated with other lower- and upper-limb muscular strength tests, it is regarded as a general index of muscular fitness in youth [34].

Among fitness tests, greater isometric muscle strength of the abdomen and back in youth predict lower levels of cardiovascular disease risk factors in young adulthood independently of cardiorespiratory fitness, adiposity, and other sociodemographic and lifestyle factors [35].

The true global burden of mental illness has only recently been understood [36]. Worldwide, about 15% of children and adolescents experience a mental disorder [37]. There is some confidence from experimental and observational studies that physical activity has mental health effects at young age [6, 38]. Current research concerning physical fitness and mental health in childhood is limited, with some evidence for positive mental health benefits from higher physical fitness. LaVigne et al. [39] demonstrated that physical fitness [a composite score of bent-knee sit-ups, sit-and-reach, flexed arm hang (girls only), pull-ups (boys only), and long jump, endurance run, shuttle run, and sprints] was associated with a range of psychological well-being indicators for both boys and girls.

In conclusion, all domains of physical fitness are significant indicators of health status at young age [1, 6, 21, 29, 35]. Thus, it is relevant to work on maintaining and developing sufficient physical fitness in children in order to contribute to their health and well-being [40].

2. Methodology

Scientific articles containing data on the associations between physical fitness, body composition, physical activity, and cognitive skills in children published up to May 2023 were included. The searches were conducted in electronic databases [(PubMed, CINAHL, and Education Resources Information Center (ERIC)]. Eligibility criteria were the following: (1) cross-sectional and longitudinal studies, reviews, systematic reviews, and meta-analyses (design criterion), (2) articles published in scientific journals, book chapters, books, conference proceedings, and theses (publish criterion), (3) children and adolescents aged up to 19 yrs (participant criterion), and (4) articles published in English and German (language criterion). No time limits were set. The papers were screened by two researchers independently, to come to a first selection (after reading title/abstract), and then to second selection (after reading full text) of relevant papers. A total of 2709 studies were identified through the databases searches, and 70 were included into this review.

2.1 Associations of physical fitness and body composition in children

Henriksson et al. [12] demonstrated that speed-agility fitness, cardiorespiratory fitness, and lower-limbs muscular strength at 4.5 yrs were negatively associated with fat mass index and body fat percentage at 5.5 yrs. Meanwhile, higher handgrip strength at 4.5 yrs was associated with higher BMI and fat-free mass index 1 year later. Body composition in this study was assessed by air-displacement plethysmography [12]. In another longitudinal study by Martins et al. [41], children in grade 1 (at 6 yrs) were followed through grade 5 (at 10 yrs). The results from 1-mile run/walk test were not associated with BMI changes, but gross motor coordination was inversely associated with changes in BMI [41]. Findings in children aged 4.6–11 yrs relate baseline $\dot{V}O_2$peak inversely to increasing (over a 3- to 5-yr period) adiposity after adjustments for age, maturity, ethnicity, initial fat mass, and increase in lean tissue mass (assessed by dual-energy X-ray absorptiometry, DEXA) [42]. Additionally, cardiorespiratory fitness seemed to be more important than absolute energy expenditure in the development of obesity [42]. Children at 7–10 yrs with cardiorespiratory fitness of the lowest tertile had a 5.5–6-fold greater chance of having overweight and obesity, as well as metabolic syndrome at 14–17 yrs than the children having better cardiorespiratory fitness levels after controlling for BMI percentile, blood pressure, and cholesterol levels [43]. In children aged 6–12 yrs (on average 8.8 yrs), BMI, parental obesity, and low performance in 20 m shuttle run were the main predictors of the 2-yr tracking of body fatness, and cardiorespiratory fitness level at baseline was a predictor of high waist circumference after 2 yrs [44].

Hruby et al. [45] followed over 1–4 yrs a large sample of 2793 children, who were at baseline 1st to 7th graders. They were classified as "fit" or "underfit" according to age- and sex-specific norms in five fitness domains. It was concluded that schoolchildren with overweight who achieve or maintain physical fitness are more likely to achieve healthy weight, and healthy-weight children who maintain fitness are more likely to maintain healthy weight [45]. This is in accordance with a study, where children aged 10–17 yrs (on average 13 yrs) with abdominal obesity had 8.5 and 6.5 increased odds of low handgrip-to-BMI ratio compared to children with normal waist circumference, both in boys and girls, respectively [46].

Freitas et al. [47] observed children on average for 7.2 yrs starting at age 8 yrs, showing that the variance in adiposity was explained to a small extent by physical fitness. More specifically, for girls, Flamingo balance at 8 and 12 yrs was a predictor of body fatness at 15 and 19 yrs (2–8%). Flexed arm hang at 8 yrs predicted waist circumference at 15 yrs by 8%. The association of flexed arm hang was negative. In boys, about 2–4% of the variance in BMI, waist circumference, and sum of skinfolds at 15 yrs was explained by the sit-ups at 8 yrs [47]. After controlling for fatness indicators, the sit-ups were negatively associated with adult fatness. Other fitness items (strength and endurance) become predictors of future fatness at later age periods. Overall, Flamingo balance and flexed arm hang were the most stable predictors of body fatness in childhood, adolescence, and young adulthood. Yet, the signal of the regression coefficients for Flamingo balance was positive in the age intervals 8–15 and 16–23 yrs but negative in the age interval of 12–19 yrs [47].

Koutedakis et al. [48] demonstrated that in children at 12.3 yrs, 20 m shuttle run test predicted lower body fat percentage (assessed by skinfolds) 2 years later after controlling for age, sex, maturation status, physical activity, cardiorespiratory fitness, and energy intake at follow-up. Twisk et al. [49] reported that baseline neuromotor fitness index including measurements of muscle strength, flexibility, speed, and coordination at 13 yrs was negatively related to sum of skinfolds at 27 yrs. In addition, among children aged 13–16 yrs, $\dot{V}O_2$peak predominantly predicted lower sum of skinfolds both in boys and girls, and smaller waist circumference in girls, but not waist-to-height ratio at 32 yrs [49]. By contrast, Barnekow-Bergkvist et al. [50] found that better performance in 9-min run at 16 yrs was associated with greater odds of high BMI in males at the age 34 yrs. Higher bench press (male) and two-hand lift (female) results at 16 yrs were associated with greater risk of high BMI at age 34. The associations for waist-to-hip ratio were less clear. The number of sit-ups predicted neither BMI nor waist-to-hip ratio [50]. In turn, Janz et al. [51] found that changes in $\dot{V}O_2$peak and handgrip strength from childhood (mean age 10.5 yrs) to adolescence at 5-yr follow-up were negatively related to fat mass (assessed by bioelectrical impedance) and waist circumference after controlling for age and sex, with even stronger associations after adding fat-free mass and sexual maturation as confounding factors. Changes in cardiorespiratory fitness and muscular strength explained 15% of the variability in 5-yr adiposity and 15% variability in the 5-yr abdominal adiposity [51]. In a study by Hasselstrøm et al. [52] children aged 15–19 yrs were observed again 8 yrs later, reporting that higher or increased $\dot{V}O_2$peak (in both sexes) and composite of strength parameters (the sum of maximal isometric contractions of trunk flexors and extensors and elbow flexors and knee extensors) (in males) were related to lower body fat percentage (sum of skinfolds) at follow-up after adjustments for age [52]. These findings are strongly supported by a study with long follow-up for 22 yrs, where a five-factor composite, physical test was used to assess the physical fitness level. It was found out that high-school students with low fitness levels were more likely to be overweight in adulthood vs. those with high fitness levels. The interpretation of outcomes is limited since potential confounding effects were not controlled [53]. The long-lasting contribution from better cardiorespiratory fitness in maintaining healthier body composition was confirmed by Kvaavik et al. [54], who observed that higher $\dot{V}O_2$peak levels at 11–15 yrs (on average 13 yrs) may provide protection against later obesity (assessed by BMI and triceps skinfold thickness), although the effects diminished over time, disappearing at 40 yrs. Controlling for educational attainment of both the parent and the study member had little impact on these associations [54]. Correspondingly, Boreham et al. [55] showed modest inverse associations between the number of laps in 20 m shuttle run at 12 and 15 yrs with sum of skinfolds at 22.5 yrs in both sexes [55]. Similarly, low fitness, such as running speed, arm pull, standing high jump, and $\dot{V}O_2$peak during adolescence predicted lower fatness during early adulthood, after controlling for baseline physical activity and fatness (sum of skinfolds) [56]. In accordance, overweight/obese boys aged 8–13 yrs with greater $\dot{V}O_2$peak levels had a lower increase in total body fat mass (assessed by DEXA) at 15 yrs after adjustments for changes in Tanner stage, age, and fat-free mass. A total of 15% higher $\dot{V}O_2$peak at baseline resulted in a 1.38 kg lower fat mass gain over 4 years [57]. Likewise, adolescents categorized as low-fit based on the composite physical fitness test score demonstrated higher BMI compared with fit peers within 3-yrs follow-up period [58]. Meanwhile, Kim et al. [59] observed that in a large sample consisting of children from kindergarten to eighth grade not all physical fitness items uniformly predicted further fatness in childhood. They identified that the associations between abdominal strength, upper body strength, flexibility, and agility test outcomes (pass vs. fail) and incidence of overweight 1 year later were attenuated after controlling for baseline BMI status, except for the endurance run in girls [59]. To the contrary to findings by Kim et al. [59], Grøntved et al. [35] demonstrated longitudinally that greater strength fitness predicted lower fatness. More precisely, greater isometric muscle strength of the abdomen and back in youth was inversely associated with lower BMI levels 12 yrs later in multivariable adjusted analyses including fitness [35].

To summarize, most research demonstrates healthy longitudinal associations between physical fitness and fatness indicators in childhood and adolescence, with some positive impact reaching even into adulthood. Yet, there is some variation in the results, including heterogeneity within physical fitness domains and gender groups. Also, there is a deficiency of studies exploring the relationships between physical fitness and fat-free mass in preschool-aged children. Therefore, further investigations are warranted to clarify the associations between muscular fitness and body composition in childhood.

2.2 Associations of physical activity, sedentary time and physical fitness in children

Physical activity is a major modifiable determinant for increasing physical fitness [23]. At early age (4–6 yrs) only vigorous physical activity, but not moderate or total physical activity, was related to the improvement in 20 m shuttle run test, agility in obstacle course, and dynamic balance on balance beam after 9 months by controlling for sociocultural confounding factors [23]. Similarly, findings in children aged 9–15 yrs (on average 12.2 yrs) indicate that light and moderate physical activity were not associated with $\dot{V}O_2$peak at 2-yr follow-up, but baseline vigorous physical activity had a positive dose–response association with cardiorespiratory fitness 2 years later after adjustment for age, sex, diet quality, accelerometer wear time, other intensities of physical activity, and baseline value of $\dot{V}O_2$peak [60].

At the same time, a study by Leppänen et al. [13] showed that both greater moderate and vigorous physical activity at 4–5 yrs were associated with higher cardiorespiratory fitness in 20 m shuttle run test, lower-limbs muscular strength and speed-agility fitness 1 year later after adjustment for age, sex, sedentary time and accelerometer wear time. Substituting 5 min/day of sedentary time, light or moderate physical activity with vigorous physical activity at 4–5 yrs was associated with higher upper- and lower-limbs muscular strength at 1-yr follow-up [13].

Associations between parent-reported physical activity (h/wk) at 4.5 yrs and fitness composite score (including predicted $\dot{V}O_2$peak, grip strength, vertical jump, sit-and-reach, and the inverse of waist circumference) at 3-yr follow-up were positive, and relations of baseline physical activity and follow-up $\dot{V}O_2$peak approached significance ($p = 0.051$) after controlling for follow-up age, sex, and household income [61]. No significant associations of sedentary time, physical activity, change in sedentary time, or change in physical activity with any of the follow-up composite or single fitness measures existed, with the only exception for sedentary time at 4.5 yrs, that negatively predicted follow-up handgrip strength after controlling for follow-up age, sex, household income, and BMI. No sex interactions were observed [61].

Day et al. [62] have investigated the longitudinal associations between organized sports activity (h/wk) and core strength parameters in young females. The authors observed that premenarcheal organized physical activity participation was a significant predictor of sit-up performance at both premenarcheal and post-menarcheal assessments after accounting for maturity, body size, and baseline values. However, participation in organized sports over a two-year circum-menarcheal period was not a strong independent predictor of strength outcomes at the postmenarcheal assessment [62].

A study in adolescents with long follow-up period reported that leisure time sports activity in females and participation in organized sports in both sexes at the age of 15–18 yrs were related to greater probability of having higher $\dot{V}O_2$peak level 18 yrs later [50]. On the contrary, in adolescents aged 15–19 yrs, increased physical activity (h/wk) was not associated with higher or increased $\dot{V}O_2$peak at 8-yr follow-up neither in males nor females by controlling for age [52].

To summarize, there is a major shortage of studies investigating the longitudinal relationships between physical activity, sedentary time, and physical fitness in childhood. Studies using questionnaires for assessment of physical activity show mixed results, meanwhile, objectively measured physical activity data reveal that a higher amount of moderate and/or intensive type of activities in childhood is a predictor of better physical fitness at later age. Differences in objective and self-reported outcomes might come from the aspect that questionnaires assessing physical activity did not collect information about its intensity, rather the frequency and duration. It is suggested that the intensity of physical activity may be a stronger predictor of physical fitness than the duration or frequency [61].

2.3 Associations of physical fitness and cognitive skills in children

Higher physical fitness is a capacity that enables easier access to and greater engagement in activities within the physical domain. Greater engagement in physical activities, in turn, provides greater opportunity to engage in problem-solving, experience multiple perspectives, support formation of meaningful relationships, and employ social skills that require impulse control and other cognitive abilities [39].

A study on the relations between physical fitness and cognitive functioning in children at early age (4–6 yrs) shows that more laps in 20 m shuttle run test and motor skills (agility and dynamic balance) predicted superior spatial working memory and/or attention at baseline, whereas 9 months later some of the positive associations between initial physical fitness measures and cognitive functions were preserved to some extent [63]. At follow-up, cardiorespiratory fitness predicted still better attention in unadjusted analysis and the relations between dynamic balance (steps on the beam) and spatial working memory turned significant after controlling for confounding factors such as age, sex, BMI, migration status, parental education, native language, linguistic region, and baseline cognitive performance. At the same time, the cross-sectional beneficial relations of agility (obstacle course) and cognition disappeared at follow-up in adjusted model [63].

Preadolescents with high cardiorespiratory fitness level on 20 m shuttle run test exhibited superior performance in a visual discrimination task [64] and performed more accurately the tasks involving inhibition compared to children in the low fitness group, whereas no group differences were observed for reaction time [65].

At adolescence (on average 14 yrs) positive indirect associations of motor skills (the sum of the performance in a 5-leaps test and a tennis ball throwing-catching combination test) and muscular fitness with mathematics performance were mediated by visuospatial working memory once adjusted for age, sex, pubertal stage, body fat percentage, learning difficulties, and mother's education. Meantime, 20 m shuttle run performance was positively associated with mathematics achievement, but the authors did not detect indirect path through cognition [66].

A study with 2-yr-follow-up indicated that boys aged 6–9 yrs, who were in the lowest third of motor competence score at baseline had worse nonverbal reasoning test score over the 2-yr follow-up than boys whose initial motor performance score was in the middle and uppermost thirds after adjusting for age and study group [17]. Secondly, it was found that a lower motor competence score, a shorter 50 m shuttle run test duration and a larger number of cubes moved in the Box and Block Test at 6–9 yrs were associated with smaller increase in the nonverbal reasoning test score during 2-yr follow-up in boys after adjustment for age and study group. None of these associations remained significant after further adjustment for baseline cognitive test (Raven's Colored Progressive Matrices) score. Thus, the associations were largely explained by baseline cognitive abilities. Accordingly, cognition at baseline may predominantly predict later cognitive functioning compared to changes in motor fitness and cardiorespiratory fitness in childhood. As a proof, a negative relationship between cardiorespiratory fitness (maximal workload on cycle ergometer/fat-free mass) at baseline and cognitive skills 2 years later disappeared after controlling for cognition at baseline. In addition, cardiorespiratory fitness was not associated with cognition in boys, and cardiorespiratory fitness and motor competence were not related to cognition in girls. As well the changes in motor competence or cardiorespiratory fitness were not associated with changes in cognition in children at follow-up [17].

Cross-sectional data imply that $\dot{V}O_2$peak at 7–9 yrs was positively associated with inhibitory control, though not with working memory [67]. At the same time, Skog et al. [68] found that most of cardiorespiratory fitness indicators were related to better cognitive functions such as working memory accuracy and/or visual learning in children at 16–19 yrs after adjustments for age and sex. Inconsistent with Pindus et al. [67], $\dot{V}O_2$peak among higher-fit adolescents was related to better flexible modulation of cognitive control processes to meet task demands than in lower-fit ones [69].

There is also longitudinal evidence about the beneficial association between $\dot{V}O_2$peak at 9-10 yrs and cognitive control. Children with higher levels of cardiorespiratory fitness demonstrated increased accuracy on a modified compatible and incompatible flanker task both at initial and 1-y follow-up test sessions, coupled with a superior ability to flexibly allocate strategies during task conditions that required different amounts of cognitive control, compared to less fit children. More fit children also gained a speed benefit at follow-up testing. These findings are supported by the structural data from magnetic resonance imaging as bilateral putamen volumes of the dorsal striatum and globus pallidus volumes predicted flanker performance at initial and follow-up testing one year later [70].

To summarize, the research reveals predominantly beneficiary associations between different physical fitness items and cognitive functions in children. However, considering some inconsistency in the results [17, 63, 65, 66] and the limited number of longitudinal studies [17, 63, 70] the conclusions regarding the causality and duration of the positive effects of fitness on children's cognition cannot be firmly drawn.

3. Conclusions

Given current evidence in children, we can conclude the existence of healthy longitudinal relations between physical fitness and fatness of some positive associations reaching into adulthood. With regards to the limited number of longitudinal studies, the associations between objectively measured physical activity and physical fitness in children are partially supported, favoring activities of moderate and/or vigorous intensity. At present, the association between sedentary behavior and physical fitness remains unclear. Better physical fitness mostly predicts superior cognitive development in children, though, there is need for clarification considering scarcity of longitudinal research, short-follow-up periods, and partially mixed results.

Therefore, continued research on physical fitness and activity, body composition, and cognition in children should be supported. Future research should apply more precise methods over BMI or waist circumference, such as DEXA, air-displacement plethysmography, bioelectrical impedance analysis, and skinfold thicknesses, in accurately assessing body composition; objective assessment of physical activity should be encouraged to precisely capture information of its intensity. Evaluating cohorts with greater variability in activity level and body composition and as soon as at the earliest stages of life should help to corroborate current findings. More studies are needed to better understand whether the associations differ in male and female, given that this could have implications for future policy recommendations.

Author details

Kirkke Reisberg[1,2*], Eva-Maria Riso[1] and Jaak Jürimäe[1]

1 Faculty of Medicine, Institute of Sports Sciences and Physiotherapy, University of Tartu, Tartu, Estonia

2 Tartu Health Care College, Tartu, Estonia

*Address all correspondence to: kirkkereisberg@nooruse.ee

References

[1] Ortega FB, Ruiz JR, Castillo MJ, Sjöström M. Physical fitness in childhood and adolescence: A powerful marker of health. International Journal of Obesity. 2008;**32**:1-11. DOI: 10.1038/sj.ijo.0803774

[2] Pizarro AN, Correia D, Lopes C, Teixeira PJ, Mota J. Active and sedentary behaviors in youth (6-14 years old): Data from the IAN-AF survey (2015-2016). Porto Biomedical Journal. 2022;7:e161. DOI: 10.1097/j.pbj.0000000000000161

[3] Barnett TA, Kelly AS, Young DR, Perry CK, Pratt CA, Edwards NM, et al. Sedentary behaviors in today's youth: Approaches to the prevention and management of childhood obesity: A scientific statement from the American Heart Association. Circulation. 2018;**138**:e142-ee59. DOI: 10.1161/CIR.0000000000000591

[4] Mintjens S, Menting MD, Daams JG, van Poppel MNM, Roseboom TJ, Gemke RJBJ. Cardiorespiratory fitness in childhood and adolescence affects future cardiovascular risk factors: A systematic review of longitudinal studies. Cardiorespiratory fitness in childhood and adolescence affects future cardiovascular risk factors: A systematic review of longitudinal studies. Sports Medicine. 2018;**48**:2577-2605. DOI: 10.1007/s40279-018-0974-5

[5] Ortega FB, Lavie CJ, Blair SN. Obesity and cardiovascular disease. Circulation Research. 2016;**118**:1752-1770. DOI: 10.1161/CIRCRESAHA.115.306883

[6] Rodriguez-Ayllon M, Cadenas-Sánchez C, Estévez-López F, Muñoz NE, Mora-Gonzalez J, Migueles JH, et al. Role of physical activity and sedentary behavior in the mental health of preschoolers, children and adolescents: A systematic review and meta-analysis. Sports Medicine. 2019;**49**:1383-1410. DOI: 10.1007/s40279-019-01099-5

[7] Wu XY, Han LH, Zhang JH, Luo S, Hu JW, Sun K. The influence of physical activity, sedentary behavior on health-related quality of life among the general population of children and adolescents: A systematic review. PLoS One. 2017;**12**:e0187668. DOI: 10.1371/journal.pone.0187668

[8] Gualdi-Russo E, Rinaldo N, Toselli S, Zaccagni L. Associations of physical activity and sedentary behaviour assessed by accelerometer with body composition among children and adolescents: A scoping review. Sustainability. 2021;**13**:335. DOI: 10.3390/su13010335

[9] Herdy AH, Ritt LE, Stein R, Araújo CG, Milani M, Meneghelo RS, et al. Cardiopulmonary exercise test: Background, applicability and interpretation. Arquivos Brasileiros de Cardiologia. 2016;**107**:467-481. DOI: 10.5935/abc.20160171

[10] Cadenas-Sánchez C, Martinez-Tellez B, Sanchez-Delgado G, Mora-Gonzalez J, Castro-Piñero J, Löf M, et al. Assessing physical fitness in preschool children: Feasibility, reliability and practical recommendations for the PREFIT battery. Journal of Science and Medicine in Sport. 2016;**19**:910-915. DOI: 10.1016/j.jsams.2016.02.003

[11] Cadenas-Sánchez C, Intemann T, Labayen I, Peinado AB, Vidal-Conti J, Sanchis-Moysi J, et al. Physical fitness reference standards for preschool children: The PREFIT project. Journal of Science and Medicine in Sport.

2019;**22**:430-437. DOI: 10.1016/j.jsams.2018.09.227

[12] Henriksson P, Leppänen MH, Henriksson H, Delisle Nyström C, Cadenas-Sánchez C, Ek A, et al. Physical fitness in relation to later body composition in pre-school children. Journal of Science and Medicine in Sport. 2019;**22**:574-579. DOI: 10.1016/j.jsams.2018.11.024

[13] Leppänen MH, Henriksson P, Nyström DC, Henriksson H, Ortega FB, Pomeroy J, et al. Longitudinal physical activity, body composition, and physical fitness in preschoolers. Medicine and Science in Sports and Exercise. 2017;**49**:2078-2085. DOI: 10.1249/MSS.0000000000001313

[14] Riso E-M, Toplaan L, Viira P, Vaiksaar S, Jürimäe J. Physical fitness and physical activity of 6-7-year-old children according to weight status and sports participation. PLoS One. 2019;**14**:e0218901. DOI: 10.1371/journal.pone.0218901

[15] Lang JJ, Chaput JP, Longmuir PE, Barnes JD, Belanger K, Tomkinson GR, et al. Cardiorespiratory fitness is associated with physical literacy in a large sample of Canadian children aged 8 to 12 years. BMC Public Health. 2018;**18**:1041. DOI: 10.1186/s12889-018-5896-5

[16] Ruiz JR, Castro-Piñero J, Artero EG, Ortega FB, Sjöström M, Suni J, et al. Predictive validity of health-related fitness in youth: A systematic review. British Journal of Sports Medicine. 2009;**43**:909-923. DOI: 10.1136/bjsm.2008.056499

[17] Haapala EA, Lintu N, Väistö J, Tompuri T, Soininen S, Viitasalo A, et al. Longitudinal associations of fitness, motor competence, and adiposity with cognition. Medicine and Science in Sports and Exercise. 2019;**51**:465-471. DOI: 10.1249/MSS.0000000000001826

[18] Marques A, Henriques-Neto D, Peralta M, Martins J, Gomes F, Popovic S, et al. Field-based health-related physical fitness tests in children and adolescents: A systematic review. Frontiers in Pediatrics. 2021;**9**:640028. DOI: 10.3389/fped.2021.640028

[19] Moradi A, Sadri Damirchi E, Narimani M, Esmaeilzadeh S, Dziembowska I, Azevedo LB, et al. Association between physical and motor fitness with cognition in children. Medicina (Kaunas, Lithuania). 2019;**55**:7. DOI: 10.3390/medicina55010007

[20] Ortega FB, Cadenas-Sánchez C, Sánchez-Delgado G, Mora-González J, Martínez-Téllez B, Artero EG, et al. Systematic review and proposal of a field-based physical fitness-test battery in preschool children: The PREFIT battery. Sports Medicine. 2015;**45**:533-555. DOI: 10.1007/s40279-014-0281-8

[21] Gómez-Bruton A, Marín-Puyalto J, Muñiz-Pardos B, Lozano-Berges G, Cadenas-Sanchez C, Matute-Llorente A, et al. Association between physical fitness and bone strength and structure in 3- to 5-year-old children. Sports Health. 2020;**12**:431-440. DOI: 10.1177/1941738120913645

[22] Faigenbaum AD, Myer GD, Fernandez IP, Carrasco EG, Bates N, Farrell A, et al. Feasibility and reliability of dynamic postural control measures in children in first through fifth grades. International Journal of Sports Physical Therapy. 2014;**9**:140-148

[23] Bürgi F, Meyer U, Granacher U, Schindler C, Marques-Vidal P, Kriemler S, et al. Relationship of physical activity with motor skills, aerobic fitness and body fat in preschool children:

A cross-sectional and longitudinal study (Ballabeina). International Journal of Obesity. 2005;**2011**(35):937-944. DOI: 10.1038/ijo.2011.54

[24] Muehlbauer T, Brueckner D, Schedler S. Effect of practice on learning a balance task in children, adolescents, and young adults. Frontiers in Psychology. 2022;**6**(13):989645. DOI: 10.3389/fpsyg.2022.989645

[25] Hirabayashi S, Iwasaki Y. Developmental perspective of sensory organization on postural control. Brain & Development. 1995;**17**:111-113. DOI: 10.1016/0387-7604(95)00009-z

[26] Ellsäßer G, Diepgen TL. Epidemiologische Analyse von Sturzunfällen im Kindesalter (<15 Jahre) Konsequenzen für die Prävention: Konsequenzen für die Prävention. Bundesgesundheitsblatt, Gesundheitsforschung, Gesundheitsschutz. 2002;**45**:267-276. (German). DOI: 10.1007/s00103-001-0371-2

[27] Docherty CL, Valovich McLeod TC, Shultz SJ. Postural control deficits in participants with functional ankle instability as measured by the balance error scoring system. Clinical Journal of Sports Medicine: Official Journal of the Canadian Academy of Sport Medicine. 2006;**16**:203-208. DOI: 10.1097/00042752-200605000-00003

[28] McGuine TA, Greene JJ, Best T, Leverson G. Balance as a predictor of ankle injuries in high school basketball players. Clinical Journal of Sport Medicine: Official Journal of the Canadian Academy of Sport Medicine. 2000;**10**:239-244. DOI: 10.1097/00042752-200010000-00003

[29] Ramírez-VélezR,Tordecilla-SandersA, Correa-Bautista JE, Peterson MD, Garcia-Hermoso A. Handgrip strength and ideal cardiovascular health among Colombian children and adolescents. The Journal of Pediatrics. 2016;**179**:82-89.e1. DOI: 10.1016/j.jpeds.2016.08.099

[30] Sartorio A, Lafortuna CL, Pogliaghi S, Trecate L. The impact of gender, body dimension and body composition on hand-grip strength in healthy children. Journal of Endocrinological Investigation. 2002;**25**:431-435. DOI: 10.1007/BF03344033

[31] Manzano-Carrasco S, Garcia-Unanue J, Lopez-Fernandez J, Hernandez-Martin A, Sanchez-Sanchez J, Gallardo L, et al. Differences in body composition and physical fitness parameters among prepubertal and pubertal children engaged in extracurricular sports: The active health study. European Journal of Public Health. 2022;**32**:i67-i72. DOI: 10.1093/eurpub/ckac075

[32] Rioux BV, Kuwornu P, Sharma A, Tremblay MS, McGavock JM, Sénéchal M. Association between handgrip muscle strength and cardiometabolic z-score in children 6 to 19 years of age: Results from the Canadian health measures survey. Metabolic Syndrome and Related Disorders. 2017;**15**:379-384. DOI: 10.1089/met.2016.0147

[33] Fredriksen PM, Mamen A, Hjelle OP, Lindberg M. Handgrip strength in 6-12-year-old children: The Health Oriented Pedagogical Project (HOPP). Scandinavian Journal of Public Health. 2018;**46**:54-60. DOI: 10.1177/1403494818769851

[34] Castro-Piñero J, Ortega FB, Artero EG, Girela-Rejón MJ, Mora J, Sjöström M, et al. Assessing muscular strength in youth: Usefulness of standing long jump as a general index of muscular fitness. Journal of

Strength and Conditioning Research. 2010;**24**:1810-1817. DOI: 10.1519/JSC.0b013e3181ddb03d

[35] Grøntved A, Ried-Larsen M, Møller NC, Kristensen PL, Froberg K, Brage S, et al. Muscle strength in youth and cardiovascular risk in young adulthood (the European Youth Heart Study). British Journal of Sports Medicine. 2015;**49**:90-94. DOI: 10.1136/bjsports-2012-091907

[36] Bruha L, Spyridou V, Forth G, Ougrin D. Global child and adolescent mental health: Challenges and advances. London Journal of Primary Care. 2018;**16**(10):108-109

[37] Polanczyk GV, Salum GA, Sugaya LS, Caye A, Rohde LA. Annual research review: A meta-analysis of the worldwide prevalence of mental disorders in children and adolescents. Journal of Child Psychology and Psychiatry. 2015;**56**:345-365. DOI: 10.1111/jcpp.12381

[38] Biddle SJH, Ciaccioni S, Thomas G, Vergeer I. Physical activity and mental health in children and adolescents: An updated review of reviews and an analysis of causality. Psychology of Sport and Exercise. 2019;**42**:146-155. DOI: 10.1016/j.psychsport.2018.08.011

[39] LaVigne T, Hoza B, Smith AL, Shoulberg EK, Bukowski W. Associations between physical fitness and children's psychological well-being. Journal of Clinical Sport Psychology. 2016;**10**:32-47. DOI: 10.1123/jcsp.2014-0053

[40] Haga M. The relationship between physical fitness and motor competence in children. Child: Care, Health and Development. 2008;**34**:329-334. DOI: 10.1111/j.1365-2214.2008.00814.x

[41] Martins D, Maia J, Seabra A, Garganta R, Lopes V, Katzmarzyk P, et al. Correlates of changes in BMI of children from the Azores islands. International Journal of Obesity. 2010;**34**:1487-1493. DOI: 10.1038/ijo.2010.56

[42] Johnson MS, Figueroa-Colon R, Herd SL, Fields DA, Sun M, Hunter GR, et al. Aerobic fitness, not energy expenditure, influences subsequent increase in adiposity in black and white children. Pediatrics. 2000;**106**:E50. DOI: 10.1542/peds.106.4.e50

[43] McMurray RG, Bangdiwala SI, Harrell JS, Amorim LD. Adolescents with metabolic syndrome have a history of low aerobic fitness and physical activity levels. Dynamic Medicine: DM. 2008;7:5. DOI: 10.1186/1476-5918-7-5

[44] Psarra G, Nassis GP, Sidossis LS. Short-term predictors of abdominal obesity in children. European Journal of Public Health. 2006;**16**:520-255. DOI: 10.1093/eurpub/cki196

[45] Hruby A, Chomitz VR, Arsenault LN, Must A, Economos CD, McGowan RJ, et al. Predicting maintenance or achievement of healthy weight in children: The impact of changes in physical fitness. Obesity (Silver Spring, Md.). 2012;**20**:1710-1717. DOI: 10.1038/oby.2012.13

[46] Palacio-Agüero A, Díaz-Torrente X, Quintiliano Scarpelli Dourado D. Relative handgrip strength, nutritional status and abdominal obesity in chilean adolescents. PLoS One. 2020;**15**:e0234316. DOI: 10.1371/journal.pone.0234316

[47] Freitas D, Beunen G, Maia J, Claessens A, Thomis M, Marques A, et al. Tracking of fatness during childhood, adolescence and young adulthood: A 7-year follow-up study in Madeira Island, Portugal. Annals of Human Biology. 2012;**39**:59-67. DOI: 10.3109/03014460.2011.638322

[48] Koutedakis Y, Bouziotas C, Flouris AD, Nelson PN. Longitudinal modeling of adiposity in periadolescent Greek schoolchildren. Medicine and Science in Sports and Exercise. 2005;**37**:2070-2074. DOI: 10.1249/01.mss.0000178099.80388.15

[49] Twisk JW, Kemper HC, van Mechelen W. Tracking of activity and fitness and the relationship with cardiovascular disease risk factors. Medicine and Science in Sports and Exercise. 2000;**32**:1455-1461. DOI:10.1097/00005768-200008000-00014

[50] Barnekow-Bergkvist M, Hedberg G, Janlert U, Jansson E. Adolescent determinants of cardiovascular risk factors in adult men and women. Scandinavian Journal of Public Health. 2001;**29**:208-217

[51] Janz KF, Dawson JD, Mahoney LT. Increases in physical fitness during childhood improve cardiovascular health during adolescence: The Muscatine study. International Journal of Sports Medicine. 2002;**23**:S15-S21. DOI: 10.1055/s-2002-28456

[52] Hasselstrøm H, Hansen SE, Froberg K, Andersen LB. Physical fitness and physical activity during adolescence as predictors of cardiovascular disease risk in young adulthood. Danish youth and sports study. An eight-year follow-up study. International Journal of Sports Medicine. 2002;**23**:S27-S31. DOI: 10.1055/s-2002-28458

[53] Jekal Y, Kim Y, Yun JE, Kim ES, Naruse M, Park JH, et al. The association of adolescent fatness and fitness with risk factors for adult metabolic syndrome: A 22-year follow-up study. Journal of Physical Activity & Health. 2014;**11**:823-830. DOI: 10.1123/jpah.2012-0068

[54] Kvaavik E, Klepp KI, Tell GS, Meyer HE, Batty GD. Physical fitness and physical activity at age 13 years as predictors of cardiovascular disease risk factors at ages 15, 25, 33, and 40 years: Extended follow-up of the Oslo youth study. Pediatrics. 2009;**123**:e80-e86. DOI: 10.1542/peds.2008-1118

[55] Boreham C, Twisk J, Neville C, Savage M, Murray L, Gallagher A. Associations between physical fitness and activity patterns during adolescence and cardiovascular risk factors in young adulthood: The Northern Ireland Young hearts project. International Journal of Sports Medicine. 2002;**23**:S22-S26. DOI: 10.1055/s-2002-28457

[56] Minck MR, Ruiter LM, Van Mechelen W, Kemper HC, Twisk JW. Physical fitness, body fatness, and physical activity: The Amsterdam Growth and Health Study. American Journal of Human Biology. 2000;**12**:593-599

[57] Byrd-Williams CE, Shaibi GQ, Sun P, Lane CJ, Ventura EE, Davis JN, et al. Cardiorespiratory fitness predicts changes in adiposity in overweight Hispanic boys. Obesity (Silver Spring, Md.). 2008;**16**:1072-1077. DOI: 10.1002/1520-6300(200009/10)12:5<593::AID-AJHB3>3.0.CO;2-U

[58] Aires L, Andersen LB, Mendonça D, Martins C, Silva G, Mota J. A 3-year longitudinal analysis of changes in fitness, physical activity, fatness and screen time. Acta Paediatrica. 2010;**99**:140-144. DOI: 10.1111/j.1651-2227.2009.01536.x

[59] Kim J, Must A, Fitzmaurice GM, Gillman MW, Chomitz V, Kramer E, et al. Relationship of physical fitness to prevalence and incidence of overweight among schoolchildren. Obesity Research. 2005;**13**:1246-1254. DOI: 10.1038/oby.2005.148

[60] Carson V, Rinaldi RL, Torrance B, Maximova K, Ball GD, Majumdar SR, et al. Vigorous physical activity and longitudinal associations with cardiometabolic risk factors in youth. International Journal of Obesity (London). 2014;**38**:16-21. DOI: 10.1038/ijo.2013.135

[61] Potter M, Spence JC, Boulé N, Stearns JA, Carson V. Behavior tracking and 3-year longitudinal associations between physical activity, screen time, and fitness among young children. Pediatric Exercise Science. 2018;**30**:132-141. DOI: 10.1123/pes.2016-0239

[62] Day MA, Dowthwaite JN, Rosenbaum PF, Roedel GG, Brocker AA, Scerpella TA. Pre-menarcheal physical activity predicts post-menarcheal lean mass and core strength, but not fat mass. Journal of Musculoskeletal & Neuronal Interactions. 2015;**15**:341-349

[63] Niederer I, Kriemler S, Gut J, Hartmann T, Schindler C, Barral J, et al. Relationship of aerobic fitness and motor skills with memory and attention in preschoolers (Ballabeina): A cross-sectional and longitudinal study. BMC Pediatrics. 2011;**11**:34. DOI: 10.1186/1471-2431-11-34

[64] Hillman CH, Castelli DM, Buck SM. Aerobic fitness and neurocognitive function in healthy preadolescent children. Medicine and Science in Sports and Exercise. 2005;**37**:1967-1974. DOI: 10.1249/01.mss.0000176680.79702.ce

[65] Hillman CH, Buck SM, Themanson JR, Pontifex MB, Castelli DM. Aerobic fitness and cognitive development: Event-related brain potential and task performance indices of executive control in preadolescent children. Developmental Psychology. 2009;**45**:114-129. DOI: 10.1037/a0014437

[66] Syväoja HJ, Kankaanpää A, Hakonen H, Inkinen V, Kulmala J, Joensuu L, et al. How physical activity, fitness, and motor skills contribute to math performance: Working memory as a mediating factor. Scandinavian Journal of Medicine & Science in Sports. 2021;**31**:2310-2321. DOI: 10.1111/sms.14049

[67] Pindus DM, Drollette ES, Scudder MR, Khan NA, Raine LB, Sherar LB, et al. Moderate-to-vigorous physical activity, indices of cognitive control, and academic achievement in preadolescents. The Journal of Pediatrics. 2016;**173**:136-142. DOI: 10.1016/j.jpeds.2016.02.045

[68] Skog H, Lintu N, Haapala HL, Haapala EA. Associations of cardiorespiratory fitness, adiposity, and arterial stiffness with cognition in youth. Physiological Reports. 2020;**8**:e14586. DOI: 10.14814/phy2.14586

[69] Pontifex MB, Raine LB, Johnson CR, Chaddock L, Voss MW, Cohen NJ, et al. Cardiorespiratory fitness and the flexible modulation of cognitive control in preadolescent children. Journal of Cognitive Neuroscience. 2011;**23**:1332-1345. DOI: 10.1162/jocn.2010.21528

[70] Chaddock L, Hillman CH, Pontifex MB, Johnson CR, Raine LB, Kramer AF. Childhood aerobic fitness predicts cognitive performance one year later. Journal of Sports Sciences. 2012;**30**:421-430. DOI: 10.1080/02640414.2011.647706

Section 2

Practical Applications to Develop Physical Fitness in Children

Chapter 3

Field-Based Measurement of Cardiorespiratory Fitness for Children and the Youth in Low and Middle Income Settings

Lenora Canizares Fernandez and Anna Czarina L. Chavez

Abstract

Cardiorespiratory fitness (CRF) has declined worldwide among the youth with 81% of adolescents not being physically active. Promotion of cardiorespiratory fitness among the youth is an important goal with the global challenge of reducing physical inactivity by 15% in the next 7 years. Assessment and monitoring though of cardiorespiratory fitness have not been standardized for children worldwide. Moreover, the gold standard of gas-analyzed cardiopulmonary exercise testing is too expensive for use in low to middle-income countries (LMICs). Submaximal exercise tests that need minimal inexpensive equipment and training for the administering staff are most appropriate for use in population studies and individual CRF assessment in LMICs. Three office-based and two field-based tests (e.g. 20 m shuttle run test) are recommended for use among children in LMICs. Validated CRF questionnaires can be used in epidemiologic studies. Health-related fitness test batteries for children have also been conducted in LMICs. There is, therefore, an urgent need to develop a standardized set of measures for CRF among children that can be implemented internationally. These should be scalable, simple, valid, reliable, easily implementable and can surmount the large geo-regional variations in assessing and reporting CRF among the youth.

Keywords: cardiorespiratory fitness, exercise test, pediatric, youth, physical activity, low to-middle income countries

1. Introduction

Cardiorespiratory fitness (CRF) is a major component of physical fitness and is the capacity of the cardiovascular and respiratory systems to provide oxygen to skeletal muscle mitochondria for energy production during physical activity [1]. Physical fitness is the more general term that pertains to the ability of the person to perform physical activities or specific exercises [2]. Physical activity (PA), on the other hand, is classically defined as "any bodily movement produced by skeletal muscles that results in energy expenditure" and exercise is a type of physical activity that is "planned to improve or maintain physical fitness [3]." Cardiorespiratory fitness and physical fitness are attributes of a person while physical activity and exercise are behaviors of a person [1]. Cardiorespiratory fitness, physical fitness and regular physical activity have all been essential components for promoting both mental and physical health from youth to adulthood among all individuals [1, 2]. Low levels of CRF among the youth predict poor cardiometabolic health, premature cardiovascular disease, lower academic achievement and lower mental health status [1]. CRF has declined among the youth throughout the world and the 2022 Global Action Plan on Physical Activity (GAPPA) likewise reported that 81% of adolescents did not meet the World Health Organization's (WHO) recommended levels of physical activity [4–6]. All countries, therefore, have been challenged to reduce physical inactivity by 15% and to reach this goal by Year 2030 [4].

Promotion of cardiorespiratory fitness and physical activity among the youth have become important goals to improve health and prevent future cardiovascular diseases globally so that assessment and monitoring of these health indices have also been recently given more attention [1]. The American Heart Association even proposes cardiorespiratory fitness being the fifth vital sign [7]. Half of the participating communities, especially among the low- to middle-income countries (LMICs), have not been able to assign a grade for Physical Fitness in the Global Matrix 4.0 Report on Physical Activity due to lack of data [6]. Recent economic challenges and the COVID-19 pandemic have further reduced the access and opportunities to provide and assess physical activity and fitness among the children and youth in LMICs [6]. These gaps highlight the need to provide evaluation tools to assess cardiorespiratory fitness and physical activity in a simple, cost-effective and adaptable manner while maintaining their validity, reliability and reproducibility. This chapter will discuss the different cardiorespiratory fitness and physical activity tests for children and adolescents that can be employed in low-resource settings.

2. Methodology

The following online databases were used as sources for published articles: PubMed, BioMed Central, American Heart Association, ResearchGate, Public Library of Science (PLOS), and Multidisciplinary Digital Publishing Institute (MDPI). Individual terms or a combination of the following keywords were utilized to select relevant literature from the years 2019–2023: fitness, exercise, physical activity, children, adolescents, youth, cardiopulmonary, cardiorespiratory, field test, battery, evaluation, assessment, low-income countries, and middle-income countries. A few related studies older than 2019 that supported findings from the relevant articles were also reviewed (2004, 2006, 2013, 2017). Systematic reviews, studies conducted on populations of low resource countries, and updated clinical guidelines were included as the main source of content for this chapter.

3. Physiology of cardiorespiratory fitness (CRF), CRF testing and correlation with physical activity

The cardiovascular and respiratory systems are inextricably linked by a chain of processes from pulmonary ventilation and diffusion to cardiac contractility, vascular circulation and muscle cell oxygen and nutrient extraction to perform physical work and activity [7]. The best indicator of this integrated cardiorespiratory fitness to perform physical work is the person's maximal oxygen consumption or aerobic capacity measured through their VO2Max. It is the oxygen consumed in liters per minute, or milliliters per kilogram per minute. Since oxygen consumption (VO2) increases with a given workload, the VO2Max is determined when VO2 reaches a plateau despite increasing work intensity [8, 9]. However, considerations for children not demonstrating a plateau during incremental exercise has prompted the use of the highest VO2 measured in the youth (VO2Peak) instead. This is analogous to the VO2Max in adults [1].

As per Fick's Principle (cardiac output = oxygen consumption ÷ arteriovenous oxygen content difference), VO2Max is the product of the maximal arteriovenous oxygen difference, and the cardiac output [9]. This explains how the body ensures adequate oxygen delivery from our lungs, to the blood, through our heart, and eventually to our tissues and working muscles during times of physical stress such as exercise [10]. Any cardiac or pulmonary condition impairing gas exchange may serve as a barrier to achieving this. To further illustrate the physiologic changes that take place in a child and adolescent, we examine cardiac output, respiration, and arteriovenous oxygen difference.

During the early phase of physical exercise, the increase in cardiac output comes from the increase both in the left ventricular stroke volume and the end-diastolic volume. As the intensity of exercise progresses, the heart rate rises. Compared to adults, children and adolescents have a smaller left ventricular stroke volume during exercise, which causes a compensatory higher heart rate response [1, 10].

In terms of respiration, tidal volume physiologically increases with progressive physical exercise. Once the tidal volume reaches approximately half the vital capacity of the lungs, minute ventilation increases through increased respiratory rate. Developmental aspects affecting the efficiency of ventilation may be observed throughout childhood and adolescence, and is said to be due to decreasing respiratory rate, increasing tidal volume, and depth of breathing [1, 10].

The arteriovenous oxygen difference pertains to the concentration between arterial and venous blood, and indicates the amount of oxygen consumed by the muscles and organ systems during exercise. During maximal exercise, the arteriovenous oxygen difference between prepubertal boys and girls is zero. Post-puberty, boys would have a higher arteriovenous oxygen difference than girls. During submaximal exercise, arteriovenous oxygen difference is higher in children versus adults. This is said to be a compensatory mechanism by children for the lower cardiac output so as to extract more oxygen from the blood [10].

4. Cardiorespiratory fitness testing through the gas-analyzed graded cardiopulmonary exercise test (CPET)

All these parameters reflecting cardiorespiratory fitness are obtained during a cardiopulmonary exercise test (CPET). CPET is non-invasive, comprehensive, and is regarded as the gold standard method for evaluating physical fitness both in children and adults [11]. It provides a breath-by-breath monitoring of oxygen and carbon dioxide during exercise and the physiologic values discussed above. It is conducted in a laboratory and expertise is needed in its performance and interpretation. The equipment is expensive and calibration and maintenance are meticulous processes requiring expertise as well [1] Reference values for the pediatric population are available, however, caution is still needed in using these values since these can vary according to the type of protocol (whether the treadmill or cycle ergometer was used for exercise) and the correction factors applied to the reference population are sometimes not applicable in certain situations [12]. Lastly, walking or cycling as the activities used in CPET protocols may not reflect the actual types of physical activities that the youth commonly do on a regular basis [12].

Due to these limitations of the CPET, other tests have been utilized to assess cardiorespiratory fitness and these shall be discussed in the following sections. Cardiorespiratory fitness, moreover, is only one of the four major components of health-related fitness and the others are muscular fitness, flexibility and body composition [1]. Muscular fitness is the integrated function of muscle strength, endurance and power to exert maximal force against an external resistance or repeatedly under submaximal loads [1, 13]. Flexibility is the ability of an individual's joint or series of joints to move through an unrestricted, pain free range of motion. Body composition, the fourth component, is the percentages of fat, muscle or fat-free tissue and total body water in the total body mass of an individual [1]. Specific tests are recommended for these other components of health-related physical fitness.

5. Cardiorespiratory fitness and physical activity correlation

Physical activity (PA) is the voluntary skeletal muscle movement producing energy expenditure and exercise is a subset of PA that is structured, planned and purposefully performed to improve or maintain one or more components of physical fitness [14]. PA is a complex behavior but is usually classified according to the four dimensions of (1) mode or type of activity, (2) frequency, (3) duration and (4) intensity of performing the activity [3, 14]. Regular physical activity, through exercise and training, improves CRF and greater CRF results to more capacity for physical activity, thus, creating a facilitative cycle of an "active-fit lifestyle [1]." The overall effect of improving both CRF and PA is the promotion of health and its related outcomes (**Figure 1**) [1, 3, 15].

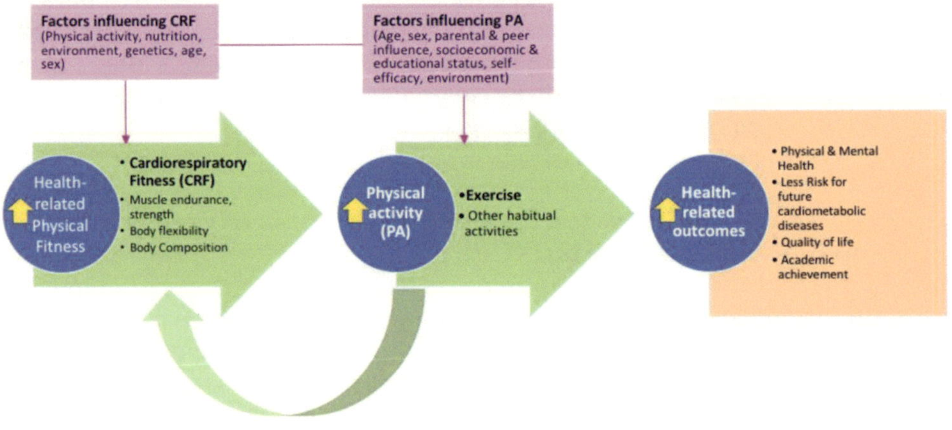

Figure 1.
"Active-fit Lifestyle" facilitative cycle of cardiorespiratory fitness, physical activity and improvement in health-related outcomes among children. CRF: cardiorespiratory fitness.

The recommended physical activity to maintain general cardiopulmonary fitness among adults is well-known [4]. For children and adolescents, differences in the recommended duration, types of activities, and even hours of sleep, may be observed. The WHO recommends physical activities for different youth age groups as follows [4]:

For children under 5 years of age, specifically for those less than 1 year old, interactive floor-based play, several times a day is encouraged. For children under 1 year old who have not achieved mobility yet, at least 30 minutes in a prone position may be done multiple times throughout the day, during waking hours. Reading and storytelling should be included when sedentary, and exposure to screens and gadgets at this age is not recommended. 14–17 hours and 12–16 hours of good quality sleep is recommended for 0–3 months and 4–11 months of age, respectively. This is inclusive of naps during the day.

For children 1–4 years old, at least 180 minutes of varied physical activities at any intensity, distributed throughout the day, is encouraged. No more than 1 hour of sedentary screen time should be allowed for this age group. Good quality sleep should be around 11–14 hours for children 1–2 years old, and 10–13 hours for children 3–4 years old.

Strollers, high chairs, and other similar restraints (including being strapped on to the caregiver) should not go beyond 1 hour at a time within a 24-hour period.

For children and adolescents aged 5–17 years, it is recommended that they do at least an average of 60 minutes per day of moderate-to-vigorous intensity (mostly aerobic) activities distributed across the week. These activities, as well as strengthening exercises, should be done at least 3 days a week.

As in children younger than 5 years, screen time must be minimized or limited in this age group especially when sedentary.

6. Measuring physical activity

There is a variety of measures for PA that are generally divided into subjective or objective categories [3]. Questionnaires, activity logs, and diaries are utilized as self-report or staff-administered methods under the subjective category while objective tests include direct observation, heart rate monitoring, using doubly labeled water, accelerometers and pedometers [2].

Since PA involves a complex behavior with multiple dimensions and domains to consider, there is not one precise, biological marker nor is there one single test to reliably encompass all its facets and dimensions. It also becomes more difficult to quantify physical activity behavior in free-living children and adolescents because only a small segment of the population performs physical activity for the sole purpose of improving fitness or health [14]. Vigorous physical activity among children is also very intermittent with 96% of activity bouts shorter than 10 seconds [14]. Estimation of energy expenditures of childhood PA often uses adult-derived standard energy costs as there no comprehensive reference values available yet for the youth [2].

Nevertheless, PA measures are often utilized, especially the self-report methods, in population surveys and epidemiologic studies since these are the most practical and remain to be valuable in formulating recommendations and policies [2].

7. How to assess cardiorespiratory fitness (CRF) in LMIC's

Gas-analyzed graded cardiopulmonary exercise test (CPET) is considered the gold standard for assessing cardiorespiratory fitness, however, the significant logistic limitations in procuring, operating and maintaining the metabolic cart and its accessories for CPET hinder its common use in low-middle income countries [1].

Non-gas analyzed tests that may be conducted in an office or on the field are the other tests recommended to assess CRF among children [1]. These are often submaximal exercise tests that estimate the energy expenditure and the CRF of the individual using equations or nomograms that have been validated with the gas-analyzed CPET [9, 16]. These submaximal exercise activities are often easy to perform with varying logistic requirement. Large measurement errors may occur and standardization of the predictive equations and nomograms for children for the different tests are not yet complete [1, 13, 16]. Nevertheless, the submaximal exercise tests that have been validated and that are easy to perform with the least needed equipment are the most appropriate to use in LMICs to assess CRF among children.

Three office-based submaximal exercise tests and two field tests are considered to be most feasible for use in low-resource settings.

7.1 Office-based exercise tests

7.1.1 45-second squat test

The 45-Second Squat Test is also known as the Ruffier-Dickson Test and has been used to classify cardiorespiratory fitness among adults and children [17]. It is simple and does not require any equipment but a timer and a device to check the heart rate.

The heart rate is measured for a full minute either with a pulse oximeter, or manually through auscultation with a stethoscope of heart sounds at the point of maximal impulse (PMI) prior to starting the test (P0). Afterwards, the subject is asked to perform 30 squats within 45 seconds. Proper positioning consists of knee flexion during squats being at approximately 90 degrees, with the subject's back as straight as possible, and the shoulders flexed forward. Heart rates are recorded at 1–2 minutes into the test, immediately once completed (P1), and after 1 minute of rest (P2) [1, 17].

The Ruffier-Dickson Index (RDI) is then calculated as follows [18]:

$$RDI = \frac{(P1 - 70) + 2(P2 - P0)}{10} \tag{1}$$

Where:

$P0$ = heart rate prior to starting the test.

$P1$ = heart rate at 1–2 minutes into the test.

$P2$ = heart rate after 1 minute of rest.

The RDI indices would correspond to certain levels of exercise endurance capacity from very poor to excellent endurance [18].

The test of 30 squats in 45 seconds is considered a moderate to vigorous impact type of activity that corresponds to ~6 peak MET in oxygen uptake and is associated with a cardiorespiratory load of 128 beats/min peak heart rate [17]. Recent studies though in the pediatric population demonstrated a low validity using the initial RDI formula [19, 20]. A revised Ruffier-Dickson index for children has been validated and commonly used in Ukraine [19].

Ruffier-Dickson index adapted for children (Ic) [19]:

$$Ic = \frac{[P1 + 2(P2 - P0)\frac{Pa}{Pp} - 70}{10} \tag{2}$$

Where:

$P0$ = heart rate prior to starting the test.

$P1$ = heart rate at 1–2 minutes into the test.

$P2$ = heart rate after 1 minute of rest.

Pa = normal population heart rate at rest for adults (or 70/minute).

Pp = normal population heart rate at rest for young patients aged 6, 7 and 8 years, respectively (or 102, 98, 93/minute, respectively).

The derived pediatric RDI (Ic), according to the age, would correspond to a certain health level assessment from low to high levels (1–5) [19].

7.1.2 3-minute step test

As with the 45-Second Squat Test, the heart rate is measured for a full minute with a pulse oximeter, or manually through auscultation with a stethoscope of heart sounds at the point of maximal impulse (PMI) prior to starting the test (T0) [1]. A metronome is set at an established cadence (in the Bruggeman study, 96 steps per minute was used) and the subjects are asked to step up and down a step of 12 inches in height for three minutes at a rhythm of "up, up" and "down, down [20]." Heart rates are likewise measured at the first, second and third minutes (T1, T2, and T3) into the test, and again after 1 minute of recovery upon completing the test (T4). The Jacks et al. VO2max predictive formula is used to calculate the subject's score using the values obtained [20].

The 3-Minute Step and 45-Second Squat Tests showed statistically significant correlations with VO2max [1, 20]. Furthermore, the Step Test shows a high Area Under the Receiver Operator Curve, illustrating its usefulness. Both tests have been found to be conducted safely at the clinic/office setting [20].

7.1.3 6-minute walk test

The 6-Minute Walk Test (6MWT) was deemed to have a relatively poor correlation with VO2Max in healthy children and adolescents to estimate CRF [1]. However, it is said to be a better indicator of the ability of patients to perform their daily activities n some clinical scenarios, and as such would correlate with quality of life measures [21].

In a systematic review by Mylius et al. of 22 studies about healthy participants aged ≤18 years, it sought to determine the reference values for the 6MWT [22]. The prediction equation found to be valid and that yielded the highest R2 value of 0.6 was as follows [22]:

$$\begin{aligned}&\text{6 Minute Walking Distance}\\&=(4.63\times\text{height in } cm)-(3.53\times\text{weight in } kg)+(10.42\times age)+56.32\end{aligned} \tag{3}$$

The systematic review by Cacau and colleagues of reference values for the 6 MWT in healthy children and adolescents also supported that current existing reference equations accounted for well-established variables in the context of exercise performance (e.g. height, heart rate, age and weight) [23, 24]. Countries without established reference values for the 6MWT should be encouraged to conduct studies to establish these because it would provide their own clinicians and researchers with a precise interpretation of the test [23].

To date, a growing number of countries have been developing their own reference values and formulas to determine the maximum distance of each age group and sex, and deemed the 6MWT a safe, well-tolerated, and understandable test to conduct both in healthy children, as well as in those with cardiopulmonary and neuromuscular disorders [23].

For this particular test, its suggestion for use may be applied in children between 4 and 12 years old, for as long as they can follow instructions and are motivated in accomplishing the test [23].

The 6MWT requires a stopwatch, a measuring tape or stick, 30 meters of a walkway with obstacles removed, two markers (cones, tape, or any available weighted or stationary object) to determine the turn-around points or end-distances that need to be covered as well as markers on the wall 3 meters apart, a print out of the Borg's Rate of Perceived Exertion scale in a size 20 font, a sphygmomanometer with an appropriately-sized cuff (must cover at least two-thirds or 70% of the upper arm), and a pulse oximeter to measure oxygen saturation and heart rate [21].

Before the test is started, the participant may be asked to sit on a chair for at least 10 minutes. At this time, the blood pressure may be measured with an appropriately-sized pediatric cuff on a sphygmomanometer, and the heart rate and oxygen saturation on a pediatric pulse oximeter. The Borg Rate of Perceived Exertion is asked while the patient is at rest [1, 24].

The participant is instructed to walk, not run or jog, continuously between the 2 endpoints marked with the stationary object, for a duration of 6 minutes. If they get tired, they may rest (lean against a wall, stop, or slow down), but are advised to continue walking until the 6 minutes are up. As soon as the participant starts walking, the timer must be started. Each time the participant returns to the starting line, mark the lap on the record sheet and the stopwatch. The additional distance covered (meters in the final partial lap) using markers on the wall 3 meters apart as distance guides, must also be recorded. Once the total distance is calculated, round it off to the nearest meter, and record it on the worksheet [21].

Standardized encouragement is provided as follows [21]:

- At the end of 1 minute: "You are doing well. You have 5 minutes to go."
- At 4 minutes remaining: "Keep up the good work. You have 4 minutes to go."
- At 3 minutes remaining: "You are doing well. You are halfway done.
- At 2 minutes remaining: "Keep up the good work. You have only 2 minutes left.
- With 1 minute remaining: "You are doing well. You only have 1 minute to go.
- With 15 seconds to go: "In a moment I'm going to tell you to stop. When I do, just stop right where you are and I will come to you."
- Finally, at 6 minutes: "Stop."

The examiner must not walk with the patient and must use an even tone in delivering the instructions. After the test, the Borg Rate of Perceived Exertion is asked and recorded again. If the participant reports any chest pain, intolerable dyspnea, leg cramps, staggering, diaphoresis, and pallor or ashen appearance, the test must be discontinued [1, 21].

7.2 Field-based exercise tests

Raghuveer and colleagues discussed different types of run tests that may easily be administered in the school setting, given a large cohort of children and adolescents, and may be used to guide population-based interventions for CRF improvement [1, 13]. Among these are the 20-meter Shuttle Run Test, the 1.5-meter Run Test, and the 12-Minute Run Test [1].

7.2.1 20-meter shuttle run test

The 20-meter shuttle run test (20mSRT) is also known as the beep test, bleep test, PACER (Progressive Aerobic Cardiovascular Endurance Run) test, and Multi-stage fitness test (MSFT) [1]. In this test, the subject is asked to run at increasing standardized paces (beginning with 5 miles/hour or 8 kilometers/hour, progressing with 0.3 miles/hour or 0.5 kilometers/hour increments each minute), between two points that are 20 meters apart. The test is stopped when the subject is no longer able to follow the set pace. The last announced stage number with its equivalent maximal aerobic speed is used to estimate the child's VO2max using a predictive equation or it can be compared to normative values from a reference population [1, 25].

The 20mSRT is able to elicit a maximal effort in most children and induces the highest peak VO2 compared to other exercises [26]. It simulates the typical youth activities of running, sprinting, jogging and agility in changes in speed and direction. It has been widely studied in both sexes and across a wide range of ethnicities and ages. The criterion validity of the 20mSRT as a measure of CRF is moderate and its reliability is high to very high with a reliability coefficient of 0.78 to 0.93 in children aged 8–18 years [25]. Test-retest differences among children are also not significant. Like other tests for CRF, it must be noted that the maximal effort by the child may be influenced by factors such as physiology (fractional utilization of oxygen, VO2 kinetics, anaerobic capacity, and agility), body mass, motivation, tolerance to discomfort, and self-efficacy [25, 26].

The other advantages of the 20mSRT are its acceptability, feasibility, scalability, the ease in its interpretation and transferability of the results to relevant and health-related situations. The 20mSRT is often included in physical fitness test batteries [26]. It can be administered in group settings such as in schools, thus, large groups of youth can be tested simultaneously. It can be conducted indoors or outdoors and the external pacing can help mitigate pacing variability. The larger time gaps at the initial stages of the test serve as a warm up for most subjects. At the end of the test, children should have a cool-down period with light to moderate intensity aerobic activities lasting for 5–10 minutes [25].

The results from the 20mSRT can either be interpreted using criterion-referenced or normative-referenced standards [25–27]. Criterion-referenced health-related standards are used to identify pediatric subjects who may need health-related interventions or to screen those at increased risk of future diseases [26]. Screening using criterion-referenced standards are also used for recruitment into military-related or highly physical jobs and for athlete identification. Leger's original predictive formula for estimating VO2 max from the 20mSRT is still regarded as the most valid equation, however, some authors noted large prediction errors may occur with VO2 max estimation [25–27]. These authors recommend reporting the number of laps completed as the basis for a child's fitness assessment [25, 26].

Norm-referenced interpretation, on the other hand, is done when the aim is to compare the subject to his/her peers as is commonly done in physical education and similar situations. Normative data are available for over 1.1 million children and youth from 50 countries for the 20mSRT [25]. Developing countries such as Bosnia, Croatia, Estonia, and Tibet have such pediatric reference values for 20mSRT available [28–31].

7.2.2 Distance or time-based run tests

In the 1.5-Mile or 2400-Meter Run Test (distance-based) the patient is instructed to complete the run in the shortest amount of time, while in the 12-Minute Run Test (time-based) and the patient is tasked to cover the greatest possible distance, with their best effort [1]. A recent meta-analysis showed moderate to high correlation of the 1.5-Mile ($r = 0.79$) and 12-Minute Run Test ($r = 0.78$) with VO2max as measured by CPET and with the 20mSRT as well [32].

7.3 Questionnaires to assess pediatric cardiorespiratory fitness

When submaximal fitness tests are not possible to conduct due to various causes, questionnaires maybe used to assess CRF [1]. Questionnaires are often used for epidemiologic and population-based studies but these methods will not be sufficient to estimate cardiorespiratory fitness in individuals [33].

Questionnaires range from those that assess physical activity to CRF as a single domain [1, 33, 34]. The World Health Organization currently recommends the Global Physical Activity Questionnaire (GPAQ) to standardize the reporting of physical activity for population-based surveys among the different countries [4]. It may not be applicable though to children, especially with the domain on occupational physical activity in the questionnaire [34]. A multi-country study across six continents has been initiated to develop and validate the Global Adolescent and Child Physical Activity Questionnaire (GAC-PAQ) and will be completed in year 2025 [35]. This will help standardize the language of physical activity assessment for children globally.

For the domain of CRF itself, the International Fitness Scale (IFIS) is one of the most validated tool in different countries for the pediatric population [33]. It is composed of five questions on physical fitness, CRF, muscular strength, speed and flexibility that uses a five-point Likert scale [36]. It is concise and can be completed in 5 minutes. IFIS response among children aged 12–18 years significantly correlated with CRF. The analysis of covariance showed adolescents reporting better fitness had higher measured fitness levels for all the variables studied ($p < 0.001$) regardless of gender, age and weight status [33].

The recent meta-analysis on the use of IFIS to predict CRF among children included two studies from LMICs and showed moderate to substantial reliability with test-retest reliability coefficients ranging from 0.40 to 0.99 [36].

7.4 CRF test batteries

Since health-related physical fitness (PF) is a multi-dimensional attribute, many proponents advocate for a battery of physical fitness tests that will reflect the features of cardiorespiratory fitness, muscle endurance and strength, flexibility, and body composition [26]. A 2021 meta-analysis identified 24 PF batteries for children and the most widely applied batteries were the "Eurofit", "FitnessGram", and "Alpha-fit [26]." All of the PF batteries contained cardiorespiratory fitness and upper body strength as components. The most common CRF tests included in the PF batteries, on the other hand, were the PACER and the 1-mile run/walk tests. Estimation of maximum aerobic capacity from these CRF tests have to be balanced with the other factors affecting physical fitness such as sex and adiposity [26].

All of the PF batteries were performed in school settings and some of the studies on PF test batteries in the meta-analysis were conducted in LMICs, hence, denoting the ease of implementation [26]. A PF battery called the Performance and Fitness (PERF-FIT) test battery was designed in South Africa for implementation primarily in low-resource settings [37]. This battery is an instructor-administered skill-related fitness test for children aged 5 to 12 years. The test combines movement skills, agility and power and utilizes task loading or progressive increase in task difficulty to all skill items. Testing equipment should not cost beyond 50 US dollars and these were composed of simple and cheap items such as tape measure, rectangular foam, and soda cans [37]. The content validity indices for the throw and catch items were 0.86 and 1.00, respectively, with the total validity score for the other items reaching 0.99 [37]. The PERF-FIT, therefore, has good validity and is easy to administer in low-resource settings [37].

Overall, the PF batteries utilized throughout the world are too varied and there are only a few studies that have validated these fitness tests in the LMICs. Global collaboration is needed to develop a universal field-based fitness test battery that can easily be implemented with non-specialized staff, low in cost, scalable, easily interpretable while remaining valid and reliable [38].

8. Use of wearable and smartphone technology to measure PA

Objective measurement of physical activity utilizes motion sensors on the subject and the rapid increase in the technology of wearable devices has benefited this field. Wearable technologies are devices with sensors, screen, processor, memory and software that have algorithms to store, filter, interpret and organize real time data of motion and physiologic events happening in the wearer. The main wearable devices to measure PA are the pedometers and accelerometers where the pedometer counts footsteps over a period of time, while the triaxial accelerometer measures acceleration in three planes during body motions [14].

A 2023 meta-analysis showed that varied wearable devices are used to measure PA for children [39]. The pedometers revealed low accuracy at slower speeds and when these were attached to certain clothing items (e.g. skirt part of dresses). Accelerometers provided more data such as the frequency, duration and intensity of PA. The ActiGraph, Actical and ActiTrainer accelerometers had the best measurement properties to assess common movement-related outcomes for school-based activities while, among the pedometers, the Yamax Digi-Walker (SW-200, SW-700 and 701) provided the best measurement for movement-related outcomes [39].

Overall, there are only a few studies on these technologies for school-based activities and most were conducted in high-resource countries [40].

A low-cost commercial smartwatch, the Xiaomi Mi Band (MB), was evaluated in some low-income countries and showed high agreement of MB step counts with subjective reports on physical activity and sleep-related measures [41]. Most of the subjects in this study, though, were adults [41].

Smartphone technology likewise offers a new avenue for physical activity surveillance among children. A 2023 systematic review gathered only cross-sectional and cohort studies that used mobile apps purposely developed for the studies or were downloadable from the Apple App Store or Android Play Store [42]. All studies were conducted in high income countries [42]. The data were not yet sufficient to assess the validity and reliability of smartphone technology for PA surveillance among children and adolescents [42].

9. Conclusion

Improvement in cardiorespiratory fitness among children and adolescents is a global goal so as to promote physical and mental health, improve quality of life and academic achievement and prevent future cardiovascular and chronic illnesses in this population [1, 4]. Assessment and monitoring of CRF are intrinsic processes in this journey of improving physical fitness. While gas-analyzed graded cardiopulmonary exercise testing is the acknowledged gold standard to assess CRF in children, simple office-based and field-based exercise tests are available for use and have been validated for individual and large-scale purposes [1]. Low- to middle-income countries can utilize these low-cost and simple sub-maximal exercise tests while also maximizing the use of readily available physical activity and physical fitness questionnaires. Wearable and smartphone technology are very popular in this age group and its rapid development also helps drive down its cost [39, 40]. More studies and urgent collaboration is needed among all countries to validate, simplify, standardize and implement these fitness tests, whether as individual tools or as a test battery, so that physical inactivity can indeed be significantly decreased among children and the youth by 2030 [38].

Conflict of interest

The authors declare no conflict of interest.

Author details

Lenora Canizares Fernandez* and Anna Czarina L. Chavez
Philippine General Hospital, University of the Philippines, Manila, Philippines

*Address all correspondence to: lcfernandezmd@yahoo.com

References

[1] Raghuveer G, Hartz J, Lubans DR, Takken T, Wiltz JL, Mietus-Snyder M, et al. Cardiorespiratory fitness in youth: An important marker of health: A scientific statement from the American Heart Association. Circulation. 2020;**142**(7):2-7, 9-11

[2] Corder K, Ekelund U, Steele RM, Wareham NJ, Brage S. Assessment of physical activity in youth. Journal of Applied Physiology. 2008. pp. 3-5, 27-29. DOI: 10.1152/japplphysiol.00094.2008

[3] Caspersen CJ, Powell KE, Christenson GM. Physical activity, exercise, and physical fitness: definitions and distinctions for health-related research. Public Health Reports. 1985;**100**(2):126-131

[4] Global Status Report on Physical Activity 2022. Geneva: World Health Organization; 2022. pp. 8-9. Licence: CC BY-NC-SA 3.0 IGO

[5] De Moraes A, Guerra P, Menezes P. The worldwide prevalence of insufficient physical activity in adolescents; a systematic review. Nutrición Hospitalaria. 2013;**28**(3):575-584

[6] Aubert S, Barnes JD, Demchenko I, Hawthorne M, Abdeta C, Abi Nader P, et al. Global Matrix 4.0 physical activity report card grades for children and adolescents: Results and analyses from 57 countries. Journal of Physical Activity & Health. 2022;**19**(11):700-728. DOI: 10.1123/jpah.2022-0456

[7] Ross R, Blair SN, Arena R, Church TS, Després JP, Franklin BA, et al. Importance of assessing cardiorespiratory fitness in clinical practice: A case for fitness as a clinical vital sign: A scientific statement from the American Heart Association. Circulation. 2016;**134**(24):e653-e699. DOI: 10.1161/CIR.0000000000000461

[8] Bartels M, Prince D. Acute medical conditions: Cardiopulmonary disease, medical frailty, and renal failure. In: Eapen B, Johns J, Kowalske K, Lew H, Miller M, Worsowicz G, editors. Braddom's Physical Medicine and Rehabilitation. 6th ed. Philadelphia: Elsevier; 2021. p. 515

[9] Takken T, Bongers BC, van Brussel M, Haapala EA, EHJ H. Cardiopulmonary exercise testing in pediatrics. Annals of the American Thoracic Society. 2017;**14**(Supplement_1):S123-S128

[10] Guazzi M, Bandera F, Ozemek C, Systrom D, Arena R. Cardiopulmonary exercise testing. Journal of the American College of Cardiology. 2017;**70**(13):1618-1636

[11] Goddard T, Sonnappa S. The role of cardiopulmonary exercise testing in evaluating children with exercise induced dyspnoea. Paediatric Respiratory Reviews, S1526054220301184. 2020. p. 2. DOI: 10.1016/j.prrv.2020.08.002

[12] Armstrong N, Welsman J. Youth cardiorespiratory fitness: Evidence, myths and misconceptions. Bulletin of the World Health Organization. 2019;**97**(11):777-782. DOI: 10.2471/BLT.18.227546

[13] IOM (Institute of Medicine). Fitness Measures and Health Outcomes in Youth. Washington, DC: The National Academies Press; 2012

[14] Trost S. State of the art reviews: Measurement of physical activity in children and adolescents. American Journal of Lifestyle Medicine. 2007;**9**(4):299-314

[15] Park H, Kim N. Predicting factors of physical activity in adolescents: A systematic review. Asian Nursing Research. 2008;**2**(2):113-128

[16] Lang JJ, Wolfe Phillips E, Orpana HM, Tremblay MS, Ross R, Ortega FB, et al. Field-based measurement of cardiorespiratory fitness to evaluate physical activity interventions. Bulletin of the World Health Organization. 2018;**96**(11):794-796

[17] Sartor F, Bonato M, Papini G, Bosio A, Mohammed RA, Bonomi AG, et al. A 45-second self-test for cardiorespiratory fitness: Heart rate-based estimation in healthy individuals. PLoS One. 2016;**11**(12):e0168154. DOI: 10.1371/journal.pone.0168154

[18] Zanevskyy I, Zanevska L. Validity of the Dickson index regarding primary school physical education. Human Movement. 2019;**20**(2):44-49. DOI: 10.5114/hm.2019.81021

[19] Zanevskyy I, Janiszewska R, Zanevska L. Validity of Ruffier test in evaluation of resistance to the physical effort. Journal of Testing and Evaluation. 2017;**45**(6):1-7. DOI: 10.1520/JTE20160380

[20] Bruggeman BS, Vincent HK, Chi X, Filipp SL, Mercado R, Modave F, et al. Simple tests of cardiorespiratory fitness in a pediatric population. Marocolo M, editor. PLoS One. 2020;**15**(9):e0238863

[21] American Thoracic Society. ATS statement: Guidelines for the six-minute walk test. American Journal of Respiratory and Critical Care Medicine. 2002;**166**(1):111-117. DOI: 10.1164/rccm.166/1/111

[22] Mylius CF, Paap D, Takken T. Reference value for the 6-minute walk test in children and adolescents: A systematic review. Expert Review of Respiratory Medicine. 2016;**10**(12):1335-1352

[23] de AP CL, de Santana-Filho VJ, Maynard LG, Neto MG, Fernandes M, Carvalho VO. Reference values for the six-minute walk test in healthy children and adolescents: A systematic review. Brazilian Journal of Cardiovascular Surgery. 2016;**31**(5):381-388. DOI: 10.5935/1678-9741.20160081

[24] de AP CL, Carvalho VO, ADS P, CRA D, Ykeda DS, de Carvalho EM, et al. Reference values for the 6-min walk distance in healthy children age 7 to 12 years in Brazil: Main results of the TC6minBrasil multi-center study. Respiratory Care. 2018;**63**(3):339-346 Available from: https://rc.rcjournal.com/content/63/3/339

[25] Tomkinson G, Lang J, Blanchard J, Léger L, Tremblay M. The 20-m shuttle run: Assessment and interpretation of data in relation to youth aerobic fitness and health. Education, Health & Behavior Studies Faculty Publications [Internet]. 2019;**31**(2):5 Available from: https://commons.und.edu/cgi/viewcontent.cgi?article=1062&context=ehb-fac

[26] Marques A, Henriques-Neto D, Peralta M, Martins J, Gomes F, Popovic S, et al. Field-based health-related physical fitness tests in children and adolescents: A systematic review. Frontiers in Pediatrics. 2021;**5**:9

[27] Léger LA, Mercier D, Gadoury C, Lambert J. The multistage 20 metre shuttle run test for aerobic fitness. Journal of Sports Sciences. 1988;**6**(2):93-101. DOI: 10.1080/02640418808729800

[28] Fan C, Sun R, Nie M, Wang M, Yao Z, Feng Q, et al. The cardiorespiratory

fitness of children and adolescents in Tibet at altitudes over 3,500 meters. PLoS One. 2021;**16**(8):e0256258. DOI: 10.1371/journal.pone.0256258

[29] Järvamägi M, Riso E-M, Reisberg K, Jürim. Development of cardiorespiratory fitness in children in the transition from kindergarten to basic school according to participation in organized sports. Frontiers in Physiology. 2022;**13**:881364. DOI: 10.3389/fphys.2022.881364

[30] Sagat P, Stefan L, Petrić V, Stemberger V, Blacević I. Normative values of cardiorespiratory fitness in Croatian children and adolescents. PLoS One. 2023;**18**(4):e0284410. DOI: 10.1371/journal.pone.0284410

[31] Pojskic H, Eslami B. Relationship between obesity, physical activity, and cardiorespiratory fitness levels in children and adolescents in Bosnia and Herzegovina: An analysis of gender differences. Frontiers in Physiology. 2018;**9**:1734. DOI: 10.3389/fphys.2018.01734

[32] Mayorga-Vega D, Bocanegra-Parrilla R, Ornelas M, Viciana J. Criterion-related validity of the distance- and time-based walk/run field tests for estimating cardiorespiratory fitness: A systematic review and meta-analysis. PLoS One. 2016;**11**(3):e0151671. DOI: 10.1371/journal.pone.0151671

[33] Ortega FB, Ruiz JR, España-Romero V, Vicente-Rodriguez G, Martínez-Gómez D, Manios Y, et al. The international fitness scale (IFIS): Usefulness of self-reported fitness in youth. International Journal of Epidemiology. 2011;**40**(3):701-711. DOI: 10.1093/ije/dyr039

[34] Keating XD, Zhou K, Liu X, Hodges M, Liu J, Guan J, et al. Reliability and concurrent validity of global physical activity questionnaire (GPAQ): A systematic review. International Journal of Environmental Research and Public Health. 2019;**16**(21):4128. DOI: 10.3390/ijerph16214128

[35] Mahidol University, Institute for Population and Social Research: [03-February-2023]. Activity Questionnaire [GAC-PAQ]: A Multi-Country Study across Six Continents [Internet]. 2023. Available from: https://ipsr.mahidol.ac.th/en/post_research/proj-6601050/. [Accessed: July 20, 2023]

[36] Pereira DA, Correia Júnior JL, Carvas Junior N, Freitas-Dias R. Reliability of questionnaire The International Fitness Scale: a systematic review and meta-analysis. Einstein (São Paulo). 2020;**18**:eRW5232. DOI: 10.31744/einstein_journal/2020RW5232

[37] Smits-Engelsman BCM, Bonney E, Neto JLC, Jelsma DL. Feasibility and content validity of the PERF-FIT test battery to assess movement skills, agility and power among children in low-resource settings. BMC Public Health. 2020;**20**(1):1139. DOI: 10.1186/s12889-020-09236-w

[38] Lang JJ, Zhang K, Agostinis-Sobrinho C, Andersen LB, Basterfield L, Berglind D, et al. Top 10 international priorities for physical fitness research and surveillance among children and adolescents: A twin-panel Delphi study. Sports Medicine (Auckland, N.Z.). 2023;**53**(2):549-564. DOI: 10.1007/s40279-022-01752-6

[39] Sousa AC, Ferrinho SN, Travassos B. The use of wearable technologies in the assessment of physical activity in preschool- and school-age youth: Systematic review. International Journal of Environmental Research and Public Health. 2023;**20**(4):3402. DOI: 10.3390/ijerph20043402

[40] Giurgiu M, Kolb S, Nigg C, et al. Assessment of 24-hour physical behaviour in children and adolescents via wearables: A systematic review of free-living validation studies. BMJ Open Sport & Exercise Medicine. 2022;**8**:e001267. DOI: 10.1136/bmjsem-2021-001267

[41] Topalidis P, Florea C, Eigl E-S, Kurapov A, Leon CAB, Schabus M. Evaluation of a low-cost commercial Actigraph and its potential use in detecting cultural variations in physical activity and sleep. Sensors. 2021;**21**:3774. DOI: 10.3390/s21113774

[42] Nasruddin NIN, Murphy J, Armstrong MEG. Physical activity surveillance in children and adolescents using smartphone technology: Systematic review. JMIR Pediatrics and Parenting. 2023;**6**:e42461. DOI: 10.2196/42461

Chapter 4

Motor Games for Learning Fundamental Motor Skills

Valentina Biino

Abstract

Active Initiation Guidelines recommend that children up to age 5 years engage in daily physical activity to develop basic motor skills for health-related fitness. However, many entering kindergarten today have low motor skills and many more are predicted to have lower motor coordination skills tomorrow. Recent studies suggest that children who do not adequately develop their movement skills and fitness levels in early childhood will fail to progress them later in life. This chapter presents a literature review of motor competence in young children and suggests game playing as a means for preschoolers to learn fundamental motor skills in locomotor and object control skills.

Keywords: game, children, preschoolers, fundamental motor skills, MVPA

1. Introduction

Two fundamental questions lie at the core of human motor learning: how can movement skills be learned and which movement skills need to be acquired. Humans have both the capacity for skilled movement and the ability to learn it. Without essential movement skills, we would be defenseless against the dangers around us and unable to expand the spectrum of body-mind development that communication with the surrounding environment demands [1, 2]. As we learn to move, we encounter and overcome obstacles; we climb, keep our balance, and manipulate objects while doing so, thus using every opportunity to explore more and more. Besides the need to survive, we sense a fundamental need to move. Without the ability to master basic motor skills adequately, we could not satisfy our need to move.

Stodden's conceptual model [3] explains the role of motor competence in children's willingness to move according to body weight and in reaction to perceived motor competence and health-related fitness. Later studies [4–6] provided longitudinal and experimental evidence to support this conceptual model. Children will have few opportunities to participate in physical activity, play and sports later in life if they lack the basic skills for running, jumping, kicking, catching, throwing and hitting. If, instead, they are provided with the necessary skills to participate in physical and recreational activities, they are more likely to be active throughout life.

There is a reciprocal relationship between the degree of competence in fundamental motor skills and participation in physical activity: higher levels of motor competence correspond to higher levels of participation in physical activity and play, with a consequent increase in active lifestyles. In addition, the fundamental motor skills underlying many of the diverse activities of daily life that make survival possible are acquired during growth and into maturity. Rosengren and colleagues [7] reported that children should be assigned exercises that focus on solving a movement task potentially related to survival (e.g., walking, running, climbing, grasping), so-called motor development tasks, or exercises that require expertise (e.g., riding a bicycle, dancing, rolling an object) which, albeit less concerned with survival, are more sensitive to expertise, the so-called motor learning tasks.

Young children can improve the quality, speed, and control of fundamental motor skills (FMS) to meet demands that go far beyond mere survival. The age of onset for mature models of FMS is between 2 and 6 years [8]. The development of motor skills concerns the movements used to move the body from one place to another and those that enable throwing and catching objects [9]. The period encompassing kindergarten and first grade primary school is when FMS can be best developed and refined.

As children acquire and perfect their FMS, they build their motor competence: they experience the changes in motor behavior and the processes that underlie such changes. Using the metaphor of the "motor development mountain", Clark and Metcalfe [10] suggested that FMS act as precursors of movement skills. It follows then that to reach "the top of the mountain", children must acquire a certain level of competence in FMS in order to be able to apply these skills in the various contexts of sports and motor activities of daily life. FMS can also be compared to real "building blocks" for the construction of increasingly advanced and complex movements required for playing games and sports and/or other physical activities [11, 12].

2. What kind of physical activity supports learning motor skills?

Motor development and motor/skill learning are central to successful outcomes in multiple domains. A domain is a category within which similar skills can be grouped. A motor skill can be defined as the means to successfully accomplish the goals of a particular skill. It is primarily determined by the quality of movement and is not necessarily relevant to a specific sport. One thing common to all motor skills is that they must be learned. A person may be categorized either as unskilled or highly skilled, depending on how well the skill has been learned and practiced [13]. People are not born possessing movement skills but rather acquire them so as to adapt to the demands of their environment.

Three aspects characterize motor skills: the perceptive requirements, the muscle coordination patterns involved, and the demands imposed by the environment. Furthermore, motor skills belong not only to the motor domain but are composites of all three domains: motor, cognitive, and perceptual [14]. Motor skill development engages children's perceptual and cognitive abilities and involves their social development as well (**Figure 1**) [15].

Motor activities that include learning FMS are essential for the development of motor competence in children, as they start to coordinate the muscles of the limbs with those of the body to generate the desired movement [11]. Children need to be provided with ample opportunities for structured practice starting in early childhood to improve their motor performance skills.

Scientific research shows that motor skills interventions are effective for improving FMS and moderate to vigorous intensity physical activity (MVPA) [16, 17].

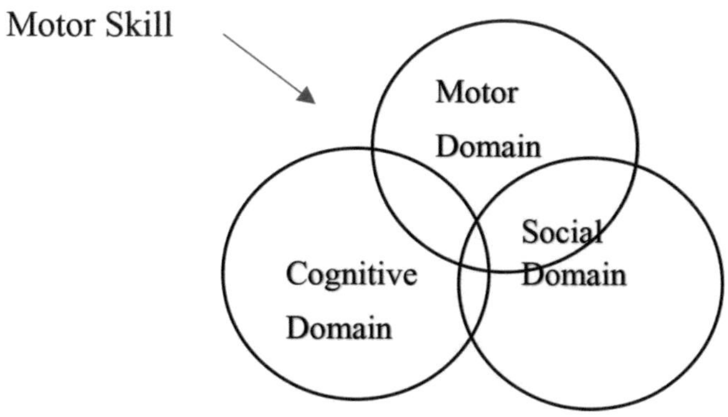

Figure 1.
Holistic approach.

Early childhood education centers should have planned movement programs in place as well as strategies to promote the development of motor skills in children. Implementing motor skills interventions is an effective strategy to improve FMS. Wadsworth and colleagues [18] reported that interventions based on FMS learning boosted MVPA. Girls and boys of all ages, and kindergarten schoolchildren in particular, generally preferred exercises that focus on motor skills (FMS group) learning or mixed (FMS + physical activity group) to free play and physical activity, demonstrating that interventions that combine both FMS and physical activity may reduce physical activity disparities in preschool children.

Yet, it is not sufficient to improve children's cognitive functioning by training a motor activity or practicing a game based only on promoting competence in FMS. Instead, exercise of basic motor skills needs to be expanded and progressed through fun games or goal setting strategies [19] such as "how many times can you hit the target on the wall by throwing a ball for 5 minutes'?" [20]. When considering a holistic approach to development, motor activities should challenge children's mental skills and the physical abilities needed to refine them [21]. Children enjoy themselves in a learning environment where they can explore and solve problems. Motor activities should therefore be designed to promote deliberate play [22], which refers to games and sports that are intrinsically motivating, provide immediate gratification, and maximize enjoyment [23]. However, regardless of the type of exercises practiced, children improve at problem solving when confronted with variety in the problems they encounter [21]. This is why it is important that the activities are varied in practice and continuously "destabilized" [24, 25]. Motivation to succeed in executing movement is inherent in children. It is related to what they have learned about themselves and how they perceive their abilities.

The key to successful mastering of motor skills in children is that they are taught, so it is crucial that children be provided with clearly stated instructions for learning the critical components of a movement. Teaching the key elements of movement will increase the chances of executing a movement successfully and developing that movement correctly and skillfully in the future. The bad habits that children have learned in early life will heavily influence their motor competence later on and will probably render the movement less effective and smooth [21].

Starting from an early age children should be provided with appropriately graded experiences, instruction, correction, as well as encouragement and feedback [26, 27]. Verbal encouragement provided by a competent adult motivates the child to marshal effort and stick to the task. Children learn early on the difference between enthused encouragement that sounds authentic and believable and generic cheering with little meaning. For this reason, a physical education teacher, given his or her competence and trained eye, can more credibly provide encouragement that strongly supports children during a game.

Moreover, muscle tension, heart rate, and sweating increase during a game. Young children with limited exposure to MVPA may perceive such sensory experience as negative (fear, anxiety) or positive (novel pleasure, fun, joy). Teachers' feedback during the initial phase of teaching an exercise or a game can help the child understand and recognize the physical activation that constitutes the core of playing a game [21].

Playing games catalyzes and promotes the development and acquisition of motor skills, reduces boredom, and promotes previously learned FMS. Developing FMS improves physical literacy, increases self-confidence, and provides a more positive attitude towards exercise. The "play now or pay later" concept [28] characterizes physical activity as a means to prevent a cascade of adverse health outcomes later in life. Physical activity may be considered a primary prevention with a positive impact on promoting an active lifestyle. Physical education teachers should therefore provide meaningful opportunities for children to participate in a variety of physical activity games through programs that are developmentally appropriate, meaningful, and enjoyable [28]. Children should progress through well-known physical activity games. For example, children who play *Hide and seek, jump rope*, or play to *One, Two, Three... Star* in Italy or *One, Two, Three... Sun* in France or *One, Two, Three... Pumpkin* in Mexico and so on, learn many abilities because in this games there are locomotor skills and stability tasks such as run, jump, leap, stop and go. Children who play the various versions of *Speedy Swapper*s or try to tag and catch opponents learn how to run, to spring or to move while chasing, fleeing or dodging opponents. Looked at it this way, the motor games that children play can provide much insight into the skills they can potentially acquire. Physical growth and regular exercise have a crucial role in the ways movement patterns can change [29].

Over the years, the preconception has been dismissed that FMS are important only for participating in sports or physical activity in general and achieving the recommended dose of daily physical activity. Neuroscience has made substantial advances in linking physical activity to cognitive performance, as well as brain structure and function [30]. Throughout growth and development, close links exist between brain activity and movement [31]. Donnelly and colleagues [32] found that participation in sports and physical activity boosts mental acuity, skills and strategies that are vital for coping with life's challenges. Previous studies have shown that regular exercise alters higher brain functions, i.e., the executive system, by improving the switching from one type of task to another, regulating the updating and tracking of representative information in working memory, and inhibiting strong habitual responses [24, 25, 33]. Furthermore, studies involving preschool children have shown that those with higher proficiency in FMS and physical activity have better working memory, attention, and inhibitory control [34]. Mastering FMS is crucial for holistic development in the physical, cognitive-perceptual and relational domains [12].

Regular participation in aerobic physical activity with a good mastery of FMS can induce lasting improvement in executive functions via three pathways: the cognitive engagement required in challenging motor activities, complex coordination tasks, and the physiological changes in the brain that aerobic exercise induces [33]. In their literature review, Donnelly and colleagues [32] reported an association between physical activity, physical fitness, cognition, and academic achievement. For instance, improvement in executive function was associated with acute bouts of physical activity and physical fitness and improvement in academic performance was associated with both acute and chronic physical activity in general [14]. In brief, providing instruction in physical education can lead to improvement in academic performance. In their review, Macdonald et al. [35] found that refinement of motor skills is positively associated with academic achievement in mathematics and reading, especially during early school years. Positive associations also emerged between academic achievement and components of gross motor competence, particularly speed and agility, upper limb coordination, and FMS proficiency levels.

Mastery of FMS is not only the starting point for any form of motor development but also for cognitive development: a real structure that progressively becomes logical, mental, thought and verbal organization. A holistic approach defines physical and mental domains not only as complementary but also as indivisible and interdependent. Children master the majority of FMS by age 6 years [36]. This skills set is a key aim in the national primary school curriculum (Department for Education. Early Years Foundation Internship Statutory Framework; Department for Education: London, UK, 2014). Despite the aim of the program and the potential for development, however, many children fail to master these skills.

Recent research [5, 22] suggests that nearly half of children leave school without having mastered the basic motor skills for successful participation in sports and physical activity. Some studies have reported a non-linear trend for motor competence across time [37, 38], with peak performance at 8–9 years of age and a plateau in locomotor skills occurring as early as 10 years Vandorpe et al., [37]. Why? What happens or what does not happen during the so-called "sampling years" [38] when children should participate in a wide range of activities centered on deliberate play for fun [23]? How is this time spent in the "hungry for skills" stage when children learn to enjoy exercising and developing movement skills?

It is far from proven that skills levels naturally reach the threshold that encourages, motivates or facilitates participation in motor games [16, 21, 39]. Stodden et al. [3] suggested that physical activity during early childhood can guide children's growth in motor competence. Children with higher levels of motor skill proficiency in FMS in middle and late childhood will more likely maintain physical activity for longer periods of time and continue to improve their motor skills. An increase in physical activity can mean more opportunities to promote motor development. From infancy onwards, depending on the level of participation in physical activity, a sort of positive spiral can be created for developing high motor competence, with more time devoted to daily physical activity to achieve higher health-related fitness levels. Chronically low motor competence levels indicate a negative attitude towards physical activity and physical fitness, with a greater predisposition to weight gain and obesity.

Furthermore, motor performance influences how a child is viewed by peers [9]. Less skilled children will generally be chosen last to join a team in group games during recess and extracurricular activities. Being chosen last or not at all can have a negative impact on a child's physical self-concept and motivation to get active and play with peers.

2.1 What are the fundamental motor skills?

Clark [10] defined FMS as the "principal patterns of coordination that underlie later movement skillfulness" (p. 251). Motor skills rely on the coordination of arms or legs and the body. Depending on speed and strength parameters, a motor skill is a learned, goal-directed activity accomplished by muscle action. This classic definition of motor skills contains the word "learned", which means that motor skills can be improved.

Three macro categories of skills are distinguished [12, 17]:

- Locomotor skills. Skills that allow you to move your body from one point in space to another using mainly the muscles of the lower limbs (e.g., walking, running, jumping, hopping, galloping).

- Interaction and object control/manipulation skills. Skills that involve a muscle sequence that allows you to interact and control/manipulate objects with your body (e.g., catching and throwing, hitting or kicking objects).

- Postural skills. Skills that stabilize certain body segments in relation to other segments, to the whole body or to external objects, while holding a body position for best executing a specific task in static and dynamic balance (**Figure 2**).

FMS are typically categorized as object control and locomotor skills [9, 32]. Some authors define balance and stability skills as the locomotor skills underlying FMS considered independently and essential for learning motor literacy [11].

Motor skills emerge and mature during preschool and primary school years. While children continue to develop these skills as they grow, focused instruction, guidance, appropriate feedback, and encouragement are essential for the acquisition of motor skills [22]. Young children in particular need to learn how to execute and correct their movements so that they can progress in developing their skills.

And in order for that to happen, teachers should illustrate the technique and state clearly how to execute a movement from the start. They should express themselves using a vocabulary shared with the children so that the technique can be described and memorized. For example, effective instruction on the execution of skipping could be given as follows:

- *"Now take a step forward and hop on the spot with the same leg, then take a step with the other leg and hop. And so on: step and hop on one leg, step and hop on the other leg".*

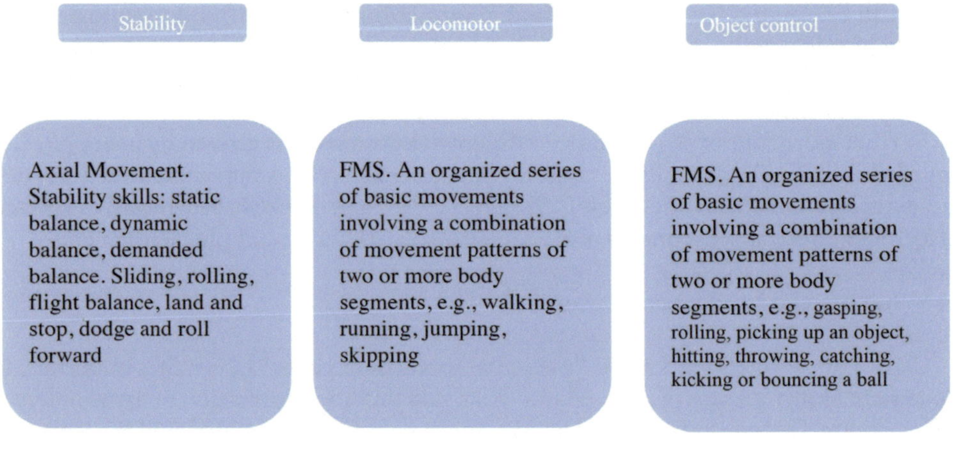

Figure 2.
Fundamental motor skills scheme.

Given that instructions can also be given during the execution of a movement, the teacher will need to keep explanation to a minimum and simplify it with keywords that accompany the movement rhythmically:

- *step-hop/step-hop*

In brief: step and hop on the same foot while moving the arms in opposition. After stepping, both feet are temporarily off the ground. The body moves forward in a rhythmic motion.

Since teaching and assessment are inseparable, the level of FMS learning is monitored to inform exercise programming. Well designed assessments are not perceived as tests but rather as part of progression through a program. As FMS emerge and mature between age 3 and 10 years, they are categorized as locomotor skills, among which gross motor skills require smooth, coordinated movements of the body in spacc. For example:

- *running.* The ability to advance steadily with springing steps so that both feet leave the ground for an instant with each stride.
- *galloping*. The ability to maintain a fast, natural, three-beat gait.
- *hopping.* The ability to hop a minimum distance on the preferred foot.
- *skipping.* The ability to skip in continuous, rhymical, alternating steps.
- *horizontal jumping.* The ability to take a horizontal jump from a standing position.
- *sliding*. The ability to slide sideways in a straight line from one point to another.

FMS include common ball handling skills:

- *Two-hand strike of a stationary ball. S*trike a stationary ball with a plastic bat.
- *One-hand forehand strike while-bouncing a ball.* Strike a bouncing ball with a plastic paddle.
- *Two-hand catch.* Catch a ball that has been thrown underhand.
- *Kick a stationary ball.* Kick a stationary ball with the preferred foot.
- *Overhand throw.* Throw a ball with the preferred hand while aiming at a point on a wall.
- *Underhand throw.* Throw a ball with the preferred hand while aiming at a point on a wall [9].

3. Relation between fundamental motor skill and cardiorespiratory fitness

Many studies suggests that motor competence (MC) and cardiorespiratory fitness (CRF) have declined in children and adolescences [38, 40–42]. This fact has made the current generation less able and fit to participate in various physical and daily life activities than previous generations. These changes in MC, CRF and Physical activity in children and adolescences have been suggested to lead to a negative circle leading to an increase risk overweight and obesity [43, 44]. MC is widely recognized as an important correlate of physical activity (PA), weight status and of a psychological and social physical benefits. It is understood that MC is a precursor to PA as learning to move is necessary for participation in PA [3]. The development of MC that includes FMS begins at birth through the acquisition of locomotor, object manipulation and stability skills, before becoming a central pillar of lifetime education. Mastery of FMS influences children's BMI and time spent sedentary already at preschool age [45]. Wadsworth et al. [18] showed that FMS learning focus even improves MVPA in younger boys and girls.

While a longitudinal study [46] has explained that a greater lean body mass could be associated to more suitable Gross Motor Coordination levels.

The question that arises is understandable: do the decline in MC and CRF levels could depend on the percentage of fat mass in children and adolescences?

Several allometric approaches [43, 46] have shown that MC is an important determinant of body composition; many batteries test used to assess MC are highly dependent on fat mass, as well as CRF scaled by BMI it depends on adiposity. But there is a positive association between MC and CRF as a function of the percentage of fat mass? The results of the Haapala study et al. [43], showed that children with poor MC levels had low CRF levels scaled by BMI, and fat mass is included in BMI; instead children with lower and higher levels of MC had similar CFF levels, scalded by lean mass. Therefore the association between MC and fat mass, in this case, is not depended on CRF.

In the educational context this evidence opens the possibility of not precluding coordination or VPA aerobic activities The aerobic exercise when it consist of running and jumping games of the rope, basketball and football modified to one heart rate was set at an average above 150 beats per minute, can represent an effective means of jointly achieving good levels of both MC and CRF.

Cardiovascular fitness, resistance, strength and flexibility are essential in developmental age as in all ages [28, 46]. Advances in studies on the cardiovascular system have made it clear how children respond and adapt to aerobic training. Today, pediatricians and educators, while continuing to be wary towards physical stress and effort in children, prescribe moderate to vigorous intensity physical activity (Moderate – to – Vigorous Physical Activity, MVPA). However, children are not little adults and cannot enjoy the same exercise routine as adults. The activity patterns of children differ greatly from those adults [21]. This is to be kept in mind in sports and school settings as appropriate or inappropriate programs can influence children's motivation to be active. To train physical efficiency in children, the scientific community suggests systematically encouraging fundamental motor skills in a playful and cooperative way. Physical activity games represent a suitable and effective means of developing coordination and physical fitness in children.

FMS need to be learned, practiced, and reinforced [47]. Improvement in motor proficiency have been attributed to FMS applied to a variety of games and sports. For example, you need to be able to run, jump, pitch and hit a ball in order to play baseball.

Unfortunately, children are sometimes more motivated by what they are capable of doing than by learning how to do a skill correctly. Prekindergarten children can hit, roll or kick a ball even when the move is made with the wrong step. Without correction, a poor motor pattern becomes a habit that is very difficult to unlearn [48]. It should be remembered therefore that the constructs of motor enjoyment and self-efficacy are

Figure 3.
Morra game.

essential precursors of long-term engagement in play and physical activity. If children know how to do things correctly, they feel better about themselves and make progress. To foster this sense of satisfaction, the correct execution of FMS must be clearly illustrated as needed while playing a game. In this way, the game situation allows for introducing increasingly complex coordination tasks. Modifying game rules to challenge children cognitively can be a daunting and demanding task, even for the most experienced teacher. This is illustrated in three modified traditional games to which a specific locomotor element is added (**Figure 3**).

The Week

A grid of small and large rectangles is drawn with chalk on the ground.

The children jump and hop in the grid or a mix inside the rectangles, depending on size or distance.

One, Two, Three...Skip

Players spread out in scatter formation. They choose one of the locomotor skills; keeping it in mind, they stand still like statue in the starting position of that locomotor skill. When the game leader calls the players, must move and perform that locomotor skill correctly.

Paper, Rock...Six

Players challenge each other in pairs in a game of *Morra*, a traditional game that trains the ability to calculate while calling out the number of the players' fingers shown in a flat hand. The player that manages to count first, grabs a handkerchief and runs away, and the other tries to catch it.

4. Conclusion

Motivating kindergarten and primary school children to engage in motor activity can be quite easy. For small children, any call to move is perceived as an invitation to play. Whether making a basket, jumping rope or knocking down cones, just doing it can be a remarkable new discovery. However, once children discover they can hit a target, score a basket or kick a ball, it's hard to get them to go back and work on the critical elements of those skills.

What is important is to remember that FMS incorporate not only the actual competence to perform physical skills but also the psychological and behavioral skills that enable engagement in physical activity. Quality early physical experiences, appropriately graded, can ensure optimal development of FMS so that children can refine their actual and perceived skills. In light of the above, the syllabus of physical activity programs needs to be examined as regards quality physical education and early childhood sports instruction to ensure can be fully developed in pre- and school-age segments of the population.

Conflict of interest

The author declare no conflict of interest.

Author details

Valentina Biino
University of Verona, Italy

*Address all correspondence to: valentina.biino@univr.it

References

[1] National Association for Sport and Physical Education. Active Start: A Statement of Physical Activity Guidelines for Children Birth to Five Years. 2nd ed. Oxon Hill, MD: AAHPERD; 2009

[2] Bernstein NA. On dexterity and its development. In: Latash ML, Turvey MT. Dexterity and Its Development, translated by Latash ML. London, New York: Routledge Taylor and Francis Group; 1996

[3] Stodden DF, Langendorfer SJ, Goodway JD, Roberton MA, Rudisill ME, GarciaC,et al.Adevelopmentalperspective on the role of motor skill competence in physical activity: An emergent relationship. Quest. 2008;**60**(2):290-306. DOI: 10.1080/00336297.2008.10483582

[4] Battaglia G, Giustino V, Tabacchi G, Lanza M, Schena F, Biino V, et al. Interrelationship between age, gender, and weight status on motor coordination in Italian children and early adolescents aged 6-13 years old. Frontiers in Pediatrics. 2021;**9**(September):1-10. DOI: 10.3389/fped.2021.738294

[5] Barnett LM, Webster EK, Hulteen RM, De Meester A, Valentini NC, Lenoir M, et al. Through the looking glass: A systematic review of longitudinal evidence, providing new insight for motor competence and health. Sports medicine (Auckland, N.Z.). 2022;**52**(4):875-920. DOI: 10.1007/s40279-021-01516-8

[6] Gallotta MC, Zimatore G, Falcioni L, Migliaccio S, Lanza M, Schena F, et al. Influence of geographical area and living setting on Children's weight status, motor coordination, and physical activity. Frontiers in Pediatrics. 2022;**9**:794284. DOI: 10.3389/fped.2021.794284

[7] Rosengren KS, Geert JP, Savelsbergh GJ. Development and learning: ATASC-based perspective of the acquisition of perceptual-motor behaviors. Infant Behavior and Development. 2003;**26**:473-494. DOI: 10.1016/j.infbeh.2003.08.001

[8] Gallahue D, Cleland-Donnelly F. Developmental Physical Education for all Children. 4th ed. Champaign, IL: Human Kinetics; 2007

[9] Dale U. Evaluation of the psychometric properties of the TGMD-3. Journal of Motor Learning and Development. 2019;**5**(1):4

[10] Clark JE, Metcalfe JS. The mountain of motor development: A metaphor. In: Clark JE, Humphrey J, editors. motor development: Research and reviews. Vol. Vol. 2. Reston, VA: NASPE Publications; 2002. pp. 163-190

[11] Logan SW, Ross SM, Chee K, Stodden DF, Robinson LE. Fundamental motor skills: A systematic review of terminology. Journal of Sports Sciences. 2018;**36**(7):781-796. DOI: 10.1080/02640414.2017.1340660

[12] Bolger LE, Bolger LA, O'Neill C, Coughlan E, O'Brien W, Lacey S, et al. Global levels of fundamental motor skills in children: A systematic review. Journal of Sports Sciences. 2021;**39**(7):717-753. DOI: 10.1080/02640414.2020.1841405

[13] Ericsson KA. The Road to Excellence: The Acquisition of Expert Performance in the Arts and Sciences, Sports, and Games. Mahwah, NJ: Lawrence Erlbaum; 1996

[14] Biino V, Bertinato L, Rossini P, Giuriato M. Influence of highly

motivational games on the executive function in adolescence. Journal of Physical Education and Sport. 2020;**20**((3)):1386-1391. DOI: 10.7752/jpes.2020.03191

[15] Edwards WH. Motor Learning and Control: From Theory to Practice. Wadsworth Cengage Learning; 2010, California State University, Sacramento. Copyright 2010 Cengage Learning, Inc. All Rights Reserved. Library of Congress Control Number: 2010922549, ISBN-13: 978-0-495-01080-7, ISBN-10: 0-495-01080-4Wadsworth, 20 Davis Drive Belmont, CA 94002-3098 USA

[16] Logan SW, Robinson LE, Wilson AE, Lucas WA. Getting the fundamentals of movement: A meta-analysis of the effectiveness of motor skill interventions in children. Child: Care, Health and Development. 2012;**38**(3):305-315. DOI: 10.1111/j.1365-2214.2011.01307.x

[17] Webster EK, Martin CK, Staiano AE. Fundamental motor skills, screen-time, and physical activity in preschoolers. Journal of Sport and Health Science. 2019;**8**(2):114-121. DOI: 10.1016/j.jshs.2018.11.006

[18] Wadsworth DD, Johnson JL, Carroll AV, Pangelinan MM, Rudisill ME, Sassi J. Intervention strategies to elicit MVPA in Preschoolers during outdoor play. International Journal of Environmental Research and Public Health. 2020;**17**(2):650. DOI: 10.3390/ijerph17020650

[19] Lee J, Zhang T, Chu T, Gu X, Zhu P. Effects of a fundamental motor skill-based afterschool program on Children's physical and cognitive health outcomes. International Journal of Environmental Research and Public Health. 2020;**17**(3):733. DOI: 10.3390/ijerph17030733

[20] Tomporowsky P, McCullik B, Pesce C. Enhancing Children's Cognition with Physical Activity Games. Human Kinetics Publishers; 2015, Printed in the United State of America. United States: Human Kinetics, P.O. Box 5076, Champaign, IL 61825-5076 800-747-4457

[21] MacNamara Á, Collins D, Giblin S. Just let them play? Deliberate preparation As the Most appropriate Foundation for Lifelong Physical Activity. Frontiers in Psychology. 2015;**6**:1548. DOI: 10.3389/fpsyg.2015.01548

[22] Côté J, Baker J, Abernethy B. Play and practice in the development of sport expertise. In: Tenenbaum G, Eklund RC, editors. Handbook of Sport Psychology. Hoboken, NJ: John Wiley & Sons; 2007. pp. 184-202

[23] Pesce C, Croce R, Ben-Soussan TD, Vazou S, McCullick B, Tomporowski PD, et al. Variability of practice as an Interface between motor and cognitive development. International Journal of Sport and Exercise Psychology. 2019;**17**(2):133-152. DOI: 10.1080/1612197X.2016.1223421

[24] Biino V, Tinagli V, Borioni F, Pesce C. Cognitively enriched physical activity may foster motor competence and executive function as early as preschool age: A pilot trial. Physical Education and Sport Pedagogy. 2021. pp. 2-19. DOI: 10.1080/17408989.2021.1990249

[25] Altunsoz IH, Goodway JD. SKIPing to motor competence: The influence of project successful kinesthetic instruction for preschoolers on motor competence of disadvantaged preschoolers. Physical Education and Sport Pedagogy. 2016. pp. 3-17. DOI: 10.1080/17408989.2015.1017453

[26] Brian AS, Goodway JD, Sutherland SL. Training teachers to SKIP:

A motor skill intervention pilot study. Research Quarterly for Exercise and Sport. 2014;**85**(S1):A42

[27] Faigenbaum AD, Myer GD. Exercise deficit disorder in youth: Play now or pay later. Current Sports Medicine Reports. 2012;**11**:196-200. DOI: 10.1249/JSR.0b013e31825da961

[28] Griffiths A, Toovey R, Morgan PE, Spittle AJ. Psychometric properties of gross motor assessment tools for children: A systematic review. BMJ Open. 2018;**8**:e021734. DOI: 10.1136/bmjopen-2018-021734

[29] Diamond A. Executive Functions. Annual Review of Psychology. 2013;**64**:135-168. DOI: 10.1146/annurev-psych-113011-143750

[30] Galdi M, D'Anna C, Pastena N, Paloma FG. Gross-motor skills for potential intelligence descriptive study in a kindergarten. Procedia - Social and Behavioral Sciences. 2015;**174**(February):3797-3804. DOI: 10.1016/j.sbspro.2015.01.1115

[31] Donnelly JE, Ed D, Co-chair F, Hillman CH, Co-chair PD, Ph D, et al. Physical activity, fitness, cognitive function, and academic achievement in children: A systematic review. In Medicine and Science in Sports and Exercise. 2017;**48**(6):1-36. DOI: 10.1249/MSS.0000000000000901.Physical

[32] Best JR. Effects of physical activity on children's executive function: Contributions of experimental research on aerobic exercise. Developmental Review. 2010;**30**:331-351. DOI: 10.1016/j.dr.2010.08.001

[33] Malambo C, Nová A, Clark C, Musálek M. Associations between fundamental movement skills, physical fitness, motor competency, physical activity, and executive functions in pre-school age children: A systematic review. Children. 2022;**9**(7):1-14. DOI: 10.3390/children9071059

[34] Macdonald K, Milne N, Orr R, Pope R. Relationships between motor proficiency and academic performance in mathematics and reading in school-aged children and adolescents: A systematic review. International Journal of Environmental Research and Public Health. 2018;**15**(8):1-23. DOI: 10.3390/ijerph15081603

[35] Eyre ELJ, Walker LJ, Duncan MJ. Fundamental movement skills of children living in England: The role of ethnicity and native English language. Perceptual and Motor Skills. 2018;**125**(1):5-20. DOI: 10.1177/0031512517745437

[36] Vandorpe B, Vandendriessche J, Lefevre J, Pion J, Vaeyens R, Matthys S, et al. The KörperkoordinationsTest für kinder: Reference values and suit ability for 6-12-year-old children in Flanders. Scandinavian Journal of Medicine & Science in Sports. 2011;**21**(3):378-388. DOI: 10.1111/j.1600-0838.2009.01067

[37] Giuriato M, Biino V, Bellafiore M, Battaglia G, Palma A, Baldari C, et al. Gross motor coordination: We have a problem! A study with the Körperkoordinations test für kinder in youth (6-13 years). Frontiers in Pediatrics. 2021;**9**(December):1-12. DOI: 10.3389/fped.2021.785990

[38] Kirk D. Physical education, youth sport and lifelong participation: The importanceof early learning experiences. European Physical Education Review. 2005;**11**:239-255. DOI: 10.1177/1356336X05056649

[39] Vandoni M, Carnevale Pellino V, Gatti A, Lucini D, Mannarino S, Larizza C, et al. Effects of

an online supervised exercise training in children with obesity during the COVID-19 pandemic. International Journal of Environmental Research and Public Health. 2022;**19**(15):9421. DOI: 10.3390/ijerph19159421

[40] Sember V, Đurić S, Starc G, Leskošek B, Sorić M, Kovač M, et al. Secular trends in skill-related physical fitness among Slovenian children and adolescents from 1983 to 2014. Scandinavian Journal of Medicine & Science in Sports. 2023. pp. 1-12. DOI: 10.1111/sms.14456

[41] Fühner T, Kliegl R, Arntz F, Kriemler S, Granacher U. An update on secular trends in physical fitness of children and adolescents from 1972 to 2015: A systematic review. Sports medicine (Auckland, N.Z.). 2021;**51**(2):303-320. DOI: 10.1007/s40279-020-01373-x

[42] Haapala EA, Gao Y, Lintu N, Väistö J, Vanhala A, Tompuri T, et al. Associations between cardiorespiratory fitness, motor competence, and adiposity in children. Translational Sports Medicine. 2021;**4**(1):56-64. DOI: 10.1002/tsm2.198 http://hdl.handle.net/10138/334831

[43] Lima RA, Pfeiffer KA, Bugge A, Møller NC, Andersen LB, Stodden DF. Motor competence and cardiorespiratory fitness have greater influence on body fatness than physical activity across time. Scandinavian Journal of Medicine & Science in Sports. 2017;**27**(12):1638-1647. DOI: 10.1111/sms.12850

[44] Duncan MJ, Hall C, Eyre E, Barnett LM, James RS. Pre-schoolers fundamental movement skills predict BMI, physical activity, and sedentary behavior: A longitudinal study. Scandinavian Journal of Medicine & Science in Sports. 2021;**31**(Suppl. 1):8-14. DOI: 10.1111/sms.13746

[45] Giuriato M, Lovecchio N, Carnevale Pellino V, Mieszkowski J, Kawczyński A, Nevill A, et al. Gross motor coordination and their relationship with body mass and physical activity level during growth in children aged 8-11 years old: A longitudinal and allometric approach. PeerJ. 2022;**10**:e13483. DOI: 10.7717/peerj.13483

[46] World Health Organization. Global Action Plan on Physical Activity 2018-2030: More Active People for a Healthier World. Geneva: World Health Organization; 2018

[47] Brian A, Goodway JD, Logan JA, Sutherland S. SKIPing with teachers: An early years motor skill intervention. Physical Education and Sport Pedagogy. 2017;**22**(3):270-282. DOI: 10.1080/17408989.2016.1176133

[48] Colvin AV, Markos NJ, Walker PJ. Teaching Fundamental Motor Skills. 3rd ed. IL, USA: Human Kinetict; 2023

Chapter 5

Making Physical Activities a Part of a Child's Life

Endang Ernandini and Jonathan Alvin Wiryaputra

Abstract

Children will grow and develop to their fullest potential by learning from others, imitating, playing, engaging in activities, and socializing. There are several benefits to engaging in regular physical activity. Engaging in exercise habits or participating in sports organizations strengthens abilities, hand-eye coordination skills, functional movement skills, as well as strength, academic performance, and self-management skills in daily life, have higher bone mineral density and lower risks of cardiovascular issues, overweight, or obesity in young adulthood. It is important to note that tests are based on movements that are enjoyable and commonly performed by children aged 5–12 years as part of their daily activities. In children's Resistance Training exercises, strength-building often involves movements such as frog jumps, bear crawls, crab walks, kangaroo hops, and one-leg hops. There is a lot of research data indicating that physical activity can benefit some children with congenital diseases, too.

Keywords: children, physical activities, play, motoric, senosric

1. Introduction

A healthy child is characterized by growth and development as they age. Parents, healthcare professionals, school teachers, and relatives—all individuals in a child's environment—must cooperate and coordinate to help children reach their optimal potential. Children will grow and develop to their fullest potential by learning from others, imitating, playing, engaging in activities, and socializing.

Physical activity (PA) plays an important role in a child's life, even into their later years, and it has a positive impact on a child's mental health [1]. Physical activity has been proven to contribute positively to social, emotional, and cognitive development [2]. Research by Iivonen and Zeng also shows that the development of motor skills is greatly influenced by physical activity [3, 4]. The development of motor skills significantly affects an individual's ability to fulfill daily life tasks. The relationship between physical activity and motor development is not unidirectional but reciprocal. To achieve their sensory and motor abilities, children require experiences from their everyday lives. Therefore, childhood is a critical period of development that will shape their future lives. The relationship is seen to be bidirectional, not unidirectional, in a child's life [5]. From the early stages, children require experiences for their sensory and motor abilities, making childhood a critical period for their development [5].

Does a child's life with different health statuses result in different physical activity needs? And what about age? Do children's needs change as they grow older?

Over the past few decades, children's physical activities have undergone dramatic changes. Motoric physical activities have been replaced by indoor activities, and sometimes even just playing with gadgets. It is rare to see children playing in fields or mountains after school, exploring the outdoors, and searching for fruits in the forest. This is likely due to the crowded and built-up environment and the increasing amount of schoolwork that requires children to spend time in front of laptops.

The World Health Organization (WHO) defines physical activity as any bodily movement produced by skeletal muscles that requires energy expenditure. Physical activity includes all activities during leisure time, work time, and when moving from one place to another. It encompasses moderate to vigorous activities, including sports. WHO has recommended specific amounts of physical activity based on age and specific populations, taking into account brain development, muscle capacity, cardiovascular and respiratory function, sleep needs, and nutritional requirements. For children under 1 year old, physical activity should be divided into various time intervals and performed on mats or the floor. Let infants engage in supervised tummy time for at least 30 minutes, divided into several intervals. When the baby is awake, it should not be confined or restrained for more than 1 hour at a time, such as when sitting in a high chair, stroller, or being carried. Their sleep needs should be fulfilled, with 14–17 hours for infants aged 0–3 months and 12–16 hours for infants aged 4–11 months. Children aged 1–2 years should spend at least 180 minutes physically active and engaging in various activities with moderate to vigorous intensity. Signs of being in the moderate intensity zone include being breathless but still able to speak. On a scale from 0 to 10, where 0 is sitting and 10 is vigorous activity, moderate intensity is around 5–6. It is not recommended to let children sit quietly, watch TV, or play with gadgets for more than 1 hour. They should fulfill their sleep needs, which range from 11 to 14 hours per day. For children aged 3–4 years, physical activity should be performed for at least 180 minutes per day, including 60 minutes of intense activity. The rule of not allowing more than 1 hour of TV watching or gadget use still applies. Quality sleep should be maintained for 10–13 hours per day, for children and adolescents aged 5–17 years, at least 60 minutes of moderate to vigorous intensity physical activity should be performed daily. These activities will strengthen their muscles and bones [6].

Motor development milestones are essential indicators of a child's physical growth and motor skills. The World Health Organization (WHO) provides a comprehensive guide for tracking motor development in children. Here is a summary of motor development milestones based on the WHO reference (**Table 1**) [6].

Thirty studies were included in the meta-analysis, resulting in a total of 21,686 participants assessing fitness in children ages 3–18 years for more than 1 year of follow-up. Does muscle fitness affect health status even in the future? Meta-analysis found the effect size to be significant, with moderate to large results, namely muscle fitness, negative for increases in body mass index, skinfold thickness, homeostasis model assessment, insulin resistance estimation, and triglycerides. Cardiovascular disease risk score ($r = -0.29$; 95% CI - 0.39 to - 0.18) and bone mineral density ($r = 0.166$; 95% CI 0.086 to 0.243). The results of the study indicate when a child starts exercising or physical activity that has been meaningfully active since childhood, will have benefits for maintaining muscle fitness, maintaining body weight so obesity does not occur, reducing the possibility of diabetes mellitus, heart attacks, and osteoporosis [7–10].

The American Academy of Pediatrics (AAP) states that the development of skills such as jumping, leaping, kicking, and throwing significantly influences

Age	Gross Motor	Fine Motor	Sensory Development
0–3 months	Lift and turn your head briefly when lying on the stomach.	Grasps objects when they touch their hands.	Shows visual and auditory responsiveness to stimuli.
	Moves arms and legs in a random manner.		Begins to follow moving objects with their eyes.
4–6 months	Rolls over from back to stomach and vice versa.	Reaches for and grabs objects voluntarily.	Reaches for and explores objects with their hands.
	Sits with support and begins to support weight on legs when standing.		Begins to develop depth perception.
7–9 months	Crawls or scoots on the floor.	Transfers objects from one hand to another.	Uses hands and mouth to explore objects through touch and taste.
	Pulls up to stand and cruises along furniture.	Begins to use thumb and fingers to pick up small items.	Shows increased awareness of their surroundings.
10–12 months	Take first independent steps (walking).	Uses a pincer grasp (thumb and forefinger) to pick up small objects.	Uses a pincer grasp to pick up small objects.
	Stands momentarily without support.	Attempts to scribble with a crayon or marker.	Begins to show an interest in exploring textures and shapes.
12–24 months	Walks confidently and begins to run.	Build a tower of two to four blocks.	
	Climbs stairs with assistance and kicks a ball forward.	Uses a spoon to feed themselves.	
24–36 months	Runs more smoothly and jumps with both feet off the ground.	Draws simple shapes like circles and lines.	
	Climbs stairs with alternate feet and pedals a tricycle.	Begins to use safety scissors.	
36–60 months	Hops on one foot and balances on each foot for a few seconds.	Draws more complex shapes and begins to write letters.	
	Throws and catches a ball with increased accuracy.	Strings beads and manipulates small objects with precision.	

Table 1.
Motor development milestone in children [6].

cardiovascular function, both during childhood and into adulthood. Engaging in exercise habits or participating in sports organizations strengthens abilities, hand-eye coordination skills, functional movement skills, as well as strength, academic performance, and self-management skills in daily life [11].

2. From free play to sport

Recent research on children's physical activity levels has shed light on the significance of achieving 12,000 steps a day. Studies have shown that encouraging children to engage in regular physical activity, such as walking, can have numerous health benefits. The recommended 12,000 steps per day for children are associated with improved cardiovascular health, increased bone density, and enhanced motor skills development. Moreover, regular physical activity can help combat the growing concern of childhood obesity and promote overall well-being. To achieve this target, it is essential to create environments that encourage and facilitate physical activity, such as safe walking paths, parks, and playgrounds. By promoting a culture of movement and play, we can empower children to lead healthier and more active lives, setting the foundation for a lifetime of positive health outcomes [12].

In my clinical experience, healthy children tend to be physically active in their daily lives. Such habits should be guided by parents and educators to be more beneficial, not only for their daily lives but also for achieving success. This applies to both typically developing children and those with special needs.

Based on observations, discussions with various cases, and research from the American Academy of Pediatrics (AAP) in Physical Activity Assessment and Counseling in Pediatric Clinical Settings, it is stated that a child's development of structured sports activities such as running, jumping, kicking, and throwing is strongly related to cardiovascular health, both in the present and as the child grows into adulthood. Engaging in structured physical activity habits enhances physical abilities in terms of hand-eye coordination, functional movement skills, strength, academic performance, self-regulation, and general life skills. This is significant for socialization [13]. It starts with free play patterns adjusted according to a child's developmental milestones, abilities, talents, and sometimes considering gender. Thus, the patterns developed from activities at home can be transformed into organized sports activities. A child's abilities will improve when exercise habits are also incorporated into their school curriculum, especially when they can join sports organizations they enjoy. They can also be encouraged to explore competition within their age group.

Programs are designed to combine free play patterns for kindergartners and first-graders with specific skill-based movements. For example, a child may be trained in the skill of running while carrying a ball and how they can develop cooperation skills with their peers. The progress of these developing abilities can be evaluated within 4 months [14].

Children with athletic talents or those engaged in sports with specialized coaches will naturally feel more motivated and challenged to further develop their physical activity and chosen sport. It is worth noting that physical activity also improves cognitive performance and academic achievement in school [15].

Specifically, one study found that children who actively participated in a sports club had a positive association with good math scores [16].

Markel DL states in his research that a child is ready to face learning and the integration of physical activity into a more diverse skill set and better concentration for achievement when they have reached the age of 6. At that stage, children can be directed toward more structured sports aiming for achievements [17].

While looking for research statements, it is known that individuals engaged in sports are more resilient to stress and less prone to suicidal ideation. However, caution must be exercised regarding the use of steroids.

There are several advantages and disadvantages of using steroids (**Table 2**).

There may be a connection between the use of Anabolic Androgenic Steroids (AAS) and poor academic performance. In a large national study, DuRant and colleagues [21] stated that students who reported below-average academic performance had a significantly higher prevalence of AAS use compared to students with average or

Advantages	Disadvantages
Better muscle development	Bulimia, anorexia
Reduce fatigue	Stunting
Better physique	Bigamerexia
	Tendency to use other substances such as alcohol, cocaine, injected drugs, cigarettes (Jesson) and having suicidal thoughts [18, 19]
	Hepatic system: Liver toxicity [20], hepatocellular adenomas
	Cardiovascular: Increased of low-density lipoprotein, Decreased high-density lipoprotein
	Reproductive system: Testicular atrophy and decreased spermatogenesis
	Musculoskeletal: stiffening of tendon, absorbs less energy, and likability to fail during activity

Table 2.
Advantages and disadvantages of steroids usage in children [21–23].

above-average academic performance. However, two other studies [22, 23] reported no relationship between academic achievement and AAS use. Further research is needed to explore this question.

3. The importance of test batteries to measure physical fitness in children

Childhood physical fitness is a crucial aspect of overall health and well-being. With the prevalence of sedentary lifestyles and the rise in childhood obesity, it is more important than ever to assess and promote physical fitness in children. Test batteries, consisting of standardized assessments, play a pivotal role in evaluating various aspects of a child's physical fitness. These batteries enable educators, healthcare professionals, and parents to gain valuable insights into a child's overall fitness level and identify areas for improvement. This article explores the significance of test batteries in measuring physical fitness in children and how they contribute to developing targeted interventions to support their health and fitness journey. Some test batteries for children aged 5–12 years (measuring physical fitness in children who are 5–12 years old with a functional and easy-to-administer test battery) [24].

The wide range of abilities in children as they grow older sometimes makes it difficult to assess their physical fitness and determine suitable testing methods for each age group and how to compare them across different age ranges. In a research report, Ingunn Fjortoft and colleagues presented an interesting review of tests that can be performed. These tests are simple and engaging while being able to evaluate physical fitness levels. It is important to note that these tests are based on movements that are enjoyable and commonly performed by children aged 5–12 years as part of their daily activities. The tests are as follows:

3.1 Standing board jump

Leg power is a crucial component of physical fitness, as it directly impacts a child's ability to perform daily activities, sports, and recreational pursuits. The Standing Board Jump provides a reliable measure of leg power, giving valuable information on a child's ability to generate force with their lower body muscles. This information can be useful in designing targeted exercise programs to improve leg strength and power [25].

The Standing Board Jump is a fitness assessment that measures a child's explosive leg power. It involves the child standing on a firm surface with feet shoulder-width apart, ready to jump. They are asked to jump forward as far as they can while swinging their arms for momentum. The distance jumped is then recorded and serves as an indicator of the child's lower body strength and power. One of the primary advantages of the Standing Board Jump is its simplicity and safety. Unlike more complex fitness tests, this assessment requires minimal equipment and space, making it easy to administer in various settings, such as schools, community centers, and sports clubs. Moreover, it is a non-invasive test that poses little risk of injury to the child, making it suitable for children of all fitness levels [25].

Cut off value for Standing Board Jump (cm) test, result: 122.54 Standard Deviations (SD) 19.41.

3.2 The 7-meter two-foot jump test

Explosive power is an essential component of physical fitness, especially in activities that involve quick bursts of energy, such as sprinting, jumping, and certain sports movements. The 7-meter two-foot jump test focuses on explosive power, providing valuable data on a child's ability to generate force rapidly, which has practical implications for their performance in various physical activities [25].

The 7-meter two-foot jump test yields objective and quantifiable results, making it an ideal tool for evaluating physical fitness in children. The distance jump can be easily measured and recorded, allowing educators, coaches, and healthcare professionals to track a child's progress over time. These objective metrics provide valuable feedback to children, motivating them to set goals and strive for continuous improvement in their physical fitness. The 7-meter two-foot jump test requires the child to jump as far as possible using both feet, with the goal of covering a distance of 7 meters (approximately 23 feet) as quickly as they can. This test evaluates lower body strength, power, and coordination, as the child must generate explosive force to propel themselves over the distance. It is a dynamic assessment that mirrors real-life movements, making it a practical and engaging way to measure a child's physical fitness [25].

Cut-off value for jumping a distance of 7 m on 2 feet as fast as possible (s) test, result: 3.87 SD 0.59.

3.3 The 7-meter one-foot jump test

Balance is a fundamental aspect of physical fitness, especially in activities that involve dynamic movements and sports participation. The 7-meter one-foot jump test challenges a child's balance and stability, as they must land and stabilize on one foot after the jump. This aspect of the test provides valuable information about a child's ability to maintain equilibrium and control over their body, which is essential for various physical activities and daily life [26].

The 7-meter one-foot jump test offers objective and measurable results, making it an excellent tool for monitoring a child's physical fitness progress over time. By recording the distance covered in each jump, educators and healthcare professionals can track improvements and set achievable fitness goals for children. This objectivity motivates children to work toward bettering their performance and maintaining an active lifestyle. The 7-meter one-foot jump test requires a child to jump as far as possible using only one foot, aiming to cover a distance of 7 meters (approximately 23 feet) as quickly as they can. This test focuses on assessing the child's explosive power and balance, as they must generate force with one leg while maintaining stability and coordination during the jump [26].

Cut off value for Jumping a distance of 7 m on 1 foot as fast as possible (s) test, result: 3.19 SD 0.37.

3.4 The tennis ball throw test

Upper body strength plays a crucial role in a child's physical development, influencing their performance in everyday tasks and athletic endeavors. The Tennis Ball Throw Test directly assesses a child's upper body strength and power, providing valuable information about their potential for engaging in sports and physical activities that require strength and agility [27].

Hand-eye coordination is a fundamental motor skill that impacts a child's ability to perform precise movements. The Tennis Ball Throw Test challenges a child's hand-eye coordination as they aim and release the tennis ball. Regular practice of this test can help enhance their coordination, benefiting them in various sports and activities throughout their lives [27].

The Tennis Ball Throw Test is a functional assessment that simulates real-life movements and sports-related skills. The child stands in a designated area, grasping a tennis ball with one hand, and attempts to throw it as far as they can. This test evaluates upper body strength, coordination, and the ability to generate force, mirroring activities like throwing, passing, and participating in various sports. The Tennis Ball Throw Test engages children in a fun and competitive activity, motivating them to participate actively in fitness assessments. The excitement of trying to throw the ball as far as possible fosters a positive attitude toward physical activity, promoting a sense of enjoyment and accomplishment in the process [27].

Cut off value for Throwing a tennis ball with one hand as far as possible (m) test, result: 11.97 SD 3.56.

3.5 The medicine ball push test

Pushing the Medicine ball requires coordination and body awareness, as the child must coordinate both hands and exert force uniformly to propel the ball forward. Regular practice of this test can enhance a child's coordination and spatial awareness, contributing to improved motor skills that benefit them in various athletic pursuits [28].

The Medicine Ball Push Test engages children in an enjoyable and interactive activity, motivating them to actively participate in fitness assessments. The challenge of pushing the ball as far as possible fosters a positive attitude toward physical activity, encouraging children to view fitness as a rewarding and enjoyable endeavor. Objective results in the Medicine Ball Push Test enable children to set and achieve fitness goals. As they record their progress over time, they are inspired to surpass their previous distances, instilling a sense of accomplishment and self-confidence. This process encourages children to take ownership of their physical fitness journey and strive for continuous improvement. The Medicine Ball Push Test is a functional evaluation that mimics real-life movements and sports-related actions. In this assessment, the child stands in a designated area and uses both hands to push a 1 kg medical ball as far as they can. This test assesses functional strength and coordination, resembling actions such as pushing heavy objects and engaging in sports that involve upper body strength [28].

Cut off value for pushing a medicine ball (1 kg) with two hands as far as possible (m) test, result: 3.34 SD 0.47.

3.6 Climbing up wall bars

Climbing up wall bars requires significant upper-body strength and endurance. As children pull their bodies upwards using their arms, shoulders, and core muscles, this test serves as an excellent indicator of their upper body strength and the ability to sustain efforts during physical activity. Wall bar climbing promotes the development of motor skills and coordination. The activity demands precise movements and coordination between the upper and lower body. Regular practice can improve a child's ability to coordinate their movements, positively impacting their overall motor skills and body awareness [29].

Climbing wall bars demands a combination of agility and flexibility as children navigate their way through the bars. The activity involves bending, twisting, and adjusting body positions to reach higher levels. This agile movement fosters flexibility and adaptability, valuable skills for various physical activities and sports. Climbing up wall bars is a comprehensive fitness assessment that engages various muscle groups and motor skills. In this test, the child ascends a series of vertical bars arranged on a wall, aiming to reach the top as quickly as possible. This activity evaluates upper body strength, grip strength, coordination, balance, and agility, making it a well-rounded measure of physical fitness [29].

The height of each column in the wall bars measures 2.55 meters, and the width is 0.75 meters [29]. Cut off value for Climbing up wall bars as fast as possible (s) test, result: 12.10 SD 2.83.

3.7 The shuttle run test

The Shuttle Run Test, also known as the 20-meter shuttle run or the beep test, involves a child running back and forth between two markers placed 20 meters apart. The child must touch the marker at each end before returning, in sync with audio cues. As the test progresses, the time between the beeps decreases, demanding increased speed and agility. The test continues until the child can no longer keep up with the pace or voluntarily stops. The Shuttle Run Test provides a direct measure of a child's speed and agility. The quick changes in direction, accelerations, and decelerations required during the test challenge a child's ability to move efficiently and responsively [30].

This evaluation is crucial for determining a child's athletic potential and identifying areas for improvement. In addition to speed and agility, the Shuttle Run Test assesses a child's cardiovascular endurance. The test is designed to increase gradually in intensity, pushing the child's heart and lungs to work harder as they continue running. A child's ability to sustain the test for longer indicates a higher level of cardiovascular fitness. The Shuttle Run Test provides objective and quantifiable results, making it an excellent tool for measuring a child's physical fitness. The total number of completed shuttles is recorded, and this data can be compared to established fitness norms to evaluate a child's fitness level in comparison to their peers [30].

Cut off value for Shuttle run as fast as possible (s) test, result: 25.87 SD 2.03.

3.8 The 20-meter sprint test

The 20-meter sprint test requires a child to run a straight line, covering a distance of 20 meters as fast as they can. The test assesses a child's speed and acceleration, making it an efficient evaluation of their anaerobic power and agility. Speed and acceleration are critical components of physical fitness, especially in activities that require quick bursts of energy, such as sports and daily life [31].

The 20-meter sprint test provides a direct measure of a child's ability to accelerate and attain maximum speed in a short distance. The 20-meter sprint test primarily relies on the anaerobic energy system, which supplies energy for short and intense bursts of activity. By pushing the body to its limits within a brief period, the test evaluates a child's anaerobic capacity, which is vital for various sports and high-intensity physical activities. The 20-meter sprint test yields objective and immediate results. The time taken to complete the sprint is recorded, providing quantifiable data that can be easily compared and tracked over time. This objectivity allows educators, coaches, and healthcare professionals to assess a child's progress and tailor fitness programs accordingly [31].

Cut off value for Running 20 m as fast as possible (s) test, result: 4.62 SD 0.40.

3.9 The reduced cooper test

The Reduced Cooper Test is an adaptation of the classic 12-minute Cooper Test, designed to better suit children and individuals with varying fitness levels. In this test, the child runs or walks for 6 minutes, covering as much distance as possible within the given time frame. The distance covered serves as an indicator of the child's cardiovascular endurance and overall physical fitness. One of the primary advantages of the Reduced Cooper Test is its versatility. Children have the option to run or walk during the 6-minute duration, allowing them to choose the pace that best suits their fitness level. This inclusivity ensures that children of all abilities can participate comfortably and confidently in the assessment [32].

The Reduced Cooper Test primarily evaluates cardiovascular endurance, a critical aspect of physical fitness that indicates the efficiency of the heart and lungs in supplying oxygen to the working muscles. By encouraging continuous movement for 6 minutes, this test challenges a child's aerobic capacity and stamina. The Reduced Cooper Test provides objective and quantifiable results. The distance covered by the child within the 6-minute timeframe is recorded, enabling educators, coaches, and healthcare professionals to compare and track progress over time. This objectivity facilitates personalized fitness planning and monitoring [32].

Cut off value for Reduced Cooper Test (6 minutes), both running or walking are allowed (m) test, result: 984.82 SD 133.47.

4. Misconception about resistance training in children

Physical activity (PA) does not only involve aerobic activities. Often, sports and even children's games involve activities of resistance training (RT). In fact, to improve performance, speed, strength, and agility, engaging in resistance training activities is necessary. However, there are often misconceptions, misunderstandings, and myths surrounding RT in children, which may cause confusion and fear [29].

Resistance training (RT), or sometimes referred to as strength training, is a component of sports designed to increase muscle strength, muscular power, and muscle endurance. RT can take various forms, ranging from bodyweight exercises to the use of equipment, which can be manual or robotic. When discussing RT, it is not limited to exercises using equipment only. In children's RT exercises, strength-building often involves movements such as frog jumps, bear crawls, crab walks, kangaroo hops, and one-leg hops [33]. Children as young as 5 years old can perform single-leg jumps (**Table 3**) [34].

Resistance training, when appropriately designed and supervised, offers numerous health benefits for children. First, it helps in developing muscular strength and endurance. As children engage in resistance exercises, their muscles adapt and grow stronger, allowing them to perform daily activities with greater ease and efficiency. Second, resistance training contributes to improved bone health. The stresses placed on bones during resistance exercises stimulate bone growth and density, reducing the risk of osteoporosis and fractures later in life. This is especially significant during childhood and adolescence, when bone development is at its peak. Moreover, resistance training positively impacts body composition. It helps to decrease body fat and increase lean muscle mass, fostering a healthier body composition, which can contribute to better overall health and reduce the risk of obesity-related issues. Additionally, resistance training has been shown to enhance motor skills and functional abilities in children. By developing muscular strength, balance, and coordination, children can improve their athletic performance, excel in sports, and develop better physical competence in daily activities [35].

Misconception	Evidence
Before reaching puberty, a child is incapable of experiencing strength gains.	Before reaching puberty, children have the capability to build strength through improved neurological recruitment of muscle fibers. Moreover, if resistance training programs are closely supervised and prioritize correct technique, children can achieve strength gains with minimal risk of injury.
Engaging in resistance training might lead young boys and girls to become "muscle bound."	Strength gains in prepubertal individuals are achieved through neurological mechanisms, while during puberty, these gains may be further boosted by muscle hypertrophy facilitated by the presence of pubertal hormones.
Youth participating in resistance training may experience a reduction in their aerobic performance.	Studies have demonstrated that incorporating both aerobic and resistance training in programs can lead to enhancements in aerobic performance. Moreover, it has been observed that combining these two types of training does not hinder strength gains in children.
Resistance training has been associated with concerns about potentially hindering growth in children.	There is no evidence to suggest that properly structured resistance training programs have adverse effects on the growth plates, linear growth, or cardiovascular health of young individuals.
The strength of children today exceeds previous levels.	Addressing strength deficiencies and developing strength reserves is crucial due to the decreasing levels of muscular fitness observed in today's youth.
1 RM testing is considered risky for young individuals.	When conducted under qualified supervision and adhering to appropriate testing guidelines, 1 RM testing can be a secure approach to assessing muscular strength in youth.

Table 3.
Misconception and evidence about resistance training in children [29, 33, 34].

Resistance training also promotes positive psychological effects in children. It can boost self-esteem and self-confidence as they achieve strength and fitness goals. Additionally, it may help reduce anxiety and stress, leading to improved mental well-being. It is essential to note that resistance training programs for children should be tailored to their age, developmental stage, and individual capabilities. Proper supervision and coaching by qualified professionals are crucial to ensure safety and maximize the health benefits of resistance training while avoiding potential risks. With the right approach, resistance training can be a valuable component of a child's overall physical development and long-term health [35].

The mechanism of strength increase caused by fitness in children is a complex interplay of various physiological processes. When children engage in fitness activities, such as resistance training, several key mechanisms come into play to facilitate strength gains. First, resistance training leads to neurological adaptations. As children perform exercises against resistance, their nervous system learns to recruit more muscle fibers simultaneously, which enhances the force production capacity of the muscles. This improved neuromuscular coordination allows children to exert more strength and power during subsequent training sessions and everyday activities. Second, resistance training stimulates muscle hypertrophy. The repetitive stress placed on muscles during resistance exercises triggers cellular responses that lead to the growth and enlargement of muscle fibers. This muscle hypertrophy contributes to increased muscle strength and endurance, as well as overall improvements in muscular fitness. Third, fitness activities promote bone remodeling and density. The mechanical loading experienced during resistance training encourages bone cells to adapt and remodel, resulting in stronger and denser bones. This is particularly crucial during childhood and adolescence, when bone growth is at its peak, as it helps in building a strong skeletal foundation for the future. Moreover, fitness activities have a positive impact on connective tissues. Tendons and ligaments adapt to the increased loading from resistance exercises, becoming more resilient and better able to withstand forces. Strengthened connective tissues provide stability and support to the muscles, reducing the risk of injuries and allowing children to perform exercises with improved efficiency. Lastly, fitness activities can influence hormonal responses [32].

Resistance training, in particular, stimulates the release of hormones such as growth hormone and testosterone, which play essential roles in muscle growth and development. These hormonal responses contribute to the overall process of strength increase in children. Overall, the mechanism of strength increase caused by fitness in children involves a combination of neurological adaptations, muscle hypertrophy, bone remodeling, enhanced connective tissues, and hormonal responses. By understanding these mechanisms, coaches, parents, and healthcare professionals can design appropriate and effective fitness programs to optimize strength gains and promote the overall well-being of children [32].

Resistance training in children, while generally safe and beneficial, does come with some potential risks that need to be carefully considered and managed. First, the risk of injury is a primary concern. Children's growing bodies may be more susceptible to overuse injuries or strain if proper technique and supervision are not emphasized during resistance training sessions. It is crucial for coaches, parents, and trainers to ensure that exercises are age-appropriate and that children are using the correct form to minimize the risk of injury. Second, there is a concern about excessive training volume and intensity. Pushing children to lift excessively heavy weights or perform intense resistance exercises beyond their capabilities may lead to physical and emotional burnout. Overtraining can negatively impact growth and development, as well as decrease motivation and interest in physical activity. Another risk is the potential for early specialization and sport-specific training. While resistance training can enhance athletic performance, focusing too much on specific sports or movements at a young age may limit a child's overall physical development and increase the risk of overuse injuries. Additionally, if resistance training programs are not appropriately designed or supervised, children may be at risk of experiencing emotional or psychological stress related to body image or performance pressure. Ensuring a positive and supportive environment during training is essential to promote a healthy relationship with exercise and physical fitness. Furthermore, resistance training in children with certain medical conditions or physical limitations should be approached with caution [36].

Proper medical evaluation and clearance should be obtained before initiating any resistance training program for children with pre-existing health conditions. To mitigate these risks, it is vital to implement evidence-based and age-appropriate resistance training programs for children. Qualified trainers and coaches who have expertise in working with young individuals should oversee the training sessions. Moreover, creating a well-rounded and balanced fitness regimen that includes a variety of activities, sports, and exercises can promote overall physical development and reduce the risk of overuse injuries. By addressing these potential risks proactively, resistance training can be a safe and effective way to promote the health and well-being of children [36].

5. Physical activity modification

There are several congenital diseases that often occur in children. Congenital heart disease (CHD) affects nearly 1% of births [37]. Indonesia records that 8 out of 1000 births experience congenital heart disease [38], Singapore 9.7 out of 1000 live births [39], and India records 13.3 out of 1000 live births [40]. With technological and scientific advancements, 90% of children with CHD who undergo surgical procedures will survive and are also likely to grow into adulthood [41]. On the other hand, many of these surviving patients will also be exposed to several complications. Data from developed countries indicate that many child patients with CHD and even adults with heart disease have obesity as a comorbidity. This obesity is thought to occur due to a sedentary lifestyle. This often happens because of activity restrictions imposed by parents and even doctors who have a limited understanding of exercise for children with CHD [42].

Currently, there is a lot of research data indicating that physical activity can benefit some CHD patients. Several studies also state that many deaths in CHD patients occur during rest. Many data also prove that structured and measured physical activity, even directed sports, will provide benefits in creating good health, endurance, strength, flexibility, and metabolism. This condition will likely reduce the frequency of relapses, hospitalizations, and even deaths [43].

Caution should still be exercised for pediatric CHD patients. International guidelines on Physical Activity (PA) in CHD focus on guidelines for patients who have undergone surgery, enabling them to engage in physical activity and even competitive sports. Before initiating PA or sports activities, several functional tests need to be considered and conducted. Simple tests that can be performed even at the community level include the 6-minute walk test. This test is performed on flat terrain. It is better to have a 30-meter track for back-and-forth walking for 6 minutes. During the test, patients should be monitored for heart rate, oxygen saturation, dyspnea, and fatigue. This test has been proven safe for patients with cardiorespiratory disorders. This test can at least be conducted for patients with moderate to severe abnormalities. As a reference, the 6MWT result for healthy boys aged 11 to 14 is 576 ± 93 m, and for girls is 545 ± 92 m [44]. Stress Test: This test is often performed using the Modified Bruce Protocol on a treadmill. A good exercise value is above 10 METs. Caution should be exercised when conducting this test in children with pulmonary hypertension, cardiomyopathy with heart failure, arrhythmia, severe outflow obstruction, prolonged QTc, and severe aortic dilation [45].

Atrial septal defect (ASD): Patients without ASD surgery, whether small, moderate, or large, without pulmonary artery hypertension (PAH), are allowed to participate in all sports. If ASD surgery is performed during childhood, physical activity can be resumed 3–6 months after surgery. Direct contact sports are not recommended until after 6 months. If surgery is performed after the age of 40, only low-intensity physical activity is allowed, especially if there are residual PAH, arrhythmias, and ventricular dysfunction [46].

Ventricular septal defect (VSD): Prudent discretion is advised, as individuals afflicted with Eisenmenger syndrome are susceptible to the potential occurrence of unforeseen mortality [47]. Patients who have not undergone surgical intervention, possess minor to moderate ventricular septal defects (VSD), and exhibit unimpaired cardiac function should be granted the opportunity to engage in a comprehensive spectrum of athletic activities. Nonetheless, in cases where pulmonary hypertension and a left-to-right shunt are present, it is judicious to restrict athletic involvement to pursuits of low intensity. Competitive sports are also not allowed. Patients who have undergone VSD closure surgery require 3–6 months of recovery and rehabilitation before participating in all areas of physical activity. However, if patients still have arrhythmias, pulmonary hypertension, and severe heart function decline, their activity should be limited to low-dynamic sport leisure level [46].

Tetralogy of fallot (TOF): Rationally, TOF, which involves various anatomical heart abnormalities and cyanotic conditions, is associated with exercise intolerance. This is confirmed by cardiopulmonary exercise test (CPET) examinations showing significant desaturation. Therefore, regardless of the TOF condition, low-intensity physical activity is allowed [47].

Attention-deficit/hyperactivity disorder (ADHD) is one of the most prevalent neurodevelopmental disorders in childhood, presenting with symptoms of hyperactivity, impulsivity, and/or inattention. The estimated prevalence of ADHD was 5.29% (95% confidence interval [CI]: 5.01–5.56) in community samples of children and adolescents from 35 countries across six continents worldwide. Difficulty in managing children with ADHD arises because they struggle to interact with their environment. Children with ADHD live in their own world. The American Psychiatric Association's Diagnostic and Statistical Manual of Mental Disorders—5th Ed (DSM-5) divides ADHD into three subtypes based on dominant symptoms: Inattention (ADHD-I), hyperactive and impulsive (ADHD-HI), and combined (ADHD-C) [48].

In a study by Luciano Acordi and colleagues, intriguing findings are reported regarding the benefits of swimming therapy for the mental health, cognition, and motor coordination of schoolchildren diagnosed with ADHD. This training spanned 8 weeks and significantly altered depression and improved cognitive abilities and attention. In terms of motor coordination and physical fitness, the aquatic program yielded satisfying results for the coordination of both limbs, flexibility, and abdominal muscle strength [49].

This research is grounded in reports about the side effects of medications for children and adolescents with ADHD. Around 20% of teenagers experience and report side effects from the medications they consume for ADHD, including mood disorders like anxiety, stress, and depression [50].

One potential explanation for the current findings is that exercise promotes neuroplasticity and neuroprotection, leading to improved cognitive function and increased gray matter volume. Another explanation, proposed by Dietrich and Audiffren, is that exercise engages arousal mechanisms involving neurotransmitter systems, aiding implicit cognitive and emotional information processing in the reticular activating system. In terms of motor coordination, physical training can alter brain functioning and enhance motor coordination [51].

The aquatic program took place in a semi-Olympic thermal swimming pool over 8 weeks, with two sessions per week, totaling 16 sessions. Each session lasted 45 minutes and included approximately 5 minutes of stretching, 25 minutes of swimming instruction, 10 minutes of recreational activity, and 5 minutes of calmness and stretching [49]. Unfortunately, the journal does not elaborate on the teaching experience, how to engage children with ADHD, or how to enhance their focus and concentration.

Parents and teachers often have misconceptions about physical activities or play before starting school lessons. They might view physical activities as energy-draining and detrimental to learning. However, research by Hermoso and colleagues surprisingly reveals that physical play has a positive impact. An intervention involving physical activities was conducted daily before the first lesson (8,00–8,30 am) for 8 weeks. Pre and postassessments were carried out, and the results showed no significant changes in attention and concentration among the students. This indicates that their attention and concentration remained sufficient for learning after physical play and before the study began. However, significant improvements were observed in language and math scores after the active play program. Positive changes were also noted in their physical condition, including fat mass, fat-free mass, muscle strength, and cardiorespiratory fitness [52].

Author details

Endang Ernandini[1*] and Jonathan Alvin Wiryaputra[2]

1 Center of Rehabilitation, Indonesia Ministry of Defense, Indonesia

2 Faculty of Military Medicine, Republic of Indonesia Defense University, Indonesia

*Address all correspondence to: ernandiniebeb@gmail.com

References

[1] Dapp LC, Gashaj V, Roebers CM. Physical activity and motor skills in children: A differentiated approach. Psychology of Sport and Exercise. 2021;**54**:101916

[2] Ahn JV, Sera F, Cummins S, Flouri E. Associations between objectively measured physical activity and later mental health outcomes in children: Findings from the UK millennium cohort study. Journal of Epidemiology and Community Health. 2018;**72**(2):94-100

[3] Iivonen S, Sääkslahti AK. Preschool children's fundamental motor skills: A review of significant determinants. Early Child Development and Care. 2014;**184**(7):1107-1126

[4] Zuur AF, Ieno EN, Walker NJ, Saveliev AA, Smith GM. Mixed effects models and extensions in ecology with R. Vol. 574. New York: Springer; 2009. p. 574

[5] Robinson LE, Stodden DF, Barnett LM, Lopes VP, Logan SW, Rodrigues LP, et al. Motor competence and its effect on positive developmental trajectories of health. Sports Medicine. 2015;**45**:1273-1284

[6] World Health Organization. 2021 physical activity factsheets for the European Union Member States in the WHO European Region (No. WHO/EURO: 2021-3409-43168-60449). World Health Organization. Regional Office for Europe; 2021

[7] Fühner T, Kliegl R, Arntz F, Kriemler S, Granacher U. An update on secular trends in physical fitness of children and adolescents from 1972 to 2015: A systematic review. Sports Medicine. 2021;**51**:303-320

[8] Zhu X, Zheng H. Factors influencing peak bone mass gain. Frontiers of Medicine. 2021;**15**:53-69

[9] Hebert JJ, Klakk H, Møller NC, Grøntved A, Andersen LB, Wedderkopp N. The prospective association of organized sports participation with cardiovascular disease risk in children (the CHAMPS study-DK). Mayo Clinic Proceedings. 2017;**92**(1):57-65

[10] Dunton G, McConnell R, Jerrett M, Wolch J, Lam C, Gilliland F, et al. Organized physical activity in young school children and subsequent 4-year change in body mass index. Archives of Pediatrics & Adolescent Medicine. 2012;**166**(8):713-718

[11] Eime RM, Young JA, Harvey JT, Charity MJ, Payne WR. A systematic review of the psychological and social benefits of participation in sport for children and adolescents: Informing development of a conceptual model of health through sport. International Journal of Behavioral Nutrition and Physical Activity. 2013;**10**(1):1-21

[12] Tudor-Locke C, Craig CL, Beets MW, Belton S, Cardon GM, Duncan S, et al. How many steps/day are enough? For children and adolescents. International Journal of Behavioral Nutrition and Physical Activity. 2011;**8**(1):1-4

[13] Matvienko O, Ahrabi-Fard I. The effects of a 4-week after-school program on motor skills and fitness of kindergarten and first-grade students. American Journal of Health Promotion. 2010;**24**(5):299-303

[14] Ruiz JR, Ortega FB, Castillo R, Martín-Matillas M, Kwak L, Vicente-Rodríguez G, et al. Physical

activity, fitness, weight status, and cognitive performance in adolescents. The Journal of Pediatrics. 2010;**157**(6):917-922

[15] Domazet SL, Tarp J, Huang T, Gejl AK, Andersen LB, Froberg K, et al. Associations of physical activity, sports participation and active commuting on mathematic performance and inhibitory control in adolescents. PLoS One. 2016;**11**(1):e0146319

[16] Merkel DL. Youth sport: Positive and negative impact on young athletes. Open access Journal of Sports Medicine. 2013;**4**:151-160

[17] Rich JD, Dickinson BP, Feller A, et al. The infectious complications of anabolic-androgenic steroid injection. International Journal of Sports Medicine. 1999;**20**:563-566

[18] Melia P, Pipe A, Greenberg L. The use of anabolic-androgenic steroids by Canadian students. Clinical Journal of Sport Medicine. 1996;**6**:9-14

[19] Ishak KG, Zimmerman HJ. Hepatotoxic effects of the anabolic/androgenic steroids. Seminars in Liver Disease. 1987;7:230-236

[20] DuRant RH, Escobedo LG, Heath GW. Anabolic-steroid use, strength training, and multiple drug use among adolescents in the United States. Pediatrics. 1995;**96**:23-28

[21] Adalf EM, Smart RG. Characteristics of steroid users in an adolescent school population. Journal of Alcohol and Drug Education. 1992;**38**(1):43-49

[22] DuRant RH, Middleman AB, Faulkner AH, et al. Adolescent anabolic-steroid use, multiple drug use, and high school sports participation. Pediatric Exercise Science. 1997;**9**:150-158

[23] Vivas A, González-Ruíz K, Benavides Rodríguez L, Camelo-Prieto DL, Correa Bautista JE, Ramírez-Vélez R. Reference Values for Standing Broad Jump in Colombian Schoolchildren the Fuprecol Study: 2767 Board# 290 June 3, 930 AM–1100 AM. 2016

[24] Fjørtoft I, Pedersen AV, Sigmundsson H, Vereijken B. Measuring physical fitness in children who are 5 to 12 years old with a test battery that is functional and easy to administer. Physical Therapy. 2011;**91**(7):1087-1095

[25] Ayán-Pérez C, Cancela-Carral JM, Lago-Ballesteros J, Martínez-Lemos I. Reliability of Sargent jump test in 4-to 5-year-old children. Perceptual and Motor Skills. 2017;**124**(1):39-57

[26] Bogdanis GC, Donti O, Papia A, Donti A, Apostolidis N, Sands WA. Effect of plyometric training on jumping, sprinting and change of direction speed in child female athletes. Sports. 2019;7(5):116

[27] Van Waelvelde H, De Weerdt W, De Cock P, Engelsman BS. Ball catching. Can it be measured? Physiotherapy Theory and Practice. 2003;**19**(4):259-267

[28] Davis KL, Kang M, Boswell BB, DuBose KD, Altman SR, Binkley HM. Validity and reliability of the medicine ball throw for kindergarten children. The Journal of Strength & Conditioning Research. 2008;**22**(6):1958-1963

[29] Kozina Z, Repko O, Kozin S, Kostyrko A, Yermakova T, Goncharenko V. Motor skills formation technique in 6 to 7-year-old children based on their psychological and physical features (rock climbing as an example). Journal of Physical Education and Sport. 2016;**16**(3):866

[30] Lang JJ, Belanger K, Poitras V, Janssen I, Tomkinson GR, Tremblay MS.